ARISTOTLE

NICOMACHEAN ETHICS

ARISTOTLE

NICOMACHEAN ETHICS

Translated
with Introduction, Notes, and Glossary, by

TERENCE IRWIN

Second Edition

Hackett Publishing Company, Inc.
Indianapolis/Cambridge

Printed in the United States of America

10 09 08 07 6 7 8 9 10

For further information, please address
Hackett Publishing Company, Inc.
P. O. Box 44937
Indianapolis, Indiana 46244–0937

www.hackettpublishing.com

Cover design by Listenberger & Associates
Interior design by Meera Dash and Abigail Coyle

Library of Congress Cataloging-in-Publication Data
Aristotle.
[Nicomachean ethics. English]
Nicomachean ethics / Aristotle : translated, with introduction, notes, and glossary by Terence Irwin.—2nd ed.
p. cm.
Includes bibliographical references.
ISBN 0-87220-465-0 —ISBN 0-87220-464-2 (pbk.)
1. Ethics. I. Irwin, Terence. II. Title.
B430.A5N5313 1999
171'.3—dc21 99-26709
CIP

ISBN-13: 978-0-87220-465-2 (cloth)
ISBN-13: 978-0-87220-464-5 (pbk.)

CONTENTS

Preface ix
Abbreviations and Conventions xi
Introduction xiii

Nicomachean Ethics 1

Book I [Happiness] 1
1. [Ends and Goods] 1
2. [The Highest Good and Political Science] 1
3. [The Method of Political Science] 2
4. [Common Beliefs] 3
5. [The Three Lives] 4
6. [The Platonic Form of the Good] 5
7. [An Account of the Human Good] 7
8. [Defense of the Account of the Good] 10
9. [How Is Happiness Achieved?] 12
10. [Can We Be Happy during Our Lifetime?] 13
11. [How Happiness Can Be Affected after One's Death] 15
12. [Praise and Honor] 15
13. [Introduction to the Virtues] 16

Book II [Virtue of Character] 18
1. [How a Virtue of Character Is Acquired] 18
2. [Habituation] 19
3. [The Importance of Pleasure and Pain] 20
4. [Virtuous Actions versus Virtuous Character] 22
5. [Virtue of Character: Its Genus] 23
6. [Virtue of Character: Its Differentia] 23
7. [The Particular Virtues of Character] 25
8. [Relations between Mean and Extreme States] 27
9. [How Can We Reach the Mean?] 29

Book III [Preconditions of Virtue] 30
1. [Voluntary Action] 30
2. [Decision] 33
3. [Deliberation] 34
4. [Wish] 36
5. [Virtue and Vice Are in Our Power] 37

[The Individual Virtues of Character] 40
6. [Bravery; Its Scope] 40
7. [Bravery; Its Characteristic Outlook] 41
8. [Conditions That Resemble Bravery] 42
9. [Feelings Proper to Bravery] 44
10. [Temperance; Its Scope] 45
11. [Temperance; Its Outlook] 47
12. [Intemperance] 48

Book IV 49
1. [Generosity] 49
2. [Magnificence] 53
3. [Magnanimity] 56
4. [The Virtue Concerned with Small Honors] 60
5. [Mildness] 61
6. [Friendliness] 62
7. [Truthfulness] 63
8. [Wit] 65
9. [Shame] 66

Book V [Justice] 67
1. [Varieties of Justice] 67
2. [Special Justice Contrasted with General] 69
3. [Justice in Distribution] 71
4. [Justice in Rectification] 72
5. [Justice in Exchange] 74
6. [Political Justice] 77
7. [Justice by Nature and by Law] 78
8. [Justice, Injustice, and the Voluntary] 79
9. [Puzzles about Justice and Injustice] 80
10. [Decency] 83
11. [Injustice to Oneself] 84

Book VI [Virtues of Thought] 86
1. [The Mean and the Virtues of Thought] 86
2. [Thought, Desire, and Decision] 87
3. [Scientific Knowledge] 87
4. [Craft Knowledge] 88
5. [Prudence] 89
6. [Understanding] 90
7. [Wisdom versus Prudence] 90
8. [Types of Prudence] 92
9. [Good Deliberation] 93
10. [Comprehension] 95
11. [Practical Thought and Particulars] 95
12. [Puzzles about Prudence and Wisdom] 96
13. [Prudence and Virtue of Character] 98

Book VII [Incontinence] 99
1. [Virtue, Vice, and Incontinence] 99
2. [Puzzles about Incontinence] 100
3. [Incontinence and Ignorance] 102
4. [Simple Incontinence] 104
5. [Bestiality and Disease] 106
6. [Incontinence and Related Conditions] 107
7. [Incontinence, Intemperance, and Softness] 109
8. [Why Intemperance Is Worse than Incontinence] 110
9. [Continence] 111
10. [Answers to Further Questions about Incontinence] 113

[Pleasure] 114
11. [Questions about Pleasure] 114
12. [Pleasure and Good] 115
13. [Pleasure and Happiness] 116
14. [Bodily Pleasures] 117

Book VIII [Friendship] 119
1. [Common Beliefs and Questions] 119
2. [The Object of Friendship] 120
3. [The Three Types of Friendship] 121
4. [Comparison between the Types of Friendship] 123
5. [State and Activity in Friendship] 124
6. [Activities Characteristic of the Different Types of Friendship] 125

7. [Friendship between Unequals] 127
8. [Giving and Receiving in Friendship] 128
9. [Friendship in Communities] 129
10. [Political Systems] 130
11. [Friendships in Political Systems] 131
12. [Friendships in Families] 132
13. [Disputes in Friendships between Equals] 134
14. [Disputes in Friendships between Unequals] 136

Book IX **137**
1. [Friends with Dissimilar Aims] 137
2. [Conflicts between Different Types of Friendships] 139
3. [Dissolution of Friendships] 140
4. [Self-love and Friendship] 141
5. [Goodwill and Friendship] 143
6. [Friendship and Concord] 144
7. [Active Benevolence and Friendship] 145
8. [Self-love and Selfishness] 146
9. [Why Are Friends Needed?] 148
10. [How Many Friends Are Needed?] 150
11. [Friends in Good and Ill Fortune] 151
12. [Shared Activity in Friendship] 152

Book X [Pleasure] **153**
1. [The Right Approach to Pleasure] 153
2. [Arguments about Pleasure] 154
3. [Pleasure Is a Good, but Not the Good] 155
4. [Pleasure Is an Activity] 157
5. [Pleasures Differ in Kind] 159

[Happiness: Further Discussion] **162**
6. [Conditions for Happiness] 162
7. [Happiness and Theoretical Study] 163
8. [Theoretical Study and the Other Virtues] 165

[From Ethics to Politics] **167**
9. [Moral Education] 167

Notes **172**
Glossary **315**
Further Reading **355**

PREFACE

This translation seeks to make Aristotle's terse and concentrated Greek fairly intelligible to those who read him in English. Those who want to read through the *Ethics* to grasp the main outlines of Aristotle's position need a translation that can be understood without detailed explanations, and I have tried to keep the needs of these readers in mind. But I have also tried to help those who want to study the *Ethics*, and not merely to read through it; these readers will also want to consult the Notes and Glossary to help them toward a fuller understanding of the text.

I have tried to present the text without too much editorial intervention (though, like other translators, I have presented the division into chapters, which is the result of intervention by previous editors). The headings in the translation are mine, with no authority in Aristotle. Readers should consult the last section of the Introduction before they turn to the translation or Notes. As they read through the *Ethics*, they may want to read through a section of the Introduction before turning to the more detailed discussion in the Notes and Glossary.

At every stage, I have benefited from the work of previous translators and commentators, and especially from the commentaries by Stewart and by Gauthier and Jolif.

The opportunity to prepare a second edition after fifteen years has allowed me to revise the translation at many points. In some places, I have changed my mind about the sense of a particular sentence, or about the best rendering of a recurrent technical term. In other places, more careful attention to the course of the argument, and to the cues that Aristotle offers in his use of particles, has led me to change my mind about the best division of sentences and paragraphs. I have revised the notes so that they now include an outline and summary of each chapter (formerly interpolated in the translation), and I have expanded them to discuss more issues of interpretation.

I am pleased to be able to repeat my earlier thanks to Daniel Devereux, Richard Kraut, Anthony Long, Alexander Nehamas, and Donald Zeyl, and especially to John Cooper and Gail Fine, for their help with the first edition. I am grateful to all the readers who provided comments and criticisms on the first edition; whether or not I agreed with them, I have tried to take account of them, and I hope that they have led me to some improvements in the present edition. Christopher Taylor, Jennifer Whiting, Gail Fine, and, especially, Katherine Woolfitt, have identified many errors in the final typescript. Since I do not imagine that the present version is beyond the need of criticism, I will be equally grateful for further comments and suggestions.

Hackett Publishing Company has made a significant contribution to philosophical publishing and to philosophical education for the last twenty years or more, and I am fortunate to have been associated with it.

T. H. Irwin
Cornell University
Ithaca, New York
August 1999

ABBREVIATIONS AND CONVENTIONS

Works of Aristotle

The works of Aristotle are cited by abbreviations of their conventional Latin or English titles.

APo	Analytica Posteriora	Posterior Analytics
APr	Analytica Priora	Prior Analytics
Catg.	Categoriae	Categories
DA	De Anima	On the Soul
DC	De Caelo	On the Heavens
DI	De Interpretatione	On Interpretation
EE	Ethica Eudemia	Eudemian Ethics
EN	Ethica Nicomachea	Nicomachean Ethics
GA	De Generatione Animalium	Generation of Animals
GC	De Generatione et Corruptione	Generation and Corruption
HA	Historia Animalium	History of Animals
IA	De Incessu Animalium	Progression of Animals
MA	De Motu Animalium	Movement of Animals
Met.	Metaphysica	Metaphysics
Metr.	Meteorologica	Meteorology
MM	Magna Moralia	Great Ethics
PA	De Partibus Animalium	Parts of Animals
Phys.	Physica	Physics
PN	Parva Naturalia	Short Natural Treatises
Poet.	De Arte Poetica	Poetics
Pol.	Politica	Politics
[Probl.]	Problemata	Problems
Rhet.	Rhetorica	Rhetoric
Top.	Topica	Topics

The *Problems* is generally regarded as spurious.

Dialogues of Plato are cited by abbreviated title and standard Stephanus pages.

Other Abbreviations

ROT	The Revised Oxford Translation (see Further Reading [1]).
OCD	*Oxford Classical Dictionary* (see [49]).[1]
OCT	Oxford Classical Text (see [8]).
DK	Diels-Kranz (see [51]).
Kaibel	Kaibel, G., ed. *Comicorum Graecorum Fragmenta* (Berlin, 1899).
Kock	Kock, T., ed. *Comicorum Atticorum Fragmenta* (Leipzig, 1880–1888).
TGF	Nauck, A., ed. *Tragicorum Graecorum Fragmenta*, ed. 2 (Leipzig, 1899).
West	West, M. L., ed. *Delectus ex Elegis et Iambis Graecis* (Oxford, 1980).
CAG	*Commentaria in Aristotelem Graeca* (Berlin, various dates).

1. Numbers in square brackets refer to items listed in Further Reading.

INTRODUCTION

1. Aristotle's Life and Works

Aristotle was born in Stagira in Macedon (now part of northern Greece; see note to i 2.§8, v 7.§1) in 384 B.C. In his lifetime the kingdom of Macedon, first under Philip and then under his son Alexander ('the Great'), conquered the Greek cities in Europe and Asia, and then went on to conquer the Persian Empire. The Macedonian rulers made elaborate efforts to present themselves as Greeks; they were not entirely successful in these efforts, and many Greeks regarded them as foreign invaders. Though Aristotle spent much of his adult life in Athens, he was not an Athenian citizen; he was closely linked to the kings of Macedon (cf. note to vii 7.§6), and he was affected by the volatile relations between the Greek cities, especially Athens, and Macedon.

Aristotle was the son of Nicomachus, a doctor who had been attached to the Macedonian court. (See MEDICINE.[2]) In 367 B.C., Aristotle came to Athens and was a member of PLATO's Academy until the death of Plato in 347. Plato's successor as head of the Academy was his nephew SPEUSIPPUS. At that time, Aristotle left Athens, first for Assos (in Asia Minor), where the pro-Macedonian TYRANT Hermeias was a patron of philosophical studies. Aristotle married Pythias, a niece of Hermeias; they had a daughter, also called Pythias. After Hermeias was killed by the Persians, Aristotle traveled farther (cf. 1155a21–2); he moved on to Lesbos in the eastern Aegean (cf. note to v 10.§7), and then back to Macedon. He was a tutor of Alexander. In 334 he returned to Athens and founded his own school, the Lyceum. After the death of Pythias, Aristotle formed an attachment to Herpyllis, and they had a son Nicomachus (named, following the Greek custom, after his grandfather). In 323 Alexander died; in the resulting outbreak of anti-Macedonian feeling in Athens, Aristotle left for Chalcis, on the island of Euboea (cf. note to ix 6.§3), where he died in 322 B.C. In his will Aristotle directed that Pythias' bones were to be placed in his grave, in accordance with her wishes; he also made provision for the support of Herpyllis and Nicomachus.[3]

2. Words in SMALL CAPITALS refer to entries in the Glossary. Numbers in square brackets refer to items listed in Further Reading. For abbreviations, see the list of Abbreviations and Conventions.

3. Aristotle's will; see ROT, p. 2464.

2. Aristotle's Works

The nearly complete modern English translation of Aristotle's extant works (in ROT) fills about 2,450 pages. Many of his works, however, have been lost, and those that survive complete are quite different in character from many of the lost works.[4] Among the lost works are dialogues, probably similar in character to some of Plato's dialogues, and other treatises designed for publication. Aristotle may refer to some of the lost works when he speaks of his POPULAR writings.

The Aristotelian corpus, as we have it, largely consists of works that appear to be closely related to Aristotle's lectures. Sometimes he seems to refer (see note to ii 7.§1) to 'visual aids' of the sort that might be present in a classroom. Sometimes the grammatically incomplete sentences and compressed allusions suggest notes that a lecturer might expand.

We cannot tell how many of his treatises Aristotle regarded as finished. We probably ought not to treat them as finished literary works. They may be more like files that Aristotle revised, expanded, summarized, or combined, for different teaching purposes, or when new ideas struck him.

In the Greek manuscripts, the corpus is arranged as follows:[5]

1. *Catg., DI, APr, APo, Top.* These are traditionally known as the 'Organon' ('instrument') because they deal with logic (in Aristotle's broad sense), which is an instrument of philosophical thinking, not a discipline with its own specific subject matter.

2. *Phys., DC, GC, Metr., DA, PN, HA, PA, MA, IA, GA.* These belong to natural philosophy, dealing with different aspects of NATURE.

3. *Met.* This deals with 'first philosophy', the study of reality in general. (*EN* i 6 discusses metaphysical topics; cf. note to §13.)

4. *EN, MM, EE, Pol.* These belong to 'practical' philosophy, which deals with ACTION rather than PRODUCTION.

5. *Rhet., Poet.* These deal with PRODUCTION rather than ACTION.[6]

Aristotle presents ETHICS as a distinct discipline, relatively independent of other areas of philosophy (notes to i 6.§13, viii 1.§6; cf. *EE* 1216b35–1217a10). Nonetheless, he often refers to, or relies on, his other

4. Ancient lists of titles of Aristotle's works are printed in ROT, p. 2386.

5. This list excludes (a) works generally agreed to be spurious that have been included in the Aristotelian corpus; (b) the lost works; (c) the *Constitution of Athens* (probably not by Aristotle himself), which was discovered after the standard arrangement of Aristotle's works was established. All of (a) and (c), and some surviving fragments, or supposed fragments, of (b), are included in ROT.

6. For Aristotle's own division of disciplines, see *PA* 640a1; *Met.* 982b11, 993b20, vi 1.

philosophical doctrines. See ACTIVITY, CAPACITY, CAUSE, ETHICS, FUNCTION, HUMAN BEING, SCIENCE, SOUL. Readers will read the *EN* with more understanding if they also read the most immediately relevant parts of Aristotle's other works. For a start, they might try: *Catg*. 1–9 (the doctrine of categories); *APo* i 1–3, ii 19 (on SCIENCE); *Top*. i (on the dialectical method practiced in ETHICS); *Phys*. ii, iii 1 (on NATURE, CAUSE, and MOVEMENT); *DA* i 1, ii 1–4 (on SOUL), ii 5–11 (on PERCEPTION), iii 4 (on UNDERSTANDING), iii 9–11 (on DESIRE and ACTION); *PA* i 1 (on NATURE); *MA* 7 (on practical INFERENCE); *Met*. i 1 (on SCIENCE), 6, 9 (on SOCRATES and PLATO), iv 1–2, ix 1–8 (on CAPACITY and ACTIVITY), xii (on GOD).

3. The Ethical Treatises

Aristotle's ethical theory is mostly contained in three treatises: the *MM*, the *EE*, and the *EN*. The titles of the last two works may reflect a tradition that Eudemus (a member of the Lyceum) and Nicomachus (the son of Aristotle and Herpyllis) edited Aristotle's lectures.

It is widely agreed that the *MM* was not written by Aristotle. But it may well be substantially authentic in content; perhaps it contains a student's notes on a course of lectures by Aristotle earlier than the courses underlying the other two treatises. The *EE* is now widely agreed to be authentic; it is usually (not universally) and reasonably taken to be earlier than the *EN*.

The three books *EN* v–vii are also, according to manuscripts of *EN* and *EE*, the three books *EE* iv–vi. The manuscripts do not say which treatise these three 'common' books originally belonged to, or how they came to belong to both treatises. Stylistic and doctrinal evidence links these books with the rest of the *EE*; but it does not follow that Aristotle did not also intend them to be part of the *EN*. If the *EE* is earlier than the *EN*, Aristotle may have used these books, perhaps revised, in his new course of lectures. A decision on this issue is related to a decision on the relative date of the two treatises. (See further the notes to vii 11.§1, x 6.§1.)

We should not infer, then, that the *EN* has reached us in exactly the form in which Aristotle intended to leave it. If it is unfinished, we can more easily understand the presence of two discussions of pleasure, and of two discussions of the VOLUNTARY in iii 1 and v 8 (a common book).

4. Outline of the *Ethics*

We can gain some idea of the contents and structure of the *EN* from this outline:

A. i 1–12. HAPPINESS, the ultimate human good.

B. i 13. Happiness requires VIRTUES of character and of thought.

C. ii 1–9. Virtue of character: the STATES of human beings that secure their happiness.

D. iii 1–5. Preconditions of virtue: VOLUNTARY action and responsibility.

E. iii 6 to v 11. The individual virtues of character.

F. vi 1–13. Virtues of thought.

G. vii 1–10. INCONTINENCE and related conditions.

H. vii 11–14. PLEASURE.

I. viii–ix. Friendship.

J. x 1–5. Pleasure.

K. x 6–8. Happiness and theoretical STUDY.

L. x 9. Ethics, moral education, and politics.

This outline suggests that in some places the standard division into books represents the natural divisions in Aristotle's argument, and in other places it does not. The division into books goes back to the early editors of Aristotle's works in antiquity. It was partly determined by the requirements of ancient book production; and so we should not be surprised if it fails to match the argument of the work.

This order is similar to the order of the *EE*, up to the end of H; shortly after H our manuscripts of the *EE* break off, and we do not know what, if anything, corresponded to J to L above. The *MM* is less similar in structure, but it covers these topics in more or less the same order up to I; it breaks off in the discussion of friendship. Hence the order of treatment in A through I is likely to be Aristotle's own order.

We can follow the development of Aristotle's argument if we examine the main themes. The following sections of this introduction briefly present the main themes, without considering all the relevant questions of interpretation; some of these questions are taken up in the Notes.

5. Happiness

Aristotle conceives ETHICS as a part of POLITICAL SCIENCE; he treats the *EN* and the *Politics* as parts of a single inquiry (*EN* x 9; cf. note to i 2.§9). Ethics seeks to discover the good for an individual and a community (*EN* i 2), and so it begins with an examination of happiness. Happiness is the right starting point for an ethical theory because, in Aristotle's view, rational agents necessarily choose and deliberate with a view to their ultimate good, which is happiness; it is the ultimate end, since we want it for its own sake, and we want other things for its sake. If it is to be the ultimate end, happiness must be COMPLETE.

To find a more definite account of happiness, Aristotle argues from the human FUNCTION, the characteristic activity that is essential to a human being, in the same way as a purely nutritive life is essential to a plant, and a life guided by sense perception and desire is essential to an animal (see notes to i 7.§12–13). Since a human being is essentially a rational agent, the function of a human being is a life guided by practical reason. The good life for a human being must be good for a being with the function of a human being; hence it must be a good life guided by practical reason, and hence it must be a life in accordance with the VIRTUE that is needed for achieving one's good. The human good, therefore, is an ACTIVITY of the SOUL in accordance with complete virtue in a complete life.

Aristotle believes that this outline of happiness (1098a20–2) is definite enough to rule out three serious errors and to point us in the right direction. He develops these points in i 5, 8–12. (1) We must reject the life devoted purely to pleasure (1095b19–20), for reasons that Aristotle makes clear only in x 2–5. This life is incomplete because it allows no essential role to rational activity; and mere pleasure without rational activity is not the good for a rational agent (cf. 1174a1–4). Since a life of pleasure can be improved on in this way, pleasure cannot be the good (1172b28–32). Hence Aristotle rejects hedonism. (2) SOCRATES' view that virtue is sufficient for happiness conflicts with common beliefs (1096a2). Virtue alone does not constitute a complete and self-sufficient life. For external misfortunes impede rational activity (1100b29–30, 1153b14–25), and therefore preclude happiness (1100a5–9). (3) Still, no matter what we have to lose as a result of being virtuous, we have better reason to choose virtue than we have to choose any combination of other goods that are incompatible with it (1100b30–1101a8). Hence Aristotle claims that virtuous activity CONTROLS happiness.

6. Virtue of Character

If virtuous activity controls happiness, we need to know what the relevant virtues are to secure happiness (i 13). Since Aristotle recognizes both rational and nonrational DESIRES, he argues that the excellent and virtuous condition of the soul will include virtues of both the rational and the nonrational parts. The virtues of the rational part are the virtues of thought, discussed in Book vi. The virtues of character are the various ways in which the nonrational elements cooperate with reason, so that human beings fulfill their function well and in accordance with complete virtue. Aristotle discusses these virtues in Books ii–v.

He defines a virtue of character as a STATE, in order to distinguish a virtue from a CAPACITY and from a FEELING (ii 5). I may have a capacity without using it properly on the right occasions; for instance, I may have medical skill even if I do not bother to use it at all, or if I use it to poison my patients. Similarly, I may have a feeling (of sympathy, hatred, anger, etc.) without guiding it properly to the right objects. To be a generous person, I must not only know how to give money on the right occasions, and have generous impulses; I must also direct my capacities and feelings to the right goals, so that I act from the right desires, for the right reasons, and on the right occasions (cf. *Met*. 1025a1–13).

Aristotle does not treat virtues as simply means to virtuous action. Actions may be virtuous even though they are not done for the virtuous person's reasons (1105a26–b9, 1144a11–20). But agents are not virtuous unless they do the virtuous action because they have decided to do it for its own sake. Aristotle assumes that in praising and valuing virtuous people we do not value simply their reliable tendency to produce virtuous actions; we also value the state of character that they display in their actions. The discussion of VOLUNTARY action shows us the circumstances in which the praiseworthy state is displayed in actions.

In arguing that a virtue of character must be a 'mean' or an 'intermediate' state, Aristotle does not recommend moderation in actions or in feelings for its own sake. He does not suggest, for instance, that if we achieve the mean in relation to anger, we will never be more than moderately angry; on the contrary, the virtuous person will be extremely angry on the occasions when extreme anger is called for. (He discusses anger more fully in iv 5.) Still, Aristotle's doctrine is more than the trivial advice that we should do what is appropriate to the occasion. For in claiming that a mean state in relation to nonrational impulses and appetites is possible and desirable, he rejects other views about the desirable condition of FEELINGS. The views he rejects include these: (1) Virtue consists in indulgence of nonrational impulses, leaving them completely unchecked. (2) Virtue requires suppression of nonrational impulses (1104b24–6). (3) Virtue is nothing more than control of nonrational impulses by rational desire. (cf. 1102b13–20). In Aristotle's view, (3) is closest to being right, but is nonetheless mistaken, because it confuses virtue with continence (see INCONTINENCE). Contrary to (3), virtue also demands harmony and agreement between the nonrational and the rational part, under the guidance of the rational part.

The task of moral education, therefore, is not merely to subject the nonrational part of the soul to practical reason. Virtuous people allow reasonable satisfaction to their appetites; they do not suppress all their fears; they do not disregard all their feelings of pride or shame or resentment (1126a3–8), or their desire for other people's good opinion. Brave people are appropriately afraid of serious danger (1115b10–20), and if the cause is not worth the danger they withdraw; but when the cause justifies their standing firm, their fear is not so strong that they have to struggle against it.

In claiming that the virtuous person makes a DECISION (iii 2–3) to do the virtuous action for its own sake, Aristotle implies that a certain pattern of desire and deliberation (1113a2–12, 1139a21–b5) is characteristic of the virtuous person.

In claiming that the mean is determined by the PRUDENT person, he refers to the intellectual virtue that is responsible for good deliberation (1140a24–31). These aspects of his definition of virtue of character imply that it is inseparable from virtue of intellect.

Aristotle illustrates and explains these different aspects of virtue of character in Books iii–vii.

7. Voluntary Action and Responsibility

Aristotle discusses VOLUNTARY action and conditions for moral responsibility (iii 1–5), because he wants to show how his account of the nature of virtue supports the common belief that we are justly praised and blamed both for virtuous and vicious actions and for being virtuous and vicious people. He agrees that the proper objects of praise and blame are the things that we ourselves, rather than necessity or fortune, are responsible for (see CAUSE; *EE* 1223a9–15); he tries to show that we are responsible for our virtuous and vicious actions and characters.

He claims that we are open to praise and blame for our voluntary actions, and that voluntary actions are those that are caused neither by force nor ignorance, but have their 'PRINCIPLE in us', insofar as we know the particular circumstances of the action (1111a22–4). These actions are the appropriate objects of praise and blame.

According to Aristotle, these criteria for voluntary action imply that nonrational animals also act voluntarily (1111a24–6). These nonrational agents, however, are not open to praise or blame. Ordinary human voluntary action is open to praise and blame, because its principle is 'in us' (1110a17–18, 1111a22–4, 1113b20–1) as rational agents. (That is why a mere bodily process, such as aging, over which we have no rational control, has no principle in us; cf. v 8.§3 and note.) Voluntary action is in our control as rational agents; hence we are justly praised and blamed for it.

It follows that we are held responsible for our actions insofar as they reflect our character, decisions, and hence (given Aristotle's analysis of DECISION in ii 2–3) our deliberation about the good. For similar reasons, Aristotle believes that our character and outlook are also open to justified and effective criticism, since we are responsible for our characters. He appeals to the process of acquisition of the virtues to show that we are responsible for becoming virtuous or vicious (iii 5). He implies that it is in our rational control (when, presumably, we pass beyond the pure habituation of early childhood, discussed in Book ii; see note to iii 5.§10) to affect the way our character develops; and insofar as this is in our rational control, we are justly held responsible for the resulting state of our character.

8. Prudence and Virtue

Why does Aristotle take prudence to be necessary for virtue of character? (See 6, Virtue of Character, above; notes to vi 12.§6, 8; 13.§2, 7.) If correct decision and prudence are expressed in action on good deliberation, then the special role of practical reason in virtue seems to be its role in deliberation. But in Aristotle deliberation seems to have a rather narrow scope, insofar as it is concerned with what 'promotes' an end (see DECISION). If 'x promotes y' is interpreted as 'x is an instrumental means to y', Aristotle claims that deliberation and prudence are concerned only with instrumental means to ends. In that case, they tell us how to find the means to happiness, but they do not tell us anything about what happiness is.

Aristotle need not, however, restrict the scope of practical reason in this way, if 'x promotes y' is not confined to instrumental means. If he allows deliberation about components of ends, prudence finds the actions that promote happiness insofar as they are parts of the happy life. Such actions are (a) to be chosen for their own sake, as being their own end, rather than (b) to be chosen simply as instrumental means to some further end. See ACTION (3), note to vi 5.§1.

The wide scope of deliberation makes it clearer why decision is an essential element in virtue and why Aristotle claims—surprisingly at first sight—that we can decide on an action for its own sake, even though decision is always about what promotes an end. For the virtuous person's decision is the result of deliberation about the composition of happiness; and this deliberation results in specific claims about which actions are noninstrumentally good components of happiness. These are the actions that the virtuous person decides on, both for their own sakes and for the sake of happiness (cf. notes to i 7.§5, vi 9.§7).

In claiming that prudence involves deliberation, Aristotle also emphasizes the importance of its grasping the relevant features of a particular situation, since this is necessary if deliberation is to result in a correct decision about what to do here and now. The right moral choice requires experience of particular situations, since general rules cannot be applied mechanically to particular situations (see notes to ix 2). The relevant aspect of prudence is a sort of PERCEPTION or intuitive UNDERSTANDING of the right aspects of particular situations (see notes to vi 8.§9, 11.§5).

9. Incontinence

After describing the virtues of character and thought, Aristotle discusses the problem of incontinence (vii 1–10). Incontinence (or 'weakness of will') is usually taken to consist in knowing that x is better than y, but choosing y nonetheless. SOCRATES, as Aristotle understands him, denies the possibility of incontinence and explains apparently incontinent behavior as the result of ignorance of the good. In i 13 and iii 2, Aristotle suggests an account of incontinence much closer to the one that Plato offers in *Republic* iv: Incontinence results when an agent's nonrational desires are stronger than his rational desire and overcome it. His full account of incontinence, however, includes both Socratic and Platonic elements in a rather puzzling combination. This is one of the most difficult parts of the *EN*; the notes on vii 3 try to set out some of the questions of interpretation.

It is clear, at any rate, that Aristotle rejects Socrates' position; he takes it to go wrong in treating the allegedly incontinent person's error as simple ignorance about what is better and worse. Contrary to Socrates' view, the incontinent person makes the right DECISION and draws the right conclusion from his practical inference. His nonrational desires cause him to choose[7] what will satisfy these desires, and to act against his correct decision.

Nonetheless, Aristotle accepts part of the Socratic account, because he thinks incontinent action must be explained by some sort of ignorance. The relevant sort of ignorance is caused by disordered nonrational desires; it is not ignorance of general principles (that we ought not to steal, for example), but of the application of these principles to particular cases. Aristotle seems to suggest that the incontinent is someone who agrees that he ought not to overindulge his appetites, agrees that eating these six cakes would be overindulgence, and hence makes the correct decision not to eat them, but nonetheless, when he eats them, fails to recognize that this is really a case of overindulgence.

One might reasonably ask (i) whether this is a satisfactory account of incontinence; (ii) why Aristotle believes that a true account ought to attribute some role to ignorance; and (iii) whether he has identified a plausible type of ignorance.

10. Pleasure

Aristotle's demand for the virtuous person to decide on the virtuous action for its own sake is connected with two further claims. (1) The virtuous person must take pleasure in virtuous action as such (1099a7–21, 1104b3–11). (2) In doing so, the virtuous person has the most pleasant life. In these claims Aristotle relies on his views about the nature of pleasure and its role in happiness.

To begin with, Aristotle identifies the life of pleasure with the life devoted to the life of rather gross sensual pleasures (i 5; see 5, Happiness, above). Books vii and x, however, contain quite elaborate discussions of the nature of pleasure and the different values of different types of pleasure (see end of 3, The Ethical Treatises, above). Aristotle believes that true judgments about pleasure imply that the virtuous person's life is also

7. On the use of pronouns, and of 'man' and 'person', see PERSON.

the most pleasant life. (On some apparent differences between the two discussions, see notes to x 3.§11, 5.§7.)

He rejects the view that pleasure is some uniform sensation to which different kinds of pleasant action are connected only causally and externally (in the way that reading many boring books might induce the same feeling of boredom). Instead he argues that the specific pleasure taken in x rather than y is internally related to doing x rather than y, and essentially depends on pursuing x for x's own sake. In that case, different pleasures—for instance, the pleasure of lying on the beach in the sun and the pleasure of solving a crossword puzzle—are not two instances of the same sensation that just happen to have different causes. The two different objects (i.e., the activities we take the pleasure in) are essential to the character of the pleasures themselves.

Aristotle tries to express this relation of a pleasure to the activity that is its object by describing the pleasure as a 'consequent end' (see note to x 4.§8) resulting from an ACTION or ACTIVITY, not from a PRODUCTION or process (see MOVEMENT), as such. The value of this pleasure depends on the value of the activity on which the pleasure follows (see notes to x 5). The virtuous person has the most pleasant life; but this life cannot be devoted exclusively to the pursuit of pleasure.

11. The Scope of the Virtues

Aristotle's Greek for 'virtue of character', *ēthikē aretē*, rendered into Latin as 'virtus moralis', is the origin of the English 'moral virtue'. Some readers, however, suggest that the Aristotelian virtues described in Books iii, iv, and v are not really moral virtues at all. If we assume that morality and moral virtue are essentially concerned with the good of others, we might think Aristotle is relatively unconcerned with morality. Some of the virtues seem to be largely self-regarding (e.g., temperance, magnanimity); some seem to involve good manners or good taste rather than strictly moral qualities (e.g., magnificence, truthfulness, wit), and only some seem to deal with the good of others (bravery, mildness, generosity). Only one virtue—justice (in its general form)—is clearly focused on the good of others in its own right (1129b25–1130a5).

This description of the virtues, however, underestimates ways in which the virtues of character as a whole display the impartial concern for others that is often ascribed to morality. The virtuous person decides on the virtuous action because it is FINE; indeed, fine action is the action that achieves the mean (see notes to iv 1.§7, 2.§7). The fine systematically promotes the good of others. This is why Aristotle takes general justice to be nothing more than the exercise of the other virtues of character (see note to v 1.§20).

Happiness, as Aristotle conceives it, requires activity in accordance with complete virtue (see note to i 7.§15). Why should complete virtue require concern for the good of others? In Aristotle's view, a human being is a political animal insofar as human capacities and aims are completely fulfilled only in a community; the individual's happiness must involve the good of fellow members of a community (1097b8–11, 1169b16–19).

Aristotle defends this claim in his discussion of FRIENDSHIP. All three of the main types of friendship (for pleasure, for advantage, and for the good) are concerned with the good of the other person; but only the best sort of friendship—friendship for the good between virtuous people—involves A's concern for B's good for B's own sake and for B's essential character (see notes to viii 3.§1–6).

In the best sort of friendship the friend is 'another himself', so that if A and B are friends, A takes the attitudes to B that A also takes to A. Aristotle uses this feature of friendship to explain why friendship is part of a complete and self-sufficient life (see ix 9 and notes). Friendship involves 'living together' (i.e., sharing the activities one counts as especially important in one's life; see note to viii 5.§3), and especially the sharing of reasoning and thinking. Friends cooperate in deliberation, decision, and action; and the thoughts and actions of each provide reasons for the future thoughts and actions of the other. If A regards B as another self, then A will be concerned about B's aims and plans, and pleased by B's successes no less than by A's own. The cooperative aspects of friendship with B more fully realize A's own capacities as a rational agent, and so promote A's happiness more fully.

For this reason Aristotle thinks that the full development of a human being requires concern for the good of others. He defends his claim initially for friendship between individuals, but also for the type of friendship that forms a CITY, the 'complete COMMUNITY' (*Pol.* 1252a1–7, b27–30) that achieves the complete life that is identified with happiness.

12. Two Conceptions of Happiness?

In x 6–8, Aristotle returns to the discussion of happiness. He argues that the human FUNCTION is especially realized by the pure intellectual activity of STUDY—the contemplation of scientific and philosophical truths, apart from any attempt to apply them to practice. Since human happiness consists in the fulfillment of the human function, study is a supremely important element in happiness. For it is the highest fulfillment of our nature as rational beings; it is the sort of rational activity that we share with the gods, who are rational beings with no need to apply reason to practice. Aristotle infers that study is the happiest life available to us, insofar as we have the rational intellects we share with the gods (see notes to x 7).

One might conclude that Aristotle actually identifies study with happiness: Study is the only noninstrumental good that is part of happiness, and the moral virtues are to be valued, from the point of view of happiness, simply as means to study. It is natural to take x 6–8 in this way; if one does, it is tempting to understand the argument in i 7 from the human FUNCTION as an argument to show that happiness is to be identified with the theoretical reasoning involved in study (see, especially, x 7.§9, 8.§8, and notes).

If this is Aristotle's view, however, two difficulties arise. (1) It is difficult to see how the purely instrumental status that seems to be ascribed to virtue of character in x 6–8 is compatible with Aristotle's repeated claims in the rest of the *EN* that virtues and virtuous actions are to be chosen for their own sake. (2) It is even difficult to see how the virtues of character are even the best instrumental means to happiness. Even if some virtuous actions are instrumental means to study, the motives demanded of the virtuous person do not seem useful for those who aim at study.

In the light of these difficulties, some readers who are convinced that x 6–8 identify happiness with study have inferred that Books i through ix defend a 'comprehensive' conception of happiness (as explained in notes to i 7.§3–8), and that x 6–8 defend an incompatible conception of happiness as study. One might argue that these are two alternative conceptions of happiness. Perhaps happiness as study is for those who are capable of it and in the conditions that allow single-minded devotion to it, and happiness as the exercise of the virtues of character is the best that is available to those who are less well endowed, or who are in less favorable circumstances.

Before we embrace any of these views about Aristotle's eventual conception of happiness, we ought to ask whether it is really certain that in x 6–8 he identifies happiness with study. The notes on these chapters suggest some grounds for uncertainty. One might take Aristotle to mean that study is the best component of happiness, but not the whole of happiness. If we were pure intellects with no other desires and no bodies, study would be the whole of our good. Since, however, we are not in fact merely intellects, our good is the good of the whole human being. Since study is not the complete good for a human being (see note to x 8.§6), it is not our complete good. Though study is the single most self-sufficient activity (insofar as it is the single activity that comes closest to being self-sufficient; see note to x 7.§4), this degree of self-sufficiency does not justify the identification of study with happiness. For Aristotle has argued that happiness must be complete, and for this reason he argues that neither virtue alone nor pleasure alone can be happiness. He should not, then, agree that study is happiness just because it is invulnerable and self-contained.

If this is Aristotle's view, study fits the account of happiness that we seem to find in the rest of the *EN*. According to this account, the virtues of character, and the actions that accord with them, deserve to be chosen for their own sakes as components of happiness. In the virtuous person, they regulate the choice of other goods, and so they also regulate choices about study. Admittedly, Aristotle does not explain how we should decide on particular occasions whether to pursue study or to prefer one of the other components of happiness; but he does not seem to retreat from his conception of happiness as a compound of rational activities that assigns a central and dominant place to the moral virtues. The *Politics* may be taken to develop this conception of happiness, since it sets study in the context of a social order regulated by the virtues of character (see, especially, *Pol.* vii 3–4, 9, 13).

13. This Edition

Modern editions of the Greek text of the *EN* are based on Greek manuscripts copied in the Byzantine period (from the tenth to the fifteenth centuries)[8] from manuscripts derived indirectly from the edition of Aristotle's works produced by Andronicus in the first century B.C. Like every other editor and translator, I deviate from, or add to, the transmitted text in various ways. Readers, especially those unused to Greek and Latin texts, should bear these points in mind:

1. The transmitted text is usually fairly sound; but numerous variations and imperfections in the manuscripts require decisions by editors and translators. I have taken the OCT (see Further Reading [8]) as the basis of the translation, and have tried to mention deviations (on points other than punctuation) in the Notes. These deviations express different judgments (a) about which reading is to be preferred in cases where the manuscripts differ, or (b) about how to emend the manuscript reading, in cases where it does not seem to give satisfactory sense, or (c) about whether some words are intrusions into the manuscripts, not part of what Aristotle actually wrote, or (d) about whether something has fallen out of the manuscripts and needs to be supplied, or (e) about whether the manuscripts have the text in the right order.

2. Readers do not always realize that the division of books into chapters does not go back to antiquity, still less to Aristotle; it inevitably reflects the views of interpreters. This is especially clear in the case of the *EN*, since modern editions of the Greek text actually print two capitulations (both of medieval origin). I have included the first (marked by Roman figures in OCT) for reference. Where the other capitulation differs, I have left an extra space.

3. Modern editions also print the division of chapters (according to the first numeration) into sections (which go back at least to the edition by Carl Zell in 1820). I have also reproduced these sections (marked

8. On ancient manuscripts, see OCD, s.v. 'Books, Greek and Roman', 'Palaeography', 'Textual criticism'.

by §), since they reflect a generally sensible view of the structure of Aristotle's argument. In cases where I do not agree with them (where my paragraphs diverge from Zell's sections), it may be useful to readers to consider the alternative interpretation implied by Zell's division. The marginal line numbering is derived from Immanuel Bekker's edition of Aristotle (1831).[9] The Notes refer to Zell sections (so that 'i 7.§3' refers to Book i, chapter 7, section 3). References are given to Zell sections (or to Bekker lines, for greater precision).

4. The headings to each chapter, book, and section are mine and have no authority in the manuscripts; these titles are enclosed in square brackets.

This translation is intended for readers who want to understand the *EN* in detail, and not merely to acquire a general impression of it. Any translator who wants to be reasonably accurate in details that matter to the philosophical reader has to face some difficulties presented by the *EN*:

1. Aristotle's writing is often compressed and allusive; to convey in English the impression made by Aristotle's Greek, a translator would have to produce a version that would be hard to understand without a detailed commentary. If, however, translators set out to make Aristotle readily intelligible to the English reader, they will have to expand, interpret, and paraphrase to an extent that intrudes on the commentator's role. I have used bracketed supplements in cases where it seemed reasonable to point out to the reader that no precise equivalent for the bracketed words appears in the Greek text. Readers should by no means suppose that everything not enclosed in brackets uncontroversially corresponds to something in Aristotle's text. If they consult the Notes, they should be able to discover cases where my rendering is free or controversial.

2. Some of Aristotle's central philosophical terms cannot easily be translated uniformly; it is difficult, for instance, to translate *archē* (see PRINCIPLE) and *logos* (see REASON) by the same English term wherever they occur. But one's choice of rendering often requires a decision about the course of the argument. (See, e.g., notes to i 4.§5–7, 7.§20.)

3. Aristotle has come to us through medieval Latin philosophy, and some English equivalents of Latin terms (such as 'substance', 'essence', 'incontinence') have come to be standard renderings for

9. For instance, '1094a10' refers to line 10 of the left-hand column of page 1094 of Bekker's edition. Since Bekker's pagination is continuous, a Bekker page and line uniquely identify a particular passage. These Bekker pages and lines are standardly used to refer to passages in Aristotle. Since they refer to pages and lines of the Greek text, they correspond only roughly to an English translation.

some of Aristotle's Greek terms. These English terms, however, no longer convey in modern English what the medieval Latin terms conveyed, and so they may be misleading. Still, an attempt to purge a translation of these terms derived from Latin would conceal an important thread in the history of philosophy. (See PRUDENCE, VOLUNTARY.) I have been reluctant to discard these traditional renderings (though sometimes I have overcome this reluctance); though they may mislead readers who do not study the terms in their context (with the help of the Glossary), they are probably no more misleading than the superficially more contemporary renderings that one might choose instead.

4. Greek tolerates longer sentences than English; hypotactic constructions (with several long subordinate clauses) are common. The paratactic character of modern English often encourages the translator to break one complex Greek sentence into two or more English sentences. Sometimes, however, the structure of an argument can be more clearly expressed in a long sentence forming a logical unit; that is why some sentences in the translation are more complex than a contemporary English sentence would normally be (see, e.g., ix 9.§5).

5. It is characteristic of Greek to begin sentences with connecting particles. Concern for English style would require omitting many of these particles in a translation. Omission of them, however, may remove important information. When Aristotle connects two clauses or sentences with 'for', he normally indicates that the second clause gives some reason for what has been said in the first clause; such information about the structure of the argument is useful to the philosophical reader. Hence the translation includes more connectives ('for', 'but', 'however', and so on) than are usual in contemporary English, and also marks Aristotle's repeated use of a given connective with a special force (see note to i 1.§1 on 'that is why', and note to vii 2.§6 on 'further').

The Notes and Glossary are essential adjuncts to the translation. The Notes list textual variations from the OCT and give the sources for Aristotle's references to other authors. They suggest alternative translations (in some important passages), or more literal translations (in cases where expansion or paraphrase is needed for the sake of intelligibility; see, e.g., note to i 7.§8). The Notes also contain some very selective discussion of the course of Aristotle's argument, and some help in understanding passages that seem both difficult and important. In particular, they seek to help readers who are trying to grasp the connection of thought between one sentence and the next.

The Notes contain only a few comments on historical events, proper names (for example, Priam, Thales, Sparta), and so on. Readers must be prepared to look these up in reference books, among which OCD is especially useful. A few references to OCD are included.

The Glossary indicates the correspondence between Greek terms and their English renderings. It also tries to explain some of Aristotle's terms and to sketch some of the philosophical doctrines and assumptions that they convey. A word in small capital letters in the Notes directs the reader to the relevant entry in the Glossary. One way to understand Aristotle better is to look up the passages cited in the entries in the Glossary and to examine them in their context.

An asterisk (*) in the translation marks the last word of a passage discussed in the Notes. Aristotle's works are cited throughout by the abbreviated titles given earlier in the list of Abbreviations and Conventions.

NICOMACHEAN ETHICS

BOOK I

[HAPPINESS]

1

[Ends and Goods]

§1 Every craft and every line of inquiry, and likewise every action and decision, seems to seek some good;* that is why some people were right to describe the good as what everything seeks.* §2 But the ends [that are sought] appear to differ; some are activities, and others are products apart from the activities.* Wherever there are ends apart from the actions, the products are by nature better than the activities. 1094a 5

§3 Since there are many actions, crafts, and sciences, the ends turn out to be many as well; for health is the end of medicine, a boat of boat building, victory of generalship, and wealth of household management. §4 But some of these pursuits are subordinate to some one capacity; for instance, bridle making and every other science producing equipment for horses are subordinate to horsemanship, while this and every action in warfare are, in turn, subordinate to generalship, and in the same way other pursuits are subordinate to further ones.* In all such cases, then,* the ends of the ruling sciences are more choiceworthy than all the ends subordinate to them, since the lower ends are also pursued for the sake of the higher. §5 Here it does not matter whether the ends of the actions are the activities themselves, or something apart from them, as in the sciences we have mentioned. 10 15

2

[The Highest Good and Political Science]

§1 Suppose, then, that the things achievable by action have some end that we wish for because of itself, and because of which we wish for the other things, and that we do not choose everything because of something else—for if we do, it will go on without limit, so that desire will prove to be empty and futile. Clearly, this end will be the good, that is to say, the best good.* 20

1094a §2 Then does knowledge of this good carry great weight for [our] way of life, and would it make us better able, like archers who have a target to 25 aim at, to hit the right mark?* §3 If so, we should try to grasp, in outline at any rate, what the good is, and which is its proper science or capacity.

§4 It seems proper to the most controlling science—the highest ruling science.* §5 And this appears characteristic of political science. §6 For it is the one that prescribes which of the sciences ought to be stud- 1094b ied in cities, and which ones each class in the city should learn, and how far; indeed we see that even the most honored capacities—generalship, household management, and rhetoric, for instance—are subordinate to 5 it. §7 And since it uses the other sciences concerned with action,* and moreover legislates what must be done and what avoided, its end will include the ends of the other sciences, and so this will be the human good. §8 For even if the good is the same for a city as for an individual, still the good of the city is apparently a greater and more complete good to acquire and preserve. For while it is satisfactory to acquire and pre- 10 serve the good even for an individual, it is finer and more divine to acquire and preserve it for a people and for cities.* And so, since our line of inquiry seeks these [goods, for an individual and for a community], it is a sort of political science.*

3

[The Method of Political Science]

Our discussion will be adequate if we make things perspicuous enough to accord with the subject matter; for we would not seek the same degree of exactness in all sorts of arguments alike, any more than in the products 15 of different crafts.* §2 Now, fine and just things, which political science examines, differ and vary so much as to seem to rest on convention only, not on nature.* §3 But [this is not a good reason, since] goods also vary in the same way, because they result in harm to many people—for some have been destroyed because of their wealth, others because of their 20 bravery.* §4 And so, since this is our subject and these are our premises, we shall be satisfied to indicate the truth roughly and in outline; since our subject and our premises are things that hold good usually [but not universally], we shall be satisfied to draw conclusions of the same sort.

Each of our claims, then, ought to be accepted in the same way [as claiming to hold good usually]. For the educated person seeks exactness 25 in each area to the extent that the nature of the subject allows; for apparently it is just as mistaken to demand demonstrations from a rhetorician as to accept [merely] persuasive arguments from a mathematician.* 1095a §5 Further, each person judges rightly what he knows, and is a good judge about that; hence the good judge in a given area is the person educated in that area, and the unqualifiedly good judge is the person educated in every area. *1095a*

This is why a youth is not a suitable student of political science; for he lacks experience of the actions in life, which are the subject and premises of our arguments. §6 Moreover, since he tends to follow his feelings, his study will be futile and useless; for the end [of political science] is action, not knowledge.* §7 It does not matter whether he is young in years or immature in character, since the deficiency does not depend on age, but results from following his feelings in his life and in a given pursuit; for an immature person, like an incontinent person, gets no benefit from his knowledge. But for those who accord with reason in forming their desires and in their actions, knowledge of political science will be of great benefit. 5 10

§8 These are the preliminary points about the student, about the way our claims are to be accepted, and about what we propose to do.*

4

[Common Beliefs]

Let us, then, begin again.* Since every sort of knowledge and decision* pursues some good, what is the good that we say political science seeks? What, [in other words,] is the highest of all the goods achievable in action? 15

§2 As far as its name goes, most people virtually agree; for both the many and the cultivated call it happiness, and they suppose that living well and doing well are the same as being happy.* But they disagree about what happiness is, and the many do not give the same answer as the wise.* 20

§3 For the many think it is something obvious and evident—for instance, pleasure, wealth, or honor. Some take it to be one thing, others another. Indeed, the same person often changes his mind; for when he has fallen ill, he thinks happiness is health, and when he has fallen into poverty, he thinks it is wealth. And when they are conscious of their own ignorance, they admire anyone who speaks of something grand and above their heads. [Among the wise,] however, some used to think that besides these many goods there is some other good that exists in its own right and that causes all these goods to be goods.* 25

§4 Presumably, then, it is rather futile to examine all these beliefs, and it is enough to examine those that are most current or seem to have some argument for them. 30

§5 We must notice, however, the difference between arguments from principles and arguments toward principles.* For indeed Plato was right to be puzzled about this, when he used to ask if [the argument] set out from the principles or led toward them*—just as on a race course the path may go from the starting line to the far end,* or back again. For we should 1095b

1095b certainly begin from things known, but things are known in two ways;* for some are known to us, some known without qualification. Presumably, then, *we* ought to begin from things known to *us*.

5 §6 That is why we need to have been brought up in fine habits if we are to be adequate students of fine and just things, and of political questions generally. §7 For we begin from the [belief] that [something is true]; if this is apparent enough to us, we can begin without also [knowing] why [it is true].* Someone who is well brought up has the beginnings, or can easily acquire them.* Someone who neither has them nor 10 can acquire them should listen to Hesiod:* 'He who grasps everything himself is best of all; he is noble also who listens to one who has spoken well; but he who neither grasps it himself nor takes to heart what he hears from another is a useless man.'

5

[The Three Lives]

But let us begin again from the point from which we digressed.* For, it would seem, people quite reasonably reach their conception of the good, 15 i.e., of happiness, from the lives [they lead]; §2 for there are roughly three most favored lives: the lives of gratification, of political activity, and, third, of study.*

The many, the most vulgar, would seem to conceive the good and happiness as pleasure, and hence they also like the life of gratification. 20 §3 In this they appear completely slavish, since the life they decide on is a life for grazing animals.* Still, they have some argument in their defense, since many in positions of power feel as Sardanapallus* felt, [and also choose this life].

§4 The cultivated people, those active [in politics], conceive the good as honor, since this is more or less the end [normally pursued] in the political life. This, however, appears to be too superficial to be what we 25 are seeking;* for it seems to depend more on those who honor than on the one honored, whereas we intuitively believe that the good is something of our own and hard to take from us.* §5 Further, it would seem, they pursue honor to convince themselves that they are good; at any rate, they seek to be honored by prudent people, among people who know them, 30 and for virtue. It is clear, then, that—in their view at any rate—virtue is superior [to honor].

§6 Perhaps, indeed, one might conceive virtue more than honor to be the end of the political life. However, this also is apparently too incomplete [to be the good]. For it seems possible for someone to possess virtue 1096a but be asleep or inactive throughout his life, and, moreover, to suffer the worst evils and misfortunes. If this is the sort of life he leads, no one would count him happy, except to defend a philosopher's paradox.*

Enough about this, since it has been adequately discussed in the popular works* as well. *1096a*

§7 The third life is the life of study, which we shall examine in what follows.* 5

§8 The moneymaker's life is in a way forced on him [not chosen for itself];* and clearly wealth is not the good we are seeking, since it is [merely] useful, [choiceworthy only] for some other end. Hence one would be more inclined to suppose that [any of] the goods mentioned earlier is the end, since they are liked for themselves. But apparently they are not [the end] either; and many arguments have been presented 10 against them.* Let us, then, dismiss them.

6

[The Platonic Form of the Good]

Presumably, though, we had better examine the universal good, and puzzle out what is meant in speaking of it.* This sort of inquiry is, to be sure, unwelcome to us, because those who introduced the Forms were friends* of ours; still, it presumably seems better, indeed only right, to destroy 15 even what is close to us if that is the way to preserve truth. We must especially do this as philosophers, [lovers of wisdom]; for though we love both the truth and our friends, reverence is due to the truth first.

§2 Those who introduced this view did not mean to produce an Idea for any [series] in which they spoke of prior and posterior [members];* that was why they did not mean to establish an Idea [of number] for [the series of] numbers. But the good is spoken of both in what-it-is [that is, 20 substance], and in quality and relative;* and what exists in its own right, that is, substance, is by nature prior to the relative,* since a relative would seem to be an appendage and coincident of being. And so there is no common Idea over these.

§3 Further, good is spoken of in as many ways as being [is spoken of]:* in what-it-is, as god and mind;* in quality, as the virtues; in quantity, as the 25 measured amount; in relative, as the useful; in time, as the opportune moment; in place, as the [right] situation; and so on. Hence it is clear that the good cannot be some common and single universal; for if it were, it would be spoken of in only one [of the types of] predication, not in them all.

§4 Further, if a number of things have a single Idea, there is also a sin- 30 gle science of them; hence [if there were an Idea of good] there would also be some single science of all goods. But, in fact, there are many sciences even of the goods under one [type of] predication; for the science of the opportune moment, for instance, in war is generalship, in disease medicine. And similarly the science of the measured amount in food is medicine, in exertion gymnastics. [Hence there is no single science of the good, and so no Idea.]

1096a35 §5 One might be puzzled about what [the believers in Ideas] really 1096b mean in speaking of the So-and-So Itself,* since Man Itself and man* have one and the same account of man; for insofar as each is man, they will not differ at all. If that is so, then [Good Itself and good have the same account of good]; hence they also will not differ at all insofar as each is good, [hence there is no point in appealing to Good Itself].

§6 Moreover, Good Itself will be no more of a good by being eternal; 5 for a white thing is no whiter if it lasts a long time than if it lasts a day.

§7 The Pythagoreans would seem to have a more plausible view about the good, since they place the One in the column of goods. Indeed, Speusippus seems to have followed them. §8 But let us leave this for another discussion.

A dispute emerges, however, about what we have said, because the 10 arguments [in favor of the Idea] are not concerned with every sort of good. Goods pursued and liked in their own right are spoken of as one species of goods, whereas those that in some way tend to produce or preserve these goods, or to prevent their contraries, are spoken of as goods because of these and in a different way. §9 Clearly, then, goods are spoken of in two ways, and some are goods in their own right, and others 15 goods because of these.* Let us, then, separate the goods in their own right from the [merely] useful goods, and consider whether goods in their own right correspond to a single Idea.

§10 But what sorts of goods may we take to be goods in their own right? Are they the goods that are pursued even on their own—for instance, prudence, seeing, some types of pleasures, and honors?* For even if we also pursue these because of something else, we may nonethe-20 less take them to be goods in their own right. Alternatively, is nothing except the Idea good in its own right, so that the Form will be futile?* §11 But if these other things are also goods in their own right, then, [if there is an Idea of good,] the same account of good will have to turn up in all of them, just as the same account of whiteness turns up in snow and in chalk.* In fact, however, honor, prudence, and pleasure have different 25 and dissimilar accounts, precisely insofar as they are goods. Hence the good is not something common corresponding to a single Idea.

§12 But how, then, is good spoken of? For it is not like homonyms resulting from chance.* Is it spoken of from the fact that goods derive from one thing or all contribute to one thing? Or is it spoken of more by analogy? For as sight is to body, so understanding is to soul, and so on for other cases.*

30 §13 Presumably, though, we should leave these questions for now, since their exact treatment is more appropriate for another [branch of] philosophy.* And the same is true about the Idea. For even if there is some one good predicated in common,* or some separable good, itself in its own right, clearly that is not the sort of good a human being can 35 achieve in action or possess; but that is the sort we are looking for now.

§14 Perhaps, however, someone might think it is better to get to know *1096b* the Idea with a view to the goods that we can possess and achieve in 1097a action; for [one might suppose that] if we have this as a sort of pattern, we shall also know better about the goods that are goods for us, and if we know about them, we shall hit on them. §15 This argument certainly has some plausibility, but it would seem to clash with the sciences. For 5 each of these, though it aims at some good and seeks to supply what is lacking, leaves out knowledge of the Idea; but if the Idea were such an important aid, surely it would not be reasonable for all craftsmen to know nothing about it and not even to look for it.

§16 Moreover, it is a puzzle to know what the weaver or carpenter will gain for his own craft from knowing this Good Itself, or how anyone 10 will be better at medicine or generalship from having gazed on the Idea Itself. For what the doctor appears to consider is not even health [universally, let alone good universally], but human health, and presumably the health of this human being even more, since he treats one particular patient at a time.*

So much, then, for these questions.

7

[An Account of the Human Good]

But let us return once again to the good we are looking for, and con- 15 sider just what it could be.* For it is apparently one thing in one action or craft, and another thing in another; for it is one thing in medicine, another in generalship, and so on for the rest. What, then, is the good of each action or craft? Surely it is that for the sake of which the other things are done; in medicine this is health, in generalship victory, in house-building 20 a house, in another case something else, but in every action and decision it is the end, since it is for the sake of the end that everyone does the other actions.* And so, if there is some end of everything achievable in action, the good achievable in action will be this end; if there are more ends than one, [the good achievable in action] will be these ends.*

§2 Our argument, then, has followed a different route to reach the same conclusion.* But we must try to make this still more perspicuous.* 25 §3 Since there are apparently many ends, and we choose some of them (for instance, wealth, flutes, and, in general, instruments) because of something else, it is clear that not all ends are complete.* But the best good is apparently something complete. And so, if only one end is complete, the good we are looking for will be this end; if more ends than one are complete, it will be the most complete end of these.* 30

§4 We say that an end pursued in its own right is more complete than an end pursued because of something else, and that an end that is never choiceworthy because of something else is more complete than ends that

1097a are choiceworthy both in their own right and because of this end. Hence an end that is always choiceworthy in its own right,* never because of something else, is complete without qualification.

§5 Now happiness, more than anything else, seems complete without 1097b qualification.* For we always choose it because of itself,* never because of something else. Honor, pleasure, understanding, and every virtue we certainly choose because of themselves, since we would choose each of them even if it had no further result; but we also choose them for the sake of hap- 5 piness, supposing that through them we shall be happy.* Happiness, by contrast, no one ever chooses for their sake, or for the sake of anything else at all.

§6 The same conclusion [that happiness is complete] also appears to follow from self-sufficiency. For the complete good seems to be self-sufficient.* What we count as self-sufficient is not what suffices for a solitary 10 person by himself, living an isolated life, but what suffices also for parents, children, wife, and, in general, for friends and fellow citizens, since a human being is a naturally political [animal].* §7 Here, however, we must impose some limit; for if we extend the good to parents' parents and children's children and to friends of friends, we shall go on without limit; but we must examine this another time.

15 Anyhow, we regard something as self-sufficient when all by itself it makes a life choiceworthy and lacking nothing; and that is what we think happiness does. §8 Moreover, we think happiness is most choiceworthy of all goods, [since] it is not counted as one good among many.* [If it were] counted as one among many,* then, clearly, we think it would be more choiceworthy if the smallest of goods were added; for the good that is added becomes an extra quantity of goods, and the larger of two goods 20 is always more choiceworthy.*

Happiness, then, is apparently something complete and self-sufficient, since it is the end of the things achievable in action.*

§9 But presumably the remark that the best good is happiness is apparently something [generally] agreed, and we still need a clearer statement of what the best good is.* §10 Perhaps, then, we shall find 25 this if we first grasp the function of a human being. For just as the good, i.e., [doing] well, for a flautist, a sculptor, and every craftsman, and, in general, for whatever has a function and [characteristic] action, seems to depend on its function,* the same seems to be true for a human being, if a human being has some function.

30 §11 Then do the carpenter and the leather worker have their functions and actions, but has a human being no function?* Is he by nature idle, without any function?* Or, just as eye, hand, foot, and, in general, every [bodily] part apparently has its function, may we likewise ascribe to a human being some function apart from all of these?*

§12 What, then, could this be? For living is apparently shared with 1098a plants, but what we are looking for is the special function of a human

being; hence we should set aside the life of nutrition and growth.* The life 1098a
next in order is some sort of life of sense perception; but this too is apparently shared with horse, ox, and every animal.*

§13 The remaining possibility, then, is some sort of life of action* of the [part of the soul] that has reason.* One [part] of it has reason as obeying reason; the other has it as itself having reason and thinking.* More- 5
over, life is also spoken of in two ways [as capacity and as activity], and we must take [a human being's special function to be] life as activity, since this seems to be called life more fully.* §14 We have found, then, that the human function is activity of the soul in accord with reason or requiring reason.*

Now we say that the function of a [kind of thing]—of a harpist, for instance—is the same in kind as the function of an excellent individual of the kind—of an excellent harpist, for instance. And the same is true with- 10
out qualification in every case, if we add to the function the superior achievement in accord with the virtue; for the function of a harpist is to play the harp, and the function of a good harpist is to play it well.* Moreover, we take the human function to be a certain kind of life, and take this life to be activity and actions of the soul that involve reason; hence the function of the excellent man is to do this well and finely. 15

§15 Now each function is completed well by being completed in accord with the virtue proper [to that kind of thing].* And so the human good proves to be activity of the soul in accord with virtue,* and indeed with the best and most complete virtue, if there are more virtues than one.* §16 Moreover, in a complete life.* For one swallow does not make a spring, nor does one day; nor, similarly, does one day or a short time 20
make us blessed and happy.

§17 This, then, is a sketch of the good; for, presumably, we must draw the outline first, and fill it in later.* If the sketch is good, anyone, it seems, can advance and articulate it, and in such cases time discovers more, or is a good partner in discovery. That is also how the crafts have improved, 25
since anyone can add what is lacking [in the outline].

§18 We must also remember our previous remarks, so that we do not look for the same degree of exactness in all areas, but the degree that accords with a given subject matter and is proper to a given line of inquiry.* §19 For the carpenter's and the geometer's inquiries about the 30
right angle are different also; the carpenter restricts himself to what helps his work, but the geometer inquires into what, or what sort* of thing, the right angle is, since he studies the truth. We must do the same, then, in other areas too, [seeking the proper degree of exactness], so that digressions do not overwhelm our main task.

§20 Nor should we make the same demand for an explanation in all 1098b
cases. On the contrary, in some cases it is enough to prove rightly that [something is true, without also explaining why it is true]. This is so, for

1098b instance, with principles, where the fact that [something is true] is the first thing, that is to say, the principle.*

§21 Some principles are studied by means of induction, some by means of perception, some by means of some sort of habituation, and oth-
5 ers by other means.* §22 In each case we should try to find them out by means suited to their nature, and work hard to define them rightly. §23 For they carry great weight* for what follows; for the principle seems to be more than half the whole,* and makes evident the answer to many of our questions.

8

[Defense of the Account of the Good]

We should examine the principle, however, not only from the conclusion
10 and premises [of a deduction], but also from what is said about it;* for all the facts harmonize with a true account, whereas the truth soon clashes with a false one.*

§2 Goods are divided, then, into three types, some called external, some goods of the soul, others goods of the body.* We say that the goods
15 of the soul are goods most fully, and more than the others, and we take actions and activities of the soul to be [goods] of the soul. And so our account [of the good] is right, to judge by this belief anyhow—and it is an ancient belief, and accepted by philosophers.

§3 Our account is also correct in saying that some sort of actions and activities are the end; for in that way the end turns out to be a good of the
20 soul, not an external good.

§4 The belief that the happy person lives well and does well also agrees with our account, since we have virtually said that the end is a sort of living well and doing well.

§5 Further, all the features that people look for in happiness appear to be true of the end described in our account.* §6 For to some people
25 happiness seems to be virtue; to others prudence; to others some sort of wisdom; to others again it seems to be these, or one of these, involving pleasure or requiring it to be added;* others add in external prosperity as well. §7 Some of these views are traditional, held by many, while others are held by a few men who are widely esteemed. It is reasonable for each group not to be completely wrong, but to be correct on one point at least, or even on most points.

30 §8 First, our account agrees with those who say happiness is virtue [in general] or some [particular] virtue; for activity in accord with virtue is proper to virtue. §9 Presumably, though, it matters quite a bit whether we suppose that the best good consists in possessing or in using—that is to say, in a state or in an activity [that actualizes the state].* For someone

may be in a state that achieves no good—if, for instance, he is asleep or inactive in some other way—but this cannot be true of the activity; for it will necessarily act and act well. And just as Olympic prizes are not for the finest and strongest, but for the contestants—since it is only these who win—the same is true in life; among the fine and good people, only those who act correctly* win the prize. 1099a 5

§10 Moreover, the life of these active people is also pleasant in itself.* For being pleased is a condition of the soul, [and hence is included in the activity of the soul]. Further, each type of person finds pleasure in whatever he is called a lover of; a horse, for instance, pleases the horse-lover, a spectacle the lover of spectacles. Similarly, what is just pleases the lover of justice, and in general what accords with virtue pleases the lover of virtue. 10

§11 Now the things that please most people conflict,* because they are not pleasant by nature, whereas the things that please lovers of the fine are things pleasant by nature. Actions in accord with virtue are pleasant by nature, so that they both please lovers of the fine and are pleasant in their own right. 15

§12 Hence these people's life does not need pleasure to be added [to virtuous activity] as some sort of extra decoration; rather, it has its pleasure within itself.* For besides the reasons already given, someone who does not enjoy fine actions is not good; for no one would call a person just, for instance, if he did not enjoy doing just actions, or generous if he did not enjoy generous actions, and similarly for the other virtues. 20

§13 If this is so, actions in accord with the virtues are pleasant in their own right. Moreover, these actions are good and fine as well as pleasant; indeed, they are good, fine, and pleasant more than anything else is, since on this question the excellent person judges rightly, and his judgment agrees with what we have said.

§14 Happiness, then, is best, finest, and most pleasant, and the Delian inscription is wrong to distinguish these things: 'What is most just is finest; being healthy is most beneficial; but it is most pleasant to win our heart's desire.'* For all three features are found in the best activities, and we say happiness is these activities, or [rather] one of them, the best one.* 25

§15 Nonetheless, happiness evidently also needs external goods to be added, as we said, since we cannot, or cannot easily, do fine actions if we lack the resources.* For, first of all, in many actions we use friends, wealth, and political power just as we use instruments. §16 Further, deprivation of certain [externals]—for instance, good birth, good children, beauty—mars our blessedness. For we do not altogether have the character of happiness* if we look utterly repulsive or are ill-born, solitary, or childless; and we have it even less, presumably, if our children or friends are totally bad, or were good but have died. 1099b 5

§17 And so, as we have said, happiness would seem to need this sort of prosperity added also. That is why some people identify happiness with good fortune, and others identify it with virtue.

9

[How Is Happiness Achieved?]

1099b This also leads to a puzzle: Is happiness acquired by learning, or habitua-
10 tion, or by some other form of cultivation? Or is it the result of some divine fate, or even of fortune?*

§2 First, then, if the gods give any gift at all to human beings, it is reasonable for them to give us happiness more than any other human good, insofar as it is the best of human goods. §3 Presumably, however, this question is more suitable for a different inquiry.

15 But even if it is not sent by the gods, but instead results from virtue and some sort of learning or cultivation, happiness appears to be one of the most divine things, since the prize and goal of virtue appears to be the best good, something divine and blessed. §4 Moreover [if happiness comes in this way] it will be widely shared; for anyone who is not deformed [in his capacity] for virtue will be able to achieve happiness
20 through some sort of learning and attention.

§5 And since it is better to be happy in this way than because of fortune, it is reasonable for this to be the way [we become] happy. For whatever is natural is naturally in the finest state possible. §6 The same is true of the products of crafts and of every other cause, especially the best cause; and it would be seriously inappropriate to entrust what is greatest and finest to fortune.*

25 §7 The answer to our question is also evident from our account. For we have said that happiness is a certain sort of activity of the soul in accord with virtue, [and hence not a result of fortune]. Of the other goods, some are necessary conditions of happiness, while others are naturally useful and cooperative as instruments [but are not parts of it].

§8 Further, this conclusion agrees with our opening remarks. For we
30 took the goal of political science to be the best good; and most of its attention is devoted to the character of the citizens, to make them good people who do fine actions.*

§9 It is not surprising, then, that we regard neither ox, nor horse, nor
1100a any other kind of animal as happy; for none of them can share in this sort of activity. §10 For the same reason a child is not happy either, since his age prevents him from doing these sorts of actions. If he is called happy, he is being congratulated [simply] because of anticipated blessedness; for,
5 as we have said, happiness requires both complete virtue and a complete life.*

§10 It needs a complete life because life includes many reversals of fortune, good and bad, and the most prosperous person may fall into a terrible disaster in old age, as the Trojan stories tell us about Priam. If someone has suffered these sorts of misfortunes and comes to a miserable end, no one counts him happy.

10

[Can We Be Happy during Our Lifetime?]

Then should we count no human being happy during his lifetime, but follow Solon's advice to wait to see the end?* §2 But if we agree with Solon, can someone really be happy during the time after he has died? Surely that is completely absurd, especially when we say happiness is an activity. *1100a10*

§3 We do not say, then, that someone is happy during the time he is dead, and Solon's point is not this [absurd one], but rather that when a human being has died, we can safely pronounce [that he was] blessed [before he died], on the assumption that he is now finally beyond evils and misfortunes.* But this claim is also disputable. For if a living person has good or evil of which he is not aware, a dead person also, it seems, has good or evil, if, for instance, he receives honors or dishonors, and his children, and descendants in general, do well or suffer misfortune.* 15 20

§4 However, this conclusion also raises a puzzle. For even if someone has lived in blessedness until old age, and has died appropriately, many fluctuations of his descendants' fortunes may still happen to him; for some may be good people and get the life they deserve, while the contrary may be true of others, and clearly they may be as distantly related to their ancestor as you please. Surely, then, it would be an absurd result if the dead person's condition changed along with the fortunes of his descendants, so that at one time he would turn out to have been happy [in his lifetime] and at another time he would turn out to have been miserable.* §5 But it would also be absurd if the condition of descendants did not affect their ancestors at all or for any length of time. 25 30

§6 But we must return to the previous puzzle, since that will perhaps also show us the answer to our present question. §7 Let us grant that we must wait to see the end, and must then count someone blessed, not as now being blessed [during the time he is dead] but because he previously was blessed. Would it not be absurd, then, if, at the very time when he is happy, we refused to ascribe truly to him the happiness he has?* Such refusal results from reluctance to call him happy during his lifetime, because of its ups and downs; for we suppose happiness is enduring and definitely not prone to fluctuate, but the same person's fortunes often turn to and fro.* §8 For clearly, if we take our cue from his fortunes, we shall often call him happy and then miserable again, thereby representing the happy person as a kind of chameleon, insecurely based. 35 1100b 5

§9 But surely it is quite wrong to take our cue from someone's fortunes. For his doing well or badly does not rest on them.* A human life, as we said, needs these added, but activities in accord with virtue control happiness, and the contrary activities control its contrary. §10 Indeed, the present puzzle is further evidence for our account [of happiness]. For no human achievement has the stability of activities in accord with virtue, since these seem to be more enduring even than our knowledge of 10

1100b15 the sciences.* Indeed, the most honorable among the virtues themselves are more enduring than the other virtues, because blessed people devote their lives to them more fully and more continually than to anything else—for this continual activity would seem to be the reason we do not forget them.

§11 It follows, then, that the happy person has the [stability] we are looking for and keeps the character he has throughout his life. For 20 always, or more than anything else, he will do and study the actions in accord with virtue, and will bear fortunes most finely, in every way and in all conditions appropriately, since he is truly 'good, foursquare, and blameless'.*

§12 Many events, however, are subject to fortune; some are minor, some major. Hence, minor strokes of good or ill fortune clearly will not 25 carry any weight for his life. But many major strokes of good fortune will make it more blessed; for in themselves they naturally add adornment to it, and his use of them proves to be fine and excellent.* Conversely, if he suffers many major misfortunes, they oppress and spoil his blessedness, 30 since they involve pain and impede many activities. And yet, even here what is fine shines through, whenever someone bears many severe misfortunes with good temper, not because he feels no distress, but because he is noble and magnanimous.*

§13 And since it is activities that control life, as we said, no blessed 35 person could ever become miserable, since he will never do hateful and 1101a base actions. For a truly good and prudent person,* we suppose, will bear strokes of fortune suitably, and from his resources at any time will do the finest actions, just as a good general will make the best use of his forces in 5 war, and a good shoemaker will make the finest shoe from the hides given to him, and similarly for all other craftsmen.

§14 If this is so, the happy person could never become miserable, but neither will he be blessed if he falls into misfortunes as bad as Priam's.* Nor, however, will he be inconstant and prone to fluctuate, since he will 10 neither be easily shaken from his happiness nor shaken by just any misfortunes.* He will be shaken from it, though, by many serious misfortunes, and from these a return to happiness will take no short time. At best, it will take a long and complete length of time that includes great and fine successes.

15 §15 Then why not say that the happy person is the one whose activities accord with complete virtue, with an adequate supply of external goods, not for just any time but for a complete life? Or should we add that he will also go on living this way and will come to an appropriate end, since the future is not apparent to us, and we take happiness to be the end, and altogether complete in every way? §16 Given these facts 20 [about the future and about happiness], we shall say that a living person who has, and will keep, the goods we mentioned is blessed, but blessed as a human being is.* So much for a determination of this question.

11

[How Happiness Can Be Affected after One's Death]

Still, it is apparently rather unfriendly and contrary to the [common] *1101a* beliefs to claim that the fortunes of our descendants and all our friends contribute nothing. §2 But since they can find themselves in many and various circumstances, some of which affect us more, some less, it is 25 apparently a long—indeed endless—task to differentiate all the particular cases. Perhaps a general outline will be enough of an answer.

§3 Misfortunes, then, even to the person himself, differ, and some have a certain gravity and weight for his life, whereas others would seem 30 to be lighter. The same is true for the misfortunes of his friends; §4 and it matters whether they happen to living or to dead people—much more than it matters whether lawless and terrible crimes are committed before a tragic drama begins or in the course of it.*

§5 In our reasoning, then, we should also take account of this difference, but even more account, presumably, of the puzzle about whether 35 the dead share in any good or evil. For if we consider this, anything good 1101b or evil penetrating to the dead would seem to be weak and unimportant, either without qualification or for them. Even if the good or evil is not so weak and unimportant, still its importance and character are not enough to make people happy who are not already happy, or to take away the 5 blessedness of those who are happy. §6 And so, when friends do well, and likewise when they do badly, it appears to contribute something to the dead, but of a character and size that neither makes happy people not happy nor anything of this sort.

12

[Praise and Honor]

Now that we have determined these points, let us consider whether hap- 10 piness is something praiseworthy, or instead something honorable; for clearly it is not a capacity [which is neither praiseworthy nor honorable].

§2 Whatever is praiseworthy appears to be praised for its character and its state in relation to something.* We praise the just and the brave person, for instance, and in general the good person and virtue, because 15 of their actions and achievements; and we praise the strong person, the good runner, and each of the others because he naturally has a certain character and is in a certain state in relation to something good and excellent. §3 This is clear also from praises of the gods; for these praises appear ridiculous because they are referred to us, but they are referred to 20 us because, as we said, praise depends on such a reference.

§4 If praise is for these sorts of things, then clearly for the best things there is no praise, but something greater and better. And indeed this is

1101b how it appears. For the gods and the most godlike* of men are [not
25 praised, but] congratulated for their blessedness and happiness. The same is true of goods; for we never praise happiness, as we praise justice, but we count it blessed, as something better and more godlike [than anything that is praised].

§5 Indeed, Eudoxus seems to have used the right sort of argument in defending the supremacy of pleasure.* By not praising pleasure, though it
30 is a good, we indicate—so he thought—that it is superior to everything praiseworthy; [only] the god and the good have this superiority since the other goods are [praised] by reference to them.

§6 [Here he seems to have argued correctly.] For praise is given to virtue, since it makes us do fine actions; but celebrations are for achievements, either of body or of soul. §7 But an exact treatment of this is
35 presumably more proper for specialists in celebrations. For us, anyhow, it
1102a is clear from what has been said that happiness is something honorable and complete.

§8 A further reason why this would seem to be correct is that happiness is a principle; for [the principle] is what we all aim at in all our other actions;* and we take the principle and cause of goods to be something honorable and divine.

13

[Introduction to the Virtues]

5 Since happiness is a certain sort of activity of the soul in accord with complete virtue, we must examine virtue; for that will perhaps also be a way to study happiness better.* §2 Moreover, the true politician* seems to have put more effort into virtue than into anything else, since
10 he wants to make the citizens good and law-abiding. §3 We find an example of this in the Spartan and Cretan legislators and in any others who share their concerns. §4 Since, then, the examination of virtue is proper for political science, the inquiry clearly suits our decision at the beginning.*

§5 It is clear that the virtue we must examine is human virtue, since
15 we are also seeking the human good and human happiness. §6 By human virtue we mean virtue of the soul, not of the body, since we also say that happiness is an activity of the soul. §7 If this is so, it is clear
20 that the politician must in some way know about the soul, just as someone setting out to heal the eyes must know about the whole body as well.* This is all the more true to the extent that political science is better and more honorable than medicine; even among doctors, the cultivated ones devote a lot of effort to finding out about the body. Hence the politician as well [as the student of nature] must study the soul.* §8 But he must
25 study it for his specific purpose, far enough for his inquiry [into virtue];

for a more exact treatment would presumably take more effort than his purpose requires.* *1102a*

§9 [We] have discussed the soul sufficiently [for our purposes] in [our] popular works as well [as our less popular],* and we should use this discussion. We have said, for instance, that one [part] of the soul is nonrational, while one has reason. §10 Are these distinguished as parts of a body and everything divisible into parts are? Or are they two [only] in definition, and inseparable by nature, as the convex and the concave are in a surface? It does not matter for present purposes.* 30

§11 Consider the nonrational [part]. One [part] of it, i.e., the cause of nutrition and growth, would seem to be plantlike and shared [with all living things]; for we can ascribe this capacity of the soul to everything that is nourished, including embryos, and the same capacity to full-grown living things, since this is more reasonable than to ascribe another capacity to them.* 1102b

§12 Hence the virtue of this capacity is apparently shared, not [specifically] human. For this part and this capacity more than others seem to be active in sleep, and here the good and the bad person are least distinct; hence happy people are said to be no better off than miserable people for half their lives. §13 This lack of distinction is not surprising, since sleep is inactivity of the soul insofar as it is called excellent or base, unless to some small extent some movements penetrate [to our awareness], and in this way the decent person comes to have better images [in dreams] than just any random person has. §14 Enough about this, however, and let us leave aside the nutritive part, since by nature it has no share in human virtue. 5 10

§15 Another nature in the soul would also seem to be nonrational, though in a way it shares in reason. For in the continent and the incontinent person we praise their reason, that is to say, the [part] of the soul that has reason, because it exhorts them correctly and toward what is best; but they evidently also have in them some other [part] that is by nature something apart from reason, clashing and struggling with reason. For just as paralyzed parts of a body, when we decide to move them to the right, do the contrary and move off to the left, the same is true of the soul; for incontinent people have impulses in contrary directions. §16 In bodies, admittedly, we see the part go astray, whereas we do not see it in the soul; nonetheless, presumably, we should suppose that the soul also has something apart from reason, countering and opposing reason. The [precise] way it is different does not matter. 15 20 25

§17 However, this [part] as well [as the rational part] appears, as we said, to share in reason. At any rate, in the continent person it obeys reason; and in the temperate and the brave person it presumably listens still better to reason, since there it agrees with reason in everything.*

§18 The nonrational [part], then, as well [as the whole soul] apparently has two parts. For while the plantlike [part] shares in reason not at 30

1102b all, the [part] with appetites and in general desires* shares in reason in a way, insofar as it both listens to reason and obeys it. This is the way in which we are said to 'listen to reason' from father or friends, as opposed to the way in which [we 'give the reason'] in mathematics.* The nonrational part also [obeys and] is persuaded in some way by reason, as is 1103a shown by correction, and by every sort of reproof and exhortation.

§19 If, then, we ought to say that this [part] also has reason, then the [part] that has reason, as well [as the nonrational part], will have two parts. One will have reason fully, by having it within itself; the other will have reason by listening to reason as to a father.*

5 The division between virtues accords with this difference. For some virtues are called virtues of thought, others virtues of character; wisdom, comprehension, and prudence are called virtues of thought, generosity and temperance virtues of character.* For when we speak of someone's character we do not say that he is wise or has good comprehension, but that he is gentle or temperate. And yet, we also praise the 10 wise person for his state, and the states that are praiseworthy are the ones we call virtues.

BOOK II

[VIRTUE OF CHARACTER]

1

[How a Virtue of Character Is Acquired]

15 Virtue, then, is of two sorts, virtue of thought and virtue of character. Virtue of thought arises and grows mostly from teaching; that is why it needs experience and time. Virtue of character [i.e., of *ēthos*] results from habit [*ethos*]; hence its name 'ethical', slightly varied from 'ethos'.*

§2 Hence it is also clear that none of the virtues of character arises in 20 us naturally. For if something is by nature in one condition, habituation cannot bring it into another condition. A stone, for instance, by nature moves downwards, and habituation could not make it move upwards, not even if you threw it up ten thousand times to habituate it; nor could habituation make fire move downwards, or bring anything that is by nature in one condition into another condition. §3 And so the virtues 25 arise in us neither by nature nor against nature. Rather, we are by nature able to acquire them, and we are completed through habit.*

§4 Further, if something arises in us by nature, we first have the capacity for it, and later perform the activity. This is clear in the case of the 30 senses; for we did not acquire them by frequent seeing or hearing, but we already had them when we exercised them, and did not get them by exercising them. Virtues, by contrast, we acquire, just as we acquire crafts, by having first activated them. For we learn a craft by producing the same product that we must produce when we have learned it; we become builders, for instance, by building, and we become harpists by playing the harp. Similarly, then, we become just by doing just actions, temperate by doing temperate actions, brave by doing brave actions. *1103a* 1103b

§5 What goes on in cities is also evidence for this. For the legislator makes the citizens good by habituating them, and this is the wish of every legislator; if he fails to do it well he misses his goal.* Correct habituation distinguishes a good political system from a bad one. 5

§6 Further, the sources and means that develop each virtue also ruin it, just as they do in a craft. For playing the harp makes both good and bad harpists, and it is analogous in the case of builders and all the rest; for building well makes good builders, and building badly makes bad ones. §7 Otherwise no teacher would be needed, but everyone would be born a good or a bad craftsman. 10

It is the same, then, with the virtues. For what we do in our dealings with other people makes some of us just, some unjust; what we do in terrifying situations, and the habits of fear or confidence that we acquire, make some of us brave and others cowardly. The same is true of situations involving appetites and anger; for one or another sort of conduct in these situations makes some temperate and mild, others intemperate and irascible. To sum it up in a single account: a state [of character] results from [the repetition of] similar activities.* 15 20

§8 That is why we must perform the right activities, since differences in these imply corresponding differences in the states.* It is not unimportant, then, to acquire one sort of habit or another, right from our youth. On the contrary, it is very important, indeed all-important. 25

2

[Habituation]

Our present discussion does not aim, as our others do, at study; for the purpose of our examination is not to know what virtue is, but to become good, since otherwise the inquiry would be of no benefit to us.* And so we must examine the right ways of acting; for, as we have said, the actions also control the sorts of states we acquire. 30

§2 First, then, actions should accord with the correct reason.* That is a common [belief], and let us assume it. We shall discuss it later, and say what the correct reason is and how it is related to the other virtues.

§3 But let us take it as agreed in advance that every account of the actions we must do has to be stated in outline, not exactly. As we also said at the beginning, the type of accounts we demand should accord with the subject matter; and questions about actions and expediency, like questions about health, have no fixed answers.* 1104a

1104a5 §4 While this is the character of our general account, the account of particular cases is still more inexact. For these fall under no craft or profession; the agents themselves must consider in each case what the opportune action is, as doctors and navigators do.* §5 The account we offer, then, in our present inquiry is of this inexact sort; still, we must try to offer help.*

§6 First, then, we should observe that these sorts of states naturally tend to be ruined by excess and deficiency. We see this happen with strength and health—for we must use evident cases [such as these] as witnesses to things that are not evident.* For both excessive and deficient exercise ruin bodily strength, and, similarly, too much or too little eating or drinking ruins health, whereas the proportionate amount produces, increases, and preserves it.

§7 The same is true, then, of temperance, bravery, and the other virtues. For if, for instance, someone avoids and is afraid of everything, standing firm against nothing, he becomes cowardly; if he is afraid of nothing at all and goes to face everything, he becomes rash. Similarly, if he gratifies himself with every pleasure and abstains from none, he becomes intemperate; if he avoids them all, as boors do, he becomes some sort of insensible person. Temperance and bravery, then, are ruined by excess and deficiency, but preserved by the mean.*

§8 But these actions are not only the sources and causes both of the emergence and growth of virtues and of their ruin; the activities of the virtues [once we have acquired them] also consist in these same actions.* For this is also true of more evident cases; strength, for instance, arises from eating a lot and from withstanding much hard labor, and it is the strong person who is most capable of these very actions. §9 It is the same with the virtues. For abstaining from pleasures makes us become temperate, and once we have become temperate 1104b we are most capable of abstaining from pleasures. It is similar with bravery; habituation in disdain for frightening situations and in standing firm against them makes us become brave, and once we have become brave we shall be most capable of standing firm.

3

[The Importance of Pleasure and Pain]

5 But we must take someone's pleasure or pain following on his actions to be a sign of his state.* For if someone who abstains from bodily pleasures enjoys the abstinence itself, he is temperate; if he is grieved by it, he is intemperate.* Again, if he stands firm against terrifying situations and enjoys it, or at least does not find it painful, he is brave; if he finds it painful, he is cowardly. For virtue of character is about pleasures and pains.*

For pleasure causes us to do base actions, and pain causes us to abstain from fine ones. §2 That is why we need to have had the appropriate upbringing—right from early youth, as Plato says*—to make us find enjoyment or pain in the right things; for this is the correct education. *1104b10*

§3 Further, virtues are concerned with actions and feelings; but every feeling and every action implies pleasure or pain;* hence, for this reason too, virtue is about pleasures and pains. §4 Corrective treatments also indicate this, since they use pleasures and pains; for correction is a form of medical treatment, and medical treatment naturally operates through contraries. 15

§5 Further, as we said earlier, every state of soul is naturally related to and about whatever naturally makes it better or worse; and pleasures and pains make people base, from pursuing and avoiding the wrong ones, at the wrong time, in the wrong ways, or whatever other distinctions of that sort are needed in an account. These [bad effects of pleasure and pain] are the reason why people actually define the virtues as ways of being unaffected and undisturbed [by pleasures and pains].* They are wrong, however, because they speak of being unaffected without qualification, not of being unaffected in the right or wrong way, at the right or wrong time, and the added qualifications. 20 25

§6 We assume, then, that virtue is the sort of state that does the best actions concerning pleasures and pains, and that vice is the contrary state.

§7 The following will also make it evident that virtue and vice are about the same things. For there are three objects of choice—fine, expedient, and pleasant—and three objects of avoidance—their contraries, shameful, harmful, and painful.* About all these, then, the good person is correct and the bad person is in error, and especially about pleasure. For pleasure is shared with animals, and implied by every object of choice, since what is fine and what is expedient appear pleasant as well. 30 35 1105a

§8 Further, pleasure grows up with all of us from infancy on. That is why it is hard to rub out this feeling that is dyed into our lives. We also estimate actions [as well as feelings]—some of us more, some less—by pleasure and pain. §9 For this reason, our whole discussion must be about these; for good or bad enjoyment or pain is very important for our actions. 5

§10 Further, it is more difficult to fight pleasure than to fight spirit—and Heracleitus tells us [how difficult it is to fight spirit].* Now both craft and virtue are in every case about what is more difficult, since a good result is even better when it is more difficult. Hence, for this reason also, the whole discussion, for virtue and political science alike, must consider pleasures and pains; for if we use these well, we shall be good, and if badly, bad. 10

§11 To sum up: Virtue is about pleasures and pains; the actions that are its sources also increase it or, if they are done badly, ruin it; and its activity is about the same actions as those that are its sources. 15

4

[Virtuous Actions versus Virtuous Character]

1105a Someone might be puzzled, however, about what we mean by saying that we become just by doing just actions and become temperate by doing temperate actions.* For [one might suppose that] if we do grammatical or 20 musical actions, we are grammarians or musicians, and, similarly, if we do just or temperate actions, we are thereby just or temperate.

§2 But surely actions are not enough, even in the case of crafts;* for it is possible to produce a grammatical result by chance, or by following someone else's instructions. To be grammarians, then, we must both pro- 25 duce a grammatical result and produce it grammatically—that is to say, produce it in accord with the grammatical knowledge in us.

§3 Moreover, in any case, what is true of crafts is not true of virtues.* For the products of a craft determine by their own qualities whether they have been produced well; and so it suffices that they have the right qualities when they have been produced.* But for actions in accord with the 30 virtues to be done temperately or justly it does not suffice that they themselves have the right qualities.* Rather, the agent must also be in the right state when he does them. First, he must know [that he is doing virtuous actions]; second, he must decide on them, and decide on them for themselves; and, third, he must also do them from a firm and unchanging state.

1105b As conditions for having a craft, these three do not count, except for the bare knowing.* As a condition for having a virtue, however, the knowing counts for nothing, or [rather] for only a little, whereas the other two conditions are very important, indeed all-important. And we achieve 5 these other two conditions by the frequent doing of just and temperate actions.

§4 Hence actions are called just or temperate when they are the sort that a just or temperate person would do. But the just and temperate person is not the one who [merely] does these actions, but the one who also does them in the way in which just or temperate people do them.

10 §5 It is right, then, to say that a person comes to be just from doing just actions and temperate from doing temperate actions; for no one has the least prospect of becoming good from failing to do them.

§6 The many, however, do not do these actions. They take refuge in arguments, thinking that they are doing philosophy, and that this is the 15 way to become excellent people. They are like a sick person who listens attentively to the doctor, but acts on none of his instructions. Such a course of treatment will not improve the state of the sick person's body; nor will the many improve the state of their souls by this attitude to philosophy.*

5

[Virtue of Character: Its Genus]

Next we must examine what virtue is. Since there are three conditions *1105b20* arising in the soul—feelings, capacities, and states—virtue must be one of these.*

§2 By feelings I mean appetite, anger, fear, confidence, envy, joy, love, hate, longing, jealousy, pity, and in general whatever implies pleasure or pain. By capacities I mean what we have when we are said to be capable 25 of these feelings—capable of being angry, for instance, or of being afraid* or of feeling pity. By states I mean what we have when we are well or badly off in relation to feelings.* If, for instance, our feeling is too intense or slack, we are badly off in relation to anger, but if it is intermediate, we are well off; the same is true in the other cases.

§3 First, then, neither virtues nor vices are feelings. For we are called 30 excellent or base insofar as we have virtues or vices, not insofar as we have feelings. Further, we are neither praised nor blamed insofar as we have feelings; for we do not praise the angry or the frightened person, and do not blame the person who is simply angry, but only the person 1106a who is angry in a particular way. We are praised or blamed, however, insofar as we have virtues or vices.* §4 Further, we are angry and afraid without decision; but the virtues are decisions of some kind, or [rather] require decision.* Besides, insofar as we have feelings, we are said to be 5 moved; but insofar as we have virtues or vices, we are said to be in some condition rather than moved.

§5 For these reasons the virtues are not capacities either; for we are neither called good nor called bad, nor are we praised or blamed, insofar as we are simply capable of feelings. Further, while we have capacities by 10 nature, we do not become good or bad by nature; we have discussed this before.*

§6 If, then, the virtues are neither feelings nor capacities, the remaining possibility is that they are states. And so we have said what the genus of virtue is.

6

[Virtue of Character: Its Differentia]

But we must say not only, as we already have, that it is a state, but also 15 what sort of state it is.*

§2 It should be said, then, that every virtue causes its possessors to be in a good state and to perform their functions well.* The virtue of eyes, for instance, makes the eyes and their functioning excellent, because it makes us see well; and similarly, the virtue of a horse makes the horse 20 excellent, and thereby good at galloping, at carrying its rider, and at

1106a standing steady in the face of the enemy. §3 If this is true in every case, the virtue of a human being will likewise be the state that makes a human being good and makes him perform his function well.

25 §4 We have already said how this will be true, and it will also be evident from our next remarks, if we consider the sort of nature that virtue has.*

In everything continuous and divisible we can take more, less, and equal, and each of them either in the object itself or relative to us; and the 30 equal is some intermediate between excess and deficiency. §5 By the intermediate in the object I mean what is equidistant from each extremity; this is one and the same for all. But relative to us the intermediate is what is neither superfluous nor deficient; this is not one, and is not the same for all.*

§6 If, for instance, ten are many and two are few, we take six as inter-35 mediate in the object, since it exceeds [two] and is exceeded [by ten] by an equal amount, [four]. §7 This is what is intermediate by numerical pro-1106b portion. But that is not how we must take the intermediate that is relative to us. For if ten pounds [of food], for instance, are a lot for someone to eat, and two pounds a little, it does not follow that the trainer will prescribe six, since this might also be either a little or a lot for the person who is to take it—for Milo [the athlete] a little, but for the beginner in gymnastics a 5 lot; and the same is true for running and wrestling. §8 In this way every scientific expert avoids excess and deficiency and seeks and chooses what is intermediate—but intermediate relative to us, not in the object.

§9 This, then, is how each science produces its product well, by focus-10 ing on what is intermediate and making the product conform to that.* This, indeed, is why people regularly comment on well-made products that nothing could be added or subtracted; they assume that excess or deficiency ruins a good [result], whereas the mean preserves it. Good craftsmen also, we say, focus on what is intermediate when they produce 15 their product. And since virtue, like nature, is better and more exact than any craft, it will also aim at what is intermediate.*

§10 By virtue I mean virtue of character; for this is about feelings and actions, and these admit of excess, deficiency, and an intermediate condition. We can be afraid, for instance, or be confident, or have appetites, or 20 get angry, or feel pity, and in general have pleasure or pain, both too much and too little, and in both ways not well. §11 But having these feelings at the right times, about the right things, toward the right people, for the right end, and in the right way, is the intermediate and best condition, and this is proper to virtue. §12 Similarly, actions also admit of excess, deficiency, and an intermediate condition.

25 Now virtue is about feelings and actions, in which excess and deficiency are in error and incur blame, whereas the intermediate condition is correct and wins praise,* which are both proper to virtue. §13 Virtue, then, is a mean, insofar as it aims at what is intermediate.

30 §14 Moreover, there are many ways to be in error—for badness is proper to the indeterminate, as the Pythagoreans pictured it, and good to

the determinate. But there is only one way to be correct. That is why error is easy and correctness is difficult, since it is easy to miss the target and difficult to hit it. And so for this reason also excess and deficiency are proper to vice, the mean to virtue; 'for we are noble in only one way, but bad in all sorts of ways.'* *1106b* 35

§15 Virtue, then, is a state that decides, consisting in a mean, the mean relative to us, which is defined by reference to reason, that is to say, to the reason by reference to which the prudent person would define it.* It is a mean between two vices, one of excess and one of deficiency. 1107a

§16 It is a mean for this reason also: Some vices miss what is right because they are deficient, others because they are excessive, in feelings or in actions, whereas virtue finds and chooses what is intermediate. 5

§17 That is why virtue, as far as its essence and the account stating what it is are concerned, is a mean, but, as far as the best [condition] and the good [result] are concerned, it is an extremity.

§18 Now not every action or feeling admits of the mean.* For the names of some automatically include baseness—for instance, spite, shamelessness, envy [among feelings], and adultery, theft, murder, among actions.* For all of these and similar things are called by these names because they themselves, not their excesses or deficiencies, are base. Hence in doing these things we can never be correct, but must invariably be in error. We cannot do them well or not well—by committing adultery, for instance, with the right woman at the right time in the right way. On the contrary, it is true without qualification that to do any of them is to be in error. 10 15

§19 [To think these admit of a mean], therefore, is like thinking that unjust or cowardly or intemperate action also admits of a mean, an excess and a deficiency. If it did, there would be a mean of excess, a mean of deficiency, an excess of excess and a deficiency of deficiency. §20 On the contrary, just as there is no excess or deficiency of temperance or of bravery (since the intermediate is a sort of extreme), so also there is no mean of these vicious actions either, but whatever way anyone does them, he is in error. For in general there is no mean of excess or of deficiency, and no excess or deficiency of a mean. 20 25

7

[The Particular Virtues of Character]

However, we must not only state this general account but also apply it to the particular cases. For among accounts concerning actions, though the general ones are common to more cases, the specific ones are truer, since actions are about particular cases, and our account must accord with these.* Let us, then, find these from the chart.* 30

§2 First, then, in feelings of fear and confidence the mean is bravery. The excessively fearless person is nameless (indeed many cases are nameless), and the one who is excessively confident is rash. The one who is excessive in fear and deficient in confidence is cowardly.

§3 In pleasures and pains—though not in all types, and in pains less than in pleasures*—the mean is temperance and the excess intemperance. People deficient in pleasure are not often found, which is why they also lack even a name; let us call them insensible.

§4 In giving and taking money the mean is generosity, the excess wastefulness and the deficiency ungenerosity. Here the vicious people have contrary excesses and defects; for the wasteful person is excessive in spending and deficient in taking, whereas the ungenerous person is excessive in taking and deficient in spending. §5 At the moment we are speaking in outline and summary, and that is enough; later we shall define these things more exactly.

§6 In questions of money there are also other conditions. Another mean is magnificence; for the magnificent person differs from the generous by being concerned with large matters, while the generous person is concerned with small. The excess is ostentation and vulgarity, and the deficiency is stinginess. These differ from the vices related to generosity in ways we shall describe later.

§7 In honor and dishonor the mean is magnanimity, the excess something called a sort of vanity, and the deficiency pusillanimity. §8 And just as we said that generosity differs from magnificence in its concern with small matters, similarly there is a virtue concerned with small honors, differing in the same way from magnanimity, which is concerned with great honors. For honor can be desired either in the right way or more or less than is right. If someone desires it to excess, he is called an honor-lover, and if his desire is deficient he is called indifferent to honor, but if he is intermediate he has no name. The corresponding conditions have no name either, except the condition of the honor-lover, which is called honor-loving.

This is why people at the extremes lay claim to the intermediate area. Moreover, we also sometimes call the intermediate person an honor-lover, and sometimes call him indifferent to honor; and sometimes we praise the honor-lover, sometimes the person indifferent to honor.* §9 We will mention later the reason we do this; for the moment, let us speak of the other cases in the way we have laid down.

§10 Anger also admits of an excess, deficiency, and mean. These are all practically nameless; but since we call the intermediate person mild, let us call the mean mildness. Among the extreme people, let the excessive person be irascible, and his vice irascibility, and let the deficient person be a sort of inirascible person, and his deficiency inirascibility.

§11 There are also three other means, somewhat similar to one another, but different. For they are all concerned with common dealings in conversations and actions, but differ insofar as one is concerned with truth telling in these areas, the other two with sources of pleasure, some of which are found in amusement, and the others in daily life in general. Hence we should also discuss these states, so that we can better observe that in every case the mean is praiseworthy, whereas the extremes are neither praiseworthy nor correct, but blameworthy. Most of these cases are also nameless, and we must try, as in the other cases also, to supply names ourselves, to make things clear and easy to follow. *1108a* 15

§12 In truth-telling, then, let us call the intermediate person truthful, and the mean truthfulness; pretense that overstates will be boastfulness, and the person who has it boastful; pretense that understates will be self-deprecation, and the person who has it self-deprecating. 20

§13 In sources of pleasure in amusements let us call the intermediate person witty, and the condition wit; the excess buffoonery and the person who has it a buffoon; and the deficient person a sort of boor and the state boorishness. 25

In the other sources of pleasure, those in daily life, let us call the person who is pleasant in the right way friendly, and the mean state friendliness. If someone goes to excess with no [ulterior] aim, he will be ingratiating; if he does it for his own advantage, a flatterer. The deficient person, unpleasant in everything, will be a sort of quarrelsome and ill-tempered person. 30

§14 There are also means in feelings and about feelings. Shame, for instance, is not a virtue, but the person prone to shame as well as [the virtuous people we have described] receives praise. For here also one person is called intermediate, and another—the person excessively prone to shame, who is ashamed about everything—is called excessive; the person who is deficient in shame or never feels shame at all is said to have no sense of disgrace; and the intermediate one is called prone to shame. 35 1108b

§15 Proper indignation is the mean between envy and spite; these conditions are concerned with pleasure and pain at what happens to our neighbors. For the properly indignant person feels pain when someone does well undeservedly; the envious person exceeds him by feeling pain when anyone does well, while the spiteful person is so deficient in feeling pain that he actually enjoys [other people's misfortunes].* 5

§16 There will also be an opportunity elsewhere to speak of these. We must consider justice after these.* Since it is spoken of in more than one way, we shall distinguish its two types and say how each of them is a mean. Similarly, we must also consider the virtues that belong to reason. 10

8

[Relations between Mean and Extreme States]

Among these three conditions, then, two are vices—one of excess, one of deficiency—and one, the mean, is virtue. In a way, each of them is

1108b opposed to each of the others, since each extreme is contrary both to the intermediate condition and to the other extreme, while the intermediate is
15 contrary to the extremes.

§2 For, just as the equal is greater in comparison to the smaller, and smaller in comparison to the greater, so also the intermediate states are excessive in comparison to the deficiencies and deficient in comparison to
20 the excesses—both in feelings and in actions. For the brave person, for instance, appears rash in comparison to the coward, and cowardly in comparison to the rash person; the temperate person appears intemperate in comparison to the insensible person, and insensible in comparison with the intemperate person; and the generous person appears wasteful in comparison to the ungenerous, and ungenerous in comparison to the wasteful person.* §3 That is why each of the extreme people tries to
25 push the intermediate person to the other extreme, so that the coward, for instance, calls the brave person rash, and the rash person calls him a coward, and similarly in the other cases.

§4 Since these conditions of soul are opposed to each other in these ways, the extremes are more contrary to each other than to the intermediate. For they are further from each other than from the intermediate, just
30 as the large is further from the small, and the small from the large, than either is from the equal.

§5 Further, sometimes one extreme—rashness or wastefulness, for instance—appears somewhat like the intermediate state, bravery or generosity. But the extremes are most unlike one another; and the things that
35 are furthest apart from each other are defined as contraries. And so the things that are further apart are more contrary.

1109a §6 In some cases the deficiency, in others the excess, is more opposed to the intermediate condition. For instance, cowardice, the deficiency, not rashness, the excess, is more opposed to bravery, whereas intemper-
5 ance, the excess, not insensibility, the deficiency, is more opposed to temperance.

§7 This happens for two reasons: One reason is derived from the object itself. Since sometimes one extreme is closer and more similar to the intermediate condition, we oppose the contrary extreme, more than this closer one, to the intermediate condition.* Since rashness, for
10 instance, seems to be closer and more similar to bravery, and cowardice less similar, we oppose cowardice, more than rashness, to bravery; for what is further from the intermediate condition seems to be more contrary to it. This, then, is one reason, derived from the object itself.

§8 The other reason is derived from ourselves. For when we ourselves have some natural tendency to one extreme more than to the other, this extreme appears more opposed to the intermediate condition. Since, for
15 instance, we have more of a natural tendency to pleasure, we drift more easily toward intemperance than toward orderliness. Hence we say that an extreme is more contrary if we naturally develop more in that direc-

tion; and this is why intemperance is more contrary to temperance, since it is the excess [of pleasure]. *1109a*

9

[How Can We Reach the Mean?]

We have said enough, then, to show that virtue of character is a mean and what sort of mean it is; that it is a mean between two vices, one of excess and one of deficiency; and that it is a mean because it aims at the intermediate condition in feelings and actions. 20

§2 That is why it is also hard work to be excellent. For in each case it is hard work to find the intermediate; for instance, not everyone, but only one who knows, finds the midpoint in a circle. So also getting angry, or giving and spending money, is easy and everyone can do it; but doing it to the right person, in the right amount, at the right time, for the right end, and in the right way is no longer easy, nor can everyone do it. Hence doing these things well is rare, praiseworthy, and fine. 25 30

§3 That is why anyone who aims at the intermediate condition must first of all steer clear of the more contrary extreme, following the advice that Calypso also gives: 'Hold the ship outside the spray and surge.'* For one extreme is more in error, the other less. §4 Since, therefore, it is hard to hit the intermediate extremely accurately,* the second-best tack, as they say, is to take the lesser of the evils. We shall succeed best in this by the method we describe. 35 1109b

We must also examine what we ourselves drift into easily. For different people have different natural tendencies toward different goals, and we shall come to know our own tendencies from the pleasure or pain that arises in us. §5 We must drag ourselves off in the contrary direction; for if we pull far away from error, as they do in straightening bent wood, we shall reach the intermediate condition. 5

§6 And in everything we must beware above all of pleasure and its sources; for we are already biased in its favor when we come to judge it. Hence we must react to it as the elders reacted to Helen, and on each occasion repeat what they said; for if we do this, and send it off, we shall be less in error.* 10

§7 In summary, then, if we do these things we shall best be able to reach the intermediate condition. But presumably this is difficult, especially in particular cases, since it is not easy to define the way we should be angry, with whom, about what, for how long. For sometimes, indeed, we ourselves praise deficient people and call them mild, and sometimes praise quarrelsome people and call them manly. 15

§8 Still, we are not blamed if we deviate a little in excess or deficiency from doing well, but only if we deviate a long way, since then we are easily noticed. But how great and how serious a deviation receives blame is 20

1109b not easy to define in an account; for nothing else perceptible is easily defined either. Such things* are among particulars,* and the judgment depends on perception.*

§9 This is enough, then, to make it clear that in every case the interme-25 diate state is praised, but we must sometimes incline toward the excess, sometimes toward the deficiency; for that is the easiest way to hit the intermediate and good condition.

Book III

[Preconditions of Virtue]

1

[Voluntary Action]

30 Virtue, then, is about feelings and actions. These receive praise or blame if they are voluntary, but pardon, sometimes even pity, if they are involuntary.* Hence, presumably, in examining virtue we must define the voluntary and the involuntary. §2 This is also useful to legislators, both for 35 honors and for corrective treatments.*

1110a §3 Now it seems that things coming about by force or because of ignorance are involuntary.*

What is forced has an external principle, the sort of principle in which the agent, or [rather] the victim,* contributes nothing*—if, for instance, a wind or people who have him in their control were to carry him off.

5 §4 But what about actions done because of fear of greater evils, or because of something fine?* Suppose, for instance, a tyrant tells you to do something shameful, when he has control over your parents and children, and if you do it, they will live, but if not, they will die.* These cases raise dispute about whether they are voluntary or involuntary.

§5 However, the same sort [of unwelcome choice] is found in throw-10 ing cargo overboard in storms.* For no one willingly throws cargo overboard, without qualification,* but anyone with any sense throws it overboard to save himself and the others.

§6 These sorts of actions, then, are mixed,* but they are more like voluntary actions. For at the time they are done they are choiceworthy, and the goal of an action accords with the specific occasion; hence we should also call the action voluntary or involuntary on the occasion when he 15 does it. Now in fact he does it willingly. For in such actions he has within him the principle of moving the limbs that are the instruments [of the action]; but if the principle of the actions is in him, it is also up to him to do them or not to do them.* Hence actions of this sort are voluntary, though presumably the actions without [the appropriate] qualification are involuntary, since no one would choose any such action in its own right.

§7 For such [mixed] actions people are sometimes actually praised, *1110a20* whenever they endure something shameful or painful as the price of great and fine results. If they do the reverse, they are blamed; for it is a base person who endures what is most shameful for nothing fine or for only some moderately fine result. In some cases there is no praise, but there is pardon, whenever someone does a wrong action because of con- 25 ditions of a sort that overstrain human nature, and that no one would endure.*

§8 But presumably there are some things we cannot be compelled to do. Rather than do them we should suffer the most terrible consequences and accept death; for the things that [allegedly] compelled Euripides' Alcmaeon to kill his mother appear ridiculous.*

§9 It is sometimes difficult, however, to judge what [goods] should be 30 chosen at the price of what [evils], and what [evils] should be endured as the price of what [goods]. It is even more difficult to abide by our judgment, since the results we expect [when we endure] are usually painful, and the actions we are compelled [to endure, when we choose] are usually shameful. That is why those who have been compelled or not com- 1110b pelled receive praise or blame.

§10 What sorts of things, then, should we say are forced? Perhaps we should say that something is forced without qualification whenever its cause is external and the agent contributes nothing. Other things are involuntary in their own right, but choiceworthy on this occasion and as the price of these [goods], and their principle is in the agent. These are 5 involuntary in their own right, but, on this occasion and as the price of these [goods], voluntary.* But they are more like voluntary actions, since the actions are particulars, and [in the case of mixed actions] these particulars are voluntary. But what sort of thing should be chosen as the price of what [good] is not easy to answer, since there are many differences in particular [conditions].

§11 But what if someone says that pleasant things and fine things force 10 us, on the ground that they are outside us and compel us? For him, then, everything must be forced, since everyone in every action aims at something fine or pleasant. Moreover, if we are forced and unwilling to act, we find it painful; but if something pleasant or fine is its cause, we do it with pleasure. It is ridiculous, then,* for him to ascribe responsibility to external causes, not to himself as being easily snared by such things;* and 15 ridiculous to hold himself responsible for his fine actions, but pleasant things responsible for his shameful actions.

§12 What is forced, then, would seem to be what has its principle outside the person forced, who contributes nothing.

§13 Everything caused by ignorance is nonvoluntary, but what is involuntary also involves pain and regret. For if someone's action was 20 caused by ignorance, but he now has no objection to the action, he has

1110b done it neither willingly, since he did not know what it was, nor unwillingly, since he now feels no pain.* Hence, among those who act because of ignorance, the agent who now regrets his action seems to be unwilling, but the agent with no regrets may be called nonwilling, since he is another case—for, since he is different, it is better if he has his own special name.

25 §14 Further, action caused by ignorance would seem to be different from action done in ignorance. For if the agent is drunk or angry, his action seems to be caused by drunkenness or anger, not by ignorance, though it is done in ignorance, not in knowledge. Certainly every vicious person is ignorant of the actions he must do or avoid, and this sort of 30 error makes people unjust, and in general bad.

§15 [This] ignorance of what is beneficial is not taken to make action involuntary. For the cause of involuntary action is not [this] ignorance in the decision, which causes vice; it is not [in other words] ignorance of the 1111a universal, since that is a cause for blame.* Rather, the cause is ignorance of the particulars which the action consists in and is concerned with,* since these allow both pity and pardon. For an agent acts involuntarily if he is ignorant of one of these particulars.

§16 Presumably, then, it is not a bad idea to define these particulars, and say what they are, and how many. They are: who is doing it; what he 5 is doing; about what or to what he is doing it; sometimes also what he is doing it with—with what instrument, for example; for what result, for example, safety; in what way, for example, gently or hard.

§17 Now certainly someone could not be ignorant of *all* of these unless he were mad. Nor, clearly, could he be ignorant of who is doing it, since he could hardly be ignorant of himself. But he might be ignorant of what he is doing, as when someone says that [the secret] slipped out while he was speaking, or, as Aeschylus said about the mysteries, that he did not 10 know it was forbidden to reveal it; or, like the person with the catapult, that he let it go when he [only] wanted to demonstrate it. Again, he might think that his son is an enemy, as Merope did;* or that the barbed spear has a button on it, or that the stone is pumice stone. By giving someone a 15 drink to save his life we might kill him; and wanting to touch someone, as they do in sparring, we might wound him.

§18 Since an agent may be ignorant of any of these particular constituents of his action, someone who was ignorant of one of these seems to have acted unwillingly, especially if he was ignorant of the most important; these seem to be what he is doing, and the result for which he does it.*

§19 Hence the agent who acts involuntarily is the one who acts in 20 accord with this specific sort of ignorance, who must also feel pain and regret for his action.*

§20 Since involuntary action is either forced or caused by ignorance, voluntary action seems to be what has its principle in the agent himself, knowing the particulars that constitute the action.*

§21 For, presumably, it is not right to say that action caused by spirit or appetite is involuntary.* §22 For, first of all, on this view none of the other animals will ever act voluntarily; nor will children.* §23 Next, among all the actions caused by appetite or spirit do we do none of them voluntarily? Or do we do the fine actions voluntarily and the shameful involuntarily? Surely [the second answer] is ridiculous, given that one and the same thing [i.e., appetite or spirit] causes [both fine and shameful actions]. §24 And presumably it is also absurd to say [as the first answer implies] that things we ought to desire* are involuntary. Indeed, we ought both to be angry at some things and to have appetite for some things—for health and learning, for instance. §25 Again, what is involuntary seems to be painful, whereas what accords with appetite seems to be pleasant. *1111a25* 30

§26 Moreover, how are errors in accord with spirit any less voluntary than those in accord with rational calculation? For both sorts of errors are to be avoided. §27 Besides, nonrational feelings seem to be no less human than rational calculation; and so actions resulting from spirit or appetite are also proper to a human being. It is absurd, then, to regard them as involuntary. 1111b

2

[Decision]

Now that we have defined the voluntary and the involuntary, the next task is to discuss decision; for decision seems to be most proper to virtue, and to distinguish characters from one another better than actions do.* 5

§2 Decision, then, is apparently voluntary, but not the same as the voluntary, which extends more widely. For children and the other animals share in voluntary action, but not in decision; and the actions we do on the spur of the moment are said to be voluntary, but not to accord with decision.* 10

§3 Those who say decision is appetite or spirit or wish or some sort of belief would seem to be wrong. For decision is not shared with nonrational animals, but appetite and spirit are shared with them. §4 Again, the incontinent person acts on appetite, not on decision,* but the continent person does the reverse, by acting on decision, not on appetite. §5 Again, appetite is contrary to decision, but not to appetite. Besides, the object of appetite is what is pleasant or painful, whereas neither of these is the object of decision.* §6 And still less is spirit decision; for actions caused by spirit seem least of all to accord with decision. 15

§7 But further, it is not wish either, though it is apparently close to it.* For we do not decide on impossible things—anyone claiming to decide on them would seem a fool;* but we do wish for impossible things—for immortality, for instance—as well as possible things. §8 Further, we 20

1111b wish [not only for results we can achieve], but also for results that are [possible, but] not achievable through our own agency*—victory for 25 some actor or athlete, for instance.* But what we decide on is never anything of that sort, but what we think would come about through our own agency. §9 Again, we wish for the end more [than for the things that promote it], but we decide on things that promote the end.* We wish, for instance, to be healthy, but we decide to do things that will make us healthy; and we wish to be happy, and say so, but we could not appropri- 30 ately say we decide to be happy, since in general the things we decide on would seem to be things that are up to us.

§10 Nor is it belief. For belief seems to be about everything, no less about things that are eternal and things that are impossible [for us] than about things that are up to us. Moreover, beliefs are divided into true and false, not into good and bad, but decisions are divided into good and bad more than into true and false.

1112a §11 Now presumably no one even claims that decision is the same as belief in general. But it is not the same as any kind of belief either. For our decisions to do good or bad actions, not our beliefs, form the characters we have. §12 Again, we decide to take or avoid something good or bad. 5 We believe what it is, whom it benefits or how; but we do not exactly believe to take or avoid. §13 Further, decision is praised more for deciding on what is right, whereas belief is praised for believing rightly.* Moreover, we decide on something [even] when we know most completely that it is good;* but [what] we believe [is] what we do not quite know. §14 Again, those who make the best decisions do not seem to be the same 10 as those with the best beliefs; on the contrary, some seem to have better beliefs, but to make the wrong decisions because of vice. §15 We may grant that decision follows or implies belief. But that is irrelevant, since it is not the question we are asking; our question is whether decision is the same as some sort of belief.

§16 Then what, or what sort of thing, is decision, since it is none of the 15 things mentioned? Well, apparently it is voluntary, but not everything voluntary is decided. §17 Then perhaps what is decided is what has been previously deliberated. For decision involves reason and thought, and even the name itself would seem to indicate that [what is decided, *prohaireton*] is chosen [*haireton*] before [*pro*] other things.*

3

[Deliberation]

Do we deliberate about everything, and is everything open to delibera- 20 tion? Or is there no deliberation about some things? §2 By 'open to deliberation', presumably, we should mean that someone with some sense, not some fool or madman, might deliberate about it.

§3 Now no one deliberates about eternal things—about the universe, for instance, or about the incommensurability of the sides and the diagonal; §4 nor about things that are in movement but always come about the same way, either from necessity or by nature* or by some other cause—the solstices, for instance, or the rising of the stars; §5 nor about what happens in different ways at different times—droughts and rains, for instance; nor about what results from fortune—the finding of a treasure, for instance. For none of these results could be achieved through our agency. 1112a 25 30

§7 We deliberate about what is up to us, that is to say, about the actions we can do; and this is what is left [besides the previous cases]. For causes seem to include nature, necessity, and fortune, but besides them mind and everything [operating] through human agency. §6 But we do not deliberate about all human affairs; no Spartan, for instance, deliberates about how the Scythians might have the best political system.* Rather, each group of human beings deliberates about the actions that they themselves can do. 33 28 29 33

§8 There is no deliberation about the sciences that are exact and self-sufficient, as, for instance, about letters, since we are in no doubt about how to write them [in spelling a word]. Rather, we deliberate about what results through our agency, but in different ways on different occasions—about, for instance, medicine and money making. We deliberate about navigation more than about gymnastics, to the extent that it is less exactly worked out, and similarly with other [crafts]. §9 And we deliberate about beliefs more than about sciences,* since we are more in doubt about them. 1112b 5

§10 Deliberation concerns what is usually [one way rather than another], where the outcome is unclear and the right way to act* is undefined. And we enlist partners in deliberation on large issues when we distrust our own ability to discern [the right answer]. 10

§11 We deliberate not about ends, but about what promotes ends.* A doctor, for instance, does not deliberate about whether he will cure, or an orator about whether he will persuade, or a politician about whether he will produce good order, or any other [expert] about the end [that his science aims at]. Rather, we lay down the end, and then examine the ways and means* to achieve it. 15

If it appears that any of several [possible] means will reach it, we examine which of them will reach it most easily and most finely;* and if only one [possible] means reaches it, we examine how that means will reach it, and how the means itself is reached, until we come to the first cause, the last thing to be discovered. For a deliberator would seem to inquire and analyze in the way described, as though analyzing a diagram. [The comparison is apt, since], §12 apparently, all deliberation is inquiry, though not all inquiry—in mathematics, for instance—is deliberation. And the last thing [found] in the analysis would seem to be the first that comes into being.* 20

1112b25 §13 If we encounter an impossible step—for instance, we need money but cannot raise it—we desist; but if the action appears possible, we undertake it.* What is possible is what we could achieve through our agency [including what our friends could achieve for us]; for what our friends achieve is, in a way, achieved through our agency, since the principle is in us. §14 [In crafts] we sometimes look for instruments, some-
30 times [for the way] to use them; so also in other cases we sometimes look for the means to the end, sometimes for the proper use of the means, or for the means to that proper use.

§15 As we have said, then, a human being would seem to be a principle of action. Deliberation is about the actions he can do, and actions are for the sake of other things; §16 hence we deliberate* about things that
1113a promote an end, not about the end. Nor do we deliberate about particulars, about whether this is a loaf, for instance, or is cooked the right amount; for these are questions for perception, and if we keep on deliberating at each stage we shall go on without end.

§17 What we deliberate about is the same as what we decide to do, except that by the time we decide to do it, it is definite; for what we
5 decide to do is what we have judged [to be right] as a result of deliberation. For each of us stops inquiring how to act as soon as he traces the principle to himself, and within himself to the guiding part; for this is the part that decides. §18 This is also clear from the ancient political systems described by Homer; there the kings would first decide and then announce their decision to the people.*

10 §19 We have found, then,* that what we decide to do is whatever action, among those up to us, we deliberate about and [consequently] desire to do. Hence also decision will be deliberative desire to do an action that is up to us; for when we have judged [that it is right] as a result of deliberation, we desire to do it in accord with our wish.*

§20 We have said in outline, then, what sorts of things decision is about, and [specifically] that we decide on things that promote the end.

4

[Wish]

15 Wish, we have said, is for the end. But some think that wish is for the good, others that it is for the apparent good.

§2 For those who say the good is wished, it follows that what someone wishes if he chooses incorrectly is not wished at all. For if it is wished, then [on this view] it is good; but what he wishes is in fact bad, if it turns
20 out that way. [Hence what he wishes is not wished, which is self-contradictory.]

§3 But for those who say the apparent good is wished, it follows that nothing is wished by nature. Rather, for each person what is wished is what seems [good to him]; but different things, and indeed contrary things, if it turns out that way, appear good to different people.* [Hence contrary things will be wished and nothing will be wished by nature.]

§4 If, then, these views do not satisfy us, should we say that, without qualification and in reality, what is wished is the good, but for each person what is wished is the apparent good? For the excellent person, then, what is wished will be what is [wished] in reality, while for the base person what is wished is whatever it turns out to be [that appears good to him]. Similarly in the case of bodies, really healthy things are healthy to people in good condition, while other things are healthy to sickly people; and the same is true of what is bitter, sweet, hot, heavy, and so on.* For the excellent person judges each sort of thing correctly, and in each case what is true appears to him.

§5 For each state [of character] has its own distinctive [view of] what is fine and pleasant. Presumably, then, the excellent person is far superior because he sees what is true in each case, being himself a sort of standard and measure.* In the many, however, pleasure would seem to cause deception, since it appears good when it is not. §6 Certainly, they choose what is pleasant because they assume it is good, and avoid pain because they assume it is evil.*

5

[Virtue and Vice Are in Our Power]

We have found, then, that we wish for the end, and deliberate and decide about things that promote it; hence the actions concerned with things that promote the end are in accord with decision and are voluntary. The activities of the virtues are concerned with these things [that promote the end].*

§2 Hence virtue is also up to us, and so also, in the same way, is vice. For when acting is up to us, so is not acting, and when no is up to us, so is yes. And so if acting, when it is fine, is up to us, not acting, when it is shameful, is also up to us; and if not acting, when it is fine, is up to us, then acting, when it is shameful, is also up to us. §3 But if doing, and likewise not doing, fine or shameful actions is up to us, and if, as we saw, [doing or not doing them] is [what it is] to be a good or bad person, being decent or base is up to us.*

§4 The claim that 'no one is willingly bad or unwillingly blessed'* would seem to be partly true but partly false. For while certainly no one is unwillingly blessed, vice is voluntary.

§5 If this is not so, we must dispute what has been said, and we must deny that a human being is a principle, begetting actions as he begets children. §6 But if what we have said appears true, and we cannot refer back to other principles apart from those that are up to us,* those things that have their principle in us are themselves up to us and voluntary.

1113b §7 There would seem to be evidence in favor of our view not only in what each of us does as a private citizen, but also in what legislators themselves do. For they impose corrective treatments and penalties on 25 anyone who does vicious actions, unless his action is forced or is caused by ignorance that he is not responsible for;* and they honor anyone who does fine actions. In all this they assume that they will encourage the second sort of person, and restrain the first. But no one encourages us to do anything that is not up to us and voluntary; people assume it is pointless to persuade us not to get hot or distressed or hungry or anything else of that sort, since persuasion will not stop it happening to us.

30 §8 Indeed, legislators also impose corrective treatments for the ignorance itself, if the agent seems to be responsible for the ignorance.* A drunk, for instance, pays a double penalty; for the principle is in him, since he controls whether he gets drunk, and his getting drunk causes his ignorance.* They also impose corrective treatment on someone who [does a vicious action] in ignorance of some provision of law that he is required 1114a to know and that is not hard [to know]. §9 And they impose it in other cases likewise for any other ignorance that seems to be caused by the agent's inattention; they assume it is up to him not to be ignorant, since he controls whether he pays attention.

§10 But presumably he is the sort of person who is inattentive.* Still, he is himself responsible for becoming this sort of person, because he has 5 lived carelessly. Similarly, an individual is responsible for being unjust, because he has cheated, and for being intemperate, because he has passed his time in drinking and the like; for each type of activity produces the corresponding sort of person.* §11 This is clear from those who train for any contest or action, since they continually practice the 10 appropriate activities. §12 [Only] a totally insensible person would not know that a given type of activity is the source of the corresponding 12 state; §13 [Hence] if someone does what he knows will make him 13 unjust, he is willingly unjust.*

11, 12 Further, it is unreasonable for someone doing injustice not to wish to 13 be unjust, or for someone doing intemperate action not to wish to be intemperate.* §14 This does not mean, however, that if he is unjust and 15 wishes to stop, he will thereby stop and be just.* For neither does a sick person recover his health [simply by wishing]; nonetheless, he is sick willingly,* by living incontinently and disobeying the doctors, if that was how it happened. At that time, then, he was free not to be sick, though no longer free once he has let himself go, just as it was up to someone to throw a stone, since the principle was up to him,* though he can no 20 longer take it back once he has thrown it. Similarly, then, the person who is [now] unjust or intemperate was originally free not to acquire this character, so that he has it willingly, though once he has acquired the character, he is no longer free not to have it [now].*

§15 It is not only vices of the soul that are voluntary; vices of the body are also voluntary for some people, and we actually censure them. For we never censure someone if nature causes his ugliness; but if his lack of training or attention causes it, we do censure him. The same is true for weakness or maiming; for everyone would pity someone, not reproach him, if he were blind by nature or because of a disease or a wound, but would censure him if his heavy drinking or some other form of intemperance made him blind. §16 Hence bodily vices that are up to us are censured, while those not up to us are not censured. If so, then in the other cases also the vices that are censured will be up to us.

§17 But someone may say that everyone aims at the apparent good, and does not control how it appears, but, on the contrary, his character controls how the end appears to him.* [We reply that] if each person is in some way responsible for his own state [of character], he is also himself in some way responsible for how [the end] appears.*

Suppose, on the other hand, that no one* is responsible for acting badly, but one does so because one is ignorant of the end, and thinks this is the way to gain what is best for oneself. In that case, one's aiming at the end is not one's own choice; one needs a sort of natural, inborn sense of sight, to judge finely and to choose what is really good. Whoever by nature has this sense in a fine condition has a good nature; for [, according to this view,] this sense is the greatest and finest thing, given that one cannot acquire it or learn it from another, but its natural character determines [his] later condition, and when it is naturally good and fine, that is true and complete good nature.* If all this is true, then, surely virtue will be no more voluntary than vice.*

§18 For how the end appears is laid down, by nature or in whatever way, for the good and the bad person alike; they trace all the other things back to the end in doing whatever actions they do.* §19 Let us suppose, then, that nature does not make the end appear however it appears to each person, but something also depends on him.* Alternatively, let us suppose that [how] the end [appears] is natural, but virtue is voluntary because the virtuous person does the other things voluntarily.* In either case, vice will be no less voluntary than virtue; for the bad person, no less than the good, is responsible for his own actions, even if not for [how] the end [appears].*

§20 Now the virtues, as we say, are voluntary. For in fact we are ourselves in a way jointly responsible for our states of character, and the sort of character we have determines the sort of end we lay down.* Hence the vices will also be voluntary, since the same is true of them.

§21 We have now discussed the virtues in common. We have described their genus in outline; they are means, and they are states. Certain actions produce them, and they cause us to do these same actions in accord with the virtues themselves, in the way that correct reason prescribes. They are up to us and voluntary.*

1114b30 §22 Actions and states, however, are not voluntary in the same way. For we are in control of actions from the beginning to the end, when we 1115a know the particulars. With states, however, we are in control of the beginning, but do not know, any more than with sicknesses, what the cumulative effect of particular actions will be. Nonetheless, since it was up to us to exercise a capacity either this way or another way, states are voluntary.

§23 Let us now take up the virtues again, and discuss them one by 5 one. Let us say what they are, what sorts of thing they are concerned with, and how they are concerned with them. It will also be clear at the same time how many of them there are.

[The Individual Virtues of Character]

6

[Bravery; Its Scope]

First let us discuss bravery. We have already made it apparent that there is a mean about feelings of fear and confidence.* §2 What we fear, clearly, is what is frightening,* and such things are, speaking without qualification, bad things; hence people define fear as expectation of something bad.*

10 §3 Certainly we fear all bad things—for instance, bad reputation, poverty, sickness, friendlessness, death—but they do not all seem to concern the brave person. For fear of some bad things, such as bad reputation, is actually right and fine, and lack of fear is shameful; for if someone fears bad reputation, he is decent and properly prone to shame, and if he has no fear of it, he has no feeling of disgrace. Some, however, 15 call this fearless person brave, by a transference of the name; for he has some similarity to the brave person, since the brave person is also a type of fearless person.

§4 Presumably it is wrong to fear poverty or sickness or, in general, [bad things] that are not the results of vice or caused by ourselves; still, someone who is fearless about these is not thereby brave. He is also called 20 brave by similarity; for some people who are cowardly in the dangers of war are nonetheless generous, and face with confidence the [danger of] losing money.*

§5 Again, if someone is afraid of committing wanton aggression on children or women,* or of being envious or anything of that sort, that does not make him cowardly. And if someone is confident when he is going to be whipped for his crimes, that does not make him brave.

25 §6 Then what sorts of frightening conditions concern the brave person? Surely the most frightening; for no one stands firmer against terrifying conditions. Now death is most frightening of all, since it is a boundary, and when someone is dead nothing beyond it seems either

good or bad for him any more. §7 Still, not even death in all conditions—on the sea, for instance, or in sickness—seems to be the brave person's concern. *1115a*

§8 In what conditions, then, is death his concern? Surely in the finest conditions. Now such deaths are those in war, since they occur in the greatest and finest danger.* §9 This judgment is endorsed by the honors given in cities and by monarchs. §10 Hence someone is called fully brave if he is intrepid in facing a fine death and the immediate dangers that bring death. And this is above all true of the dangers of war. 30 35

§11 Certainly the brave person is also intrepid on the sea and in sickness, but not in the same way as seafarers are. For he has given up hope of safety, and objects to this sort of death [with nothing fine in it], but seafarers' experience makes them hopeful. §12 Moreover, we act like brave men on occasions when we can use our strength, or when it is fine to be killed; and neither of these is true when we perish from shipwreck or sickness. 1115b 5

7

[Bravery; Its Characteristic Outlook]

Now what is frightening is not the same for everyone. We say, however, that some things are too frightening for a human being to resist;* these, then, are frightening for everyone, at least for everyone with any sense. What is frightening, but not irresistible for a human being, varies in its seriousness and degree; and the same is true of what inspires confidence. 10

§2 The brave person is unperturbed, as far as a human being can be. Hence, though he will fear even the sorts of things that are not irresistible, he will stand firm against them, in the right way, as reason prescribes, for the sake of the fine, since this is the end aimed at by virtue.*

§3 It is possible to be more or less afraid of these frightening things, and also possible to be afraid of what is not frightening as though it were frightening. §4 The cause of error may be fear of the wrong thing, or in the wrong way, or at the wrong time, or something of that sort; and the same is true for things that inspire confidence. 15

§5 Hence whoever stands firm against the right things and fears the right things, for the right end, in the right way, at the right time, and is correspondingly confident, is the brave person; for the brave person's actions and feelings accord with what something is worth, and follow what reason prescribes.

§6 Every activity aims at actions in accord with the state of character. Now to the brave person bravery is fine; hence the end it aims at is also fine, since each thing is defined by its end.* The brave person, then, aims at the fine when he stands firm and acts in accord with bravery. 20

§7 Among those who go to excess the excessively fearless person has no name—we said earlier that many cases have no names.* He would be 25

1115b some sort of madman, or incapable of feeling distress, if he feared nothing, neither earthquake nor waves, as they say about the Celts.*

The person who is excessively confident about frightening things is
30 rash. §8 The rash person also seems to be a boaster, and a pretender to bravery.* At any rate, the attitude to frightening things that the brave person really has is the attitude that the rash person wants to appear to have; hence he imitates the brave person where he can. §9 That is why most of them are rash cowards; for, rash though they are on these [occasions for imitation], they do not stand firm against anything frightening.
1116a7 §12 Moreover, rash people are impetuous, wishing for dangers before
8, 9 they arrive, but they shrink from them when they come. Brave people, on the contrary, are eager when in action, but keep quiet until then.*

1115b34 §10 The person who is excessively afraid is the coward, since he fears
35 the wrong things, and in the wrong way, and so on. Certainly, he is also
1116a deficient in confidence, but his excessive pain distinguishes him more clearly. §11 Hence, since he is afraid of everything, he is a despairing sort. The brave person, on the contrary, is hopeful, since [he is confident and] confidence is proper to a hopeful person.

5 §12 Hence the coward, the rash person, and the brave person are all concerned with the same things, but have different states related to them;
7 the others are excessive or defective, but the brave person has the intermediate and right state.

10 §13 As we have said, then, bravery is a mean about what inspires confidence and about what is frightening in the conditions we have described; it chooses and stands firm because that is fine or because anything else is shameful. Dying to avoid poverty or erotic passion or something painful is proper to a coward, not to a brave person. For shirking
15 burdens is softness, and such a person stands firm [in the face of death] to avoid an evil, not because standing firm is fine.*

8

[Conditions That Resemble Bravery]

Bravery, then, is something of this sort. But five other sorts of things are also called bravery.*

The bravery of citizens comes first, since it looks most like bravery. For citizens seem to stand firm against dangers with the aim of avoiding
20 reproaches and legal penalties and of winning honors; that is why the bravest seem to be those who hold cowards in dishonor and do honor to brave people. §2 That is how Homer also describes them when he speaks of Diomede and Hector: 'Polydamas will be the first to heap dis-
25 grace on me', and 'For some time Hector speaking among the Trojans will say, "The son of Tydeus fled from me."'* §3 This is most like the

[genuine] bravery described above, because it results from a virtue; for it *1116a* is caused by shame and by desire for something fine, namely honor,* and by aversion from reproach, which is shameful.

§4 In this class we might also place those who are compelled by their 30 superiors. However, they are worse to the extent that they act because of fear, not because of shame, and to avoid pain, not disgrace. For their commanders compel them, as Hector does; 'If I notice anyone shrinking back 35 from the battle, nothing will save him from being eaten by the dogs.'* §5 Commanders who strike any troops who give ground, or who post 1116b them in front of ditches and suchlike, do the same thing, since they all compel them.* The brave person, however, must be moved by the fine, not by compulsion.

§6 Experience about a given situation also seems to be bravery; that is 5 why Socrates actually thought that bravery is scientific knowledge.* Different people have this sort [of apparent courage] in different conditions. In wartime professional soldiers have it; for there seem to be many groundless alarms in war, and the professionals are the most familiar with these.* Hence they appear brave, since others do not know that the alarms are groundless. §7 Moreover, their experience makes them most capable in attack and defense, since they are skilled in the use of their 10 weapons, and have the best weapons for attack and defense. §8 The result is that in fighting nonprofessionals they are like armed troops against unarmed, or trained athletes against ordinary people; for in these contests also the best fighters are the strongest and physically fittest, not the bravest. 15

§9 Professional soldiers, however, turn out to be cowards whenever the danger overstrains them* and they are inferior in numbers and equipment. For they are the first to run, whereas the citizen troops stand firm and get killed; this was what happened at the temple of Hermes.* For the citizens find it shameful to run, and find death more choiceworthy than 20 safety at this cost. But the professionals from the start were facing the danger on the assumption of their superiority; once they learn their mistake, they run, since they are more afraid of being killed than of doing something shameful. That is not the brave person's character.

§10 Spirit is also counted as bravery; for those who act on spirit also 25 seem to be brave—as beasts seem to be when they attack those who have wounded them—because brave people are also full of spirit.* For spirit is most eager to run and face dangers; hence Homer's words, 'put strength in his spirit', 'aroused strength and spirit', and 'his blood boiled'.* All 30 these would seem to signify the arousal and the impulse of spirit.

§11 Now brave people act because of the fine, and their spirit cooperates with them. But beasts act because of pain; for they attack only because they have been wounded or frightened, (since they keep away from us in a forest). They are not brave, then, since distress and spirit drives them in an impulsive rush to meet danger, foreseeing none of the 35

1117a terrifying prospects. For if they were brave, hungry asses would also be brave, since they keep on feeding even if they are beaten;* and adulterers also do many daring actions because of lust.

5 §12 Human beings as well as beasts find it painful to be angered, and pleasant to exact a penalty. But those who fight for these reasons are not brave, though they are good fighters; for they fight because of their feelings, not because of the fine nor as reason prescribes. Still, they have 4 something similar [to bravery]. The [bravery] caused by spirit would 5 seem to be the most natural sort, and to be [genuine] bravery once it has also acquired decision and the goal.*

9, 10 §13 Hopeful people are not brave either; for their many victories over many opponents make them confident in dangers. They are somewhat similar to brave people, since both are confident. But whereas brave people are confident for the reason given earlier, the hopeful are confident because they think they are stronger and nothing could happen to 15 them; §14 drunks do the same sort of thing, since they become hopeful. When things turn out differently from how they expected, they run away. The brave person, on the contrary, stands firm against what is and appears frightening to a human being; he does this because it is fine to stand firm and shameful to fail.

§15 Indeed, that is why someone who is unafraid and unperturbed in emergencies seems braver than [someone who is unafraid only] when he 20 is warned in advance; for his action proceeds more from his state of character, because it proceeds less from preparation.* For if we are warned in advance, we might decide what to do [not only because of our state of character, but] also by reason and rational calculation; but in emergencies [we must decide] in accord with our state of character.*

§16 Those who act in ignorance also appear brave, and indeed they are close to hopeful people, though inferior to them insofar as they lack 25 the self-esteem of hopeful people. That is why the hopeful stand firm for some time, whereas if ignorant people have been deceived and then realize or suspect that things are different, they run. That was what happened to the Argives when they stumbled on the Spartans and took them for Sicyonians.*

§17 We have described, then, the character of brave people and of those who seem to be brave.

9

[Feelings Proper to Bravery]

30 Bravery is about feelings of confidence and fear—not, however, about both in the same way, but more about frightening things. For someone is brave if he is undisturbed and in the right state about these, more than if he is in this state about things inspiring confidence.

§2 As we said, then, standing firm against what is painful makes us call people brave; that is why bravery is both painful and justly praised, since it is harder to stand firm against something painful than to refrain from something pleasant. §3 Nonetheless, the end that bravery aims at seems to be pleasant, though obscured by its surroundings. This is what happens in athletic contests. For boxers find that the end they aim at, the crown and the honors, is pleasant, but, being made of flesh and blood, they find it distressing and painful to take the punches and to bear all the hard work; and because there are so many of these painful things, the end, being small, appears to have nothing pleasant in it. *1117a* 35 1117b 5

§4 And so, if the same is true for bravery, the brave person will find death and wounds painful, and suffer them unwillingly, but he will endure them because that is fine or because failure is shameful.* Indeed, the truer it is that he has every virtue and the happier he is, the more pain he will feel at the prospect of death. For this sort of person, more than anyone, finds it worthwhile to be alive, and knows he is being deprived of the greatest goods, and this is painful. But he is no less brave for all that; presumably, indeed, he is all the braver, because he chooses what is fine in war at the cost of all these goods. §5 It is not true, then, in the case of every virtue that its active exercise is pleasant; it is pleasant only insofar as we attain the end. 10 15

§6 But presumably it is quite possible for brave people, given the character we have described, not to be the best soldiers.* Perhaps the best will be those who are less brave, but possess no other good; for they are ready to face dangers, and they sell their lives for small gains. 20

§7 So much for bravery. It is easy to grasp what it is, in outline at least, from what we have said.

10

[Temperance; Its Scope]

Let us discuss temperance next; for bravery and temperance seem to be the virtues of the nonrational parts. Temperance, then, is a mean concerned with pleasures, as we have already said; for it is concerned less, and in a different way, with pains. Intemperance appears in this same area too. Let us, then, now distinguish the specific pleasures that concern them. 25

§2 First, let us distinguish pleasures of the soul from those of the body. Love of honor and of learning, for instance, are among the pleasures of the soul; for though a lover of one of these enjoys it, only his thought, not his body, is at all affected. Those concerned with such pleasures are called neither temperate nor intemperate. The same applies to those concerned with any of the other nonbodily pleasures; for lovers of tales, storytellers, 30 35

1117b those who waste their days on trivialities, are called babblers, but not
1118a intemperate. Nor do we call people intemperate if they feel pain over money or friends.

§3 Temperance, then, will be about bodily pleasures, but not even about all of these. For those who find enjoyment in objects of sight, such
5 as colors, shapes, a painting, are called neither temperate nor intemperate, even though it would also seem possible to enjoy these either rightly or excessively and deficiently. §4 The same is true for hearing; no one is ever called intemperate for excessive enjoyment of songs or playacting, or temperate for the right enjoyment of them.

10 §5 Nor is this said about someone enjoying smells, except coincidentally.* For someone is called intemperate not for enjoying the smell of apples or roses or incense, but rather for enjoying the smell of perfumes or cooked delicacies. For these are the smells an intemperate person enjoys because they remind him of the objects of his appetite. §6 And
15 we can see that others also enjoy the smells of food if they are hungry.* It is the enjoyment of the things [that he is reminded of by these smells] that is proper to an intemperate person, since these are the objects of his appetite.

§7 Nor do other animals find pleasures from these senses, except coin-
20 cidentally. What a hound enjoys, for instance, is not the smell of a hare, but eating it; but the hare's smell made the hound perceive it. And what a lion enjoys is not the sound of the ox, but eating it; but since the ox's sound made the lion perceive that it was near, the lion appears to enjoy the sound. Similarly, what pleases him is not the sight of 'a deer or a wild goat',* but the prospect of food.

25 §8 The pleasures that concern temperance and intemperance are those that are shared with the other animals, and so appear slavish and bestial.* These pleasures are touch and taste.*

§9 However, they seem to deal even with taste very little or not at all. For taste discriminates flavors—the sort of thing that wine tasters
30 and cooks savoring food do; but people, or intemperate people at any rate, do not much enjoy this. Rather, they enjoy the gratification that comes entirely through touch, in eating and drinking and in what are called the pleasures of sex. §10 That is why a glutton actually prayed
1118b for his throat to become longer than a crane's, showing that he took pleasure in the touching.* And so the sense that concerns intemperance is the most widely shared, and seems justifiably open to reproach, since we have it insofar as we are animals, not insofar as we are human beings.

§11 To enjoy these things, then, and to like them most of all, is bestial.
5 For indeed the most civilized of the pleasures coming through touch, such as those produced by rubbing and warming in gymnasia, are excluded from intemperance, since the touching that is proper to the intemperate person concerns only some parts of the body, not all of it.

11

[Temperance; Its Outlook]

Some appetites seem to be shared [by everyone], while others seem to be *1119a* additions that are distinctive [of different people]. The appetite for nour- 10 ishment, for instance, is natural, since everyone who lacks nourishment, dry or liquid, has an appetite for it, sometimes for both; and, as Homer says, the young in their prime [all] have an appetite for sex.* Not everyone, however, has an appetite for a specific sort of food or drink or sex, or for the same things. §2 That is why an appetite of this type seems to be distinctive of [each of] us. Still, this also includes a natural element, since different sorts of people find different sorts of things more pleasant, and there are some things that are more pleasant for everyone than things chosen at random would be.

§3 In natural appetites few people are in error, and only in one direc- 15 tion, toward excess. Eating indiscriminately or drinking until we are too full is exceeding the quantity that accords with nature; for [the object of] natural appetite is the filling of a lack. That is why these people are called 'gluttons', showing that they glut their bellies past what is right;* that is 20 how especially slavish people turn out.

§4 With the pleasures that are distinctive of different people, many make errors and in many ways; for people are called lovers of something if they enjoy the wrong things, or if they enjoy something in the wrong way. And in all these ways intemperate people go to excess. For some of 25 the things they enjoy are hateful, and hence wrong; distinctive pleasures that it is right to enjoy they enjoy more than is right, and more than most people enjoy them.

§5 Clearly, then, with pleasures excess is intemperance, and is blameworthy. With pains, however, we are not called temperate, as we are called brave, for standing firm against them, or intemperate for not 30 standing firm. Rather, someone is intemperate because he feels more pain than is right at failing to get pleasant things; and even this pain is produced by the pleasure [he takes in them]. And someone is temperate because he does not feel pain at the absence of what is pleasant, or at refraining from it.

§6 The intemperate person, then, has an appetite for all pleasant 1119a things, or rather for the most pleasant of them, and his appetite leads him to choose these at the cost of the other things. That is why he also feels pain both when he fails to get something and when he has an appetite for it, since appetite involves pain. It would seem absurd, however, to suffer 5 pain because of pleasure.

§7 People who are deficient in pleasures and enjoy them less than is right are not found very much. For that sort of insensibility is not human; indeed, even the other animals discriminate among foods, enjoying some

1119a but not others. If someone finds nothing pleasant, or preferable to any-
10 thing else, he is far from being human. The reason he has no name is that he is not found much.

§8 The temperate person has an intermediate state in relation to these [bodily pleasures]. For he finds no pleasure in what most pleases the intemperate person, but finds it disagreeable; he finds no pleasure at all in the wrong things. He finds no intense pleasure in any [bodily pleasures],
15 suffers no pain at their absence, and has no appetite for them, or only a moderate appetite, not to the wrong degree or at the wrong time or anything else at all of that sort.* If something is pleasant and conducive to health or fitness, he will desire this moderately and in the right way; and he will desire in the same way anything else that is pleasant, if it is no obstacle to health and fitness, does not deviate from the fine, and does not exceed his means. For the opposite sort of person likes these pleasures
20 more than they are worth; that is not the temperate person's character, but he likes them as correct reason prescribes.

12

[Intemperance]

Intemperance is more like a voluntary condition than cowardice; for it is caused by pleasure, which is choiceworthy, whereas cowardice is caused by pain, which is to be avoided.* §2 Moreover, pain disturbs and ruins the nature of the sufferer, while pleasure does nothing of the sort; intem-
25 perance, then, is more voluntary. That is why it is also more open to reproach. For it is also easier to acquire the habit of facing pleasant things, since our life includes many of them and we can acquire the habit with no danger; but with frightening things the reverse is true.

§3 However, cowardice seems to be more voluntary than particular cowardly actions. For cowardice itself involves no pain, but the particular
30 actions disturb us because of the pain [that causes them], so that people actually throw away their weapons and do all the other disgraceful actions. That is why these actions even seem to be forced [and hence involuntary].*

§4 For the intemperate person the reverse is true. The particular actions are the result of his appetite and desire, and so they are voluntary; but the whole condition is less voluntary [than the actions], since no one has an appetite to be intemperate.

1119b §5 We also apply the name of intemperance to the errors of children, since they have some similarity.* Which gets its name from which does not matter for our present purposes, but clearly the posterior is called after the prior.

§6 The name would seem to be quite appropriately transferred. For
5 the things that need to be tempered are those that desire shameful things

and tend to grow large. Appetites and children are most like this; for children also live by appetite, and desire for the pleasant is found more in them than in anyone else. *1119b*

§7 If, then, [the child or the appetitive part] is not obedient and subordinate to its rulers, it will go far astray. For when someone lacks understanding, his desire for the pleasant is insatiable and seeks indiscriminate satisfaction. The [repeated] active exercise of appetite increases the appetite he already had from birth, and if the appetites are large and intense, 10 they actually expel rational calculation. That is why appetites must be moderate and few, and never contrary to reason. §8 This is the condition we call obedient and temperate. And just as the child's life must follow the instructions of his guide, so too the appetitive part must follow 15 reason.*

§9 Hence the temperate person's appetitive part must agree with reason; for both [his appetitive part and his reason] aim at the fine, and the temperate person's appetites are for the right things, in the right ways, at the right times, which is just what reason also prescribes.

So much, then, for temperance.

Book IV

1

[Generosity]

Next let us discuss generosity. It seems, then, to be the mean about wealth; for the generous person is praised not in conditions of war, nor in those in which the temperate person is praised, nor in judicial verdicts, but in the 25 giving and taking of wealth, and more especially in the giving.* §2 By wealth we mean anything whose worth is measured by money.

§3 Both wastefulness and ungenerosity are excesses and deficiencies about wealth. Ungenerosity is always ascribed to those who take wealth 30 more seriously than is right. But when wastefulness is attributed to someone, several vices are sometimes combined. For incontinent people and those who spend money on intemperance are called wasteful. §4 Since these have many vices at the same time, they make wasteful people seem the basest.

These people, however, are not properly called wasteful.* §5 For the wasteful person is meant to have the single vicious feature of ruining his 1120a property; for someone who causes his own destruction ['lays waste' to himself, and so] is wasteful, and ruining one's own property seems to be a sort of self-destruction, on the assumption that our living depends on our property. This, then, is how we understand wastefulness.

§6 Whatever has a use can be used either well or badly; riches are 5 something useful; and the best user of something is the person who has

1120a the virtue concerned with it. Hence the best user of riches will be the person who has the virtue concerned with wealth; and this is the generous person.*

§7 Using wealth seems to consist in spending and giving, whereas taking and keeping seem to be possessing rather than using. That is why it is more proper to the generous person to give to the right people than to take from the right sources and not from the wrong sources.*

For it is more proper to virtue to do good than to receive good, and more proper to do fine actions than not to do shameful ones;* §8 and clearly [the right sort of] giving implies doing good and doing fine actions, while [the right sort of] taking implies receiving well or not doing something shameful. Moreover, thanks go to the one who gives, not to the one who fails to take, and praise goes more [to the giver]. §9 Besides, not taking is easier than giving, since people part with what is their own less readily than they avoid taking what is another's. §10 Further, those who are called generous are those who give [rightly]. Those who avoid taking [wrongly] are not praised for generosity, though they are praised nonetheless for justice, while those who take [rightly] are not much praised at all. §11 Besides, generous people are loved more than practically any others who are loved because of their virtue; that is because they are beneficial; and they are beneficial in their giving.

§12 Actions in accord with virtue are fine, and aim at the fine. Hence the generous person will also aim at the fine in his giving, and will give correctly; for he will give to the right people, the right amounts, at the right time, and all the other things that are implied by correct giving. §13 Moreover, he will do this with pleasure,* or at any rate without pain; for action in accord with virtue is pleasant or at any rate painless, and least of all is it painful.

§14 If someone gives to the wrong people, or does not aim at the fine, but gives for some other reason, he will not be called generous, but some other sort of person. Nor will he be called generous if he finds it painful to give; for such a person would choose wealth over fine action, and that is not how the generous person chooses.

§15 Nor will the virtuous person take wealth from the wrong sources; since he does not honor wealth, this way of taking it is not for him. §16 Nor will he be ready to ask for favors; since he is the one who benefits others, receiving benefits readily is not for him.

1120b §17 He will, however, acquire wealth from the right sources—from his own possessions, for instance—regarding taking not as fine, but as necessary to provide something to give. Nor will he neglect his own possessions, since he wants to use them to assist people. And he will avoid giving to just anyone, so that he will have something to give to the right people, at the right time, and where it is fine.

§18 It is also very definitely proper to the generous person to exceed so much in giving that he leaves less for himself, since it is proper to a generous person not to look out for himself. §19 However, ['exceed' must be explained;] in speaking of generosity we refer to what accords with one's means. For what is generous does not depend on the quantity of what is given, but on the state [of character] of the giver, and the generous state gives in accord with one's means. Hence one who gives less than another may still be more generous, if he has less to give. 1120b 10

§20 Those who have not acquired their means by their own efforts, but have inherited it, seem to be more generous; for they have had no experience of shortage, and, besides, everyone likes his own work more than [other people's], as parents and poets do.*

It is not easy for a generous person to grow rich, since he is ready to spend, not to take or keep, and honors wealth for the sake of giving, not for itself. §21 Indeed, that is why fortune is denounced, because those who most deserve to grow rich actually do so least. This is only to be expected, however, since someone cannot possess wealth, any more than other things, if he pays no attention to possessing it. 15

§22 Still, he does not give to the wrong people, at the wrong time, and so on. For if he did, he would no longer be acting in accord with generosity, and if he spent his resources on the wrong sort of giving, he would have nothing left to spend for the right purposes. §23 For, as we have said, the generous person is the one who spends in accord with his means, and for the right purposes, whereas the one who exceeds his means is wasteful. That is why tyrants are not called wasteful, since it seems they will have difficulty exceeding their possessions in giving and spending. 20 25

§24 Since generosity, then, is a mean concerned with the giving and the taking of wealth, the generous person will both give and spend the right amounts for the right purposes, in small and large matters alike, and do this with pleasure. He will also take the right amounts from the right sources. For since the virtue is a mean about both giving and taking, he will do both in the right way; for decent giving implies decent taking, and the other sort of taking is contrary to the decent sort. Hence the states that imply each other are present at the same time in the same subject, whereas the contrary states clearly are not. 30 1121a

§25 If the generous person finds that his spending deviates from what is fine and right, he will feel pain, but moderately and in the right way; for it is proper to virtue to feel both pleasure and pain in the right things and in the right way.*

§26 The generous person is also an easy partner to have common dealings with matters of money; §27 for he can easily be treated unjustly, since he does not honor money, and is more grieved if he has failed to spend what it was right to spend than if he has spent what it was wrong to spend—here he does not please Simonides.* 5

1121a §28 The wasteful person is in error here too, since he feels neither pleasure nor pain at the right things or in the right way; this will be more evident as we go on.

10 §29 We have said, then, that wastefulness and ungenerosity are excesses and deficiencies in two things, in giving and taking—for we also count spending as giving. Now wastefulness is excessive in giving and 15 not taking, but deficient in taking. Ungenerosity is deficient in giving and excessive in taking, but in small matters.

§30 Now the different aspects of wastefulness are not very often combined; for it is not easy to take from nowhere and give to everyone, since private citizens soon outrun their resources in giving, and private citizens are the ones who seem to be wasteful. §31 However, such a person 20 seems to be quite a lot better than the ungenerous person, since he is easily cured, both by growing older and by poverty, and is capable of reaching the intermediate condition.* For he has the features proper to the generous person, since he gives and does not take, though he does neither rightly or well. If, then, he is changed, by habituation or some other means, so that he does them rightly and well, he will be generous; for 25 then he will give to the right people and will not take from the wrong sources. This is why the wasteful person seems not to be base in his character; for excess in giving without taking is proper to a foolish person, not to a vicious or ignoble one. §32 Someone who is wasteful in this way seems to be much better than the ungenerous person, both for the reasons just given and because he benefits many, whereas the ungenerous person benefits no one, not even himself.

30 §33 Most wasteful people, however, as we have said, [not only give wrongly, but] also take from the wrong sources, and to this extent are ungenerous.* §34 They become acquisitive because they wish to spend, but cannot do this readily, since they soon exhaust all they have; hence 1121b they are compelled to provide from elsewhere. At the same time they care nothing for the fine, and so take from any source without scruple; for they have an urge to give,* and the way or source does not matter to them.

§35 This is why their ways of giving are not generous either, since they 5 are not fine, do not aim at the fine, and are not done in the right way. Rather, these people sometimes enrich people who ought to be poor, and would give nothing to people with sound characters, but would give much to flatterers or to those providing some other pleasure. That is why most of these people are also intemperate. For since they part with money 10 readily, they also spend it lavishly on intemperance; and because their lives do not aim at the fine, they decline toward pleasures.

§36 If, then, the wasteful person has been left without a guide, he changes into this;* but if he receives attention, he might reach the intermediate and the right state.

§37 Ungenerosity, however, is incurable, since old age and every incapacity seem to make people ungenerous.* And it comes more naturally to human beings than wastefulness; for the many are money-lovers rather than givers. §38 Moreover, it extends widely and has many species, since there seem to be many ways of being ungenerous. For it consists in two conditions, deficiency in giving and excess in taking; but it is not found as a whole in all cases. Sometimes the two conditions are separated, and some people go to excess in taking, whereas others are deficient in giving. *1121b15* 20

§39 For the people called misers, tightfisted, skinflints and so on, are all deficient in giving, but they do not go after other people's goods and do not wish to take them. With some people the reason for this is some sort of decency in them, and a concern to avoid what is shameful. For some people seem—at least, this is what they say—to hold on to their money so that they will never be compelled to do anything shameful.* These include the cheeseparer, and everyone like that; he is so called from his excessive refusal to give anything. Others keep their hands off other people's property because they are afraid,* supposing that it is not easy for them to take other people's property without other people taking theirs too; hence, they say, they are content* if they neither take from others nor give to them. 25 30

§40 Other people, by contrast, go to excess in taking, by taking anything from any source—those, for instance, who work at degrading occupations,* pimps and all such people, and usurers who lend small amounts at high interest; for all of these take the wrong amounts from the wrong sources. 1122a

§41 Shameful love of gain is apparently their common feature, since they all put up with reproaches for some gain—more precisely, for a small gain. §42 For those who take the wrong things from the wrong sources on a large scale—such as tyrants who sack cities and plunder temples—are called wicked, impious, and unjust, but not ungenerous. §43 The ungenerous, however, include the gambler and the robber,* since these are shameful lovers of gain. For in pursuit of gain both go to great efforts and put up with reproaches; the robber faces the greatest dangers to get his haul, while the gambler takes his gains from his friends, the very people he ought to be giving to. Both of them, then, are shameful lovers of gain, because they wish to acquire gains from the wrong sources; and all these methods of acquisition are ungenerous. 5 10

§44 It is plausibly said that ungenerosity is contrary to generosity. For it is a greater evil than wastefulness; and error in this direction is more common than the error of wastefulness, as we have described it. §45 So much, then, for generosity and the vices opposed to it. 15

2

[Magnificence]

Next, it seems appropriate to discuss magnificence also. For it seems to be, like generosity, a virtue concerned with wealth, but it does not extend, 20

1122a as generosity does, to all the actions involving wealth, but only to those involving heavy expenses, and in them it exceeds generosity in its large scale. For, just as the name [*megaloprepeia*] itself suggests, magnificence is expenditure that is fitting [*prepousa*] in its large scale [*megethos*]. §2 But large scale is large relative to something; for the expenses of the captain of 25 a warship and of the leader of a delegation are not the same.* Hence what is fitting is also relative to oneself, the circumstances, and the purpose.

§3 Someone is called magnificent only if he spends the worthy amount on a large purpose, not on a trivial or an ordinary purpose like the one who 'gave to many a wanderer';* for the magnificent person is generous, but generosity does not imply magnificence.*

30 §4 The deficiency falling short of this state is called stinginess. The excess is called vulgarity, poor taste, and such things. These are excesses not because they spend an excessively great amount on the right things, but because they show off in the wrong circumstances and in the wrong way. We shall discuss these vices later.

§5 The magnificent person, in contrast to these, is like a scientific 35 expert, since he is able to observe what will be the fitting amount, and to 1122b spend large amounts in an appropriate way. §6 For, as we said at the start, a state is defined by its activities and its objects; now the magnificent person's expenditures* are large and fitting; so also, then, must the results be, since that is what makes the expense large and fitting to the 5 result. Hence the result must be worthy of the expense, and the expense worthy of, or even in excess of, the result.

§7 In this sort of spending the magnificent person will aim at the fine; for that is a common feature of the virtues.* §8 Moreover, he will spend gladly and readily, since it is stingy to count every penny. §9 He will think more about the finest and most fitting way to spend than about the 10 cost or about the cheapest way to do it.

§10 Hence the magnificent person must also be generous; for the generous person will also spend what is right in the right way. But it is in this spending that the large scale of the magnificent person, his greatness, is found, since his magnificence is a sort of large scale of generosity in these things; and from an expense that is equal [to a nonmagnificent person's] 15 he will make the result more magnificent. For a possession and a result have different sorts of excellence; the most honored [and hence most excellent] possession is the one worth most—for example, gold—but the most honored result is the one that is great and fine, since that is what is admirable to behold.* Now what is magnificent is admirable, and the excellence of the result consists in its large scale.*

20 §11 This sort of excellence is found in the sorts of expenses called honorable, such as expenses for the gods—dedications, temples, sacrifices, and so on, for everything divine—and in expenses that provoke a good competition for honor, for the common good,* if, for instance, some

city thinks a splendid chorus or warship or a feast for the city must be provided. *1122b*

§12 But in all cases, as we have said, we fix the right amount by reference to the agent [as well as the task]—by who he is and what resources he has; for the amounts must be worthy of these, fitting the producer as well as the result. 25

§13 That is why a poor person could not be magnificent; he lacks the means for large and fitting expenditures. If he tries to be magnificent, he is foolish; for he spends more than what is worthy and right for him, whereas correct spending accords with virtue. §14 Large spending befits those who have the means, acquired through their own efforts or their ancestors or connections, or are well born or reputable, and so on; for each of these conditions includes greatness and reputation for worth. 30

§15 This, then, above all is the character of the magnificent person, and magnificence is found in these sorts of expenses, as we have said, since these are the largest and most honored. 35

It is found also in those private expenses that arise only once, such as a wedding and the like, and in those that concern the whole city, or the people in it with a reputation for worth—the receiving of foreign guests and sending them off, gifts and exchanges of gifts. For the magnificent person spends money on the common good, not on himself, and the gifts have some similarity to dedications. 1123a 5

§16 It is also proper to the magnificent person to build a house befitting his riches, since this is also a suitable adornment.* He spends more readily on long-lasting results, since these are the finest. In each case he spends on what is fitting. §17 For what suits gods does not suit human beings, and what suits a temple does not suit a tomb. 10

And since each great expense is great in relation to a particular kind of object, the most magnificent will be a great expense on a great object, and the [magnificent] in a particular area will be what is great in relation to the particular kind of object.* §18 Moreover, greatness in the results is not the same as greatness in an expense, since the finest ball or oil bottle has the magnificence proper to a gift for a child, but its value is small and paltry.* §19 That is why it is proper to the magnificent person, whatever kind of thing he produces, to produce it magnificently, since this is not easily exceeded, and to produce something worthy of the expense. 15

§20 This, then, is the character of the magnificent person.

The vulgar person who exceeds [the mean] exceeds by spending more than is right, as has been said. For in small expenses he spends a lot, and puts on an inappropriate display. He gives his club a dinner party in the style of a wedding banquet,* and when he supplies a chorus for a comedy, he brings them onstage dressed in purple, as they do at Megara.* In all this he aims not at the fine, but at the display of his wealth and at the 20 25

1123a admiration he thinks he wins in this way. Where a large expense is right, he spends a little, and he spends a lot where a small expense is right.*

§21 The stingy person will be deficient in everything. After spending the largest amounts, he will refuse a small amount, and so destroy a fine 30 result. Whatever he does, while he is doing it he will hesitate and consider how he can spend the smallest possible amount; he will even moan about spending this, and will always think he is doing something on a larger scale than is right.

§22 These states, vulgarity and stinginess, are vices. But they do not bring reproaches, since they do no harm to one's neighbors* and are not too disgraceful.

3

[Magnanimity]

35 Magnanimity seems, even if we go simply by the name, to be concerned 1123b with great things.* Let us see first the sorts of things it is concerned with. §2 It does not matter whether we consider the state itself or the person who acts in accord with it.

§3 The magnanimous person, then, seems* to be the one who thinks himself worthy* of great things and is really worthy of them. For if someone is not worthy of them but thinks he is, he is foolish, and no virtuous person is foolish or senseless; hence the magnanimous person is the one 5 we have mentioned. §4 For if someone is worthy of little and thinks so, he is temperate, but not magnanimous; §5 for magnanimity is found in greatness, just as beauty is found in a large body, and small people can be attractive and well proportioned, but not beautiful.*

§6 Someone who thinks he is worthy of great things, but is not worthy of them, is vain; but not everyone who thinks he is worthy of greater things than he is worthy of is vain.

10 §7 Someone who thinks he is worthy of less than he is worthy of is pusillanimous,* whether he is worthy of great or of moderate things, or of little and thinks himself worthy of still less. The one who seems most pusillanimous is the one who is worthy of great things; for consider how little he would think of himself if he were worthy of less.

§8 The magnanimous person, then, is at the extreme insofar as he makes great claims. But insofar as he makes them rightly, he is intermedi- 15 ate; for what he thinks he is worthy of accords with his real worth, whereas the others are excessive or deficient. §12 The pusillanimous 25 person is deficient both in relation to himself [i.e., his worth] and in relation to the magnanimous person's estimate of his own worth. §13 The vain person makes claims that are excessive for himself, but not for the magnanimous person.*

§9 If, then, he thinks he is worthy of great things, and is worthy of them, especially of the greatest things, he has one concern above all.

§10 Worth is said to [make one worthy of] external goods; and we would suppose that the greatest of these is the one we award to the gods, the one above all that is the aim of people with a reputation for worth, the prize for the finest [achievements]. All this is true of honor, since it is the greatest of external goods. Hence the magnanimous person has the right concern with honors and dishonors. §11 And even without argument it appears that magnanimous people are concerned with honor; for the great think themselves worthy of honor most of all, but in accord with their worth.* *1123b* 20

§14 Since the magnanimous person is worthy of the greatest things, he is the best person. For in every case the better person is worthy of something greater, and the best person is worthy of the greatest things; and hence the truly magnanimous person must be good.*

Greatness in each virtue also seems proper to the magnanimous person.* §15 Surely* it would not at all fit a magnanimous person to run away [from danger when a coward would], swinging his arms [to get away faster], or to do injustice. For what goal will make him do shameful actions, given that none [of their goals] is great to him? And if we examine particular cases, we can see that the magnanimous person appears altogether ridiculous if he is not good. Nor would he be worthy of honor if he were base; for honor is the prize of virtue, and is awarded to good people. 30 35

§16 Magnanimity, then, would seem to be a sort of adornment* of the virtues; for it makes them greater, and it does not arise without them. That is why it is difficult to be truly magnanimous, since it is not possible without being fine and good. 1124a

§17 The magnanimous person, then, is concerned especially with honors and dishonors.* When he receives great honors from excellent people, he will be moderately pleased, thinking he is getting what is proper to him, or even less. For there can be no honor worthy of complete virtue; but still he will accept honors [from excellent people], since they have nothing greater to award him. But if he is honored by just anyone, or for something small, he will altogether disdain it; for that is not what he is worthy of. And similarly he will disdain dishonor; for it will not be justly attached to him. 5 10

§18 As we have said, then, the magnanimous person is concerned especially with honors. Still, he will also have a moderate attitude to riches and power and every sort of good and bad fortune, however it turns out. He will be neither excessively pleased by good fortune nor excessively distressed by ill fortune, since he does not even regard honor as the greatest good. For positions of power and riches are choiceworthy for their honor; at any rate their possessors wish to be honored on account of them. Hence the magnanimous person, given that he counts honor for little, will also count these other goods for little; that is why he seems arrogant.* 15 20

1124a §19 The results of good fortune, however, also seem to contribute to magnanimity. For the wellborn and the powerful or rich are thought worthy of honor, since they are in a superior position, and everything superior in some good is more honored. That is why these things also make people more magnanimous, since some people honor their possessors for 25 these goods.* In reality, however, it is only the good person who is honorable. §20 Still, anyone who has both virtue and these goods is more readily thought worthy of honor.

Those who lack virtue but have these other goods are not justified in thinking themselves worthy of great things, and are not correctly called magnanimous; that is impossible without complete virtue. §21 They 30 become arrogant and wantonly aggressive when they have these other goods.* For without virtue it is hard to bear the results of good fortune 1124b suitably, and when these people cannot do it, but suppose they are superior to other people, they think less of everyone else, and do whatever they please. They do this because they are imitating the magnanimous person though they are not really like him. They imitate him where they 5 can; hence they do not act in accord with virtue, but they think less of other people. §22 For the magnanimous person is justified when he thinks less of others, since his beliefs are true; but the many think less of others with no good reason.*

§23 He does not face dangers in a small cause; he does not face them frequently, since he honors few things; and he is no lover of danger.* But he faces dangers in a great cause, and whenever he faces them he is unsparing of his life, since he does not think life at all costs is worth living.

10 §24 He is the sort of person who does good but is ashamed when he receives it; for doing good is proper to the superior person, but receiving it is proper to the inferior.* He returns more good than he has received; for in this way the original giver will be repaid, and will also have incurred a new debt to him, and will be the beneficiary.

§25 Magnanimous people seem to remember the good they do, but not what they receive, since the recipient is inferior to the giver, and the 15 magnanimous person wishes to be superior. And they seem to find pleasure in hearing of the good they do, and none in hearing of what they receive—that also seems to be why Thetis does not tell Zeus of the good she has done him,* and the Spartans do not tell of the good they have done the Athenians, but only of the good received from them.*

§26 Again, it is proper to the magnanimous person to ask for nothing, or hardly anything, but to help eagerly.

20 When he meets people with good fortune or a reputation for worth, he displays his greatness,* since superiority over them is difficult and impressive, and there is nothing ignoble in trying to be impressive with them. But when he meets ordinary people* he is moderate, since superiority over them is easy, and an attempt to be impressive among inferiors is as vulgar as a display of strength against the weak.

§27 He stays away from what is commonly honored, and from areas where others lead; he is inactive and a delayer, except for some great honor or achievement. His actions are few, but great and renowned.* *1124b* 25

§28 Moreover, he must be open in his hatreds and his friendships, since concealment is proper to a frightened person.* He is concerned for the truth* more than for people's opinion. He is open in his speech and actions, since his thinking less of other people makes him speak freely. And he speaks the truth, except [when he speaks less than the truth] to the many, [because he is moderate], not because he is self-deprecating.* 30

§29 He cannot let anyone else, except a friend, determine his life. For that would be slavish; and this is why all flatterers are servile and inferior people are flatterers.* 1125a

§30 He is not prone to marvel, since he finds nothing great, or to remember evils, since it is proper to a magnanimous person not to nurse memories, especially not of evils, but to overlook them. 5

§31 He is no gossip. For he will not talk about himself or about another, since he is not concerned to have himself praised or other people blamed. Nor is he given to praising people. Hence he does not speak evil even of his enemies, except [when he responds to their] wanton aggression.*

§32 He especially avoids laments or entreaties about necessities or small matters, since these attitudes are proper to someone who takes these things seriously. 10

§33 He is the sort of person whose possessions are fine and unproductive rather than productive and advantageous, since that is more proper to a self-sufficient person.

§34 The magnanimous person seems to have slow movements, a deep voice, and calm speech. For since he takes few things seriously, he is in no hurry, and since he counts nothing great, he is not strident; and these [attitudes he avoids] are the causes of a shrill voice and hasty movements.* 15

This, then, is the character of the magnanimous person. §35 The deficient person is pusillanimous, and the person who goes to excess is vain. [Like the vulgar and the stingy person] these also seem not to be evil people, since they are not evildoers, but to be in error.

For the pusillanimous person is worthy of goods, but deprives himself of the goods he is worthy of, and would seem to have something bad in him because he does not think he is worthy of the goods. Indeed he would seem not to know himself; for if he did, he would aim at the things he is worthy of, since they are goods. For all that, such people seem hesitant rather than foolish. But this belief of theirs actually seems to make them worse. For each sort of person seeks what [he thinks] he is worth; and these people hold back from fine actions and practices, and equally from external goods, because they think they are unworthy of them. 20 25

1125a §36 Vain people, by contrast, are foolish and do not know themselves, and they make this obvious. For they undertake commonly honored 30 exploits, but are not worthy of them, and then they are found out. They adorn themselves with clothes and ostentatious style and that sort of thing; and since they want everyone to know how fortunate they are, they talk about it, thinking it will bring them honor.

§37 Pusillanimity is more opposed than vanity to magnanimity; for it arises more often, and is worse.*

35 §38 Magnanimity, then, as has been said, is the virtue concerned with honor, and [specifically] with great honor.*

4

[The Virtue Concerned with Small Honors]

1125b But, as we said in the first discussion, [just as there is a virtue for small-scale giving], there would also seem to be a virtue concerned with honor that seems to be related to magnanimity in the way that generosity is related to magnificence.* For it abstains, just as generosity does, from any- 5 thing great, but forms the right attitude in us on medium and small matters.

§2 Just as the taking and giving of money admits of a mean, an excess and a deficiency, so also we can desire honor more or less than is right, 10 and we can desire it from the right sources and in the right way.* §3 For we blame the honor-lover for aiming at honor more than is right, and from the wrong sources; and we blame someone indifferent to honor for deciding not to be honored even for fine things. §4 Sometimes, however, we praise the honor-lover for being manly and a lover of the fine; and again we praise the indifferent person for being moderate and temperate, as we said in the first discussion.

Clearly, since we speak in several ways of loving something, what we 15 refer to as love of honor is not the same attitude in every case.* When we praise it, we refer to loving honor more than the many do. When we blame it, we refer to loving honor more than is right. Since the mean has no name, the extremes look like the only contestants, as though they had the field to themselves.* Still, if there is excess and deficiency, there is also an intermediate condition.

20 §5 Since people desire honor both more and less than is right, it is also possible to desire it in the right way. This state, therefore, a nameless mean concerned with honor, is praised. In relation to love of honor, it appears as indifference to honor; in relation to indifference, it appears as love of honor; in relation to both, it appears in a way as both. §6 The 25 same would seem to be true of the other virtues too; but in this particular case the extreme people appear to be opposed [only to each other] because the intermediate person has no name.

5

[Mildness]

Mildness is the mean concerned with anger. Since the mean is nameless, *1125b* and the extremes are practically nameless too, we call the intermediate condition mildness, inclining toward the deficiency, which is also nameless.* §2 The excess might be called a kind of irascibility; for the 30 relevant feeling is anger, though its sources are many and varied.

§3 The person who is angry at the right things and toward the right people, and also in the right way, at the right time, and for the right length of time, is praised. This, then, will be the mild person, if mildness is praised.* For [if mildness is something to be praised,] being a mild person means being undisturbed, not led by feeling, but irritated wherever 35 reason prescribes, and for the length of time it prescribes. §4 And he 1126a seems to err more in the direction of deficiency, since the mild person is ready to pardon, not eager to exact a penalty.

§5 The deficiency—a sort of inirascibility or whatever it is—is blamed. 5 For people who are not angered by the right things, or in the right way, or at the right times, or toward the right people, all seem to be foolish. §6 For such a person seems to be insensible and to feel no pain, and since he is not angered, he does not seem to be the sort to defend himself. Such willingness to accept insults to oneself and to overlook insults to one's family and friends is slavish.*

§7 The excess arises in all these ways—in anger toward the wrong 10 people, at the wrong times, more than is right, more hastily than is right, and for a longer time—but they are not all found in the same person. For they could not all exist together; for evil destroys itself as well as other things, and if it is present as a whole it becomes unbearable.

§8 Irascible people get angry quickly, toward the wrong people, at the wrong times, and more than is right; but they stop soon, and this is their 15 best feature. They do all this because they do not contain their anger, but their quick temper makes them pay back the offense without concealment, and then they stop.

§9 Choleric people are quick-tempered to extreme, and irascible about everything and at everything; that is how they get their name.

§10 Bitter people are hard to reconcile, and stay angry for a long time, 20 since they contain their [angry] spirit. It stops when they pay back the offense; for the exaction of the penalty produces pleasure in place of pain, and so puts a stop to the anger. But if this does not happen, they hold their grudge. For no one else persuades them to get over it, since it is not 25 obvious; and digesting anger in oneself takes time. This sort of person is most troublesome to himself and to his closest friends.

§11 The people we call irritable are those who are irritated by the wrong things, more severely and for longer than is right, and are not reconciled until [the offender has suffered] a penalty and corrective treatment.*

1126a30 §12 We regard the excess as more opposed than the deficiency to mildness. For it is more widespread, since it comes more naturally to human beings* to exact a penalty from the offender [than to overlook an offense]; and, moreover, irritable people are harder to live with.

§13 These remarks also make clear a previous point of ours. For it is hard to define how, against whom, about what, and how long we should 35 be angry, and up to what point someone is acting correctly or in error. For someone who deviates a little toward either excess or deficiency is not 1126b blamed; for sometimes we praise deficient people and say they are mild, but sometimes we say that people who get irritated are manly because we think they are capable of ruling others.* How far, then, and in what way must someone deviate to be open to blame? It is not easy to answer in a [general] account; for the judgment depends on particular cases, and [we make it] by perception.*

5 §14 However, this much at least is clear: The intermediate state is praiseworthy,* and in accord with it we are angry toward the right people, about the right things, in the right way, and so on. The excesses and deficiencies are blameworthy, lightly if they go a little way, more if they go further, and strongly if they go far. Clearly, then, we must keep to the 10 intermediate state. §15 So much, then, for the states concerned with anger.

6

[Friendliness]

In meeting people, living together, and common dealings in conversations and actions, some people seem to be ingratiating; these are the ones who praise everything to please us and never cross us, but think they 15 must cause no pain to those they meet.* §2 In contrast to these, people who oppose us on every point and do not care in the least about causing pain are called cantankerous and quarrelsome.

§3 Clearly, the states we have mentioned are blameworthy, and the state intermediate between them is praiseworthy; in accord with it one 20 accepts or objects to things when it is right and in the right way. §4 This state has no name, but it would seem to be most like friendship; for the character of the person in the intermediate state is just what we mean in speaking of a decent friend, except that the friend is also fond of us.

§5 It differs from friendship in not requiring any special feeling* or any fondness for the people we meet. For this person takes each thing in the right way because that is his character, not because he is a friend or an 25 enemy. For he will behave this way to new and old acquaintances, to familiar companions and strangers without distinction, except that he will also do what is suitable for each; for the proper ways to spare or to hurt the feelings of familiar companions are not the proper ways to treat strangers.* 1126b

§6 We have said, then, that in general he will treat people in the right way when he meets them. [More exactly] he will aim to avoid causing pain or to share pleasure, but will always refer to the fine and the beneficial.* §7 For he would seem to be concerned with the pleasures 30 and pains that arise in meeting people; and if it is not fine, or it is harmful, for him to share one of these pleasures, he will object and will decide to cause pain instead. Further, if the other person will suffer no slight disgrace or harm from doing an action, and only slight pain if he is crossed, the virtuous person will object to the action and not accept it.

§8 When he meets people with a reputation for worth, his attitude will 35 be different from his attitude to just anyone; he will take different atti- 1127a tudes to those he knows better and those he knows less well; and similarly with the other differences, according what is suitable to each sort of person. What he will choose in itself is to share pleasure and avoid causing pain.* But he will be guided by consequences, if they are greater—that 5 is to say, by the fine and the expedient;* and to secure great pleasure in the future he will cause slight pain.

§9 This, then, is the character of the intermediate person, though he has no name.

Among those who share pleasure the person who aims to be pleasant with no ulterior purpose* is ingratiating; the one who does it for some advantage in money and what money can buy is the flatterer. The one 10 who objects to everything is, as we have said, the cantankerous and quarrelsome person. However, the extremes appear to be opposite [only] to each other, because the intermediate condition has no name.*

7

[Truthfulness]

The mean that corresponds to boastfulness* is also concerned with practically these same [conditions of social life]; and it too is nameless. It is a 15 good idea to examine the nameless virtues as well as the others. For if we discuss particular aspects of character one at a time, we will acquire a better knowledge of them; and if we survey the virtues and see that in each case the virtue is a mean, we will have more confidence in our belief that the virtues are means. As concerns social life, then, having discussed those who aim at giving pleasure or pain when they meet people, let us now discuss those who are truthful and false, both in words and in 20 actions—that is to say, in their claims [about themselves].

§2 The boaster* seems to claim qualities that win reputation, though he either lacks them altogether or has less than he claims. §3 The self-deprecator, by contrast, seems to disavow or to belittle his actual qualities.

1127a §4 The intermediate person is straightforward, and therefore truthful in
25 what he says and does, acknowledging the qualities he has without exaggerating or belittling.*

§5 Each of these things may be done with or without an ulterior purpose; and someone's character determines what he says and does and the way he lives, if he is not acting for an ulterior purpose. §6 Now in itself [when no ulterior purpose is involved], falsehood is base and blameworthy, and truth is fine and praiseworthy; in this way the truthful person, like
30 other intermediate people, is praiseworthy, and both the tellers of falsehoods are blameworthy, the boaster to a higher degree. Let us discuss each type of blameworthy person; but first let us discuss the truthful person.

§7 For we do not mean someone who is truthful in agreements in mat-
1127b ters of justice and injustice, since these concern a different virtue, but someone who is truthful both in what he says and in how he lives, when nothing about justice is at stake, simply because that is his state of character. §8 Someone with this character seems to be a decent person.
5 For a lover of the truth who is truthful even when nothing is at stake will be still keener to tell the truth when something is at stake, since he will avoid falsehood as shameful [when something is at stake], having already avoided it in itself [when nothing was at stake]. This sort of person is praiseworthy. §9 He inclines to tell less, rather than more, than the truth; for this appears more suitable, since excesses are oppressive.

10 §10 If someone claims to have more than he has, with no ulterior purpose, he certainly looks as though he is a base person, since otherwise he would not enjoy telling falsehoods; but apparently he is pointlessly foolish* rather than bad. §11 Among those who do it with an ulterior purpose, the one who does it for the reputation or honor is not to be blamed too much as a boaster.* But the one who does it for money or for means to making money is more disgraceful.

15 §12 It is not a person's capacity, but his decision, that makes him a boaster; for his state of character makes a person a boaster, just as it makes a person a liar.* And [boasters differ in their states of character]; one is a boaster because he enjoys telling falsehoods in itself, another because he pursues reputation or gain.

§13 Boasters who aim at reputation, then, claim the qualities that win praise or win congratulation for happiness. Boasters who aim at profit
20 claim the qualities that gratify other people and that allow someone to avoid detection when he claims to be what he is not—a wise diviner or doctor,* for instance. That is why most [boasters] claim these sorts of things and boast about them; for they have the features just mentioned.

§14 Self-deprecators underestimate themselves in what they say, and so appear to have more cultivated characters. For they seem to be avoid-
25 ing bombast, not looking for profit, in what they say. The qualities that win reputation are the ones that these people especially disavow, as Socrates also used to do.*

§15 Those who disavow small qualities that they obviously have are called humbugs, and people more readily think less of them. Sometimes, indeed, this even appears a form of boastfulness, as the Spartans' [austere] dress does; for the extreme deficiency, as well as the excess, is boastful.* §16 But those who are moderate in their self-deprecation and confine themselves to qualities that are not too commonplace or obvious appear sophisticated. 1127b 30

§17 It is the boaster [rather than the self-deprecator] who appears to be opposite to the truthful person, since he is the worse [of the two extremes].

8

[Wit]

Since life also includes relaxation, and in this we pass our time with some form of amusement, here also it seems possible to behave appropriately in meeting people, and to say and listen to the right things and in the right way. The company we are in when we speak or listen also makes a difference. §2 And, clearly, in this case also it is possible to exceed the intermediate condition or to be deficient. 1128a

§3 Those who go to excess in raising laughs seem to be vulgar buffoons.* They stop at nothing to raise a laugh, and care more about that than about saying what is seemly and avoiding pain to the victims of the joke. Those who would never say anything themselves to raise a laugh, and even object when other people do it, seem to be boorish and stiff. Those who joke in appropriate ways are called witty, or, in other words, agile-witted. For these sorts of jokes seem to be movements of someone's character, and characters are judged, as bodies are, by their movements. 5 10

§4 Since there are always opportunities at hand for raising a laugh, and most people enjoy amusements and jokes more than they should, buffoons are also called witty because they are thought cultivated; nonetheless, they differ, and differ considerably, from witty people, as our account has made clear. 15

§5 Dexterity* is also proper to the intermediate state. It is proper to the dexterous person to say and listen to what suits the decent and civilized person. For some things are suitable for this sort of person to say and listen to by way of amusement; and the civilized person's amusement differs from the slavish person's. §6 This can also be seen from old and new comedies; for what people used to find funny was shameful abuse, but what they now find funny instead is innuendo, which is considerably more seemly.* 20 25

§7 Then should the person who jokes well be defined by his making remarks not unsuitable for a civilized person, or by his avoiding pain and even giving pleasure to the hearer? Perhaps, though, this [avoiding pain

1128a and giving pleasure] is indefinable, since different people find different things hateful or pleasant.* §8 The remarks he is willing to hear made are of the same sort, since those he is prepared to hear made seem to be those he is prepared to make himself.*

30 §9 Hence he will not be indiscriminate in his remarks. For since a joke is a type of abuse, and legislators prohibit some types of abuse, they would presumably be right to prohibit some types of jokes too. §10 Hence the cultivated and civilized person, as a sort of law to himself,* will take this [discriminating] attitude. This, then, is the character of the intermediate person, whether he is called dexterous or witty.

35 The buffoon cannot resist raising a laugh, and spares neither himself nor anyone else if he can cause laughter, even by making remarks that the 1128b sophisticated person would never make, and some that the sophisticated person would not even be willing to hear made.

The boor is useless when he meets people in these circumstances. For he contributes nothing himself, and objects to everything; §11 but relaxation and amusement seem to be necessary in life.

5 §12 We have spoken, then, of three means in life, all concerned with common dealings in certain conversations and actions. They differ insofar as one is concerned with truth, the others with what is pleasant. One of those concerned with pleasure is found in amusements, and the other in our behavior in the other aspects of life when we meet people.

9

[Shame]

10 It is not appropriate to treat shame as a virtue; for it would seem to be more like a feeling than like a state [of character].* It is defined, at any rate, as a sort of fear of disrepute. §2 Its expression is similar to that of fear of something terrifying; for a feeling of disgrace makes people blush, 15 and fear of death makes them turn pale. Hence both [types of fear] appear to be in some way bodily [reactions], which seem to be more characteristic of feelings than of states.

§3 Further, the feeling of shame is suitable for youth, not for every time of life. For we think it right for young people to be prone to shame, since they live by their feelings,* and hence often go astray, but are 20 restrained by shame; and hence we praise young people who are prone to shame. No one, by contrast, would praise an older person for readiness to feel disgrace, since we think it wrong for him to do any action that causes a feeling of disgrace.

§4 For a feeling of disgrace is not proper to the decent person either, if it is caused by base actions; for these should not be done. §5 If some actions are really disgraceful and others are base [only] in [his] belief, that 25 does not matter, since neither should be done, and so he should not feel disgrace. §6 On the contrary; being the sort of person who does any disgraceful action is proper to a vicious person. *1128b*

If someone's state [of character] would make him feel disgrace if he were to do a disgraceful action, and because of this he thinks he is decent, that is absurd. For shame is concerned with what is voluntary, and the decent person will never willingly do base actions.

§7 Shame might, however, be decent on an assumption; if one were to do [disgraceful actions], one would feel disgrace; but this does not apply to the virtues.* If we grant that it is base to feel no disgrace or shame at disgraceful actions, it still does not follow that to do such actions and then to feel disgrace at them is decent. 30

Continence is not a virtue either. It is a sort of mixed state. We will explain about it in what we say later. Now let us discuss justice. 35

Book V

[Justice]

1

[Varieties of Justice]

The questions we must examine about justice and injustice are these: What sorts of actions are they concerned with? What sort of mean is justice? What are the extremes between which justice is intermediate? §2 Let us investigate them by the same line of inquiry as we used in the topics discussed before. 1129a 5

§3 We see that the state everyone means in speaking of justice is the state that makes us just agents—[that is to say], the state that makes us do justice and wish what is just.* In the same way they mean by injustice the state that makes us do injustice and wish what is unjust. That is why we also should first assume these things as an outline.* 10

§4 For what is true of sciences and capacities is not true of states. For while one and the same capacity or science seems to have contrary activities, a state that is a contrary has no contrary activities. Health, for instance, only makes us do healthy actions, not their contraries; for we say we are walking in a healthy way if [and only if] we are walking in the way a healthy person would. 15

§5 Often one of a pair of contrary states is recognized from the other contrary; and often the states are recognized from their subjects. For if, for instance, the good state is evident, the bad state becomes evident too; and moreover the good state becomes evident from the things that have it, and the things from the state. For if, for instance, the good state is thickness of flesh, the bad state must be thinness of flesh, and the thing that produces the good state must be what produces thickness of flesh. 20

1129a25 §6 If one of a pair of contraries is spoken of in more ways than one, it follows, usually, that the other is too. If, for instance, the just is spoken of in more ways than one, so is the unjust.

§7 Now it would seem that justice and injustice are both spoken of in more ways than one, but since their homonymy is close, the difference is 30 unnoticed, and is less clear than it is with distant homonyms where the distance in appearance is wide (for instance, the bone below an animal's neck and what we lock doors with are called keys homonymously).*

§8 Let us, then, find the number of ways an unjust person is spoken of. Both the lawless person and the overreaching and unfair* person seem to be unjust; and so, clearly, both the lawful and the fair person will be just. 1129b Hence the just will be both the lawful and what is fair, and the unjust will be both the lawless and the unfair.

§9 Since the unjust person is an overreacher, he will be concerned with goods—not with all goods, but only with those involved in good and bad fortune, goods which are, [considered] without qualification, always good, but for this or that person not always good.* Though human beings 5 pray for these and pursue them, they are wrong; the right thing is to pray that what is good without qualification will also be good for us, but to choose [only] what is good for us.

§10 Now the unjust person [who chooses these goods] does not choose more in every case; in the case of what is bad without qualification 10 he actually chooses less. But since what is less bad also seems to be good in a way, and overreaching aims at more of what is good, he seems to be an overreacher. §11 In fact he is unfair; for unfairness includes [all these actions], and is a common feature [of his choice of the greater good and of the lesser evil].

§12 Since, as we saw, the lawless person is unjust and the lawful person is just, it clearly follows that whatever is lawful is in some way just; for the provisions of legislative science are lawful, and we say that each of 15 them is just.* §13 In every matter that they deal with, the laws aim either at the common benefit of all, or at the benefit of those in control, whose control rests on virtue or on some other such basis.* And so in one way what we call just is whatever produces and maintains happiness and its parts for a political community.*

20 §14 Now the law instructs us to do the actions of a brave person—for instance, not to leave the battle-line, or to flee, or to throw away our weapons; of a temperate person—not to commit adultery or wanton aggression; of a mild person—not to strike or revile another; and similarly requires actions in accord with the other virtues, and prohibits 25 actions in accord with the vices. The correctly established law does this correctly, and the less carefully framed one does this worse.

§15 This type of justice, then, is complete virtue, not complete virtue without qualification, but complete virtue in relation to another. And that is why justice often seems to be supreme among the virtues, and 'neither the evening star nor the morning star is so marvellous', and the proverb says, 'And in justice all virtue is summed up.'* *1129b* 30

Moreover, justice is complete virtue to the highest degree because it is the complete exercise of complete virtue.* And it is the complete exercise because the person who has justice is able to exercise virtue in relation to another, not only in what concerns himself; for many are able to exercise virtue in their own concerns, but unable in what relates to another.

§16 That is why Bias seems to have been correct in saying that ruling will reveal the man; for a ruler is automatically related to another, and in a community.* §17 That is also why justice is the only virtue that seems to be another person's good, because it is related to another; for it does what benefits another, either the ruler or the fellow member of the community.* 1130a 5

§18 The worst person, therefore, is the one who exercises his vice toward himself and his friends as well [as toward others].* And the best person is not the one who exercises virtue [only] toward himself, but the one who [also] exercises it in relation to another, since this is a difficult task.*

§19 This type of justice, then, is the whole, not a part, of virtue, and the injustice contrary to it is the whole, not a part, of vice. 10

§20 Our discussion makes clear the difference between virtue and this type of justice. For virtue is the same as justice, but what it is to be virtue is not the same as what it is to be justice.* Rather, insofar as virtue is related to another, it is justice, and insofar as it is a certain sort of state without qualification, it is virtue.

2

[Special Justice Contrasted with General]

But we are looking for the type of justice, since we say there is one, that consists in a part of virtue, and correspondingly for the type of injustice that is a part of vice. 15

§2 A sign that there is this type of justice and injustice is this: If someone's activities accord with the other vices—if, for instance, cowardice made him throw away his shield, or irritability made him revile someone, or ungenerosity made him fail to help someone with money—what he does is unjust, but not overreaching. But when someone acts from overreaching, in many cases his action accords with none of these vices—certainly not all of them; but it still accords with some type of wickedness, since we blame him, and [in particular] it accords with injustice.* §3 Hence there is another type of injustice that is a part of the whole, and a way of being unjust that is a part of the whole that is contrary to law. 20

1130a25 §4 Further, if A commits adultery for profit and makes a profit, but B commits adultery because of his appetite, and spends money on it to his own loss, B seems intemperate rather than overreaching, but A seems unjust, not intemperate. Clearly, then, this is because A acts to make a profit.

30 §5 Further, we can refer every other unjust action to some vice—to intemperance if someone committed adultery, to cowardice if he deserted his comrade in the battle-line, to anger if he struck someone. But if he made an [unjust] profit, we can refer it to no other vice except injustice.

§6 It is evident, then, that there is another type of injustice, special injustice, apart from injustice as a whole, and that it is synonymous with 1130b injustice as a whole, since the definition is in the same genus. For both have their area of competence in relation to another, but special injustice is concerned with honor or wealth or safety (or whatever single name will include all these), and aims at the pleasure that results from making a 5 profit, whereas the concern of injustice as a whole is whatever concerns the excellent person.*

§7 Clearly, then, there is more than one type of justice, and there is another type besides [the type that is] the whole of virtue; but we must still grasp what it is, and what sort of thing it is.

§8 The unjust is divided into the lawless and the unfair, and the just 10 into the lawful and the fair.* The injustice previously described, then, is concerned with the lawless. §9 But the unfair is not the same as the lawless; it is related to it as part to whole, since whatever is unfair is lawless, but not everything lawless is unfair. Hence also the unfair type of injustice and the unfair way of being unjust are not the same as the law- 15 less type, but differ as parts from wholes. For unfair injustice is a part of the whole of injustice, and, similarly, fair justice is a part of the whole of justice. Hence we must describe special as well as general justice and injustice, and equally this way of being just or unjust.

20 §10 Let us, then, set aside the type of justice and injustice that accords with the whole of virtue, justice being the exercise of the whole of virtue, and injustice of the whole of vice, in relation to another.* And it is evident how we must distinguish the way of being just or unjust that accords with this type of justice and injustice.* For most lawful actions, we might say, are those produced by virtue as a whole;* for the law prescribes living in accord with each virtue, and forbids living in accord with each 25 vice.* §11 Moreover, the actions producing the whole of virtue are the lawful actions that the laws prescribe for education promoting the common good. We must wait till later, however, to determine whether the education that makes an individual an unqualifiedly good man is a task for political science or for another science; for, presumably, being a good man is not the same as being every sort of good citizen.*

30 §12 Special justice, however, and the corresponding way of being just

have one species that is found in the distribution of honors or wealth or anything else that can be divided among members of a community who share in a political system; for here it is possible for one member to have a share equal or unequal to another's. A second species concerns rectification in transactions. *1130b* 1131a

§13 This second species has two parts, since one sort of transaction is voluntary, and one involuntary. Voluntary transactions (for instance, selling, buying, lending, pledging, renting, depositing, hiring out) are so called because their principle is voluntary. Among involuntary transactions some are secret (for instance, theft, adultery, poisoning, pimping, slave-deception, murder by treachery, false witness), whereas others involve force (for instance, imprisonment, murder, plunder, mutilation, slander, insult). 5

3

[Justice in Distribution]

Since the unjust person is unfair, and what is unjust is unfair, there is clearly an intermediate between the unfair [extremes].* §2 This is the fair; for in any action where too much and too little are possible, the fair [amount] is also possible. §3 And so, if the unjust is unfair, the just is fair (*ison*), as seems true to everyone even without argument. And since the equal (*ison*) [and fair] is intermediate, the just is some sort of intermediate. 10

§4 Since the equal involves at least two things [equal to each other], it follows that the just must be intermediate and equal, and related to something, and for some people. Insofar as it is intermediate, it must be between too much and too little; insofar as it is equal, it involves two things; and insofar as it is just, it is just for some people. §5 Hence the just requires four things at least; the people for whom it is just are two, and the [equal] things involved are two. 15 20

§6 Equality for the people involved will be the same as for the things involved, since [in a just arrangement] the relation between the people will be the same as the relation between the things involved. For if the people involved are not equal, they will not [justly] receive equal shares; indeed, whenever equals receive unequal shares, or unequals equal shares, in a distribution, that is the source of quarrels and accusations.

§7 This is also clear from considering what accords with worth. For all agree that the just in distributions must accord with some sort of worth, but what they call worth is not the same; supporters of democracy say it is free citizenship, some supporters of oligarchy say it is wealth, others good birth, while supporters of aristocracy say it is virtue.* 25

§8 Hence the just [since it requires equal shares for equal people] is in some way proportionate. For proportion is special to number as a whole, 30

1131a not only to numbers consisting of [abstract] units,* since it is equality of ratios and requires at least four terms. §9 Now divided proportion clearly requires four terms. But so does continuous proportion, since here 1131b we use one term as two, and mention it twice. If, for instance, line A is to line B as B is to C, B is mentioned twice; and so if B is introduced twice, the terms in the proportion will be four.*

5 §10 The just also requires at least four terms, with the same ratio [between the pairs], since the people [A and B] and the items [C and D] involved are divided in the same way. §11 Term C, then, is to term D as A is to B, and, taking them alternately, B is to D as A is to C. Hence there will also be the same relation of whole [A and C] to whole [B and D]; this is the relation in which the distribution pairs them, and it pairs them justly if this is how they are combined.

10 §12 Hence the combination of term A with C and of B with D is the just in distribution, and this way of being just is intermediate, whereas the unjust is contrary to the proportionate. For the proportionate is intermediate, and the just is proportionate.

§13 This is the sort of proportion that mathematicians call geometrical, since in geometrical proportion the relation of whole to whole is the same 15 as the relation of each [part] to each [part]. §14 But this proportion [involved in justice] is not continuous, since there is no single term for both the person and the item. The just, then, is the proportionate, and the unjust is the counterproportionate. Hence [in an unjust action] one term becomes more and the other less; and this is indeed how it turns out in practice, since the one doing injustice has more of the good, and the vic-20 tim has less.

§15 With an evil the ratio is reversed, since the lesser evil, compared to the greater, counts as a good; §16 for the lesser evil is more choiceworthy than the greater, what is choiceworthy is good, and what is more choiceworthy is a greater good.

§17 This, then, is the first species of the just.

4

[Justice in Rectification]

25 The other species is rectificatory, found in transactions both voluntary and involuntary. §2 This way of being just belongs to a different species from the first.

For the just in distribution of common assets will always accord with 30 the proportion mentioned above; for [just] distribution from common funds will also accord with the ratio to one another of different people's deposits. Similarly, the way of being unjust that is opposed to this way of being just is what is counterproportionate.

§3 The just in transactions, by contrast, though it is a sort of equality (and the unjust a sort of inequality), accords with numerical proportion, not with the [geometrical] proportion of the other species. For here it does not matter if a decent person has taken from a base person, or a base person from a decent person, or if a decent or a base person has committed adultery. Rather, the law looks only at differences in the harm [inflicted], and treats the people involved as equals, if one does injustice while the other suffers it, and one has done the harm while the other has suffered it. 1132a 5

§4 And so the judge tries to restore this unjust situation to equality, since it is unequal.* For [not only when one steals from another but] also when one is wounded and the other wounds him, or one kills and the other is killed, the action and the suffering are unequally divided [with profit for the offender and loss for the victim]; and the judge tries to restore the [profit and] loss to a position of equality, by subtraction from [the offender's] profit.* 10

§5 For in such cases, stating it without qualification, we speak of profit for the attacker who wounded his victim, for instance, even if that is not the proper word for some cases; and we speak of loss for the victim who suffers the wound. §6 At any rate, when what was suffered has been measured, one part is called the [victim's] loss, and the other the [offender's] profit. Hence the equal is intermediate between more and less. Profit and loss are more and less in contrary ways, since more good and less evil is profit, and the contrary is loss. The intermediate area between [profit and loss], we have found, is the equal, which we say is just. Hence the just in rectification is the intermediate between loss and profit. 15

§7 That is why parties to a dispute resort to a judge, and an appeal to a judge is an appeal to the just; for the judge is intended to be a sort of living embodiment of the just.* Moreover, they seek the judge as an intermediary, and in some cities they actually call a judge a 'mediator', assuming that if they are awarded an intermediate amount, the award will be just. If, then, the judge is an intermediary, the just is in some way intermediate. 20

§8 The judge restores equality, as though a line [AB] had been cut into unequal parts [AC and CB], and he removed from the larger part [AC] the amount [DC] by which it exceeds the half [AD] of the line [AB], and added this amount [DC] to the smaller part [CB].* And when the whole [AB] has been halved [into AD and DB], then they say that each person has what is properly his own, when he has got an equal share. 25

§9 The equal [in this case] is intermediate, by numerical proportion, between the larger [AC] and the smaller line [CB]. This is also why it is called just (*dikaion*), because it is a bisection (*dicha*), as though we said bisected (*dichaion*), and the judge (*dikastes*) is a bisector (*dichastes*). §10 For when [the same amount] is subtracted from one of two equal things and added to the other, then the one part exceeds the other by the two parts; for if a part had been subtracted from the one, but not added to the other, the larger part would have exceeded the smaller by just one part. Hence the 30 1132b

1132b larger part exceeds the intermediate by one part, and the intermediate from which [a part] was subtracted [exceeds the smaller] by one part.

§11 In this way, then, we will recognize what we must subtract from the one who has more and add to the one who has less [to restore equality]; for to the one who has less we must add the amount by which the
5 intermediate exceeds what he has, and from the greatest amount [held by the one who has more] we must subtract the amount by which it exceeds the intermediate. §12 Let lines AA', BB', and CC' be equal; let AE be subtracted from AA' and CD be added to CC', so that the whole line DCC' will exceed the line EA' by the parts CD and CF [where CF equals AE]; it follows that DCC' exceeds BB' by CD.*

11 §13 These names 'loss' and 'profit' are derived from voluntary exchange. For having more than one's own share is called making a profit, and having less than what one had at the beginning is called suf-
15 fering a loss, in buying and selling, for instance, and in other transactions permitted by law. §14 And when people get neither more nor less, but precisely what belongs to them, they say they have their own share and make neither a loss nor a profit. Hence the just is intermediate between a certain kind of loss and profit, since it is having the equal amount both
20 before and after [the transaction].*

5

[Justice in Exchange]

Some people, however, think reciprocity is also just without qualification. This was the Pythagoreans' view, since their definition stated without qualification that what is just is reciprocity with another.

25 §2 The truth is that reciprocity suits neither distributive nor rectificatory justice, §3 though people take even Rhadamanthys' [primitive] conception of justice to describe rectificatory justice: 'If he suffered what he did, upright justice would be done.'* §4 For in many cases reciprocity conflicts [with rectificatory justice]. If, for instance, a ruling official [exercising his office] wounded someone else, he must not be wounded in
30 retaliation, but if someone wounded a ruling official, he must not only be wounded but also receive corrective treatment. §5 Moreover, the voluntary or involuntary character of the action makes a great difference.

§6 In communities for exchange, however, this way of being just, reciprocity that is proportionate rather than equal, holds people together; for a city is maintained by proportionate reciprocity. For people seek to
1133a return either evil for evil, since otherwise [their condition] seems to be slavery,* or good for good, since otherwise there is no exchange; and they are maintained [in a community] by exchange. §7 Indeed, that is why they make a temple of the Graces prominent, so that there will be a return of benefits received. For this is what is special to grace; when someone

has been gracious to us, we must do a service for him in return, and also ourselves take the lead in being gracious again.* 1133a5

§8 It is diagonal combination that produces proportionate exchange. Let A be a builder, B a shoemaker, C a house, D a shoe. The builder must receive the shoemaker's product from him, and give him the builder's own product in return. If, then, first of all, proportionate equality is found, and, next, reciprocity is also achieved, the proportionate return will be reached. Otherwise it is not equal, and the exchange will not be maintained, since the product of one may well be superior to the product of the other. These products, then, must be equalized. 10

§9 This is true of the other crafts also; for they would have been destroyed unless the producer produced the same thing, of the same quantity and quality as the thing affected underwent. For no community [for exchange] is formed from two doctors. It is formed from a doctor and a farmer, and, in general, from people who are different and unequal and who must be equalized.* 15

§10 This is why all items for exchange must be comparable in some way. Currency came along to do exactly this, and in a way it becomes an intermediate, since it measures everything, and so measures excess and deficiency—[for instance,] how many shoes are equal to a house.* Hence, as builder is to shoemaker, so must the number of shoes be to a house; for if this does not happen, there will be no exchange and no community. §11 But proportionate equality will not be reached unless they are equal in some way. Everything, then, must be measured by some one measure, as we said before. 20 25

In reality, this measure is need, which holds everything together; for if people needed nothing, or needed things to different extents, there would be either no exchange or not the same exchange.* And currency has become a sort of pledge of need, by convention; in fact it has its name (*nomisma*) because it is not by nature, but by the current law (*nomos*), and it is within our power to alter it and to make it useless. 30

§12 Reciprocity will be secured, then, when things are equalized, so that the shoemaker's product is to the farmer's as the farmer is to the shoemaker. However, they must be introduced into the figure of proportion not when they have already exchanged and one extreme has both excesses, but when they still have their own; in that way they will be equals and members of a community, because this sort of equality can be produced in them.* Let A be a farmer, C food, B a shoemaker, and D his product that has been equalized; if this sort of reciprocity were not possible, there would be no community. 1133b 5

§13 Now clearly need holds [a community] together as a single unit, since people with no need of each other, both of them or either one, do not exchange, as they exchange whenever another requires what one has oneself, such as wine, when they allow the export of corn. This, then, must be equalized. 10

1133b §14 If an item is not required at the moment, currency serves to guarantee us a future exchange, guaranteeing that the item will be there for us if we need it; for it must be there for us to take if we pay. Now the same thing happens to currency [as other goods], and it does not always count 15 for the same; still, it tends to be more stable. Hence everything must have a price; for in that way there will always be exchange, and then there will be community.

Currency, then, by making things commensurate as a measure does, equalizes them; for there would be no community without exchange, no exchange without equality, no equality without commensuration. And so, though things so different cannot become commensurate in reality, they 20 can become commensurate enough in relation to our needs.

§15 Hence there must be some single unit fixed [as current] by a stipulation. This is why it is called currency; for this makes everything commensurate, since everything is measured by currency. Let A, for instance, be a house, B ten minae, C a bed. A is half of B if a house is worth five 25 minae or equal to them; and C, the bed, is a tenth of B. It is clear, then, how many beds are equal to one house—five. §16 This is clearly how exchange was before there was currency; for it does not matter whether a house is exchanged for five beds or for the currency for which five beds are exchanged.

30 §17 We have now said what it is that is unjust and just. And now that we have defined them, it is clear that doing justice is intermediate between doing injustice and suffering injustice, since doing injustice is having too much and suffering injustice is having too little.*

1134a Justice is a mean, not as the other virtues are, but because it is about an intermediate condition, whereas injustice is about the extremes.* Justice is the virtue in accord with which the just person is said to do what is just in accord with his decision, distributing good things and bad, both between himself and others and between others. He does not award too much of 5 what is choiceworthy to himself and too little to his neighbor (and the reverse with what is harmful), but awards what is proportionately equal; and he does the same in distributing between others.

§18 Injustice, on the other hand, is related [in the same way] to the unjust. What is unjust is disproportionate excess and deficiency in what is beneficial or harmful; hence injustice is excess and deficiency because it 10 concerns excess and deficiency. The unjust person awards himself an excess of what is beneficial, [considered] without qualification, and a deficiency of what is harmful, and, speaking as a whole, he acts similarly [in distributions between] others, but deviates from proportion in either direction. In an unjust action getting too little good is suffering injustice, and getting too much is doing injustice.

15 §19 So much, then, for the nature of justice and the nature of injustice, and similarly for just and unjust in general.

6

[Political Justice]

Since it is possible to do injustice without thereby being unjust, what sort *1134a* of injustice must someone do to be unjust by having one of the different types of injustice, by being a thief or adulterer or brigand, for instance?*

Perhaps it is not the type of action that makes the difference [between merely doing injustice and being unjust]. For someone might lie with a 20 woman and know who she is, but the principle might be feelings rather than decision. §2 In that case he is not unjust, though he does injustice—not a thief, for instance, though he stole, not an adulterer though he committed adultery, and so on in the other cases.

§3 Now we have previously described the relation of reciprocity to the 25 just.* §4 But we must recognize that we are inquiring not only into the just without qualification,* but also into the politically just. This belongs to those who share in common a life aiming at self-sufficiency, who are free and either proportionately or numerically equal.* Hence those who lack these features have nothing politically just in their relations, though they have something just insofar as it is similar to the politically just.

For the just belongs to those who have law in their relations. Law 30 belongs to those among whom injustice is [possible]; for the judicial process is judgment that distinguishes the just from the unjust. Where there is injustice there is also doing injustice, though where there is doing injustice there need not also be injustice.* And doing injustice is awarding to oneself too many of the things that, [considered] without qualification, are good, and too few of the things that, [considered] without qualification, are bad.

§5 That is why we allow only reason, not a human being, to be ruler.* 35 For a human being awards himself too many goods and becomes a tyrant; 1134b a ruler, however, is a guardian of the just, and hence of the equal [and so must not award himself too many goods].

§6 If a ruler is just, he seems to profit nothing by it. For since he does not award himself more of what, [considered] without qualification, is good if it is not proportionate to him, he seems to labor for another's ben- 5 efit. That is why justice is said, as we also remarked before, to be another person's good.* §7 Hence some payment [for ruling] should be given; this is honor and privilege. The people who are not satisfied with these rewards are the ones who become tyrants.*

§8 The just for a master and a father is similar to this, not the same. For 10 there is no unqualified injustice in relation to what is one's own; one's own possession, or one's child until it is old enough and separated, is as though it were a part of oneself.* §9 Now no one decides to harm himself. Hence there is no injustice in relation to them,* and so nothing politically unjust or just either. For we found that the politically just must accord with law, and belong to those who are naturally suited for law, and 15

1134b hence to those who have equality in ruling and being ruled.* [Approximation to this equality] explains why relations with a wife more than with children or possessions allow something to count as just;* for that is the just in households. Still, this too is different from the politically just.

7

[Justice by Nature and by Law]

One part of the politically just is natural, and the other part legal. The nat-
20 ural has the same validity everywhere alike, independent of its seeming so or not. The legal originally makes no difference [whether it is done] one way or another, but makes a difference whenever people have laid down the rule—that a mina is the price of a ransom, for instance, or that a goat rather than two sheep should be sacrificed. The legal also includes laws passed for particular cases (for instance, that sacrifices should be offered to Brasidas)* and enactments by decree.

25 §2 Now some people think everything just is merely legal. For the natural is unchangeable and equally valid everywhere—fire, for instance, burns both here and in Persia—whereas they see that the just changes [from city to city].

§3 This is not so, though in a way it is so. With us, though presumably
30 not at all with the gods,* there is such a thing as the natural, but still all is changeable; despite the change there is such a thing as what is natural and what is not.

§4 Then what sort of thing, among those that [are changeable and hence] admit of being otherwise, is natural, and what sort is not natural, but legal and conventional, if both natural and legal are changeable? It is clear in other cases also, and the same distinction [between the natural and the unchangeable] will apply; for the right hand, for instance, is
35 naturally superior, even though it is possible for everyone to become ambidextrous.*

1135a §5 The sorts of things that are just by convention and expediency are like measures. For measures for wine and for corn are not of equal size everywhere, but in wholesale markets they are bigger, and in retail smaller. Similarly, the things that are just by human [enactment] and not
5 by nature differ from place to place, since political systems also differ.* Still, only one system is by nature the best everywhere.*

§6 Each [type of] just and lawful [action] is related as a universal to the corresponding particulars; for the [particular] actions that are done are many, but each [type] is one, since it is universal.*

§7 An act of injustice is different from the unjust, and an act of justice
10 from the just. For the unjust is unjust by nature or enactment; when this has been done, it is an act of injustice,* but before it is done it is only unjust. The same applies to an act of justice [in contrast to the just]. Here, however, the general [type of action contrary to an act of injustice] is more

usually called a just act, and what is called an act of justice is the [specific type of just act] that rectifies an act of injustice. 1135a

Later we must examine each of these actions, to see what sorts of species, and how many, they have, and what they are concerned with. 15

8

[Justice, Injustice, and the Voluntary]

Given this account of just and unjust actions, one does injustice or does justice whenever one does them willingly. Whenever one does them unwillingly, one neither does justice nor does injustice, except coincidentally, since the actions one does are coincidentally just or unjust.*

§2 An act of injustice and a just act are defined by the voluntary and the involuntary. For when the action is voluntary, the agent is blamed, and thereby also it is an act of injustice. And so something will be unjust without thereby being an act of injustice, if it is not also voluntary. 20

§3 As I said before, I say that an action is voluntary just in case it is up to the agent, who does it in knowledge, and [hence] not in ignorance of the person, instrument, and goal (for instance, whom he is striking, with what, and for what goal),* and [does] each of these neither coincidentally nor by force* (if, for instance, someone seized your hand and struck another [with it], you would not have done it willingly, since it was not up to you). But [a further distinction must be drawn about knowledge. For] it is possible that the victim is your father, and you know he is a human being or a bystander, but do not know he is your father.* The same distinction must be made for the goal and for the action as a whole. 25 30

Actions are involuntary, then, if they are done in ignorance; or they are not done in ignorance, but they are not up to the agent; or they are done by force. For we also do or undergo many of our natural [actions and processes], such as growing old and dying, in knowledge, but none of them is either voluntary or involuntary.* 1135b

§4 Both unjust and just actions may also be coincidental in the same way. For if someone returned a deposit unwillingly and because of fear, we ought to say that he neither does anything just nor does justice, except coincidentally.* Similarly, if someone is under compulsion and unwilling when he fails to return the deposit, we should say that he coincidentally does injustice and does something unjust. 5

§5 In some of our voluntary actions we act on a previous decision, and in some we act without previous decision. We act on a previous decision when we act on previous deliberation, and we act without previous decision when we act without previous deliberation. 10

§6 Among the three ways of inflicting harms in a community, actions done with ignorance are errors if someone does neither the action he supposed, nor to the person, nor with the instrument, nor for the result he

1135b supposed. For he thought, for instance, that he was not hitting, or not hit-
15 ting this person, or not for this result; but coincidentally the result that was achieved was not what he thought (for instance, [he hit him] to graze, not to wound), or the victim or the instrument was not the one he thought.

§7 If, then, the infliction of harm violates reasonable expectation, the action is a misfortune. If it does not violate reasonable expectation, but is done without vice, it is an error. For someone is in error if the principle of the cause is in him, and unfortunate when it is outside.*

20 §8 If he does it in knowledge, but without previous deliberation, it is an act of injustice; this is true, for instance, of actions caused by spirit and other feelings that are natural or necessary for human beings. For when someone inflicts these harms and commits these errors, he does injustice and these are acts of injustice; but he is not thereby unjust or wicked,
25 since it is not vice that causes him to inflict the harm. But whenever his decision is the cause, he is unjust and vicious.*

§9 That is why it is right to judge that actions caused by spirit do not result from forethought [and hence do not result from decision], since the principle is not the agent who acted on spirit, but the person who provoked him to anger.* §10 Moreover the dispute is not about whether [the action caused by anger] happened or not, but about whether it was
30 just, since anger is a response to apparent injustice. For they do not dispute about whether it happened or not, as they do in commercial transactions, where one party or the other must be vicious, unless forgetfulness is the cause of the dispute. Rather [in cases of anger] they agree about the fact and dispute about which action was just; but [in commercial transactions] the [cheater] who has plotted against his victim knows very well [that
1136a what he is doing is unjust].* Hence [in cases of anger the agent] thinks he is suffering injustice, while [in transactions the cheater] does not think so.

§11 If [the cheater's] decision causes him to inflict the harm, he does injustice, and this is the sort of act of injustice that makes an agent unjust,* if it violates proportion or equality. In the same way, a person is just if his decision causes him to do justice; one [merely] does justice if one merely does it voluntarily.

5 §12 Some involuntary actions are to be pardoned, and some are not. For if someone's error is not only committed in ignorance, but also caused by ignorance, it is to be pardoned. But if, though committed in ignorance, it is caused not by ignorance but by some feeling that is neither natural nor human, it is not to be pardoned.*

9

[Puzzles about Justice and Injustice]

10 If we have adequately defined suffering injustice and doing injustice, some puzzles might be raised.

First of all, are those bizarre words of Euripides correct, where he says: '"I killed my mother—a short tale to tell." "Were both of you willing or both unwilling?"'?* Is it really possible to suffer injustice willingly, or is it always involuntary, as doing injustice is always voluntary? And is it always one way or the other, or is it sometimes voluntary and sometimes involuntary? *1136a* 15

§2 The same question arises about receiving justice. Since doing justice is always voluntary [as doing injustice is], it is reasonable for the same opposition to apply in both cases, so that both receiving justice and suffering injustice will be either alike voluntary or alike involuntary. But it seems absurd in the case of receiving justice as well [as in the case of suffering injustice] for it to be always voluntary, since some people receive justice, but not willingly. 20

§3 We might also raise the following puzzle: Does everyone who has received something unjust suffer injustice, or is it the same with receiving as it is with doing? For certainly it is possible, in the case both of doing and of receiving, to have a share in just things coincidentally; and clearly the same is true of unjust things, since doing something unjust is not the same as doing injustice, and suffering something unjust is not the same as suffering injustice. The same is true of doing justice and receiving it; for it is impossible to suffer injustice if no one does injustice and impossible to receive justice if no one does justice. 25 30

§4 Now if doing injustice is simply harming someone willingly (and doing something willingly is doing it with knowledge of the victim, the instrument, and the way), and the incontinent person harms himself willingly, he suffers injustice willingly. Hence someone can do injustice to himself; and one of our puzzles was just this, whether someone can do injustice to himself. §5 Further, someone's incontinence might cause him to be willingly harmed by another who is willing, so that it would be possible to suffer injustice willingly. 1136b

Perhaps, however, our definition [of doing injustice] was incorrect, and we should add to 'harming with knowledge of the victim, the instrument, and the way', the further condition 'against the wish of the victim'. §6 If so, someone is harmed and suffers something unjust willingly, but no one suffers injustice willingly. For no one wishes it, not even the incontinent, but he acts against his wish; for no one wishes for what he does not think is excellent, and what the incontinent does is not what he thinks it is right [and hence excellent] to do.* 5

§7 And if someone gives away what is his own, as Homer says Glaucus gave to Diomede 'gold for bronze, a hundred cows' worth for nine cows' worth',* he does not suffer injustice. For it is up to him to give them, whereas suffering injustice is not up to him, but requires someone to do him injustice. 10

§8 Clearly, then, suffering injustice is not voluntary.

1136b15 Two further questions that we decided to discuss still remain: If A distributes to B more than B deserves, is it A, the distributor, or B, who has more, who does injustice? And is it possible to do injustice to oneself?

§9 For if the first alternative is possible, and A rather than B does 20 injustice, it follows that if A knowingly and willingly distributes more to B than to himself, A does injustice to himself. And indeed this is what a moderate person seems to do; for the decent person tends to take less than his share.

Perhaps, however, it is not true without qualification that he takes less. For perhaps he overreaches for some other good,* such as reputation or the unqualifiedly fine. Moreover, our definition of doing injustice allows us to solve the puzzle. For since he suffers nothing against his own wish, 25 he does not suffer injustice, at least not from his distribution, but, at most, is merely harmed.

§10 But it is evidently the distributor who does injustice, and the one who has more does not always do it. For the one who does injustice is not the one who has an unjust share, but the one who willingly does what is unjust, that is to say, the one who has the principle of the action; this is the 30 distributor, not the recipient. §11 Besides, doing is spoken of in many ways, and there is a way in which inanimate things, or hands, or servants at someone else's order, kill; the recipient, then, does not do injustice, but does something that is unjust.

§12 Further, if the distributor judged in ignorance, he does not do injustice in violation of what is legally just, and his judgment is not unjust; in a way, though, it is unjust, since what is legally just is different from what is primarily just. If, however, he judged unjustly, and did it 1137a knowingly, he himself as well [as the recipient] is overreaching—for gratitude or to exact a penalty.

§13 And so someone who has judged unjustly for these reasons has also got more, exactly as though he got a share of the [profits of] the act of injustice. For he gave judgment about some land, for instance, on this condition [that he would share the profits], and what he got was not land, but money.

5 §14 People think doing injustice is up to them; that is why they think that being just is also easy. But it is not. For lying with a neighbor's wife, wounding a neighbor, bribing, are all easy and up to us, but being in a certain state when we do them is not easy, and not up to us.*

10 §15 Similarly, people think it takes no wisdom to know the things that are just and unjust, because it is not difficult to comprehend what the laws speak of. But these are not the things that are just, except coincidentally. Knowing how actions must be done, and how distributions must be made, if they are to be just, takes more work than it takes to know about 15 healthy things. And even in the case of healthy things, knowing about

honey, wine, hellebore, burning, and cutting is easy, but knowing how 1137a these must be distributed to produce health, and to whom and when, takes all the work that it takes to be a doctor.

§16 For the same reason they think doing injustice is no less proper to the just than to the unjust person, because the just person is no less, and even more, able to do each of the actions.* For he is able to lie with a 20 woman, and to wound someone; and the brave person, similarly, is able to throw away his shield, and to turn and run this way or that. But doing acts of cowardice or injustice is not doing these actions, except coincidentally; it is being in a certain state when we do them. Similarly, practicing medicine or healing is not cutting or not cutting, giving drugs or not giv- 25 ing them, but doing all these things in a certain way.

§17 Just things belong to those who have a share in things that, [considered] without qualification, are good, who can have an excess or a deficiency of them.* Some (as, presumably, the gods) can have no excess of them; others, the incurably evil, benefit from none of them, but are harmed by them all; others again benefit from these goods up to a point; 30 and this is why the just is something human.*

10

[Decency]

The next task is to discuss how decency is related to justice and how the decent is related to the just.* For on examination they appear as neither the same without qualification nor as states of different kinds. Sometimes we praise what is decent and the decent person, so that even when we 35 praise someone for other things we transfer the term 'decent' and use it 1137b instead of 'good',* making it clear that what is more decent is better. But sometimes, when we reason about the matter, it appears absurd for what is decent to be something apart from what is just, and still praiseworthy. For [apparently] either what is just is not excellent or what is decent is not excellent,* if it is something other than what is just; or else, if they are 5 both excellent, they are the same.

§2 These, then, are roughly the claims that raise the puzzle about the decent; but they are all correct in a way, and none is contrary to any other. For the decent is better than one way of being just, but it is still just, and not better than the just by being a different kind of thing. Hence 10 the same thing is just and decent; while both are excellent, what is decent is superior.

§3 The puzzle arises because the decent is just, but is not the legally just, but a rectification of it. §4 This is because all law is universal, but in some areas no universal rule can be correct; and so where a universal 15 rule has to be made, but cannot be correct, the law chooses the [universal rule] that is usually [correct], well aware of the error being made. And the

1137b law is no less correct on this account; for the source of the error is not the law or the legislator, but the nature of the object itself, since that is what the subject matter of actions is bound to be like.*

20 §5 And so, whenever the law makes a universal rule, but in this particular case what happens violates the [intended scope of] the universal rule, on this point the legislator falls short, and has made an error by making an unqualified rule. Then it is correct to rectify the deficiency; this is what the legislator would have said himself if he had been present there, and what he would have prescribed, had he known, in his legislation.

25 §6 That is why the decent is just, and better than a certain way of being just—not better than the unqualifiedly just, but better than the error that results from the omission of any qualification [in the rule]. And this is the nature of the decent—rectification of law insofar as the universality of law makes it deficient.*

This is also the reason why not everything is guided by law. For on some matters legislation is impossible, and so a decree is needed. 30 §7 For the standard applied to the indefinite is itself indefinite, as the lead standard is in Lesbian building, where it is not fixed, but adapts itself to the shape of the stone;* similarly, a decree is adapted to fit its objects.

§8 It is clear from this what is decent, and clear that it is just, and better 35 than a certain way of being just. It is also evident from this who the 1138a decent person is; for he is the one who decides on and does such actions, not an exact stickler for justice in the bad way, but taking less than he might even though he has the law on his side. This is the decent person, and his state is decency; it is a sort of justice, and not some state different from it.

11

[Injustice to Oneself]

Is it possible to do injustice to oneself or not? The answer is evident from what has been said.*

5 First of all, some just actions are the legal prescriptions in accord with each virtue; we are legally forbidden, for instance, to kill ourselves.* §2 Moreover, if someone illegally and willingly inflicts harm on another, not returning harm for harm, he does injustice (a person acting willingly 10 is one who knows the victim and the instrument). Now if someone murders himself because of anger, he does this willingly, in violation of correct reason, when the law forbids it; hence he does injustice. §3 But injustice to whom? Surely to the city, not to himself, since he suffers it willingly, and no one willingly suffers injustice. That is why the city both penalizes him and inflicts further dishonor on him for destroying himself, on the ground that he does injustice to the city.*

§4 Now consider the type of injustice that belongs to an agent who is only unjust, not base generally. Clearly the corresponding type of unjust action is different from the first type. For this second type of unjust person is wicked in the same [special] way as the coward is, not by having total wickedness; hence his acts of injustice do not accord with total wickedness either. In this case also one cannot do injustice to oneself. For if one could, the same person could lose and get the same thing at the same time. But this is impossible; on the contrary, what is just or unjust must always involve more than one person. *1138a15* 20

§5 Moreover, doing injustice is voluntary, and results from a decision, and strikes first; for a victim who retaliates does not seem to do injustice. But if someone does injustice to himself, he does and suffers the same thing at the same time. Further, on this view, it would be possible to suffer injustice willingly.

§6 Besides, no one does injustice without doing one of the particular acts of injustice. But no one commits adultery with his own wife, or burgles his own house, or steals his own possessions. 25

And in general the puzzle about doing injustice to oneself is also solved by the distinction about voluntarily suffering injustice.

§7 It is also evident that both doing and suffering injustice are bad, since one is having more, one having less, than the intermediate amount, just as in the case of health in medicine and fitness in gymnastics [both more and less than the intermediate amount are bad].* But doing injustice is worse; for it is blameworthy, involving vice that is either complete and unqualified or close to it (since not all voluntary doing of injustice is combined with [the state of] injustice).* Suffering injustice, however, involves no vice or injustice. 30 35

§8 In its own right, then, suffering injustice is less bad; and though it might still be coincidentally a greater evil, that is no concern of a craft. Rather, the craft says that pleurisy is a worse illness than a stumble, even though a stumble might sometimes coincidentally turn out worse—if, for instance, someone stumbled and by coincidence was captured by the enemy or killed because he fell. 1138b 5

§9 It is possible for there to be a sort of justice, by similarity and transference, not of a person to himself, but of certain parts of a person—not every kind of justice, but the kind that belongs to masters or households. For in these discussions the part of the soul that has reason is distinguished from the nonrational part. People look at these and it seems to them that there is injustice to oneself, because in these parts it is possible to suffer something against one's own desires.* Hence it is possible for those parts to be just to each other, as it is for ruler and ruled.*

§10 So much, then, for our definitions of justice and the other virtues of character. 10

BOOK VI

[VIRTUES OF THOUGHT]

1

[The Mean and the Virtues of Thought]

1138b Since we have said previously that we must choose the intermediate con-
20 dition, not the excess or the deficiency, and that the intermediate condition is as the correct reason says, let us now determine what it says.* For in all the states of character we have mentioned, as well as in the others, there is a target that the person who has reason focuses on and so tightens or relaxes; and there is a definition of the means, which we say are between
25 excess and deficiency because they accord with the correct reason.

§2 To say this is admittedly true, but it is not at all clear.* For in other pursuits directed by a science, it is equally true that we must labor and be idle neither too much nor too little, but the intermediate amount pre-
30 scribed by correct reason. But knowing only this, we would be none the wiser about, for instance, the medicines to be applied to the body, if we were told we must apply the ones that medical science prescribes and in the way that the medical scientist applies them.

§3 That is why our account of the states of the soul, in the same way, must not only be true as far as it has gone, but we must also determine what the correct reason is, that is to say,* what its definition is.

35 §4 After we divided the virtues of the soul, we said that some are vir-
1139a tues of character and some of thought. And so, having finished our discussion of the virtues of character, let us now discuss the others as follows, after speaking first about the soul.

5 §5 Previously, then, we said there are two parts of the soul, one that has reason, and one nonrational.* Now we should divide in the same way the part that has reason. Let us assume there are two parts that have reason: with one we study beings whose principles do not admit of being otherwise than they are, and with the other we study beings whose principles admit of being otherwise.* For when the beings are of different
10 kinds, the parts of the soul naturally suited to each of them are also of different kinds, since the parts possess knowledge by being somehow similar and appropriate [to their objects].

§6 Let us call one of these the scientific part, and the other the rationally calculating part; for deliberating is the same as rationally calculating, and no one deliberates about what cannot be otherwise. Hence the ration-
15 ally calculating part is one part of the part of the soul that has reason.

§7 Hence we should find the best state* of the scientific part and the best state of the rationally calculating part; for this state is the virtue of each of them. Now a thing's virtue is relative to its own proper function, [and so we must consider the function of each part].*

2

[Thought, Desire, and Decision]

There are three [capacities] in the soul—sense perception, understanding, desire*—that control action and truth. §2 Of these three, sense perception is clearly not the principle of any action, since beasts have perception, but no share in action.* *1139a* 20

As assertion and denial are to thought, so pursuit and avoidance are to desire. Now virtue of character is a state that decides; and decision is a deliberative desire. If, then, the decision is excellent, the reason must be true and the desire correct, so that what reason asserts is what desire pursues. This, then, is thought and truth concerned with action. §3 The thought concerned with study, not with action or production, has its good or bad state in being true or false; for truth is the function of whatever thinks. But the function of what thinks about action is truth agreeing with correct desire.* 25 30

§4 The principle of an action—the source of motion, not the goal—is decision;* the principle of decision is desire and goal-directed reason.* That is why decision requires understanding and thought, and also a state of character; for acting well* or badly requires both thought and character. 35

§5 Thought by itself moves nothing; what moves us is goal-directed thought concerned with action.* For this thought is also the principle of productive thought; for every producer in his production aims at some [further] goal,* and the unqualified goal is not the product, which is only the [qualified] goal of some [production], and aims at some [further] goal. [An unqualified goal is] what we achieve in *action*, since acting well is the goal, and desire is for the goal. That is why* decision is either understanding combined with desire or desire combined with thought; and this is the sort of principle that a human being is. 1139b 5

§6 We do not decide to do what is already past; no one decides, for instance, to have sacked Troy. For neither do we deliberate about what is past, but only about what will be and admits of being or not being; and what is past does not admit of not having happened. That is why Agathon is correct to say 'Of this alone even a god is deprived—to make what is all done to have never happened'.* 10

The function of each of the understanding parts, then, is truth. And so the virtues of each part will be the states that best direct it toward the truth.*

3

[Scientific Knowledge]

Then let us begin again, and discuss these states of the soul.* Let us say, then, that there are five states in which the soul grasps the truth in its 15

1139b affirmation or denials. These are craft, scientific knowledge, prudence, wisdom, and understanding; for belief and supposition admit of being false.

§2 What science is, is evident from the following, if we must speak 20 exactly and not be guided by [mere] similarities.* For we all suppose that what we know scientifically does not even admit of being otherwise; and whenever what admits of being otherwise escapes observation, we do not notice whether it is or is not, [and hence we do not know about it]. Hence what is known scientifically is by necessity. Hence it is everlasting; for the things that are by unqualified necessity are all everlasting, and everlasting things are ingenerable and indestructible.

25 §3 Further, every science seems to be teachable, and what is scientifically knowable is learnable. But all teaching is from what is already known, as we also say in the *Analytics*;* for some teaching is through induction, some by deduction, [which both require previous knowledge]. Induction [leads to] the principle, i.e., the universal,* whereas deduction 30 proceeds from the universal. Hence deduction has principles from which it proceeds and which are not themselves [reached] by deduction. Hence they are [reached] by induction.

§4 Scientific knowledge, then, is a demonstrative state, and has all the other features that in the *Analytics** we add to the definition. For one has scientific knowledge whenever one has the appropriate sort of confidence, 35 and knows the principles; for if one does not know them better than the conclusion, one will have scientific knowledge [only] coincidentally.

So much for a definition of scientific knowledge.

4

[Craft Knowledge]

1140a What admits of being otherwise includes what is produced and what is achieved in action.* §2 Production and action are different; about them we rely also on [our] popular discussions. And so the state involving reason and concerned with action is different from the state involving reason 5 and concerned with production. Nor is one included in the other;* for action is not production, and production is not action.

§3 Now building, for instance, is a craft, and is essentially a certain state involving reason concerned with production; there is no craft that is not a state involving reason concerned with production, and no such state 10 that is not a craft. Hence a craft is the same as a state involving true reason concerned with production.

§4 Every craft is concerned with coming to be, and the exercise of the craft is the study* of how something that admits of being and not being comes to be, something whose principle is in the producer and not in the product. For a craft is not concerned with things that are or come to be by necessity; nor with things that are by nature, since these have their principle in themselves.* *1140a* 15

§5 Since production and action are different, craft must be concerned with production, not with action.

In a way craft and fortune are concerned with the same things, as Agathon says: 'Craft was fond of fortune, and fortune of craft.'* 20

§6 A craft, then, as we have said, is a state involving true reason concerned with production. Lack of craft is the contrary state involving false reason and concerned with production. Both are concerned with what admits of being otherwise.

5

[Prudence]

To grasp what prudence is, we should first study the sort of people we call prudent. It seems proper to a prudent person to be able to deliberate finely* about things that are good and beneficial for himself, not about some restricted area*—about what sorts of things promote health or strength, for instance—but about what sorts of things promote living well in general.* 25

§2 A sign of this is the fact that we call people prudent about some [restricted area] whenever they calculate well to promote some excellent end, in an area where there is no craft.* Hence where [living well] as a whole is concerned, the deliberative person will also be prudent. 30

§3 Now no one deliberates about things that cannot be otherwise or about things that cannot be achieved in his action. Hence, if science involves demonstration, but there is no demonstration of anything whose principles admit of being otherwise (since every such thing itself admits of being otherwise); and if we cannot deliberate about things that are by necessity; it follows that prudence is not science nor yet craft knowledge. It is not science, because what is achievable in action admits of being otherwise; and it is not craft knowledge, because action and production belong to different kinds. 35 1140b

§4 The remaining possibility, then, is that prudence is a state grasping the truth, involving reason, concerned with action about things that are good or bad for a human being. For production has its end in something other than itself, but action does not, since its end is acting well itself.* 5

§5 That is why Pericles and such people are the ones whom we regard as prudent, because they are able to study what is good for themselves and for human beings; we think that household managers and politicians are such people.* 10

This is also how we come to give temperance (*sōphrosunē*) its name, because we think that it preserves prudence (*sōzousan tēn phronēsin*).*

1140b §6 It preserves the [right] sort of supposition. For the sort of supposition that is corrupted and perverted by the pleasant or painful is not every 15 sort—not, for instance, the supposition that the triangle does or does not have two right angles—but suppositions about what is achievable in action. For the principles of things achievable in action are their goal, but if someone is corrupted because of pleasure or pain, no [appropriate] principle can appear to him, and it cannot appear that this is the right 20 goal and cause of all his choice and action; for vice corrupts the principle.* And so prudence must be a state grasping the truth, involving reason, and concerned with action about human goods.*

§7 Moreover, there is virtue [or vice in the use] of craft, but not [in the use] of prudence. Further, in a craft, someone who makes errors voluntarily is more choiceworthy; but with prudence, as with the virtues, the 25 reverse is true. Clearly, then, prudence is a virtue, not craft knowledge.*

§8 There are two parts of the soul that have reason. Prudence is a virtue of one of them, of the part that has belief; for belief is concerned, as prudence is, with what admits of being otherwise.

Moreover, it is not only a state involving reason. A sign of this is the fact that such a state can be forgotten, but prudence cannot.*

6

[Understanding]

30 Scientific knowledge is supposition about universals, things that are by necessity. Further, everything demonstrable and every science have principles, since scientific knowledge involves reason. Hence there can be neither scientific knowledge nor craft knowledge nor prudence about the 35 principles of what is scientifically known. For what is scientifically known is demonstrable, [but the principles are not]; and craft and pru- 1141a dence are about what admits of being otherwise. Nor is wisdom [exclusively] about principles;* for it is proper to the wise person to have a demonstration of some things.

§2 [The states of the soul] by which we always grasp the truth and 5 never make mistakes, about what can or cannot be otherwise, are scientific knowledge, prudence, wisdom, and understanding. But none of the first three—prudence, scientific knowledge, wisdom—is possible about principles. The remaining possibility, then, is that we have understanding about principles.*

7

[Wisdom versus Prudence]

10 We ascribe wisdom in crafts to the people who have the most exact expertise in the crafts.* For instance, we call Pheidias a wise stoneworker and

Polycleitus a wise bronze worker; and by wisdom we signify precisely virtue in a craft. §2 But we also think some people are wise in general, not wise in some [restricted] area, or in some other [specific] way (as Homer says in the *Margites*: 'The gods did not make him a digger or a ploughman or wise in anything else').* Clearly, then, wisdom is the most exact [form] of scientific knowledge. 1141a 15

§3 Hence the wise person must not only know what is derived from the principles of a science, but also grasp the truth about the principles. Therefore wisdom is understanding plus scientific knowledge; it is scientific knowledge of the most honorable things that has received [understanding as] its coping stone.*

For it would be absurd for someone to think that political science or prudence is the most excellent science;* for the best thing in the universe is not a human being [and the most excellent science must be of the best things]. 20

§4 Moreover,* if what is good and healthy for human beings and for fish is not the same, whereas what is white or straight is always the same, everyone would also say that the content of wisdom is the same in every case, but the content of prudence* is not. For the agent they would call prudent is the one who studies well each question about his own [good], and he is the one to whom they would entrust such questions.* That is why prudence is also ascribed to some of the beasts, the ones that are evidently capable of forethought about their own life.* 25

It is also evident that wisdom is not the same as political science.* For if people are to say that science about what is beneficial to themselves [as human beings] counts as wisdom, there will be many types of wisdom [corresponding to the different species of animals]. For if there is no one medical science about all beings, there is no one science about the good of all animals, but a different science about each specific good. [Hence there will be many types of wisdom, contrary to our assumption that it has always the same content.] It does not matter if human beings are the best among the animals; for there are other beings of a far more divine nature than human beings—most evidently, for instance, the beings composing the universe. 30 1141b

§5 What we have said makes it clear that wisdom is both scientific knowledge and understanding about the things that are by nature most honorable. That is why people say that Anaxagoras or Thales* or that sort of person is wise, but not prudent, whenever they see that he is ignorant of what benefits himself. And so they say that what he knows is extraordinary, amazing, difficult, and divine, but useless, because it is not human goods that he looks for. 5

§6 Prudence, by contrast, is about human concerns, about things open to deliberation. For we say that deliberating well is the function of the prudent person more than anyone else; but no one deliberates about 10

1141b things that cannot be otherwise, or about things lacking any goal that is a good achievable in action.* The unqualifiedly good deliberator is the one whose aim accords with rational calculation in pursuit of the best good for a human being that is achievable in action.*

15 §7 Nor is prudence about universals only. It must also acquire knowledge of particulars, since it is concerned with action and action is about particulars.* That is why in other areas also some people who lack knowledge but have experience are better in action than others who have knowledge. For someone who knows that light meats are digestible and 20 [hence] healthy,* but not which sorts of meats are light, will not produce health; the one who knows that bird meats are light and healthy* will be better at producing health. And since prudence is concerned with action, it must possess both [the universal and the particular knowledge] or the [particular] more [than the universal]. Here too, however, [as in medicine] there is a ruling [science].*

8

[Types of Prudence]

Political science and prudence are the same state, but their being is not the same.*

25 §2 One type of prudence about the city is the ruling part; this is legislative science. The type concerned with particulars [often] monopolizes the name 'political science' that [properly] applies to both types in common.* This type is concerned with action and deliberation, since [it is concerned with decrees and] the decree* is to be acted on as the last thing [reached in deliberation]. Hence these people are the only ones who are said to be politically active; for these are the only ones who put [political science] into practice, as hand-craftsmen put [a craft] into practice.

30 §3 Similarly, prudence concerned with the individual himself seems most of all to be counted as prudence; and this [type of prudence often] monopolizes the name 'prudence' that [properly] applies [to all types] in common. Of the other types, one is household science, another legislative, another political, one type of which is deliberative and another judicial.

§4 In fact knowledge of what is [good] for oneself is one species [of 1142a prudence].* But there is much difference [in opinions] about it.* The one who knows about himself, and spends his time on his own concerns, seems to be prudent, while politicians seem to be too active.* Hence Euripides says, 'Surely I cannot be prudent, since I could have been inac- 5 tive, numbered among all the many in the army, and have had an equal share.... For those who go too far and are too active....'* For people seek what is good for themselves, and suppose that this [inactivity] is the right action [to achieve their good]. Hence this belief has led to the view that these are the prudent people.* Presumably, however, one's own welfare requires household management and a political system. Further, [another reason for the difference of opinion is that] it is unclear, and should be examined, how one must manage one's own affairs. *1142a* 10

§5 A sign of what has been said [about the unclarity of what prudence requires] is the fact that whereas young people become accomplished in geometry and mathematics, and wise within these limits, prudent young people do not seem to be found.* The reason is that prudence is concerned with particulars as well as universals, and particulars become known from experience, but a young person lacks experience, since some length of time is needed to produce it. 15

§6 Indeed [to understand the difficulty and importance of experience] we might consider why a child can become accomplished in mathematics, but not in wisdom or natural science. Surely it is because mathematical objects are reached through abstraction,* whereas in these other cases the principles* are reached from experience. Young people, then, [lacking experience], have no real conviction in these other sciences, but only say the words,* whereas the nature of mathematical objects is clear to them. 20

§7 Further, [prudence is difficult because it is deliberative and] deliberation may be in error about either the universal or the particular.* For [we may wrongly suppose] either that all sorts of heavy water are bad or that this water is heavy.

§8 It is apparent that prudence is not scientific knowledge; for, as we said, it concerns the last thing [i.e., the particular], since this is what is achievable in action.* §9 Hence it is opposite to understanding.* For understanding is about the [first] terms,* [those] that have no account of them; but prudence is about the last thing, an object of perception, not of scientific knowledge. This is not the perception of special objects,* but the sort by which we perceive that the last among mathematical objects is a triangle; for it will stop there too.* This is another species [of perception than perception of special objects]; but it is still perception more than prudence is.* 25 30

9

[Good Deliberation]

Inquiry and deliberation are different, since deliberation is a type of inquiry. We must also grasp what good deliberation is,* and see whether it is some sort of scientific knowledge, or belief, or good guessing, or some other kind of thing.

§2 First of all, then, it is not scientific knowledge. For we do not inquire for what we already know; but good deliberation is a type of deliberation, and a deliberator inquires and rationally calculates. 1142b

1142b Moreover, it is not good guessing either. For good guessing involves no reasoning, and is done quickly; but we deliberate a long time, and it is 5 said that we must act quickly on the result of our deliberation, but deliberate slowly.* §3 Further, quick thinking is different from good deliberation, and quick thinking is a kind of good guessing.

Nor is good deliberation just any sort of belief. Rather, since the bad deliberator is in error, and the good deliberator deliberates correctly, good deliberation is clearly some sort of correctness.

10 But it is not correctness in scientific knowledge or in belief. For there is no correctness in scientific knowledge,* since there is no error in it either; and correctness in belief consists in truth, [but correctness in deliberation does not].* Further, everything about which one has belief is already determined, [but what is deliberated about is not yet determined].

However, good deliberation requires reason; hence the remaining possibility is that it belongs to thought. For thought is not yet assertion; [and this is why it is not belief]. For belief is not inquiry, but already an asser-15 tion; but in deliberating, either well or badly, we inquire for something and rationally calculate about it.

§4 But good deliberation is a certain sort of correctness in deliberation. That is why we must first inquire what [this correctness] is and what it is [correctness] about.* Since there are several types of correctness, clearly good deliberation will not be every type.* For the incontinent or base person will use rational calculation to reach what he proposes to see, and so 20 will have deliberated correctly [if that is all it takes], but will have got himself a great evil.* Having deliberated well seems, on the contrary, to be some sort of good; for the sort of correctness in deliberation that makes it good deliberation is the sort that reaches a good.*

§5 However, we can reach a good by a false inference, as well [as by correct deliberation], so that we reach the right thing to do, but by the 25 wrong steps, when the middle term is false.* Hence this type of deliberation, leading us by the wrong steps to the right thing to do, is not enough for good deliberation either.

§6 Further, one person may deliberate a long time before reaching the right thing to do, while another reaches it quickly. Nor, then, is the first condition enough for good deliberation; good deliberation is correctness that accords with what is beneficial, about the right thing, in the right way, and at the right time.

§7 Further, our deliberation may be either good without qualification 30 or good only to the extent that it promotes some [limited] end.* Hence unqualifiedly good deliberation is the sort that correctly promotes the unqualified end [i.e., the highest good], while the [limited] sort is the sort that correctly promotes some [limited] end.* If, then, having deliberated well is proper to a prudent person, good deliberation will be the type of correctness that accords with what is expedient for promoting the end about which prudence is true supposition.*

10

[Comprehension]

Comprehension, i.e. good comprehension, makes people, as we say, comprehend and comprehend well.* It is not the same as scientific knowledge in general. Nor is it the same as belief, since, if it were, everyone would have comprehension. Nor is it any one of the specific sciences [with its own specific area], in the way that medicine is about what is healthy or geometry is about magnitudes. For comprehension is neither about what always is and is unchanging nor about just anything that comes to be. It is about what we might be puzzled about and might deliberate about. That is why it is about the same things as prudence, but not the same as prudence. 1143a 5

§2 For prudence is prescriptive, since its end is what action we must or must not do, whereas comprehension only judges.* (For comprehension and good comprehension are the same; and so are people with comprehension and with good comprehension.) Comprehension is neither having prudence nor acquiring it. 10

§3 Rather, it is similar to the way learning is called comprehending when someone applies scientific knowledge. In the same way comprehension consists in the application of belief to judge someone else's remarks on a question that concerns prudence, and moreover it must judge them finely since judging well is the same as judging finely. §4 That is how the name 'comprehension' was attached to the comprehension that makes people have good comprehension. It is derived from the comprehension found in learning; for we often call learning comprehending.* 15

11

[Practical Thought and Particulars]

The [state] called consideration makes people, as we say, considerate and makes them have consideration; it is the correct judgment of the decent person.* A sign of this is our saying that the decent person more than others is considerate, and that it is decent to be considerate about some things. Considerateness is the correct consideration that judges what is decent; and correct consideration judges what is true. 20

§2 It is reasonable that all these states tend in the same direction.* For we ascribe consideration, comprehension, prudence, and understanding to the same people, and say that these have consideration, and thereby understanding, and that they are prudent and comprehending. For all these capacities are about the last things, i.e., particulars.* Moreover, someone has comprehension and good consideration, or has considerateness, in being able to judge about the matters that concern the prudent 25 30

1143a person; for the decent is the common concern of all good people in relations with other people.

§3 [These states are all concerned with particulars because] all the things achievable in action are particular and last things. For the prudent person also must recognize [things achievable in action], while compre-
35 hension and consideration are concerned with things achievable in action, and these are last things.

§4 Understanding is also concerned with the last things, and in both directions.* For there is understanding, not a rational account, both about
1143b the first terms and about the last.* In demonstrations understanding is about the unchanging terms that are first. In [premises] about action understanding is about the last term, the one that admits of being otherwise, and [hence] about the minor premise.* For these last terms are
5 beginnings of the [end] to be aimed at, since universals are reached from particulars.*

§5 We must, therefore, have perception of these particulars, and this
9, 10 perception is understanding.* §6 That is why understanding is both beginning and end; for demonstrations [begin] from these things and are about them.*

6 §5 That is why these states actually seem to grow naturally,* so that, whereas no one seems to have natural wisdom,* people seem to have natural consideration, comprehension, and judgment. §6 A sign [of their apparent natural character] is our thinking that they also correspond to someone's age, and the fact that understanding and consideration belong to a certain age, as though nature were the cause. And so we must attend to the undemonstrated remarks and beliefs of experienced and older people or of prudent people, no less than to demonstrations. For these people see correctly because experience has given them their eye.

15 §7 We have said, then, what prudence and wisdom are; what each is about; and that each is the virtue of a different part of the soul.*

12

[Puzzles about Prudence and Wisdom]

One might, however, go through some puzzles about what use they are.*
20 For wisdom is not concerned with any sort of coming into being, and hence will not study any source of human happiness. Admittedly, pru-
25, 26 dence will study this; but what do we need it for? For knowledge of what is healthy or fit (i.e., of what results from the state of health, not of what
27 produces it) makes us no readier to act appropriately if we are already
21 healthy; for having the science of medicine or gymnastics makes us no readier to act appropriately. Similarly, prudence is the science of what is just and what is fine, and what is good for a human being; but this is how
25 the good man acts; and if we are already good, knowledge of them makes

us no readier to act appropriately, since virtues are states [activated in actions].* *1143b*

§2 If we concede that prudence is not useful for this, should we say it is useful for becoming good? In that case it will be no use to those who are already excellent.* Nor, however, will it be any use to those who are not. For it will not matter to them* whether they have it themselves or take the advice of others who have it. The advice of others will be quite adequate for us, just as it is with health: we wish to be healthy, but still do not learn medical science. 28 30

§3 Besides, it would seem absurd for prudence, inferior as it is to wisdom, to control it [as a superior. But this will be the result], since the science that produces also rules and prescribes about its product.* 35

We must discuss these questions; for so far we have only raised the puzzles about them.

§4 First of all, let us state that both prudence and wisdom must be choiceworthy in themselves, even if neither produces anything at all; for each is the virtue of one of the two [rational] parts [of the soul].* 1144a

§5 Secondly, they do produce something. Wisdom produces happiness, not in the way that medical science produces health, but in the way that health produces [health].* For since wisdom is a part of virtue as a whole, it makes us happy because it is a state that we possess and activate. 5

§6 Further, we fulfill our function* insofar as we have prudence and virtue of character; for virtue makes the goal correct, and prudence makes the things promoting the goal [correct].* The fourth part of the soul, the nutritive part, has no such virtue [related to our function], since no action is up to it to do or not to do. 10

§7 To answer the claim that prudence will make us no better at achieving fine and just actions,* we must begin from a little further back [in our discussion]. We begin here: we say that some people who do just actions are not yet thereby just, if, for instance, they do the actions prescribed by the laws either unwillingly or because of ignorance or because of some other end, not because of the actions themselves, even though they do the right actions, those that the excellent person ought to do.* Equally, however, it would seem to be possible for someone to do each type of action in the state that makes him a good person, that is to say, because of decision and for the sake of the actions themselves.* 15 20

§8 Now virtue makes the decision correct;* but the actions that are naturally to be done to fulfill the decision are the concern not of virtue, but of another capacity.* We must grasp them more perspicuously before continuing our discussion.

§9 There is a capacity, called cleverness, which is such as to be able to do the actions that tend to promote whatever goal is assumed* and to attain them.* If, then, the goal is fine, cleverness is praiseworthy, and if the goal is base, cleverness is unscrupulousness. That is why both prudent and unscrupulous people are called clever.* 25

1144a §10 Prudence is not cleverness,* though it requires this capacity. [Prudence,] this eye of the soul, requires virtue in order to reach its fully developed state,* as we have said and as is clear. For inferences about actions have a principle, 'Since the end and the best good is this sort of thing' (whatever it actually is—let it be any old thing for the sake of argument).* And this [best good] is apparent only to the good person; for vice perverts us and produces false views about the principles of actions. Evidently, then, we cannot be prudent without being good.

13

[Prudence and Virtue of Character]

We must, then, also examine virtue over again.* For virtue is similar [in this way] to prudence; as prudence is related to cleverness, not the same but similar, so natural virtue is related to full virtue.* For each of us seems to possess his type of character to some extent by nature; for in fact we are just, brave, prone to temperance, or have another feature, immediately from birth. But still we look for some further condition to be full goodness, and we expect to possess these features in another way. For these natural states belong to children and to beasts as well [as to adults], but without understanding they are evidently harmful.* At any rate, this much would seem to be clear: Just as a heavy body moving around unable to see suffers a heavy fall because it has no sight, so it is with virtue. [A naturally well-endowed person without understanding will harm himself.]

§2 But if someone acquires understanding, he improves in his actions; and the state he now has, though still similar [to the natural one], will be fully virtue. And so, just as there are two sorts of conditions, cleverness and prudence, in the part of the soul that has belief, so also there are two in the part that has character, natural virtue and full virtue. And of these full virtue cannot be acquired without prudence.*

§3 That is why* some say that all the virtues are [instances of] prudence, and why the inquiries Socrates used to undertake* were in one way correct, and in another way in error. For insofar as he thought all the virtues are [instances of] prudence,* he was in error; but insofar as he thought they all require prudence, what he used to say was right.

§4 Here is a sign of this: Whenever people now define virtue, they all say what state it is and what it is related to, and then add that it is the state in accord with the correct reason.* Now the correct reason is the reason in accord with prudence; it would seem, then, that they all in a way intuitively believe that the state in accord with prudence is virtue.

§5 But we must make a slight change. For it is not merely the state in accord with the correct reason, but the state involving the correct reason, that is virtue.* And it is prudence that is the correct reason in this area. Socrates, then, used to think the virtues are [instances of] reason because he thought they are all [instances of] knowledge, whereas we think they involve reason. *1144b30*

§6 What we have said, then, makes it clear that we cannot be fully good without prudence, or prudent without virtue of character. And in this way we can also solve the dialectical argument that someone might use to show that the virtues are separated from one another.* For, [it is argued], since the same person is not naturally best suited for all the virtues, someone will already have one virtue before he gets another. This is indeed possible in the case of the natural virtues. It is not possible, however, in the case of the [full] virtues that someone must have to be called good without qualification; for one has all the virtues if and only if one has prudence, which is a single state.* 35 1145a

§7 And it is clear that, even if prudence were useless in action, we would need it because it is the virtue of this part of the soul,* and because the decision will not be correct without prudence or without virtue*—for [virtue] makes us achieve the end, whereas [prudence] makes us achieve the things that promote the end.* 5

§8 Moreover, prudence does not control wisdom or the better part of the soul, just as medical science does not control health.* For medical science does not use health, but only aims to bring health into being; hence it prescribes for the sake of health, but does not prescribe to health. Besides, [saying that prudence controls wisdom] would be like saying that political science rules the gods because it prescribes about everything in the city. 10

BOOK VII

[INCONTINENCE]

1

[Virtue, Vice, and Incontinence]

Let us now make a new start, and say that there are three conditions of character to be avoided—vice, incontinence, and bestiality. The contraries of two of these are clear; we call one virtue and the other continence. 15

The contrary to bestiality is most suitably called virtue superior to us, a heroic, indeed divine, sort of virtue. Thus Homer made Priam say that Hector was remarkably good; 'nor did he look as though he were the child of a mortal man, but of a god.'* §2 And so, if, as they say, human beings become gods because of exceedingly great virtue, this is clearly the sort of state that would be opposite to the bestial state. For indeed, just as a beast has neither virtue nor vice, so neither does a god, but the god's state is more honorable than virtue, and the beast's belongs to some kind different from vice.* 20 25

§3 Now it is rare that a divine man exists. (This is what the Spartans

1145a habitually call him; whenever they very much admire someone, they say 30 he is a divine man.) Similarly, the bestial person is also rare among human beings. He is most often found in foreigners; but some bestial features also result from diseases and deformities. We also use 'bestial' as a term of reproach for people whose vice exceeds the human level.

35 §4 We must make some remarks about this condition later. We have discussed vice earlier. We must now discuss incontinence, softness, and 1145b self-indulgence, and also continence and resistance; for we must not suppose that continence and incontinence are concerned with the same states as virtue and vice, or that they belong to a different kind.

§5 As in the other cases, we must set out the appearances,* and first of 5 all go through the puzzles. In this way we must prove the common beliefs about these ways of being affected*—ideally, all the common beliefs, but if not all, most of them, and the most important.* For if the objections are solved, and the common beliefs are left, it will be an adequate proof.

§6 Continence and resistance seem to be good and praiseworthy con- 10 ditions, whereas incontinence and softness seem to be base and blameworthy conditions.* The continent person seems to be the same as one who abides by his rational calculation; and the incontinent person seems to be the same as one who abandons it. The incontinent person knows that his actions are base, but does them because of his feelings, whereas the continent person knows that his appetites are base, but because of reason does not follow them.

15 People think the temperate person is continent and resistant. Some think that every continent and resistant person is temperate, while others do not. Some people say the incontinent person is intemperate and the intemperate incontinent, with no distinction; others say they are different.

§7 Sometimes it is said that a prudent person cannot be incontinent; but sometimes it is said that some people are prudent and clever, but still incontinent.

20 Further, people are called incontinent about spirit, honor, and gain.

These, then, are the things that are said.

2

[Puzzles about Incontinence]

We might be puzzled about what sort of correct supposition someone has when he acts incontinently.*

First of all, some say he cannot have knowledge [at the time he acts]. For it would be terrible, Socrates used to think,* for knowledge to be in some- 25 one, but mastered by something else, and dragged around like a slave.* For Socrates used to oppose the account [of incontinence] in general, in the belief that there is no incontinence; for no one, in Socrates' view, supposes while he acts that his action conflicts with what is best; our action conflicts with what is best only because we are ignorant [of the conflict].* 1145b

§2 This argument, then, contradicts things that appear manifestly.* If ignorance causes the incontinent person to be affected as he is, we must look for the type of ignorance that it turns out to be; for it is evident, at any rate, that before he is affected the person who acts incontinently does not think [he should do the action he eventually does].* 30

§3 Some people concede some of [Socrates' points], but reject some of them. For they agree that nothing is superior to knowledge, but they deny the claim that no one's action conflicts with what has seemed better to him. That is why they say that when the incontinent person is overcome by pleasure he has only belief, not knowledge. 35

§4 If, however, he has belief, not knowledge, and the supposition that resists is not strong, but only a weak one, such as people have when they are in doubt, we will pardon failure to abide by these beliefs against strong appetites. In fact, however, we do not pardon vice, or any other blameworthy condition [and incontinence is one of these]. 1146a

§5 Then is it prudence that resists, since it is the strongest? This is absurd. For on this view the same person will be both prudent and incontinent; but no one would say that the prudent person is the sort to do the worst actions willingly. Besides, we have shown earlier that the prudent person acts [on his knowledge], since he is concerned with the last things, [i.e., particulars] and that he has the other virtues.* 5

§6 Further,* if the continent person must have strong and base appetites, the temperate person will not be continent nor the continent person temperate. For the temperate person is not the sort to have either excessive or base appetites; but [the continent person] must have both. For if his appetites are good, the state that prevents him from following them must be base, so that not all continence is excellent. If, however, the appetites are weak and not base, continence is nothing impressive; and if they are base and weak, it is nothing great. 10 15

§7 Further, if continence makes someone prone to abide by every belief, it is bad, if, for instance, it makes him abide by a false as well [as true] belief. And if incontinence makes someone prone to abandon every belief, there will be an excellent type of incontinence. Take, for instance, Neoptolemus in Sophocles' *Philoctetes*.* For he is praiseworthy for his failure to abide by [his promise to tell the lies] that Odysseus had persuaded him [to tell]; [he breaks his promise] because he feels pain at lying. 20

§8 Further, the sophistical argument is a puzzle. For [the sophists] wish to refute an [opponent, by showing] that his views have paradoxical results,* so that they will be clever in encounters.* Hence the inference that results is a puzzle; for thought is tied up, whenever it does not want to stand still, because the conclusion is displeasing, but it cannot advance, because it cannot solve the argument.* §9 A certain argument, then, concludes that foolishness combined with incontinence is virtue. For 25

1146a incontinence makes someone act contrary to what he supposes [is right];
30 but since he supposes that good things are bad and that it is wrong to do them, he will do the good actions, not the bad.

§10 Further, someone who acts to pursue what is pleasant because this is what he is persuaded and decides to do* seems to be better than someone who acts not because of rational calculation, but because of incontinence. For the first person is the easier to cure, because he might be 35 persuaded to act otherwise; but the incontinent person illustrates the 1146b proverb 'If water chokes us, what must we drink to wash it down?' For if he had been persuaded to do the action he does, he would have stopped when he was persuaded to act otherwise; but in fact, though already persuaded to act otherwise, he still acts [wrongly].

§11 Further, is there incontinence and continence about everything? If so, who is simply incontinent?* For no one has all the types of inconti- 5 nence, but we say that some people are simply incontinent.

§12 These, then, are the sorts of puzzles that arise.* We must undermine some of these claims, and leave others intact; for the solution* of the puzzle is the discovery [of what we are seeking].

3

[Incontinence and Ignorance]

First, then, we must examine whether the incontinent has knowledge or 10 not, and in what way he has it. Second, what should we take to be the range of incontinence and continence—every pleasure and pain, or some definite subclass? Are the continent and the resistant person the same or different? Similarly we must deal with the other questions that are relevant to this study.

15 §2 We begin* by examining whether continence and incontinence differ from other things by their range or by their attitudes.* In other words, is the incontinent person incontinent because of a specific range of actions, or because of a specific attitude, or because of both? Next, is there incontinence and continence about everything, or not?*

For the simply incontinent person is not incontinent about everything, 20 but he has the same range as the intemperate person.* Nor is he incontinent simply by being inclined toward these things—that would make incontinence the same as intemperance.* Rather, he is incontinent by being inclined toward them in this way. For the intemperate person acts on decision when he is led on, since he thinks it is right in every case to pursue the pleasant thing at hand; the incontinent person, however, thinks it is wrong to pursue this pleasant thing, yet still pursues it.*

25 §3 It is claimed that the incontinent person's action conflicts with the true belief, not with knowledge.* But whether it is knowledge or belief

that he has does not matter for this argument. For some people with belief *1146b* are in no doubt, but think they have exact knowledge.

§4 If, then, it is the weakness of their conviction that makes people with belief, not people with knowledge, act in conflict with their supposition, it follows that knowledge will [for these purposes] be no different from belief; for, as Heracleitus makes clear,* some people's convictions 30 about what they believe are no weaker than other people's convictions about what they know.

§5 But we speak of knowing in two ways; we ascribe it both to someone who has it without using it and to someone who is using it.* Hence it will matter whether someone has the knowledge that his action is wrong, without attending* to his knowledge, or he both has it and attends to it. 35 For this second case seems extraordinary, but wrong action when he does not attend to his knowledge does not seem extraordinary.

§6 Further, since there are two types of premises, someone's action 1147a may well conflict with his knowledge if he has both types of premises, but uses only the universal premise and not the particular premise.* For it is particulars that are achievable in action.* There are also different types of universal,* one type referring to the agent himself, and the other refer- 5 ring to the object. Perhaps, for instance, someone knows that dry things benefit every human being, and that he himself is a human being, or that this sort of thing is dry; but he either does not have or does not activate the knowledge that this particular thing is of this sort. These ways [of knowing and not knowing], then, make such a remarkable difference that it seems quite intelligible [for someone acting against his knowledge] to have the one sort of knowledge, but astounding if he has the other sort.*

§7 Further, human beings may have knowledge in a way different 10 from those we have described. For we see that having without using includes different types of having; hence some people, such as those asleep or mad or drunk, both have knowledge in a way and do not have it.* Moreover, this is the condition of those affected by strong feelings.* 15 For spirited reactions, sexual appetites, and some conditions of this sort clearly [both disturb knowledge and] disturb the body as well, and even produce fits of madness in some people. Clearly, then [since incontinents are also affected by strong feelings], we should say that they have knowledge in a way similar to these people.

§8 Saying the words that come from knowledge is no sign [of fully having it].* For people affected in these ways even recite demonstrations 20 and verses of Empedocles. And those who have just learned something do not yet know it, though they string the words together; for it must grow into them, and this takes time. And so we must suppose that those who are acting incontinently also say the words in the way that actors do.

§9 Further, we may also look at the cause in the following way, refer- 25 ring to [human] nature.* For one belief is universal; the other is about particulars, and because they are particulars, perception controls them. And

1147a in the cases where these two beliefs result in one belief,* it is necessary, in one case, for the soul to affirm what has been concluded,* but, in the case of beliefs about production, to act at once on what has been concluded. If, 30 for instance, everything sweet must be tasted, and this, some one particular thing, is sweet, it is necessary for someone who is able and unhindered also to act on this at the same time.*

§10 Suppose, then, that someone has the universal belief hindering him from tasting;* he has the second belief, that everything sweet is pleasant and this is sweet,* and this belief is active;* but it turns out that appe- 35 tite is present in him.* The belief, then, [that is formed from the previous two beliefs] tells him to avoid this,* but appetite leads him on, since it is capable of moving each of the [bodily] parts.*

1147b The result, then, is that in a way reason and belief make him act incontinently. The [second] belief is contrary to the correct reason, but only coincidentally, not in its own right.* §11 For the appetite, not the belief, is contrary [in its own right to the correct reason]. That is also why beasts 5 are not incontinent, because they have no universal supposition, but [only] appearance and memory of particulars.*

§12 How is the ignorance resolved, so that the incontinent person recovers his knowledge?* The same account that applies to someone drunk or asleep applies here too, and is not special to this way of being affected. We must hear it from the natural scientists.

10 §13 Since the last premise is a belief about something perceptible,* and controls action, this is what the incontinent person does not have when he is being affected.* Or [rather] the way he has it is not knowledge of it, but, as we saw, [merely] saying the words,* as the drunk says the words of Empedocles.*

And since the last term does not seem to be universal, or expressive of 15 knowledge in the same way as the universal term,* even the result Socrates was looking for would seem to come about. §14 For the knowledge that is present when someone is affected by incontinence, and that is dragged about because he is affected,* is not the sort that seems to be fully knowledge, but it is only perceptual knowledge.*

So much, then, for knowing and not knowing, and for how it is possible to know and still to act incontinently.

4

[Simple Incontinence]

20 Next we must say whether anyone is simply incontinent, or all incontinents are incontinent in some particular way; and if someone is simply incontinent, we must say what sorts of things he is incontinent about.

First of all, both continence and resistance and incontinence and softness are evidently about pleasures and pains.

§2 Some sources of pleasure are necessary; others are choiceworthy in their own right, but can be taken to excess.* The necessary ones are the bodily conditions, i.e., those that concern food, sexual intercourse, and the sorts of bodily conditions that we took temperance and intemperance to be about. Other sources of pleasure are not necessary, but are choiceworthy in themselves, such as victory, honor, wealth, and similar good and pleasant things. *1147b25* 30

When people go to excess, against the correct reason in them, in the pursuit of these sources of pleasure, we do not call them simply incontinent, but add the qualification that they are incontinent about wealth, gain, honor, or spirit, and not simply incontinent. For we assume that they are different, and called incontinent [only] because of a similarity, just as the Olympic victor named Human* was different, since for him the common account [of human being] was only a little different from his special one, but it was different nonetheless. 35 1148a

A sign in favor of what we say is the fact that incontinence is blamed not only as an error but as a vice, either unqualified or partial,* while none of these conditions is blamed as a vice.

§3 Now consider the people concerned with the bodily gratifications, those that we take temperance and intemperance to be about. Some of these people go to excess in pursuing these pleasant things and avoiding painful things—hunger, thirst, heat, cold, and all the objects of touch and taste—not, however, because they have decided on it, but against their decision and thought. These are the people called simply incontinent, not with the added condition that they are incontinent about, for instance, anger. 5 10

§4 A sign of this is the fact that people are also called soft about these [bodily] pleasures, but not about any of the non-necessary ones.

This is also why we include the incontinent and the intemperate person, and the continent and the temperate person, in the same class, but do not include any of those who are incontinent in some particular way. It is because incontinence and intemperance are, in a way, about the same pleasures and pains. In fact they are about the same things, but not in the same way; the intemperate person decides on them, but the incontinent person does not.* That is why, if someone has no appetites, or slight ones, for excesses, but still pursues them and avoids moderate pains, we will take him to be more intemperate than the person who does it because he has intense appetites. For think of the lengths he would go to if he also acquired vigorous appetites and felt severe pains at the lack of necessities. 15 20

§5 Some pleasant things are naturally choiceworthy, some naturally the contrary, some in between, as we divided them earlier. Hence some appetites and pleasures are for fine and excellent kinds of things, such as wealth, profit, victory, and honor. About all these and about the things in between people are blamed not for feeling an appetite and love for them, but for doing so in a particular way, namely to excess. 25

1148a30 Some people are overcome by, or pursue, some of these naturally fine and good things to a degree that goes against reason; they take honor, or children, or parents (for instance) more seriously than is right. For though these are certainly good and people are praised for taking them seriously, still excess about them is also possible. It is excessive if one fights, as 1148b Niobe did [for her children], even with the gods, or if one regards his father as Satyrus, nicknamed the Fatherlover, did—for he seemed to be excessively silly about it. There is no vice* here, for the reason we have given, since each of these things is naturally choiceworthy for itself, though excess about them is bad and to be avoided.

5 §6 Similarly, there is no incontinence here either, since incontinence is not merely to be avoided, but also blameworthy [and these conditions are not]. But because this way of being affected is similar to incontinence, people call it incontinence, adding the qualification that it is incontinence about this or that. Just so they call someone a bad doctor or a bad 10 actor, though they would never call him simply bad, since each of these conditions is not vice, but only similar to it by analogy. It is clear, likewise, that the only condition we should take to be continence or incontinence is the one concerned with what concerns temperance and intemperance. We speak of incontinence about spirit because of the similarity [to simple incontinence], and hence add the qualification that someone is incontinent about spirit, as we do in the case of honor or gain.

5

[Bestiality and Disease]

15 Some things are naturally pleasant, and some of these are pleasant without qualification, whereas others correspond to differences between kinds of animals and of human beings. Other things are not naturally pleasant, but deformities or habits or base natures make them pleasant; and we can see states that are about each of these that are similar to [states that are about naturally pleasant things].

20 §2 By bestial states I mean, for instance, the female human being* who is said to tear pregnant women apart and devour the children; or the pleasures of some of the savage people around the Black Sea who are reputed to enjoy raw meat and human flesh, while some trade their children to each other to feast on; or what is said about Phalaris.*

25 §3 These states are bestial. Other states result from attacks of disease, and in some cases from fits of madness—for instance, the person who sacrificed his mother and ate her, and the one who ate the liver of his fellow slave. Others result from diseased conditions or from habit—for instance, plucking hairs, chewing nails, even coal and earth, and besides these sex- 30 ual intercourse between males. For in some people these result from [a

diseased] nature, in others from habit, as, for instance, in those who have suffered wanton [sexual] assault since their childhood. *1148b*

§4 If nature is the cause, no one would call these people incontinent, any more than women would be called incontinent for being mounted rather than mounting.* The same applies to those who are in a diseased state because of habit.

§5 Each of these states, then, is outside the limits of vice, just as bestiality is. If someone who has them overcomes them or is overcome by them, that is not simple [continence or] incontinence, but the type so called from similarity, just as someone who is overcome by spirit should be called incontinent in relation to his feeling, but not [simply] incontinent. For among all the excesses of foolishness, cowardice, intemperance, and irritability some are bestial, some diseased. 1149a 5

§6 If, for instance, someone's natural character makes him afraid of everything, even the noise of a mouse, he is a coward with a bestial sort of cowardice. Another person was afraid of a weasel because of an attack of disease. Among foolish people also, those who naturally lack reason and live only by sense perception,* as some races of distant foreigners do, are bestial. Those who are foolish because of attacks of disease, such as epilepsy, or because of fits of madness, are diseased. 10

§7 Sometimes it is possible to have some of these conditions without being overcome—if, for instance, Phalaris had an appetite to eat a child or for some bizarre sexual pleasure, but restrained it. It is also possible to be overcome by these conditions and not merely to have them. 15

§8 One sort of vice is human, and this is called simple vice; another sort is called vice with an added condition, and is said to be bestial or diseased vice, but not simple vice. Similarly, then, it is also clear that one sort of incontinence is bestial, another diseased, but only the incontinence corresponding to human intemperance is simple incontinence. 20

§9 It is clear, then, that incontinence and continence apply only within the range of intemperance and temperance, and that for other things there is another form of incontinence, so called by transference* of the name, and not simply.

6

[Incontinence and Related Conditions]

Moreover, let us observe that incontinence about spirit is less shameful than incontinence about appetites. For spirit would seem to hear reason a bit, but to mishear it. It is like overhasty servants who run out before they have heard all their instructions, and then carry them out wrongly, or dogs who bark at any noise at all, before looking to see if it is a friend. In the same way, since spirit is naturally hot and hasty, it hears, but does not 25 30

1149a hear the instruction, and rushes off to exact a penalty. For reason or appearance has shown that we are being slighted or wantonly insulted; and spirit, as though it had inferred that it is right to fight this sort of 35 thing, is irritated at once.* Appetite, however, only needs reason or perception to say that this is pleasant, and it rushes off for gratification.

1149b And so spirit follows reason in a way, but appetite does not. Therefore [incontinence about appetite] is more shameful. For if someone is incontinent about spirit, he is overcome by reason in a way; but if he is incontinent about appetite, he is overcome by appetite, not by reason.

5 §2 Further, it is more pardonable to follow natural desires, since it is also more pardonable to follow those natural appetites that are common to everyone and to the extent that they are common.* Now spirit and irritability are more natural than the excessive and unnecessary appetites. It is just as the son said in his defense for beating his father: 'Yes, and he 10 beat his father, and his father beat *his* father before that'; and pointing to his young son, he said, 'And he will beat me when he becomes a man; it runs in our family'.* Similarly, the father being dragged by his son kept urging him to stop at the front door, since that was as far as he had dragged his own father.

§3 Further, those who plot more are more unjust. Now the spirited 15 person does not plot, and neither does spirit; it is open. Appetite, however, is like what they say about Aphrodite, 'trick weaving Cypris',* and what Homer says about her embroidered girdle: 'Blandishment, which steals the wits even of the very prudent'.* If, then, incontinence about appetite is more unjust and more shameful than incontinence about 20 spirit, it is simple incontinence, and vice in a way.

§4 Further, no one feels pain when he commits wanton aggression; but whatever someone does from anger, he feels pain when he does it, whereas the wanton aggressor does what he does with pleasure. Now if whatever more justly provokes anger is more unjust, incontinence caused by appetite is more unjust, since spirit involves no wanton aggression.

25 §5 It is clear, then, how incontinence about appetites is more shameful than incontinence about spirit, and that continence and incontinence are about bodily appetites and pleasures.

§6 Now we must grasp the varieties of these appetites and pleasures.* As we said at the beginning, some appetites are human and natural in 30 kind and degree, some bestial, some caused by deformities and diseases. Temperance and intemperance are concerned only with the first of these. This is also why we do not call beasts either temperate or intemperate, except by transference of the name, if one kind of animal exceeds another altogether in wanton aggression, destructiveness, and ravenousness. For 35 beasts have neither decision nor rational calculation, but are outside 1150a [rational] nature, as the madmen among human beings are.*

§7 Bestiality is less grave than vice, but more frightening; for the best part is not corrupted, as it is in a human being, but absent altogether.*

Hence a comparison between the two is like a comparison between an inanimate and an animate being to see which is worse. For in each case the badness of something that lacks an internal principle of its badness is less destructive than the badness of something that has such an internal principle; and understanding is such an internal principle.* It is similar, then, to a comparison between the injustice [of a beast] and an unjust human being; for in a way each [of these] is worse, since a bad human being can do innumerably more bad things than a beast. *1150a* 5

7

[Incontinence, Intemperance, and Softness]

Let us now consider the pleasures and pains arising through touch and taste, the appetites for these pleasures, and the aversions from these pains. Earlier we defined temperance and intemperance as being about these. Now it is possible for someone to be in the state in which he is overcome, even by [pleasure and pains] which most people overcome; and it is possible to overcome even those that overcome most people.* The person who is prone to be overcome by pleasures is incontinent; the one who overcomes is continent; the one overcome by pains is soft; and the one who overcomes them is resistant. The state of most people is in between, though indeed they may lean more toward the worse states. 10 15

§2 Now some pleasures are necessary and some are not. [The necessary ones are necessary] to a certain extent, but their excesses and deficiencies are not. The same is true for appetites and pains. One person pursues excesses of pleasant things because they are excesses and because he decides on it,* for themselves and not for some further result. He is intemperate; for he is bound to have no regrets, and so is incurable, since someone without regrets is incurable.* The one who is deficient is his opposite, while the intermediate one is temperate. The same is true of the one who avoids bodily pains not because he is overcome, but because he decides on it. 20

§3 One of those who do not [act on] decision is led on because of pleasure; the other is led on because he is avoiding the pain that comes from appetite; hence these two differ from each other.* 25

Now it would seem to everyone that someone who does a shameful action from no appetite or a weak one is worse than if he does it from an intense appetite; and, similarly, that if he strikes another not from anger, he is worse than if he strikes from anger.* For [if he can do such evil when he is unaffected by feeling], what would he have done if he had been strongly affected? That is why the intemperate person is worse than the incontinent. 30

One of the states mentioned [i.e., the decision to avoid pain] is more a species of softness, whereas the other person is intemperate.*

1150a §4 The continent person is opposite to the incontinent, and the resis-
35 tant to the soft.* For resistance consists in holding out, and continence in overcoming, but holding out is different from overcoming, just as not being defeated differs from winning; hence continence is more choiceworthy than resistance.

1150b §5 Someone who is deficient in withstanding what most people withstand, and are capable of withstanding, is soft and self-indulgent;* for self-indulgence is a kind of softness. This person trails his cloak to avoid
5 the labor and pain of lifting it, and imitates an invalid, though he does not think he is miserable—he is [merely] similar to a miserable person.

§6 It is similar with continence and incontinence also. For it is not surprising if someone is overcome by strong and excessive pleasures or pains; indeed, this is pardonable, provided he struggles against them—
10 like Theodectes' Philoctetes bitten by the snake, or Carcinus' Cercyon in the *Alope*, and like those who are trying to restrain their laughter and burst out laughing all at once, as happened to Xenophantus.* But it is surprising if someone is overcome by what most people can resist, and is incapable of withstanding it, not because of his hereditary nature or
15 because of disease (as, for instance, the Scythian kings' softness is hereditary, and as the female is distinguished [by softness] from the male).

§7 The lover of amusements also seems to be intemperate, but in fact he is soft. For amusement is a relaxation, since it is a release, and the lover of amusement is one of those who go to excess here.

20 §8 One type of incontinence is impetuosity, while another is weakness. For the weak person deliberates, but then his feeling makes him abandon the result of his deliberation; but the impetuous person is led on by his feelings because he has not deliberated.* For some people are like those who do not get tickled themselves if they tickle someone else first; if they see and notice something in advance, and rouse themselves and their
25 rational calculation, they are not overcome by feelings, no matter whether something is pleasant or painful.* Quick-tempered and volatile people are most prone to be impetuous incontinents. For in quick-tempered people the appetite is so fast, and in volatile people so intense, that they do not wait for reason, because they tend to follow appearance.*

8

[Why Intemperance Is Worse than Incontinence]

30 The intemperate person, as we said, is not prone to regret, since he abides by his decision [when he acts]. But every incontinent is prone to regret. That is why the truth is not what we said in raising the puzzles, but in fact the intemperate person is incurable, and the incontinent curable.* For vice resembles diseases such as dropsy or consumption, while incontinence is more like epilepsy; vice is a continuous bad condition, but incontinence is

not. For the incontinent is similar to those who get drunk quickly from a little wine, and from less than it takes for most people.* And in general incontinence and vice are of different kinds. For the vicious person does not recognize that he is vicious, whereas the incontinent person recognizes that he is incontinent. 1151a3 4, 5 1150b3 5

§2 Among the incontinent people themselves, those who abandon themselves [to desire, i.e., the impetuous] are better than those [i.e., the weak] who have reason but do not abide by it. For the second type are overcome by a less strong feeling, and do not act without having deliberated, as the first type do. 1151a

§3 Evidently, then, incontinence is not a vice, though presumably it is one in a way. For incontinence is against one's decision, but vice accords with decision. All the same, incontinence is similar to vice in its actions. Thus Demodocus attacks the Milesians: 'The Milesians are not stupid, but they do what stupid people would do';* in the same way incontinents are not unjust, but will do injustice. 5 10

§4 Moreover, the incontinent person is the sort to pursue excessive bodily pleasures against correct reason, but not because he is persuaded [it is best]. The intemperate person, however, is persuaded, because he is the sort of person to pursue them. Hence the incontinent person is easily persuaded out of it, while the intemperate person is not.

For virtue preserves the principle, whereas vice corrupts it; and in actions the end we act for is the principle, as the assumptions are the principles in mathematics.* Reason does not teach the principles either in mathematics or in actions; [with actions] it is virtue, either natural or habituated, that teaches correct belief about the principle.* The sort of person [with this virtue] is temperate, and the contrary sort intemperate. 15 20

§5 But there is also someone who because of his feelings abandons himself against correct reason. They overcome him far enough so that his actions do not accord with correct reason, but not so far as to make him the sort of person to be persuaded that it is right to pursue such pleasures without restraint. This, then, is the incontinent person. He is better than the intemperate person, and is not bad without qualification, since the best thing, the principle, is preserved in him.* Another sort of person is contrary to him. [This is the continent person,] who abides [by reason] and does not abandon himself, not because of his feelings at least. It is evident from this that the continent person's state is excellent, and the incontinent person's state is base. 25

9

[Continence]

Then is someone continent if he abides by just any sort of reason and any sort of decision, or must he abide by the correct decision?* And is some- 30

1151a one incontinent if he fails to abide by just any decision and any reason, or must it be reason that is not false, and the correct decision? This was the puzzle raised earlier.

Perhaps in fact the continent person abides, and the incontinent fails to abide, by just any decision coincidentally, but abides by the true reason 35 and the correct decision in itself.* For if someone chooses or pursues one 1151b thing because of a second, he pursues and chooses the second in itself and the first coincidentally. Now when we speak of something without qualification, we speak of it in itself. Hence in one way [i.e., coincidentally] the continent person abides by just any belief, and the incontinent abandons it; but, [speaking] without qualification, the continent person abides by the true belief and the incontinent person abandons it.

5 §2 Now there are some other people who tend to abide by their belief.* These are the people called stubborn, who are hard to persuade into something and not easy to persuade out of it. These have some similarity to continent people, just as the wasteful person has to the generous, and the rash to the confident. But they are different on many points. For the continent person is not swayed because of feeling and appetite; [but he is 10 not inflexible about everything] since he will be easily persuaded whenever it is appropriate. But stubborn people are not swayed by reason; for they acquire appetites, and many of them are led on by pleasures.

§3 The stubborn include the opinionated, the ignorant, and the boorish. The opinionated are as they are because of pleasure and pain. For 15 they find enjoyment in winning [the argument] if they are not persuaded to change their views, and they feel pain if their opinions are voided, like decrees [in the Assembly]. Hence they are more like incontinent than like continent people.

§4 There are also some people who do not abide by their resolutions, but not because they are incontinent—Neoptolemus, for instance, in Sophocles' *Philoctetes*.* Though certainly it was pleasure that made him 20 abandon his resolution, it was a fine pleasure; for telling the truth was pleasant to him,* but Odysseus had persuaded him to lie. [He is not incontinent;] for not everyone who does something because of pleasure is either intemperate or base or incontinent, but only someone who does it because of a shameful pleasure.*

§5 There is also the sort of person who enjoys bodily things less than is 25 right, and does not abide by reason; hence the continent person is intermediate between this person and the incontinent.* For the incontinent fails to abide by reason because of too much [enjoyment]; the other person fails because of too little; but the continent person abides and is not swayed because of too much or too little. If continence is excellent, then 30 both of these contrary states must be base, as indeed they appear. However, the other state is evident in only a few people on a few occasions;

and hence continence seems to be contrary only to incontinence, just as *1151b*
temperance seems to be contrary only to intemperance.

§6 Now many things are called by some name because of similarity [to genuine cases]; this has happened also to the continence of the temperate person, because of similarity.* For the continent and the temperate person 35
are both the sort to do nothing against reason because of bodily pleasures, but the continent person has base appetites, whereas the temperate per- 1152a
son lacks them. The temperate person is the sort to find nothing pleasant against reason, but the continent is the sort to find such things pleasant but not to be led by them.*

The incontinent and the intemperate person are similar too; though 5
they are different, they both pursue bodily sources of pleasure. But the intemperate person [pursues them because he] also thinks it is right, while the incontinent person does not think so.

10

[Answers to Further Questions about Incontinence]

Nor can the same person be at once both prudent and incontinent.* For we have shown that a prudent person must also at the same time be 8
excellent in character, [and the incontinent person is not].* §2 However, 10
a clever person may well be incontinent. Indeed, the reason people sometimes seem to be prudent but incontinent is that [really they are only 11
clever and] cleverness differs from prudence in the way we described in 12, 13
our first discussion; though they are closely related in definition, they dif- 14
fer in [so far as prudence requires the correct] decision.*

Moreover, someone is not prudent simply by knowing; he must also 8, 9
act on his knowledge. But the incontinent person does not. §3 He is not 14
in the condition of someone who knows and is attending [to his knowledge, as he would have to be if he were prudent], but in the condition of 15
one asleep or drunk.*

He acts willingly; for in a way he acts in knowledge both of what he is doing and of the end he is doing it for.* But he is not base, since his decision is decent; hence he is half base. Nor is he unjust, since he is not a plotter. For one type of incontinent person [i.e., the weak] does not abide by the result of his deliberation, while the volatile [i.e., impetuous] person is not even prone to deliberate at all.*

In fact the incontinent person is like a city that votes for all the right 20
decrees and has excellent laws, but does not apply them, as in Anaxandrides' taunt, 'The city willed it, that cares nothing for laws'. §4 The base person, by contrast, is like a city that applies its laws, but applies bad ones.*

Incontinence and continence are about what exceeds the state of most 25
people; the continent person abides [by reason] more than most people

1152a are capable of doing, the incontinent person less.*

The [impetuous] type of incontinence found in volatile people is more easily cured than the [weak] type of incontinence found in those who deliberate but do not abide by it. And incontinents through habituation 30 are more easily cured than the natural incontinents; for habit is easier than nature to change.* Indeed the reason why habit is also difficult to change is that it is like nature; as Eunenus says, 'Habit, I say, is longtime training, my friend, and in the end training is nature for human beings.'*

35 §5 We have said, then, what continence and incontinence, resistance and softness are, and how these states are related to each other.

[PLEASURE]

11

[Questions about Pleasure]

1152b Pleasure and pain are proper subjects of study for the political philosopher, since he is the ruling craftsman of the end that we refer to in calling something bad or good without qualification.* §2 Further, we must also 5 examine them because we have laid it down that virtue and vice of character are about pains and pleasures, and because most people think happiness involves pleasure—that is why they also call the blessed person by that name (*makarios*) from enjoyment (*chairein*).*

§3 Now it seems to some people that no pleasure is a good, either in its own right or coincidentally, on the ground that the good is not the same 10 as pleasure.* To others it seems that some pleasures are good, but most are bad. A third view is that even if every pleasure is a good, the best good still cannot be pleasure.

§4 The reasons for thinking it is not a good at all are these:* Every pleasure is a perceived becoming toward [the fulfillment of something's] nature;* but no becoming is of the same kind as its end—for instance, no 15 [process of] building is of the same kind as a house. Further, the temperate person avoids pleasures. Further, the prudent person pursues what is painless, not what is pleasant. Further, pleasures impede prudent thinking,* and impede it more the more we enjoy them; no one, for instance, can think about anything during sexual intercourse. Further, every good 20 is the product of a craft, but there is no craft of pleasure. Further, children and animals pursue pleasure.

§5 To show that not all pleasures are excellent things, people say that some are shameful and reproached, and that some are harmful, since some pleasant things cause disease.

§6 To show that the best good is not pleasure, people say that pleasure is not an end, but a becoming.

These, then, are roughly the things said about it.

12

[Pleasure and Good]

These arguments, however, do not show that pleasure is not a good, or even that it is not the best good.* This will be clear as follows. *1152b25*

First of all, since what is good may be good in either of two ways, as good without qualification or as good for some particular thing or person, this will also be true of natures and states, and hence also of processes and becomings.* And so, among the [processes and becomings] that seem bad, some are bad without qualification but for some person not bad, and for this person actually choiceworthy. Some are not choiceworthy for him either, except sometimes and for a short time, not on each occasion.* Some are not even pleasures, but appear to be; these are the [processes], for instance, in sick people that involve pain and are means to medical treatment.* 30

§2 Further, since one sort of good is an activity and another sort is a state, the processes that restore us to our natural state are pleasant coincidentally. Here the activity in the appetites belongs to the rest of our state and nature.* For there are also pleasures without pain and appetite, such as the pleasures of studying, those in which our nature lacks nothing. 35 1153a

A sign [that supports our distinction between pleasures] is the fact that we do not enjoy the same thing when our nature is being refilled as we enjoy when it is eventually fully restored.* When it is fully restored, we enjoy things that are pleasant without qualification, but when it is being refilled, we enjoy even the contrary things. For we even enjoy sharp or bitter things, though none of these is pleasant by nature or pleasant without qualification. Hence [these pleasures] are not pleasures [without qualification] either; for as pleasant things differ from one another, so the pleasures arising from them differ too.* 5

§3 Further, it is not necessary for something else to be better than pleasure, as the end, some say, is better than the becoming.* For pleasures are not becomings, nor do they all even involve a becoming. They are activities, and an end [in themselves], and arise when we exercise [a capacity], not when we are coming to be [in some state].* And not all pleasures have something else as their end, but only those in people who are being led toward the completion of their nature. 10

That is why it is also a mistake to call pleasure a perceived becoming.* It should instead be called an activity of the natural state, and should be called not perceived, but unimpeded.* The reason it seems to some people to be a becoming is that it is fully good [and hence an activity]; for they think activities are becomings, though in fact these are different things. 15

§4 To say that pleasures are bad because some pleasant things cause disease is the same as saying that some healthy things are bad for money-making.* To this extent both are bad; but that is not enough to make them bad, since even study is sometimes harmful to health. 20

1153a §5 Neither prudence nor any state is impeded by the pleasures arising from it, but only by alien pleasures.* For the pleasures arising from study and learning will make us study and learn all the more.

25 §6 The fact that pleasure is not the product of a craft is quite reasonable; for a craft does not belong to any other activity either, but to a capacity.* And yet, the crafts of perfumery and cooking do seem to be crafts of pleasure.

§7 The claim that the temperate person avoids pleasure, that the prudent person pursues the painless life, and that children and beasts pursue pleasure—all these are solved by the same reply.* For we have explained 30 in what ways pleasures are good, and in what ways not all are good without qualification;* and it is these pleasures [that are not good without qualification] that beasts and children pursue, whereas the prudent person pursues painlessness in relation to these.* These are the pleasures that involve appetite and pain and the bodily pleasures (since these involve appetite and pain) and their excesses, whose pursuit makes the intemperate person intemperate. That is why the temperate person avoids these 35 pleasures [but not all pleasures], since there are pleasures of the temperate person too.

13

[Pleasure and Happiness]

1153b Moreover, it is also agreed that pain is an evil, and is to be avoided; for one kind of pain is bad without qualification, and another is bad in a particular way, by impeding [activities]. But the contrary to what is to be avoided, insofar as it is bad and to be avoided, is a good; hence pleasure 5 must be a good.* For the solution Speusippus used to offer—[that pleasure is opposite both to pain and to the good] as the greater is contrary both to the lesser and to the equal—does not succeed.* For he would not say [as his solution requires] that pleasure is essentially an evil.*

§2 Besides, just as one science might well be the best good, even though some sciences are bad, some pleasure might well be the best good, even though most pleasures are bad.* Indeed, presumably, if each state 10 has its unimpeded activities, and happiness is the activity—if the activity is unimpeded—of all states or of some one of them, it follows that some unimpeded activity is most choiceworthy. But pleasure is this, [namely, an unimpeded activity];* and so some type of pleasure might be the best good* even if most pleasures turn out to be bad without qualification.

15 That is why all think the happy life is pleasant and weave pleasure into happiness, quite reasonably. For no activity is complete if it is impeded, and happiness is something complete. That is why the happy person needs to have goods of the body and external goods added [to good activities], and needs fortune also, so that he will not be impeded in these ways.

§3 Some maintain, on the contrary, that we are happy when we are broken on the wheel, or fall into terrible misfortunes, provided that we are good.* Whether they mean to or not, these people are talking nonsense.* 1153b 20

§4 And because happiness needs fortune added, some believe good fortune is the same as happiness. But it is not. For when it is excessive, it actually impedes happiness; and then, presumably, it is no longer rightly called *good* fortune, since the limit [up to which it is good] is defined in relation to happiness.*

§5 The fact that all, both beasts and human beings, pursue pleasure is some sign of its being in some way the best good: 'No rumor is altogether lost which many peoples [spread]. . . .'* §6 But since the best nature and state neither is nor seems to be the same for all, they also do not all pursue the same pleasure, though they all pursue pleasure. Presumably in fact they do pursue the same pleasure, and not the one they think or would say they pursue; for all things by nature have something divine [in them].* 25 30

However, the bodily pleasures have taken over the name because people most often aim at them, and all share in them; and so, since these are the only pleasures they know, people suppose that they are the only pleasures.* 35 1154a

§7 It is also apparent that if pleasure is not a good and an activity, it will not be true that the happy person lives pleasantly. For what will he need pleasure for if it is not a good?* Indeed, it will even be possible for him to live painfully; for pain is neither an evil nor a good if pleasure is not, and why then would he avoid it? Nor indeed will the life of the excellent person be more pleasant if his activities are not also more pleasant. 5

14

[Bodily Pleasures]

Those who maintain that some pleasures, such as the fine ones, are highly choiceworthy, but the bodily pleasures that concern the intemperate person are not, should examine bodily pleasures.* 10

§2 If what they say is true, why are the pains contrary to these pleasures deplorable? For it is a good that is contrary to an evil. Then are the necessary [bodily pleasures] good only in the way that what is not bad is good? Or are they good up to a point? [Surely they are good up to a point.] For though some states and processes allow no excess of the better, and hence no excess of pleasure [in them] either, others do allow excess of the better, and hence also allow excess of the pleasure in them. Now the bodily goods allow excess. The base person is base because he pursues the excess, but not because he pursues the necessary pleasures; for all enjoy delicacies and wines and sexual relations in some way, though not all in the right way. 15

1154a20 The contrary is true of pain. For the base person avoids pain in general, not [only] an excess of it. For not [all] pain is contrary to excess [of pleasure], except to someone who pursues the excess [of pleasure].

§3 We must, however, not only state the true view, but also explain the false view; for an explanation of that promotes confidence.* For when we 25 have an apparently reasonable explanation of why a false view appears true, that makes us more confident of the true view. Hence we should say why bodily pleasures appear more choiceworthy.

§4 First, then, it is because bodily pleasure pushes out pain. Excesses of pain make people seek a cure in the pursuit of excessive pleasure and 30 of bodily pleasure in general. And these cures become intense—that is why they are pursued—because they appear next to their contraries.

Indeed these are the two reasons why pleasure seems to be no excellent thing, as we have said.* First, some pleasures are the actions of a base nature—either base from birth, as in a beast, or base because of habit, such as the actions of base human beings. Secondly, others are cures of 1154b something deficient, and it is better to be in a good state than to be coming into it. In fact these* pleasures coincide with our restoration to complete health, and so are excellent coincidentally.

§5 Further, bodily pleasures are pursued because they are intense, by people who are incapable of enjoying other pleasures. Certainly, these people induce some kinds of thirst in themselves. What they do is not a 5 matter for reproach, whenever [the pleasures] are harmless,* but it is base whenever they are harmful. These people do this because they enjoy nothing else, and many people's natural constitution makes the neutral condition painful to them.

For an animal is always suffering,* as the natural scientists also testify, since they maintain that seeing and hearing are painful. However, we are used [to seeing and hearing] by now, so they say, [and so feel no intense 10 pain]. §6 Indeed, the [process of] growth makes young people's condition similar to an intoxicated person's and [hence] youth is pleasant. Naturally volatile people, by contrast, are always requiring a cure, since their constitution causes their body continual turmoil, and they are always having intense desires. A pain is driven out by its contrary pleasure, 15 indeed by any pleasure at all that is strong enough; and this is why such people become intemperate and base.

§7 Pleasures without pains, however, have no excess.* These are pleasant by nature and not coincidentally. By coincidentally pleasant things I mean pleasant things that are curative; for the [process of] being cured coincides with some action of the part of us that remains healthy, and 20 hence undergoing a cure seems to be pleasant. Things are pleasant by nature, however, when they produce action of a healthy nature.

§8 The reason why no one thing is always pleasant is that our nature is not simple, but has more than one constituent, insofar as we are perishable; hence the action of one part is against nature for the other nature in *1154b* us, and when they are equally balanced, the action seems neither pleasant nor painful. For if something has a simple nature the same action will 25 always be the most pleasant.

That is why the god always enjoys one simple pleasure [without change].* For activity belongs not only to change but also to unchangingness, and indeed there is pleasure in rest more than in change. 'Variation in everything is sweet'* (as the poet says) because of some inferiority; for 30 just as it is the inferior human being who is prone to variation, so also the nature that needs variation is inferior, since it is not simple or decent.

§9 So much, then, for continence and incontinence and for pleasure and pain, what each of them is, and in what ways some [aspects] of them are good and others bad. It remains for us to discuss friendship as well.*

Book VIII

[Friendship]

1

[Common Beliefs and Questions]

After that, the next topic is friendship; for it is a virtue, or involves virtue. 1155a

Further, it is most necessary for our life.* For no one would choose to 5 live without friends even if he had all the other goods.* Indeed rich people and holders of powerful positions, even more than other people, seem to need friends. For how would one benefit from such prosperity if one had no opportunity for beneficence, which is most often displayed, and most highly praised, in relation to friends? And how would one guard 10 and protect prosperity without friends, when it is all the more precarious the greater it is?

§2 But in poverty also, and in the other misfortunes, people think friends are the only refuge.* Moreover, the young need friends to keep them from error. The old need friends to care for them and support the actions that fail because of weakness. And those in their prime need friends to do fine actions; for 'when two go together . . .',* they are more 15 capable of understanding and acting.

§3 Further, a parent would seem to have a natural friendship for a child, and a child for a parent, not only among human beings but also among birds and most kinds of animals. Members of the same species,* 20 and human beings most of all, have a natural friendship for each other; that is why we praise friends of humanity.* And in our travels we can see how every human being is akin and beloved to a human being.

§4 Moreover, friendship would seem to hold cities together, and legislators would seem to be more concerned about it than about justice. For 25

1155a concord would seem to be similar to friendship, and they aim at concord among all, while they try above all to expel civil conflict, which is enmity.* Further, if people are friends, they have no need of justice, but if they are just they need friendship in addition; and the justice that is most just seems to belong to friendship.*

30 §5 But friendship is not only necessary, but also fine.* For we praise lovers of friends, and having many friends seems to be a fine thing. Moreover, people think that the same people are good and also friends.

§6 Still, there are quite a few disputed points about friendship.*

For some hold it is a sort of similarity and that similar people are 35 friends. Hence the sayings, 'similar to similar', and 'birds of a feather', and so on. On the other side, it is said that similar people are all like the proverbial potters, quarreling with each other.*

1155b On these questions some people inquire at a higher level, more proper to natural science.* Euripides says that when earth gets dry it longs passionately for rain, and the holy heaven when filled with rain longs passionately to fall into the earth;* and Heracleitus says that the opponent cooperates, the finest harmony arises from discordant elements, and all things come to be in struggle.* Others, such as Empedocles, oppose this view, and say that similar aims for similar.*

§7 Let us, then, leave aside the puzzles proper to natural science, since they are not proper to the present examination, and let us examine the 10 puzzles that concern human [nature], and bear on characters and feelings.* For instance, does friendship arise among all sorts of people, or can people not be friends if they are vicious? And is there one species of friendship, or are there more? Some people think there is only one species because friendship allows more and less. But here their confidence rests 15 on an inadequate sign; for things of different species also allow more and less. We have spoken about these earlier.*

2

[The Object of Friendship]

Perhaps these questions will become clear once we find out what it is that is lovable.* For, it seems, not everything is loved, but [only] the lovable, and this is either good or pleasant or useful. However, it seems that the 20 useful is the source of some good or some pleasure; hence the good and the pleasant are lovable as ends.

§2 Now do people love the good, or the good for themselves? For sometimes these conflict; and the same is true of the pleasant. Each one, it seems, loves the good for himself; and while the good is lovable without 25 qualification, the lovable for each one is the good for himself. In fact, each one loves not what *is* good for him, but what *appears* good for him; but this will not matter, since [what appears good for him] will be what appears lovable.* *1155b*

§3 There are these three causes, then, of love.* Now love for an inanimate thing is not called friendship, since there is no mutual loving, and no wishing of good to it. For it would presumably be ridiculous to wish good things to wine; the most you wish is its preservation so that you can have it. To a friend, however, it is said, you must wish goods for his own sake.* If you wish good things in this way, but the same wish is not returned by the other, you would be said to have [only] goodwill for the other. For friendship is said to be *reciprocated* goodwill. 30

§4 But perhaps we should add that friends are aware of the reciprocated goodwill. For many a one has goodwill to people whom he has not seen but supposes to be decent or useful, and one of these might have the same goodwill toward him. These people, then, apparently have goodwill to each other, but how could we call them friends, given that they are unaware of their attitude to each other? [If they are to be friends], then, they must* have goodwill to each other, wish goods and be aware of it, from one of the causes mentioned above.* 35 1156a 5

3

[The Three Types of Friendship]

Since these causes differ in species, so do the types of loving and types of friendship.* Hence friendship has three species, corresponding to the three objects of love. For each object of love has a corresponding type of mutual loving, combined with awareness of it.*

But those who love each other wish goods to each other [only] insofar as they love each other.* Those who love each other for utility love the other not in his own right, but insofar as they gain some good for themselves from him. The same is true of those who love for pleasure; for they like a witty person not because of his character, but because he is pleasant to them. 10

§2 Those who love for utility or pleasure, then, are fond of a friend because of what is good or pleasant for themselves, not insofar as the beloved is who he is,* but insofar as he is useful or pleasant. Hence these friendships as well [as the friends] are coincidental, since the beloved is loved not insofar as he is who he is, but insofar as he provides some good or pleasure. 15

§3 And so these sorts of friendships are easily dissolved, when the friends do not remain similar [to what they were]; for if someone is no longer pleasant or useful, the other stops loving him. 20

What is useful does not remain the same, but is different at different times.* Hence, when the cause of their being friends is removed, the friendship is dissolved too, on the assumption that the friendship aims at

1156a these [useful results]. §4 This sort of friendship seems to arise espe-
25 cially among older people, since at that age they pursue the advantageous, not the pleasant, and also among those in their prime or youth who pursue the expedient.*

Nor do such people live together very much. For sometimes they do not even find each other pleasant. Hence they have no further need to meet in this way if they are not advantageous [to each other]; for each finds the 30 other pleasant [only] to the extent that he expects some good from him. The friendship of hosts and guests is taken to be of this type too.*

§5 The cause of friendship between young people seems to be pleasure. For their lives are guided by their feelings, and they pursue above all what is pleasant for themselves and what is at hand. But as they grow 35 up [what they find] pleasant changes too. Hence they are quick to become friends, and quick to stop; for their friendship shifts with [what they find] 1156b pleasant, and the change in such pleasure is quick. Young people are prone to erotic passion, since this mostly accords with feelings, and is caused by pleasure; that is why they love and quickly stop, often changing in a single day.

5 These people wish to spend their days together and to live together; for this is how they gain [the good things] corresponding to their friendship.

§6 But complete friendship is the friendship of good people similar in virtue; for they wish goods in the same way to each other insofar as they are good, and they are good in their own right.* [Hence they wish goods 10 to each other for each other's own sake.] Now those who wish goods to their friend for the friend's own sake are friends most of all; for they have this attitude because of the friend himself, not coincidentally.* Hence these people's friendship lasts as long as they are good; and virtue is enduring.*

Each of them is both good without qualification and good for his friend, since good people are both good without qualification and advan-15 tageous for each other.* They are pleasant in the same ways too, since good people are pleasant both without qualification and for each other.* [They are pleasant for each other] because each person finds his own actions and actions of that kind pleasant, and the actions of good people are the same or similar.

§7 It is reasonable that this sort of friendship is enduring, since it 20 embraces in itself all the features that friends must have. For the cause of every friendship is good or pleasure, either unqualified or for the lover; and every friendship accords with some similarity. And all the features we have mentioned are found in this friendship because of [the nature of] the friends themselves. For they are similar in this way [i.e., in being good].* Moreover, their friendship also has the other things—what is good without qualification and what is pleasant without qualification;

and these are lovable most of all. Hence loving and friendship are found *1156b* most of all and at their best in these friends.

§8 These kinds of friendships are likely to be rare, since such people 25 are few. Further, they need time as well, to grow accustomed to each other;* for, as the proverb says, they cannot know each other before they have shared their salt as often as it says,* and they cannot accept each other or be friends until each appears lovable to the other and gains the other's confidence. §9 Those who are quick to treat each other in 30 friendly ways wish to be friends, but are not friends, unless they are also lovable, and know this. For though the wish for friendship comes quickly, friendship does not.

4

[Comparison between the Types of Friendship]

This sort of friendship, then, is complete both in time and in the other ways. In every way each friend gets the same things and similar things 35 from each, and this is what must be true of friends. Friendship for plea- 1157a sure bears some resemblance to this complete sort, since good people are also pleasant to each other. And friendship for utility also resembles it, since good people are also useful to each other.*

With these [incomplete friends] also, the friendships are most enduring whenever they get the same thing—pleasure, for instance—from each 5 other, and, moreover, get it from the same source, as witty people do, in contrast to the erotic lover and the boy he loves.

For the erotic lover and his beloved do not take pleasure in the same things; the lover takes pleasure in seeing his beloved, but the beloved takes pleasure in being courted by his lover.* When the beloved's bloom is fading,* sometimes the friendship fades too; for the lover no longer finds pleasure in seeing his beloved, and the beloved is no longer courted 10 by the lover. Many, however, remain friends if they have similar characters and come to be fond of each other's characters from being accustomed to them.* §2 Those who exchange utility rather than pleasure in their erotic relations are friends to a lesser extent and less enduring friends.*

Those who are friends for utility dissolve the friendship as soon as the 15 advantage is removed; for they were never friends of each other, but of what was expedient for them.*

Now it is possible for bad people as well [as good] to be friends to each other for pleasure or utility, for decent people to be friends to base people, and for someone with neither character to be a friend to someone with any character. Clearly, however, only good people can be friends to each other because of the other person himself;* for bad people find no enjoy- 20 ment in one another if they get no benefit.

1157a §3 Moreover, the friendship of good people is the only one that is immune to slander. For it is not easy to trust anyone speaking against someone whom we ourselves have found reliable for a long time; and among good people there is trust, the belief that he would never do injustice, and all the other things expected in a true friendship. But in the other 25 types of friendship [distrust] may easily arise.

§4 [These must be counted as types of friendship.] For people include among friends [not only the best type, but] also those who are friends for utility, as cities are—since alliances between cities seem to aim at expediency—and those who are fond of each other, as children are, for pleasure. 30 Hence we must presumably also say that such people are friends, but say that there are more species of friendship than one.*

On this view, the friendship of good people insofar as they are good is friendship primarily and fully, but the other friendships are friendships by similarity.* For insofar as there is something good, and [hence] something similar to [what one finds in the best kind], people [in the incomplete friendships] are friends; for what is pleasant is good to lovers of pleasure. §5 But these [incomplete] types of friendship are not very regularly combined, and the same people do not become friends for both 35 utility and pleasure. For things that [merely] coincide with each other are not very regularly combined.

1157b §6 Friendship has been assigned, then, to these species.* Base people will be friends for pleasure or utility, since they are similar in that way. But good people will be friends because of themselves, since they are friends insofar as they are good. These, then, are friends without qualifi- 5 cation; the others are friends coincidentally and by being similar to these.*

5

[State and Activity in Friendship]

Just as, in the case of the virtues, some people are called good in their state of character, others good in their activity, the same is true of friendship.* For some people find enjoyment in each other by living together, and provide each other with good things. Others, however, are asleep or separated by distance, and so are not active in these ways, but are in the 10 state that would result in the friendly activities; for distance does not dissolve the friendship without qualification, but only its activity. But if the absence is long, it also seems to cause the friendship to be forgotten; hence the saying, 'Lack of conversation has dissolved many a friendship'.

15 §2 Older people and sour people do not appear to be prone to friendship. For there is little pleasure to be found in them, and no one can spend his days with what is painful or not pleasant, since nature appears to avoid above all what is painful and to aim at what is pleasant.

§3 Those who welcome each other but do not live together would seem to have goodwill rather than friendship. For nothing is as proper to friends as living together; for while those who are in want desire benefit, blessedly happy people [who want for nothing], no less than the others, desire to spend their days together, since a solitary life fits them least of all.* But people cannot spend their time with each other if they are not pleasant and do not enjoy the same things, as they seem to in the friendship of companions. *1157b* 20

§4 Now the friendship of good people is friendship most of all, as we have often said. For what is lovable and choiceworthy seems to be what is good or pleasant without qualification, and what is lovable and choiceworthy to each person seems to be what is good or pleasant to himself;* and both of these make one good person lovable and choiceworthy to another good person. 25

§5 Loving would seem to be a feeling, but friendship a state. For loving is directed no less toward inanimate things, but reciprocal loving requires decision, and decision comes from a state; and [good people] wish good to the beloved for his own sake in accord with their state, not their feeling.* 30

Moreover, in loving their friend they love what is good for themselves; for when a good person becomes a friend he becomes a good for his friend. Each of them loves what is good for himself, and repays in equal measure the wish and the pleasantness of his friend; for friendship is said to be equality. And this is true above all in the friendship of good people. 35 1158a

6

[Activities Characteristic of the Different Types of Friendship]

Among sour people and older people, friendship is found less often, since they are worse-tempered and find less enjoyment in meeting people, so that they lack the features that seem most typical and most productive of friendship.* That is why young people become friends quickly, but older people do not, since they do not become friends with people in whom they find no enjoyment—nor do sour people. These people have goodwill to each other, since they wish goods and give help in time of need; but they scarcely count as friends, since they do not spend their days together or find enjoyment in each other, and these things seem to be above all typical of friendship. 5 10

§2 No one can have complete friendship for many people, just as no one can have an erotic passion for many at the same time; for [complete friendship, like erotic passion,] is like an excess, and an excess is naturally directed at a single individual.* And just as it is difficult for many people

1158a to please the same person intensely at the same time, it is also difficult, presumably, for many to be good. §3 [To find out whether someone is 15 really good], one must both have experience of him and be on familiar terms with him, which is extremely difficult.* If, however, the friendship is for utility or pleasure, it is possible for many people to please;* for there are many people of the right sort, and the services take little time.*

§4 Of these other two types of friendship, the friendship for pleasure is more like [real] friendship; for they get the same thing from each other, 20 and they find enjoyment in each other, or [rather] in the same things. This is what friendships are like among young people; for a generous [attitude] is found here more [than among older people], whereas it is mercenary people who form friendships for utility.

Moreover, blessedly happy people have no need of anything useful, but do need sources of pleasure.* For they want to spend their lives with companions, and though what is painful is borne for a short time, no one 25 could continuously endure even the Good Itself if it were painful to him.* That is why they seek friends who are pleasant. But, presumably, they must also seek friends who are good as well [as pleasant], and good for them too; for then they will have everything that friends must have.

§5 Someone in a position of power appears to have separate groups of 30 friends; for some are useful to him, others pleasant, but the same ones are not often both.* For he does not seek friends who are both pleasant and virtuous, or useful for fine actions, but seeks one group to be witty, when he pursues pleasure, and the other group to be clever in carrying out instructions; and the same person rarely has both features.*

§6 Though admittedly, as we have said, an excellent person is both pleasant and useful, he does not become a friend to a superior [in power 35 and position] unless the superior is also superior in virtue; otherwise he does not reach [proportionate] equality by having a proportionate superior. And this superiority both in power and in virtue is not often found.

1158b §7 The friendships we have mentioned involve equality, since both friends get the same and wish the same to each other, or exchange one thing for another—for instance, pleasure for benefit.* But, as we have 5 said, they are friendships to a lesser extent, and less enduring.

They seem both to be and not to be friendships, because of their similarity and dissimilarity to the same thing. For, on the one hand, insofar as they are similar to the friendship of virtue, they are apparently friendships; for that type of friendship includes both utility and pleasure, and one of these types includes utility, the other pleasure. On the other hand, 10 the friendship of virtue is enduring and immune to slander, whereas these change quickly, and differ from it in many other ways as well; to that extent they are apparently not friendships, because of their dissimilarity to that best type.

7

[Friendship between Unequals]

A different species of friendship is the one that rests on superiority*—of a father toward his son, for instance, and in general of an older person toward a younger, of a man toward a woman, and of any sort of ruler toward the one he rules. These friendships also differ from each other. For friendship of parents to children is not the same as that of rulers to ruled; nor is friendship of father to son the same as that of son to father, or of man to woman as that of woman to man. For each of these friends has a different virtue and a different function, and there are different causes of love. Hence the ways of loving are different, and so are the friendships. *1158b* 15

§2 Now each does not get the same thing from the other, and must not seek it; but whenever children accord to their parents what they must accord to those who gave them birth, and parents accord what they must do to their children, their friendship is enduring and decent. 20

In all the friendships that rest on superiority, the loving must also be proportional; for instance, the better person, and the more beneficial, and each of the others likewise, must be loved more than he loves; for when the loving accords with the comparative worth of the friends, equality is achieved in a way, and this seems to be proper to friendship. 25

§3 Equality, however, does not appear to be the same in friendship as in justice.* For in justice equality is equality primarily in worth and secondarily in quantity; but in friendship it is equality primarily in quantity and secondarily in worth. 30

§4 This is clear if friends come to be separated by some wide gap in virtue, vice, wealth, or something else; for then they are friends no more, and do not even expect to be. This is most evident with gods, since they have the greatest superiority in all goods. But it is also clear with kings, since far inferior people do not expect to be their friends; nor do worthless people expect to be friends to the best or wisest. 35 1159a

§5 Now in these cases there is no exact definition of how long people are friends. For even if one of them loses a lot, the friendship still endures; but if one is widely separated [from the other], as a god is [from a human being], it no longer endures. 5

§6 This raises a puzzle: Do friends really wish their friend to have the greatest good, to be a god, for instance?* For [if he becomes a god], *he* will no longer have friends, and hence no longer have goods,* since friends are goods. If, then, we have been right to say that one friend wishes good things to the other for the sake of the other *himself,* the other must remain whatever sort of being he is. Hence it is to the other as a human being that a friend will wish the greatest goods—though presumably not all of them, since each person wishes goods most of all to himself.* 10

8

[Giving and Receiving in Friendship]

1159a15 Because the many love honor they seem to prefer being loved to loving.* That is why they love flatterers. For the flatterer is a friend in an inferior position, or [rather] pretends to be one, and pretends to love more than he is loved; and being loved seems close to being honored, which the many certainly pursue.*

§2 It would seem, however, that they choose honor coincidentally, not 20 in its own right. For the many enjoy being honored by powerful people because they expect to get whatever they need from them, and so enjoy the honor as a sign of this good treatment. Those who want honor from decent people with knowledge are seeking to confirm their own view of themselves, and so they are pleased because the judgment of those who say 25 they are good makes them confident that they are good.* Being loved, on the contrary, they enjoy in its own right. That is why it seems to be better than being honored, and friendship seems choiceworthy in its own right.*

§3 But friendship seems to consist more in loving than in being loved.* A sign of this is the enjoyment a mother finds in loving.* For sometimes 30 she gives her child away to be brought up, and loves him as long as she knows about him; but she does not seek the child's love, if she cannot both [love and be loved]. She would seem to be satisfied if she sees the child doing well, and she loves the child even if ignorance prevents him from returning to her what is due to a mother.

35 §4 Friendship, then, consists more in loving; and people who love their friends are praised; hence, it would seem, loving is the virtue of 1159b friends.* And so friends whose love accords with the worth of their friends are enduring friends and have an enduring friendship. §5 This above all is how unequals as well as equals can be friends, since this is how they can be equalized.*

Equality and similarity, and above all the similarity of those who are similar in being virtuous, is friendship.* For virtuous people are endur- 5 ingly [virtuous] in their own right, and enduring [friends] to each other. They neither request nor provide assistance that requires base actions, but, you might even say, prevent this. For it is proper to good people to avoid error themselves and not to permit it in their friends.

Vicious people, by contrast, have no firmness, since they do not even 10 remain similar to what they were. They become friends for a short time, enjoying each other's vice.* §6 Useful or pleasant friends, however, last longer, for as long as they supply each other with pleasures or benefits.*

The friendship that seems to arise most from contraries is friendship for utility, of poor to rich, for instance, or ignorant to knowledgeable; for 15 we aim at whatever we find we lack, and give something else in return.* Here we might also include the erotic lover and his beloved, and the beautiful and the ugly. That is why an erotic lover also sometimes *1159b* appears ridiculous, when he expects to be loved in the same way as he loves; that would presumably be a proper expectation if he were lovable in the same way, but it is ridiculous when he is not.*

§7 Presumably, however, contrary seeks contrary coincidentally, not in 20 its own right, and desire is for the intermediate.* For what is good for the dry, for instance, is to reach the intermediate, not to become wet, and the same is true for the hot, and so on. Let us, then, dismiss these questions, since they are rather extraneous to our concern.

9

[Friendship in Communities]

As we said at the beginning,* friendship and justice would seem to be 25 about the same things and to be found in the same people. For in every community there seems to be some sort of justice, and some type of friendship also. At any rate, fellow voyagers and fellow soldiers are called friends, and so are members of other communities. And the extent of their community is the extent of their friendship, since it is also the 30 extent of the justice found there. The proverb 'What friends have is common' is correct, since friendship involves community.*

§2 But, whereas brothers and companions have everything in common, what people have in common in other types of community is limited, more in some communities and less in others, since some friendships are also closer than others, some less close.* 35

§3 What is just is also different, since it is not the same for parents 1160a toward children as for one brother toward another, and not the same for companions as for fellow citizens, and similarly with the other types of friendship. Similarly, what is unjust toward each of these is also different, and becomes more unjust as it is practiced on closer friends.* It is more shocking, for instance, to rob a companion of money than to rob a fellow 5 citizen, to fail to help a brother than a stranger, and to strike one's father than anyone else. Justice also naturally increases with friendship, since it involves the same people and extends over an equal area.

§4 All the communities [mentioned], however, would seem to be parts of the political community.* For people keep company for some advan- 10 tage and to supply something contributing to their life. And the political community as well [as the others] seems both to have been originally formed and to endure for advantage;* for legislators also aim at advantage, and the common advantage is said to be just.*

§5 Now the other types of community aim at partial advantage.* Sea 15 travellers, for instance, seek the advantage proper to a journey, in making money or something like that, while fellow soldiers seek the advantage proper to war, desiring either money or victory or a city; and the same is

1160a true of fellow members of a tribe or deme.* Some communities—religious 20 societies and dining clubs—seem to arise for pleasure, since these are, respectively, for religious sacrifices and for companionship.*

But all these communities would seem to be subordinate to the political community, since it aims not at some advantage close at hand, but at advantage for the whole of life.* . . . [We can see this in the arrangements that cities make for religious festivals. For] in performing sacrifices and 25 arranging gatherings for these, people both accord honors to the gods and provide themselves with pleasant relaxations.* For the long-established sacrifices and gatherings appear to take place after the harvesting of the crops, as a sort of first-fruits, since this was the time when people used to be most at leisure [and the time when relaxation would be most advantageous for the whole of life].*

30 §6 All the types of community, then, appear to be parts of the political community, and these sorts of communities imply the appropriate sorts of friendships.

10

[Political Systems]

There are three species of political system (*politeia*), and an equal number of deviations, which are a sort of corruption of them.* The first political system is kingship; the second aristocracy; and since the third rests on property (*timēma*), it appears proper to call it a timocratic system, though 35 most people usually call it a polity.* §2 The best of these is kingship and the worst timocracy.

1160b The deviation from kingship is tyranny. For, though both are monarchies, they show the widest difference, since the tyrant considers his own advantage, but the king considers the advantage of his subjects. For 5 someone is a king only if he is self-sufficient and superior in all goods; and since such a person needs nothing more, he will consider the subjects' benefit, not his own. For a king who is not like this would be only some sort of titular king. Tyranny is contrary to this; for the tyrant pursues his own good. It is more evident that [tyranny] is the worst [deviation than that timocracy is the worst political system]; but the worst is contrary to the best; [hence kingship is the best].

10 §3 The transition from kingship is to tyranny. For tyranny is the degenerate condition of monarchy, and the vicious king becomes a tyrant.

The transition from aristocracy [rule of the best people] is to oligarchy [rule of the few], resulting from the badness of the rulers. They distribute the city's goods contrary to people's worth, so that they distribute all or 15 most of the goods to themselves, and always assign ruling offices to the same people, counting wealth for most. Hence the rulers are few, and they are vicious people instead of the most decent.

The transition from timocracy is to democracy [rule by the people], since these border on each other. For timocracy is also meant to be rule by the majority, and all those with the property-qualification are equal; [and majority rule and equality are the marks of democracy]. Democracy is the least vicious [of the deviations]; for it deviates only slightly from the form of a [genuine] political system. *1160b* 20

These, then, are the most frequent transitions from one political system to another, since they are the smallest and easiest.

§4 Resemblances to these—indeed, a sort of pattern of them—can also be found in households.* For the community of a father and his sons has the structure of kingship, since the father is concerned for his children. Indeed that is why Homer also calls Zeus father,* since kingship is meant to be paternal rule. 25

Among the Persians, however, the father's rule is tyrannical, since he treats his sons as slaves.* The rule of a master over his slaves is also tyrannical, since it is the master's advantage that is achieved in it. This, then, appears a correct form of rule, whereas the Persian form appears erroneous, since the different types of rule suit different subjects. 30

§5 The community of man and woman appears aristocratic. For the man's rule in the area where it is right accords with the worth [of each], and he commits* to the woman what is fitting for her. If, however, the man controls everything, he changes it into an oligarchy; for then his action does not accord with the worth [of each], or with the respect in which [each] is better. Sometimes, indeed, women rule because they are heiresses; these cases of rule do not accord with virtue, but result from wealth and power, as is true in oligarchies. 35 1161a

§6 The community of brothers is like a timocratic [system], since they are equal except insofar as they differ in age. That is why, if they differ very much in age, the friendship is no longer brotherly. 5

Democracy is found most of all in dwellings without a master, since everyone there is on equal terms; and also in those where the ruler is weak and everyone is free [to do what he likes].*

11

[Friendships in Political Systems]

Friendship appears in each of the political systems, to the extent that justice appears also.* A king's friendship to his subjects involves superior beneficence. For he benefits his subjects, since he is good and attends to them to ensure that they do well, as a shepherd attends to his sheep; hence Homer also called Agamemnon shepherd of the peoples.* 10 15

§2 A father's friendship resembles this, but differs in conferring a greater benefit, since the father is the cause of his children's being, which seems to be the greatest benefit, and of their nurture and education. These

1161a benefits are also ascribed to ancestors; and by nature a father is ruler over sons, ancestors over descendants, and a king over subjects.

20 §3 All these are friendships of superiority. That is why parents are also honored. And what is just is not the same in each of these friendships, but it accords with worth; for so does the friendship.

§4 The friendship of man to woman is the same as in an aristocracy. 25 For it accords with virtue, in assigning more good to the better, and assigning what is fitting to each. The same is true of what is just here.

§5 The friendship of brothers is similar to that of companions, since they are equal and of an age, and such people usually have the same feelings and characters. Friendship in a timocracy is similar to this. For there the citizens are meant to be equal and decent, and so rule in turn and on 30 equal terms. The same is true, then, of their friendship.

§6 In the deviations, however, justice is found only to a slight degree; and hence the same is true of friendship.* There is least of it in the worst deviation; for in a tyranny there is little or no friendship.

For where ruler and ruled have nothing in common, they have no 35 friendship, since they have no justice either.* This is true for a craftsman 1161b in relation to his tool, and for the soul in relation to the body.* For in all these cases the user benefits what he uses, but there is neither friendship nor justice toward inanimate things.* Nor is there any toward a horse or cow, or toward a slave, insofar as he is a slave. For master and slave have 5 nothing in common, since a slave is a tool with a soul, while a tool is a slave without a soul.*

§7 Insofar as he is a slave, then, there is no friendship with him. But there is friendship with him insofar as he is a human being.* For every human being seems to have some relation of justice with everyone who is capable of community in law and agreement;* hence [every human being seems] also [to have] friendship [with every human being], to the extent that [every human being] is a human being.*

§8 Hence there are friendships and justice to only a slight degree in 10 tyrannies also, but to a much larger degree in democracies; for there people are equal, and so have much in common.

12

[Friendships in Families]

As we have said, then, every friendship is found in a community. But we should set apart the friendship of families and that of companions.* The friendship of citizens, tribesmen, voyagers, and suchlike are more like 15 friendships in a community, since they appear to reflect some sort of agreement;* and among these we may include the friendship of host and guest.

§2 Friendship in families also seems to have many species, but they all seem to depend on paternal friendship. For a parent is fond of his children because he regards them as something of himself; and children are fond of a parent because they regard themselves as coming from him.* *1161b*

A parent knows better what has come from him than the children know that they are from the parent; and the parent regards his children as his own more than the product regards the maker as its own. For a person regards what comes from him as his own, as the owner regards his tooth or hair or anything; but what has come from him regards its owner as its own not at all, or to a lesser degree.* The length of time also matters. For a parent becomes fond of his children as soon as they are born, but children become fond of the parent when time has passed and they have acquired some comprehension or [at least] perception. And this also makes it clear why mothers love their children more [than fathers do].* 20 25

§3 A parent, then, loves his children as [he loves] himself. For what has come from him is a sort of other himself; [it is other because] it is separate.* Children love a parent because they regard themselves as having come from him. Brothers love each other because they have come from the same [parents]. For the same relation to the parents makes the same thing for both of them;* hence we speak of the same blood, the same stock, and so on. Hence they are the same thing in a way, in different [subjects]. 30

§4 Being brought up together and being of an age contributes largely to friendship; for 'two of an age' [get on well], and those with the same character are companions. That is why the friendship of brothers and that of companions are similar. Cousins and other relatives are akin by being related to brothers, since that makes them descendants of the same parents [i.e., the parents of these brothers]. Some are more akin, others less, by the ancestor's being near to or far from them. 35 1162a

§5 The friendship of children to a parent, like the friendship of human beings to a god, is friendship toward what is good and superior.* For the parent conferred the greatest benefits on his children, since he is the cause of their being and nurture and of their education once they have been born. §6 This sort of friendship also includes pleasure and utility, more than the friendship of unrelated people does, to the extent that [parents and children] have more of a life in common.* 5

Friendship between brothers has the features of friendship between companions, especially when [the companions] are decent, or in general similar.* For brothers are that much more akin to each other [than ordinary companions], and are fond of each other from birth; they are that much more similar in character when they are from the same parents, nurtured together and educated similarly; and the proof of their reliability over time is fullest and firmest. §7 Among other relatives too the features of friendship are proportional [to the relation]. 10 15

The friendship of man and woman also seems to be natural. For human beings form couples more naturally than they form cities, to the extent that the household is prior to the city, and more necessary, and

1162a20 childbearing is shared more widely among the animals.* For the other animals, the community goes only as far as childbearing. Human beings, however, share a household not only for childbearing, but also for the benefits in their life.* For the difference between them implies that* their functions are divided, with different ones for the man and the woman; hence each supplies the other's needs by contributing a special function to the common good. For this reason their friendship seems to include both utility and pleasure.

25 And it may also be friendship for virtue, if they are decent. For each has a proper virtue, and this will be a source of enjoyment for them.* Children seem to be another bond, and that is why childless unions are more quickly dissolved; for children are a common good for both, and what is common holds them together.

30 §8 How should a man conduct his life toward his wife, or, in general, toward a friend? That appears to be the same as asking how they are to conduct their lives justly. For what is just is not the same for a friend toward a friend as toward a stranger, or the same toward a companion as toward a classmate.*

13

[Disputes in Friendships between Equals]

35 There are three types of friendship, as we said at the beginning, and within each type some friendships rest on equality, while others are in 1162b accord with superiority.* For equally good people can be friends, but also a better and a worse person; and the same is true of friends for pleasure or utility, since they may be either equal or unequal in their benefits. Hence equals must equalize in loving and in the other things, because of their equality; and unequals must make the return that is proportionate to the types of superiority.

5 §2 Accusations and reproaches arise only or most often in friendship for utility.* And this is reasonable. For friends for virtue are eager to benefit each other, since this is proper to virtue and to friendship; and if this is what they strain to achieve, there are no accusations or fights.* For no one 10 objects if the other loves and benefits him; if he is gracious, he retaliates by benefiting the other. And if the superior gets what he aims at, he will not accuse his friend of anything, since each of them desires what is good.

§3 Nor are there many accusations among friends for pleasure. For 15 both of them get what they want at the same time if they enjoy spending their time together; and someone who accused his friend of not pleasing him would appear ridiculous, since he is free to spend his days without the friend's company.

§4 Friendship for utility, however, is liable to accusations. For these friends deal with each other in the expectation of gaining benefits. Hence they always require more, thinking they have got less than is fitting; and *1162b* they reproach the other because they get less than they require and deserve. And those who confer benefits cannot supply as much as the 20 recipients require.

§5 There are two ways of being just, one unwritten, and one governed by rules of law. And similarly one type of friendship of utility would seem to depend on character, and the other on rules.* Accusations arise most readily if it is not the same sort of friendship when they dissolve it 25 as it was when they formed it.

§6 Friendship dependent on rules is the type that is on explicit conditions.* One type of this is entirely mercenary and requires immediate payment. The other is more generous and postpones the time [of repayment], but in accordance with an agreement [requiring] one thing in return for another. In this sort of friendship it is clear and unambiguous what is owed, but the postponement is a friendly aspect of it. That is why some cities do not allow legal actions in these cases, but think that people who 30 have formed an arrangement on the basis of trust must put up with the outcome.

§7 Friendship [for utility] that depends on character is not on explicit conditions. Someone makes a present or whatever it is, as to a friend, but expects to get back as much or more, since he assumes that it is not a free gift, but a loan.

§8 If one party does not dissolve the friendship on the terms on which he formed it, he will accuse the other.* This happens because all or most 35 people wish for what is fine, but decide to do what is beneficial;* and while it is fine to do someone a good turn without aiming to receive one 1163a in return, it is beneficial to receive a good turn.

§9 We should, if we can, make a return worthy of what we have received, [if the other has undertaken the friendship] willingly.* For we should never make a friend of someone who is unwilling, but must suppose that we were in error at the beginning, and received a benefit from the wrong person; for since it was not from a friend, and this was not why 15 he was doing it, we must dissolve the arrangement as though we had received a good turn on explicit conditions. And we will agree to repay if we can. If we cannot repay, the giver would not even expect it. Hence we should repay if we can. We should consider at the beginning who is doing us a good turn, and on what conditions, so that we can put up with it on these conditions, or else decline it.

§10 It is disputable whether we must measure [the return] by the ben- 10 efit accruing to the recipient, and make the return proportional to that, or instead by the good turn done by the benefactor. For a recipient says that what he got was a small matter for the benefactor, and that he could have gotten it from someone else instead, and so he belittles it. But the benefactor says it was the biggest thing he had, that it could not be gotten from 15 anyone else, and that he gave it when he was in danger or similar need.

1163a §11 Since the friendship is for utility, surely the benefit to the recipient must be the measure [of the return]. For he was the one who required it, and the benefactor supplies him on the assumption that he will get an 20 equal return. Hence the aid has been as great as the benefit received, and the recipient should return as much as he gained, or still more, since that is finer.

But in friendships in accord with virtue, there are no accusations. Rather, the decision of the benefactor would seem to be the measure, since the controlling element in virtue and character lies in decision.*

14

[Disputes in Friendships between Unequals]

25 There are also disputes in friendships in accord with superiority, since each friend expects to have more than the other, but whenever this happens the friendship is dissolved.

For the better person thinks it is fitting for him to have more, on the ground that more is fittingly allotted to the good person. And the more beneficial person thinks the same. For it is wrong, they say, for someone to have an equal share if he is useless; the result is a public service, not a 30 friendship, if the benefits from the friendship do not accord with the worth of the actions. [The superior party says this] because he notices that in a financial community the larger contributors gain more, and he thinks the same thing is right in a friendship.*

But the needy person, the inferior party in the friendship, takes the opposite view, saying it is proper to a virtuous friend to supply his needy 35 [friends]. For what use is it, as they say, to be an excellent or powerful person's friend if you are not going to gain anything by it?

1163b §2 Well, each of them would seem to be correct in what he expects, and it is right for each of them to get more from the friendship—but not more of the same thing. Rather, the superior person should get more honor, and the needy person more profit, since honor is the reward of virtue and beneficence, while profit is what supplies need.*

5 §3 This also appears to be true in political systems. For someone who provides nothing for the community receives no honor, since what is common is given to someone who benefits the community, and honor is something common. For it is impossible both to make money off the com-10 munity and to receive honor from it at the same time; for no one endures the smaller share of everything. Hence someone who suffers a monetary loss [by holding office] receives honor in return, while someone who accepts gifts [in office] receives money [but not honor]; for distribution that accords with worth equalizes and preserves the friendship, as we have said.*

This, then, is how we should treat unequals. If we benefit from them in money or virtue,* we should return honor, and thereby make what return *1163b15* we can. §4 For friendship seeks what is possible, not what accords with worth, since that is impossible in some cases, as it is with honor to gods and parents. For no one could ever make a return in accord with their worth, but someone who attends to them as far as he is able seems to be a decent person.

That is why it might seem* that a son is not free to disown his father, 20 but a father is free to disown his son. For a debtor should return what he owes, and since, no matter what a son has done, he has not made a worthy return for what his father has done for him, he is always the debtor. But the creditor is free to remit the debt, and hence the father is free to remit.

At the same time, however, it presumably seems that no one would ever withdraw from a son, except from one who was far gone in vice. For, quite apart from their natural friendship, it is human not to repel aid. The 25 son, however, if he is vicious, will want to avoid helping his father, or will not be keen on it. For the many wish to receive benefits, but they avoid doing them because they suppose it is unprofitable. So much, then, for these things.

BOOK IX

[FRIENDSHIP]

1

[Friends with Dissimilar Aims]

In all friendships of friends with dissimilar aims, proportion equalizes and preserves the friendship, as we said; in political friendship, for 35 instance, the cobbler receives a worthy exchange for his shoes, and so do the weaver and the others.* §2 Here money is supplied as a common 1164a measure; everything is related to this and measured by it.

In erotic friendships, however, sometimes the lover charges that he loves the beloved deeply and is not loved in return; and in fact perhaps 5 he has nothing lovable in him. The beloved, however, often charges that previously the lover was promising him everything, and now fulfills none of his promises.

§3 These sorts of charges arise whenever the lover loves his beloved for pleasure while the beloved loves his lover for utility, and they do not both provide these. For if the friendship has these causes, it is dissolved whenever they do not get what they were friends for; for each was not 10 fond of the other himself, but only of what the other had, which was unstable.* That is why the friendships are also unstable. Friendship of character, however, is friendship in itself,* and endures, as we have said.

1164a §4 Friends quarrel when they get results different from those they
15 want; for when someone does not get what he aims at, it is like getting nothing. It is like the person who promised the lyre player a reward, and a greater reward the better he played; in the morning, when the player asked him to deliver on his promise, the other said he had paid pleasure in return for pleasure.* Now if this was what each of them had wished, it would be quite enough. But if one wished for delight and the other for
20 profit, and one has got his delight and the other has not made his profit, things are not right in their common dealings.* For each person sets his mind on what he finds he requires, and this will be his aim when he gives what he gives.

§5 Who should fix the worth [of a benefit], the giver or the one who has already received it?* [Surely the latter.] For the giver would seem to entrust [the judgment] to the one who has received. This is what Protago-
25 ras is said to have done; for whenever he taught anything at all, he used to tell the pupil to estimate how much the knowledge was worth, and that was the amount he used to collect.* In such cases, however, some prefer the rule 'Payment to a man . . .'.*

§6 But those who take the money first, and then do nothing that they
30 said they would do, because their promises were excessive, are reasonably accused, since they do not carry out what they agreed to.* §7 And presumably the sophists are compelled to make excessive promises. For no one would pay them money for the knowledge they really have; hence they take the payment, and then do not do what they were paid to do, and reasonably are accused.*

35 But where no agreement about services is made, friends who give services because of the friend himself are not open to accusation, as we have
1164b said, since this is the character of the friendship that accords with virtue. And the return should accord with the decision [of the original giver], since decision is proper to a friend and to virtue.*

And it would seem that the same sort of return should also be made to those who have shared philosophy in common with us. For its worth is not
5 measured by money, and no equivalent honor can be paid; but it is enough, presumably, to do what we can, as we do toward gods and parents.*

§8 If the giving is not of this sort, but on some specified condition, presumably the repayment must be, ideally, what each of them thinks accords with the worth of the gift. But if they do not agree on this, then it would seem not merely necessary, but also just, for the party who benefits
10 first to fix the repayment. For if the other receives in return as much benefit as the first received, or as much as he would have paid for the pleasure, he will have got the worthy return from him.

Indeed this is also how it appears in buying and selling. §9 And in some cities there are actually laws prohibiting legal actions in voluntary bargains, on the assumption that if we have trusted someone we must
15 dissolve the community with him on the same terms on which we formed

it. The law does this because it supposes that it is more just for the recipient to fix repayment than for the giver to fix it. For usually those who have something and those who want it do not put the same price on it, since, to the giver, what he owns and what he is giving appears to be worth a lot. But nonetheless the return is made in the amount fixed by the initial recipient. Presumably, however, the price must be not what it appears to be worth when he has got it, but the price he put on it before he got it.* 1164b 20

2

[Conflicts between Different Types of Friendships]

Here are some other questions that raise a puzzle. Must you accord [authority in] everything to your father, and obey him in everything? Or must you trust the doctor when he is sick, and should you vote for a military expert to be general?* Similarly, should you do a service for your friend rather than for an excellent person, and return a favor to a benefactor rather than do a favor for a companion, if you cannot do both?* 25

§2 Surely it is not easy to define all these matters exactly.* For they include many differences of all sorts—in importance and unimportance, and in the fine and the necessary.* §3 Still, it is clear that not everything should be rendered to the same person, and usually we should return favors rather than do favors for our companions, just as we should return a loan to a creditor rather than lend to a companion.* 30

§4 But presumably this is not always true. If, for instance, someone has ransomed you from pirates, should you ransom him in return, no matter who he is? Or if he does not need to be ransomed, but asks for his money back, should you return it, or should you ransom your father instead? Here it seems that you should ransom your father, rather than even yourself. 35 1165a

§5 As we have said, then, we should, generally speaking, return what we owe. But if making a gift [to B] outweighs [returning the money to A] by being finer or more necessary, we should incline to [making the gift to B] instead.* For sometimes even a return of a previous favor is not fair [but an excessive demand], whenever [the original giver] knows he is benefiting an excellent person, but [the recipient] would be returning the benefit to someone he thinks is vicious. For sometimes you should not even lend in return to someone who has lent to you. For he expected repayment when he lent to a decent person, whereas you have no hope of it from a bad person. If that is really so, then, the demand [for reciprocity] is not fair; and even if it is not so, but you think it is so, your refusal of the demand seems not at all absurd. 5 10

§6 As we have often said, then, arguments about acting and being affected are no more definite than their subject matter. Clearly, then, we

1165a15 should not render the same things to everyone, and we should not render everything to our fathers, just as we should not make all our sacrifices to Zeus.*

§7 And since different things should be rendered to parents, brothers, companions, and benefactors, we should accord to each what is proper and suitable. This is what actually appears to be done; for instance, kins-20 folk are the people invited to a wedding, since they share the same family, and hence share in actions that concern it; and for the same reason it is thought that kinsfolk more than anyone must come to funerals.

§8 It seems that we must supply means of support to parents more than anyone. For we suppose that we owe them this, and that it is finer to supply those who are the causes of our being than to supply ourselves in this way. And we should accord honor to our parents, just as we should to 25 the gods, but not every sort of honor; for we should not accord the same honor to a father as to a mother, nor accord to them the honor due to a wise person or a general.* We should accord a father's honor to a father, and likewise a mother's to a mother.

§9 We should accord to every older person the honor befitting his age, by standing up, giving up seats, and so on. With companions and broth-30 ers we should speak freely, and have everything in common. To kinsfolk, fellow tribesmen, fellow citizens, and all the rest we should always try to accord what is proper, and should compare what belongs to each, as befits closeness of relation, virtue, or usefulness.

§10 Admittedly, this comparison is easier with people of the same kind, and more difficult with people of different kinds. But such difficulty 35 is no reason for giving up the comparison; rather, we should define as far as we can.

3

[Dissolution of Friendships]

1165b There is also a puzzle about dissolving or not dissolving friendships with friends who do not remain the same. With friends for utility or pleasure perhaps there is nothing absurd in dissolving the friendship whenever they are no longer pleasant or useful. For they were friends of pleasure or 5 utility; and if these give out, it is reasonable not to love. We might, however, accuse a friend if he really liked us for utility or pleasure, and pretended to like us for our character. For, as we said at the beginning, friends are most at odds when they are not friends in the way they think they are.

§2 And so, if we mistakenly suppose we are loved for our character, 10 when our friend is doing nothing to suggest this, we must hold ourselves responsible. But if we are deceived by his pretense, we are justified in accusing him—even more justified than in accusing debasers of the currency, to the extent that his evildoing debases something more precious.

§3 But if we accept a friend as a good person, and then he becomes vicious, and seems so, should we still love him?* Surely we cannot, if not everything, but only the good, is lovable. The bad is not lovable, and must not be loved; for we ought neither to love the bad nor to become similar to a base person, and we have said that similar is friend to similar.*

1165b 15

Then should the friendship be dissolved at once [as soon as the friend becomes bad]? Surely not with every sort of person, but only with an incurably vicious person. If someone can be set right, we should try harder to rescue his character than his property, insofar as character is both better and more proper to friendship. Still, the friend who dissolves the friendship seems to be doing nothing absurd. For he was not the friend of a person of this sort; hence, if the friend has altered, and he cannot save him, he leaves him.

20

§4 But if one friend stayed the same and the other became more decent and far excelled his friend in virtue, should the better person still treat the other as a friend?* Surely he cannot. This becomes clear in a wide separation, such as we find in friendships beginning in childhood. For if one friend still thinks as a child, while the other becomes a man of the best sort, how could they still be friends, if they neither approve of the same things nor find the same things enjoyable or painful? For they do not even find it so in their life together, and without that they cannot be friends, since they cannot live together—we have discussed this.

25

30

§5 Then should the better person regard the other as though he had never become his friend? Surely he must keep some memory of the familiarity they had. Just as we think we must do kindnesses for friends more than for strangers, so also we should accord something to past friends because of the former friendship, whenever it is not excessive vice that causes the dissolution.*

35

4

[Self-love and Friendship]

The defining features of friendship that are found in friendships to one's neighbors would seem to be derived from features of friendship toward oneself.* For a friend is taken to be someone who wishes and does goods or apparent goods to his friend for the friend's own sake; or one who wishes the friend to be and to live for the friend's own sake—this is how mothers feel toward their children, and how friends who have been in conflict feel [toward each other]. Others take a friend to be one who spends his time with his friend, and makes the same choices; or one who shares his friend's distress and enjoyment—and this also is especially true of mothers. And people define friendship by one of these features.*

1166a

5

§2 Each of these features is found in the decent person's relation to himself, and it is found in other people, insofar as they suppose they are

10

1166a decent. As we have said, virtue and the excellent person would seem to be the standard in each case.*

§3 For the excellent person is of one mind with himself, and desires 15 the same things in his whole soul.* Hence he wishes goods and apparent goods to himself, and achieves them in his actions, since it is proper to the good person to reach the good by his efforts. He wishes and does them for his own sake, since he does them for the sake of his thinking part, and that is what each person seems to be.* Moreover, he wishes himself to live and to be preserved. And he wishes this for his rational part* more than for any other part.

20 §4 For being is a good for the good person, and each person wishes for goods for himself. And no one chooses to become another person even if that other will have every good when he has come into being; for, as it is, the god has the good [but no one chooses to be replaced by a god].* Rather [each of us chooses goods] on condition that he remains whatever he is; and each person would seem to be the understanding part, or that most of all. [Hence the good person wishes for goods for the understanding part.]

§5 Further, such a person finds it pleasant to spend time with himself, 25 and so wishes to do it. For his memories of what he has done are agreeable, and his expectations for the future are good, and hence both are pleasant. And besides, his thought is well supplied with topics for study. Moreover, he shares his own distresses and pleasures, more than other people share theirs. For it is always the same thing that is painful or pleasant, not different things at different times. This is because he practically never regrets [what he has done].*

30 The decent person, then, has each of these features in relation to himself, and is related to his friend as he is to himself, since the friend is another himself. Hence friendship seems to be one of these features, and people with these features seem to be friends.

§6 But is there friendship toward oneself, or not? Let us dismiss that 35 question for the present. However, there seems to be friendship insofar as someone is two or more parts. This seems to be true from what we have 1166b said, and because an extreme degree of friendship resembles one's friendship to oneself.*

§7 The many, base though they are, also appear to have these features. But perhaps they share in them only insofar as they approve of them- 5 selves and suppose they are decent. For no one who is utterly base and unscrupulous either has these features or appears to have them.

§8 Indeed, even base people hardly have them.* For they are at odds with themselves, and have an appetite for one thing and a wish for another, as incontinent people do. For they do not choose things that seem to be good for them, but instead choose pleasant things that are 10 actually harmful; and cowardice or laziness causes others to shrink from doing what they think best for themselves.* And those who have done many terrible actions hate and shun life* because of their vice, and destroy themselves. *1166b*

§9 Besides, vicious people seek others to pass their days with, and shun themselves. For when they are by themselves they remember many disagreeable actions, and anticipate others in the future; but they manage to forget these in other people's company. These people have nothing lovable about them, and so have no friendly feelings for themselves. 15

Hence such a person does not share his own enjoyments and distresses. For his soul is in conflict, and because he is vicious one part is distressed at being restrained, and another is pleased [by the intended action]; and so each part pulls in a different direction, as though they were tearing him apart.* §10 Even if he cannot be distressed and pleased at the same time, still he is soon distressed because he was pleased, and wishes these things had not become pleasant to him; for base people are full of regret.* 20 25

Hence the base person appears not to have a friendly attitude even toward himself, because he has nothing lovable about him.

If this state is utterly miserable, everyone should earnestly shun vice and try to be decent; for that is how someone will have a friendly relation to himself and will become a friend to another.

5

[Goodwill and Friendship]

Goodwill would seem to be a feature of friendship, but still it is not friendship.* For it arises even toward people we do not know, and without their noticing it, whereas friendship does not. We have also said this before. 30

Nor is it loving, since it lacks intensity and desire, which are implied by loving. §2 Moreover, loving requires familiarity, but goodwill can also arise in a moment, as it arises, for instance, [in a spectator] for contestants.* For [the spectator] acquires goodwill for them, and wants what they want, but would not cooperate with them in any action; for, as we said, his goodwill arises in a moment and his fondness is superficial. 35 1167a

§3 Goodwill, then, would seem to be a beginning of friendship, just as pleasure coming through sight is a beginning of erotic passion.* For no one has erotic passion for another without previous pleasure in his appearance. But still enjoyment of his appearance does not imply erotic passion for him; passion consists also in longing for him in his absence and in an appetite for his presence. Similarly, though people cannot be friends without previous goodwill, goodwill does not imply friendship; for when they have goodwill, people only wish goods to the other, and will not cooperate with him in any action, or go to any trouble for him.* Hence we might transfer [the name 'friendship'], and say that goodwill is 5 10

1167a inactive friendship, and that when it lasts some time and they grow accustomed* to each other, it becomes friendship.

It does not, however, become friendship for utility or pleasure; for 15 these aims do not produce goodwill either.* For a recipient of a benefit does what is just when he returns goodwill for what he has received. But those who wish for another's welfare because they hope to enrich themselves through him would seem to have goodwill to themselves, rather than to him. Likewise, they would seem to be friends to themselves rather than to him, if they attend to him because he is of some use to them.*

§4 But in general goodwill results form some sort of virtue and 20 decency, whenever one person finds another to be apparently fine or brave or something similar. As we said, this also arises in the case of contestants.

6

[Friendship and Concord]

Concord also appears to be a feature of friendship. That is why it is not merely sharing a belief, since this might happen among people who do 25 not know each other. Nor are people said to be in concord when they agree on just anything, on astronomical questions, for instance, since concord on these questions is not a feature of friendship. Rather, a city is said to be in concord when [its citizens] agree on what is advantageous, make the same decision, and act on their common resolution.

30 §2 Hence concord concerns questions for action, and, more exactly, large questions where both or all can get what they want. A city, for instance, is in concord whenever all the citizens resolve to make offices elective, or to make an alliance with the Spartans, or to make Pittacus ruler, when he himself is also willing.*

But whenever each person wants the same thing all to himself, as the people in the *Phoenissae* do, they are in conflict.* For it is not concord 35 when each merely has the same thing in mind, whatever it is. Rather, each must also have the same thing in mind for the same person; this is true, 1167b for instance, whenever both the common people and the decent party* want the best people to rule, since when that is so both sides get what they seek.

Concord, then, is apparently political friendship, as indeed it is said to be; for it is concerned with advantage and with what affects life [as a whole].*

5 §3 This sort of concord is found in decent people. For they are in concord with themselves and with each other, since they are practically of the same mind;* for their wishes are stable, not flowing back and forth like a tidal strait.* They wish for what is just and advantageous, and also seek it in common.

10 Base people, however, cannot be in concord, except to a slight degree,

just as they can be friends only to a slight degree; for they seek to overreach in benefits [to themselves], and shirk labors and public services. And since each wishes this for himself, he interrogates and obstructs his neighbor; for when people do not look out for the common good, it is ruined. The result is that they are in conflict, trying to compel one another to do what is just, but not wishing to do it themselves. *1167b* 15

7

[Active Benevolence and Friendship]

Benefactors seem to love their beneficiaries more than the beneficiaries love them [in return], and this is discussed as though it were an unreasonable thing to happen. In most people's view, this is because the beneficiaries are debtors and the benefactors creditors: The debtor in a loan wishes the creditor did not exist, while the creditor even attends to the safety of the debtor. So also, then, a benefactor wants the beneficiary to exist because he expects gratitude in return, whereas the beneficiary is not attentive about making the return. 20 25

Now Epicharmus might say that most people say this because they 'take a bad person's point of view'.* Still, it would seem to be a human point of view, since the many are indeed forgetful, and seek to receive benefits more than to give them.

§2 However, it seems that the cause is more proper to [human] nature, and the case of creditors is not even similar.* For they do not love their debtors, but in wishing for their safety simply seek repayment. Benefactors, however, love and like their beneficiaries even if they are of no present or future use to them. §3 The same is true of craftsmen; for each likes his own product more than it would like him if it acquired a soul.* Presumably this is true of poets most of all, since they dearly like their own poems, and are fond of them as though they were their children. 30 35 1168a

§4 This, then, is what the case of the benefactor resembles; here the beneficiary is his product, and hence he likes him more than the product likes its producer. The reason for this is that being is choiceworthy and lovable for all, and we are insofar as we are actualized, since we are insofar as we live and act. Now the product is, in a way, the producer in his actualization; hence the producer is fond of the product, because he loves his own being.* This is natural, since what he is potentially is what the product indicates in actualization. 5

§5 At the same time, the benefactor's action is fine for him,* so that he finds enjoyment in the person he acts on; but the person acted on finds nothing fine in the agent, but only, at most, some advantage, which is less pleasant and lovable. 10

§6 What is pleasant is actualization in the present, expectation for the future, and memory of the past; but what is most pleasant is the [action 15

1168a we do] insofar as we are actualized, and this is also most lovable. For the benefactor, then, his product endures, since the fine is long-lasting; but for the person acted on, the useful passes away.

Besides, memory of fine things is pleasant, while memory of [receiving] useful things is not altogether pleasant, or is less pleasant—though the reverse would seem to be true for expectation.

20 Moreover, loving is like production, while being loved is like being acted on; and [the benefactor's] love and friendliness are the result of his greater activity.

§7 Further, everyone is fond of whatever has taken effort to produce; for instance, people who have made money themselves are fonder of it than people who have inherited it. And while receiving a benefit seems to 25 take no effort, giving one is hard work. This is also why mothers love their children more [than fathers do], since giving birth is more effort for them, and they know better that the children are theirs.* And this also would seem to be proper to benefactors.

8

[Self-love and Selfishness]

There is also a puzzle about whether one ought to love oneself or some- 30 one else most of all; for those who like themselves most are criticized and denounced as self-lovers, as though this were something shameful.* Indeed, the base person seems to go to every length for his own sake, and all the more the more vicious he is; hence he is accused, for instance, of doing nothing [for any end apart] from himself.* The decent person, on the contrary, acts for what is fine, all the more the better he is, and for his 35 friend's sake, disregarding his own [interest].

1168b §2 The facts, however, conflict with these claims, and that is not unreasonable.* For it is said that we must love most the friend who is most a friend; and one person is a friend to another most of all if he wishes goods to the other for the other's sake, even if no one will know about it. But these are features most of all of one's relation to oneself; and so too are all 5 the other defining features of a friend, since we have said that all the features of friendship extend from oneself to others.*

All the proverbs agree with this too, speaking, for instance, of 'one soul', 'what friends have is common', 'equality is friendship', and 'the knee is closer than the shin'.* For all these are true most of all in someone's relations with himself, since one is a friend to himself most of all. 10 Hence he should also love himself most of all.

It is not surprising, then, that there is a puzzle about which view we ought to follow, since both inspire some confidence. §3 Presumably, then, we must divide these sorts of arguments, and distinguish how far 15 and in what ways those on each side are true. Perhaps, then, it will become clear, if we grasp how those on each side understand self-love.

§4 Those who make self-love a matter for reproach ascribe it to those who award the biggest share in money, honors, and bodily pleasures to themselves. For these are the goods desired and eagerly pursued by the many on the assumption that they are best. That is why they are also contested.* Those who overreach for these goods gratify their appetites and in general their feelings and the nonrational part of the soul; and this is the character of the many. That is why the application of the term ['self-love'] is derived from the most frequent [kind of self-love], which is base. This type of self-lover, then, is justifiably reproached. *1168b* 20

§5 And plainly it is the person who awards himself these goods whom the many habitually call a self-lover. For if someone is always eager above all to do* just or temperate actions or any other actions in accord with the virtues, and in general always gains for himself what is fine, no one will call him a self-lover or blame him for it. 25

§6 This sort of person, however, more than the other sort, seems to be a self-lover. At any rate he awards himself what is finest and best of all, and gratifies the most controlling part of himself, obeying it in everything. And just as a city and every other composite system seems to be above all its most controlling part, the same is true of a human being; hence someone loves himself most if he likes and gratifies this part.* 30

Similarly, someone is called continent or incontinent because his understanding is or is not the master, on the assumption that this is what each person is.* Moreover, his own voluntary actions seem above all to be those involving reason.* Clearly, then, this, or this above all, is what each person is, and the decent person likes this most of all. 35 1169a

That is why he most of all is a self-lover, but a different kind from the self-lover who is reproached. He differs from him as much as the life guided by reason differs from the life guided by feelings,* and as much as the desire for what is fine differs from the desire for what seems advantageous.* 5

§7 Those who are unusually eager to do fine actions are welcomed and praised by everyone. And when everyone strains to achieve what is fine and concentrates on the finest actions, everything that is right will be done for the common good, and each person individually will receive the greatest of goods, since that is the character of virtue.* And so the good person must be a self-lover, since he will both help himself and benefit others by doing fine actions. But the vicious person must not love himself, since he will harm both himself and his neighbors by following his base feelings. 10

§8 For the vicious person, then, the right actions conflict with those he does. The decent person, however, does the right actions, since every understanding chooses what is best for itself and the decent person obeys his understanding. 15

§9 It is quite true that, as they say, the excellent person labors for his friends and for his native country, and will die for them if he must; he will sacrifice money, honors, and contested goods in general, in achieving the 20

1169a fine for himself.* For he will choose intense pleasure for a short time over slight pleasure for a long time; a year of living finely over many years of
25 undistinguished life; and a single fine and great action over many small actions. This is presumably true of one who dies for others; he does indeed choose something great and fine for himself. He is also ready to sacrifice money as long as his friends profit; for the friends gain money, while he gains the fine, and so he awards himself the greater good.

30 §10 He treats honors and offices in the same way; for he will sacrifice them all for his friends, since this is fine and praiseworthy for himself. It is not surprising, then, that he seems to be excellent, since he chooses the fine at the cost of everything. It is also possible, however, to sacrifice actions to his friend, since it may be finer to be responsible for his friend's doing the action than to do it himself.*

35 §11 In everything praiseworthy, then, the excellent person awards
1169b more of the fine to himself. In this way, then, we must be self-lovers, as we have said. But in the way the many are, we ought not to be.*

9

[Why Are Friends Needed?]

There is also a dispute about whether the happy person will need friends or not.* For it is said that blessedly happy and self-sufficient people have
5 no need of friends. For they already have [all] the goods, and hence, being self-sufficient, need nothing added. But your friend, since he is another yourself, supplies what your own efforts cannot supply. Hence it is said, 'When the god gives well, what need is there of friends?'*

§2 It would seem absurd, however, to award the happy person all the
10 goods, without giving him friends; for having friends seems to be the greatest external good.* And if it is more proper to a friend to confer benefits than to receive them, and it is proper to the good person and to virtue to do good, and it is finer to benefit friends than to benefit strangers, the excellent person will need people for him to benefit.* Indeed, that is why there is a question about whether friends are needed more in good
15 fortune than in ill fortune; for it is assumed that in ill fortune we need people to benefit us, and in good fortune we need others for us to benefit.

§3 Presumably it is also absurd to make the blessed person solitary. For no one would choose to have all [other] goods and yet be alone, since a human being is a political [animal], tending by nature to live together
20 with others.* This will also be true, then, of the happy person; for he has the natural goods, and clearly it is better to spend his days with decent friends than with strangers of just any character. Hence the happy person needs friends.

§4 Then what are those on the other side saying, and on what point are they correct? Perhaps they say what they say because the many think that
25 it is the useful people who are friends.* Certainly the blessedly happy

person will have no need of these, since he has [all] goods. Similarly, he will have no need, or very little, of friends for pleasure; for since his life is pleasant, it has no need of imported pleasures.* Since he does not need these sorts of friends, he does not seem to need friends at all. *1169b*

§5 This conclusion, however, is presumably not true. For we said at the beginning that happiness is a kind of activity; and clearly activity comes into being, and does not belong [to someone all the time], as a possession does. Now if being happy consists in living and being active; the activity of the good person is excellent, and [hence] pleasant in itself, as we said at the beginning; what is our own is pleasant; and we are able to observe our neighbors more than ourselves, and to observe their actions more than our own; it follows that a good person finds pleasure in the actions of excellent people who are his friends, since these actions have both the naturally pleasant [features—they are good, and they are his own]. The blessed person, therefore, will need virtuous friends, given that he decides to observe virtuous actions that are his own, and the actions of a virtuous friend are of this sort.* 30 35 1170a

Further, it is thought that the happy person must live pleasantly.* But the solitary person's life is hard, since it is not easy for him to be continuously active all by himself; but in relation to others and in their company it is easier. §6 Hence his activity will be more continuous. It is also pleasant in itself, as it must be in the blessedly happy person's case. For the excellent person, insofar as he is excellent, enjoys actions in accord with virtue, and objects to actions caused by vice, just as the musician enjoys fine melodies and is pained by bad ones. 5 10

§7 Further, good people's life together allows the cultivation of virtue, as Theognis says.*

If we examine the question more from the point of view of [human] nature,* an excellent friend would seem to be choiceworthy by nature for an excellent person. For, as we have said, what is good by nature is good and pleasant in itself for an excellent person. 15

For animals, life is defined by the capacity for perception, but for human beings, it is defined by the capacity for perception or understanding; moreover, every capacity refers to an activity, and a thing is present fully in its activity; hence living fully would seem to be perceiving or understanding.*

Now life is good and pleasant in itself; for it has definite order, which is proper to the nature of what is good.* What is good by nature is also good for the decent person; that is why life would seem to be pleasant for everyone. §8 But we must not consider a life that is vicious and corrupted, or filled with pains; for such a life lacks definite order, just as its proper features do. (The truth about pain will be more evident in what follows.)* 20 25

§9 Life itself, then, is good and pleasant, as it would seem, at any rate, from the fact that everyone desires it, and decent and blessed people

1170a desire it more than others do—for their life is most choiceworthy for them, and their living is most blessed.

30 Now someone who sees perceives that he sees; one who hears perceives that he hears; one who walks perceives that he walks; and similarly in the other cases also there is some [element] that perceives that we are active; so that if we are perceiving, we perceive that we are perceiving, and if we are understanding, we perceive that we are understanding.* Now perceiving that we are perceiving or understanding is the same as perceiving that we are, since we agreed that being is perceiving or understanding.

1170b Perceiving that we are alive is pleasant in itself. For life is by nature a good, and it is pleasant to perceive that something good is present in us. Living is also choiceworthy, for a good person most of all, since being is 5 good and pleasant for him; for he is pleased to perceive something good in itself together [with his own being].

§10 The excellent person is related to his friend in the same way as he is related to himself, since a friend is another himself.* Therefore, just as his own being is choiceworthy for him, his friend's being is choiceworthy for him in the same or a similar way. We agreed that someone's own being is choiceworthy because he perceives that he is good, and this sort 10 of perception is pleasant in itself. He must, then, perceive his friend's being together [with his own], and he will do this when they live together and share conversation and thought.* For in the case of human beings what seems to count as living together is this sharing of conversation and thought, not sharing the same pasture, as in the case of grazing animals.

15 If, then, for the blessedly happy person, being is choiceworthy, since it is naturally good and pleasant, and if the being of his friend is closely similar to his own, his friend will also be choiceworthy.* What is choiceworthy for him he must possess, since otherwise he will in this respect lack something.* Anyone who is to be happy, then, must have excellent friends.

10

[How Many Friends Are Needed?]

20 Then should we have as many friends as possible?* Or is it the same as with the friendship of host and guest, where it seems to be good advice to 'have neither many nor none'?* Is this also good advice in friendship, to have neither no friends nor excessively many?

25 §2 With friends for utility the advice seems very apt, since it is hard work to return many people's services, and life is too short for it. Indeed, more [such] friends than are adequate for one's own life are superfluous, and a hindrance to living finely; hence we have no need of them. A few friends for pleasure are enough also, just as a little seasoning on food is enough.

30 §3 Of excellent people, however, should we have as many as possible as friends, or is there some proper measure of their number, as of the

number in a city? For a city could not be formed from ten people, but it *1170b* would be a city no longer if it had a hundred thousand.* Presumably, though, the right quantity is not just one number, but anything between certain defined limits. Hence there is also some limit defining the number 1171a of friends. Presumably, this is the largest number with whom you could live together, since we found that living together seems to be most characteristic of friendship.

§4 Clearly you cannot live with many people and distribute yourself among them.* Further these many people must also be friends to one another, if they are all to spend their days together; and this is hard work 5 for many people to manage. §5 It also becomes difficult for many to share one another's enjoyments and distresses as their own, since you are quite likely to find yourself sharing one friend's pleasure and another friend's grief at the same time.

Presumably, then, it is good not to seek as many friends as possible, and good to have no more than enough for living together; indeed it even 10 seems impossible to be an extremely close friend to many people. That is why it also seems impossible to be passionately in love with many people, since passionate erotic love tends to be an excess of friendship, and one has this for one person; hence also one has extremely close friendship for a few people.

§6 This would seem to be borne out in what people actually do. For the friendship of companions is not found in groups of many people, and 15 the friendships celebrated in song are always between two people. By contrast, those who have many friends and treat everyone as close to them seem to be friends to no one, except in the way fellow citizens are friends; these people are regarded as ingratiating.* Certainly it is possible to have a fellow citizen's friendship for many people, and still to be a truly decent person, not ingratiating; but it is impossible to be many people's friend for their virtue and for themselves. We have reason to be sat- 20 isfied if we can find even a few such friends.

11

[Friends in Good and Ill Fortune]

Have we more need of friends in good fortune or in ill fortune?* For in fact we seek them in both; for in ill fortune we need assistance, and in good fortune we need friends to live with and to benefit, since then we wish to do good. Certainly it is more necessary to have friends in ill fortune; that is why useful friends are needed here. But it is finer to have 25 them in good fortune. That is why we also seek decent friends; for it is more choiceworthy to do good to them and spend our time with them.

§2 The very presence of friends is also pleasant, in ill fortune as well as good fortune; for we have our pain lightened when our friends share our 30 distress. Indeed, that is why one might be puzzled about whether they

1171a take a part of it from us, as though helping us to lift a weight, or, alternatively, their presence is pleasant and our awareness that they share our distress makes the pain smaller. Well, we need not discuss whether it is this or something else that lightens our pain; at any rate, what we have mentioned does appear to occur.

35 §3 However, the presence of friends would seem to be a mixture [of 1171b pleasure and pain]. For certainly the sight of our friends in itself is pleasant, especially when we are in ill fortune, and it gives us some assistance in removing our pain. For a friend consoles us by the sight of him and by conversation, if he is dexterous, since he knows our character and what gives us pleasure and pain.*

5 §4 Nonetheless, awareness of his pain at our ill fortune is painful to us; for everyone tries to avoid causing pain to his friends. That is why someone with a manly nature tries to prevent his friend from sharing his pain.* Unless he is unusually immune to pain, he cannot endure pain coming to his friends; and he does not allow others to share his mourning 10 at all, since he is not prone to mourn himself either. Females, however, and effeminate men enjoy having people to wail with them; they love them as friends who share their distress. But in everything we clearly must imitate the better person.

§5 In good fortune, by contrast, the presence of friends makes it pleasant to pass our time and to notice that they take pleasure in our own 15 goods. That is why it seems that we must eagerly call our friends to share our good fortune, since it is fine to do good. But we must hesitate to call them to share our ill fortune, since we must share bad things with them as little as possible; hence the saying 'My misfortune is enough'. We should 20 invite them most of all whenever they will benefit us greatly, with little trouble to themselves.*

§6 Conversely, it is presumably appropriate to go eagerly, without having to be called, to friends in misfortune. For it is proper to a friend to benefit, especially to benefit a friend in need who has not demanded it, since this is finer and pleasanter for both friends. In good fortune he should come eagerly to help him, since friends are needed for this also; 25 but he should be slow to come to receive benefits, since eagerness to be benefited is not fine. Presumably, though, one should avoid getting a reputation for being a killjoy, as sometimes happens, by refusing benefits.

Hence the presence of friends is apparently choiceworthy in all conditions.

12

[Shared Activity in Friendship]

30 What the erotic lover likes most is the sight of his beloved, and this is the sort of perception he chooses over the others, supposing that this above

all is what makes him fall in love and remain in love. In the same way, surely, what friends find most choiceworthy is living together. For friendship is community, and we are related to our friend as we are related to ourselves. Hence, since the perception of our own being is choiceworthy, so is the perception of our friend's being. Perception is active when we live with him; hence, not surprisingly, this is what we seek.* *1171b* 35 1172a

§2 Whatever someone [regards as] his being, or the end for which he chooses to be alive, that is the activity he wishes to pursue in his friend's company. Hence some friends drink together, others play dice, while others do gymnastics and go hunting, or do philosophy. They spend their days together on whichever pursuit in life they like most; for since they want to live with their friends, they share the actions in which they find their common life. 5

§3 Hence the friendship of base people turns out to be vicious. For they are unstable, and share base pursuits; and by becoming similar to each other, they grow vicious. But the friendship of decent people is decent, and increases the more often they meet.* And they seem to become still better from their activities and their mutual correction. For each molds the other in what they approve of, so that '[you will learn] what is noble from noble people'. 10

§4 So much, then, for friendship. The next task will be to discuss pleasure.* 15

Book X

[Pleasure]

1

[The Right Approach to Pleasure]

The next task, presumably, is to discuss pleasure. For it seems to be especially proper to our [animal] kind; that is why, when we educate children, we steer them by pleasure and pain.* Besides, enjoying and hating the right things seems to be most important for virtue of character. For pleasure and pain extend through the whole of our lives, and are of great importance for virtue and the happy life, since people decide on pleasant things, and avoid painful things. 20 25

§2 Least of all, then,* it seems, should these topics be neglected, especially since they arouse much dispute. For some say pleasure is the good, while others, on the contrary, say it is altogether base.* Presumably, some [who say it is base] say so because they are persuaded that it is so. Others, however, say it because they think it is better for the conduct of our lives to present pleasure as base even if it is not. For, they say, the many lean toward pleasure and are slaves to pleasures, and that is why we must 30

1172a lead them in the contrary direction, because that is the way to reach the intermediate condition.*

35 §3 Surely, however, this is wrong. For arguments about actions and feelings are less credible than the facts; hence any conflict between argu-
1172b ments and perceptible [facts] arouses contempt for the arguments, and moreover undermines the truth as well [as the arguments].* For if someone blames pleasure, but then has been seen to seek it on *some* occasions, the reason for his lapse seems to be that he regards *every* type of pleasure as something to seek; for the many are not the sort to make distinctions.*

5 §4 True arguments, then, would seem to be the most useful, not only for knowledge but also for the conduct of life. For since they harmonize with the facts, they are credible, and so encourage those who comprehend them to live by them.

Enough of this, then; let us now consider what has been said about pleasure.

2

[Arguments about Pleasure]

10 Eudoxus thought that pleasure is the good,* because he saw that all [animals], both rational and nonrational, seek it, and in everything, he says, what is choiceworthy is good, and what is most choiceworthy is supreme. The fact that all are drawn to the same thing [i.e., pleasure], indicates, in
15 his view, that it is best for all, since each [kind of animal] finds its own good, just as it finds its own nourishment; and what is good for all, what all aim at, is the good. These arguments of his were found credible because of his virtuous character, rather than on their own [merits]. For since he seemed to be outstandingly temperate, he did not seem to be saying this because he was a friend of pleasure; rather, it seemed that what he said was how it really was.

§2 He thought it was no less evident from consideration of the con-
20 trary. For pain in itself, he said, is something to be avoided* for all, so that, similarly, its contrary is choiceworthy for all. Now what is most choiceworthy is what we choose not because of, or for the sake of, anything else; and it is agreed that this is the character of pleasure, since we never ask anyone what his end is in being pleased, because we assume that pleasure is choiceworthy in itself.

Moreover, [he argued], when pleasure is added to any other good, to
25 just or temperate action, for instance, it makes that good more choiceworthy; and good is increased by the addition of itself.

§3 This [last] argument, at least, would seem to present pleasure as one good among others, no more a good than any other. For the addition of any other good makes a good more choiceworthy than it is all by itself. Indeed Plato uses this sort of argument to undermine the claim of plea-
30 sure to be the good.* For, he argues, the pleasant life is more choicewor-

thy when combined with prudence* than it is without it; and if the mixed [good] is better, pleasure is not the good, since nothing can be added to the good to make it more choiceworthy. Nor, clearly, could anything else be the good if it is made more choiceworthy by the addition of anything that is good in itself. §4 Then what is the good that meets this condition, and that we share in also? That is what we are looking for. *1172b* 35

But when some object that what everything aims at is not good, surely there is nothing in what they say.* For if things seem [good] to all, we say they are [good];* and if someone undermines confidence in these, what he says will hardly inspire more confidence in other things. For if [only animals] without understanding desired these things, there would be something in the objection;* but if prudent [animals]* also desire them, how can there be anything in it? And presumably even in inferior [animals] there is something superior to themselves* that seeks their own proper good. 1173a 5

§5 The argument [against Eudoxus] about the contrary would also seem to be incorrect.* For they argue that if pain is an evil, it does not follow that pleasure is a good, since evil is also opposed to evil, and both are opposed to the neutral condition [without pleasure or pain]. The objectors' general point here is right, but what they say in the case mentioned is false. For if both pleasure and pain were evils, we would also have to avoid both, and if both were neutral, we would have to avoid neither, or else avoid both equally. Evidently, however, we avoid pain as an evil and choose pleasure as a good; hence this must also be the opposition between them. 10

3

[Pleasure Is a Good, but Not the Good]

Again, if [as the objectors argue] pleasure is not a quality, it does not follow [as they suppose] that it is not a good.* For virtuous activities and happiness are not qualities either.* 15

§2 They say that the good is definite, whereas pleasure is indefinite because it admits of more and less.* If their judgment rests on the actual condition of being pleased, it must also hold for justice and the other virtues, where evidently we are said to have a certain character more and less, and to act more and less in accord with the virtues;* for we may be more [and less] just or brave, and may do just or temperate actions more and less. If, on the other hand, their judgment rests on the [variety of] pleasures, then surely they fail to state the reason [why pleasures admit of more and less], namely that some are unmixed [with pain] and others are mixed.* 20

§3 Moreover, just as health admits of more and less, though it is definite, why should pleasure not be the same? For not every [healthy per- 25

1173a son] has the same proportion [of bodily elements], nor does the same person always have the same, but it may be relaxed and still remain up to a certain limit, and may differ in more and less. The same is quite possible, then, for pleasure also.

30 §4 They hold that what is good is complete, whereas processes and becomings are incomplete, and they try to show that pleasure is a process and a becoming. It would seem, however, that they are wrong, and pleasure is not even a process.* For quickness or slowness seems to be proper to every process—if not in itself (as, for instance, with the universe), then in relation to something else. But neither of these is true of pleasure. For 1173b though certainly it is possible to become pleased quickly, as it is possible to become angry quickly, it is not possible to be pleased quickly, even in relation to something else, whereas this is possible for walking and growing and all such things [i.e., for processes]. It is possible, then, to pass quickly or slowly into pleasure, but not possible to be [quickly or slowly] in the corresponding activity, i.e., to be pleased quickly [or slowly].*

5 §5 And how could pleasure be a becoming? For one random thing, it seems, does not come to be from any other; what something comes to be from is what it is dissolved into. Hence whatever pleasure is the becoming of, pain should be the perishing of it.

§6 They do indeed say that pain is the emptying of the natural [condition, and hence the perishing], and that pleasure is its refilling [and hence the becoming].* Emptying and filling happen to the body; if, then, plea-10 sure is the refilling of something natural, what has the refilling will also have the pleasure. Hence it will be the body that has pleasure. This does not seem to be true, however. The refilling, then, is not pleasure, though someone might be pleased while a refilling is going on, and pained when he is becoming empty.*

This belief [that pleasure is refilling] seems to have arisen from pains 15 and pleasures in connection with food; for first we are empty and suffer pain, and then take pleasure in the refilling. §7 The same is not true, however, of all pleasures; for pleasures in mathematics, and among pleasures in perception those through the sense of smell, and many sounds, sights, memories, and expectations as well, all arise without [previous] 20 pain. In that case what will they be comings-to-be of? For since no emptiness of anything has come to be, there is nothing whose refilling might come to be.

§8 To those who cite the disgraceful pleasures [to show that pleasure is not a good], we might reply that these [sources of disgraceful pleasures] are not pleasant.* For if things are healthy or sweet or bitter to sick people, we should not suppose that they are also healthy, or sweet, or bitter, except to them, or that things appearing white to people with eye disease are white, except to them. Similarly, if things are pleasant to people in bad condition, we should not suppose that they are also pleasant, except to these people.*

§9 Or else we might say that pleasures are choiceworthy, but not if they come from these sources, just as wealth is desirable, but not if you have to betray someone to get it, and health is desirable, but not if it requires you to eat anything and everything.* *1173b25*

§10 Or perhaps pleasures differ in species. For those from fine sources are different from those from shameful sources; and we cannot have the just person's pleasure without being just, any more than we can have the musician's without being musicians, and similarly in the other cases.* 30

§11 The difference between a friend and a flatterer seems to indicate that pleasure is not good, or else that pleasures differ in species.* For in dealings with us the friend seems to aim at what is good, but the flatterer at pleasure; and the flatterer is reproached, whereas the friend is praised, 1174a on the assumption that in their dealings they have different aims.

§12 And no one would choose to live with a child's [level of] thought for his whole life, taking as much pleasure as possible in what pleases children, or to enjoy himself while doing some utterly shameful action, even if he would never suffer pain for it.*

Moreover, there are many things that we would be eager for even if 5 they brought no pleasure—for instance, seeing, remembering, knowing, having the virtues. Even if pleasures necessarily follow on them, that does not matter; for we would choose them even if no pleasure resulted from them.*

§13 It would seem to be clear, then, that pleasure is not the good, that 10 not every pleasure is choiceworthy, and that some are choiceworthy in themselves, differing in species or in their sources [from those that are not].*

Let this suffice, then, for discussion of the things said about pleasure and pain.*

4

[Pleasure Is an Activity]

What, then, or what kind of thing, is pleasure? This will become clearer if we take it up again from the beginning.* For seeing seems to be complete at any time, since it has no need for anything else to complete its form by 15 coming to be at a later time. And pleasure is also like this, since it is some sort of whole, and no pleasure is to be found at any time that will have its form completed by coming to be for a longer time.*

§2 That is why pleasure is not a process either. For every process, such as constructing a building,* takes time, and aims at some end, and is com- 20 plete when it produces the product it seeks, or, [in other words, is complete] in this whole time [that it takes].* Moreover, each process is incomplete during the processes that are its parts, i.e., during the time it goes on; and it consists of processes that are different in form from the whole process and from one another.*

1174a For laying stones together and fluting a column are different processes; 25 and both are different from the [whole] production of the temple. For the production of the temple is a complete production, since it needs nothing further [when it is finished] to achieve the proposed goal; but the production of the foundation or the triglyph is an incomplete production, since [when it is finished] it is [the production] of a part.* Hence [processes that are parts of larger processes] differ in form; and we cannot find a process complete in form at any time [while it is going on], but [only], if at all, in the whole time [that it takes].*

30 §3 The same is true of walking and the other [processes]. For if locomotion is a process from one place to another, it includes locomotions differing in form—flying, walking, jumping, and so on. And besides these differences, there are differences in walking itself. For the place from which and the place to which are not the same in the whole racecourse as they are in a part of it, or the same in one part as in another; nor is travel-1174b ling along one line the same as travelling along another, since what we cover is not just a line, but a line in a [particular] place, and this line and that line are in different places.*

Now we have discussed process exactly elsewhere.* But, at any rate, a process, it would seem, is not complete at every time; and the many [con-5 stituent] processes are incomplete, and differ in form, since the place from which and the place to which make the form of a process [and different processes begin and end in different places].

§4 The form of pleasure, by contrast, is complete at any time. Clearly, then, it is different from a process, and is something whole and complete. This also seems true because a process must take time, but being pleased 10 need not; for what is present in an instant is a whole.* This also makes it clear that it is wrong to say that pleasure is a process or a becoming.* For this is not said of everything, but only of what is divisible and not a whole; for seeing, or a point, or a unit, has no coming to be, and none of these is either a process or a becoming. But pleasure is a whole; hence it too has no coming to be.

15 §5 Every perceptual capacity is active in relation to its perceptible object, and completely active when it is in good condition in relation to the finest of its perceptible objects.* For this above all seems to be the character of complete activity, whether it is ascribed to the capacity or to the subject that has it. Hence for each capacity the best activity is the activity of the subject in the best condition in relation to the best object of the capacity.

20 This activity will also be the most complete and the most pleasant. For every perceptual capacity and every sort of thought and study has its pleasure; the most pleasant activity is the most complete; and the most complete is the activity of the subject in good condition in relation to the most excellent object of the capacity. Pleasure completes the activity.

§6 But the way in which pleasure completes the activity is not the way in which the perceptible object and the perceptual capacity complete it when they are both excellent—just as health and the doctor are not the cause of being healthy in the same way.* 1174b25

§7 Clearly a pleasure arises that corresponds to each perceptual capacity, since we say that sights and sounds are pleasant; and clearly it arises most of all whenever the perceptual capacity is best, and is active in relation to the best sort of object. When this is the condition of the perceptible object and of the perceiving subject, there will always be pleasure, when the producer and the subject to be affected are both present.* 30

§8 Pleasure completes the activity—not, however, as the state does, by being present [in the activity], but as a sort of consequent end, like the bloom on youths.* Hence as long as the objects of understanding or perception and the subject that judges or attends are in the right condition, there will be pleasure in the activity. For as long as the subject affected and the productive [cause] remain similar and in the same relation to each other, the same thing naturally arises. 1175a

§9 Then how is it that no one is continuously pleased? Is it not because we get tired? For nothing human is capable of continuous activity, and hence no continuous pleasure arises either, since pleasure is a consequence of the activity.* Some things delight us when they are new to us, but later delight us less, for the same reason. For at first our thought is stimulated and intensely active toward them, as our sense of sight is when we look closely at something; but later the activity becomes lax and careless, so that the pleasure fades also. 5 10

§10 Why does everyone desire pleasure? We might think it is because everyone also aims at being alive.* Living is a type of activity, and each of us is active toward the objects he likes most and in the ways he likes most. The musician, for instance, activates his hearing in hearing melodies; the lover of learning activates his thought in thinking about objects of study; and so on for each of the others. Pleasure completes their activities, and hence completes life, which they desire. It is reasonable, then, that they also aim at pleasure, since it completes each person's life for him, and life is choiceworthy. 15

§11 But do we choose life because of pleasure, or pleasure because of life? Let us set aside this question for now, since the two appear to be combined and to allow no separation; for pleasure never arises without activity, and, equally, it completes every activity.* 20

5

[Pleasures Differ in Kind]

Hence pleasures also seem to differ in species.* For we suppose that things of different species are completed by different things. That is how

1175a it appears, both with natural things and with artifacts—for instance, with 25 animals, trees, a painting, a statue, a house, or an implement. Similarly, activities that differ in species are also completed by things that differ in species. §2 Now activities of thought differ in species from activities of the capacities for perception, and so do these from each other; so also, then, do the pleasures that complete them.

30 This is also apparent from the way each pleasure is proper to the activity that it completes.* For the proper pleasure increases the activity; for we judge each thing better and more exactly when our activity involves pleasure. If, for instance, we enjoy doing geometry, we become better geometers, and understand each question better; and similarly lovers of 35 music, building, and so on improve at their proper function when they 1175b enjoy it. Each pleasure increases the activity; what increases it is proper to it; and since the activities are different in species, what is proper to them is also different in species.

§3 This is even more apparent from the way some activities are impeded by pleasures from others. For lovers of flutes, for instance, cannot pay attention to a conversation if they catch the sound of someone 5 playing the flute, because they enjoy flute playing more than their present activity; and so the pleasure proper to flute playing destroys the activity of conversation.

§4 The same is true in other cases also, whenever we are engaged in two activities at once. For the more pleasant activity pushes out the other 10 one, all the more if it is much more pleasant, so that we no longer even engage in the other activity. Hence if we are enjoying one thing intensely, we do not do another very much. It is when we are only mildly pleased that we do something else; for instance, people who eat nuts in theatres do this most when the actors are bad.

15 §5 Since, then, the proper pleasure makes an activity more exact, longer, and better, whereas an alien pleasure damages it, clearly the two pleasures differ widely. For an alien pleasure does virtually what a proper pain does. The proper pain destroys activity, so that if, for instance, writing or rational calculation has no pleasure and is in fact painful for us, we 20 do not write or calculate, since the activity is painful. Hence the proper pleasures and pains have contrary effects on an activity; and the proper ones are those that arise from the activity in itself. And as we have said, the effect of alien pleasures is similar to the effect of pain, since they ruin the activity, though not in the same way as pain.

25 §6 Since activities differ in degrees of decency and badness, and some are choiceworthy, some to be avoided, some neither, the same is true of pleasures; for each activity has its own proper pleasure. Hence the pleasure proper to an excellent activity is decent, and the one proper to a base activity is vicious; for, similarly, appetites for fine things are praiseworthy, 30 and appetites for shameful things are blameworthy. And in fact the pleasure in an activity is more proper to it than the desire for it. For the desire

is distinguished from it in time and in nature; but the pleasure is close to the activity, and so little distinguished from it that disputes arise about whether the activity is the same as the pleasure. *1175b*

§7 Still, pleasure would seem to be neither thought nor perception, since that would be absurd. Rather, it is because [pleasure and activity] are not separated that to some people they appear the same.* Hence, just as activities differ, so do the pleasures. Sight differs from touch in purity, as hearing and smell do from taste; hence the pleasures also differ in the same way. So also do the pleasures of thought differ from these [pleasures of sense]; and both sorts have different kinds within them. 35 1176a

§8 Each kind of animal seems to have its own proper pleasure, just as it has its own proper function; for the proper pleasure will be the one that corresponds to its activity. This is apparent if we also study each kind; for a horse, a dog, and a human being have different pleasures, and, as Heracleitus says, an ass would choose chaff over gold, since asses find food more pleasant than gold.* Hence animals that differ in species also have pleasures that differ in species; and it would be reasonable for animals of the same species to have the same pleasures also. 5

§9 In fact, however, the pleasures differ quite a lot, in human beings at any rate. For the same things delight some people, and cause pain to others; and while some find them painful and hateful, others find them pleasant and lovable. The same is true of sweet things. For the same things do not seem sweet to a feverish and to a healthy person, or hot to an enfeebled and to a vigorous person; and the same is true of other things. 10 15

§10 But in all such cases it seems that what is really so is what appears so to the excellent person. If this is right, as it seems to be, and virtue, i.e., the good person insofar as he is good, is the measure of each thing, then what appear pleasures to him will also really be pleasures, and what is pleasant will be what he enjoys.*

And if what he finds objectionable appears pleasant to someone, that is not at all surprising; for human beings suffer many sorts of corruption and damage. It is not pleasant, however, except to these people in these conditions. §11 Clearly, then, we should say that the pleasures agreed to be shameful are not pleasures at all, except to corrupted people.* 20

But what about those pleasures that seem to be decent? Of these, which kind, or which particular pleasure, should we take to be the pleasure of a human being? Surely it will be clear from the activities, since the pleasures are consequences of these. Hence the pleasures that complete the activities of the complete and blessedly happy man, whether he has one activity or more than one, will be called the fully human pleasures to the fullest extent. The other pleasures will be human in secondary, or even more remote ways, corresponding to the character of the activities. 25

[Happiness: Further Discussion]

6

[Conditions for Happiness]

1176a30 We have now finished our discussion of the types of virtue; of friendship; and of pleasure.* It remains for us to discuss happiness in outline, since we take this to be the end of human [aims]. Our discussion will be shorter if we first take up again what we said before.

§2 We said, then, that happiness is not a state. For if it were, someone 35 might have it and yet be asleep for his whole life, living the life of a plant, 1176b or suffer the greatest misfortunes. If we do not approve of this, we count happiness as an activity rather than a state, as we said before.*

Some activities are necessary, i.e., choiceworthy for some other end,* while others are choiceworthy in their own right. Clearly, then, we should 5 count happiness as one of those activities that are choiceworthy in their own right, not as one of those choiceworthy for some other end. For happiness lacks nothing, but is self-sufficient.*

§3 An activity is choiceworthy in its own right if nothing further apart from it is sought from it. This seems to be the character of actions in accord with virtue; for doing fine and excellent actions is choiceworthy 10 for itself. But pleasant amusements also [seem to be choiceworthy in their own right];* for they are not chosen for other ends, since they actually cause more harm than benefit, by causing neglect of our bodies and possessions. Moreover, most of those people congratulated for their happiness resort to these sorts of pastimes. That is why people who are witty 15 participants in them have a good reputation with tyrants, since they offer themselves as pleasant [partners] in the tyrant's aims, and these are the sort of people the tyrant requires.* And so these amusements seem to have the character of happiness because people in supreme power spend their leisure in them.*

§4 These sorts of people, however, are presumably no evidence. For virtue and understanding, the sources of excellent activities, do not 20 depend on holding supreme power. Further, these powerful people have had no taste of pure and civilized pleasure, and so they resort to bodily pleasures.* But that is no reason to think these pleasures are most choiceworthy, since boys also think that the things they honor are best. Hence, just as different things appear honorable to boys and to men, it is reasonable that in the same way different things appear honorable to base and to decent people.*

25 §5 As we have often said, then, what is honorable and pleasant is what is so to the excellent person. To each type of person the activity that accords with his own proper state is most choiceworthy; hence the activity in accord with virtue is most choiceworthy to the excellent person [and hence is most honorable and pleasant].*

§6 Happiness, then, is not found in amusement; for it would be absurd if the end were amusement, and our lifelong efforts and sufferings aimed at amusing ourselves. For we choose practically everything for some other end—except for happiness, since it is [the] end; but serious work and toil aimed [only] at amusement appears stupid and excessively childish. Rather, it seems correct to amuse ourselves so that we can do something serious, as Anacharsis says;* for amusement would seem to be relaxation, and it is because we cannot toil continuously that we require relaxation. Relaxation, then, is not [the] end; for we pursue it [to prepare] for activity. But the happy life seems to be a life in accord with virtue, which is a life involving serious actions, and not consisting in amusement. *1176b* 30 35 1177a

§7 Besides, we say that things to be taken seriously are better than funny things that provide amusement, and that in each case the activity of the better part and the better person is more serious and excellent; and the activity of what is better is superior, and thereby has more the character of happiness.* 5

§8 Besides, anyone at all, even a slave, no less than the best person, might enjoy bodily pleasures; but no one would allow that a slave shares in happiness, if one does not [also allow that the slave shares in the sort of] life [needed for happiness].* Happiness, then,* is found not in these pastimes, but in the activities in accord with virtue, as we also said previously. 10

7

[Happiness and Theoretical Study]

If happiness is activity in accord with virtue, it is reasonable for it to accord with the supreme virtue, which will be the virtue of the best thing. The best is understanding, or whatever else seems to be the natural ruler and leader,* and to understand what is fine and divine, by being itself either divine or the most divine element in us. Hence complete happiness will be its activity in accord with its proper virtue;* and we have said that this activity is the activity of study.* 15

§2 This seems to agree with what has been said before, and also with the truth.* For this activity is supreme, since understanding is the supreme element in us, and the objects of understanding are the supreme objects of knowledge. 20

Further, it is the most continuous activity, since we are more capable of continuous study than any continuous action.*

§3 Besides, we think pleasure must be mixed into happiness; and it is agreed that the activity in accord with wisdom is the most pleasant of the activities in accord with virtue. Certainly, philosophy seems to have remarkably pure and firm pleasures, and it is reasonable for those who have knowledge to spend their lives more pleasantly than those who seek it. 25

1177a §4 Moreover, the self-sufficiency we spoke of will be found in study more than in anything else.* For admittedly the wise person, the just person, and the other virtuous people all need the good things necessary for
30 life. Still, when these are adequately supplied, the just person needs other people as partners and recipients of his just actions; and the same is true of the temperate person, the brave person, and each of the others. But the wise person is able, and more able the wiser he is, to study even by him-
1177b self; and though he presumably does it better with colleagues, even so he is more self-sufficient than any other [virtuous person].

§5 Besides, study seems to be liked because of itself alone, since it has no result beyond having studied.* But from the virtues concerned with action we try to a greater or lesser extent to gain something beyond the action itself.

5 §6 Besides, happiness seems to be found in leisure; for we deny ourselves leisure so that we can be at leisure, and fight wars so that we can be at peace.* Now the virtues concerned with action have their activities in politics or war, and actions here seem to require trouble. This seems completely true for actions in war, since no one chooses to fight a war, and no
10 one continues it, for the sake of fighting a war; for someone would have to be a complete murderer if he made his friends his enemies so that there could be battles and killings. But the actions of the politician also deny us leisure; apart from political activities themselves, those actions seek positions of power and honors, or at least they seek happiness for the politi-
15 cian himself and for his fellow citizens, which is something different from political science itself, and clearly is sought on the assumption that it is different.*

§7 Hence among actions in accord with the virtues those in politics and war are preeminently fine and great; but they require trouble, aim at some [further] end, and are choiceworthy for something other than them-
20 selves.* But the activity of understanding, it seems, is superior in excellence because it is the activity of study, aims at no end apart from itself, and has its own proper pleasure, which increases the activity. Further, self-sufficiency, leisure, unwearied activity (as far as is possible for a human being), and any other features ascribed to the blessed person, are
25 evidently features of this activity. Hence a human being's complete happiness will be this activity, if it receives a complete span of life, since nothing incomplete is proper to happiness.*

§8 Such a life would be superior to the human level. For someone will live it not insofar as he is a human being, but insofar as he has some divine element in him.* And the activity of this divine element is as much superior to the activity in accord with the rest of virtue as this element is
30 superior to the compound.* Hence if understanding is something divine in comparison with a human being, so also will the life in accord with understanding be divine in comparison with human life. We ought not to follow the makers of proverbs and 'Think human, since you are human',

or 'Think mortal, since you are mortal'.* Rather, as far as we can, we ought to be pro-immortal, and go to all lengths to live a life in accord with our supreme element; for however much this element may lack in bulk, by much more it surpasses everything in power and value.* 1177b 1178a

§9 Moreover, each person seems to be his understanding, if he is his controlling and better element.* It would be absurd, then, if he were to choose not his own life, but something else's. And what we have said previously will also apply now. For what is proper to each thing's nature is supremely best and most pleasant for it; and hence for a human being the life in accord with understanding will be supremely best and most pleasant, if understanding, more than anything else, is the human being.* This life, then, will also be happiest. 5

8

[Theoretical Study and the Other Virtues]

The life in accord with the other kind of virtue [i.e., the kind concerned with action] is [happiest] in a secondary way, because the activities in accord with this virtue are human.* For we do just and brave actions, and the other actions in accord with the virtues, in relation to other people, by abiding by what fits each person in contracts, services, all types of actions, and also in feelings; and all these appear to be human conditions. §2 Indeed, some feelings actually seem to arise from the body; and in many ways virtue of character seems to be proper to feelings. 10 15

§3 Besides, prudence is inseparable from virtue of character, and virtue of character from prudence.* For the principles of prudence accord with the virtues of character; and correctness in virtues of character accords with prudence. And since these virtues are also connected to feelings, they are concerned with the compound. Since the virtues of the compound are human virtues, the life and the happiness in accord with these virtues is also human. The virtue of understanding, however, is separated [from the compound]. Let us say no more about it, since an exact account would be too large a task for our present project. 20

§4 Moreover, it seems to need external supplies very little, or [at any rate] less than virtue of character needs them.* For let us grant that they both need necessary goods, and to the same extent; for there will be only a very small difference, even though the politician labors more about the body and suchlike. Still, there will be a large difference in [what is needed] for the [proper] activities [of each type of virtue]. For the generous person will need money for generous actions; and the just person will need it for paying debts, since wishes are not clear, and people who are not just pretend to wish to do justice. Similarly, the brave person will need enough power, and the temperate person will need freedom [to do intemperate actions], if they are to achieve anything that the virtue 25 30

1178a requires.* For how else will they, or any other virtuous people, make their virtue clear?

35 §5 Moreover, it is disputed whether decision or action is more in control of virtue, on the assumption that virtue depends on both.* Well, certainly it is clear that the complete [good] depends on both;* but for actions many external goods are needed, and the greater and finer the actions the more numerous are the external goods needed.

1178b

§6 But someone who is studying needs none of these goods, for that activity at least; indeed, for study at least, we might say they are even hindrances. Insofar as he is a human being, however, and [hence] lives together with a number of other human beings, he chooses to do the actions that accord with virtue.* Hence he will need the sorts of external goods [that are needed for the virtues], for living a human life.

5

§7 In another way also it appears that complete happiness is some activity of study. For we traditionally suppose that the gods more than anyone are blessed and happy; but what sorts of actions ought we to ascribe to them? Just actions? Surely they will appear ridiculous making contracts, returning deposits, and so on. Brave actions? Do they endure what [they find] frightening and endure dangers because it is fine? Generous actions? Whom will they give to? And surely it would be absurd for them to have currency or anything like that. What would their temperate actions be? Surely it is vulgar praise to say that they do not have base appetites. When we go through them all, anything that concerns actions appears trivial and unworthy of the gods.* Nonetheless, we all traditionally suppose that they are alive and active, since surely they are not asleep like Endymion. Then if someone is alive, and action is excluded, and production even more, what is left but study? Hence the gods' activity that is superior in blessedness will be an activity of study. And so the human activity that is most akin to the gods' activity will, more than any others, have the character of happiness.*

10

15

20

25 §8 A sign of this is the fact that other animals have no share in happiness, being completely deprived of this activity of study. For the whole life of the gods is blessed, and human life is blessed to the extent that it has something resembling this sort of activity; but none of the other animals is happy, because none of them shares in study at all.* Hence happiness extends just as far as study extends, and the more someone studies, the happier he is, not coincidentally but insofar as he studies, since study is valuable in itself. And so [on this argument] happiness will be some kind of study.*

30

§9 But happiness will need external prosperity also, since we are human beings; for our nature is not self-sufficient for study, but we need a healthy body, and need to have food and the other services provided.* Still, even though no one can be blessedly happy without external goods,

35

1179a

we must not think that to be happy we will need many large goods. For self-sufficiency and action do not depend on excess. *1179a*

§10 Moreover, we can do fine actions even if we do not rule earth and sea; for even from moderate resources we can do the actions that accord with virtue.* This is evident to see, since many private citizens seem to do decent actions no less than people in power do—even more, in fact. It is enough if moderate resources are provided; for the life of someone whose activity accords with virtue will be happy. 5

§11 Solon surely described happy people well, when he said they had been moderately supplied with external goods, had done what he regarded as the finest actions, and had lived their lives temperately.* For it is possible to have moderate possessions and still to do the right actions. And Anaxagoras would seem to have supposed that the happy person was neither rich nor powerful, since he said he would not be surprised if the happy person appeared an absurd sort of person to the many.* For the many judge by externals, since these are all they perceive. §12 Hence the beliefs of the wise would seem to accord with our arguments.* 10 15

These considerations, then, produce some confidence. But the truth in questions about action is judged from what we do and how we live, since these are what control [the answers to such questions]. Hence we ought to examine what has been said by applying it to what we do and how we live;* and if it harmonizes with what we do, we should accept it, but if it conflicts we should count it [mere] words. 20

§13 The person whose activity accords with understanding and who takes care of understanding would seem to be in the best condition, and most loved by the gods.* For if the gods pay some attention to human beings, as they seem to, it would be reasonable for them to take pleasure in what is best and most akin to them, namely understanding; and reasonable for them to benefit in return those who most of all like and honor understanding, on the assumption that these people attend to what is beloved by the gods, and act correctly and finely. Clearly, all this is true of the wise person more than anyone else; hence he is most loved by the gods. And it is likely that this same person will be happiest; hence, by this argument also, the wise person, more than anyone else, will be happy. 25 30

[From Ethics to Politics]

9

[Moral Education]

We have now said enough in outlines about happiness and the virtues, and about friendship and pleasure also.* Should we, then, think that our decision [to study these] has achieved its end? On the contrary, the aim of studies about action, as we say, is surely not to study and know about a 35 1179b

1179b given thing, but rather to act on our knowledge.* §2 Hence knowing about virtue is not enough, but we must also try to possess and exercise virtue, or become good in any other way.

5 §3 Now if arguments were sufficient by themselves to make people decent, the rewards they would command would justifiably have been many and large, as Theognis says,* and rightly bestowed. In fact, however, arguments seem to have enough influence to stimulate and encourage the civilized ones among the young people, and perhaps to make virtue take possession of a well-born character that truly loves what is 10 fine; but they seem unable to turn the many toward being fine and good.

§4 For the many naturally obey fear, not shame; they avoid what is base because of the penalties, not because it is disgraceful. For since they live by their feelings, they pursue their proper pleasures and the sources 15 of them, and avoid the opposed pains, and have not even a notion of what is fine and [hence] truly pleasant, since they have had no taste of it.

§5 What argument, then, could reform people like these? For it is impossible, or not easy, to alter by argument what has long been absorbed as a result of one's habits.* But, presumably, we should be satisfied to achieve some share in virtue if we already have what we seem to need to become decent.*

20 §6 Now some think it is nature that makes people good; some think it is habit; some that it is teaching. The [contribution] of nature clearly is not up to us, but results from some divine cause in those who have it, who are the truly fortunate ones.* Arguments and teaching surely do not prevail 25 on everyone, but the soul of the student needs to have been prepared by habits for enjoying and hating finely, like ground that is to nourish seed.* §7 For someone who lives in accord with his feelings would not even listen to an argument turning him away, or comprehend it [if he did listen]; and in that state how could he be persuaded to change? And in 30 general feelings seem to yield to force, not to argument. §8 Hence we must already in some way have a character suitable for virtue, fond of what is fine and objecting to what is shameful.

It is difficult, however, for someone to be trained correctly for virtue from his youth if he has not been brought up under correct laws; for the many, especially the young, do not find it pleasant to live in a temperate 35 and resistant way.* That is why laws must prescribe their upbringing and practices; for they will not find these things painful when they get used to them.

1180a §9 Presumably, however, it is not enough if they get the correct upbringing and attention when they are young; rather, they must continue the same practices and be habituated to them when they become men. Hence we need laws concerned with these things also, and in gen- 5 eral with all of life. For the many yield to compulsion more than to argument, and to sanctions more than to the fine.*

§10 That is why legislators must, in some people's view, urge people toward virtue and exhort them to aim at the fine—on the assumption that *1180a* anyone whose good habits have prepared him decently will listen to them—but must impose corrective treatments and penalties on anyone who disobeys or lacks the right nature, and must completely expel an 10 incurable. For the decent person, it is assumed, will attend to reason because his life aims at the fine, whereas the base person, since he desires pleasure, has to receive corrective treatment by pain, like a beast of burden. That is why it is said that the pains imposed must be those most contrary to the pleasures he likes.

§11 As we have said, then, someone who is to be good must be finely 15 brought up and habituated, and then must live in decent practices, doing base actions neither willingly nor unwillingly. And this will be true if his life follows some sort of understanding and correct order that prevails on him.

§12 Now a father's instructions lack this power to prevail and compel; and so in general do the instructions of an individual man, unless he is a 20 king or someone like that. Law, however, has the power that compels; and law is reason that proceeds from a sort of prudence and understanding.* Besides, people become hostile to an individual human being who opposes their impulses, even if he is correct in opposing them, whereas a law's prescription of what is decent is not burdensome.

§13 And yet, it is only in Sparta, or in a few other cities as well, that the 25 legislator seems to have attended to upbringing and practices. In most other cities they are neglected, and an individual lives as he wishes, 'laying down the rules for his children and wife', like a Cyclops.*

§14 It is best, then, if the community attends to upbringing, and 30 attends correctly. But if the community neglects it, it seems fitting for each individual to promote the virtue of his children and his friends—to be able to do it, or at least to decide to do it.* From what we have said, however, it seems he will be better able to do it if he acquires legislative science.* For, clearly, attention by the community works through laws, and 35 decent attention works through excellent laws; and whether the laws are 1180b written or unwritten, for the education of one or of many, seems unimportant, as it is in music, gymnastics, and other practices. For just as in a city the provisions of law and the types of character [found in that city] have influence, similarly a father's words and habits have influence, and 5 all the more because of kinship and because of the benefits he does; for his children are already fond of him and naturally ready to obey.*

§15 Further, education adapted to an individual is actually better than a common education for everyone, just as individualized medical treatment is better. For though generally a feverish patient benefits from rest and starvation, presumably some patient does not; nor does the boxing 10 instructor impose the same way of fighting on everyone.* Hence it seems that treatment in particular cases is more exactly right when each person gets special attention, since he then more often gets the suitable treatment.

1180b Nonetheless a doctor, a gymnastics trainer, and everyone else will give 15 the best individual attention if they also know universally what is good for all, or for these sorts. For sciences are said to be, and are, of what is common [to many particular cases]. §16 Admittedly someone without scientific knowledge may well attend properly to a single person, if his experience has allowed him to take exact note of what happens in a given case, just as some people seem to be their own best doctors, though 20 unable to help anyone else at all.* Nonetheless, presumably, it seems that someone who wants to be an expert in a craft and a branch of study should progress to the universal, and come to know that, as far as possible; for that, as we have said, is what the sciences are about.*

§17 Then perhaps also someone who wishes to make people better by 25 his attention, many people or few, should try to acquire legislative science, if laws are a means to make us good. For not just anyone can improve the condition of just anyone, or the person presented to him; but if someone can, it is the person with knowledge, just as in medical science and the others that require attention and prudence.

30 §18 Next, then, should we examine whence and how someone might acquire legislative science? Just as in other cases [we go to the practitioner], should we go to the politicians, since, as we saw, legislative science seems to be a part of political science?* Or does the case of political science appear different from the other sciences and capacities? For evidently, in the other cases, the same people, such as doctors or painters, who 35 transmit the capacity to others actively practice it themselves. By contrast, 1181a it is the sophists who advertise that they teach politics but none of them practices it. Instead, those who practice it are the political activists, and they seem to act on some sort of capacity and experience rather than thought.*

For evidently they neither write nor speak on such questions, though 5 presumably it would be finer to do this than to compose speeches for the law courts or the Assembly; nor have they made politicians out of their own sons or any other friends of theirs.* §19 But it would be reasonable for them to do this if they were able; for there is nothing better than the political capacity that they could leave to their cities, and nothing better that they could decide to produce in themselves, or, therefore, in their closest friends.

10 Nonetheless, experience would seem to contribute quite a lot; otherwise people would not have become better politicians by familiarity with politics.* That is why those who aim to know about political science would seem to need experience as well.

§20 By contrast, those of the sophists who advertise [that they teach political science] appear to be a long way from teaching; for they are altogether ignorant about the sort of thing political science is, and the sorts of 15 things it is about.* For if they had known what it is, they would not have taken it to be the same as rhetoric, or something inferior to it, or thought it an easy task to assemble the laws with good reputations and then legislate. For they think they can select the best laws, as though the selection itself did not require comprehension, and as though correct judgment were not the most important thing, as it is in music. *1181a*

[They are wrong;] for those with experience in each area judge the products correctly and comprehend the ways and means of completing them, and what fits with what; for if we lack experience, we must be satisfied with noticing that the product is well or badly made, as with painting. Now laws would seem to be the products of political science; how, then, could someone acquire legislative science, or judge which laws are best, from laws alone? §21 For neither do we appear to become experts in medicine by reading textbooks. 20 1181b

And yet doctors not only try to describe the [recognized] treatments, but also distinguish different [bodily] states, and try to say how each type of patient might be cured and must be treated.* And what they say seems to be useful to the experienced, though useless to the ignorant. Similarly, then, collections of laws and political systems might also, presumably, be most useful if we are capable of studying them and of judging what is done finely or in the contrary way, and what sorts of [elements] fit with what. Those who lack the [proper] state [of experience] when they go through these collections will not manage to judge finely, unless they can do it all by themselves [without training], though they might come to comprehend them better by going through them. 5 10

§22 Since, then, our predecessors have left the area of legislation uncharted, it is presumably better to examine it ourselves instead, and indeed to examine political systems in general, and so to complete the philosophy of human affairs, as far as we are able.* 15

§23 First, then, let us try to review any sound remarks our predecessors have made on particular topics.* Then let us study the collected political systems, to see from them what sorts of things preserve and destroy cities, and political systems of different types; and what causes some cities to conduct politics well, and some badly.* For when we have studied these questions, we will perhaps grasp better what sort of political system is best; how each political system should be organized so as to be best; and what habits and laws it should follow.* 20

Let us discuss this, then, starting from the beginning.

NOTES

Book I

1

1.§1–5. Subordinate and superordinate ends and goods

(a) §1–2. Goods are found in the ends of different activities; some, but not all, of these ends, are results distinct from the activities themselves.

§1 Every craft . . . some good: Aristotle may intend to divide these four types of goal-directed pursuits along the line indicated in §2. CRAFTS are types of PRODUCTION, aimed at some goal beyond their own exercise; a LINE OF INQUIRY also aims at some result beyond its own exercise. ACTION, by contrast, includes ACTIVITY that does not aim at any end beyond itself. In including action and DECISION as well as craft and inquiry among goal-directed pursuits, Aristotle makes it clear from the beginning that actions chosen for their own sakes are among the things chosen for the sake of some end, and hence (as he will go on to argue) for the sake of some ultimate end. The rest of the *Ethics* seeks to explain how this is possible, and why it matters. In 'seems to seek' Aristotle points out that he begins with an APPEARANCE.

The *EN* seeks to describe and understand the highest good and to prescribe ways to achieve it. Here Aristotle explains what sort of thing the highest good will be, assuming for the moment that there is one (see ch. 2, 7). He calls it 'the good', 1094a22; for 'highest' see 1095a16. In this chapter Aristotle distinguishes subordinate and superordinate CRAFTS and SCIENCES, with subordinate and superordinate ENDS; in ch. 2 he argues that the highest superordinate end is the highest good. The argument is fuller at 1097a15.

that is why . . . everything seeks: 'That is why' (*diho*) normally marks a transition from the exposition of Aristotle's own view to the explanation of familiar facts or commonly shared views in the light of his own view. Here he refers to the view of EUDOXUS; see 1172b9. The claim that he endorses might be: (a) There is some one end that everything seeks, and this is the ultimate good. (b) 'Good' is to be defined as 'what everything seeks'. (c) 'Good' is to be defined as 'what something seeks'. (d) If something seeks x, x is good. (e) If everything seeks x, x is good. (f) If A seeks x, A seeks x as good (i.e., taking it to be good). Eudoxus accepts (a) and (e), and Aristotle himself endorses (e); see x 2.§4 and note. At present, however, he is entitled only to (f).

If 'action and decision' refers to action on a decision, then he need not mean that every single thing we do aims at some good; for some of the things we do are not ACTIONS on a DECISION (cf. 1111b9–15).

§2 But the ends . . . from the activities: Cf. *Met.* 1050a21–b2. Here and in a16 the difference between ACTIVITIES with and without further products (see FUNCTION) corresponds to the later distinction between PRODUCTION and ACTION. In a5 'action' must have the sense noted in ACTION (2).

(b) §3–5. Disciplines and activities are subordinate to higher disciplines and higher ends. In these cases the higher ends are higher goods.

§4 But some of . . . further ones: 'Sciences' is supplied except in 'sciences we have mentioned', a18. Aristotle refers to all the 'actions, crafts, and sciences' of a7. None of these disciplines meets his most stringent conditions for a SCIENCE. In a13 read *ton auton de tropon* (OCT: *kata ton auton dē tropon*).

1094a14 In all such cases, then: Read *en hapasais dē* (OCT: *en hapasais de*).

2

2.§1–8. The highest good

(a) §1–3. If there is a highest end, and therefore a highest good, this will be a goal to guide our life as a whole.

§1 Suppose, then . . . best good: Does Aristotle intend this to give an argument for the existence of a 'best good' or highest end that we want only for its own sake and not for the sake of something else? One interpretation of the argument is this: (1) If we choose everything because of something else, desire will be empty and futile. (2) Desire is not empty and futile. (3) Therefore we do not choose everything because of something else. (4) Therefore we choose something for its own sake. (5) This is the best good.

This interpretation requires us to take choosing everything for the sake of something else as the only other option besides choosing things for the sake of a highest end. It does not seem to be the only other option, however. If we grant that we must choose something for its own sake (not everything for the sake of something else), we need not also grant that there is just one thing that we choose for its own sake. (If all roads end somewhere, there may not be some one place where they all end.) The argument does not justify us in dismissing the possibility of choosing several things for their own sakes, without choosing everything for the sake of just one end.

If, then, Aristotle offers the argument in (1)–(5) above, he argues invalidly. But we need not take the passage to contain an argument for a highest end. In this chapter he only explores the consequences of admitting the existence of a highest end. In ch. 7 he argues more directly for a highest end, and in particular considers the possibility of several ends pursued for their own sakes; see notes to 7.§1–2.

§2 Then does . . . right mark?: This might mean: (1) If we know about the highest good, we will have a target to aim at. (2) We already have a target to aim at, and if we know about the highest good, we are more likely to hit it. Perhaps (1), suggesting that the highest good gives us a definite target, is preferable; cf. *EE* 1214b6–15; Plato, *Rep.* 519c2.

(b) §4–8. The highest end is the concern of political science, which studies the overall good for the city and for the individual.

§4 It seems . . . ruling science: The argument is this: (1) The highest good is the all-inclusive end. (2) The all-inclusive end is the end of political science. (3) Therefore the highest good is the end of political science. This suggests an argument for the existence of the highest good. If there is such a thing as political science, and if it has an end, that end will be the highest good.

§7 the other sciences concerned with action: Retain *praktikais* (OCT deletes). The sciences concerned with *praxis* (ACTION in the strictest sense) are concerned with activities that are worth pursuing for their own sakes. The supreme science does not make these activities purely instrumental; it includes them in the activities that it prescribes as the highest good. This passage introduces the important idea that the highest good is an ordered compound of noninstrumental goods, explained further in 7.§1–5.

§8 for a people and for cities: 'People' (*ethnos*) is used to refer to (1) a nation, either the Greek people or (more often) a non-Greek nation (e.g., the Persians, the Scythians), or to (2) a national group—for instance, Greeks living in several contiguous cities or villages sharing common traditions (e.g., the Arcadians). The Macedonians, Aristotle's own people (see Introduction [1]), were an *ethnos* rather than a *polis*, whereas Athens (including the whole territory of Attica) was a *polis*, a CITY. Perhaps Aristotle uses the singular 'people' and plural 'cities' because he is thinking of the Greek people in the various Greek cities. In that case, he might be referring to the ambitions of Philip and Alexander of Macedon.

a sort of political science: The LINE OF INQUIRY in the *Ethics* is sometimes called 'ETHICS' (*ēthika*). On political science see vi 8.§1–2 and notes, *EE* 1218b12–16. In calling this inquiry 'a sort of political science', Aristotle probably means that it is concerned with the basic principles of politics (cf. 1152b2), since it seeks to give an account of the highest good for individuals and for communities (cf. *Pol.* vii 1–2); it does not discuss constitutions, government, and other more narrowly political questions (which are taken up in the *Pol.*).

3

3.§1–8. The method of political science

(a) §1–4. We must approach political science with realistic expectations, since its subject matter does not allow the highest degree of exactness.

§1 Our discussion . . . different crafts: Having introduced political science and set himself the task (1094a22, 'Then surely . . .') of saying what its end is, Aristotle explains how he will proceed, and how he expects his success to be judged. Hence he now describes the method of ETHICS, and the limitations of the method. On fitting the subject matter, cf. 1098a28, 1137b19.

§2 Now, fine and just . . . not on nature: People see that what is JUST and FINE depends on circumstances; for instance, it is USUALLY but not always just to pay your debts (Plato, *Rep.* 331a). (Less probably, 'difference and variation' might be taken to refer to differences of opinion about what things are just and fine.) These people (see PROTAGORAS) infer that there is no objective truth about what is just and fine. They think that these rest on convention (lit., 'are by convention', *nomos*; see LAW), and not on NATURE.

§3 But [this is . . . their bravery: The supplement suggests the connection of thought. Aristotle seems to be objecting to the argument from variation to convention. He answers that similar variations apply to goods, without inclining us to infer that goods are merely conventional. Aspirin, for instance, is not always good for a headache, but it is not a matter of convention that it is good for headaches on those occasions when it is. Hence the argument from variation to convention is invalid. See Plato, *Pr.* 334a–c, *Tht.* 172a, 177a–179b, and notes to iii 4.§4, v 7.§2–6.

§4 Each of our claims, . . . mathematician: Aristotle turns from a comment on the method of ethics to a comment on the sort of education required to appreciate the difference between ethical inquiry and the sort of inquiry that might be expected to result in a demonstration (see SCIENCE).

(b) §5–8. Since political science is inexact, we appreciate its conclusions properly only if we have the appropriate experience and maturity.

§5 This is why a youth . . . not knowledge: Two reasons are given for excluding a YOUTH from these lectures ('student', lit., 'hearer') on ethics. The first ('for he lacks . . .') is closely connected with the remarks about the EDUCATED person. The second ('Moreover, . . .') relies more generally on the practical character of ETHICS (1), which has also been assumed in the restriction of ethics to USUAL truths. On upbringing, cf. 1095b4, 1179b25.

§8 These are . . . propose to do: This sentence summarizes chs. 1–3 in reverse order, suggesting that Aristotle regards them all as his introduction to the treatise.

4

4.§1–7. Ethical arguments must begin from common beliefs

(a) §1–3. What is the highest good? Common beliefs agree that it is happiness, but disagree about what happiness is.

§1 Let us, then, begin again: Aristotle returns to the question raised in ch. 2, and asks what the good pursued by political science might be. As usual, we begin with APPEARANCES. See *EE* i 6.

knowledge and decision: The four items mentioned in 1.§1 are reduced here to two.

§2 As far . . . being happy: Everyone thinks the good is HAPPINESS, *eudaimonia*; Aristotle argues for this in i 7.§5–8. In identifying *eudaimonia* with 'living well' (or 'having a good life', *eu zēn*) and 'doing well' (or 'acting well' or 'faring well', *eu prattein*; see ACTION), he suggests that *eudaimonia* (a) involves one's life as a whole, and (b) consists in action. He examines both (a) and (b) further in i 9–10. He does not find it natural to speak of someone being *eudaimōn* for a few minutes and then ceasing to be *eudaimōn*. (Contrast: 'I was happy when I heard the news, but my mood changed when its implications began to sink in'.) In these contexts 'welfare' may suggest the connotations of '*eudaimonia*' better than 'happiness' does.

But they disagree . . . as the wise: We need some clearer account (see REASON) and DEFINITION of happiness—of the types of states and activities it consists in; and we begin with a survey of some common views.

§3 [Among the wise,] . . . to be goods: The Platonic Form of the good exists IN ITS OWN RIGHT and hence is independent of its sensible instances. Aristotle discusses this conception of the good in ch. 6.

(b) §4–7. In examining these common beliefs, we must begin from starting points that are familiar to us, and argue from these to ethical principles. To be familiar with the appropriate starting points, we need a good upbringing.

§5 We must . . . toward principles: To justify beginning with appearances, Aristotle adds a further remark on method. First he distinguishes arguments *from* PRINCIPLES, (or 'beginnings', *archai*), from arguments *toward* principles.

For indeed Plato . . . toward them: In 'used to ask' (the Greek imperfect tense) Aristotle indicates a recollection of what the historical PLATO said. He normally uses the present tense to refer to Plato's writings. Cf 1144b19 on SOCRATES. Aristotle's description of Plato's puzzle reminds us of *Rep.* 510bc, 533cd, where Plato distinguishes arguments leading to an account of a general principle (which Plato identifies with the Form of the good) from arguments applying this general principle. The metaphor of the stadium also suggests this argument to and from a single set of principles.

far end: Lit., 'limit'. Aristotle thinks of a Greek stadium, in which the midpoint of the race is at the end farthest from the starting line.

For we should . . . two ways: After he distinguishes two directions of argument in relation to the same *archai*, Aristotle now implicitly distinguishes two kinds of *archai*. In saying that we should begin (*archein*) from x, he implies that x is an *archē* for us; and since we should begin from what we know, and things are known in two ways, there are two sorts of *archai*.

The two sorts of *archai* differ, in that one sort is 'known to us', one sort 'known WITHOUT QUALIFICATION', or (as Aristotle elsewhere puts it, e.g., *APo* 71b33–72a5) 'known by nature'. 'Known to us' means 'known as far as we are concerned' or 'known in our view', and hence 'familiar to us'. Hence in saying that something is known to us Aristotle is not saying that it is true (cf. *Met.* 1029b8–10). At one time, it was 'known to' astronomers that the sun rotates round the earth.

'Known by nature' means 'is naturally such as to be known' or 'has a nature to be known', whether or not someone actually knows it. (Similarly, we might say someone is a natural marathon runner even if she has never run a marathon.) A truth is known by nature even if no one believes it or has the concepts to express it.

Now that he has distinguished these two sorts of *archai* and these two ways in which *archai* can be known, Aristotle can answer Plato's question about whether he is going to or from the *archai*. He answers: In this inquiry, we are going from the *archai* known to us (the beginnings) on the way to *archai* known by nature (the theoretical principles).

§7 For we begin . . . is true]: Lit., 'For the *archē* is the that, and if this appears adequately, he will not at all need in addition the because'. The translation tries to make it clear that this *archē* is the beginning that is 'known to us', not the theoretical principle we are arguing toward. We start from 'the that', accepted moral beliefs. These include (if we may judge from examples given in ch. 5) not only particular beliefs such as 'I ought to keep this promise', but also general claims such as 'Honor is worth having only from the right people'. These beliefs are true or nearly true, but they need defense and justification from 'the because', a first principle that explains why they are true. We do not need the 'because' to begin our inquiry; the 'because' is what we are looking for.

An alternative interpretation of the passage is this: 'In ethics, there is no because. Our only *archē* is the "that" and we do not look for any "because" in addition.' This interpretation is rather doubtful; it would be surprising if Aristotle had introduced his standard distinction between 'known to us' and 'known without qualification' without meaning to suggest, as he normally does, that we ought to be looking for principles that are known without qualification. For further discussion of principles in ethics, see 7.§18–21, and notes.

Someone who . . . acquire them: The 'beginnings' that we have or can easily acquire from good upbringing are (on the interpretation preferred so far) the starting points of our inquiry, not the theoretical principles we are seeking. See 1095a2, 1179b25, EDUCATION.

Aristotle has so far given two reasons why we need a good upbringing. (1) 3.§5–7: We need to learn to control our feelings and impulses, so that we can benefit from instruction about morality. (2) In our present passage, he takes good upbringing to be necessary for the appropriate stock of moral beliefs that are necessary for moral inquiry.

Hesiod: *Works and Days* 293, 295–7. 'Listens to one . . . ' perhaps suggests what Aristotle has in mind in saying we can acquire the starting points.

5

5.§1–8. The 'three lives' embody common beliefs about the highest good.

§1 But let us begin . . . digressed: Three traditional ways of life are discussed, since they embody three conceptions of the good and of happiness; cf. *EE* 1214a31, 1215a32–b14. The criticisms of the three lives reflect Aristotle's own criteria for the good: (1) The good involves distinctively human activities, not those of 'grazing animals', §3. (2) It must be our own, not heavily dependent on external conditions. (3) It must be complete ('However, this also . . .', §6). For defense of these criteria, see (1) 1097b33, 1118b1, 1170b12, 1174a1; (2) 1099b13; (3) 1097a28.

§1–2 For, it would seem, . . . of study: Aristotle's sentences have been rearranged. Lit.: 'For they would seem to conceive, not unreasonably, the good and happiness from the lives, the many and most vulgar as pleasure, whence they also like the life of gratification. For the most favored lives are roughly three, the one just mentioned, the political life, and, third, the life of study. Now the many appear completely slavish . . . '

(a) §3. The life of gratification allows no scope for distinctively human activities.

§3 In this they appear . . . grazing animals: The life of pleasure is rather brusquely dismissed as SLAVISH. Aristotle discusses it more fully when he has examined pleasure; see note to x 6.§3.

Sardanapallus: An Assyrian king (669–626 B.C.) who lived in legendary luxury; cf. Aristotle, *Protrepticus* fr. 16 (Ross).

(b) §4–5. One form of the life of political activity, focused on honor, has too superficial a conception of the good.

§4 This, however, . . . we are seeking: The proper value of HONOR is more fully discussed in the account of magnanimity; see note to iv 3.§1. On the inadequacy of honor, see 1159a22.

whereas we . . . from us: What is 'our own' (or 'PROPER to us') must be some genuine intrinsic feature of ourselves, not simply the product of other people's attitudes toward us. In saying that we 'intuitively believe' this (lit., 'divine'; cf. Plato, *Rep.* 505a1), Aristotle implies that we have not yet given a reason for our conviction; it is a 'that' without a 'because' (cf. note to 4.§7).

(c) §6. A superior form of the life of political activity, focused on virtue, does not allow for the place of other goods in happiness.

§6 If this is the sort . . . philosopher's paradox: The dialectical (see ETHICS [4]) term 'philosopher's paradox' (lit., 'thesis' or 'position') is explained at *Top.* 104b18. This conception of virtue and happiness is implied in the views of SOCRATES in *Gorg.* 470e, 507c (cf. *Rep.* 354a), and accepted by his professed followers, the Cynics. Cf. notes to ii 3.§5, vii 13.§3. Aristotle is himself committed to the claim (cf. *Rep.* 361d) that virtue makes someone happier than he would be by living any other way, but not to the claim that virtue alone is sufficient for happiness.

popular works: Perhaps the *Protrepticus*, which may have been alluded to in §3; see POPULAR.

(d) §7. Consideration of the third life, the life of study, is postponed.

§7 The third . . . follows: This life is fully described and discussed in x 6–8.

(e) §8. Footnote: The life of moneymaking is not parallel to the 'three lives'.

§8 The moneymaker's . . . forced . . . itself]: If the supplement gives the right sense for 'forced', it is used in a broader sense than at iii 1.§3, 10; cf. *EE* 1215a25–37.

and many . . . against them: Perhaps yet another reference to Aristotle's own POPULAR works. In a9 read *kai* (OCT: *kaitoi*).

6

6.§1–16. A philosophical conception of the good: the Platonic conception of the Form (Idea) of the good

§1 Presumably, though, . . . speaking of it: Aristotle mentioned the Platonic belief in a universal and separated Form of the good at 1095a26, and now proceeds to criticize it at length (cf. *EE* i 8, *MM* i 1). Much of the discussion is important for Aristotle's general criticism of Plato (cf. esp. *Met.* i 9), but less important for ethics. Aristotle is primarily concerned to argue against the view that goodness is a single property. If it were one, then knowledge of what is good for human beings would ultimately rest on knowledge of the single type of goodness found throughout the universe, such as is expressed in Plato's Form of the good (*Rep.* 508–9, 517c, 534bc). The effect of Aristotle's claim that goods are HOMONYMOUS is to sever ethical argument from general cosmological theories about goodness (cf. 1155b1–10).

Aristotle groups his objections as follows (the letters correspond to the lettered sections in the following notes): In §2–4 (a)–(c) he discusses the Form as a universal. In §5–7 (d)–(f) he discusses the separation of the Form. In §8–12 (g)–(h) he argues that the evident diversity of goods precludes any universal Form of the good. In §13–16 (i)–(k) he argues that the Form is in any case irrelevant to ethics.

Aristotle's objections are brief and cryptic; a full understanding of this chapter (as opposed to the rest of the *Ethics*) requires a grasp of some of his major metaphysical doctrines. The notes on this chapter give only the sketchiest idea of some of the main points.

friends: Cf. note to ix 1.§7.

(a) §2. There is no universal for an ordered series.

§2 Those who . . . [members]: Aristotle may intend this argument: (1) The common property of being a member of some numerical series (i.e., one with relations of prior and posterior among its members) is the property of having some place within the series. (2) A Form for such a series would therefore have to be (i) the property of having a place within a series, and (ii) independent of, and hence prior to, the series. (3) But (i) and (ii) are inconsistent. (4) But the categories (see note to §3) form a numerical series. (5) Hence there cannot be any Form common to the categories.

But the good . . . relative: SUBSTANCE ('what-it-is') and relative (e.g., double, half) are two of the categories, discussed more fully in the next argument.

(b) §3. There is no universal good across the categories.

§3 Further, good . . . spoken of]: Aristotle evaluates the Platonic claims in the light of his own doctrine of the different types of predication (*katēgoria*) usually called 'categories' (cf. *Catg.* 4, *Top.* i 9, *Met.* v 7, vii 1). The categories exemplify the fact that being is HOMONYMOUS. Each category answers the question 'What is it?' at the most general level about items of a certain sort (e.g., this man, this white color, *Top.* 103b27–39). In Aristotle's view, there is no general answer to the question 'What is it?' for every being; on the contrary, the categories provide the most general answers that are available to this question. Since the goodness of any thing depends on the kind of thing it is, goodness can be no more of a unified property than being is. If the categories indicate ten ways of being a being, they must also indicate ten different ways of being good (cf. *Top.* 107a3).

in what-it-is . . . mind: Probably Aristotle means not just that god and mind (or 'UNDERSTANDING', *nous*) are examples of goods that are SUBSTANCES, but that they are what it is to be good in the category of substance.

(c) §4. There is no single Idea across different sciences.

(d) §5. It is useless for understanding goodness.

§5 One might be . . . So-and-So Itself: Aristotle now objects to the separation of the Forms as both paradigms and instances of the properties to which they correspond. In the Platonic view the Form of just is perfectly just and is separable from sensible just things. See *Met.* 987a32, 1078b9–1079a4, 1086a24–b13; Plato, *Phd.* 74.

Man Itself and man: The second 'man' here probably refers to the universal that is immanent in particulars. (Less probably, it means 'a man', i.e., a particular man.) Aristotle accuses Plato of pointlessly introducing separated, independent Forms when the immanent universals (good, man, etc.) recognized by Aristotle are all that we need if we want to understand the natures of things.

(e) §6. The eternity of the Form is irrelevant.

(f) §7. Even the Pythagorean view is more plausible.

(g) §8–11. There is no Form even for intrinsic goods.

§9 Clearly, then, . . . because of these: At this stage in the argument Aristotle takes the defender of Forms to claim only that there is a single Form for all intrinsic goods (i.e., things that are good IN THEIR OWN RIGHT).

§10 for instance, prudence, . . . honors: 'PRUDENCE' here may have the more general sense of 'rational awareness' (characteristic of, e.g., Plato's *Phil.*).

Alternatively, . . . the Form will be futile: The Form will be useless for its intended explanatory role, since it will not explain the goodness of anything else besides itself.

§11 chalk: The term Aristotle actually uses, *psimuthion*, refers to lead carbonate ('white lead') produced from lead and used for whitening.

(h) §12. Goods are not homonymous by chance, but their connections do not require the existence of a Form.

§12 For . . . homonyms resulting from chance: See HOMONYMY, note to v 1.§7.

Is it spoken of from . . . other cases: On the first suggestion ('all referring . . . ') cf. *Met.* 1003a27, *EE* 1236a14, b20. On analogy; cf. 1097b25, *Phys.* 191a8, *Met.* 1048a37. These two cases have been illustrated in previous arguments. Reference to one thing is illustrated by instrumental goods and the goods to which they are means. Analogy is illustrated by intrinsic goods; sight is intrinsically good for the eye, and so on. Cases of analogy also support Aristotle's contention that goods differ 'insofar as they are goods'; seeing is the good of the eye because the eye's function is to see, cutting is the good of a knife because the knife's function is to cut, and so on.

(i) §13. The Form has no bearing on action.

§13 Presumably, . . . [branch of] philosophy: Aristotle is concerned not to introduce nonethical discussions into ethics, if he can reasonably avoid them. Cf. note to viii 1.§6. The discipline alluded to here is 'first philosophy', the subject matter of the *Metaphysics*, which studies 'being insofar as it is being' (see *Met.* iv 1). In that work Aristotle discusses the issues about homonymy (iv 2), and also criticizes Plato's theory of Ideas at length (e.g., in i 6, 9, vii 13–16, xiii 4–5).

some one good predicated in common: Read *hen ti kai* (OCT: *hen ti to*).

(j) §14–15. The sciences do not refer to the Form.

(k) §16. The Form does not help the practice of the sciences.

§16 For what . . . a time: Elsewhere Aristotle gives a less one-sided view of the role of UNIVERSAL and PARTICULAR in CRAFTS. Cf. vi, x 9, *Met.* 981a1–b20.

7

7.§1–8. A new approach to the good should avoid these objections to other views. We begin from plausible criteria for the good, and we find that happiness meets these criteria.

(a) §1. The good is the ultimate end.

§1 But let us return . . . could be: Aristotle begins from the diversity of goods that we must recognize when we reject the Platonic attempt to find unity in goods. He wants to show that this diversity does not require us to reject unity in the human good.

For it is apparently . . . other actions: This description of different goods recalls the reference to analogy in 6.§12. After these illustrations of diversity in goodness, Aristotle focuses (in 'but in every action and decision . . . ') on the aspect of unity in the different cases.

And so, . . . these ends: The first part of this sentence repeats the conclusion drawn at the beginning of ch. 2 above. The second part, allowing the possibility of many goods constituting the end, helps to explain why the beginning of ch. 2 was expressed in conditional form. Aristotle now makes it clear that he has not proved that there is just one end of human action. Instead of '[the good achievable in action'] one might prefer '[the goods . . .]'.

(b) §2–5. The good is complete.

§2 Our argument, . . . conclusion: Aristotle seems to refer back to the conclusion reached at the beginning of i 2; see previous note. He has reached the conclusion by a different route, since he has now relied only on the connection between ends and goods (beginning from the points about analogy in ch. 6), and has said nothing about the hierarchy of ends that he introduced in ch. 1. So far he has not chosen between the two possibilities mentioned at the end of §1.

But we must . . . perspicuous: More perspicuity is needed, because ch. 2 simply referred to some hierarchies of ends, and did not explain why we must recognize a single end. In §3–8, Aristotle tries to explain this point, by arguing that (1) the good satisfies some formal criteria (see note to i 5.§1), and (2) happiness is the good, 1095a17, because it satisfies these criteria. They are formal criteria because Aristotle thinks (cf. Plato, *Phil.* 20d, and note to x 2.§3) they are reasonable conditions for us to apply to the good even before we consider the claims of specific candidates claiming to be the good.

The formal criteria require the good to be (a) complete (§3–5), (b) self-sufficient (§6–7), and (c) most choiceworthy (§8), not counted as one good among many. Here (a) follows from our choosing the good only for its own sake and not also for the sake of something else; if there were some more complete end than the good, we would choose the good for the sake of that. The other two criteria explain what is required by completeness.

§3 Since there are . . . ends are complete: See HAPPINESS (2). 'Complete' renders *teleion*, cognate with *telos*, 'end'. Some prefer to translate *teleion* by 'final' or 'perfect'. But the close connection between being *teleion* and the other criteria for happiness, and its use in 1098a18, 1101a13, support the translation 'complete'.

And so, if only . . . most complete end of these: What is 'the most complete of these'? Cf. 1098a17, 1099a30; *EE* 1219a35. Two possible answers: (a) Exclusive: We look for the single most complete end, excluding the other ends that are less complete. (b) Inclusive: The most complete end is the one that includes the other ends; we are not to pursue an unordered collection of ends, but the complete single end that is the whole formed by them. If we accept the exclusive answer, it is difficult to see how this conclusion that we must seek the most complete end follows from what Aristotle has said; if we accept the inclusive answer, we do not face this difficulty.

§4 always choiceworthy in its own right: This might mean (a) 'both always choiceworthy, and also choiceworthy in its own right', or (b) 'choiceworthy in itself on those occasions when we choose it'. Aristotle must intend (a); for (b) would not distinguish this case from the preceding case ('and an end that is never . . . ').

§5 Now happiness, . . . qualification: Though Aristotle has said (4.§1) that everyone agrees that the highest good is happiness, he thinks it is worth pointing out the grounds for this agreed view. Our views about happiness, and especially about its relation to other noninstrumental goods, suggest that it plays the role in practical thought that is appropriate for the highest good.

we always choose it because of itself: For the reason just given (note to §4), this must mean 'we always choose it, and always because of itself'.

Honor, pleasure, . . . shall be happy: This passage requires us to choose between two interpretations. (a) A comprehensive conception: The highest good, chosen only for its own sake, is composed of the noninstrumental goods that are chosen both for their own sakes and for the sake of the highest good. Cf. 1174a4. To choose them for the sake of happiness is not to choose them purely as instrumental means, since the 'for the sake of' relation, as Aristotle understands it, includes the relation of part to whole. See DECISION (2). Aristotle develops the conception he introduced in 2.§7 when he described the end of political science as including the ends of other sciences concerned with actions. (b) An exclusive conception: Every good that is chosen both for itself and for the sake of the highest good is separate from (not a part of), and strictly instrumental to, the highest good, even though it is also chosen for its own sake, and hence not for the sake of happiness. The claim in 2.§7 about the inclusive character of the end of political science simply means that political science 'embraces' the ends of the other sciences by using them.

Many have claimed that the exclusive conception in (b) gains powerful support from the discussion of happiness and theoretical study in x 6–8. See esp. notes to x 7.§5–7. Even if this claim is correct, it does not decide the question about Aristotle's view in Book i.

(c) §6–7. The good is self-sufficient.

§6 The same . . . self-sufficient: See HAPPINESS (3), note to x 7.§4. Two possible views of the self-sufficiency of happiness: (a) Inclusive: It is self-sufficient because it includes all noninstrumental goods chosen for the sake of happiness. (b) Exclusive: It is self-sufficient because it includes everything needed for the highest good, even though it does not include the other noninstrumental goods.

What we count . . . political [animal]: On the social character of human beings and of human happiness, see 1142a9, 1157b18, 1158a23, 1169b16, 1170b12, 1172a6, 1178b5; *Pol.* 1253a7, 1280b33. In saying that the highest good must be sufficient for other people as well as the individual happy person, Aristotle implies that a person's good is social not only in the weak sense that (i) it requires some contribution by other people, but also in the strong sense that (ii) it includes the happiness of these other people. We would satisfy (i) if our good required, say, only the services of other people who might be our slaves whose own good would not be realized through our good. We satisfy (ii) only if our relations to some other people achieve their good as well as our own. Aristotle argues for this strong conclusion about happiness from a claim about the political nature of human beings. He defends this claim further in his account of friendship in the *EN* and in his account (in the *Pol.*) of the city (*polis*) as the community that fulfills human nature.

If this is the right way to understand the social character of happiness, this passage supports the inclusive rather than the exclusive conception of the relation of happiness to other noninstrumental goods (see note on §5). For Aristotle implies that happiness must be self-sufficient by including all the goods that are needed to fulfill the capacities of human nature.

(d) §8. The good is most choiceworthy, not being counted as one good among many.

§8 [since] . . . many: Lit., 'not being counted together'. My translation fits an inclusive conception of happiness (see note on §5). The alternative translation 'if it is not counted with other goods' would fit an exclusive conception.

[If it were] counted as one among many: Lit., 'being counted together'. The alternative translation 'when it is counted with other goods' (and 'is more choiceworthy' and 'is added' in the next clauses) would fit an exclusive conception.

for the good . . . more choiceworthy: For this argument, see note to ix 9.§10, 1172b26, *MM* 1184a8–30. Two possibilities: (a) An inclusive conception: The argument seeks to show that happiness is comprehensive (including all noninstrumental goods) by arguing that if it were not comprehensive, we would face the absurd consequences that there could be a greater good (i.e., the combination of happiness with some other noninstrumental good) than happiness itself. (b) An exclusive conception: The argument seeks to show that happiness does not embrace all intrinsic goods, by pointing out that we can identify a greater good than happiness (i.e., the combination of happiness with some other noninstrumental good); in contrast to the inclusive conception, the exclusive conception takes this combination to be perfectly possible.

Happiness, then, . . . action: This sentence shows that the previous argument about addition was intended to show that happiness is self-sufficient. It is easy to see how this is so, if we accept an inclusive conception; for the discussion of self-sufficiency in §6–7 seemed to imply an inclusive conception of happiness, and this is exactly the conception that is spelled out in §8 (according to interpretation [a] above). It is less easy to see how an exclusive conception connects §8 with the discussion of self-sufficiency in §6–7.

The demand for completeness must not be taken to imply the maximum quantity of each noninstrumental good; see 1100b22–8, 1101b1–9.

7.§9–16. An account of the good: It is the excellent fulfillment of the human function, and hence it is activity of the soul in accord with complete virtue in a complete life.

(a) §9–10. The good of F depends on the function of F.

§9 But presumably . . . best good is: Aristotle now begins his own account of the good, which ought to satisfy the formal criteria just presented. So far the statement of the formal criteria has not made it clear what sort of life satisfies them (though Aristotle has implied that the 'three lives' of ch. 5 do not satisfy them; see note to i 5.§1).

§10 seems to depend on its function: Lit., 'seems to be in its function'. 'In' in Aristotle is often ambiguous between 'consists in' and 'depends on'; cf. *Phys.* 210a14–24. Since Aristotle takes good performance, not mere performance, of the function to be necessary for doing well, 'depends on' seems to be needed here.

The examples of craftsmen suggest that the function of some kind F is the goal-directed activity that is essential to F; a sculptor, for instance, is one who essentially aims at sculpting the relevant material into a particular shape.

In this passage Aristotle appeals to the function of F to identify what is good for F. (Contrast *EE* 1218b37–1219a6, Plato, *Rep.* 352d-353b, which explain the virtue, i.e. the goodness—of F by reference to the function of F.) What is good for Pheidias, insofar as he is a sculptor, is the sculpting activity. It does not follow that what is good for Pheidias is sculpting activity.

(b) §11–14. The distinctive human function

§11 Then do . . . no function: Some have taken this question to be rhetorical and have taken Aristotle to be arguing inductively from these examples of human beings with functions to the conclusion that a human being has a function. The inductive argument would be remarkably feeble, and there is no reason to doubt that Aristotle is asking a genuine question.

idle, without any function: Just one word in Greek, *argon*, literally 'without *ergon*'.

Or, just as . . . of these: Some have also taken this to be a rhetorical question that really argues: Since the parts of a human being have functions, the whole must have a function too. This would also be a feeble argument; we should probably take the question as a genuine question that Aristotle does not think he has answered yet.

§12 What, then, . . . and growth: To find the function of a human being, Aristotle considers different kinds of life. He assumes that (1) a human being is essentially a living being, and (2) a living being is essentially organized for goal-directed activities. Because of (2), living beings have functions, according to the conception of function applied to craftsmen and organs in §10–11. The examples in §11 show that Aristotle does not take intention to be necessary for the goal-directed activity that he identifies with a function.

The different kinds of life that Aristotle describes here correspond to the different kinds of SOUL distinguished in *DA* ii 1–3. Soul, as Aristotle conceives it, is relevant here because a creature's soul is its essence.

The life . . . every animal: In attributing a life of sense PERCEPTION to nonrational animals, Aristotle does not mean to deny that they are also essentially living creatures that engage in nutrition and growth. He means that the activities in their life—including those relevant to nutrition and growth—are controlled by their sensory states, and therefore by their desire (see *DA* 414b1–6, 433b31–434a10).

§13 life of action: This life of ACTION will be a life that includes other activities besides reasoning (just as a nonrational animal's life includes more than just perception). But it is essentially guided by reasoning, as a dog's activities are guided by perception. When Aristotle seeks to identify the 'special' human function, he is not trying to identify one specific activity that is peculiar to human beings. (If that were his aim, why pick on reasoning? Why not mention the use of cosmetics, the building of skyscrapers, the use of weapons of mass destruction?) He is trying to identify the type of activity that is essential to human beings, as distinct from other living creatures. Cf. note to ix 4.§3.

'Life of action' might be understood as (1) a life of rational action, as opposed to the goal-directed movements of nonrational animals; (2) a life including rational action that is its own end in contrast to STUDY (according to Aristotle's narrow use of 'action'; see i 2.§7, note); (3) a life of goal-directed activity that is its own end, in a broad sense of 'activity' that may include study (cf. *Pol.* 1325b16–30).

the [part of the soul] that has reason: Lit., 'what has reason'. The supplement (confirmed by 'of it' in the next sentence) indicates that Aristotle anticipates the division of the soul that he explains more fully in i 13.§15–19.

One [part] . . . and thinking: As 13.§15–19 explains, the part that obeys reason is nonrational desire. This is different in human beings from nonrational desire in nonrational animals, because it is capable of agreeing with practical reason. Here Aristotle anticipates the account of VIRTUE of character that he begins in Book ii.

Moreover, life . . . fully: By insisting that the human function requires activity, not merely a STATE, which is a sort of CAPACITY, Aristotle answers the first objection he raised in 5.§6 to the identification of happiness with virtue.

§14 in accord . . . requiring reason: These two relations to reason belong to (a) the part of the soul that is inherently rational, and (b) the part that obeys reason.

(c) §14–17. Function, virtue, and the human good

§14 And the same . . . play it well: Here (as in §10, '[doing] well') 'well' must be understood to include more than competent or skillful performance. Playing well is achieving one's good as a harpist, i.e., one's good insofar as one is considered simply as a harpist. Similarly, the virtue that makes someone do well as a human being is the virtue that makes him achieve his own good as a human being; this matters more than his good as a harpist, since his essential function is to be a human being, not to be a harpist. Aristotle needs this connection between virtue, doing well, and achieving one's own good, if he is to argue legitimately from the actions of a good and virtuous human being to the good of a human being.

§14–15 Moreover, we take the human . . . that kind of thing]: OCT deletes the whole passage.

§15 And so . . . with virtue: A human being's good requires him to perform the function of a human being. But simply performing the function will not ensure his good; many people may live human lives, and in doing so perform human functions to some extent, and still may be badly off in their lives (*EE* 1215b27–31). In that case 'performing one's function' cannot be a sufficient account of a person's good. Aristotle sees this, and replies that in such cases people are not performing the human function well. He therefore insists that to achieve our good we must perform the human function well, and that to perform it well is to perform it in the way that accords with virtue. Aristotle still needs to answer further questions.

(1) What is a virtue? What states of a person meet the conditions for being virtues that are implied here? Aristotle is not entitled to assume that the states commonly called virtues really promote happiness; he must show that they really promote happiness. He tries to show this through (a) the division of the soul (see note to i 13.§8); (b) the general account of virtue of character (ii 6); and (c) its application to the individual virtues in iii 6 through iv 9. A virtue is the state that allows the full, rationally controlled, harmonious realization of human capacities. (Cf. 1170a13 ff.)

(2) Why is it so important to be virtuous? It is not made clear here, but it is assumed in i 8 and gradually explained in i 9–10, that the active expression of the virtues is a component of happiness that we never have good reason to sacrifice for the sake of any other good, even though it does not by itself guarantee happiness. Virtue has this dominant place in happiness because (a) happiness requires a life in accord with reason, performing the human function well; and (b) the life of virtue is this sort of life, since it achieves the best sort of rational control over our lives. A proper defense of (b) requires a full account of the virtues; Aristotle summarizes his defense in ix 4.

and indeed . . . more virtues than one: See note on §3 above. Here again we must explain why Aristotle says 'most complete' rather than 'all'. An exclusive or an inclusive answer might be given.

§16 complete life: See 1101a6, 1177b25; *EE* 1219b5; *MM* 1185a5. Complete virtue needs a complete life (which need not, however, be a whole lifetime; see 1101a6–13) because virtuous activities need time to develop and to express themselves fully. This is especially clear with friendship, 1157a10, 1158a14, and with prudence, 1143b7. Here the enduring character of virtue is important; see notes to i 10.§10, vi 5.§8, viii 3.§6.

7.§17–23. Attention to the appropriate method for ethics will prevent us from asking inappropriate questions about this account of the good.

§17 This, then, . . . later: One might take either x 6–8 (which refers back to i 7) or, more generally, the rest of the *EN* to fill in some details of this sketch.

§18 We must . . . of inquiry: The comment on filling in details prompts Aristotle to add a word about the degree to which we can reasonably expect details to be filled in. Hence he presents a third discussion of method (cf. 1094b11, 1095a28). First, he applies his remarks in ch. 3 about exactness to the discussion of the highest good.

§19 what, or what sort: See DEFINITION (3).

§20 Nor should . . . the principle: The rendering of *archē* by 'principle' assumes that this passage on *archai* is concerned with theoretical principles known without qualification (in this case, the account of happiness), and not (as in 1095b6) with the starting points in our inquiry. Starting points are beliefs that need some further explanation. Theoretical principles provide the necessary explanation, and so a further explanation cannot be given for them.

§21 Some principles . . . other means: This translation assumes that Aristotle is still considering theoretical principles. Alternatively, one might suppose that he is considering *archai* more generally (including both starting points and theoretical principles).

Which of these means is most appropriate for ethical principles? Aristotle discusses habituation (see EDUCATION) further in the following books. In 'some sort of habituation', he may mean to indicate that he does not have in mind habituation, as we might ordinarily conceive it. See note to vi 13.§2; EDUCATION (5).

§23 For they carry great weight: Aristotle recalls his claim about knowledge of the final good, 1094a23.

for the principle . . . whole: A Greek proverb; i.e., 'Well begun is more than half done'.

8

8.§1–17. This account of the good accords with the relevant common beliefs.

(a) §1. The relevance of common beliefs

§1 We should . . . about it: Aristotle adds a further remark on method, suggesting a way to evaluate his claim to have found a principle. In 'from the conclusion and premises' he refers to deductive INFERENCE, which he claims to have used in arguing from general formal features of the good and from the human function. The premises of this argument do not oppose common beliefs, but they do not simply have the status of common beliefs in his account. Following the method of considering APPEARANCES (see ETHICS [7]), we appeal to common beliefs to confirm our claims about happiness.

for all . . . false one: Aristotle seems to assume rather hastily that the beliefs he will consider are true. For a more discriminating attitude see 1145b1–7.

(b) §2. Our account matches the common division of goods.

§2 Goods are divided, . . . body: By 'goods of the soul' Aristotle does not mean just 'good for the soul'; all three types of goods are good for the soul. He means 'goods that depend on the condition of the soul, rather than on the body or on conditions outside the agent'. Goods of the soul are preferable for the reason given in 1099b11–25.

(c) §3–4. Our account fits common views about the end and about happiness.

(d) §5–7. Our account explains the variety of conceptions of happiness.

§5 Further, all . . . our account: Some common views about happiness are set out in *Rhet*. i 5.

§6 involving pleasure or requiring it to be added: Lit., 'with pleasure or not without pleasure'. Aristotle seems to be distinguishing (a) life consisting in activities that are sources of pleasure in themselves, and (b) life consisting in activities that are not in themselves sources of pleasure, plus added sources of pleasure. The same distinction is assumed at 1099a15.

(e) §8–9. The view that identifies virtue with happiness is only partly correct.

§9 Presumably, . . . the state]: Aristotle explains his disagreement with the view discussed in 5.§6. Happiness requires not only virtue, but also activities that actualize the virtue in the appropriate circumstances, which he discusses further in ch. 10.

act correctly: 'Correctly' implies success (as in 'getting the correct answer' in an arithmetic test).

(f) §10–13. We can also explain the partial truth in the view that identifies happiness with pleasure.

§10 Moreover, . . . pleasant in itself: On PLEASURE, cf. 1104b3, note to x 5.§1.

§11 Now the things . . . conflict: The sources of pleasure conflict with one another. If I have an excessive desire for food, I may make myself sick by overeating, and so interfere with my other pleasures. On 'pleasant by nature' cf. 1153a5, 1176a19.

§12 Hence these people's life . . . pleasure within itself: Cf. 1169b26.

(g) §14. Our account shows how happiness satisfies the traditional ideals.

§14 Happiness, then, . . . heart's desire: This inscription at the temple of Delos is discussed at the beginning of the *EE*, 1214b1–8. See also Theognis 225.

and we say happiness . . . the best one: On this identification of happiness with one activity, rather than with all these activities, cf. note to 7.§4.

(h) §15–17. Happiness requires external goods as well as virtue and pleasure.

§15 Nonetheless, . . . resources: Aristotle corrects the impression that we might gain from his emphasis on good activities that happiness depends entirely on us and on what we choose. He certainly believes that this is the decisive element in happiness, but he also insists that the types of activities required by happiness also depend on external GOODS as resources. In 'For first of all' and 'Further' he describes two roles of external goods that he discusses more fully in chapters 9 and 10.

§16 character of happiness: Hence we are not good candidates for happiness. Cf. 1176b16, 1177a6, 1178b23.

9

9.§1–11. Happiness consists in our activities, not in good luck, but it depends on luck and external circumstances.

(a) §1–6. We achieve happiness by our own action, not by luck.

§1 This also . . . fortune: This puzzle recalls Plato, *Meno* 71a1–4, 100b2–4.

§6 and it would . . . fortune: Aristotle defends the intuitive conviction stated in 5.§4, that happiness is something of our own, not something we passively receive from other people or from external circumstances. He argues that happiness depends largely on our own actions; we are not at the mercy of FORTUNE for the major components of our happiness. Happiness partly consists in virtuous actions; and being virtuous—so Aristotle will argue in iii 5—is up to us, not entirely dependent on fortune.

(b) §7–11. Since happiness requires complete virtue in a complete life, it is not entirely independent of good and bad luck.

§8 Further, this . . . fine actions: Since political science aims at the best good, and seeks to secure it through education of character, its practice presupposes that happiness consists primarily in character and action, not in fortune.

§9 It is not surprising . . . complete life: Children, animals, and happiness; see note to x 6.§7, 1178b27; *Phys.* 197b6. A different reason is given in *EE* 1219b5.

10

10.§1–16. Happiness is not completely stable, but it is stable enough to justify us in calling people happy during their lifetime.

(a) §1–2. Solon's suggestion to call no one happy until he is dead cannot mean that someone is happy when he is dead.

§1 Then should . . . end: The reference to Priam and the Trojan War leads naturally into the discussion of Solon. In Herodotus i 30–2, Solon advises the prosperous and overconfident Croesus not to judge people's happiness (especially his own) during their lifetime, but to wait until they are dead, to see how their lives end. This advice is especially appropriate with Priam, whose life went well until near its end.

(b) §3–5. It is not clear that someone's past happiness is fixed, even after his death.

§3 We do not . . . and misfortunes: Aristotle makes it clear that Solon does not mean that if someone dies in 1901, he is happy in 1902 (immortality is not being considered here), but that only in 1902 can we justifiably pronounce that he was happy until he died in 1901. Solon's suggestion is reasonable if we consider the differences between Aristotle's conception of HAPPINESS (1) and a conception that may seem more natural to us. Solon thinks of happiness as complete success; and someone lacks this complete success if his success does not last for his entire life. Since external conditions beyond his control can interfere with his success, we are wise to wait until the end of his life, when we can be sure that these have not interfered, before we say that he was happy.

§4 But this claim . . . suffer misfortune: Apparently, the end of a person's life may be too soon to tell if he was or was not really successful in his aims. A happy person, according to the conception that Aristotle considers, is one who succeeds in fulfilling the aims that he sets himself; and if these include, e.g., the welfare of his children, then his success, and hence his happiness, depends on what happens after his death, when his children succeed or fail.

Surely, then, . . . to have been miserable: Queen Victoria died in 1901; her descendant Czar Nicholas was deposed in 1917. The absurdity that Aristotle considers here is not (a) 'Victoria has now become unhappy' (said in 1917), which he certainly thinks is absurd (a14–15, 'we do not say . . . '). He considers the different absurdity (b) 'It has now [in 1917] become true that Victoria was [before 1901] unhappy'. What was true of her in her lifetime cannot be affected by every fluctuation of fortune after her death (though it can be altered by some such fluctuations; see previous note).

(c) §6–8. It is a mistake to refuse to ascribe happiness to someone during his lifetime.

§7 Would it . . . happiness he has: Aristotle rejects the excessively cautious attitude that refuses to ascribe happiness until all the evidence is in, after someone's death.

for we suppose . . . to and fro: Aristotle concedes that the excessively cautious attitude he has rejected would be reasonable, if happiness consisted primarily in good fortune; for in that case happiness would be as unstable as fortune. If, then, we agree that a person can be called happy while alive, we implicitly reject the view that happiness consists primarily in good fortune; and so Aristotle proceeds in §9 to present a different view of happiness.

(d) §9–11. The life of virtuous activity meets the legitimate demand for happiness to be stable.

§9 For his . . . does not rest on them: Or 'does not consist in them'. (The Greek has simply 'in'; cf. iii 1.§15, note.) In Aristotle's view, Solon's worry is mostly, but not entirely, wrong. A virtuous person's main aim will be to exercise his virtues in his life. He can succeed in this, and hence achieve the main component of his happiness, independently of fortune. However, some conditions of happiness do depend on fortune, and here, Aristotle admits, happiness is not entirely stable.

§10 For no human . . . the sciences: On the stability of virtue, cf. 1105a33, 1140b29, 1156b12, 1159b2, 1164a12, 1172b9. The virtues deal with a person's life as a whole, and so he has reason to exercise them in all his dealings. This continuous exercise is supported by friendship. See 1170a7 (cf. 1154b20, 1175a3, 1177a21), 1172a1–8.

§11 'good, foursquare, and blameless': From Simonides. Cf. Plato, *Pr.* 339b.

(e) §12–14. The happiness of the virtuous person is not entirely stable, because it is not immune to external circumstances. But even bad luck cannot make him miserable.

§12 But many major . . . fine and excellent: The role for external goods suggested in 'add adornment', *sunepikosmein*, is illustrated in 1123a7, 1124a1.

And yet, . . . and magnanimous: See 1123b29. Because the virtuous person does not overestimate external goods, he will not be crushed by misfortune and will see no reason to give up his virtuous actions. See 1166a29. On making the best of available resources, see *Pol.* 1332a19.

§13 For a . . . prudent person: Here 'PRUDENT', which usually translates *phronimos*, translates the cognate *emphrōn*.

§14 If this . . . Priam's: Here Aristotle uses 'blessed' (*makarios*) as well as 'happy' (*eudaimōn*). In some places (see *EE* 1215a10, 1215b11–14) being *makarios* seems to indicate a higher degree of well-being (more suitable to gods than to human beings) than the merely *eudaimōn* person possesses. But it is difficult to see any distinction between the uses of '*makarios*' and '*eudaimōn*' in this chapter. When Aristotle says that the happy person could not become miserable even in misfortune, he probably means not (a) that he will remain happy, though not blessed, but (b) that he will be neither happy nor unhappy, but simply not happy. The end of §14, implying that we can lose happiness and regain it, supports (b).

1101a10 nor shaken by just any misfortunes: Read *outh'hupo* (OCT: *oud'hupo*).

(f) §15–16. Hence a virtuous person can be called happy in his lifetime, even though he is not assured of happiness throughout his life.

§15–16 Or should we . . . human being is: A different punctuation yields the translation: 'Or should we add . . . appropriate end? Since the future . . . , we shall say . . . human being is.' A more important question is whether Aristotle answers yes or no to the question 'Or should we add . . . ?' (however we punctuate it). If he answers yes, he decides after all that we cannot call a person happy while he is alive. If he answers no, he decides that we can call a person happy while he is alive, keeping in mind that we are speaking of human happiness, which is subject to the fluctuations of fortune. The answer no fits the argument of the chapter better; see especially §14 and note.

11

11.§1–6. Solon's suggestion is partly correct; for what happens after someone's death can affect his happiness slightly.

(a) §1–4. Postmortem misfortunes differ in degree and in their impact on one's past happiness.

§4 much more . . . course of it: In Aeschylus' *Agamemnon*, for instance, the crimes of Agamemnon (who sacrificed his daughter) and of Atreus (who killed the sons of his brother Thyestes and served them up for Thyestes to eat) are mentioned, but they affect us less than the murder of Agamemnon, which happens during the play.

(b) §5–6. But in any case their impact is slight.

12

12.§1–8. The difference between praise and honor suggests that virtue (an object of praise) is inferior to happiness (an object of honor).

(a) §2–3. Objects of praise

§2 Whatever . . . to something: On praise, cf. *MM* 1183b20–38. Praise is accorded to what is FINE (3) because it is the agent's own achievement, resulting from his own voluntary effort under human conditions (hence it is inappropriate to the gods; 1178b16). Congratulation, however, belongs to success in action; this is what distinguishes happiness from virtuous action, which is not sufficient by itself for the complete success required in happiness (cf. 1177b18).

(b) §4–7. The best good is above praise.

§4 godlike: Or 'divine'. Cf. 1145a18–27.

§5 Indeed, Eudoxus . . . of pleasure: See 1094a2, 1172b9. Aristotle is endorsing EUDOXUS' claim that some goods are too good to be praised, not the argument for hedonism that Eudoxus derives from this claim.

(c) §8. Happiness is above praise because it is the principle.

§8 for [the . . . other actions: Lit., 'for for the sake of this we do all the other things'. The antecedent of 'this' is probably 'principle' (*archē*), and Aristotle's implicit premise is that we do all our actions for the sake of happiness. It is the PRINCIPLE because our deliberation (see DECISION) begins from our conception of happiness as the highest good; and we aim at it as the END, since we try to find the action that will best realize our conception of happiness.

13

13.§1–19. The soul and the virtues

(a) §1–4. A discussion of happiness requires a discussion of virtue.

§1 Since happiness . . . happiness better: Aristotle refers back to his definition of happiness in 7.§15–16. In 'a certain sort' (*tis*) he may allude to the parts of the definition that he leaves out here: (a) the demand for the best and most complete virtue, and (b) the demand for a complete life. He has discussed (b) in chs. 9–11. It is reasonable to consider (a) when we have examined the specific virtues and seen that there are a number of them (as 7.§15 suggested). Hence the next task is to discuss virtue.

In his account of happiness Aristotle has not yet said what the virtues are; see note to i 7.§15. We still want to see whether happiness requires justice or injustice, kindness or cruelty, bravery or cowardice. Aristotle begins his answer to that question, according to the suggestion in 1098a3, by considering the human SOUL, and especially its division into rational and nonrational parts (see DESIRE). The condition that promotes happiness will be the proper relation between the rational and the nonrational parts.

§2 the true politician: Aristotle recognizes that his conception of political science and of the politician does not entirely fit the common conception of what politicians do.

§4 Since, then, . . . beginning: This was the decision announced in ch. 2, to pursue political science.

(b) §5–8. A discussion of virtue requires a discussion of the soul.

§7 If this . . . body as well: Cf. Plato, *La.* 189e–190c (adapted by Aristotle).

Hence . . . [as the student of nature] . . . soul: The account of the SOUL in the *De Anima* belongs to Aristotle's natural philosophy.

§8 for a more exact . . . requires: Cf. 3.§1–4 above. Here Aristotle emphasizes the irrelevance, not the impossibility, of EXACTNESS.

(c) §9–10. The soul is divided into rational and nonrational parts.

§9 [We] have . . . less popular]: Or perhaps ' . . . even in the POPULAR works'.

§10 Are these distinguished . . . present purposes: For this question about parts of the soul see *DA* 413b13–32, 432a15–b8, 433a31–b13. By 'two [only] in definition' (*logos*) Aristotle means what he means when he speaks of things that are 'the same, but their being is not the same'; cf. note to v 1.§20.

(d) §11–14. One sort of nonrational part operates without our awareness, and is therefore irrelevant to ethics.

§11 Consider the nonrational . . . capacity to them: In this section it is useful to remember that Aristotle ascribes SOULS to plants as well as to animals. 'Full-grown' translates *teleion*, also translated 'COMPLETE'.

(e) §15–19. Another sort of nonrational part includes nonrational desires; it is capable of agreeing or disagreeing with the rational part.

§17 At any rate, . . . reason in everything: On this important difference between continence and virtue, cf. 1111b14, 1115b10, 1119a11, 1151b34, and note to ii 3.§1.

§18 the [part] with appetites and, in general, desires: Aristotle does not mean that the nonrational part is the only part that has DESIRES; for the rational part has the type of rational desire that Aristotle calls 'wish' (*boulēsis*). He means that the desires of the nonrational part are 'simply' desires, i.e., they lack the rational element that is essential to desire for the good.

This is . . . in mathematics: Alternatively, 'in the way in which we 'take account' (lit., 'have *logos*' (reason, account) of father or friend, not in the way in which we [give an account] . . . '

§19 If, then, . . . a father: Aristotle has now explained the two ways of acting 'in accord with reason' introduced in 7.§13. The nonrational part that includes desires is not inherently rational, but is capable of following the reason in the inherently rational part.

(f) §19. Different types of virtue are required for the nonrational part (capable of agreeing with the rational part) and for the rational part.

The division . . . virtues of character: This does not mean the virtues of character involve only the nonrational part. On the contrary, they all require PRUDENCE, which belongs to the rational part. Moreover, some of the virtues of thought—prudence, good deliberation, understanding, and consideration—require the right training of the nonrational part too; see vi 9, 11.

Book II

1

1.§1–8. Virtues of character do not belong to us by nature, but are acquired by habituation.

§1 Virtue of character . . . from 'ethos': Aristotle plays on the similarity between *ēthos* (character) and *ethos* (habit). On habit, see EDUCATION (1). For etymological speculations, cf. 1112a16, 1132a30, 1140b11, 1152b7; they are part of the appeal to ordinary language, which in turn is part of Aristotle's appeal to APPEARANCES.

(a) §2–4. Virtue of character is not a natural condition, since a natural condition is not changed by habituation.

§3 Rather, we are by nature . . . habit: NATURE is not neutral, equally suited for virtue or vice, but appropriately completed by virtue. See COMPLETE.

(b) §4. We acquire crafts and virtues by practice, but we do not acquire natural conditions in that way.

(c) §5. Legislators are concerned with virtue, and hence with habituation.

§5 For the legislator . . . his goal: On the proper role of the legislator, see LAW.

(d) §6–8. We acquire virtues by learning to do the actions that are required by the virtues.

§7 To sum it up . . . similar activities: The translation and supplement assume that 'similar' means 'similar to each other', i.e., that habituation involves the repetition of the same sort of activity in the same conditions. Alternatively, 'similar' might mean 'similar to the state resulting from them', assuming that, e.g., brave actions are similar to bravery.

§8 That is . . . in the states: The account of moral EDUCATION strongly stresses habituation; the activities of the virtues (e.g., standing firm as an activity of bravery) must be practiced, if we are to acquire the right STATE of character. Habituation is needed because we need more than just the learning of instructions, 1103a15; nonrational desires must also be trained. However, these activities are not caused by the state of which they are activities; although we do what the brave person does when we are being trained, we do not do it because of our bravery until the habituation is completed and we have become brave. (See ii 4.) We do not learn simply to repeat the actions until they become automatic or 'second nature' (cf. 1152a32). We must also acquire the virtuous person's state and motive, 1105a32. Hence habituation must include more than simply becoming accustomed to a type of action.

2

2.§1–9. The right method of habituation

(a) §1. The aim of ethical theory is practical.

§1 Our present . . . benefit to us: On practical results, see ETHICS (1). Aristotle says that finding true theories is not our end; he does not deny, but assumes, that they are a means to our end. True theories are all the more important when the practical purpose of ethics is considered; see note to x 1.§3.

(b) §2. Virtuous actions must accord with the correct reason. This general formula needs to be explained in more detail if it is to be practically helpful.

§2 First, then, . . . correct reason: Aristotle begins with an APPEARANCE, a common belief about virtue, which he gradually explains and defends; see 1107a1, 1138b18, 1144b21. On 'the correct reason' see REASON (2).

(c) §3–5. Ethics is inexact both at the universal and at the particular level, but we must give as much practical help as we can.

§3 But let us take . . . fixed answers: Aristotle refers back to the discussion of inexactness in i 3.§1–4. The lack of fixed answers reflects the fact that ethics requires us to rely on usual principles. In 'actions we must do', read *prakteōn* (OCT: *praktōn*).

§4 While this . . . navigators do: This is a new source of inexactness, in addition to the source mentioned in §3. Not only are some ethical principles merely usual, but they are also impossible to apply in practice by any systematic craft.

§5 The account . . . offer help: Aristotle suggests that the *Ethics* itself will offer as much help as possible for dealing with practical questions. He returns to this practical aim in, for instance, ii 9; iv 5.§13–14; ix 2.§2–6.

(d) §6–7. Habituation must avoid excess and deficiency and must aim at a mean in the actions that promote a virtue.

§6 for we must . . . not evident: For this maxim cf. Anaxagoras, DK 59 B 21a.

§7 Similarly, if he gratifies . . . by the mean: The doctrine expounded in ii 6 is anticipated here. So far, however, Aristotle only argues that virtue is acquired by a mean—neither total repression (insensibility; see 7.§3 below) nor total indulgence of a natural desire or FEELING. He later argues that virtue consists in an intermediate condition too.

(e) §8–9. We must also aim at a mean in the actions that actualize the virtue.

§8 But these actions . . . same actions: In §6–7 Aristotle has been concerned with finding the mean in the actions through which we acquire a virtue. He now extends his claim about the mean to the actions that we perform when we have acquired the virtue.

3

3.§1–11. The importance of pleasure and pain in moral training

(a) §1. Virtue is about pleasure and pain.

§1 But we must take . . . state: In 'But . . . ' Aristotle shows that he wants to correct a misunderstanding that might arise from his emphasis on actions in ch. 2. He does not mean to suggest that virtue consists simply in the correct actions. It also requires the appropriate attitudes, which are described in this chapter and the next. Virtue requires the right kind of pleasure (1099a7) as a 'consequent' (cf. 1174b33). It is not simply that the virtuous person gets pleasure from virtuous action (he has come to feel the pleasure that in the early stages of his training was the result of some external reward); he must also take pleasure in the fact that the actions are virtuous—hence 'enjoys this [abstinence] itself'. See note to x 5.§1.

if he is grieved . . . intemperate: We might think that Aristotle is referring here to the continent (see INCONTINENT) person described at 1102b27, who suffers a conflict between the rational and nonrational parts of his soul. Here, however, Aristotle says that the person who is grieved at being denied the intemperate satisfaction of bodily appetites is intemperate, not continent. The two cases should be distinguished. (1) The continent person has been trained to have some of the virtuous person's desires, and hence he does not resent abstinence from improper pleasures; his trouble is just that he also has strong appetites for these pleasures. (2) The intemperate person may find that he has to refrain from an improper pleasure (e.g., if he sees that he cannot avoid detection if he commits adultery), and will be grieved and resentful if he has to deny himself such pleasures.

For virtue . . . and pains: This is the general thesis of this chapter. It is defended by the series of points that follow in the rest of the chapter. §6 and §11 repeat the thesis.

(b) §1–2. Pleasure and pain turn us in the right or wrong direction.

§2 as Plato says: See Plato, *Rep.* 401e; *Laws* 653e.

(c) §3–4. Feelings imply pleasure and pain.

§3 but every feeling . . . pain: On FEELINGS, see 5.§2.

(d) §5–6. Pleasure and pain lead us astray.

§5 These [bad . . . pleasures and pains]: This probably refers to the views of SPEUSIPPUS (cf. Plato, *Phil.* 42e–51a; 1153a31) or the Cynics (cf. note to i 5.§6).

(e) §7. Pleasure is involved in every sort of choice.

§7 For there are three . . . and painful: On these three possible objects of choice, cf. 1126b29, 1155b18, FINE.

(f) §8–9. Pleasure is our earliest motive.

(g) §10. It is difficult to resist pleasure.

§10 Heracleitus . . . spirit]: The supplement implies that Aristotle alludes to a remark by Heracleitus on resisting spirit (see DESIRE). See DK 22 B 85.

4

4.§1–6. Our account of habituation requires us to distinguish doing the virtuous actions from having the virtuous character.

(a) §1. Puzzle: How can we do the right actions without being in the right state? Examples from the crafts.

§1 Someone might be . . . temperate actions: On this puzzle, see note to ii 1.§8. The puzzle arises because Aristotle has emphasized the similarity between the actions that we learn to do in habituation and the actions that we do when we are virtuous. We may suppose that if the actions are the same, their motive must be the same too, so that we can learn to be virtuous only if we already have the motive of the virtuous person. This is a practical analogue of the puzzle about learning that Meno raises at Plato (*Meno* 80a–e, discussed by Aristotle in *APo* 71a20–b8). In reply, Aristotle explains why his account of habituation does not self-defeatingly assume the existence of the state that is supposed to result from the habituation. The objector's argument (1) rests on an alleged feature of the crafts, and hence (2) assumes that virtues are analogous to crafts in the relevant ways.

(b) §2. A parallel between virtues and crafts

§2 But surely . . . crafts: Aristotle's first reply challenges (1) (from previous note), and argues that the crafts do not support the objection.

(c) §3–5. A contrast between virtues and crafts

§3 Moreover, . . . virtues: The second reply is independent of the first, and challenges (2) (from note for §1, above), insisting on an important difference between virtues and crafts. It contrasts the value of acting from craft knowledge—purely instrumental value, simply a means to the right product—with the value of acting from virtue.

For the products . . . have been produced: Lit., 'the things coming to be by crafts have the well in themselves . . . ' Aristotle is not taking back the point he has made in the first reply, that someone might produce a good product accidentally. He means that the goodness and badness of production is determined by its usefulness for producing the product; a better method of production is better because it is better at producing the right sort of product.

But for actions . . . right qualities: The value of virtuous action, as opposed to a craftsman's production (the process), is not simply determined by its efficiency in producing a product; it also has its characteristic motive. The value of virtue is intrinsic; virtuous action is not valuable simply as a means to some further result (e.g., acting kindly is not simply a means to making someone feel better). The intrinsic value of virtue reflects the virtuous person's motive, shown by the second condition in a32. The demand for a specific motive differentiates virtue from craft, and hence differentiates the training required for each of them; this is Aristotle's answer to the puzzle raised in the chapter. Virtuous action versus production; see note to ii 6.§9, ACTION (3).

As conditions . . . knowing: A new paragraph is suitable here because Aristotle passes from (a) the contrast between products produced well and actions done well, to (b) the contrast between good craftsmen and virtuous agents. The two contrasts are connected, because an action is done well only if a good agent does it from the right state (whereas a product can be produced well even if a good craftsman does not produce it).

(d) §6. The importance of habituation

§6 They are like a sick . . . philosophy: Aristotle sometimes cites MEDICINE to illustrate people's lazy and unrealistic attitude to moral theory and instruction. Cf. iii 5.§14.

5

5.§1–6. The genus of virtue of character: It is a state.

(a) §1–2. The difference between feelings, capacities, and states

§1 Next . . . one of these: Aristotle sets out to define virtue by elimination. The three 'conditions' are the different conditions of soul concerned with action. Neither FEELINGS nor CAPACITIES are the same as virtues, because they are the raw material of virtue; they require training and organization, as 1104a20 implied. In this chapter Aristotle gives the genus of virtue; in ch. 6 he gives the differentia (see DEFINE).

§2 1105b25 or of being afraid: Read *phobēthenai* (OCT: *lupēthēnai*).

By states I mean . . . to feelings: 'STATE', *hexis*, lit., 'having', is formed from *echein*, 'to have'. (Hence the Latin *habitus* is a suitable translation, though the English 'habit' is misleading.) 'Well/badly off' translates *echein* with the adverb, lit., 'have well/badly'. (Greek says, 'How do you have?' for the English 'How do you do?' or 'How are you?') Here Aristotle argues that a state is not *merely* a capacity. He does not deny, but indeed believes, that a state is a *type* of capacity; see, e.g., 'able to' in 1104a32–b3, indicating the type of capacity that is included in the state of character.

(b) §3–4. Virtues are not simply feelings.

§3 Further, we are . . . have virtues or vices: Praise and blame are proper to VOLUNTARY actions; here Aristotle introduces a question that he discusses further in iii 1. In iii 5 he considers whether praising virtue and blaming vice is ever justified.

The contrast between being 'simply (*haplōs*; see UNQUALIFIED) angry' and being 'angry in a particular way' is also connected to issues about voluntariness. Aristotle assumes that it is up to us to modify our feelings so that they are appropriate; that is why we are praised for being angry appropriately.

§4 but the virtues . . . require decision: After introducing praise and blame, and hence questions about the VOLUNTARY, Aristotle mentions DECISION, already introduced in 4.§3 and discussed in iii 2–4.

(c) §5. Virtues are not capacities.

§5 we have discussed this before: See ii 1.§2–4.

(d) §6. Hence they are states.

6

6.§1–20. The differentia of virtue of character: It is an intermediate state.

(a) §1–3. Human virtue realizes the human function.

§1 But we must . . . what sort of state it is: 'What' often marks the genus, and 'what sort' the differentia; cf. DEFINITION (3).

§2 It should be . . . functions well: The connection between virtue and FUNCTION was urged in 1098a7; cf. 1139a16; Plato, *Rep*. 352d. As i 13 argued, a virtue will require the right relation among different parts of the soul, so that someone's actions are guided by reason. Here Aristotle expands his earlier suggestion (in 1104a26) that guidance by reason requires neither total repression nor total indulgence of nonrational desires. Hence the connection between virtue and function leads directly into the doctrine of the mean.

(b) §4–8. The numerical mean must be distinguished from the mean relative to us, which is the aim of the expert in athletic training.

§4 We have . . . virtue has: Aristotle warns us not to suppose that his appeal to a mean is intended to offer a precise, quantitative test for virtuous action that we can really apply to particular cases—as though, e.g., we could decide that there is a proper, moderate degree of anger to be displayed in all conditions, or in all conditions of a certain precisely described type. The point of the doctrine, and of Aristotle's insistence on the 'intermediate relative to us', is that no such precise quantitative test can be found. It cannot be found because virtue accords with correct reason, as its relation to the FUNCTION of a human being requires; correct reason may require extreme anger at extreme injuries and slight anger at trivial offenses; in both cases moderate anger would be wrong. To find the mean relative to us is to find the state of character that correct reason requires, neither suppressing nor totally indulging nonrational desires.

§5 the same for all. . . . not the same for all: 'All' in the Greek might be either masculine (i.e., 'for everyone') or neuter (i.e., 'in all cases'). The latter is more probable, since relativity to different persons is irrelevant to some of Aristotle's examples. When Aristotle speaks of the mean 'relative to us', he probably means not 'relative to different people', but 'relative to human beings (as opposed to other sorts of things)', i.e., appropriate for human nature. In this way the doctrine of the mean is closely connected with claims about the human function.

(c) §9–14. The virtuous person, like the expert in a craft, aims at the mean. The special concern of virtue is the mean in feelings and actions.

§9 This, then, . . . product conform to that: 'Product' translates *ergon*, translated

'FUNCTION' in 16–24. Here Aristotle argues, as he often does, from crafts to virtues—from the way in which a craft achieves its *ergon*, product, to the way in which virtue achieves its *ergon*, function. On the different sorts of 'achievement' involved here, see note to ii 4.§3.

And since virtue, . . . intermediate: On nature and craft, cf. *PA* 639b19; *Phys.* 194a21. Though in certain respects virtue is less EXACT than some crafts (cf. 2.§4), it differs from craft insofar as a craft is a CAPACITY that can be used well or badly, whereas virtue is the direction of a capacity to the right use (5.§5). Hence we may expect virtue to focus more precisely on the right end, and therefore (since such a focus requires aiming at the mean) to aim at the mean.

§12 are in error . . . wins praise: Read *hē men huperbolē kai hē elleipsis hamartanetai kai psegetai.* (OCT deletes *psegetai* and reads: *hē men huperbolē hamartanetai kai hē elleipsis.*)

'for we are noble . . . sorts of ways': Author unknown.

(d) §15–17. The definition of virtue: It is a mean, guided by prudence.

§15 Virtue, . . . define it: Parts of this definition have been anticipated at 1105a31, 1103b21. The reference to the PRUDENT person might be derived from 1106b8–16, by taking the prudent person to correspond to the craftsman finding the mean. But the defense of the definition mostly comes later. See 1111b5, 1138b18, 1144b21.

(e) §18–20. Clarification of the definition; some descriptions of actions imply vice and therefore preclude any mean.

§18 Now not every . . . the mean: §17, indicating that we need to be careful about the sense in which virtue is a mean and an extremity, prompts this clarification. (In §20 'since the intermediate is a sort of extreme' Aristotle repeats the point of §17.) We cannot find a virtue by taking just any description of a type of action or feeling and claiming that there is a virtue in finding the mean in that; for the action or feeling may be a vicious one. How, then, do we decide which actions and feelings are suitable raw material for the doctrine of the mean? Aristotelian virtues include mean conditions of natural desires and tendencies. But they also include mean conditions of desires and tendencies (e.g., love of honor) that develop in normal forms of social life, and Aristotle must assume that such desires and tendencies should not be eliminated by altering the normal forms of social life. On the other hand, the fact that vicious desires tend to arise in normal forms of social life is not a reason for cultivating a mean condition of them (e.g., if legally enforced monogamy encourages the development of adulterous desires). Apparently, then, Aristotle must rely on some initial judgment about the goodness or badness of different desires, and the forms of social life that encourage or allow them, before he can say which desires are the appropriate material for virtue, and for which desires a mean condition should be cultivated. These initial judgments may be disputable, as we can see by considering some of the social virtues discussed in Book iv.

For the names . . . among actions: Does Aristotle's theory justify him in his confidence that some types of action, in any circumstances, are always wrong? See note to iv 6.§8. We might say that we would not *call* anything theft or murder unless we thought it wrong. Aristotle might say the same of adultery (it is the unjust use of a wife who justly belongs to another man).

7

7.§1–16. The definition of virtue as a mean applies to the specific virtues of character.

§1 However, . . . accord with these: See PARTICULAR. Aristotle is primarily concerned to offer accounts of virtues that are more 'particular' in the sense of describing specific virtues; these virtues are not themselves token actions (Leonidas' last stand at Thermopylae) or states (Leonidas' bravery). But when Aristotle adds 'since actions are about particular cases', he seems to refer to token actions. He intends his account of specific virtues to be helpful in practical questions, as he promised in 2.§5.

Let us, . . . chart: Aristotle probably has a table of the different means and extremes on a chart in his classroom. Cf. *EE* 1220b37, *DI* 22a22. This chapter anticipates the detailed argument of iii 6 through v, and in some ways makes its aim clearer. (1) The virtues are classified into groups. (2) Aristotle seeks to show that for every genuine virtue of character the doctrine of the mean explains why it is a virtue. (3) In some cases this is fairly easy, where (as with bravery) Aristotle can find a trio of mean, excess, and deficiency already recognized in ordinary beliefs. But sometimes it is hard, where we do not naturally think of a trio, and have no names for some of the alleged members. This is why Aristotle's remarks on the 'nameless' virtues are important (see 1107b2, VIRTUE). He wants to show that his doctrine applies here too, and hence that the trio is recognizable even where common beliefs have not yet recognized it.

(a) §2–3. Virtues concerned with feelings

§3 and in pains less than in pleasures: Read *hētton de peri* (OCT: *hētton de kai peri*).

(b) §4–9. Virtues concerned with external goods

§8 This is why . . . indifferent to honor: This comment explains why Aristotle thinks it important to identify virtues that have no name to distinguish them clearly from the extremes. The absence of a clear way to distinguish them from the extremes leads to two mistakes. (1) The person at the extreme claims to have the virtue. When Aristotle says the extreme people lay claim to the intermediate area, he means not (a) they agree that virtue is a mean and claim 'We have the mean state', but (b) they claim that the virtue (which Aristotle takes to be a mean state) is the state (in fact extreme) they have. (2) We (not the extreme people) refer to the intermediate person by the name of one of the extremes. In case (1) the speaker does not correctly identify the genuinely virtuous state. In case (2) we correctly identify it, but we use a misleading name. Cf. note on iv 4.§4.

(c) §10–13. Virtues concerned with social life

(d) §14–16. Mean states that are not virtues

§15 Proper indignation . . . [other people's misfortunes]: These mean states are not discussed further in the *EN*. Cf. *EE* iii 7. They are also discussed in *Rhet*. ii 6, 9–10.

(e) §16. Justice

§16 There will . . . elsewhere . . . these: 'These' might be the states mentioned in §15 (in which case the reference might be to *Rhet*. ii) or all the virtues of character mentioned (looking forward to Books iii and iv).

8

8.§1–8. Different virtues involve different relations between the mean state and the extremes.

(a) §1–3. The mean state is opposed to each extreme.

§2 For the brave . . . wasteful person: The doctrine of the mean explains disputes about the virtues, and tells us, as a good theory should (1154a22), why people make mistakes about the virtues. Those who do not fully understand the requirements of the virtue identify it with one extreme, which is then open to legitimate criticism from the other extreme; cf. 1125b4–18; *Rhet.* 1367a32–b7.

(b) §4–5. Each extreme is more opposed to the other extreme than to the mean state.

(c) §6–8. In some cases one extreme is more opposed than the other is to the mean state.

§7 Since sometimes one extreme . . . intermediate condition: How is one extreme nearer than the other to the mean? Perhaps Aristotle means that the rash person has the same sort of attitude to fears that the brave person has, but goes too far with it, whereas the coward has not developed the right sort of attitude at all. Cf. 1121a20, 1122a13, 1125a32, 1127b31.

9

9.§1–9. Since it is difficult to reach the mean, we must try to give practical advice, even though it is imprecise.

(a) §3–4. We must avoid the extreme that is more opposed to the mean.

§3 That is why . . . spray and surge': Aristotle offers practical advice, as he promised (1104a10), stressing that his doctrine does not offer precise answers to particular questions. See ETHICS (8), PERCEPTION. The quotation (Circe's advice, not Calypso's) is derived inaccurately from Homer, *Od.* xii 219.

§4 1109a34 extremely accurately: (*akrōs*). This is a pun on *akrōs*, 'extremely', and *akron*, 'extreme' (as opposed to intermediate); cf. perhaps 1107a8, 23 (the mean is, in one sense, an extremity).

(b) §4–5. We must avoid the extreme that we drift into more easily.

(c) §6. We must be especially careful with pleasures.

§6 Hence we must react . . . less in error: In Homer (*Il.* iii 156) the Trojan elders comment on Helen's beauty: 'Her face is uncannily like the faces of the immortal goddesses. But, beautiful though she is, let her depart in the ships; may she not be left behind to cause grief to us and our children' (158–60).

(d) §7–9. This advice is necessarily inexact; in particular cases we must rely on perception.

§8 Such things: This might refer back to 'nothing else perceptible' just mentioned, or it might include the circumstances and degrees mentioned just before that. The sense is the same in either case.

are among particulars: Lit., 'are in particulars'.

and the judgment depends on perception: Lit., 'the judgment (or 'discrimination') is in perception'. For 'in' indicating dependence, see notes to i 7.§10, i 10.§9, iii 1.§15. On PERCEPTION, cf. iii 3.§16; iv 5.§13; vi 8.§9, 11.4–5.

Book III

1

1.§1–3. Introduction to the discussion of responsibility

(a) §1–2. The relevance of voluntary action; it is required for praise and blame, and hence for virtue.

§1 Virtue, then, . . . they are involuntary: The chapters on voluntary action and responsibility (iii 1–5) continue the discussion of virtues of character. Aristotle has said that virtue is praiseworthy (1101b14, 1106a2), and now argues that the praise is justified. Moreover, he has made DECISION essential to virtue, 1107a1; in iii 2–3 he discusses its nature and its relation to the voluntary. Most important, Aristotle has assumed that if happiness consists in virtuous activity, it will, to this extent, be up to us, not dependent on FORTUNE, 1099b13–25. He needs to show that virtue is up to us; he turns to this task in iii 5.

§2 This is also . . . corrective treatments: This reference to legislators reflects the close relation between legislation (see LAW) and EDUCATION for virtue.

(b) §3. Initial account of involuntary action; it results from force or ignorance.

§3 Now it seems . . . involuntary: We begin with APPEARANCES, the two conditions that 'seem' to make action involuntary. Aristotle argues (§21–27) that there are no other reasonable conditions of involuntariness.

1.§3–12. Clarification of the conditions for force

(a) §3. Initial statement; forced action requires (i) external principle, and (ii) no contribution by the agent.

the agent, or [rather] the victim: In speaking of the 'victim' (lit., 'the one affected', *ho paschōn*; see FEELING), Aristotle probably means that if I break a window because the wind blows me into it, I am a passive victim rather than an agent. Less probably, this might be translated 'or the one having the feeling' (cf. 'feelings and actions', 1109b30).

contributes nothing: Do I contribute nothing if you force me to do something I already want to do? We might say (a) yes, since my wanting makes no difference to what actually happens; (b) no, since my wanting is a contribution, though it happens not to be used in this case. Aristotle probably intends (b); cf. 1110b11–13, 18–24, 1111a32; *EE* 1224b8. 'Force' is not always used in the narrow sense defined here; cf. notes to i 5.§8, iii 12.§3.

(b) §4–5. Actions under duress sometimes seem forced, but sometimes do not.

§4 But what about actions . . . something fine: In §4–12 Aristotle rejects two possible claims about these disputed actions. (1) They are forced, and hence involuntary. (2) They are not forced but they are involuntary, so that Aristotle's initial two conditions for involuntariness do not exhaust the possibilities. In §10 Aristotle clearly intends to answer (1). He does not answer (2) so explicitly, but he answers it implicitly by arguing that these disputed actions count as voluntary.

Suppose, for instance, a tyrant . . . will die: Actions done under duress in response to such threats are against one's will, and so are offered as apparent cases of involuntary actions.

§5 However, the same . . . storms: To show that actions responding to threats are not forced, Aristotle cites the abandoning of cargo in a storm. (This might be an extremely unattractive option, since loans were often made in anticipation of the sale of a cargo; the borrower would face ruin as well as the loss of a cargo, as Antonio does in *The Merchant of Venice*. See OCD, s.v. 'Maritime loans'.) Aristotle takes this to be a clear case of voluntary action; we clearly have a choice about whether to do it, and a sensible person would choose to do it.

For no one . . . without qualification: To do F willingly 'WITHOUT QUALIFICATION' is to find F itself desirable. Aristotle contrasts this with doing F willingly only in certain circumstances, such as those he describes. He marks the same contrast when he speaks of choosing to do F 'in itself', *kath'hauto* (a19, b3). Cf. 1151b2.

(c) §6. Actions under duress are mixed, since they have some voluntary and some involuntary aspects. But, taken as a whole, they are voluntary, since their principle is in the agent.

§6 These sorts . . . are mixed: Aristotle concedes something to the view that actions under duress are involuntary; for he treats them as a mixture of voluntary and involuntary. He seems to mean that in an action such as abandoning cargo in a storm we can distinguish an involuntary element (abandoning the cargo) and a voluntary element (abandoning it in a storm to save one's life). This conception of 'mixture' raises a question: Does it not imply that all actions chosen as means to ends are mixed? If I buy a cup of tea, my action seems to contain an involuntary element (parting with my money) and a voluntary element (parting with it to drink a cup of tea). But Aristotle does not seem to intend these nonreluctant instrumental actions to be mixed.

To see what Aristotle means in speaking of mixed actions, perhaps we should attend to his examples, and add further elements to those he explicitly mentions. (i) One aspect of a mixed action is repugnant (not merely unwelcome) even though I recognize that I have to do it. (ii) The circumstances in which I choose it are extreme circumstances that I would prefer to avoid.

Now in fact . . . or not to do them: The fact that the PRINCIPLE is in the agent convinces Aristotle that the actions are really voluntary, and up to the agent. In speaking of the principle, he means not only that the agent's state of mind is the temporal origin of the action, but also that it explains the character of the action. If I am forced (in Aristotle's narrow sense) to strike you a hard blow, because someone else hits your nose with my fist, the strength of the blow does not reflect my view that it would be best to strike you hard; but if I perform a mixed action, the character of my action reflects my view of what is best in these bad circumstances.

(d) §7–9. These mixed actions are praised and blamed. Sometimes they are pardoned; but even then we recognize that duress does not always remove blame. This treatment of mixed actions presupposes that they are voluntary.

§7 In some . . . would endure: On overstraining, cf. 1115b8, 1116b16, 1121b26. In §8, on Alcmaeon, Aristotle implies that we are 'compelled' to do these actions that overstrain human nature. 'Compel' here translates *anankazein* (necessitate).

Such compulsion must be distinguished from force (*bia*). Cf. note to x 9.§9. I am not forced to do these mixed actions that I am compelled to do, because it is my choice that makes me do them; if I say 'I had no choice', I mean that there was no reasonable alternative, not that my choice made no difference or that I was psychologically incapable of refraining from making the choice I made.

§8 But presumably . . . appear ridiculous: Aristotle counters a false inference that someone might make from his previous remark about pardon and overstraining. He insists that we cannot always accept the agent's claim 'I had no choice' or 'I couldn't avoid it'. Amphiaraus, the father of Alcmaeon, had been compelled against his will by his wife Eriphyle to join the expedition of the Seven against Thebes. Foreseeing his death in the expedition, he ordered Alcmaeon to kill Eriphyle, and threatened him with his curse if he failed to carry out the order. Alcmaeon's situation is, therefore, similar to that of Orestes, who had to choose between killing his mother and disobeying his father. The play of Euripides that Aristotle refers to, the *Alcmaeon* (see TGF fr. 69), has been lost; the quotation from it in v 9.§1 suggests that the play may have presented some discussion of Alcmaeon's plea of involuntariness. In Aristotle's view, even though Alcmaeon faced serious consequences if he failed to kill his mother, and even though those consequences would often justify the claim that he had no choice, they do not justify such a claim when the alternative is killing his mother. Aristotle does not believe we literally have no choice about compelled actions.

(e) §10. Mixed actions, therefore, are not forced, and they do not raise any difficulty for our account of force.

§10 These are involuntary . . . voluntary: Aristotle reasserts the reason he gave in §6 for taking these mixed actions to be voluntary. The PRINCIPLE of this particular action is our choice based on the belief that, for instance, it is better to refuse to kill this innocent person than to save ten other people by killing him. Since a person's belief and choice explains this particular action, the action is voluntary.

(f) §11–12. The pleasant and the fine do not force us, and therefore actions aiming at the pleasant or the fine are not involuntary.

§11 It is ridiculous . . . snared by such things: This explains why Aristotle believes it is unreasonable to suppose we are forced by pleasant and fine things. It is up to us to choose whether to act on our judgment that something is pleasant or fine, and hence our beliefs and our choices are the principle of the action. In b13, read *geloion dē* (OCT: *geloion de*).

1.§13–19. Clarification of the type of ignorance that makes an action involuntary

(a) §13. Actions done because of ignorance but without regret are nonvoluntary, but not involuntary.

§13 For if someone's . . . no pain: The distinction between the nonvoluntary and the involuntary is irrelevant to the agent's relation to his action; for in either case he is not responsible for it. But it is relevant to his character. If he is pleased at something he has done because of ignorance, he shows what sorts of actions he is willing and prepared to do, and is rightly blamed or praised for his attitude to these actions. This passage is one that shows that Aristotle is concerned with more than responsibility for actions; cf. note to §3 above.

(b) §14–15. Actions done in ignorance but not because of ignorance are not involuntary.

§15 [This] ignorance . . . cause for blame: The translation and supplements assume: (1) 'Ignorance of what is beneficial', 'ignorance in the decision', and 'ignorance of the universal' all refer to the same thing; (2) This is the type of ignorance ascribed to the drunken and angry people described here. Aristotle is thinking of someone whose anger makes him think it is all right to shoot the offender (cf. 1149a25), not of someone whose anger blinds him to the fact that he is shooting, or that he is shooting this person.

In these cases, the cause of the wrong action is the fault in the agent's character, not the agent's ignorance. Hence it is not action because of ignorance of the sort that removes us from blame (see further 1113b30 on ignorance of fact).

which the action consists in and is concerned with: Lit., 'which the action is in and about'. Perhaps 'which the action depends on . . . '; for 'in', cf. note to ii 9.§6.

(c) §16–19. Actions done because of ignorance of particulars are involuntary.

§17 Again, . . . as Merope did: This alludes to Euripides' lost play, *Cresphontes*. Cf. *Poet*. 1454a5.

§18 what he is . . . does it: In a18 read *[ho] kai hou heneka* (OCT; *kai hou heneka*).

§19 Hence the agent . . . regret for his action: This section ends the explanation of 'because of ignorance' that Aristotle began in §13.

1.§20–27. Definition of the voluntary

(a) §20. Action done with knowledge of the particulars is voluntary.

§20 what has its principle . . . constitute the action: The reference to an internal principle recalls §6 and §10, and implies the absence of force. Though Aristotle has not described the nature of this principle fully, he implies that it includes an agent's desires and choices. Here knowledge of the particulars seems to be a necessary condition for the principle's being in the agent. Cf. note to v 8.§3.

(b) §21–27. Reply to an alleged counterexample to the definition: to act on a nonrational desire is not to act involuntarily.

§21 For, presumably, . . . is involuntary: Aristotle's implicit reference to desire in his appeal to an internal principle provokes an objection. He considers an opponent who argues that the definition just given is insufficient, because we can act on an internal principle and with knowledge, but still involuntarily, if we act on a nonrational DESIRE. This objection revives some of the issues raised in §11–12 above.

§22 For, first . . . children: This reply to the objection relies on the assumption that nonrational animals and children are clearly voluntary agents.

§24 ought to desire: Aristotle endorses the principle 'ought implies can'. On 'ought' (*dei*), see RIGHT.

2

2.§1–17. Voluntary action and decision

(a) §1–2. Virtue requires not only voluntary action, but action on decision.

§1 for decision . . . actions do: After insisting that nonrational desire counts as an internal principle that makes an action voluntary, Aristotle argues (cf. 1107a1) that it is not enough for virtue. Rational wish and deliberation are needed for someone to have a correct conception of what makes virtuous action FINE and good in itself. Probably this is why Aristotle thinks virtue requires decision.

§2 and the actions we do on the spur of the moment . . . decision: These actions need to be carefully distinguished from actions that in some way result from a decision; cf. note to 8.§15 below.

(b) §3–6. Decision is not appetite or spirit.

§4 Again, the incontinent . . . not on decision: This is an important claim about incontinence. Since decision requires (as we are about to learn) both wish for the end and deliberation about the means, what does the incontinent lack? Later (see vi 9.§4 and note) Aristotle makes it clear that it is possible for an incontinent to act on deliberation; hence he fails to act on a decision because he fails to act on a wish, i.e., a rational desire. Instead of acting on wish he acts on appetite. Cf. 2.§7, 3.§19, and notes.

§5 Besides, the object of appetite . . . object of decision: The point is not that we do not consider pleasure and pain when we make a decision, but that we are concerned with them only insofar as they contribute to good and bad.

(c) §7–9. It is not wish.

§7 But further . . . close to it: Though Aristotle rejects the identification of decision with wish, he does not deny that wish is necessary for decision. In 3.§19, 4.§1, and 5.§1, he implies (without making it completely explicit) that a decision must be based on a wish, not on the nonrational DESIRES—spirit and appetite.

For we do not decide on impossible . . . a fool: The explanatory clause 'anyone claiming . . . ' shows that Aristotle means that we do not decide to do what we *think* is impossible; cf. 'what is up to us', b30.

achievable through our own agency: Lit., 'through us'. Agency, however, is clearly intended. If you force me to stand between you and someone firing shots at you, you are not protected 'through me' in the sense that concerns Aristotle here.

victory . . . athlete, for instance: Prizes were awarded to the best actors in the Athenian dramatic festivals. Cf. 1166b35.

§9 Again, . . . things that promote the end: Lit., 'things toward the end', *ta pros to telos.* These are not confined to 'means to the end', as commonly understood. Aristotle is not concerned only with actions that are purely instrumental to an end; a person can also decide on something as a good in itself that promotes a further good in itself by being a part of the further good. See DECISION (2), note to vi 5.§1.

(d) §10–15. It is not belief.

§13 Further, decision . . . believing rightly: Delete *ē tō(i) orthōs* in a6 and *alēthōs* in a7 (retained in OCT). On correctness of belief and desire, see vi 2.§2–3, 1142b11.

Moreover, we decide . . . is good: Alternatively, and less probably, Aristotle might mean that knowing is a necessary condition for deciding.

(e) §16–17. Decision requires deliberation.

§17 and even the name . . . other things: 'Before' might indicate temporal or preferential priority, i.e., either (a) choosing before something else (i.e., action), or (b) choosing one action in preference to another. The previous remark on prior deliberation suggests that Aristotle has (a) in mind here.

3

3.§1–20. Deliberation and decision

(a) §1–2. The scope of deliberation is confined to what a sensible person would deliberate about.

(b) §3–7. We deliberate only about things that are up to us.

§4 either . . . or by nature: In a24, read *eite phusei* (OCT: *eite kai phusei*).

§6 But we do not . . . best political system: The transposition of this passage from its place in the mss. (and OCT) gives a better sequence of thought. This is an example of something that comes about through human effort but is not an appropriate object of deliberation for every group of human beings.

(c) §8–10. We deliberate only in cases that raise a question about what to do.

§9 about beliefs more than about sciences: Read *peri tas doxas* (OCT: *peri tas technas*, 'about crafts').

§10 the right way to act: Read *[to hōs dei] adihoriston* (OCT: no supplement).

(d) §11–16. We deliberate about what promotes an end, not about ends.

§11 We deliberate . . . promotes ends: Aristotle has been saying what deliberation is not about; he now turns to a more positive description. On this restriction to what promotes ends, see 1111b27, *Rhet.* 1355b10. To deliberate about action we must begin with some conception of an end; but finding things that promote it may show us actions that are FINE and good in themselves, and hence ends in themselves. This is how the PRUDENT person deliberates.

ways and means: Lit., 'how and through what things it will be'. 'Means' is a convenient translation here, but may mislead us in the way noted in note to 2.§9 above.

most easily and most finely: This suggests that considerations of efficiency are not the only ones to be counted in deliberation. It is proper to the virtuous and PRUDENT person to aim at what is FINE. Cf. vi 5.§1, note.

§11–12 For a deliberator . . . comes into being: The geometer considers how to construct a complex figure by analyzing it into simpler figures, until he finds the first one that he should draw.

§13 but if the action . . . undertake it: The decision seems to be the last mental event preceding the action; once we find that an action is possible, we undertake it (lit., 'put their hand to acting'). Hence the beliefs and desires described in 1147a25–31 should be part of the deliberation.

§16 hence we deliberate: In b33 read *ouk ar'an* (OCT: *ou gar an*).

(e) §17–20. Decision results from wish and decision, and hence it is also about what promotes an end.

§18 This is also . . . to the people: This Homeric reference (cf. *Il.* ii 48–141; *Od.* xxiv 412–71) seems to illustrate the claim that the deciding part of an agent is also the guiding (or 'leading') part—the one that guides our actions. The decision of the Homeric kings was normally final; the people simply endorsed it. (They did not always endorse it, just as we do not always act on our decisions.)

§19 We have found, then: Read *ontos dē* (OCT: *ontos de*).

we desire . . . wish: Read *boulēsin* (OCT: *bouleusin*, 'deliberation'). This passage and 1113b3–5 make it fairly clear that DECISION requires wish, not just any sort of DESIRE.

4

4.§1–6. Wish: rational desire for the end

(a) §1–3. According to one view, wish is for the good; according to another view, it is for the apparent good.

§3 But for those who say . . . appear good to different people: The exact point of §2–3 is obscured by the ambiguity of 'wished' (*boulēton*, cf. CHOICEWORTHY) between (a) what is wished and (b) what deserves to be wished. Two points might be relevant here. (1) When I wish for health (for instance), I wish for it 'as good', i.e., I want it because I believe it is good, not because I believe it appears good. (2) The proper object of wish—i.e., the suitable object for the well-informed person—is the good, but each person thinks that what appears good to him is the proper object of wish. Similarly what is known by nature (1095b3) is what the fully informed person thinks he knows. Probably Aristotle's main point here is (2). See also note to viii 2.§2.

(b) §4–6. Solution: The good person is the appropriate measure of the proper object of wish.

§4 Similarly in the case of . . . hot, heavy, and so on: In 'healthy to . . . ' the Greek dative is translated 'to', though it was previously translated 'for'. It is not clear whether Aristotle is saying (i) Broccoli is really healthy for healthy people, and antibiotics are really unhealthy for them, but antibiotics are really healthy for sick people, and broccoli is really unhealthy for them; or (ii) Healthy people judge correctly that broccoli is healthy for them, but sick people judge incorrectly that drinking a lot is healthy for them, though in fact it is not. The sensory examples that follow, and the demands of the argument as a whole, suggest that here Aristotle has (ii) in mind. Cf. notes to viii 2.§2; x 3.§8, 5.§10–11.

§5 Presumably, . . . standard and measure: The excellent person as standard; 1166a12, 1170a21, and notes to x 5.§10. Aristotle replies here to PROTAGORAS' principle, Plato, *Tht.* 152a (cf. 1094b15). We might take Aristotle's claim in two ways. (a) Ontological: The good person's approval constitutes something as good, and it is not good independently of being chosen. (b) Epistemological: Things are good independently of being chosen, and the good person is the one who can be relied on to approve of the things that are genuinely good. The end of §4 suggests that Aristotle has (b) rather than (a) in mind.

§5–6 In the many, . . . assume it is evil: On the errors of the many, see PLEASURE (4). In b1 read *hairountai goun* (OCT: *hairountai oun*).

5

5.§1–20. Virtue and vice are in our power.

(a) §1–6. The actions that proceed from virtue and vice are in our power.

§1 The activities of the virtues . . . the end]: These activities are probably those that result from having a virtue; they are not simply the brave actions (e.g.) that a nonbrave person might also do (cf. ii 4.§4–5, note). Less probably, Aristotle has in mind the actions that precede a virtue and develop it. See note to §3. Here Aristotle turns to one major task of his discussion of voluntary action (see note to 1.§1 above)—to show that being virtuous is up to us, something that we can determine by our own voluntary action and decision. He argues first that since 'the activities of the virtues' are up to us, being virtuous is also up to us.

§3 But if doing, . . . decent or base is up to us: Aristotle argues: (1) It is up to us to do fine or shameful actions. (2) Doing fine or shameful actions = being virtuous or vicious. (3) Hence it is up to us to be virtuous or vicious. The question is whether both (1) and (2) can be true, if 'doing fine or shameful actions' is understood in the same way in both premises.

We might object: 'All that has been shown in chs. 1–3 is that (a) virtuous actions (those that a virtuous or a nonvirtuous person might do; see note to §1 above) are up to us. It has not been shown that (b) virtuous actions from the virtuous person's motive are up to us. Hence step (1) is true only if understood as (a). But step (2) is true only if understood as (b). Hence there is a fatal equivocation.'

The objector's claim about step (2) is surely correct. Hence Aristotle must persuade us that we have sufficient reason to believe (1), understood as (b). The rest of the chapter seeks to persuade us of this. To agree with Aristotle's claim, we must agree that the relevant mental states—wish and decision—are up to us. This claim is defended in 1113b21–1114a3.

§4 'no one . . . unwillingly blessed': Quoted from Epicharmus; see DK 23 B 7.

§6 and we cannot refer . . . up to us: In b20 read *tas eph'hēmin*. Some mss. (followed by OCT) read *tas en hēmin* ('those that are in us'). The choice between the two readings is not clear; but cf. note to §14 below for support for 'up to us'.

The previous sentence shows that Aristotle takes 'we are the principles of our actions' and 'the principles of our actions are in us' to be equivalent. Here, as in 1.§6, 10, Aristotle takes x's having its principle in me to imply that x is up to me and that I do x voluntarily.

What does he mean by saying that we cannot find principles apart from those up to us (or in us)? We might take him to deny determinism (the doctrine that every event has sufficient causal conditions in some previous event); for if my internal principle itself had some cause, would this not provide a principle apart from the principle in me? We need not accept this indeterminist interpretation, however. If Aristotle takes a principle to be explanatory as well as causal, he may mean that only my internal principle really explains the character of my action; if my internal principle itself has some cause determining it, that determining cause does not explain the character of my action. If this is Aristotle's position, his claim about internal principles does not commit him to indeterminism.

(b) §7–9. Our practices of reward and punishment presuppose that virtue and vice are in our power.

§7 caused by ignorance . . . not responsible for: On 'responsible', see CAUSE. In 1114a1 below, 'caused by' translates *dia*. No sharp difference should be assumed.

§8 Indeed, legislators . . . responsible for the ignorance: Aristotle supplements, but does not reject, the treatment of ignorance of fact at 1110b18–1111a2. He does not claim that we are responsible for the action caused by ignorance, but only that we are responsible for the ignorance that caused the action.

A drunk, . . . causes his ignorance: This law was apparently not common in Greek states, but (according to *Pol.* 1274b18–23) peculiar to Pittacus (c.650–570 B.C., ruler of Mytilene; cf. ix 6.§2). It might be taken to suggest that the drunk person is responsible both for being drunk and for what he does when he is drunk (since he is punished for both). Aristotle need not endorse this view; the double punishment might be taken as a warning to avoid getting drunk (as the comment in the *Politics* suggests).

(c) §10–16. Virtue and vice, no less than health and sickness, are in our power.

§10 But presumably . . . inattentive: Aristotle has argued that legal practices show we are held responsible for our mental state. An objector now argues: 'These legal practices are unjustified. For (a) our mental states are simply the effects of the characters we have, and hence (b) we are not responsible for them.' Aristotle accepts (a), but denies that (b) follows from (a).

Still, he is himself . . . corresponding sort of person: Here Aristotle replies to the objector as follows. (1) We were in control of forming our characters. (2) Hence we are responsible for the characters we have. (3) Hence we are responsible for the mental states formed by these characters. If he believes (1), Aristotle must assume that childhood training does not form our character to an extent that puts it beyond our control.

§13 [Hence] if . . . willingly unjust: In the mss. (and OCT) this sentence follows 'not to wish to be intemperate' in §13. The transposition gives a clearer sequence of thought. In this sentence Aristotle argues that it is reasonable to hold people (other than the totally insensible) responsible for their bad character, since they form it knowingly.

Further, it is unreasonable . . . wish to be intemperate: Less probably, 'Moreover, it is unreasonable [to expect] someone doing injustice not to wish to be unjust . . . ' (which would imply, implausibly, that everyone who does injustice wishes to be unjust). Probably Aristotle is answering the objection that people who do injustice do not always wish (*boulesthai*) to be unjust, and therefore (the objector assumes) are not responsible for being unjust or for doing injustice. Aristotle answers that their attitude is unreasonable, and no excuse for their behavior.

§14 This does not . . . will be just: To grasp Aristotle's point, we must recall the narrow sense attached to 'wish' in iii 2. If I simply wish I were healthier or less lazy, that does not mean I seriously intend to do anything about it; hence Aristotle warns that merely wishing I were just does not by itself mean I will become just. In saying this, Aristotle does not say that (i) an unjust person cannot form a serious intention and decision to become just, or that (ii) such an intention and decision will always be ineffective. Hence he does not say, in this passage, that there is no hope for a vicious person.

nonetheless, . . . willingly: In a15 read *kaitoi ei* (OCT: *kai ei*). MEDICINE serves as an example of people's readiness to shift responsibility from themselves; cf. ii 4.§6, note.

the principle was up to him: In a19 read *hē gar archē ep' autō(i)* (OCT accepts the unnecessary emendation *en autō[i]*).

though once . . . have it [now]: Here again we might easily take Aristotle to be saying that the vicious person's condition is irreversible, and that he cannot improve his condition once he has become vicious. The parallel with the stone, however, suggests a more limited claim. If I have thrown a stone and broken a window, I cannot now make it true that I have not thrown the stone or that I have not broken the window, but I can retrieve the stone and I can repair the window. Similarly, if I have become vicious, I cannot make this not have happened; hence, I must reckon with the fact that I have become vicious, if I am considering how to improve. While this claim implies that the effects of vice are serious, it does not commit Aristotle to the further claim that they make the vicious person's condition hopeless. Cf. vii 7.§2.

(d) §17. Our conception of the end is up to us.

§17 But someone may say . . . the end appears to him: Aristotle considers this argument: (i) The character we form depends on our appearance of the good. (ii) But our appearance of the good depends on the character we already have. (iii) Hence we are not in control of the appearance. (iv) Hence we are not in control of the character we form. (v) Hence we are not responsible for the formation of our characters. Aristotle denies that (iii) follows from (ii).

[We reply . . . how [the end] appears: This is the first reply to the argument just presented. Aristotle insists that the character forming our appearances is itself malleable and hence the appearance is in our control. In 'if each person . . . ', Aristotle clearly accepts the antecedent of the conditional.

(e) §17. If we are not responsible for acting badly, vice and virtue are equally beyond our control.

Suppose, on the other hand, that no one: Read *ei de mēdeis* (OCT: *ei de mē, oudeis*, 'Otherwise, no one . . . '). According to this reading, Aristotle's second reply to the opponent's argument in §17 points out the unacceptable consequences of denying responsibility for evildoing altogether.

for [, according . . . good nature: This all explains the previous claim that someone who has this sense has a *good* nature; 'given that . . . ' explains the claim that this gift is greatest and finest. In b9 read *ei par'* (OCT: *kai ho par'*).

If all . . . than vice: This is the result that we are forced into if we accept the conclusion that no one is responsible for acting badly; we must take all actions, good or bad, to be the inevitable results of natural conditions that are beyond our control.

(f) §18–20. If the end or the means are in our control, virtue and vice are in our control.

§18 For how the end . . . actions they do: §18 might be taken as a defense of the argument presented in §17. But it is also part of the argument in §19, when Aristotle explains his own position.

§19 Let us . . . depends on him: Aristotle repeats the first reply he offered in §17, affirming that our conception of the end depends on us, and that this is why our character also depends on us.

Alternatively, . . . other things voluntarily: Here Aristotle seems to concede a point to his opponent. He sets aside his first reply, and argues that, nonetheless, virtue may turn out to be voluntary. Even if we are not responsible for the appearance of the end (i.e., if Aristotle's first reply is rejected), we still need not embrace the position whose consequences are expounded at the end of §17. For we can allow that the virtuous and the vicious person share the same conception of the end, for which neither is responsible, and differ in their conception of 'the other things'—presumably, the things promoting the end. Given the wide scope of 'things promoting the end' (see DECISION [2]), differences about these may make the difference between virtue and vice. In offering this reply Aristotle assumes that the 'fixed' conception of the end will be rather schematic (with its specific content to be filled in by deliberation), and not as determinate as it is taken to be at the end of §17.

for the bad . . . the end [appears]: Lit., 'for similarly to the bad person also belongs the because of (*dia*) himself in the actions, even if not in the end'.

§20 Now the virtues, . . . end we lay down: Lit., 'If, then, the virtues . . . ' But Aristotle clearly endorses it; he is reasserting his first reply (in b1–3). Does he mean to claim that everyone, no matter what his nature or upbringing may be, is fairly held responsible for his character? Cf. vii 5, 1149b27–1150a8. In saying that we are jointly responsible, Aristotle acknowledges that we are not the sole causes of our states since nature and upbringing contribute also.

5.§21–23. Summary of the account of virtue of character

§21 We have now discussed . . . up to us and voluntary: This passage summarizes the whole of ii 1 through iii 5, showing again that iii 1–5 is part of the discussion of virtue of character in general. In b28 after *kath'hautas*, insert *kai houtōs . . . prostaxē(i)* from b29–30 (OCT keeps manuscript order).

6

6.§1–6. The scope of bravery

§1 First let us . . . fear and confidence: BRAVERY and temperance are the first two virtues to be discussed because they are the two primary virtues concerned with FEELINGS (1117a24). See Plato, *La.*, *Ch.*, *Rep.* iv, *St.* 306e–end. The structure of bravery is more complex than that of some virtues (for generosity, cf. 1121a16, b17), since it involves the correct training of two feelings, not (as with temperance) of just one. Someone could train himself not to be excessively afraid, and still have no positive confidence or enthusiasm for facing dangers in a good cause. Since confidence also affects someone's readiness to face danger, it must also be trained if someone is to acquire the right attitude toward danger.

§2 frightening: Or 'fearful (*phoberon*). This term covers actual, possible, and appropriate objects of fear; see CHOICEWORTHY.

hence people define . . . bad: See Plato, *Pr.* 358d.

(a) §3–5. Bravery is not about every sort of fear and danger.

§4 for some people . . . losing money: In saying that cowards can be generous, Aristotle seems to challenge his belief in the inseparability of the virtues; see 1144b32, VIRTUE.

§5 on children or women: In a22 read *gunaikas* (OCT: *gunaika*, singular, '. . . is afraid of one's wife or children suffering wanton aggression').

(b) §6–12. Bravery is concerned with the fear of death, and primarily with the fear of death in war.

§8 Surely in the finest . . . finest danger: In his historical circumstances, Aristotle regards death in war as the FINEST way to die. The reason he gives is that here (as opposed to death in a shipwreck) someone has a chance to display his abilities in action; he does not just keep a stiff upper lip. But, probably, Aristotle also assumes that the conditions are fine insofar as it is fine to defend one's city and its common good (contrast the attitude of mercenaries, 1116b5).

7

7.§1–13. Bravery and the corresponding vices

(a) §1. The brave person is not completely free of fear.

§1 too frightening for a human being to resist: Lit., 'beyond a human being'. They involve 'overstraining'; see 1110a25, 1116b16.

(b) §2–5. But he faces dangers with the appropriate confidence on the right occasions.

§2 The brave person . . . aimed at by virtue: The brave person is not expected to be fearless; he will not fear the danger less than it warrants. Nor does he force himself to act despite a strong desire to run away (this would make him analogous to the CONTINENT person; see INCONTINENT). When he has the right degree of fear it does not overcome or paralyze him.

(c) §6. He aims at the fine.

§6 Now to the brave person . . . by its end: The brave person's judgment is correct, given the principle in 1113a29, 1166a12, 1176a15. The argument here assumes also that if a virtue is FINE, the end that defines it (actions in accord with its state of character) is also fine.

(d) §7–9. The vice of excessive confidence and deficient fear: fearlessness

§7 Among those who go . . . have no names: See 1107a34, VIRTUE.

He would be . . . about the Celts: For this view about the northern peoples, cf. *Pol.* 1327b23–7; Plato, *Rep.* 435e.

§8 The rash person . . . pretender to bravery: On boasters, see 1127a20.

§12 Moreover, rash . . . until then: In the mss. (and OCT) this passage comes at the end of §12 after 'the intermediate and right state'. The transposition connects it better with the context.

(e) §10–12. The vice of excessive fear and deficient confidence: cowardice

(f) §13. The brave person's concern with the fine is a crucial differentiating feature.

§13 For shirking burdens is softness . . . is fine: On softness (*malakia*), see 1145a35, 1150b1.

8

8.§1–17. Other conditions are sometimes called bravery, but must be distinguished from genuine bravery.

§1 Bravery, then, . . . also called bravery: Aristotle has explained that bravery demands the proper training of the feelings, and demands the right motives; action must be for the sake of the fine. He now considers the APPEARANCES (see

ETHICS [7]). He explains why commonly accepted types of bravery are not genuine bravery, and why they can easily seem to be.

(a) §1–5. The bravery of citizens

§2 That is how Homer . . . fled from me"': Homer, *Il.* xxii 100 (Hector on Polydamas); viii 148–9 (Diomede on Hector).

§3 for it is caused . . . honor: On SHAME, see also iv 9. These citizen soldiers aim at honor, which is FINE. But they do not aim at the fine, as the virtuous person does. If they aimed at the fine, they would recognize that the action itself is fine whether or not it receives honor. On the inadequacy of HONOR, see 1095b23, 1159a22.

§4 as Hector . . . dogs': Aristotle inaccurately recalls Homer, *Il.* xv 348–51, combining it with ii 391–3 (a sign of his quoting from memory).

§5 Commanders who strike . . . compel them: The juxtaposition of these two examples may be significant. 'Strike . . . ' may refer to the use of whips by Persian commanders at Thermopylae (Herodotus vii 223); Greeks often thought of barbarians as lacking true bravery. The second example, however, may refer to the tactics of Spartan commanders (Anon., *in EN* = CAG xx 165.1–3); since Spartans were conventionally regarded (though not by Plato and Aristotle) as models of bravery, the suggestion that, in this instance, they are no better than barbarians might strike Aristotle's readers as surprising.

(b) §6–9. Experience and expertise

§6 Experience about . . . bravery is scientific knowledge: Aristotle mentions the fact about experience as an explanation of SOCRATES' mistaken conception of bravery. He does not accuse Socrates of identifying bravery with experience. See Plato, *La.* 192e–196d, *Pr.* 349e–351b.

In wartime professional soldiers . . . familiar with these: The 'professional soldiers' ('professional' supplied) are mercenaries. These are not paid volunteers defending their own city for pay, but foreigners hired by a city, and with no further attachment or loyalty to it. (Machiavelli objects to their use in similar terms: see *Prince*, ch. 12.)

§9 Professional . . . danger overstrains them: On overstraining, cf. 1115b8, 1110a25.

For they are the first . . . temple of Hermes: This incident happened near Coronea in Boeotia, in 353 B.C. The mercenaries deserted the Coronean citizens.

(c) §10–12. How spirited people differ from brave people

§10 Spirit is also . . . full of spirit: On spirit (*thumos*), see DESIRE. This passage (cf. 1111b18, 1149a25) makes clear the connection between *thumos* and spirited, self-assertive, and impulsive feelings and actions.

hence Homer's . . . blood boiled: See Homer, *Il.* xi 11; xiv 151; xvi 529; v 470; xv 232, 594; *Od.* xxiv 318–9. The last phrase is not Homeric, but may belong to a lost epic (cf. [Theocritus] xx 15).

§11 hungry asses . . . beaten: Allusion to Homer, *Il.* xi 558–62. The following remark on adulterers suggests that Aristotle would not count Don Giovanni as brave.

§12 The [bravery] caused . . . decision and the goal: In the mss. (and OCT) this sentence comes before §12. This distinction between the natural basis of a virtue and the complete virtue itself is explained further in vi 13.§1–2.

(d) §13–15. How hopeful people differ from brave people

§15 Indeed, that is . . . less from preparation: Aristotle assumes that 'emergencies (lit., 'sudden things', or 'things done on the spur of the moment'; cf. iii 2.§2) are matters for decision. Someone's decision to meet danger forms his STATE of character, so that when a danger arises suddenly he does not need still further deliberation to cause him to act.

For if . . . [we must decide] in accord with our state of character: The Greek has no verb in the last clause; 'decide' seems the only plausible verb to understand. Aristotle implies that the virtuous person's action sometimes results from his decision even if deliberation and decision do not immediately precede it; see 1142b2, 1144b26, 1150b19, DECISION (4).

(e) §16–17. Why ignorance may be mistaken for bravery

§16 That was what happened . . . Sicyonians: This happened in 392 B.C. The Spartans were wearing shields taken from their fleeing Sicyonian allies. When the Argives (together with the mercenaries fighting on their side) realized they were dealing with the more formidable Spartans, they ran (Xenophon, *Hellenica* iv 4.10).

9

9.§1–7. Since the brave person values life, brave action involves pain and loss, though it also involves the pleasure proper to the virtue.

§4 And so, if the same . . . failure is shameful: Aristotle does not mean that the end pursued in bravery really is small, or that the brave person does not take pleasure in it. He means that the end is surrounded by evils that the brave person regrets, and that might lead someone who is not a brave person to overlook the pleasure to be found in brave action.

§6 But presumably . . . best soldiers: This section follows logically on the end of §4. On soldiers, cf. note to 8.§6. Here Aristotle stresses again that the brave person is not unafraid. He is free from paralyzing fear in cases where he sees that it is fine to face dangers, and he sees this only when he thinks some worthwhile cause is at stake. Cf. 1124b6.

10

10.§1–11. The pleasures relevant to temperance

(a) §2. Nonbodily pleasures are not relevant.

(b) §3–7 Not all the pleasures of the senses are relevant.

§5 Nor is this . . . except coincidentally: See *EE* 1231a6.

§6 And we can see . . . if they are hungry: The intemperate person enjoys these things even if he is not hungry.

§7 'a deer . . . goat': Homer, *Il.* iii 24.

(c) §8–11. Only the pleasures of taste and touch—especially those of touch—are relevant.

§8 The pleasures . . . and bestial: Why does Aristotle limit temperance to this narrow range of desires? Probably he thinks that this range indicates desires that develop in relative independence of those he excludes from temperance. We have them as part of the nature we share with other animals (1118b1), apart from our particular social environment or our individual choices and rational preferences. Aristotle rejects the view that there is some common explanation of overindulgence of desires as a whole, and hence he refuses to treat overindulgence as a single vice. Different forms of overindulgence associated with different desires need separate training; a reduction in someone's desire to listen to music will not necessarily reduce his excessive liking for whiskey. Aristotle's view of the scope of a virtue partly rests on such psychological assumptions as these. For similar arguments about incontinence, see vii 4, note to vii 9.§1.

These pleasures are touch and taste: In saying that the pleasures are touch and taste, Aristotle identifies pleasure with the activity enjoyed (as when we say, 'Listening to music is one of my chief pleasures in life').

§10 That is why a glutton . . . touching: According to *EE* 1231a17, *Probl.* 950a3, he was Philoxenus (cf. Aristophanes, *Frogs* 934).

11

11.§1–8. The extreme states and the mean

(a) §1–2. Common versus distinctive appetites

§1 as Homer says, . . . for sex: Homer, *Il.* xxiv 130–1.

(b) §3–5. Errors in relation to different appetites

§3 That is why . . . what is right: The word rendered 'gluttons' might also be rendered 'ravenous about their bellies'.

(c) §6. The excess: intemperance

(d) §7. The deficiency: insensibility

(e) §8. Temperance is the mean state in relation to these appetites and pleasures.

§8 For he finds no pleasure in what . . . anything else at all of that sort: Aristotle stresses a point he stressed about bravery; see 1115b12. The temperate person does not have to restrain or overcome intense, wayward appetites; that is what the CONTINENT person does. His appetites agree with his rational decision about the right extent of indulgence; see 1102b27, 1152a1.

12

12.§1–10. Two further notes on intemperance

(a) §1–4. Intemperance compared with cowardice; aspects of voluntariness and involuntariness in each of these vices

§1 Intemperance is more . . . to be avoided: The different degrees of resemblance to involuntary actions and conditions depend on the extent of pleasure and pain (cf. 1110b11, 1111a32). Cowardice seems more voluntary than cowardly actions because it is less painful; cowardice is a source of pain in particular circumstances. Intemperance, however, is a source of pleasure in particular circumstances, so that particular intemperate actions seem more voluntary than the state of being intemperate.

§3 That is why . . . seem to be forced . . . involuntary]: Here 'seem' reports a common belief that Aristotle presumably rejects, given his own account of force; see note to iii 1.§3.

(b) §5–9. Different, but related, uses of 'intemperance'

§5 We also apply the name . . . some similarity: Aristotle appeals to the relation between 'intemperate' (or 'unrestrained', *akolastos*) and 'temper' (or 'check', *kolazein*; see CORRECTIVE TREATMENT and TEMPERANCE) to make his point about CHILDREN.

§8 And just as the child's . . . follow reason: The 'guide' (*paidagōgos*) was the slave who took a child to school and elsewhere, mentioned by St. Paul in *Galatians* 3:24. Cf. 1121b11.

Book IV

1

1.§1–11. The scope of generosity

(a) §1–2. It is concerned with wealth.

§1 but in the giving and taking . . . giving: 'Take' and 'acquire' both translate *lambanein* and cognates.

(b) §3–5. The vices opposed to generosity involve the misuse of wealth.

§4 These . . . not properly called wasteful: As often (cf. note to iii 10.§8), Aristotle wants to distinguish virtues and vices more sharply than they are commonly distinguished; see GENEROSITY.

(c) §6–11. Generosity involves the correct use of wealth, especially in giving rather than in taking.

§6 Whatever has a use . . . generous person: Generosity is the first of the virtues concerned with external goods (cf. v 1.§9). These goods must be used well if they are to benefit the person who has them; and the different virtues dealing with external goods are the states of character that use them well. The generous person is the one who takes and gives money correctly. Aristotle does not say much about where he takes it from and to whom he gives it; but cf. 1120a5, b3; 1121b5; 1122a10. The answer will come partly from the requirements of justice (1120a20), but even more from the requirements of friendship (cf. ix 2). The FINE goal pursued by the generous person will reflect his desire to benefit friends and fellow citizens. He is not indiscriminately openhanded or charitable.

§7 That is why . . . wrong sources: The next paragraph (§7–11) gives five reasons: (1) 'For it is more proper . . . to (§8) doing something shameful'; (2) 'Moreover, thanks go . . . [to the giver]'; (3) §9 'Besides, not taking . . . is another's'; (4) §10 'Further, . . . praised at all'; (5) §11 'Besides, generous . . . their giving'.

For it is more proper . . . shameful ones: Aristotle does not explain here why a virtue has this active aspect. But see ix 7. The connection that he assumes between RIGHT action (in the previous sentence) and FINE action in this one suggests that we achieve the MEAN (and hence what is right) by finding actions that are fine (and hence promote a common good). Cf. note to 2.§7 below.

1.§12–23. The outlook of the generous person

(a) §12–14. In his giving he aims at the fine and takes pleasure in the action.

§12–13 aim at the fine . . . give correctly . . . with pleasure: These are the three conditions that the virtuous person's characteristically virtuous action must satisfy.

(b) §15–17. His attitude to acquisition is neither grasping nor wasteful.

(c) §18–20. He is unstinting in his giving.

§20 Those who have not acquired . . . parents and poets do: Cf. Plato, *Rep.* 330bc; 1161b18, 1167b34.

(d) §20–23. He is neither concerned to be wealthy nor indiscriminate in his giving.

(e) §24–28. He achieves the mean in the appropriate pleasures and pains.

§25 If the generous . . . right way: Probably Aristotle is not thinking of lapses by the generous person, in which he knowingly refuses to give to a worthy cause, but is thinking of cases in which the generous person's reasonable and praiseworthy giving has an inappropriate result (if, for instance, he gives money to someone who—contrary to reasonable expectation—misuses it). External success in virtuous actions that reach their intended result is part of HAPPINESS.

§27 and is more grieved . . . does not please Simonides: This seems to refer not to any surviving poem of Simonides, but to the poet's reputation for avarice. Cf. *Rhet*. 1391a6–12, 1405b23–8.

1.§29–36. Wastefulness: the vice of excess

(a) §30–32. Wastefulness without ungenerosity

§31 However, such . . . the intermediate condition: Aristotle supports his general view that often one extreme is 'more contrary' to the mean than the other, for the two reasons given in ii 8. This wasteful person has the desirable trait and motive, which need not be cultivated further to produce generosity, while the ungenerous person does not have it at all. Hence (a25) Aristotle notes that this wasteful person does not even seem to be base. This view rests on the degree of benefit or harm done to other people by the vices; see 1121a29, 1123a32. The tendency of a virtue to benefit others is not often stressed by Aristotle, but here he plainly takes it for granted (see FINE [4]).

(b) §33–36. Wastefulness combined with ungenerosity

§33 Most wasteful people, . . . are ungenerous: Someone who is prone to intemperance is also prone to wastefulness and susceptible to flatterers (1127a7). Though Aristotle wanted to distinguish wastefulness from intemperance and from vice in general (1119b31), he is equally concerned to show the connections between different vices.

§34 for they have an urge to give: 'Urge' translates *epithumia*, usually rendered 'appetite' (see DESIRE). Aristotle implies that it is an irrational and indiscriminate desire.

§36 If, then, the wasteful . . . changes into this: On being 'without a guide' (*apaidagōgētos*), cf. note to iii 12.§8.

1.§37–45. Ungenerosity: the vice of deficiency

§37 since old age . . . ungenerous: On the effects of old age, see YOUTH.

(a) §39. Ungenerosity in giving too little

§39 For some people . . . compelled to do anything shameful: This is the sort of compulsion that is present in some voluntary action, as explained in iii 1.§6–9.

Others keep their hands . . . afraid: On this sort of fear, cf. 1115a20. Virtue requires some confidence in one's own ability and in FORTUNE (1178a28). This sort of confidence belongs to magnanimity.

hence, they say, they are content: In b30 read *areskein* (OCT: *areskei*, 'hence, they are content').

(b) §40–43. Ungenerosity in taking too much, or taking from the wrong sources

§40 those, . . . degrading occupations: 'Degrading' renders *aneleutheron*, also translated 'ungenerous'; see GENEROUS.

§43 the gambler and the robber: Delete *kai ho lēstēs* (OCT retains).

(c) §44. Ungenerosity is worse than wastefulness.

2

2.§1–10. Magnificence compared to generosity

(a) §1–3. Magnificence must be on a large scale.

§2 But large scale . . . not the same: Aristotle has in mind the tasks facing someone who has to provide for the expenses of the warship or delegation. These are two *leitourgiai*, 'public services' (1163a29, 1167b12; see OCD, s.v. 'liturgy, Greek'). In Athens these services were imposed on wealthy citizens at their own expense (cf. 1122b22, three services). A public-spirited citizen would be keen to overfulfill his task in a way that would benefit the community (e.g., he might outfit a warship to sail and fight better than the average), and this would be a legitimate source of honor. For someone else, overfulfillment in a pointlessly extravagant way would be an opportunity to display his wealth; he might decorate his ship expensively without making it a better warship (1123a19–27). The opportunities for virtue and temptations to vice offered by *leitourgiai*, and even more generally by benefactions to the public, are Aristotle's concern in the discussion of magnificence (*megaloprepeia*, from 'great' and 'fitting, appropriate').

§3 'gave . . . wanderer': Homer, *Od.* xvii 420.

for the . . . does not imply magnificence: Why is generosity a virtue distinct from magnificence? Is it simply because not all generous people are wealthy enough for large benefactions? This would not be a very good reason for distinguishing two STATES. Probably Aristotle means that if a generous person came into money, his generous desires would not be enough to make him magnificent; for without further practice and habituation he would lack the judgment and tact that are needed for suitable large benefactions. On the connections between the virtues, see vi 13.§6 and note.

(b) §4. The vices of deficiency and excess

(c) §5–9. Magnificence achieves the mean and aims at the fine.

§6 now the magnificent person's expenditures: Read *hai de*. OCT: *hai dē*.

§7 In this . . . the fine; . . . common feature of the virtues: This claim about the general connection between virtuous action and the FINE supports the suggestion (see note to 1.§7) that fine action is necessary for reaching the MEAN proper to the virtues.

(d) §10. Magnificence requires generosity.

§10 For a possession and a result . . . excellence; . . . admirable to behold: 'Result' translates *ergon* (see FUNCTION). 'Excellence' translates *aretē*, usually translated 'virtue'. The point of this paragraph is that the magnificent person has the judgment that produces FINE results on a grand scale.

and the excellence . . . large scale: In b18 delete *megaloprepeia* (OCT keeps).

2.§11–20. The proper sphere of magnificence: honorable expenditure

(a) §11–15. The primary sphere: public expenditure

§11 provoke . . . common good: These expenses that 'provoke a good competition for honor' (*euphilotimēta*) give a proper focus for one's pursuit of HONOR. Aristotle recognizes that this is a reasonable motive when it has the right object; cf. 1169a8. On *philotimia*, love of honor, see iv 4.

In 'common good', 'good' is supplied (as in §15, 1123a5).

(b) §15–20. The secondary sphere: private expenditure

§16 adornment: Cf. 1100b26, 1124a1.

§17 the most magnificent . . . particular kind of object: The translation and supplement assume the manuscript text in a12, without the OCT's supplement *haplōs*.

§18 paltry: This translates *aneleutheron*, usually rendered 'ungenerous'.

2.§20–22. The vices opposed to magnificence

(a) §20. Vulgarity

§20 He gives his club . . . wedding banquet: This is a private dining club in which each member takes his turn in providing dinner for the club. Lavish spending by one member might provoke a pointless competition among the richer members, and would embarrass the poorer members, who could not keep up with the Joneses' dinner parties.

and when he supplies . . . Megara: Purple was an expensive dye in the ancient world. To pay for purple costumes for a chorus would be a pointless display, doing nothing for the choral performance itself; it would be like bringing them on in mink coats.

Where a large . . . small expense is right: Sometimes a large expense may be appropriate but inconspicuous, and here the vulgar person will stint. A warship might look seaworthy, but be unsafe if it meets bad weather. A vulgar person will gamble on the chance of good weather (since people will not notice how much he has spent if they simply look at the outside of the ship), whereas the magnificent person will equip the ship for bad weather.

(b) §21. Stinginess

(c) §22. Conclusion

§22 they do no harm to one's neighbors: This does not seem altogether true;

see the examples considered in notes to §20 above. Aristotle seems entitled to say, at most, that these vices do not involve a positive intent to harm one's neighbors.

3

3.§1–16. *The essential characteristics of magnanimity*

§1 Magnanimity . . . great things: 'Magnanimity' is the traditional Latinized form of *megalopsuchia* (lit., 'having a great soul'), and captures some aspects of it fairly well. The *megalopsuchos* will not be calculating, suspicious, ungenerous, or prone to nurse petty grievances, 1125a3. *Megalopsuchia* is concerned with HONOR in its different aspects: (a) how and for what a person honors and esteems himself; (b) what he expects others to honor him for; (c) which other people he honors and for what; and (d) which other people he wants to honor him.

The magnanimous person takes the right attitude to honor. Aristotle rejects the view of life that aims exclusively and indiscriminately at honor from other people's good opinion (cf. 1095b23, 1159a22–5). But he does not want the virtuous person to ignore honor altogether. It is a genuine good, 1123b20; the virtuous person demands it for himself for his virtue, accords it to others for their virtue, and listens to others when they are qualified to honor him. He does not isolate himself from other people's opinions; nor does he try to make himself agreeable by taking their opinions of him more seriously than they deserve, or by honoring them more than they deserve. Here magnanimity is closely connected with truthfulness; cf. 1124b30, with iv 7.

Aristotle's virtue of magnanimity is often taken to be opposed to the Christian virtue of humility. (Mill, for instance, in *On Liberty*, ch. 3, contrasts 'pagan self-assertion' with 'Christian self-denial'.) But it is not clearly correct to oppose the two virtues. Aristotle certainly opposes lying about one's own merits or other people's, if one acts from a desire to ingratiate oneself with others; but a genuine virtue of humility does not obviously require the actions and attitudes that Aristotle condemns. See, especially Aquinas, *Summa Theologiae* 2–2 q129 a3 ad 4.

(a) §3–13. The virtue and the opposed vices

§3 The magnanimous person, then, seems: In this chapter in particular, Aristotle uses 'seem' (*dokein*) to refer to commonly held beliefs (or APPEARANCES) about the magnanimous person. He does not assume that all these common beliefs identify essential, or even genuine, features of the virtuous person (see note to §34 below). But his account of the virtue tries to explain the various common beliefs; even if he thinks they are false beliefs, he tries to show how, given his account of the virtue, it is intelligible that people hold them (following the principle stated in vii 14.§3).

worthy: Sometimes 'deserving' is an appropriate translation of *axios*. But here 'worthy' is better, since Aristotle is concerned with an objectively valuable quality rather than with the basis of an entitlement. I may deserve and be entitled to unemployment pay because I am out of work, but being out of work is hardly part of my WORTH.

§5 just as beauty . . . not beautiful: On this aesthetic shortcoming of small people, cf. *Poet.* 1450b35.

§7 Someone . . . pusillanimous: 'Pusillanimous' captures the opposition to 'magnanimous' suggested by the Greek. It involves some misuse of the word, given its current English sense, which covers part of what is conveyed by the Greek *mikropsuchia* (lit., 'little-souledness').

§12–13 The pusillanimous . . . for the magnanimous person: These two sections fit better after §8 than in the place where the manuscripts put them, after §11.

§11 And even without argument . . . their worth: Retain *hoi megaloi*, deleted by OCT. Aristotle appeals to common beliefs about greatness. These beliefs suggest that greatness involves honor, even without the argument just given to connect worth and honor.

(b) §14–16. Magnanimity requires outstanding virtue.

§14 For in every case . . . must be good: The magnanimous person demands honor for himself for the right reasons; but what is most worthy of honor is virtue; hence the magnanimous person must be virtuous. Magnanimity will make the virtues greater (1124a2), because his self-esteem and his true perception of the proper basis of this self-esteem will make him want to deserve his own esteem. Since the magnanimous person values virtue above all, he will not be attracted by the rewards of cowardice or injustice, 1123b31; nor will he be shattered by strokes of adverse FORTUNE, 1100b32, 1124a12–20.

Greatness in each . . . magnanimous person: This last sentence of §14 seems to belong with §15. The first part of §14 argues from the fact that the magnanimous person deserves the greatest things to the conclusion that he has great virtue. The end of §14 and §15 argues for the same conclusion, but from common beliefs (see note to §3 above) about the magnanimous person.

§15 Surely: Read *oudamōs g'*. OCT: *oudamōs t'*.

§16 adornment: Cf. 1100b26, 1123a7.

3.§17–34. Further characteristics of the magnanimous person

(a) §17. He has a discriminating attitude to honor.

§17 The magnanimous . . . dishonors: This section (§17–34) deals with commonly recognized features of the magnanimous person that Aristotle takes to be explained by the primary features that he has already discussed.

(b) §18–22. His discriminating attitude to external goods distinguishes him from pretenders to magnanimity.

§18 that is why he seems arrogant: Here is a clear case in which Aristotle does not endorse the view that he reports as what 'seems'.

§19 That is why these . . . for these goods: Here also, in giving an account of common beliefs, Aristotle is careful not to endorse the common view that wealth by itself is appropriately honored. But he agrees that when wealth is honored, the honor makes magnanimous people more magnanimous, since it stimulates them to do more to deserve honor and to show that they deserve it; see note to §14 above.

§21 when they have these other goods: Read *hubristai ta toiauta*. OCT: *hubristai kai hoi ta toiauta*.

§22 For the magnanimous person is justified when he thinks less . . . no good reason: 'Think less' renders *kataphronein*, which may mean 'look down', 'disdain', 'despise'. But it may simply connote (i) a recognition of comparative merit, without (ii) contempt for others. Nonmagnanimous people display (ii), but the magnanimous person displays only (i). For (i), cf. Thucydides ii 62.3–4.

(c) §23. He is discriminating but fearless in his attitude to danger.

§23 He does not face . . . lover of danger: Read *mikrokindunos oude puknokindunos, dia to oliga timan, oude philokindunos.* OCT: *mikrokindunos oude philokindunos, dia to oliga timan*. This attitude to danger is evidence of bravery. The magnanimous person would not be braver if he faced any danger indiscriminately; see 1117b17, 1169a22.

(d) §24–26. He prefers the active over the passive aspects of friendship.

§24 He is the sort . . . to the inferior: He is the benefactor in unequal FRIENDSHIPS. On the proper conduct of these, cf. note to viii 14.§2. For the explanation of his attitude, see 1168a10.

(e) §26–34. His outlook is reflected in his everyday dealings with other people.

§25 Thetis . . . done him: Homer, *Il.* i 504–10.

and the Spartans . . . from them: According to Anon., *in EN* = CAG xx 189.12–18, Aristotle follows the account by his nephew Callisthenes, a historian, of an incident in 369 B.C., when the Spartans asked for Athenian help against Thebes.

§26 displays his greatness: Lit., 'is great'.

ordinary people: Lit., 'intermediate'.

§27 He stays away . . . great and renowned: He seeks honor, for the appropriate sorts of actions, but he is not concerned about competing for honor with others. Cf. ix 8.§5, 7.

§28 Moreover, he must be open . . . frightened person: He is not ready to sacrifice virtue to curry favor with others for his security or profit; nor does he think so much of the penalties of honesty that he is afraid of them.

He is concerned for the truth: In b27, read *melein* (OCT: *amelein*).

And he speaks the truth . . . self-deprecating: He avoids displaying his own greatness in a way that humiliates inferior people, b19. His reason is contrasted with the self-deprecating person's reason, though their behavior may be similar; see 1127b22. A less probable translation would be: 'except for the things he says because of self-deprecation to the many' (which would imply that the magnanimous person sometimes does speak in a self-deprecating way).

§29 He cannot let . . . flatterers: Lit., 'he cannot live in relation to another . . .' Cf. note to x 6.§8; *EE* 1233b36; *Pol.* 1254a8–17; b21, *Met.* 982b25. Having our own ends determined not by our own choices and values, but by the use someone else can make of us, is repugnant to the magnanimous person; it is an aspect of SLAVERY that Aristotle also sees in flattery (see iv 6). The magnanimous person makes an exception for his friend because the best kind of friendship allows virtuous people to share their ends; see 1156b7–24.

§31 except . . . aggression: Lit., 'except because of wanton aggression'. He will respond to WANTON AGGRESSION (cf. 1126a7), but he has no reason to suppose he will commit it himself; it is for those who counterfeit magnanimity, 1124a29. (Less probable translation: 'except to commit wanton aggression on others'.)

§34 The magnanimous . . . hasty movements: Some have supposed that Aristotle is satirizing the magnanimous person here. But the whole account does not suggest this. 'Seems' (see note to §3 above, and APPEARANCE) suggests a popular stereotype. Aristotle is not necessarily fully endorsing it, or insisting that you cannot be magnanimous unless you have a deep voice. He suggests that his account explains why this stereotype is intelligibly associated with magnanimity.

3.§35–38. The vices opposed to magnanimity

(a) §35. Pusillanimity

(b) §36–37. Vanity

§37 Pusillanimity is more opposed . . . worse: On different degrees of opposition to the mean, cf. 1109a5; note to iv 1.§31.

(c) §38. Conclusion

§38 Magnanimity, . . . great honor: The emphasis falls on 'great'. This conclusion of the treatment of magnanimity prepares for the immediately following discussion of the virtue concerned with small honors.

4

4.§1–6. The virtue concerned with small honors

(a) §1. It must be distinguished from magnanimity.

§1 But, as we said in the first discussion, . . . magnificence: Cf. 1107b25.

(b) §2–4. The excess and the deficiency

§2 Just as the taking . . . right way: Recognition of a nameless virtue (see 1107a34) confirms the doctrine of the mean. If we see only a choice between love of honor and indifference to honor, we find ourselves praising both on different occasions. Hence the state that we ought to cultivate cannot be either of them; the reasonable state must be intermediate between them.

§4 Clearly, since . . . every case: Cf. 1118b22.

Since the mean . . . to themselves: This illustrates the importance of identifying a mean in cases where it has no established names (see note to ii 7.§8). In this case the extremes seem to have the field to themselves, because we readily think the only contenders for the virtue are love of honor and indifference to honor, even though, in different contexts, we recognize the errors of each. We do not recognize, until Aristotle points it out, that we need not oscillate uneasily between these two extreme attitudes. See further, 6.§9.

(c) §5–6. The mean state in relation to honor

5

5.§1–15. Mildness

(a) §1–4. The mean state concerned with anger

§1 Mildness is the mean . . . nameless: Mildness is another virtue concerned with FEELINGS, as bravery and temperance were. Like bravery (1116b23), it is concerned with spirit, *thumos* (see DESIRE), especially as displayed in ANGER. But it is discussed at this stage, with the next three virtues, because they all concern ways of getting on with other people. Aristotle is concerned with anger especially insofar as it tends to offend and antagonize others, and with lack of anger insofar as it reflects an unreasonable (and, in a wider sense than Aristotle allows, cowardly) fear of offending others.

§3 if mildness is praised: Less probably, 'since . . . '. Aristotle means that if we are to use 'mild' in a favorable sense, we must take it to indicate the state he describes, not the extreme state of deficient anger.

(b) §5–6. The vice of deficiency

§6 Such willingness . . . slavish: On accepting insults, cf. note to 3.§31 above. On slavishness, cf. note to v 5.§6, SLAVE.

(c) §7–12. The vice of excess and its different forms

§11 penalty and corrective treatment: Read *timōrias kai*. OCT: *timōrias ē*.

§12 1126a30 comes more naturally to human beings: Lit., 'is more human'.

(d) §13–15. The difficulty of finding the mean in relation to anger

§13 but sometimes . . . ruling others: On manliness, see MAN. We incline to think that someone who complains about ill treatment is a properly self-respecting and self-assertive person who will be able to dominate others.

§13 and [we make it] by perception: Read *kai tē(i) aisthēsei* with the mss. Lit., 'the judgment is in particulars and by perception'. OCT emends to *kan tē(i) aisthēsei* ('in perception'). Cf. ii 9.§8.

§14 The intermediate state is praiseworthy: Perhaps 'praised' (*epainetos*) is ambiguous, as *-tos* endings often are; see CHOICEWORTHY.

6

6.§1–9. Friendliness in social intercourse

(a) §1–2. The vices of excess and deficiency

§1 In meeting people, . . . they meet: The sources of the vices opposed to friendliness are very similar to the sources of the vices opposed to mildness. These sources are the excessive concern of the ingratiating person (lit., 'pleaser'), and the excessive indifference of the cantankerous person, to other people's opinions. These attitudes in turn may result from the wrong attitude to honor—the attitude that the magnanimous person avoids. The attitude expressed in irascible and ill-tempered people is a source of indifference to honor that is not considered in iv 3–4.

(b) §3–9. The mean state. The friendly person takes the right attitude to causing pleasure and pain in others.

§5 in not requiring any special feeling: Lit., 'because it is without feeling'. See FRIENDSHIP (6).

for the proper . . . strangers: We do not owe to strangers either the degree of delicacy in sparing feelings, or the degree of frankness in pointing out defects, that would be appropriate between friends. A less probable translation: 'For it is not equally proper to spare the feelings of familiar companions and of strangers, nor equally proper to cause them pain' (i.e., it is more proper to spare the feelings of friends, and less proper to cause pain to friends).

§6 [More exactly], . . . fine and the beneficial: Consideration of what is fine and what is beneficial is prior to consideration of pleasure, and even to consideration of future pleasure against present pleasure, 1127a5. For the three aims of action, see ii 3.§7; viii 2.§1; *Top.* 104b30.

§8 What he will . . . causing pain: 'IN ITSELF' marks the contrast between the action considered without reference to its longer-term consequences and the action with the consequences considered (see next sentence). Cf. the example of throwing cargo overboard, iii 1.§5, where 'without qualification' (see UNQUALIFIED) marks the contrast marked here by 'in itself'.

But he will . . . expedient: Aristotle suggests how the virtuous person will consider PARTICULAR cases (see note to ix 2.§5). He will not be guided by rules that require or forbid actions of certain types without regard to consequences. If he considers the fine and the expedient in general, he will have to consider the action from the point of view of each virtue, supporting the claim in 1144b32. This general method does not prevent Aristotle from being confident in some particular cases; cf. 1107a11.

(c) §9. The vices of excess and deficiency show the wrong attitudes to causing pleasure and pain.

§9 1127a8 with no ulterior purpose: Lit., 'not because of something else'. Cf. 1127a26 (lit., 'not for the sake of something'). It does not follow that the ingratiating person is unselfish. He may still be currying favor with you, but he is not out for your money or political influence, as the flatterer is, but only for your favor. Cf. note to ix 10.§6.

However, the extremes . . . has no name: Cf. 4.§6, note, above. Once again, the lack of a name for the mean condition causes people not to notice that the virtue should be identified with a mean rather than with one of the two extremes.

7

7.§1–17. Truthfulness in social relations

(a) §1–6. In this case also there is a mean state, though it is nameless.

§1 The mean that corresponds to boastfulness: OCT adds *kai eironeias* after *alazoneias*. But the end of the chapter supports the manuscript text.

§2 1127a21 boaster: Cf. 1115b29.

§4 The intermediate . . . belittling: The truthfulness that concerns Aristotle here is not honesty in general, but honesty about oneself. The motives for deviating from it are similar to the motives that cause the extremes about honor, and are related to the sources of the vices in iv 5 and 6. Hence truthfulness is characteristic of the magnanimous person, 1124b27.

(b) §7–9. The mean state: the right attitude toward telling the truth about oneself

(c) §10–13. The vice of excess: boastfulness

§10 1127b11 pointlessly foolish: Lit., 'vain' (*mataios*, also 'futile' in 1094a27).

§11 as a boaster: In b12 read *hōs alazōn* (OCT: *hōs ho alazōn*).

§12 It is not a person's capacity, . . . liar: These different people have the same capacity for exaggeration, but different states of character because they decide to use their capacities in different ways. Cf. 1106a2–10, 1117a4, 1152a13–14; *Met.* 1004b24; *Top.* 165a30; *Rhet.* 1355b17.

§13 a wise diviner or doctor: Read *sophon [ē] iatron* (OCT: *sophon iatron*). Cf. MEDICINE.

(d) §14–17. The vice of deficiency: self-deprecation

§14 The qualities . . . Socrates also used to do: This refers to SOCRATES' frequent disavowal of knowledge about the virtues, which was often regarded as self-deprecation (*eirōneia*; hence 'Socratic irony', Plato, *Rep.* 337a). Aristotle does not say, however, that Socrates had the vice of self-deprecation; if Socrates' disavowals of knowledge were sincere and truthful, no self-deprecation was expressed.

§15 Sometimes, indeed, this even . . . is boastful: The Spartans were ostentatiously austere in their dress, because they wanted to display their indifference to mere comfort.

8

8.§1–12. Wit

(a) §1–3. There is a mean in relaxation and amusements.

§3 Those who go to excess . . . buffoons: The term rendered by 'buffoon' (*bōmolochos*) originally signifies someone who 'hangs around altars (*bōmoi*)' to steal bits of sacrificial meat. Hence the term applies to someone who plays tricks and tells jokes to ingratiate himself with another. Hence his motives are very similar to those of the flatterer or ingratiating person. Similarly, the 'boorish' (lit., 'rustic', as opposed to urbane) people (cf. 1156b13) show the crusty indifference of the ill-tempered people in iv 6. The proper sort of wit is an Aristotelian virtue because it reflects the right attitude to pleasing others; this in turn reflects the right valuation of other people's good opinion of us. See 1156a13, 1158a31, 1176b14.

(b) §4–10. Characteristics of the mean state and of the witty person

§5 Dexterity: This trait has a wider scope than wit; cf. 1171b3.

§6 This can also . . . more seemly: The 'shameful abuse' (Aristotle perhaps means that one ought to be ashamed of abusing someone in such terms), *aischrologia*, characteristic of old comedy, is shameful because it is expressed in obscene language and because it expresses vulgar personal insults. This combination is readily illustrated from the plays of Aristophanes. For Aristotle's attitude, cf. *Pol.* 1336b3–6. The New Comedy of Menander reflects the difference Aristotle describes (though he is probably not using 'new comedy' in any technical sense).

§7 Then should . . . hateful or pleasant: The second definition, referring to what gives pleasure or pain to the hearer, seems more precise than the first. But Aristotle raises a doubt about it in 'Perhaps, though . . . '; he implies that the witty person's jokes may displease some people—either humorless boors or those who prefer buffoons. Hence the first definition is more suitable, since it limits the sorts of people whose reactions are to be considered.

§8 he is prepared to make himself: In a29 read *kan poiein* (OCT: *kai poiein*, 'he makes').

§10 a sort of law to himself: This phrase is used in later moral philosophy to express the essential character of moral agency (see St. Paul, *Romans* 2:16; Butler,

Sermons, ii). Though Aristotle uses it casually and without theoretical emphasis, it conveys an important aspect of the virtuous character. Virtuous people do not need the instructions of external laws, because their own understanding guides their actions correctly.

(c) §10–12. The vices of excess and deficiency

9

9.§1–8. Shame

(a) §1–3. Shame is not a virtue but a feeling appropriate for some people.

§1 It is not appropriate . . . character]: In this chapter 'shame' translates *aidōs*, and 'disgrace' indicates *aischunē* or a cognate; Aristotle's argument, however, seems to depend on the identification of *aidōs* with *aischunē*. See SHAME.

§3 since they live by their feelings: On YOUTH, cf. i 3.§7, iii 12.§6. (A different aspect of living by one's feelings appears in ix 8.§6.)

(b) §4–8. Shame is not appropriate for the virtuous person.

§7 Shame might, . . . to the virtues: The assumed situation that would warrant shame is so far from anything that the virtuous person would do that it is pointless for him to acquire a tendency to be ashamed in that situation. Line 1124b10 is not an exception to Aristotle's claim here, since it is not concerned with base actions.

Aristotle is concerned here with retrospective shame at actions we have done, and, reasonably enough, denies it to the virtuous person. He does not consider the anticipatory shame of 1115a16, where I am properly ashamed when I even think of the possibility of doing a wrong action. He need not be rejecting that type of shame here, since it will apparently be a motive for the virtuous person (though not one of his virtues).

BOOK V

1

1.§1–11. The two types of justice

(a) §1–6. Justice is a state of character, and hence may be studied by reference to its contrary.

§3 We see . . . wish what is just: On Books v–vii and their relation to the *EN* and *EE*, see Introduction (3). We begin with some standard dialectical (see ETHICS [4]) forms of argument. See *Top.* 106a9, 145b34, 147a17. 'Makes us just agents' (lit., 'from which people are doers (*praktikoi*) of just things') probably includes the two components distinguished as DOING JUSTICE and wishing what is just.

That is why . . . an outline: The fact that these are common beliefs gives us a reason to take them as our starting point.

(b) §7–11. The two types of justice—general and special justice—are clear from their contraries.

§7 Now it would . . . 'keys' homonymously): Aristotle distinguishes two types of HOMONYMY. (1) Some homonyms are 'distant', and have only the name in common, as in the example of 'key'. (The collarbone is called 'key' (*kleis*) in Greek.) Probably this is what Aristotle has in mind in 'homonyms resulting from chance' 1096b27. (2) Some are connected, and have more than the name in common; they also have connected definitions. Aristotle argues that the different types of justice are homonyms of the second type; indeed, the connection between their definitions is close enough to mislead us into denying that they are homonyms.

§8 overreaching and unfair: On fairness (*ison*, *isotēs*), see EQUAL.

§9 goods—not with . . . not always good: These are external goods dependent on FORTUNE; see 1098b12, 1099a31, 1153b24; *EE* 1248b38. In 'without qualification'(*haplōs*—see UNQUALIFIED), Aristotle means that it is true to say 'wealth is good for a human being', without any condition, qualification, or reservation. But this is true only in the sense that a human being can use wealth well, and if he uses it well, it will promote his happiness. Even though wealth is good for a human being, speaking without qualification, it may still be bad for this or that particular vicious human being (we now no longer speak without qualification) who uses his wealth to make himself more intemperate and less happy. Only the good person will use these goods of fortune so that they are reliably good for him. (Hence these types of unqualified goods are different from those mentioned in 1113a23, 1155b24, 1157b27.)

Aristotle should have mentioned an important point about these goods of fortune. They are in limited supply, and therefore matters of competition (1168b19; *EE* 1248b28). In many cases, one person gets more of them by depriving someone else of them. Hence the person who overreaches is unfair because he profits by another's inappropriate and undeserved loss. See note to ix 6.§3.

1.§12–20. General justice

(a) §12–14. It is concerned with the observance of law, which prescribes actions appropriate to all the virtues.

§12 Since, as we saw, . . . each of them is just: Aristotle does not say here that every system of positive law is just. *Nomimon* is ambiguous between 'legal' and 'lawful' (see CHOICEWORTHY for this sort of ambiguity); but the reference to 'legislative science' ('science' supplied) shows that Aristotle is thinking of the correct laws, not of every sort of positive law, as defining general justice. Cf. 1130b22.

§13 In every matter . . . some other such basis: Or: 'Now the laws deal with every matter, aiming either . . . .' Aristotle refers to his division between correct and deviant political systems, described further in viii 10. 'Some other such basis' refers to the different bases on which different ruling groups rest their position. In b16, read *pasin ē tois kuriois ē kat'aretēn ē* . . . (OCT: *pasin ē tois aristoisē tois kuriois ē* . . .).

And so in one way . . . political community: On the parts of happiness, cf. *EE* 1214b27; *Rhet.* 1360b19; *MM* 1184a26. For this account of justice, cf. *Pol.* 1283a38.

(b) §15–20. And so general justice requires complete virtue of character.

§15 And that is why . . . summed up': Here and in §16–17 'that is why' cites a common belief that is explained by Aristotle's account of justice. Here he quotes Euripides' lost play *Melanippe* (TGF fr. 486) and Theognis 147 (which continues, 'and every man, being just, is good').

complete exercise of complete virtue: Read *tēs teleias aretēs teleia chrēsis estin.* (OCT omits *teleia.*)

§16 That is why Bias . . . a community: Bias (sixth century B.C.) was one of the Seven Sages (on whom, see DK 10; OCD s.v.). This remark does not seem to be attributed to Bias elsewhere.

§17 That is also why . . . of the community: Aristotle alludes to Thrasymachus' claim in Plato, *Rep.* 343c, that justice is good for other people, but harmful to the just person himself (cf. 1134b5). Aristotle accepts the first part of Thrasymachus' claim, but not the second part (though he does not argue against it here).

§18 The worst . . . toward others]: Cf. 1160a5.

And the best . . . difficult task: On virtue and difficulty, cf. 1102b32. In a7 read *all' ho* (OCT: *alla*).

§20 For virtue . . . to be justice: This is a standard way (cf. 1102a30, 1141b24; *DA* 427a2) of indicating that two distinct DEFINITIONS are satisfied by one thing because of its different properties. Because virtue as a whole benefits others in the ways described, it can properly be called justice.

2

2.§1–13. Special justice contrasted with general

(a) §1–6. Special injustice is a specific vice, not vice in general.

§2 But when someone . . . with injustice: Aristotle has a good case for recognizing a specific vice of injustice, distinct from the other virtues. If I wrongly avoid military service because I am afraid of the dangers, I am moved by cowardice. If I avoid it because I am willing to take advantage unfairly of others who accept military service and defend me, I need not be moved by cowardice. I am moved by a motive that seems close to overreaching (since that includes unfair avoidance of harm, 1129b7). Should we not count this as injustice in a more specific sense than Aristotle's general sense?

If so, does Aristotle adequately capture the specifically unjust character of this action? He seems to restrict special injustice too narrowly when he refers it to the desire for gain (unless our case of avoiding military service could be covered by a wide use of 'gain'; cf. 1130b1). Nor is 'gain' sufficient for injustice. Aristotle wants to say that the unjust person wants gain that is unfair, at the expense of what is justly due to another. His definition does not fully capture that aspect of special injustice.

§6 It is evident, . . . excellent person: The order is chiastic. Aristotle claims (a) special injustice is distinct from general, but (b) the two types of injustice have definitions in the same genus. In his support he mentions (b) the definition that refers to another, and (a) the different concerns of each type of injustice. In describing the concerns of special injustice, Aristotle gives examples, and adds '(or whatever single name . . .)'. The name he suggests later is 'profit'; see note to 4.§5 below.

(b) §7–9. Special justice, as opposed to general, is especially concerned with fairness.

§8 The unjust . . . the fair: Aristotle reintroduces his earlier distinction between lawfulness and fairness, to explain the differences between different types of injustice. He argues from contraries, in the way described in 1129a17. His overall argument is this: (1) 1129a26–b11: Justice and injustice are homonymous because one type of each is connected with lawfulness, and the other type with fairness. (2) 1129b11–1130a13: The type connected with lawfulness is the whole of virtue. (3) 1130a14–32: The type of injustice connected with overreaching is a part of vice. (4) 1130a32–b7: Hence the special justice that avoids overreaching is a part of virtue.

(c) §10–11. We need not discuss general justice in detail.

§10 Let us, then, set aside . . . to another: We need not here take on the task of subdividing general justice. Its subdivisions are those of virtue as a whole, i.e., the particular virtues that have been described in Books iii–iv.

And it is evident . . . this type of justice and injustice: Aristotle argues that the general justice prescribed by law is virtue and vice as a whole. He gives two reasons. (a) In the sentence 'For most lawful . . . each vice', he maintains that the laws prescribe actions that are the characteristic expression of virtues. (b) In the sentence, 'Moreover, the actions . . . common good', he remarks that the laws prescribe actions that characteristically produce the virtues.

For most . . . virtue as a whole: Read *prattomena* (OCT: *prostattomena*). On 'lawful', see note to 1.§12 above. Since Aristotle thinks positive law is fallible in its moral prescriptions, he emphasizes that not every good citizen (i.e., a citizen matching the ideal of a given system of positive law) is a genuinely good man.

for the law . . . each vice: The broad scope of 'in accord with' (*kata*) makes it hard to say whether, in Aristotle's view, laws prescribe being virtuous or simply action in conformity to virtue.

§11 We must wait . . . good citizen: This sentence is a parenthetical promissory note, prompted by the mention of moral education. The question about EDUCATION is considered again in x 9 (but not in the surviving parts of the *EE*; see Introduction [2]) and in *Pol.* vii. On the distinction between the virtues of a man and of a citizen, see *Pol.* iii 4.

(d) §12–13. But we need a detailed description of special justice.

3

3.§1–17. Justice in distribution

(a) §1–5. Justice requires equality.

§1 Since the unjust . . . unfair [extremes]: Aristotle's word, *ison*, is translated 'fair' or 'equal' or 'fair and equal' as seems appropriate. Here he moves from fairness, which is characteristic of all types of special justice, to the different types of equality that embody that fairness in different types of special justice.

(b) §6–7. Equality involves treatment proportionate to worth.

§7 For all agree . . . virtue: Different political systems agree on the importance of distributive justice and equality, and all insist that distribution should be equal to WORTH (cf. 1123b2). But they differ on what counts as the sort of worth relevant in just distributions of powers and offices. (Greek cities normally regard public offices as rewards and advantages; they are sources of honor, and usually also of profit without any necessary dishonesty.) Cf. *Pol.* iii 9.

(c) §8–17. Hence justice requires proportionate treatment.

§8 For proportion . . . [abstract] units: Aristotle contrasts (a) 'The number 3 is the successor of 2' with (b) 'There is a large number of people in the room'. In (b) the number consists of people, not of abstract units as in (a). Cf. *Phys*. 219b5, 224a2.

§9 If, for instance, . . . will be four: If line A is 3 inches, line B 6 inches and line C 12 inches, the proportion of A to B is the same as that of B to C.

4

4.§1–14. Justice in rectification

(a) §1–3. It is different from justice in distribution, since it involves numerical equality.

(b) §4–7. Judges seek to rectify by reaching a mean between gain and loss.

§4 And so the judge . . . unequal: In Athens, and in some other Greek cities, the 'judges' are the members of large popular juries, whose president is not a trained or authoritative legal official. Here Aristotle is not discussing their punitive function, but only one sort of injustice that they have to correct.

and the judge tries to restore the [profit and] loss to a position of equality . . . profit: Or 'tries to restore equality by inflicting a loss . . . profit'. Rectification and adjustment are appropriate even in cases where no definite sum of profit and loss can be identified, as it can be in financial transactions. 'Profit' has to be taken in the wide sense that was suggested in 2.§6. It is used as the single name that Aristotle suggests would be useful. Aristotle explains and defends the broad use of 'profit' in §13–14.

§7 a sort of . . . just: Lit., 'a just ensouled'.

(c) §8–12. How numerical equality is restored

§8 The judge restores . . . smaller part [CB]: Aristotle is thinking of a single line like this:

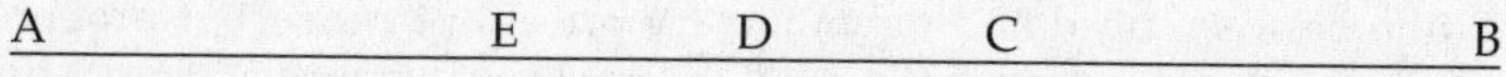

A E D C B

On this line AD = DB and ED = DC. In a32, 'For when . . . to the other', Aristotle assumes that the offender begins with AD, the victim with BD, and the offender takes DC off the victim, adding DC to AD (AD = BD); then 'the one part (AC) exceeds the other (CB) by the two parts (ED and DC)'. Restoration of equality requires us not only to take DC from the offender (who then still exceeds the victim by ED; 'for it a part . . . by just one part'), but also to restore DC to the victim (who would otherwise fall short of BD by DC; 'Hence the larger . . . one part').

§12 Let lines AA', . . . exceeds BB' by CD: This illustration involves these lines:

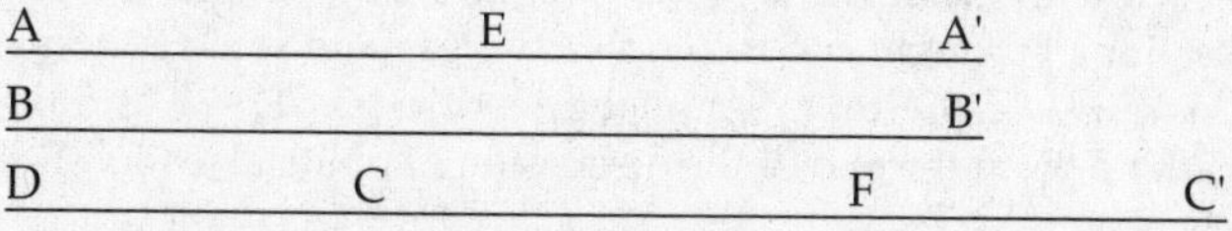

A E A'

B B'

D C F C'

Here CF = AE. This differs from the previous illustration in that we need not assume that DC = CF (and hence DC = AE), i.e., we need not assume that the offender gains exactly what the victim loses.

At the end of §12 the mss. add a sentence that also occurs as the first sentence of 5.§9. The translation (following OCT) deletes it here.

(d) §13–14. A note on 'profit' and 'loss'

§13–14 These names 'loss' . . . [the transaction]: §13–14 return to the general use of 'loss' and 'profit' that was introduced in §5–6.

5

5.§1–16. Justice in exchange

(a) §1–9. It requires proportionate, not simple, reciprocity.

§3 though people take even Rhadamanthys' . . . justice would be done': Rhadamanthys judged people in Hades after their death; cf. Plato, *Gorg.* 523e. Aristotle quotes an otherwise unknown passage of Hesiod (fr. 286; the previous line is 'If someone sows bad things, he will reap bad gains').

§6 since otherwise . . . slavery: Failure to retaliate shows lack of concern (thought to be characteristic of a SLAVE) for one's own status and worth; cf. note to iv 5.§6.

§7 Indeed, that is why . . . being gracious again: As usual, 'that is why' introduces a familiar belief or practice that Aristotle's theory explains. 'Grace' (*charis*) includes grace, gratitude, thanks, and favor; see CULTIVATED.

§9 For no community . . . must be equalized: A COMMUNITY requires members who are dissimilar enough to gain from it; see *Pol.* 1261b22–34.

(b) §10–16. Money secures proportionate reciprocity in exchange.

§10 equal to a house: In a23–4 delete *ē trophēn* ('or food'; OCT keeps).

§11 In reality, this measure is need, . . . same exchange: Cf. Plato, *Rep.* 369b–d. Currency (see LAW) is a 'pledge' of need to the extent that my need for a bed is a reason to pay you money for it. Aristotle does not go into much detail about the correlation between need and the monetary price. But the sort of proportion described in 1133a32 suggests that A and C achieve equality when the price that A pays for the shoes corresponds to his need for them. Need should not be identified with demand; A's need for C's shoes does not change even though C may increase demand for his shoes by restricting production or buying out his competitors. On exchange, cf. 1163b32.

§12 However, they must be introduced . . . produced in them: On the right way to fix price and value, cf. 1164b20.

5.§17–19. The connection between justice and the doctrine of the mean

§17 We have now . . . having too little: Aristotle summarizes his account of justice, and connects it with the doctrine of the mean. Here and in the next several sections, the connection of thought is not completely clear, and some editors have proposed transpositions of the text. Some suggest that 5.§17–19 and 6.§1–2 should be placed after 6.§5, at the end of the discussion of political justice. But see note on 6.§3.

Justice is a mean, . . . about the extremes: Justice 'is about (lit., 'is of') an intermediate condition', because the intermediate condition relevant to justice is determined by the way in which just actions and states of affairs are intermediate and

EQUAL—between suffering undue harm for another's benefit and gaining undue benefit by another's harm. In the case of the other virtues, the property of being intermediate belongs to the state of the virtuous person, not to the corresponding ACTIVITIES. In the case of justice, this property belongs to the activities. In pointing out this difference, Aristotle does not deny that the state of character which is justice is a mean in the ordinary sense, between grabbing benefits at other people's expense (DOING INJUSTICE) and acquiescence in suffering harm from reluctance to assert one's claim against another (suffering injustice); cf. 1138a28.

6

6.§1–2. Unjust action must be distinguished from unjust character.

§1 Since it is possible . . . or brigand, for instance: This passage introduces the question about unjust actions and being unjust that is discussed more fully in ch. 8. See 1136a2.

6.§3–9. Political justice

(a) §3–4. Conditions for political justice: freedom and equality

§3 Now we have . . . to the just: This discussion of political justice does not seem to be closely connected with either of the previous two sections (5.§17–19 and 6.§1–2). The lack of connection makes rearrangement of the ms. text attractive. Two points, however, support the order in the mss. (1) 6.§4 alludes to the distinction introduced in 6.§1–2. (2) 'Previously' in §3 suggests that the discussion of reciprocity has not immediately preceded.

§4 the just without qualification: See 1129b2.

This belongs . . . numerically equal: At the beginning of his general remarks on justice in political society (in a *polis*; see POLITICAL), Aristotle distinguishes this type of justice from the types found in other COMMUNITIES (cf. viii 9–11). For the account of the *polis*, see *Pol.* 1252b27, 1278b15, 1280b40.

Where there is . . . also be injustice: The distinction between doing injustice and injustice itself (i.e., being unjust) has been drawn in ii 4 and in §1–2 above. It is explained more fully in ch. 8 below.

(b) §5–7. Political justice requires the rule of law, to prevent injustice by rulers.

§5 That is why . . . to be ruler: The character of unjust explains the common practice (indicated by 'That is why . . . ') of distrusting unchecked political power vested in a single ruler. Aristotle connects the rule of LAW with the impersonal and impartial rule of reason (which will be correct reason when the law is correct); cf. *Pol.* 1287a18–32.

§6 That is why . . . another person's good: On this common belief, cf. note to v 1.§17.

§7 The people . . . tyrants: On tyrants, see viii 10.§2; *Pol.* 1266b38–1267a17.

(c) §8–9. Relations within a family do not raise questions of political justice, but they raise analogous questions.

§8 For there is no unqualified injustice . . . part of oneself: These cases allow only a derivative sort of injustice, partially resembling the injustice that is properly so called. On parts of oneself, cf. 1161b18.

§9 Hence there is no injustice in relation to them: In b13 read *auta* (OCT: *hauton*, 'himself').

For we found . . . equality in ruling and being ruled: This equality includes an equal right to rule and be ruled. Aristotle takes this to be characteristic of free citizens; *Pol.* 1283b14.

[Approximation . . . relations with a wife . . . as just: On justice between husband and wife, cf. 1162a16, WOMAN.

7

7.§1–5. Justice by nature and by law

(a) §1–2. The diversity of laws persuades some people that there is no such thing as natural justice.

§1 (for instance, . . . Brasidas): Brasidas was a Spartan general (see Thucydides v 11) who after his death received sacrifices in Amphipolis as a liberator; his cult is introduced as an example of a strictly local observance initiated by DECREE. (See OCD, s.v. 'Hero-cult'.) Amphipolis was close to Stagira, Aristotle's birthplace; that may be why the example occurs to Aristotle here.

(b) §3–5. Natural justice, however, allows some variation in different circumstances; hence the existence of variation does not count against the existence of natural justice.

§3 though presumably . . . the gods: What is natural for them is also invariable.

§4 Then what sort of thing, . . . become ambidextrous: Aristotle returns to the question about LAW and NATURE that was raised at 1094b16 (cf. *Top.* 173a7, PROTAGORAS), and answers it more confidently than clearly by the comparison with the right hand; cf. *PA* 666b35, 671b28, 672a24, 684a25; *MM* 1194b30. Natural facts about a human being make it easier and more beneficial, Aristotle thinks, to use the right hand more than the left, though it is possible to disregard this natural advantage and to use both hands equally. Analogously, human communities can survive under many sorts of laws and conceptions of justice, but it remains true that human nature and the human good make one conception of justice the correct one.

In b33, read *homoiōs? dēlon de kai epi tōn allōn kai ho* (OCT: *homoiōs, dēlon. kai epi tōn allōn ho*).

§5 Similarly, . . . since political systems also differ: The 'since' expresses Aristotle's view that the content of law both should, and characteristically does, reflect the character of the political system; *Pol.* 1289a11–25.

Still, only one . . . best everywhere: Aristotle describes the best political system in *Pol.* vii. In saying that it is the best everywhere, he does not mean that every city should try to achieve it.

7.§6–7. Just actions may be understood as universals and as particulars.

§6 Each [type . . . is universal: §6–7 are a note that has no obvious connection with the preceding discussion of political justice. It introduces the discussion of voluntary and involuntary that follows in ch. 8. Aristotle contrasts action types ('universals', such as killing an innocent victim) and determinate action tokens ('particulars', such as Smith's killing the innocent victim Jones yesterday). He insists, as he insisted in iii 1.§6, that what is voluntary or involuntary is a determinate action token.

§7 when this has . . . of injustice: What has been done is a particular action token, which can be considered as voluntary or involuntary. 'Before it is done', the properties of the universal action type define a possible act of injustice.

8

8.§1–5. Just actions, justice, and the voluntary

(a) §1–2. Acts of injustice must be voluntary.

§1 Given this account . . . just or unjust: This chapter repeats some of the distinctions drawn in iii 1, now in a specifically juridical context (cf. 1109b34). Cf. also *EE* ii 6–10, esp. 9.

(b) §3. Voluntary action must be up to the agent and must rest on the appropriate knowledge.

§3 As I said . . . for what goal): Lit., 'I call voluntary, as had also been said before, whatever among the things up to him someone does knowing and not being ignorant either of whom or by what or for the sake of what (e.g. . . .)'. 'Up to the agent' does not occur in the definition of the voluntary in iii 1 (but cf. *EE* 1225b7–11), where Aristotle seems to take it to be equivalent to the other conditions that he specifies.

and [does] . . . force: Less probably, 'and [knows] . . . ' If Aristotle refers to coincidental knowledge, he presumably explains it in b28–31. He explains doing something coincidentally in 1135b2–8.

But . . . know he is your father: The supplement assumes that in 'But . . . ' (*de*, answering *men* in a23) Aristotle points out that the list in a25 is not discriminating enough. For I could know one thing about my victim and be ignorant of something else; what I have done voluntarily to him depends on what I knew about him.

For we also . . . or involuntary: This sentence explains why 'up to the agent' is needed in the definition of voluntary. These natural processes that are neither voluntary nor involuntary were not explicitly considered in iii 1. But they are not necessarily counterexamples to the account in iii 1. If Aristotle means beliefs and desires to be the PRINCIPLE of voluntary action, these natural processes do not count as voluntary. See note to iii 1.§20.

(c) §4. Coincidentally just and unjust actions

§4 Both unjust . . . except coincidentally: I do an unjust action COINCIDENTALLY if (i) the action is in fact unjust, and (ii) its being unjust does not explain my doing it; it is no part of my reason (cf. 1138b3; *Met.* 1025a25, 1027a1). If I do an unjust action because of ignorance (i.e., I break my promise without realizing I am doing it), it is easy to see why Aristotle thinks it is only doing injustice coincidentally. But suppose I know it is unjust and either (a) I don't care but I do it for some other reason, or (b) I do care but still do it because I am threatened with death if I don't do it. Aristotle seems to think that (b) counts as doing injustice coincidentally; but what about (a)? And is the account of (b) consistent with 1110a4–b9? Cf. *EE* 1225a3–33. For coincidences, cf. 1154b17, 1157a35.

(d) §5. Voluntary action versus action on decision

8.§6–12. Different ways of violating justice

(a) §6–7. Errors result in involuntary actions.

§7 If, then, the infliction . . . it is outside: Misfortunes and errors are two subclasses of the class of errors introduced in §6; §7 uses 'error' for a species rather than for the genus.

(b) §8–12. Only the wrong decision makes an agent unjust. This distinction explains why we pardon some unjust actions, but not others.

§8 But when his decision . . . unjust and vicious: This is the third of the three types of harm mentioned in §6.

§9 That is why . . . provoked him to anger: The distinction between doing injustice and being unjust (i.e., having an unjust decision) explains the common practice of treating actions resulting from spirit (see DESIRE; here Aristotle has anger especially in mind) differently from those resulting from decision.

§10 Rather [in cases . . . is unjust]: Aristotle is contrasting disputes involving acts of injustice and anger with disputes involving unjust DECISION and character. To illustrate the second kind of case he mentions deliberate and premeditated fraudulent transactions.

§11 and this . . . agent unjust: This is the answer to the question raised in 6.§1.

§12 For if someone's error . . . not to be pardoned: For 'in ignorance' and 'caused by ignorance', cf. iii 1.§14–15. Here Aristotle distinguishes actions done in ignorance and caused by a vice or a human feeling from those caused by a feeling that is neither natural nor human; cf. 1148b15–1149a10, 1149b4, 1149b27–1150a1. We can see why people are not blamed for such states (cf. 1113b21–1114a3), but why should they not be pardoned for acting on them? Perhaps Aristotle means that an agent moved by these states will not respond suitably to pardon as an ordinary rational agent would.

9

9.§1–17. Puzzles about justice and injustice

(a) §1–3. Can someone suffer injustice voluntarily?

§1 First of all, . . . both unwilling: Aristotle quotes from Euripides' *Alcmaeon* (TGF fr. 68), already cited at iii 1.§8. He quotes an exchange between two speakers, the first of whom is Alcmaeon.

(b) §4–8. The incontinent person may seem to suffer injustice voluntarily, but in fact he does not.

§6 If so, someone is harmed . . . excellent] to do: The argument is odd. For it seems that on Aristotle's own account the incontinent suffers harm (e.g., if he ruins his health by overindulgence, knowing he should not) against his wish (his rational DESIRE); hence he seems to satisfy the conditions for suffering injustice. Aristotle replies that the incontinent person does not wish to suffer injustice; but this reply seems inadequate, since he does not normally take wishing to be necessary for voluntariness (though cf. 1169a1).

§7 as Homer . . . cows' worth: Homer, *Il.* vi 236.

(c) §8–13. Is it possible to do injustice to oneself?

§9 he overreaches for some other good: Speaking of OVERREACHING for what is fine without qualification (see UNQUALIFIED) is an oxymoron, since such a desire does not match Aristotle's account of overreaching and is not vicious at all; cf. note to ix 8.§5. 'Overreach'(*pleonektein*) is closely related to 'having more' (*pleon echein*); cf. Plato, *Rep*. 349b.

(d) §14–16. Being just requires more than simply doing just actions.

§14 People think . . . and not up to us: This section does not seem closely connected with what has preceded, except that it returns to the distinction between doing justice and being just that was set out in ch. 8 and in ii 4. In saying that it is not up to us to be in a certain state when we act, Aristotle does not deny that it is up to us to form a state of character. He just means that we cannot choose to act, here and now, from a state of character that we have not yet formed in ourselves. Cf. iii 5.§13–14 and notes.

In §14–16 Aristotle refers to two features that distinguish the virtuous person from someone who simply does virtuous actions. (1) He responds flexibly to particular situations, more accurately than someone who just has true beliefs about actions that are virtuous. (2) He does the right actions from the right STATE and motive. Aristotle thinks (2) explains (1) because the right state includes PRUDENCE, which responds flexibly and correctly to particular situations; cf. 1114b14, 1180b20.

§16 For the same reason . . . able to do each of the actions: This puzzle concerns the difference between CRAFT (a CAPACITY) and VIRTUE (a STATE). Cf. note to vi 5.§7.

(e) §17. The scope of justice explains some of the difficulties and disputes.

§17 Just things . . . deficiency of them: This section also appears to be rather loosely connected with its surroundings. Aristotle suggests that we can understand some of the questions that arise about justice if we keep in mind the fact that it involves external goods. Since they can be misused, some judgment is needed about their proper use and appropriate distribution; and this is why the disputes characteristic of justice arise.

and this . . . something human: Justice is suitable for normal human beings, not for gods.

10

10.§1–8. Puzzles about decency and justice

(a) §1. Decency appears to conflict with justice.

§1 The next task . . . to the just: This discussion of DECENCY may be out of place; ch. 11 resumes the topics of ch. 9, and ch. 10 seems to interrupt the sequence. It is relevant, however, to 9.§14–16; for decency about particular cases will be part of the just person's character, and sensitivity to the relevant considerations will be expected of the just person.

we transfer . . . instead of 'good': See HOMONYMY. As the *EN* itself often makes clear, it is common to use 'decent' to refer, by meiosis, to goodness in general.

or what is decent is not excellent: In b4–5 delete *ou dikaion* (OCT keeps; 'or what is decent is not just').

(b) §2–7. Decency does not really conflict with justice, correctly understood.

§4 since that . . . bound to be like: On the subject matter of ethics, cf. 1094b12, 1098a28.

§6 That is why . . . makes it deficient: In his usual way Aristotle tries to remove the puzzles raised by common views of decency, and to show why the beliefs causing the puzzles are true up to a point (see ETHICS [7]), and how his account explains them (marked by 'That is why . . . '). If we confine justice too strictly to law-observance (cf. 1129b11), justice and decency appear to conflict, to the disadvantage of justice. Aristotle's own view of justice, however (1129b17), shows that it is what the law aims at, not necessarily what it achieves; hence justice and decency need not conflict.

§7 as the lead . . . the stone: Probably Aristotle refers to a flexible lead ruler that could be made to fit the shape of an irregular stone, and hence could be used to find a second stone to fit next to the first in a dry stone wall. For this purpose, having a rigid ruler would be useless for building. The point is that the rule or standard should be adaptable to fit the specific circumstances.

(c) §8. Definition of decency

11

11.§1–6. Puzzles about injustice to oneself

(a) §1–3. General injustice

§1 Is it possible . . . been said: Here we return to the questions discussed in ch. 9.

we are legally . . . kill ourselves: In a6 read *ouk ea(i)* ('does not allow') (OCT: *ou keleuei*, 'does not command'). In a7 delete *ha de mē keleuei, apagoreuei* (retained by OCT; 'and what it does not command, it forbids').

§3 That is why . . . does injustice to the city: The specific form of 'dishonor' (*atimia*) that Aristotle has in mind is the loss of the status of a free citizen (see Aeschines, *in Ctesiphontem* 244), and hence the withdrawal of civil rights.

(b) §4–6. Special injustice

11.§7–8. Is it worse to do injustice or to suffer it?

§7 It is also evident . . . intermediate amount are bad]: The account of doing and suffering injustice reflects Aristotle's application of the doctrine of the mean. Cf. 1133b33.

But doing injustice . . . state of] injustice): Aristotle reverts to the distinction drawn in ch. 8.

11.§9. Can there be justice and injustice within a single person?

§9 For in these discussions . . . for ruler and ruled: Cf. 1166b19; Plato, *Rep.* 442d–444e. In b11, 'against one's own desires', read *heautou* (OCT: *heautōn*; 'their own desires').

Book VI

1

1.§1–7. A full account of virtue of character requires an account of the virtues of thought.

(a) §1–3. To explain the definition of virtue as a mean involving the correct reason, we must give an account of the correct reason.

§1 Since we have . . . determine what it says: The general formula in the account of the virtues needs to be made more precise; cf. 1103b21, *EE* 1220a13–29, 1222b5–9, 1249a22–b7. In 1107a1 Aristotle has already suggested that some reference to PRUDENCE will be needed to explain what the correct reason (see REASON [2]) is and what it aims at. Here the search for an account of the correct reason leads naturally into a discussion of the virtues of thought (1103a3), which includes prudence. This discussion is begun in 1138b35.

§2 true, but it is not at all clear: This formula is characteristic of the *EE*; see 1216b32, 1220a16.

§3 that is to say: Lit., 'and'.

(b) §4–7. An account of the correct reason requires an account of the virtues of the rational parts of the soul.

§5 Previously, . . . one nonrational: Aristotle returns to the division of the soul that he introduced in i 7 and i 13.

Now we should . . . being otherwise: Aristotle distinguishes the part of the soul concerned with SCIENCE from the part concerned with nonscientific rational calculation about non-NECESSARY states of affairs. In fact not all of these states of affairs are matters of rational calculation and deliberation, as 1112a26–b9 makes clear.

In a8 read *ta hōn endechontai* (OCT: *ta endechomena*; 'beings that admit of being otherwise').

§7 the best state: This is how the *EE* introduces the discussion of virtue; see 1218b38.

Now a thing's virtue . . . function of each part]: Aristotle still keeps the argument of i 7 (or *EE* ii 1, the corresponding passage) in mind, and returns to the connection between virtue and FUNCTION, as he did in the account of virtue of character (1106a15). The supplement tries to make it clear that this sentence introduces the argument of ch. 2 (and hence it is a bit misleading to mark a chapter break here).

2

2.§1–6. Virtue of character requires correct decision, and therefore requires both correct thought and correct desire.

(a) §1–3. The role of thought in action

§1 sense perception, understanding, desire: In this chapter Aristotle seems not to distinguish UNDERSTANDING (*nous*) from THOUGHT (*dianoia*) and REASON (*logos*). Contrast 6.§1–2, 11.§5.

§2 Of these . . . no share in action: Here and in the rest of the chapter, 'action' is used in a restricted sense, confined to rational action on a DECISION. See ACTION (2). This narrow use of 'action' is typical of the *EE*.

§3 for truth . . . correct desire: Aristotle explains why practical thought must be concerned with truth.

(b) §4–5. The relation of thought and desire in a correct decision

§4 The principle . . . decision: The inquiry into correct reason leads into a discussion of the right decision. We need virtue of thought to find the true reasoning, and we need the right sort of character if we are to follow true reasoning in our actions. Aristotle does not say that a virtue of character is separable from true reasoning. His point is that the character must agree with true reasoning if we are to have a genuine virtue of character. The rest of Book vi looks for the true reasoning that is needed.

In 'the source of motion, not the goal' (lit., 'that from which the motion [is] but not that for the sake of which (*hou heneka*) [the motion is]'), Aristotle refers to the efficient and final CAUSES. 'Goal' translates both *telos* and *hou heneka*.

the principle of decision . . . goal-directed reason: Aristotle does not make it clear whether (a) desire is prior to all reasoning, and goal-directed reasoning is subordinate to this desire, or (b) goal-directed reasoning may itself produce the relevant desire. See note to §5. This issue is complicated by the fact that the DESIRE required for decision is not nonrational desire, but rational wish (*boulēsis*) aiming at the good (cf. iii 3.§19 and note). 'Goal-directed reason' might refer to the reasoning on the basis of which we come to believe that x is good for its own sake and hence form a wish for x.

acting well: Or 'doing well' (i.e., faring well). The Greek *eupraxia* (see ACTION) is cognate with *eu prattein* ('do well'; cf. i 4.§2).

§5 Thought by itself . . . concerned with action: Thought moves us to action only when it is for the sake of some end. Aristotle might mean: (a) Thought moves us when it is directed toward some end that we already desire. (b) Thought moves us when it is directed toward some end that we recognize as worthy of desire. If he intends (a), he implies that thought moves us only if we already desire an end. If he intends (b), he allows thought to move us even in the absence of a prior desire. See note to §4.

Whichever interpretation is right, Aristotle does not say that thought moves us to action only if it depends on a desire that is independent of thought; for wish is not necessarily independent of thought. Hence he does not commit himself to a Humean view of the relation between reason and desire (see Hume, *Treatise* ii 3.3).

In speaking of 'thought concerned with action' Aristotle uses *'praxis'* in its narrowest sense, referring to action done for its own sake. See ACTION (3).

For this thought . . . [further] goal: Aristotle anticipates (as he did in i 1) the division between PRODUCTION and ACTION, which he explains in vi 4–5. Production aims at some product that is itself subordinate to some end pursued for its own sake, which is the end of action.

and desire is for the goal. That is why . . . : A different punctuation: 'Now desire is for the goal. That is why . . . '

(c) §6. The virtues of thought that are relevant to correct decision

§6 That is why Agathon . . . never happened': Agathon (TGF fr. 5) was an Athenian tragic poet (end of fifth century B.C.). He is a character in Plato's *Symposium*.

The function . . . toward the truth: Since practical thought is concerned with action and decision, it must be concerned with deliberation, and hence must belong to the rationally calculating part. Aristotle returns to the division into two rational parts at 1139a6–16.

3

3.§1. The virtues of thought

§1 Then let us . . . soul: This section goes better with ch. 2. It introduces the discussion of the particular virtues of thought. In 'begin again' Aristotle alludes to the discussion of the particular virtues of character, and promises to do the same for the virtues of thought.

3.§2–4. Scientific knowledge

(a) §2. It is about necessary facts.

§2 What science is, . . . similarities: Aristotle indicates that he is speaking in the strictest sense, so that practical 'sciences' do not count. See SCIENCE (2).

(b) §3. Its principles cannot be scientifically known.

§3 But all teaching . . . *Analytics*: See *APo* i 1. In 'already known', *progignōskomenōn*, the verb represented by 'know', *gignōskein*, has a wider scope than *epistasthai*, the verb corresponding to *epistēmē*, scientific knowledge. We can *gignōskein* (i.e., grasp, be acquainted with) something without scientific knowledge of it.

Induction [leads to] the principle, i.e., the universal: In b28 read *tēs archēs* (OCT: *he archē*; 'is the beginning'). Aristotle may be alluding to the literal sense of 'INDUCTION', i.e., 'leading on'.

(c) §4. It requires demonstration from indemonstrable principles.

§4 *Analytics*: See *APo* i 3.

4

4.§1–6. Craft

(a) §1–2. The difference between production and action

§1 What admits . . . action: Aristotle begins to draw the important distinction between ACTION and PRODUCTION by describing production and the CRAFT that is concerned with it. For the distinction see *MM* 1197a3; Plato, *Ch.* 163b. Much of Aristotle's discussion here is an implicit reply to SOCRATES' identification of virtue with craft knowledge. See 1140b21–5.

§2 Nor is one included in the other: In a5 read *kai oude* (OCT: *diho oude*; 'that is why one is not included . . . ').

(b) §3–6. Craft is concerned with production.

§4 and the exercise of the craft is the study: In a11 read *technazein theōrein* (OCT: *technazein kai theōrein*).

nor with things . . . in themselves: On natural things, see CRAFT, NATURE.

§5 as Agathon . . . of craft': Agathon, TGF fr. 6.

5

5.§1–4. Prudence

(a) §1–2. It requires deliberation about living well.

§1 deliberate finely: 'Finely' (*kalōs*) is often used more or less equivalently to 'well'. In its narrower sense, however, it is the characteristic aim of the virtues of character (see FINE), and Aristotle may intend this narrower sense here, as in the account of deliberation at 1112b17.

some restricted area: Or 'partial' (*kata meros*).

what sorts of things promote living well in general: For 'promote' (*pros*), see note to iii 2.§9, DECISION (2). 'Living well' is equivalent to 'happiness'; see 1095a19. On the general scope of prudence, see 1094b6 (for the connection with POLITICAL SCIENCE see 1141b23), 1160a21; Plato, *Pr.* 318e. The prudent person does not simply find means to ends that are taken for granted. He begins with the very indefinite conception of the end as 'living well', and his deliberation shows him the FINE actions and states that living well consists in.

§2 A sign . . . no craft: Cf. 1112a34; *Rhet.* 1357a1. The common use of 'prudent' for deliberation outside the area of a craft is justified; for since prudence is concerned with living well in general, it must be concerned with ACTION (3), not with production; hence it cannot be a craft.

(b) §3. It is neither scientific knowledge nor craft.

(c) §4–5. It is concerned with action, not production.

§4 For production . . . acting well itself: This sentence explains why prudence is concerned with ACTION (in the narrow sense) and not with production. If it is concerned with living well in general, it must also be concerned with the unqualified end, which is action, the end of production (1139b1–4). Hence it is concerned with acting well (*eupraxia*; see note on 2.§4 above).

What does Aristotle mean by distinguishing action from production? He will face serious difficulties if he does not allow the same event to be both an action (insofar as it is done for its own sake) and a production (insofar as it is done for the sake of some end external to it). Many events that are virtuous actions, and as such decided on for themselves, are also productions; consider, for instance, a magnificent person's effort to have a suitable warship equipped. Similar questions arise about the relation between MOVEMENTS and ACTIVITIES. Cf. note to x 7.§7.

5.§5–8. Defense of the account of prudence

(a) §5. It fits the character of people recognized as prudent.

§5 That is why Pericles . . . such people: Aristotle appeals to APPEARANCES (see ETHICS [7]) to confirm his account. The account in turn vindicates the appearances, showing that they are reasonable if they rest on something like Aristotle's conception of prudence. Aristotle is not committed to endorsing all the appearances (he rejects some appearances about prudence at 1141b28). Here he appeals to recognized examples of prudent people. Pericles' prudent judgment on political and strategic questions is often emphasized by Thucydides (see esp. i 139.4; ii 65; perhaps ii 65.8 on Pericles' incorruptibility explains Aristotle's claim that such people know what is good for themselves).

(b)§5–6.Itfitstherecognizedconnectionbetweenprudenceandtemperance.

This is also . . . *phronēsin*): Aristotle's fanciful etymology (cf. Plato, *Cra.* 411e) indicates the special connection of prudence—as opposed to some other virtues of thought—to character. The special connection results from the fact that prudence is about action, and hence about actions to be chosen for their own sakes. Prudence requires knowledge of noninstrumental goods; but any conviction about noninstrumental goods must compete with conceptions of good that we form from our uneducated desire for pleasure; cf. 1113a33. In a badly educated person, the pleasure-based conceptions of good prevent the formation of the convictions required for prudence.

Here Aristotle suggests that repeated mistaken indulgence in the wrong pleasures will result in our losing our belief in their wrongness; cf. 1144a31. Repeated INCONTINENCE degenerates into intemperance; cf. 1114a15.

§6 For the principles . . . their goal . . . corrupts the principle: Aristotle begins with 'principles' in the plural, but he seems to have in mind just one principle, which is the goal, i.e., the ultimate end. He seems to be referring to an agent's conception of the final good, i.e., of happiness. Cf. vi 12.§10; vii 8.§5.

And so prudence . . . human goods: The argument relies on the common belief that temperance preserves prudence. Since what temperance preserves is true supposition about action, and especially about noninstrumental goods achievable in action, this is the sort of supposition that prudence must be.

(c) §7–8. It fits the common belief that prudence cannot be misused or forgotten.

§7 Moreover, there is virtue . . . not craft knowledge: Aristotle rejects the attempt to identify prudence with a craft. He attributes the position he rejects to Socrates in Plato's early dialogues. See 1137a19; *MM* 1197a18; *Rhet.* 1355b2; *Met.* 1025a6; Plato, *HMi.* 375d–376c, *Rep.* 333e. The same point of disagreement with Socrates is expressed in Aristotle's distinction between CAPACITIES and STATES.

§8 A sign . . . prudence cannot: On forgetting, see 1100b11. Since prudence is about human goods, we do not find ourselves with no occasion to use it, so that we might come to forget it. Aristotle probably also refers to the close connection of prudence with character and habit, and hence with the virtuous person's immediate response to situations; I do not have to remember that I ought to be angry about injustice.

6

6.§1–2. Understanding

(a) §1. There must be a virtue of thought concerned with principles.

§1 Nor is wisdom [exclusively] about principles: The supplement seems to be required by 7.§3 (see note), which implies that wisdom includes understanding.

(b) §2. This virtue must be understanding.

§2 The remaining . . . understanding about principles: Here 'UNDERSTANDING' has its strictest use (3a). When SCIENTIFIC KNOWLEDGE is also spoken of in the strictest way, so that it requires demonstration, understanding a truth excludes having scientific knowledge of it, since no further account or REASON (1140b33) can be given of the PRINCIPLES of which we have understanding. See also 1142a25, 1143a35.

7

7.§1–5. Wisdom

(a) §1–3. It embraces scientific knowledge and understanding.

§1 We ascribe wisdom . . . exact expertise in the crafts: Here EXACTNESS implies that a piece of work is complete and finished in detail.

§2 (as Homer . . . anything else'): Aristotle, like other ancient readers, ascribes the comic epic *Margites* to Homer (here he quotes fr. 2)

§3 Therefore wisdom . . . coping stone: Here Aristotle implies that wisdom includes understanding (cf. note on 6.§1). He defends his narrow use of 'wisdom', which confines it to scientific knowledge and understanding, and thereby to necessary truths. These are also the subject matter of theoretical STUDY. The common use of 'wisdom' applies it to many more areas. But common sense also agrees that wisdom requires exact knowledge; since Aristotle thinks exact knowledge is confined to scientific knowledge and understanding, he claims that common sense implicitly supports his restricted use of 'wisdom'.

(b) §3–5. In contrast to prudence, wisdom is concerned with the highest realities.

For it would . . . most excellent science: 'Science' is supplied from here to the end of 8.§3 (the Greek has only feminine adjectives without nouns). (But in §5 below 'scientific knowledge' translates *epistēmē*.) Though it is hard to avoid speaking, as Aristotle himself speaks, of political science and MEDICAL science, these disciplines do not meet Aristotle's strictest criteria for a SCIENCE.

§4 Moreover: In a22 read *ei d'* (OCT: *ei dē*; 'If, then . . . ').

the content of wisdom . . . the content of prudence: Lit., 'the wise', 'the prudent' (and 'what is white', lit., 'the white').

For . . . would call . . . would entrust such questions: In a26 read *phaien an* and *epitrepseian an* (OCT: *phēsin . . . epitrepsei*; 'one says . . . will entrust').

That is why . . . their own life: On animal prudence, cf. *Met.* 980b21; *GA* 753a7–17.

It is also . . . political science: Unlike Plato, Aristotle sharply distinguishes the subject matter of wisdom and of prudence. Wisdom not only has no immediate practical end; it does not even study the same things, because the things studied by prudence are not necessary states of affairs. The objects of demonstrative science are the most honorable (or 'valuable', *timion*). They deserve most HONOR because (a) they are the necessary and unchanging principles of the universe, and necessity and unchangingness are the marks of divine realities (see GOD [6]); and (b) they are thoroughly intelligible to reason because the truths about them are necessary and exceptionless, not exposing reason to ignorance or mistake (cf. 1139b21 on the non-necessary). Hence demonstrative scientific knowledge of necessary truths is the fullest expression of a human being's capacity for rational thought, hence the best ACTIVITY, and hence the highest VIRTUE of thought; in demonstration rational inference by itself can reach justified true conclusions starting from necessary premises, with no exceptions or qualifications.

§5 Anaxagoras or Thales: See 1179a15; *EE* 1216a11; *Pol.* 1259a6; Plato, *Tht.* 174a.

7.§6–7. Prudence contrasted with wisdom

(a) §6. It is concerned with action.

§6 Prudence, by contrast, . . . achievable in action: From here to the end of ch. 8 divisions into chapters and sections are not clear, and the connection of thought is not entirely obvious. (This was also true in Book v, another book originally belonging to the *EE*.) In this section Aristotle returns to the discussion of prudence, interrupted at the end of ch. 5; he has already said something about the differences between wisdom and prudence, and now he emphasizes the differences by expanding his description of prudence.

The unqualifiedly good deliberator . . . achievable in action: The topic of good deliberation is resumed in ch. 9.

(b) §7. Hence it must consider particulars.

§7 Nor is prudence . . . is about particulars: Aristotle introduces a new feature of prudence—its close connection with PARTICULARS. He describes this feature more fully in 8.§7–9 and 11.§2–6.

In this passage, 'particulars' seems to refer to relatively determinate types (e.g., 'bird meat' as opposed to 'light meat') rather than to particular instances (individuals, e.g., this piece of chicken), though no doubt Aristotle also means that the prudent person needs familiarity with particular instances too. Such information will be a source of useful specific descriptions; see note to 11.§4.

How is this concern with particulars related to the claim that prudence is a deliberative virtue? If particulars are determinate types, identification of particulars is part of good deliberation. If they are particular instances, they are not themselves discovered by deliberation, but perception of them is required for successful deliberation, so that good deliberation must include good perception; see iii 3.§16.

§7 For someone . . . [hence] healthy: The supplement makes it explicit that Aristotle is giving an example of someone who knows why light meat is healthy; this grasp of the CAUSE is characteristic of CRAFT and SCIENCE. By contrast, the one who knows only that chicken is light and healthy does not know why it is healthy, but can identify healthy meat.

bird meats are light and healthy: Retain *koupha kai* (OCT deletes).

Here too, however . . . [science]: Cf. 1180b11–28. Aristotle wants to correct a false impression that might be created by his previous remarks; he does not mean that general principles are unimportant for the prudent person. Prudence must include a ruling science (cf. 1094a27, 1152b2); and at once he proceeds to explain this.

8

8.§1–9. The range of prudence: universals and particulars

(a) §1–3. Different applications of prudence, to the individual and to the community

§1 their being is not the same: See note to v 1.§20.

§2 One type . . . both types in common: Aristotle does not explain how this discussion of types of prudence is connected with the preceding section. The connection, however, is fairly clear. Aristotle continues the thought of the last sentence of ch. 7, which counterbalanced his remarks about prudence and particulars by emphasizing the universal, comprehensive scope of prudence; this was the scope he claimed for POLITICAL SCIENCE in 1094a26 (cf. *EE* 1218b12). In this section, he rejects a common, but unduly restricted conception of prudence and political science which (a) confines prudence to concern for my own good and no one else's, and (b) confines political science to the political and legislative process. In (a) we neglect the connection between the agent's good and other people's

(1097b9) that makes ethics inseparable from political science. In (b) we neglect the principles that should guide political action.

In b26 read *hōs kath'hekasta* (OCT: *hōs ta kath'hekasta*).

1141b27 decree: DECREES are to be contrasted with laws, which belong to the legislative form of prudence.

(b) §4. Prudence must consider the individual's good with reference to a community.

§4 In fact knowledge . . . [of prudence]: Here as in §1, the connection with what precedes is inexplicit, but fairly clear. Once again Aristotle emphasizes the universal scope of prudence, and argues against the assumptions that underlie a common restrictive view.

In b34 delete *gnōseōs* ('one species of knowledge'; OCT retains).

But there is . . . about it: Or 'It is very different [from the other species]'.

too active: Or 'busybodies' (*polupragmones*), a standard pejorative term for overinvolvement in politics (especially on the side disapproved of by the speaker). Cf. Plato, *Gorg.* 485e–486d. Aristotle neither endorses the ordinary political life (cf. 1095b22, 1179a1; *Pol.* vii 3–4) nor recommends withdrawal from political concerns.

Hence Euripides . . . too active: These lines are spoken by Odysseus in Euripides' lost play *Philoctetes* (TGF fr. 787–8), before he engaged in the morally dubious tricks involved in stealing Philoctetes' bow (if the plot resembled that of Sophocles' *Philoctetes* on this point). Odysseus regrets having abandoned the quiet life of an ordinary soldier.

1142a7 For people seek . . . prudent people: The common view about prudent people is understandable once we see it rests on a false belief about the human good. See ETHICS (7).

(c) §5–7. Since prudence must take account of these various considerations, it is difficult to acquire and depends on experience.

§5 A sign of what has been said . . . to be found: The reference of 'what has been said' is not clear. The supplement assumes that §5–6 are meant to explain and illustrate the previous sentence, 'Moreover . . . '. In explaining the different views about prudence, Aristotle mentions the difficulty of its subject matter. Part of the difficulty is the need for experience of particulars, which leads us back to the topic of 7.§7. Other possible views: (1) §5–6 are out of place, and the text should be rearranged so that they follow 7.§7. (2) They are a digression, interrupting the sequence of thought connecting §4 and §7.

§6 reached through abstraction: Abstraction (*aphairesis*, removal) involves the removal in thought, i.e., ignoring, of all the features of an object except those relevant to the particular question. For instance, the nongeometrical properties of physical objects are abstracted when we study them geometrically (i.e., insofar as they are geometrical objects). See *Phys.* 193b31–4; *Met.* 1077b17–1078a31. Since these disciplines attend to fewer properties of physical objects, they demand less detailed empirical familiarity with the objects, and especially demand less than is demanded by natural science.

principles: Or 'beginnings' (*archai*). The translation and supplement assume that Aristotle is referring to the theoretical principles of the science, not to the starting points in perception.

Young people, . . . only say the words: Cf. vii 3.§8.

§7 Further, [prudence . . . or the particular: Again the connection of thought is inexplicit. The supplement suggests that §7 continues the argument of §5–6, supporting the claim in §4 about the difficulty of the questions that concern prudence.

In this sentence the PARTICULARS Aristotle has in mind seem to be particular instances (e.g., this water here, as in the next sentence), rather than determinate types (cf. 1141b15).

(d) §8–9. Since prudence must consider particulars, it is different from scientific knowledge and understanding.

§8 It is apparent . . . achievable in action: The reference of 'as we said' is not clear. Since he has just remarked in §7 that prudence is concerned with particulars, he returns to the topic of 7.§7, which also leads him back to the discussion of UNDERSTANDING in ch. 6. The 'last thing' that concerns prudence is (as the supplement suggests) last as one proceeds from the more general to the more particular (cf. notes to 11.§2–3 below, 1146a9).

§9 Hence it is opposite to understanding: Or perhaps 'Hence it corresponds to understanding' (in that both are concerned with things that cannot be further defined—though for quite different reasons).

For understanding is about the [first] terms: Understanding grasps the primary terms in a demonstrative science. ('Terms', *horoi*, might refer to the things defined or to the DEFINITIONS.) These come first in a demonstrative science (not in a practical science) because they are the most universal. Prudence is concerned with terms that come last in a practical science (not in a demonstrative science) because they are the most particular. Aristotle does not deny his normal claim that prudence also grasps the first principles in practical affairs; for this claim, cf. 1140b18, 1142b33. He omits his normal claim about prudence grasping general principles, because he is focusing on a point of contrast between prudence and theoretical understanding.

This is not the perception of special objects: Having said that prudence is concerned with particulars, Aristotle argues that it must include some sort of PERCEPTION, since this is how we become aware of particulars. To specify the sort of perception he has in mind, he contrasts it with the ordinary perception of 'special objects' ('objects' supplied in this paragraph), i.e., color, sound, etc., which are 'proper sensibles', the objects proprietary to sight, hearing, etc. See *DA* ii 6.

but the sort . . . stop there too: We have to recognize, without being given any further reason, that the triangle is the last, i.e., the simplest, mathematical figure. In 'stop there too' Aristotle means that unless we can recognize something without being given a further argument, we will face an infinite regress. He made this point about deliberation and perception in iii 3.§16.

In a28 retain *en tois mathēmatikois* (OCT deletes).

This is another . . . prudence is: Lit., 'But this is more (or 'rather') perception than prudence, but another species of it.' The translation and supplement assume that Aristotle is contrasting (a) the perception of a triangle as the last figure with both (b) perception of proper sensibles, and (c) the perception proper to prudence. He recognizes that (c) is less like (a) than (b) is. He may have in mind the fact that the perception proper to prudence requires grasp of a more elaborate range of theoretical judgments (those that figure in ethical deliberation) than we need for either (a) or (b).

In a30 read *ē [hē] phronēsis* (OCT: no supplement, hence 'is more perception than [it is] prudence').

9

9.§1–8. Good deliberation

(a) §1–3. Since it involves inquiry, it must be distinguished from the intellectual states that result from completed inquiry.

§1 We . . . good deliberation is: Aristotle returns to the 'unqualifiedly good deliberator' who was introduced in the discussion of prudence in 7.§6. The whole of ch. 9 is an explanation of the description of the good deliberator at the end of 7.§6. It does not draw on any of the points made in 7.§7–8.§9; this is another sign of the rather loose organization of this part of Book vi. Cf. notes to 10.§1 and 11.§2.

§2 For good guessing . . . deliberate slowly: Deliberation, and hence DECISION, requires a process that takes time and precedes the action. Cf. 1117a20.

§3 1142b10 no correctness in scientific knowledge: There is no proper subset of scientific knowledge that is correct, since scientific knowledge must be correct.

1142b11 [but correctness . . . not]: For the supplement, see 1112a5.

(b) §4–7. Correctness in deliberation requires the correct conclusion and the correct process, aiming at the correct end.

§4 what [this correctness] . . . [correctness] about: In b16 delete *hē boulē* (OCT retains; 'what deliberation is and what it is about').

Since there are . . . every type: Since there are different types of CORRECTNESS, the correctness of the prudent person's deliberation must be distinguished from the other types. Aristotle shows that good deliberation is not simply the discovery of the most effective means to ends that are taken for granted.

For the incontinent . . . great evil: This passage makes it clear that it is possible to act incontinently as a result of deliberation about the satisfaction of one's bad appetite. But though the incontinent acts on deliberation, he does not act on a DECISION; see iii 2.§4. He does not act on decision, because the DESIRE that originates the deliberation is a nonrational appetite rather than the rational wish that is required for decision (see iii 3.§19). By 'what he proposes to see', Aristotle probably means 'the result he looks for'.

In contrast to the incontinent person, the vicious person acts on a decision, and hence on a wish (vii 8.§3). Simply acting on some sort of decision and wish is not sufficient for good deliberation.

for the sort of correctness . . . reaches a good: A vicious person might deliberate correctly about ways to make money dishonestly. In one respect, then, he reaches a good, since wealth is a good. In another respect, however, he fails to reach a good, since wealth is not a good for him, given that he is vicious (see v 1.§9). This second respect is the one Aristotle has in mind here.

§5 However, we can reach . . . term is false: The good deliberator, and therefore the prudent and virtuous person, must reach the correct conclusion by the right method. If my deliberation tells me correctly that I ought not to steal now, but does not tell me this for the right reasons (if, for instance, it tells me I ought not to steal simply because I am likely to be found out, or because my victim is a friend of mine), it is not good deliberation.

§7 Further, our . . . [limited] end: Lit., 'Further, it is possible to have deliberated well both without qualification and toward some end'.

Hence unqualifiedly good . . . [limited] end: The 'unqualified end' is unqualified because it is the end for a human being, not just in relation to some limited aim or imperfection of a particular human being; cf. 1139b2.

§7 what is expedient for promoting the end about which prudence is true supposition: It is grammatically possible, though implausible, to take 'what is expedient . . . ' rather than 'the end' to be the antecedent of 'about which' (so that Aristotle does not affirm that prudence is correct supposition about the end). The more probable rendering requires Aristotle to affirm that prudence is correct supposition about the unqualified end. His saying this has been taken to conflict with his claim that prudence is concerned only with deliberation about what promotes the end (see 5.§1). We need not believe there is any conflict, however, if we bear in mind the broad scope of 'promoting the end' (*pros to telos*; see DECISION), and hence of deliberation. As a result of deliberating about what promotes happiness, we discover its constituents, and so we have a more precise conception of happiness. This precise conception is probably what Aristotle has in mind when he says that prudence is true supposition about the end. Deliberation both precedes this true conception of the end and follows it (since a fairly precise conception of happiness is the basis for further deliberation about what to do). This passage does not make it clear whether Aristotle is thinking about the deliberation that forms the correct supposition about the end, or about the deliberation that follows it; he may well have both in mind. Cf. 1144a8, 31.

10

10.§1–4. Comprehension

(a) §1. It has the same subject matter as prudence.

§1 Comprehension, . . . comprehend well: As 11.§2 shows, this chapter fits at the end of ch. 8, as part of the survey of intellectual virtues that leads up to the discussion of particulars in ch. 11. It does not fit so naturally at the end of ch. 9 (though deliberation is mentioned in 1143a6), which did not fit naturally at the end of ch. 8 (see note on 9.§1).

(b) §2–4. In contrast to prudence, it is not prescriptive.

§2 For prudence is prescriptive . . . judges: Cf. *EE* 1220a9, b6. Comprehension says, 'If you apologize to him, he will be less resentful'. Prudence says, 'Since you must remove his resentment, you must apologize to him'. Aristotle does not mean that prudence produces imperatives rather than statements; the distinction between prudence and comprehension does not rest on a grammatical distinction.

§4 It is derived . . . call learning comprehending: The Greek *manthanein* used here is applied both to the process of learning and to the grasping of the subject that we have learned; it is this grasping that is identified with comprehension.

11

11.§1. Consideration and considerateness

§1 The [state] called consideration . . . decent person: This section should really be a separate chapter parallel to the chapters on the other intellectual virtues. Here Aristotle describes the connection between 'consideration' (*gnōmē*; or 'good judgment') and 'considerateness' (*sungnōmē*; see PARDON) and their relation to the decency that is described in v 10.

11.§2–7. The application of practical thought to particulars

(a) §2–3. Different virtues are needed to grasp particulars.

§2 It is reasonable . . . direction: This begins a new chapter, in which Aristotle sums up some of his remarks on the intellectual virtues and draws some conclusions. He does not refer back to ch. 9 (on good deliberation), which, as we saw, fits better after 7.§6 than after ch. 8.

For all . . . last things, i.e., particulars: Lit., 'last things and particulars'. Cf. note to 8.§8.

(b) §4–6. The special role of understanding in grasping particulars

§4 Understanding is also . . . in both directions: 'In both directions' indicates that here 'last' indicates both the last things as you go toward the more universal (hence in a36 they are the 'first terms') and the last things as you go from universal to particular (hence 'last' in a36). As in 8.§9, Aristotle contrasts (a) understanding in demonstrative science with (b) the way in which prudence is aware of particulars. In 1142a25 he called (b) a type of perception that he opposed to understanding. Here he calls (b) a type of understanding. He calls it understanding because it is analogous to (a), insofar as no further account or reason can be given for our grasp of the particular, just as none can be given for our grasp of a first principle of demonstration. Though the terms used here are different from those in 1142a25, the same basic contrast is drawn between prudence and understanding.

both about the first terms and about the last: Here 'first' and 'last' mark the same contrast as the one Aristotle has just marked by using 'last in both directions'.

In [premises] . . . minor premise: Lit., 'of the last and the admitting and of the other premise (*protasis*)'. In speaking of the minor premise, Aristotle presupposes the account of practical INFERENCE at 1147a25–31; cf. 1144a31. Understanding is needed to find the relevant features of particular situations, so that general principles can be applied to them. If, for instance, a general principle says 'Excessive display in equipping warships should be avoided', some grasp of what would be excessive in this particular case, in outfitting this warship, is needed (cf. iii 3.§16).

For these last . . . reached from particulars: Lit., 'for these are the *archai* of that for the sake of which; for universals are from (or "out of", *ek*) particulars'. We might translate *archai* 'principles' rather than 'beginnings'. But the following clause suggests that Aristotle is thinking of the process of acquiring universals, not of the PRINCIPLES that are our basic premises. If we use understanding of particulars to identify the appropriate features of particular situations, we will form more useful and determinate rules; see note to 7.§7. This will be a process of induction; see INFERENCE.

§5 We must, . . . perception is understanding: If this is the role that Aristotle has in mind for understanding of particulars, the state that he calls 'understanding' here is the same as the one that he called 'perception' (as opposed to understanding) in 8.§9. In the earlier passage, he was careful to point out that it was not ordinary perception; now he seems to have decided that the difference from ordinary perception is best captured by calling it 'understanding'.

§6 That is why understanding . . . about them: In the mss. this sentence comes in §6, after 'as though nature were the cause'. OCT deletes it as spurious, perhaps correctly. If it is genuine, it fits best at this point in §5. The translation assumes that Aristotle means: In practical (as opposed to theoretical) reasoning we begin from understanding exercised in particular situations, and we form generalizations that will be applicable to particular situations. This interpretation requires us to take 'demonstrations' rather loosely, since Aristotle normally contrasts demonstrative science with ethical reasoning (as in §4).

(c) §5–7. These virtues of thought concerned with particulars develop through experience.

§5 That is why . . . to grow naturally: Aristotle does not concede that these states really grow naturally, or that age implies prudence. He means that the important fact that EXPERIENCE is needed for prudence (cf. 8.§5–6) explains the mistaken view that prudence grows naturally.

no one seems to have natural wisdom: Wisdom requires demonstration, which requires teaching (1139b25).

§7 We have said, . . . part of the soul: The reference to the two parts of the soul recalls 2.§6. Aristotle suggests that the point of the discussion in chs. 8–11 has been to make clear the contrast between wisdom and prudence.

12

12.§1–3. Puzzles about prudence and wisdom

(a) §1. How do they contribute to being virtuous?

§1 One might, . . . use they are: The discussion of these puzzles takes up all of chs. 12 and 13.

For knowledge . . . in actions: The translation departs from the structure of the Greek. Lit.: 'What do we need it for, if prudence is that about the just things and fine things and good things for a human being, and these are the things it belongs to the good man to do, but we are no more prone to act by knowing them, if the virtues are states, just as neither the healthy things nor the fit things (as many as are spoken of not by producing but by being from the state)—for we are no more prone to act by having the medical and gymnastic?'

This puzzle rests on the assumption that just as (1): (a) I can do what is healthy and hence (b) be healthy, without (c) knowing medicine, so also (2): (a) I can do what is virtuous and hence (b) be virtuous, without (c) having prudence. Aristotle challenges the alleged parallel between (1) and (2). He denies that (2b) follows from (2a), if (2a) is understood so as not to require prudence; see 1144a11.

(b) §2. How does prudence help us to become virtuous?

§2 If we concede . . . excellent: This puzzle assumes that prudence is analogous to a specialized CRAFT whose products are useful to me, but whose practice I can leave to someone else; though I value the product of MEDICINE, I need not be a doctor myself. This objection reflects failure to distinguish prudence and virtue from craft (cf. 1105a26–b5).

In b28 read *chrēsimon* ('is not useful') (OCT: *phronimon*, 'prudent').

Nor, however, . . . matter to them: In 1143b30 read *mē ousi* (OCT: *mē echousi*) and *autois echein* (OCT: *autous echein*).

(c) §3. Does prudence control wisdom?

§3 Besides, it would . . . its product: This puzzle relies on the assumption, accepted by Aristotle, that prudence produces wisdom; see note to 13.§8.

12.§3–9. Wisdom, prudence, and virtue of character

(a) §3–6. The value of wisdom and prudence

§4 First of all, . . . [of the soul]: In reply to the first puzzle (in §1), Aristotle maintains the intrinsic value of wisdom and prudence. These are part of the formal CAUSE of happiness. We say, 'He is healthy because his body is in a healthy condition, which is . . . (giving details)'; we thereby say what health consists in. Similarly we say, 'He is happy because he is wise and . . . (adding the other components)'; we thereby say what happiness consists in.

§5 1144a4 health produces [health]: Less probably: 'health produces [happiness]'.

§6 Further, we fulfill our function: Aristotle returns to the connection between virtue and FUNCTION, recalled at the beginning of this book; see 1.§7, 2.§6. Despite the loose structure of some of the middle sections of Book vi, Aristotle has a fairly clear plan in mind.

for virtue . . . goal [correct]: For this division of labor between virtue and prudence, cf. 1144a20, 1145a4, 1178a16. We might take it to imply that (a) prudence finds what promotes a goal, and (b) this goal has already been fixed by virtue independently of prudence. Claim (a) is correct, provided that we take account of the wide scope of 'PROMOTES'. When we take account of this, however, we raise doubts about (b). For if deliberation about happiness produces a conception of the nature (components) of happiness, it produces the virtuous person's correct conception of the end (see note to 9.§7). If, contrary to (b) above, prudence itself helps to fix the goal that virtue aims at, we should not suppose that the virtue of character that makes the end correct is independent of prudence. On this question about virtue, cf. *EE* ii 11 (it is not anticipated so explicitly in the earlier books of the *EN*).

(b) §7. Virtue of character requires the correct decision.

§7 To answer . . . fine and just actions: The answer seems to come first in §10, where Aristotle says that prudence requires cleverness. A fuller answer comes in 13.§2. For 'better at achieving' (*praktikōteroi*) one might substitute 'more prone to do'.

To answer the puzzle, Aristotle goes back to the account of virtue of character as involving the correct decision, which causes one to choose the virtuous actions for their own sakes.

we say that some people . . . either unwillingly or because of ignorance or because of some other end, . . . ought to do: 'Unwillingly' might refer to force, or to the conditions mentioned in 1135b4–8. Ignorance is, of course, in Aristotle's view, another source of unwilling and involuntary action.

Equally, however, . . . because of decision and for the sake of the actions themselves: See 1105a32 (cf. 1134a20, 1135b35). We can now understand (see note on §4) why a decision, and hence deliberation about what promotes an end, is necessary for choosing the correct actions for their own sakes (i.e., as part of the conception of happiness that one has reached by deliberation).

(c) §8–10. Prudence requires both cleverness and virtue of character.

§8 Now virtue makes the decision correct: We might take this in either of two ways. (1) Aristotle is repeating what he said in §6 when he said that virtue makes the goal right; hence he means, strictly speaking, that virtue makes our decision aim at the right goal. In that case, the role he attributes to cleverness is the same as the role he attributed to prudence in §6: finding what promotes the end. Prudence differs from cleverness only because our deliberative ability is called 'prudence' only if it serves the correct end. (2) When he says that virtue makes the decision correct, he includes the roles that he ascribed to virtue and to prudence in §6, since both of these are required for a correct decision. The role he attributes to cleverness is not the deliberative task of finding what promotes an end. See notes to 13.§2, 7.

but the actions . . . another capacity: Cf. *EE* 1227b40. We should not suppose that this capacity is entirely separate from virtue; since prudence requires CLEVERNESS, and virtue requires prudence, it follows that virtue requires cleverness. See notes to 12.§6, ix 11.§3. In 'the actions . . . fulfil the decision', Aristotle does not speak of things that 'promote the end'; these are found by deliberation, and precede a decision. He seems to have in mind nondeliberative facility in finding ways to carry out a decision already made. He never says that cleverness involves deliberation.

§9 to be able to do . . . goal is assumed: Here Aristotle speaks of actions that promote a goal, whereas he has just spoken of those that promote the fulfillment of a decision; he is presumably referring to the same actions in different ways. Once again, he takes the mark of cleverness to be resourcefulness in action, not in deliberation.

and to attain them: Or perhaps 'to hit on them' (i.e., to discover or identify them). Read *tunchanein autōn*. (OCT unnecessarily emends to *tunchanein autou*, i.e., 'achieve the goal'.) Cf. *EE* 1227b40. If the role of cleverness is nondeliberative, Aristotle perhaps makes room for it in iii 3.§16, where he recognizes the limits of deliberation. In that case, he returns here to the concern of prudence with particulars, which he discussed in ch. 11.

both prudent . . . clever: Read *kai tous panourgous* (OCT: *kai panourgous*).

§10 Prudence is not cleverness: Read *ouch hē deinotēs* (OCT: *ouch hē dunamis*).

[Prudence,] . . . developed state: Lit., 'The state comes to be for this eye of the soul not without virtue'. Aristotle relies on his standard contrast between CAPACITY and STATE (cf. ii 5.§5) to make it clear that prudence requires our capacities to be turned in the right direction. Until someone is virtuous he has only an aptitude for prudence, not prudence itself. Cleverness in action is not sufficient for prudence, which also requires the right ends that belong to virtue, and hence requires the correct decision (1152a10). Aristotle does not mean, however, that the prudent person is simply a clever person who has also been well brought up. He has the right end because he has deliberated 'well' in the way explained in ch. 9.

For inferences . . . sake of argument): Cf. note to 11.§4. Here Aristotle considers the major premise. Only the good person has the correct conception of what the highest good consists in. He reaches this conception by good deliberation; cf. note to 1142b32. The demanding conditions for good deliberation (see esp. 9.§5) explain why even continent and incontinent people cannot have the right conception of the good, even though their decision is in some way correct (cf. vii 8.§5). For the bad effects of vice, cf. 1140b11.

13

13.§1–8. The connection between virtue of character and prudence

(a) §1–2. Full virtue, as opposed to natural virtue, requires prudence.

§1 We must, . . . again: It is rather misleading to mark a chapter division here, since the argument is continuous. Having argued that prudence requires virtue, Aristotle now considers the other direction of dependence, and argues that virtue requires prudence.

For virtue . . . natural virtue . . . full virtue: Cf. 1117a4, 1127b14, 1151a18, 1179b21–6; NATURE (1). Aristotle refers to natural aptitudes, not to genuine virtues (cf. 1103a23).

But still we look . . . evidently harmful: Without prudence someone will lack full (see CONTROLLING) virtue, because he will lack the appropriate discernment and flexibility in less familiar situations (cf. 1137a9, 1180b20).

§2 And so, . . . acquired without prudence: The condition that Aristotle contrasts with mere natural aptitude is full virtue of character, which includes prudence. (He also calls this 'habitual virtue,' 1151a18–19). Virtue of character is not simply the result of good upbringing without prudence (cf. 1095b4–9). Since virtue of character includes prudence, Aristotle cannot regard the process he calls 'habituation' as complete until the person being habituated has acquired prudence.

(b) §3–7. Virtue of character and prudence require each other.

§3 That is why: As usual, this connective (see note to i 1.§1) indicates facts or beliefs that Aristotle claims to make intelligible.

Socrates used to undertake: 'Used to' (Greek imperfect tense) indicates Aristotle's intention to speak of the historical SOCRATES; cf. note to i 4.§5. Socrates examines and (many readers believe, in agreement with Aristotle) defends the identification of every virtue with knowledge of good and evil, in the *La.* and *Pr.* Plato rejects this doctrine in *Rep.* iv.

[instances of] prudence: Lit., 'prudences'. Perhaps '[forms of] prudence'. The same question arises where '[instances of]' is supplied in §5.

§4 Whenever people now . . . the correct reason: Aristotle now answers the question about the correct reason that he raised in ch. 1 (cf. 1103b32). The correct reason is specified by prudence (1107a1); the description of prudence has explained more fully what the content of the correct reason will be. Aristotle still has not explained as fully as some might wish what the correct reason will prescribe. The reader needs to be convinced that someone who deliberates in the way prescribed in Book vi and who accepts the conception of happiness in Book i will decide on the virtues described in Books iii–iv.

§5 For it is not . . . that is virtue: In distinguishing (a) 'in accord with (*kata*) the correct reason' from (b) 'involving (*meta*) the correct reason', Aristotle probably means to distinguish (a) actions on the virtuous person's decision from (b) actions, based on instinctive reactions and FEELINGS, that are not actions on decision, but still would not be what they are without his rational reflection and decision (cf. 1117a22). The same distinction is drawn in 'reason . . . involves reason' (b29–30) and 'prudence . . . require prudence' (b20). Cf. notes to i 7.§13, 8.§6, 13.§18–19. Prudence is a necessary part, not the whole, of virtue.

§6 And in this way . . . one another: Though Aristotle rejects the Socratic belief in the unity and identity of all the virtues, he thinks (a) each virtue is inseparable from prudence (1107a1, 1138b18–34, 1178a16–19), and since (b) prudence is inseparable from all the virtues, it follows that (c) each virtue is inseparable from all the other virtues. We have seen why he believes (a); but (b) and (c) seem to neglect the role of external conditions in some of the virtues (magnificence and magnanimity, for instance); cf. 1122a28, 1123b5, 1125b4 (and for a different sort of exception see 1115a20). To cope with these cases (b) and (c) seem to need revision (as Aquinas suggests in *ST* 1–2 q65 a1 ad 1). Cf. *MM* 1199b35–1200a11.

for one has . . . single state: Read *mia(i) ousē(i) huparchousē(i)* (OCT: *mia(i) huparchousē(i)*). Lit., 'for at the same time as prudence, being one, being present, all will be present'.

§7 And it is clear . . . part of the soul: We return to the first puzzle (12.§1). Though Aristotle has officially been answering the second and third puzzles until now, he has also made his answer to the first more convincing by suggesting how prudence is the virtue of a rational part of the soul.

and because . . . without virtue: The translation implies that this is a second reason why we would need prudence even if it did not affect our action; we would need it in order to have the right decision, and hence the right character. Alternatively, instead of 'because (*hoti*) the decision . . . ' one might translate 'that' (*hoti*), making a second 'that' clause dependent on 'And it is clear' (parallel to the *hoti* in a3). This gives an inferior sequence of thought, since it now becomes difficult to see what the point of the remark about decision is meant to be at this stage in the chapter.

for [virtue] . . . promote the end: This clause takes up the previous 'without prudence or without virtue', in chiastic order. By 'achieve the end', Aristotle probably means 'achieve the right grasp of the end' (which he previously expressed by saying that virtue makes the end correct), rather than 'attain the end we were aiming at'. The issues raised above about the relation between virtue and prudence arise again here (cf. notes to 12.§6, 8). Here again, it is difficult to maintain, consistently with Aristotle's other remarks in chs. 12–13, that virtue, quite independently of prudence, fixes the right end, and then prudence finds what promotes it. For Aristotle has just insisted that virtue (which makes the end correct) requires prudence (which makes the things promoting the end correct); hence, it seems, we cannot make the end correct without making the things promoting the end correct. This conclusion is reasonable if prudent deliberation about what promotes the ultimate end (i.e., what constitutes happiness, fixing our conception of happiness) results in a correct conception of the end (i.e., of what constitutes happiness). On virtue and prudence, cf. 1178a16.

(c) §8. The relation of prudence to wisdom

§8 Moreover, prudence . . . control health: Wisdom has its place in a life organized and planned by prudence, but it is not thereby of less value than prudence. The place of wisdom in happiness is explained in x 6–8.

BOOK VII

1

1.§1–5. Introduction to the discussion of incontinence

(a) §1–3. Conditions superior to virtue and inferior to vice.

§1 Thus Homer . . . a god': Homer, *Il.* xxiv 258–9.

§2 And so, if, . . . different from vice: On the gods, cf. 1178b10. On becoming gods, cf. 1159a5, 1166a19.

(b) §4. Conditions between virtue and vice: continence and incontinence

(c) §5. The method of inquiry

§5 As in . . . appearances: This passage is one of the clearest statements of Aristotle's method; see ETHICS (4). The rest of the discussion of incontinence is clearly organized around the puzzles (*aporiai*; see ETHICS [5]) that Aristotle proceeds to raise.

ways of being affected: This translates *pathē*, usually rendered by 'FEELINGS'. Here Aristotle refers broadly to the conditions he has just mentioned, which are not simply feelings.

ideally, . . . most important: Aristotle takes the common beliefs seriously, but he does not promise to defend them all; incontinence is one case in which he does not think they can all be defended. The reader needs to ask how Aristotle decides how a specific belief is one of the 'most important' (or 'CONTROLLING', *kurion*) beliefs that need to be preserved.

1.§6–7. Common beliefs about incontinence

§6 Continence and . . . conditions: It is reasonable to begin a new chapter here, where Aristotle turns to a survey of the relevant common beliefs.

2

2.§1–11. Puzzles arising from the common beliefs about incontinence

(a) §1–5. In what sense does the incontinent person correctly grasp what he ought to do?

§1 We might . . . acts incontinently: Or 'how, when someone has a correct supposition, he acts incontinently'. The translation in the text is supported by the fact that §1–5 discuss the various ways in which the incontinent person might have a correct supposition. 'SUPPOSITION' is the generic term for a cognitive state. Aristotle thinks it important to decide exactly what sort of cognitive state, and about what, the incontinent is in. 'Knowledge' in this discussion renders *epistēmē*.

Socrates used to think: As in vi 13.§2–5, Aristotle uses the Greek imperfect tense to refer to the historical SOCRATES.

dragged around like a slave: See Plato, *Pr.* 352b–c. Aristotle indicates (cf. previous note) that he takes this Platonic dialogue to reflect the views of the historical Socrates.

for no one . . . the conflict]: Aristotle reports the Socratic argument (*Pr.* 353c–357e) to show that the presence of knowledge ensures I will not act against what I know to be best. Socrates relies on knowledge because it is firm and not liable to change (but cf. *Pr.* 358b). If at time t1 I have true belief that x is better than y, and at later time t2 I do y rather than x, then, in Socrates' view, I must have changed my mind between t1 and t2 so that at t2 I believe that y is better than x.

§2 contradicts things that appear manifestly: We might take 'manifestly' with 'contradicts' or (more plausibly) with 'appear'. If he is saying that these things appear manifestly, Aristotle is not necessarily asserting that they are true, but only that they seem obviously true.

If ignorance . . . eventually does]: This sentence shows that, while Aristotle rejects the Socratic position as it stands, he allows that some modification of it may be correct. In particular, he suggests that ignorance of a certain type may explain incontinence. On 'affected', see FEELING.

§5 For on this view . . . other virtues: In these two sentences Aristotle summarizes some of his claims about PRUDENCE in Book vi. Prudence requires right action and virtue, and so is incompatible with incontinence; 1144a29, 1152a6.

(b) §6. Must the incontinent person have bad desires?

§6 Further: 'Further' (*eti*) marks a shift from the puzzles about right supposition in §1–5 to a more varied set of puzzles, marked by repeated use of 'further' in §6–11.

(c) §7–9. Is incontinence sometimes desirable?

§7 Take, . . . *Philoctetes*: Sophocles, *Philoctetes* 895–916.

§8 Further, the sophistical . . . paradoxical results: An argument put forward by a SOPHIST is put forward to confuse the opponent, not because the sophist himself thinks it raises any genuine puzzle. Nonetheless, it may raise a genuine puzzle that deserves to be examined. A good example of the kind of argumentation that Aristotle has in mind is provided by Plato's *Euthydemus*.

in encounters: Read *entuchōsin* (OCT: *epituchōsin*; 'when they succeed').

for thought is tied up . . . solve the argument: On this effect of puzzles, cf. *Met.* 995a28.

(d) §10. Is incontinence worse than intemperance?

§10 Further, someone . . . persuaded and decides to do: This is the intemperate person. The restricted scope of DECISION (1) is important; cf. 1146b22.

(e) §11. What is the range of incontinence?

§11 If so, . . . simply incontinent: He is said to be incontinent 'simply' (or 'without qualification'; see UNQUALIFIED), without mention of any specific area of incontinence (in the American idiom, 'incontinent, period').

2.§12–3.§1. The right approach to the puzzles

§12 These, . . . that arise: 2.§12 and 3.§1 form a small section of their own, concluding the discussion of the puzzles and listing the questions to be discussed next.

1146b7 solution: Lit., 'loosing'. The metaphor of binding is continued from 1146a24. Cf. *EE* 1215a7.

3

3.§2. The difference between incontinence and intemperance

§2 We begin: Aristotle follows a chiastic order in discussing the puzzles he has just mentioned; the first he discusses is the last one he mentioned.

by their attitudes: Lit., 'by how'. Read *pōs* (OCT: *hōs*).

Next, is there . . . or not: This question is rather intrusive, and some editors delete it, perhaps correctly.

For the simply incontinent . . . intemperate person: If the previous question really belongs in the text, the present sentence has two functions: (1) It answers the previous question (again proceeding in chiastic order). (2) It rules out the second of the three possibilities mentioned above; Aristotle argues that the distinctive feature of the incontinent cannot be simply his attitude (since one can take the same attitude in actions that do not manifest simple incontinence).

Nor is he . . . as intemperance: This argues against the first of the three possibilities mentioned; incontinence cannot be distinguished purely by the range of incontinent actions, since that does not distinguish it from intemperance.

For the intemperate . . . pursues it: Aristotle often emphasizes the crucial difference between the DECISION of the vicious person and of the incontinent person. In 'thinks it wrong', he implies that (as he says elsewhere) the incontinent person in some way makes the correct decision (only in some way; cf. vi 13.§7 and note).

3.§3–14. In what sense does the incontinent person have or lack the appropriate knowledge?

(a) §3–4. The difference between knowledge and belief is irrelevant to this question.

§3 It is claimed . . . with knowledge: We now turn to the first of the questions announced in §1.

§4 as Heracleitus makes clear: Aristotle might be referring to some remark of Heracleitus that we cannot identify. More probably, however, he is referring to the rather dogmatic and oracular style of Heracleitus' short and paradoxical remarks, which lack the sort of supporting argument that might support a claim to knowledge.

(b) §5–6. To understand incontinence we must grasp the various ways in which knowledge may be merely potential.

§5 But we speak . . . using it: In the rest of the chapter Aristotle discusses various ways of knowing and not knowing. In §5–8 he discusses different cases that do not completely fit incontinents, but eventually help us to understand some aspects of incontinents' state of mind. The cases discussed in §5–8 all show how someone can fail to draw the right conclusion about a particular case. They do not entirely fit the incontinent; he must draw the right conclusion, since he makes the right DECISION (1148a9, 1150b30, 1151a25, 1152a17). But they will nonetheless turn out to be relevant.

1146b33 attending: See STUDY.

§6 particular premise: Lit., 'partial' (*kata meros*), mentioning particulars (*kath'hekasta*).

For it is particulars . . . in action: Since the particular premise specifies the relevant particulars, it is not surprising if we fail to act when we lack the appropriate particular premise.

There are also . . . universal: These are not universal premises, but universal terms or concepts (e.g., 'healthy' or 'dry') that may appear in either the universal or the particular premises that have just been mentioned.

astounding if he has the other sort: It is quite intelligible if someone fails to choose this piece of food if he knows that dry food is healthy for a human being, that he is a human being, and that chicken is dry, but does not know that this piece is chicken. It is astounding, however, if he has all this knowledge and still fails to choose it.

(c) §7–8. One type of potential knowledge is especially relevant to incontinence.

§7 For we see . . . do not have it: Someone may know French but, because of his present condition, have no access to his knowledge; he does not apply the knowledge in the normal way.

those affected by strong feelings: Lit., 'those in affections' (*pathē*); see FEELING.

§8 Saying the words . . . having it]: Aristotle is suggesting that incontinents are analogous to the people he has just mentioned. He considers an objection: 'The cases are not analogous. For if I'm asleep, my knowledge is unavailable to me because I don't draw any conclusions at all. But the incontinent draws the right conclusions from his knowledge.' Aristotle answers the objection by querying the last claim; he remarks that simply saying the right words is not proof of really *drawing* the right conclusion.

Here Aristotle is describing the state the incontinent is in when he is overcome by his incontinent desire, not the state he is in before he is overcome (see 2.§2 on the importance of this distinction). In §9 he reverts to the time before the incontinent is overcome.

(d) §9–11. When someone acts incontinently, the normal connection between universal and particular beliefs is disrupted by appetite.

§9 Further, we may . . . nature: Aristotle discusses the question from a natural (i.e., psychological; see NATURE) point of view, referring to the structure of practical INFERENCE; cf. *DA* 431a15, *MA* 7, *Rhet.* 1392b19.

result in one belief: This one belief appears to be the affirmation of the conclusion of the practical inference (e.g., 'this must be tasted'). This is referred to in 'what has been concluded'.

it is necessary, . . . has been concluded: Lit., (following the Greek word order), 'it is necessary that the thing that has been concluded, in the one case the soul affirms, and in productive does at once'. In 'in the one case' Aristotle probably refers to purely theoretical beliefs that have no immediate bearing on action; in these cases one stops short at affirming the conclusion. After 'productive', the most likely supplement is 'beliefs'; a less likely one would be 'premises'. It is puzzling that Aristotle uses 'PRODUCTIVE' here, referring to instrumental reason, where we might expect a more general reference to ACTION; perhaps he is influenced by his choice of example.

The Greek makes it clear that 'the thing that has been concluded' is the object both of 'affirms' and 'does'. Practical inferences require the mental drawing of a conclusion in a belief (cf. 'result in one belief' above). This passage, therefore, conflicts with the view that Aristotle regards the conclusion of a practical inference as an action rather than a belief in some proposition. (Some have ascribed such a view to Aristotle on the strength of *MA* 7.)

it is necessary . . . at the same time: Probably 'unhindered' refers to external hindrances as in *Met.* 1048a10–24, *DA* 417a27. In that case, an incontinent desire does not prevent someone from acting 'unhindered'; hence Aristotle seems to imply that the incontinent acts 'at once' on the conclusion of correct practical inference. How, then, can his conclusion fail to have its usual effect on action? This is the question Aristotle tries to answer in his account of how incontinence happens. The account is brief and obscure, and the notes suggest only one possible interpretation.

§10 the universal belief hindering him from tasting: We may call this belief 'the good major premise'. It corresponds to 'Everything sweet must be tasted' in the previous example. In the present case, Aristotle does not say exactly what the universal belief says. Most probably it is 'Nothing pleasant must be tasted' (i.e., one must not taste anything pleasant); this is probably not meant to be realistic, but just to bring out the main point about incontinence (since the incontinent has misguided appetites that need to be restrained). Alternatively, it might be 'Nothing sweet must be tasted'.

he has the second belief, that everything sweet is pleasant and this is sweet: This is the 'good minor premise' attached to the good major premise just stated. Less probably, (i) 'Everything sweet is pleasant' and (ii) 'This is sweet' might be taken as two distinct beliefs. In that case one might take (i) as the 'bad major premise' of a rival inference; this leads to further differences of interpretation at later stages of the account.

this belief is active: Probably this refers to the whole good minor premise. (If we accept the less probable view mentioned in the previous note, it will refer only to (ii).) Aristotle makes it clear that the first three cases of actual and potential knowledge (1146b31–1147a10) do not apply to the incontinent at this stage.

but it turns out that appetite is present in him: He has an appetite (i.e., a nonrational DESIRE; for its role in incontinence, cf. i 13.§15–18, iii 2.§4) for the pleasant. Hence the belief that is his good minor premise focuses both his good major premise (expressing his rational desire) and his appetite on this particular thing (e.g., a sweet cake).

The belief, then, . . . tells him to avoid this: The supplement implies that this belief is belief in the good conclusion formed from the good major and good minor premises. (It is less likely to be the belief in the good major premise only; how could Aristotle say that the good major premise tells the agent to avoid this particular thing?) The incontinent person draws and believes the good conclusion. Hence, he has formed the correct decision (cf. note to iii 3.§13). Further, given the end of §9, he must immediately act. Probably Aristotle means that his acting consists in his trying to avoid tasting this sweet thing.

but appetite . . . [bodily] parts: Despite his having drawn the good conclusion, his appetite moves him to taste the sweet thing, since his belief in the good minor premise has made him aware of the opportunity for pleasure.

The [second] belief . . . own right: The supplement implies that Aristotle has in mind the incontinent's belief in the good minor premise. This causes his incontinent action (since without it his appetite for pleasure would not be aware of this present opportunity for pleasure), but simply holding this belief is not opposed to the correct reason (since it is actually a premise leading to the good conclusion).

§11 That is also why beasts . . . particulars: On beasts, see ANIMAL. Nonrational animals, in Aristotle's view, cannot form universal beliefs of the sort exemplified in the good major premise.

(e) §12–14. Hence the incontinent person lacks a certain kind of knowledge.

§12 How is the ignorance . . . knowledge: §12 does not seem to fit into its context. So far Aristotle has said nothing to explain or defend the claim that the incontinent is ignorant. His explanation and defense comes in §13–14.

§13 Since the last premise is a belief about something perceptible: The last premise (*protasis*) is probably the whole good minor premise, i.e., 'Everything sweet is pleasant, and this is sweet'. See note to §10 above for other possible views. Less probably, '*protasis*' might be translated 'proposition' rather than 'premise'; in that case, it would refer to the good conclusion.

this is what the incontinent person does not have when he is being affected: If the previous 'Since . . . ' gives a reason for this, Aristotle must assume that if the incontinent person had the good minor premise when he is being affected (sc. by incontinence), he would not act incontinently. He seems to assume this because he also assumes that (i) if he had the good minor premise, he would also have the good conclusion, and (ii) if he had the good conclusion, he would act on it (see end of §9).

We may be surprised, however, by Aristotle's claim. For (a) the incontinent must have had the good minor premise in order to reach the good conclusion, which he must have reached for 'tells him to avoid this' to be true (see note to §10); and (b) he must still believe the good minor premise in order to act incontinently, since the good minor premise shows him that this particular thing is pleasant. In reply to (a), Aristotle concedes that the incontinent had the good minor premise, but denies that he still has it when he is being affected. In reply to (b), Aristotle probably means to distinguish (1) believing a proposition, from (2) believing it as part of an inference, and insists that only (2) counts as having a major or minor premise. I have an inference, in his view, only when I 'combine' (*sumtheōrein*) two beliefs properly (§9 above: 'these two beliefs result in one belief'; cf. *APr* 67a37). If I fail to combine them, I no longer have the beliefs as premises, even though I still believe them. In the incontinent, then, the belief that initially constituted the good minor premise becomes disconnected from the good major premise, and no longer constitutes the good minor premise; it is now connected with his appetite for pleasure, not with his rational desire.

Or [rather] the way . . . words: Aristotle answers an objection to his claim that the incontinent lacks the good minor premise. The objector points out that the incontinent says all the right words (the good minor premise and—Aristotle seems to concede—the good conclusion). Aristotle replies that the incontinent is now no longer genuinely inferring the good conclusion, but simply saying the words without believing them.

as the drunk . . . Empedocles: Aristotle recalls the discussion of ignorance in §7–8 above. This sentence would appropriately introduce §12, which also refers to the examples in §7–8.

And since the last term . . . universal term: The 'last term' (for 'term', cf. note to vi 8.§9) is probably what has just been called the 'last premise', i.e., the good minor premise. Similarly, the 'universal term' is probably the good major premise.

§14 dragged about . . . affected: The belief that constitutes the good minor premise is dragged about because it is detached from the good major premise and is attached to appetite instead. Socrates is, therefore, correct in thinking that some kind of ignorance is needed to explain incontinence.

is not the sort . . . perceptual knowledge: 'Fully knowledge' probably refers to the good conclusion, expressing the agent's knowledge that he ought not to taste this sweet thing. This knowledge, in contrast to the knowledge expressed in the good minor premise, is not dragged about (from rational desire to appetite) in the incontinent; for he does not connect it with his appetite, but simply loses it.

4

4.§1–6. Simple incontinence versus qualified incontinence

(a) §2. Different types of pleasure

§2 Some sources . . . choiceworthy in their own right, . . . excess: Cf. 1110b3, 1129b1; see UNQUALIFIED. Continence and incontinence have a limited range for the same reason that temperance has; see note to iii 10.§8.

(b) §2. Qualified forms of incontinence

Olympic victor named Human: The winning boxer in the Olympics of 456 B.C. was called Anthropos (see HUMAN BEING). Aristotle and his school compiled a list of victors in the Olympic games (for chronological purposes); see Diogenes Laertius v 21.

1148a3 a vice, either unqualified or partial: The last phrase might, less plausibly, be attached to 'incontinence' rather than to 'vice'. In that case it will presumably refer to two types of simple incontinence.

(c) §3–4. Simple incontinence and intemperance are about the same types of pleasures and pains.

§4 1148a17 the intemperate person decides . . . does not: Cf. 1119a1; 1146b22; 1150a19–23, b29; 1151a7, 22; 1152a4, 15–24. The intemperate person has a settled DECISION and policy of pursuing the bodily pleasures before him; this is what he mistakenly regards as the good to be pursued, 1113a28. Hence he does not suffer the conflicts of the incontinent; but cf. 1166b5–29. Since the incontinent has a correct decision, and violates it by his incontinent action, he suffers conflicts.

(d) §5–6. Some forms of qualified incontinence are not blameworthy.

§5 1148b2 vice: Here 'VICE' translates *'mochthēria'*, but in 1148a3, b10, it renders *'kakia'*. Aristotle does not seem to intend any distinction.

5

5.§1–9. Simple incontinence contrasted with bestial and diseased states

(a) §2. Bestiality

§2 the female human being: This use of *anthrōpos* seems to indicate disapproval; cf. *MM* 1188b33.

what is said about Phalaris: Phalaris was TYRANT of Acragas in Sicily (570–549 B.C.). He is supposed to have roasted his enemies alive in a bronze bull (perhaps, in the light of the previous example and §7 below, Aristotle implies that they were roasted to be eaten). 'Is said' might indicate reservations about the truth of the story.

(b) §3. Disease

(c) §4–7. These conditions allow only qualified vice, and hence qualified incontinence.

§4 If nature . . . rather than mounting: Aristotle relies on the association between 'incontinence' (*akrasia*) and being overcome or failure to control (*kratein*). He means that WOMEN are by nature the passive partners in sexual intercourse.

§6 naturally lack reason and live only by sense perception: This is the mark of nonrational ANIMALS (cf. 1147b5).

(d) §8–9. Simple vice and simple incontinence

§9 transference: See HOMONYMY.

6

6.§1–5. Simple incontinence contrasted with incontinence about spirit

(a) §1. Simple incontinence is less closely related to reason.

§1 1149a33 and spirit, . . . at once: When we act on spirit (*thumos*; evidently Aristotle has ANGER especially in mind here) we have some beliefs about the RIGHTNESS of what we are doing, and we are not simply moved by pleasure or pain. For this contrast, cf. 1146b23, 1151a23, 1152a6. 'As though' indicates that we are not acting on a genuine DECISION here; see 1111b18. Pleasure by itself, however, provides a reason for action.

This description of spirit recalls Plato's remarks about it in *Rep.* iv (e.g., 440b–441c).

(b) §2. It is less natural, and hence less pardonable.

§2 Further, it is more pardonable . . . are common: The actions considered here are pardonable not because they are involuntary, but because they reflect pardonable lapses in human nature (1110a23), expressing tendencies that we recognize as appropriate for a human being (1115b8), though they have misled someone on this occasion. No such excuse can be given for the excessive appetites of the incontinent person. (The point here is different from the point at 1136a5, where Aristotle refers to involuntary but unpardoned actions.)

It is just as the son . . . our family: The last scene of Aristophanes' *Clouds* (from 1321) illustrates the conflicts between fathers and sons mentioned here and in the next example.

(c) §3. It involves more plotting.

§3 'trick weaving Cypris': Author unknown.

'Blandishment . . . prudent': See Homer, *Il.* xiv 214, 217 (from the episode in which Hera seduces Zeus, and distracts him from the course of the fighting around Troy).

(d) §4. It more justly provokes anger.

6.§6–7. The range of pleasures proper to intemperance, and hence to incontinence

§6 Now we must grasp . . . and pleasures: This is an appropriate place to begin a new chapter. §6–7 are the first stage of a comparison between intemperance and incontinence that extends into ch. 7.

1149b34 For beasts . . . madmen among human beings are: Having decision and RATIONAL CALCULATION is necessary for the possibility of virtue, vice, or incontinence. The comment on madmen suggests that someone incapable of being moved by decision is also incapable of any of these states.

§7 Bestiality . . . absent altogether: Cf. *Pol.* 1253a31.

For in each . . . internal principle: Lit., 'for always the badness of what lacks a principle is less destructive, and understanding is a principle'. Even inanimate things, if they are natural, have an internal PRINCIPLE of some of their movements (see NATURE); and so do beasts. But only rational agents have an internal principle that explains their goodness and badness; it is subject to their choice and DECISION.

7

7.§1–8. Incontinence and the vices corresponding to it

(a) §1–2. Intemperance and softness

§1 Now it is possible . . . overcome most people: See ETHICS (4), 1118b23, 1125b14, 1150b12, 1151a5, 1152a7. Deviations from the average or most frequent are what we remark most easily in calling someone incontinent, just as when we call someone tall. However, Aristotle recognizes that the average is not the proper norm for complete virtue.

§2 because they . . . on it: In a19–20 read *hē(i) kath'huperbolas kai dia prohairesin* (OCT: *ē kath' . . . ē dia . . .*).

He is intemperate; for . . . incurable: The 'for' explains why 'intemperate', *akolastos,* is the right name for him. Aristotle relies on the association of *akolastos* with *kolazein* and CORRECTIVE TREATMENT (see also TEMPERANCE). He means, 'He is also *akolastos,* incorrigible, because he is incurable and hence incorrigible'. He has 'no regrets', because he acts on his firm and settled DECISION. See 1105a33, 1110b19, 1148a17; but cf. 1166a29, b6–25.

(b) §3. Intemperance is worse than incontinence.

§3 One of those . . . differ from each other: The sequence of thought in the next few paragraphs is not easy to follow. (One might wonder whether the mss. text is in the right order.) Here Aristotle shifts from the two vices—intemperance (resulting from the decision to pursue pleasure) and its negative counterpart (resulting from the decision to avoid pain)—to incontinence and its negative counterpart, which do not include a mistaken decision.

Now it would seem . . . strikes from anger: The translation marks a new paragraph here, to indicate that this contrast seems to oppose incontinence (and similar states) to vice (a state involving decision). It does not seem to be concerned with the two states (not involving decision) just mentioned.

One of the states . . . intemperate: The supplement assumes that the two states referred to here are the negative counterpart of intemperance and intemperance itself (mentioned at the end of §2). Aristotle calls the negative counterpart 'more a species of softness', to indicate that 'softness' is not really the correct name for it; for 'softness' is his name for the negative counterpart of incontinence (mentioned at the beginning of §3).

(c) §4–7. Incontinence contrasted with softness

§4 The continent . . . soft: Aristotle now returns to the two states mentioned at the beginning of §3. Softness here is softness properly so called (as opposed to the 'species of softness' that is the negative counterpart of intemperance, mentioned at the end of §3). On softness, see 1116a14, 1145a35, 1148a11, 1179b33; *Rhet.* 1384a2.

It implies inability, reluctance, or refusal to undertake necessary pains and burdens; it often includes a suggestion of effeminacy (cf. 1150b15).

§5 1150b2 self-indulgent: The term used, *trupheros*, is cognate with *truphē*, 'luxury'; cf. 1145a35; *Pol.* 1295b17, 1310a23.

§6 Theodectes' . . . Carcinus' . . . Xenophantus: See TGF p. 803 (Theodectes), p. 797 (Carcinus); these are two fourth-century dramatists. Aristotle may be referring to the Xenophantus who was a musician in the court of Alexander.

(c) §8. Two types of incontinence: impetuosity and weakness

§8 One type . . . has not deliberated: Cf. 1151a1–3, 1152a17. It is easy to see how the weak incontinent conforms to the account given in 1147a31–5. But how does the impetuous incontinent conform to it? If he does not deliberate, how can he make the correct decision? See 1117a20, DECISION (4). He can make the right decision because of his previous deliberation even if he does not deliberate afresh on this occasion.

For some people . . . pleasant or painful: If A tickles B, A will expect B to tickle A back, and if A expects this, A will not find it so ticklish. Cf. [*Probl.*] 965a11. 'Notice something in advance' marks the point of comparison with impetuous people.

Quick-tempered and volatile . . . appearance: In Aristotle's physiological theory (see [*Probl.*] 30; *PN* 453a19), excessively hot black bile (*melaina cholē*) makes someone easily excitable and prone to strong feelings when he is excited. This is the 'volatile' (*melancholikos*) person; cf. 1154b11. (Aristotle's description shows why 'melancholy', in its contemporary English sense, would be misleading.) Ajax (in Sophocles' play) is an example of a volatile person, liable to abrupt changes of feelings that are strong and violent while they last.

8

8.§1–5. Why intemperance is worse than incontinence

(a) §1–3. Intemperance, unlike incontinence, is incurable.

§1 That is why . . . curable: Aristotle answers the puzzle he raised in 2.§10. On incurability, cf. 1114a16, 1121a20, 1121b33, 1165b18, 1180a9. Aristotle seems to think that if the incontinent deliberates better (or, in the case of the impetuous person, if he deliberates at all on these occasions, 1152a27), he will see that it is not worthwhile to abandon his decision for the pleasure offered by incontinent action; and this conclusion is supposed to cure the incontinence.

For the incontinent . . . for most people: The mss. (and OCT) have this sentence at the end of §2.

§3 Thus Demodocus . . . would do: Demodocus (sixth century B.C.), fr. 1 (West).

(b) §4–5. Intemperance, unlike incontinence, destroys principles.

§4 in actions the end . . . in mathematics: The assumptions in a demonstrative science are the basic PRINCIPLES grasped by UNDERSTANDING, with no more basic principles (see vi 6.§2, 11.§4; *APo* 72a14–24; *EE* 1227a5–13).

Reason does not teach . . . principle: If Aristotle's overall position about reason and principles is consistent, his claim in this passage needs to be reconciled with his comments on the role of prudence; see 1144a8, 1144b3, 1145a4. In stressing the limits of reason in ethical principles, Aristotle insists that more than purely cognitive training is needed. But habituated virtue itself requires prudence (see note to vi 13.§1). Aristotle allows reason a role in forming the grasp of principles.

§5 since the best . . . in him: The incontinent has the right principle because he has the right wish and makes the right DECISION, insofar as he reaches the right conclusion, before he is affected by the feelings that result in incontinence. Presumably, frequent incontinence would expose him to the corrupting effects of pleasure; cf. vi 5.§6 and note.

This claim that the incontinent has the right principle needs to be compared with the claim at vi 12.§10 that only the virtuous person grasps the right principle. Perhaps the two claims can be reconciled if we recognize that (i) the incontinent reaches the right conclusion in his decision, but (ii) he does not reach it by exactly the right deliberation, and therefore has an incomplete conception of the ultimate end; see vi 9 on good deliberation.

9

9.§1–6. Continence

(a) §1. Continence requires the correct decision.

§1 Then is someone continent . . . correct decision: Here Aristotle answers the puzzle about continence raised in 2.§7–9.

Perhaps in fact . . . decision in itself: Aristotle seems to mean: 'It is true that the incontinent and the continent differ in their tendency to abide by their decision; hence this difference distinguishes them COINCIDENTALLY. But it is not the real basis of the distinction between them, and hence it is not how they differ IN THEIR OWN RIGHT. A person is continent because of abiding by the correct decision, and incontinent because of failing to abide by it; hence a reference to the correct decision is necessary if we are to grasp the real distinction.' On choosing coincidentally, cf. iii 1.§5–7. If I do not choose F in itself, then I do not choose F without qualification (see UNQUALIFIED), but only with the qualification that F is a means to G. Here what the continent person abides by in itself and for its own sake is his true decision; it is because it is true that he abides by it. Since his true decision is his decision, he abides coincidentally by his decision, but he does not abide by it because it is his decision.

Why does Aristotle insist on this basis for distinguishing the incontinent and the continent? Why not say that the person who abides by the right principles and the person who abides by the wrong principles are continent in just the same way? For his justification, see the note to iii 10.§8. The claims about pleasure and good, and about the corrupting effects of pleasure, will not apply in the same way to a 'continent' or 'incontinent' about bad principles. If I don't always follow my intemperate desire, it will not be because the pleasure at hand is too attractive (for the pleasure is what the intemperate decision decides on); nor will repeated failure to follow the intemperate decision make me more prone to intemperance. Since different psychological explanations and treatments are required, these are different conditions.

(b) §2–3. Hence, continence must be distinguished from undesirable stubbornness.

§2 Now there are . . . their belief: The distinction he has just drawn between continence and incontinence, referring essentially to the correct decision, prompts Aristotle to mention other people who might be confused with continent people if we do not bear in mind the real basis for the genuinely continent person's sticking to his views. As usual, Aristotle wants to identify the underlying state, not simply to classify types of behavior.

(c)§4.Similarly,incontinencemustbedistinguishedfromdesirableconditions that are easily confused with it.

§4 There are also . . . *Philoctetes*: To reinforce his claims about the correct basis for distinguishing incontinence from continence, Aristotle returns to the example of Neoptolemus, mentioned in 2.§7.

for telling . . . pleasant to him: In b20, read *hēdu* (OCT: *kalon*, 'was fine to him').

for not everyone . . . shameful pleasure: Aristotle resists the conclusion that Neoptolemus displayed a desirable form of incontinence. (Modern writers have drawn a parallel conclusion from Huckleberry Finn's protection of a slave despite telling himself he was acting wrongly, or from a Nazi soldier moved by pity to fail in his duty, as he conceived it, to kill Jews.) In his view, once we understand Neoptolemus' motives, we see that he did not act incontinently at all.

(d) §5. The vice of deficiency corresponding to continence

§5 There is also . . . incontinent: This section is not directly connected with the previous one, but it is relevant to Aristotle's main aim of distinguishing continence from states that might be confused with it. Here he turns to someone who irrationally refrains from the right bodily pleasures. This person is similar to the continent person in avoiding the excessive pleasures that the incontinent pursues; but he is not continent, because he does not act from the continent person's reasons and motives.

(e) §6. The difference between continence and temperance

§6 Now many . . . similarity: Pursuing his aim of distinguishing continence correctly from other states, Aristotle takes up the common beliefs, mentioned in vii 1.§6, that reflect some uncertainty about the difference between temperance and continence. Aristotle argues that we can clearly distinguish continence from temperance, once we recognize the different mental conditions involved.

The temperate . . . led by them: On this difference between temperance and continence, see the note to iii 11.§8.

10

10.§1–4. Incontinence and prudence

(a) §1–2. Incontinent people are not prudent.

§1 Nor can . . . incontinent: Aristotle turns to the common belief mentioned in 1.§7, just after the belief discussed in 9.§6. This chapter turns from the discussion of continence to a series of loosely connected remarks on incontinence.

For we have . . . is not]: In vi 12.§9–13.§3 Aristotle has examined the relation between cleverness and prudence.

§2 However, a clever . . . requires the correct] decision: This passage is transposed from its place in the mss. and OCT (following 'But the incontinent person does not' in the next paragraph). The transposition makes a better connection both with §1 and with §3. 'Account' (*logos*) might be replaced by 'reason' (less plausibly, if the description of cleverness in the note to vi 12.§9 is correct). On difference in decision, see 1127b14.

(b) §3–4. Nor are they vicious.

§3 He is not in . . . or drunk: Aristotle reverts to the description of incontinence in 3.§12.

He acts willingly . . . doing it for: The voluntary character of action on knowledge is explored in v 8.§3, iii 1.§16. Aristotle qualifies the claim that the incontinent acts in knowledge with 'in a way'. This may be intended to allude to the incontinent's loss of the good minor premise when he is under the influence of his misguided feelings; see note to 3.§13.

For one type . . . deliberate at all: Aristotle returns to the division between impetuous and weak incontinence that he drew at 7.§8.

§3–4 In fact the incontinent . . . bad ones: This and the next paragraph interrupt the contrast between the two types of incontinence. But this paragraph fits reasonably into its context; it continues to clarify the claim that the incontinent person is better than the intemperate. Anaxandrides was a fourth century comic dramatist; see fr. 67 (Kock).

10.§4–5. Different types of incontinence

§4 Incontinence and . . . incontinent person less: This remark (cf. 7.§1) does not seem to be connected with the context. It interrupts the discussion of impetuous and weak incontinence.

The [impetuous] . . . to change: This passage seems to follow most intelligibly on the remarks about impetuous and weak incontinence in §3; it strengthens the suggestion in §3 that the impetuous incontinent is less bad because he is less of a 'plotter', since he does not deliberate. Incontinence caused by nature and by habit have not been distinguished earlier.

Indeed the reason . . . human beings': This note on habit helps to explain Aristotle's emphasis on the importance of habituation in (e.g.) ii 1, iii 5, x 9. Aristotle quotes Euenus (fifth century SOPHIST), fr. 9 (West).

11

11.§1–6. Questions about pleasure and good

(a) §1–2. The importance of pleasure

§1 Pleasure and . . . without qualification: The discussion of pleasure follows naturally on the account of the virtues, to which the account of incontinence was an appropriate supplement. However, Aristotle discusses pleasure again in x 1–5 with no reference to the treatment in vii. This is one reason for thinking that the three books including the treatment of pleasure were originally written for the *EE*; see Introduction (3). But Aristotle may have meant them to be part of the *EN* too. Though the two discussions overlap in places, Book vii discusses and rebuts antihedonist arguments in some detail (not repeated in Book x), and Aristotle may have thought this discussion worth keeping. See notes to vii 13.§2, x 5.§7, 6.§1.

§2 Further, we must . . . (*chairein*): On the virtues, see 1104b3, 1172a21; *EE* 1220a37, 1221b32. On happiness, see 1098b25.

(b) §3. Objections to pleasure

§3 Now it seems . . . same as pleasure: After noticing the general tendency (attributed to 'most people' in §2) to connect happiness with pleasure and enjoyment, Aristotle notices a contrary tendency in the views of 'some people'. In this book Aristotle especially attacks the arguments against pleasure. In Book x he accepts some objections to the claims of pleasure.

(c) §4. Arguments to show that pleasure is not a good

§4 The reasons . . . these: We may label the objections in §4–6 as follows: (1a) Pleasure as becoming. (1b) Temperance and pleasure. (1c) Prudence and pleasure. (1d) Pleasure as impediment. (1e) Pleasure and craft. (1f) Animals and children. (2a) Shameful pleasures. (2b) Harmful pleasures. (3) Pleasure not an end. He answers these objections in the following discussion.

Every pleasure . . . nature: Something's nature is not necessarily its original state; here Aristotle takes it to be a thing's complete perfect state, which it grows and develops into. See NATURE (2).

Further, . . . prudent thinking: Or 'intelligent thinking'. (*Phronein* may have a general sense here. See PRUDENCE.)

(d) §5. Arguments to show that not all pleasures are good

(e) §6. Argument to show that pleasure is not the best good

12

12.§1–7. Pleasure and good: replies to objections

(a) §1–2. Unqualified versus coincidental pleasures

§1 These arguments, . . . best good: Aristotle does not agree that pleasure is the final good; he only claims these objections do not, by themselves, show it is not. For an objection Aristotle accepts, see 1172b26–35.

First of all, . . . and becomings: Aristotle applies his distinction between types of goods to types of pleasures; see UNQUALIFIED. The difference between processes and becomings (see MOVEMENT) is not exploited in vii; see note to x 2.§4.

1152b31 not on each occasion: Read *aei d'ou* (OCT: *haplōs d'ou*; 'not without qualification').

Some are not . . . treatment: Aristotle often distinguishes real from apparent goods. Here he suggests, more puzzlingly, that an analogous distinction can be applied to pleasures. Cf. 1113a31, 1173b20, 1176a22.

§2 Further, since . . . nature: The pleasure that we feel in recovery should not be identified with the process of recovery or the replenishment of an appetite or a lack. In recovery it is not the process but the ACTIVITY of the healthy part (the rest of our nature, i.e., the part undisturbed by the illness) that is the source of pleasure; the pleasure itself neither is nor requires any process of recovery.

we do not enjoy the same thing . . . eventually fully restored: In a2 delete *hēdei* (OCT retains). In a3 read *kai [ēdē]* (OCT: *kai* alone).

for as pleasant . . . differ too: This passage distinguishes the activity in which pleasure is taken, from the pleasure that is taken in it.

(b) §3. Pleasures are not becomings.

§3 Further, it is not . . . becoming: This is an answer to objection (3) (see note to 11.§4).

They are activities, . . . some state]: This is Aristotle's alternative to his opponents' view of pleasure as a becoming or process (cf. note to x 3.§4). His view is fully developed in x 4.

That is why . . . becoming: This paragraph answers objection (1a) (see note to 11.§4).

It should instead be called an activity . . . unimpeded: In 'an activity' the indefinite article corresponds to nothing in the Greek, but the context seems to require it. Since §2 has distinguished the activity enjoyed from the pleasure taken in it (see note to §2 above), Aristotle probably does not intend to identify pleasure with unimpeded activity as a whole. Probably he means not that the pleasure taken in running is the unimpeded activity of running, but that the pleasure is an unimpeded activity additional to the running. If this is his view, it is not very different from the view in Book x. Cf. notes to 13.§2, x 4.§8.

(c) §4. Pleasures may still be good even if they have bad results.

§4 To say that pleasures . . . moneymaking: This paragraph answers objection (2b) (see note to 11.§4).

(d) §5. The pleasure proper to an activity does not impede it.

§5 Neither prudence . . . alien pleasures: Answer to (1d) (see note to 11.§4).

(e) §6. Pleasure and craft

§6 The fact that pleasure . . . capacity: Answer to (1e) (see note to 11.§4).

(f) §7. The virtuous person does not avoid all pleasures, but only inappropriate ones.

§7 The claim . . . same reply: Consideration of the variety of pleasures answers (1b), (1c), and (1f) (see note to 11.§4).

in what ways pleasures . . . without qualification: In a29–30 read *pōs agathai kai pōs ouk agathai [haplōs]* (OCT: *pōs agathai haplōs kai pōs ouk agathai*; 'in what ways pleasures are good without qualification, and in what ways they are not good').

the prudent person . . . these: In claiming that the prudent person is discriminating, and does not reject pleasure altogether, Aristotle rejects the exaggerated view (perhaps held by SPEUSIPPUS) previously rejected in 1104b24; cf. note to iii 10.§8.

13

13.§1–7. Pleasure and happiness

(a) §1. The badness of pain supports the view that pleasure is good.

§1 Moreover, it is also agreed . . . pleasure must be a good: This section continues the reply to objections, coming back to objection (1) (see note to 11.§4). Aristotle now begins to argue more positively. In b2, 'bad in a particular way, by impeding [activities]', read *pē(i), tō(i)* (OCT: *tō(i) pē(i)*).

For the solution . . . does not succeed: Aristotle replies to an objection to his previous claim that the contrary to what is bad is good. Speusippus, in Aristotle's view, misapplies the doctrine of the mean to pleasure and pain; he takes pleasure and pain to be the extremes, and the good to consist in a state intermediate between them.

For he would not . . . essentially an evil: If Speusippus were right, pleasure and pain would both have to be essentially bad, as the excess and the deficiency are. But—Aristotle answers—we have no reason to accept this claim about pleasure. Hence pleasure and pain are not the sorts of extremes that allow us to appeal to the doctrine of the mean to find an intermediate state.

(b) §2. The account of happiness as unimpeded activity allows some pleasure to be the best good.

§2 Besides, just as . . . pleasures are bad: Further reply to objection (3) (see note to 11.§1).

Indeed, presumably, . . . an unimpeded activity]: Lit., 'Presumably it is also necessary, if there are unimpeded activities of each state, whether the activity of all of them is happiness, or of some one of them, if it is unimpeded, for it to be most choiceworthy; and pleasure is this'. Some possible interpretations apart from the one assumed in the translation: (1) We might take the antecedent of 'this' to be 'most choiceworthy' rather than 'an unimpeded activity'. (2) We might take the antecedent of 'this' to be 'unimpeded activity' rather than 'an unimpeded activity'. Then the argument would be: (a) Happiness is a type of unimpeded activity. (b) Pleasure is identical to unimpeded activity. (c) Therefore, happiness is a type of pleasure.

We have seen, however, that Aristotle does not seem to endorse (b); see note on 12.§3 above. Probably the argument is meant to show not that pleasure is the highest good, but that, for all the objections have shown, it still might be; cf. note to x 3.§11. Pleasure meets one necessary condition for happiness, since it is an unimpeded activity; and the possibility remains open that the right sort of pleasure might be the activity that is happiness. Aristotle's own view on this question is explained only when he explains more fully the relation between the activity that is pleasure and the activity in which the pleasure is taken; see 1175a19. Nothing in Book vii requires him to deny that these two activities are different; cf. note to 12.§2.

and so some type of pleasure might be the best good: If we prefer one of the alternative interpretations of the previous clauses (see previous note), we will prefer 'would be' to 'might be'.

(c) §3–4. Happiness requires pleasure and good fortune in addition to virtue.

§3 Some maintain, . . . are good: Aristotle rejects the identification of happiness with virtue; cf. 1095b31. The virtuous person who is tortured can be brave, but he is hindered from activating his other capacities; hence his activity cannot be complete. On FORTUNE, see 1099a31; *EE* viii 2; *Phys*. 197b25.

Whether they . . . nonsense: Lit., 'Willingly (see VOLUNTARY) or unwillingly, they are saying nothing.' Aristotle dismisses this view even more brusquely than in 1096a1.

§4 For when it . . . to happiness: Good fortune is subject to the limits that apply to the goods described in v 1.§9 (see note).

(d) §5–6. The universal pursuit of pleasure supports the view that some pleasure is the good.

§5 No 'rumor . . . [spread] . . . ': Hesiod, *Works and Days* 763–4. Hesiod continues: 'She (sc. rumor) also is a goddess' (or 'a sort of goddess').

§6 for all things . . . divine [in them]: See GOD (4).

However, the bodily . . . only pleasures: This is a footnote, anticipating an objection to the argument just given. Aristotle warns against a one-sided choice of examples of pleasures. His account of correct pleasures is developed more fully in Book x.

(e) §7. The significance of pleasure for happiness implies that it is a good.

§7 It is also . . . not a good: Aristotle returns to objection (1) (see note to 11.§4), and so passes from considering whether pleasure is the good to considering whether it is a good. He assumes that happiness is the highest good including all goods (HAPPINESS [2]). Hence, if pleasure is not a good, we ought not to expect happiness to include pleasure. In that case, our view will conflict with the common belief that happiness must include pleasure and exclude pain.

In a1, read *mē [hē]* (OCT: *mē*). In a2, read *kai energeia* (OCT: *kai hē energeia*).

14

14.§1–8. Bodily pleasures, and their degree of goodness

(a) §1–2. They are good, within the proper limits.

§1 Those who maintain . . . examine bodily pleasures: The discussion of bodily pleasures in this chapter is a further reply to objection (2) (see note to 11.§4).

(b) §3–4. It is easy to pursue bodily pleasures to excess; that is why people mistakenly regard pleasure as bad in itself.

§3 We must, . . . promotes confidence: On this procedure, see ETHICS (7). Since the whole discussion is organized around the common beliefs about pleasure that were introduced in ch. 11, it is reasonable for Aristotle to show that his theory can account for the beliefs that he rejects.

§4 Indeed these . . . have said: This paragraph is a parenthetical remark. Aristotle comments that the very features that make bodily pleasures desirable to some people also lead some theorists—who generalize mistakenly from bodily pleasures to all pleasures (see 13.§6)—to infer that no pleasures are good.

1154b1 In fact these: Read *hai dē* (OCT: *hai de*).

(c) §5–7. Bodily pleasures are intense, because of our natural imperfections.

§5 whenever [the pleasures] are harmless: Alternatively, 'whenever [the thirsts] . . . '.

For an animal is always suffering: Perhaps Aristotle is quoting or paraphrasing Anaxagoras here. This paragraph (to the end of §6) explains the claim that some people's natural constitution makes them so restless that they cannot bear a neutral condition without pain or pleasure. Aristotle mentions three cases. (a) Normal people are used to the pains involved in natural processes and exertions. (b) Young people find these natural processes pleasant because they happen so quickly (cf. *[Probl.]* 955a1–17). (c) Volatile people (see note to 7.§8) find that the natural processes are abnormally painful.

§7 Pleasures . . . no excess: The discussion of pleasures that involve pain and restoration leads Aristotle to contrast such pleasures with ones that do not involve these conditions.

(d) §8. These natural imperfections explain our pursuit of variety in pleasures.

§8 That is why the god . . . [without change]: The GOD is better than we are because he can attain all at once what we can obtain only to some degree over time. COMPLETE human happiness must be complex, and must include various activities if we are to approximate to the happiness that is complete all at once. Cf. *Met.* 1072b14–20.

'Variation . . . sweet': Euripides, *Orestes* 234.

(e) §9. Conclusion of discussion of incontinence and pleasure

§9 So much, . . . friendship as well: This conclusion is equally suitable for the *EE* and the *EN*.

BOOK VIII

1

1.§1–5. Common beliefs about friendship

(a) §1–4. Friendship is necessary in a wide range of circumstances.

§1 Further, . . . most necessary . . . life: 'Necessary' does not imply that Aristotle will confine himself to the instrumental value of friendship. Many of his examples illustrate the noninstrumental value we attach to friendship. He means that friendship is a necessary part of any tolerable human life. The ways in which friendship is necessary are discussed in §1–4; §5 turns to the ways in which it is a virtue or involves virtue, by considering how it is fine.

For no one . . . all the other goods: This suggests that friendship is not merely instrumental. Aristotle defends this attitude to friendship in ix 9.

§2 But in poverty . . . only refuge: Friendship is not merely appealing when everything else is going well; it is also necessary in other material circumstances, and at different stages of life.

'when two go together . . . ': Homer, *Il.* x 224 (Homer continues: 'one person alone has inferior wits').

§3 Members of the same species: Lit., 'members of the same race'. But the rest of the paragraph shows that Aristotle has species in mind (i.e., friendship among dogs or human beings, rather than friendship among greyhounds or Greeks).

that is . . . humanity: In the rest of Books viii and ix Aristotle does not discuss friendship directed toward other people in general, or to people one does not know. Moreover, such an attitude does not have a prominent, explicit place in his ethical theory. It is all the more remarkable that he takes its praiseworthiness for granted here.

§4 Moreover, friendship . . . which is enmity: On friendship and justice, see chs. 9–11. On concord, see ix 6.

and the justice . . . friendship: Perhaps this refers to decency, discussed in v 10. At any rate, decency illustrates what Aristotle has in mind.

(b) §5. It is fine as well as necessary.

§5 But friendship . . . fine: 'Fine' repeats the claim in 'a virtue, or involves virtue' in 1155a4. Friendship might be necessary for a good life, as FORTUNE and pleasure are, without being admirable and praiseworthy (cf. 1101b11, 1109b31), as a person's own achievement; hence Aristotle is careful to insist that friendship is also praiseworthy. See 1159a23; 1169a8, 35.

1.§6–7. Puzzles about friendship

(a) §6. Is it based on similarity or on difference?

§6 Still, . . . about friendship: It is reasonable to begin a new chapter here. Following his normal practice (cf. the discussions of incontinence and of pleasure), Aristotle, having set out the common beliefs, turns to the puzzles (see ETHICS [5]).

'Similar to . . . each other: See Homer, *Od.* xvii 218; Hesiod, *Works and Days* 225. (No known source for 'birds of a feather'.)

On these questions . . . natural science: Aristotle largely ignores the disputes referred to here, but he alludes to them in 8.§6–7 below. Cf. Plato, *Lys.* 214a.

Euripides . . . earth: Euripides, TGF fr. 898.

Heracleitus . . . struggle: DK 22 B 80.

Others, . . . Empedocles, . . . similar: DK 31 B 22, 62, 90.

(b) §7. Puzzles relevant to ethical discussion

§7 Let us, then, leave . . . characters and feelings: In his ethical argument Aristotle prefers to avoid digressions into cosmology or other nonethical areas, thinking them inappropriate; cf. 1096b31, 1159b23; *GC* 316a11–14; *EE* 1217a3, 1218b33.

We have . . . earlier: This sentence might refer to ii 8, or to *Catg.* 6b10–7. It may have been added by a later editor.

2

2.§1–4. Conditions for friendship

(a) §1–2. The object of friendship: the lovable

§1 Perhaps these . . . lovable: 'Lovable' renders *philēton,* which might be rendered 'what is loved', 'what can be loved', 'proper object of love', 'what deserves to be loved'. On this ambiguity, see CHOICEWORTHY. For the three objects of love, see 1104b30.

§2 Now do people love . . . will be what appears lovable: Aristotle distinguishes (a) what is lovable without qualification, (b) what is lovable for (or 'to'; cf. notes to iii 4.§4; x 3.§8) each person, and (c) what appears lovable to each person. This division needs to be compared with iii 4. See also UNQUALIFIED, 1156b13.

(b) §3. Friendship requires reciprocal goodwill.

§3 There are these three causes, then, of love: Lit., 'There being three things because of (*dia*) which they love'. The different types of friendship are 'for' (*dia*) character, utility, and pleasure. Here *'dia'* might refer either to the final or to the efficient CAUSE of the friendship. (Cf. 'They're hanging men and women for the wearing of the green', clearly with an efficient-causal rather than a final-causal sense.) Most probably it refers to both; since the remark that these are the causes of love summarizes the account of how they are the objects of love, 'causes' ought to include the aim of the friendship as well as the origin; 1156a31, 1172b21 associate *'dia'* clearly with the final cause.

For it would presumably . . . own sake: The contrast with wine seems to make two points. (1) We cannot really wish good to it; that is, we cannot wish for its welfare. It has no choices, desires or aims of its own. Its good consists simply in its being preserved for our use. (2) Since it has no choices, etc., of its own, we cannot wish goods to it for its own sake. We wish goods to our friend for his own sake, insofar as we regard a friend's having certain aims and desires as a good reason (under certain conditions) for us to satisfy them. This is the same attitude that we take to our own aims and desires.

When Aristotle says that 'it is said' we must wish goods to our friend for his own sake, he does not thereby endorse this common belief. We must consider how far the different kinds of friendship meet this condition. See next note.

(c) §4. It also requires mutual knowledge of reciprocal goodwill.

§4 [If they are to be friends], then, they must: The translation assumes that 'they must' refers (a) to the people (just mentioned) who have mutual goodwill. Alternatively, we might take it to refer (b) to friends in general. If (b) is right, Aristotle asserts here that wishing good to the friend for his own sake is a necessary condition for friendship. If (a) is right, he does not go so far (see previous note); he just says what needs to be added to mutual goodwill to create friendship. The decision between (a) and (b) matters for deciding whether Aristotle takes the same view about goodwill in this chapter and in ix 5.

from one of the causes mentioned above: Lit., 'because of (*dia*) one of the three things mentioned above'. This might mean: (1) Any of the three causes mentioned is a basis for goodwill. (2) One (and perhaps only one) is a basis for goodwill.

3

3.§1–5. Incomplete types of friendship

(a) §1–3. Friendships for utility and pleasure are coincidental.

§1 Since these causes . . . of friendship: The connection of thought would be clearer if these three sentences formed the end of ch. 2, and ch. 3 began with the next paragraph.

For each object . . . awareness of it: Aristotle justifies the threefold division of friendship from the description of friendship in ch. 2, except that he does not mention goodwill here (see next note).

But those . . . each other: Some editors punctuate so as to make this sentence part of the previous one (in which case 'But' should be replaced by 'and'). It is better, however, to take it as the beginning of a new topic, the discussion of the extent to which all three types of friendship are really genuine friendships. In pointing out that different types of friends wish good to the other in different ways, Aristotle suggests that in the incomplete friendships (those for utility and pleasure) goodwill is not fully present. In these, A wishes good to B only insofar as B is useful or pleasant to A, not for B's own sake. 1167a10–21 seems to exclude UNQUALIFIED goodwill from the incomplete friendships; cf. 1156b8; 1157a15, 18; 1164a10.

The three types of friendship are literally 'because of (*dia*; see note to 2.§4) the pleasant', 'because of the useful', and 'because of being such' (*poios*, i.e., a certain sort of person).

§2 not insofar as the beloved is who he is: Read *ouch hē(i) ho philoumenos estin hosper estin*, as in the next sentence. (OCT omits *hosper estin*, with the mss.; even if this is right, the supplement seems to give the right sense.) Aristotle takes (1) A loves B for who B is, (2) A loves B in B's own right, not coincidentally, and (3) A loves B for B's own sake, to imply one another. (The implication between (3) and (1)/(2) is less obvious; but see previous note.)

(b) §3–4. Friendship for utility

§3 What is useful . . . different times: We ought to begin a new paragraph here. In the rest of §3 and in §4, Aristotle defends the claim in the first sentence of §3, as it applies to friendship for utility. In §5 he defends the claim, as it applies to friendship for pleasure.

§4 This sort . . . older people . . . expedient: See YOUTH.

The friendship of hosts . . . this type too: If A is an Athenian and B is a Spartan, each is the *xenos* of the other, if A provides B with hospitality in Athens and B does the same for A in Sparta, and they provide each other with other sorts of reciprocal mutual aid. Hence *xenos* may be translated both 'host' and 'guest'. See OCD, s.v. 'Friendship, ritualized'.

(c) §5. Friendship for pleasure

3.§6–9. Complete friendship

(a) §6. Friendship for virtue is noncoincidental.

§6 But complete . . . good in their own right: Here Aristotle applies the general claim in 3.§1 (see note) that 'those who love each other wish goods to each other [only] insofar as they love each other' to the case of friendship for virtue.

[Hence they . . . not coincidentally: The supplement indicates what Aristotle must be taking for granted in claiming that friends for virtue love each other for their own sake. This feature of friendship has not been mentioned since 2.§3. Aristotle now concludes that in the best kind of friendship three conditions coincide. (1) A loves B for B's own sake. (2) A loves B for what B really is. (3) A loves B because B has a virtuous character. He suggests again (see 3.§2, note) that each of these conditions implies the other two.

He defends the connection between (2) and (3) in 'they are good in their own right' (i.e., their good character is an essential property of them). To connect (1) and (2) he seems to assume that A would not find B worth loving for B's own sake if he did not love B for himself, for what B essentially is, and A would not love B for what B essentially is if B were not essentially good (cf. 1157a18).

Hence these people's . . . virtue is enduring: See 1100b11. Complete stability is not guaranteed; see 1165b23.

Each of them is both . . . advantageous for each other: Cf. note to 2.§2 above.

They are pleasant . . . each other: On pleasure, see 1099a7, 1176a10.

(b) §7. It is stable.

§7 For they are . . . good]: In b22, read *homoioi* (OCT: *homoia*).

(c) §8–9. It is rare.

§8 Further, they need . . . each other: Lit., 'time and accustoming are needed'; cf. 1157a11, 1158a15, 1167a11.

for, as the proverb says, . . . it says: Lit., 'before they have poured out together the salts spoken of'. Greeks spoke of table companions as sharing 'salt and table'; hence the proverb means that people must share many meals before they can know each other (for the precise amount of salt, see *EE* 1238a2).

4

4.§1–6. Similarities between complete and incomplete friendship

(a) §1–2. The stability of incomplete friendships rests on their similarity to complete friendship.

§1 This sort of friendship . . . useful to each other: The account of complete friendship between virtuous people has two roles. (1) It explains how the inferior forms of friendship are not fully friendships, since they lack the essential element of goodwill. (2) It explains why they are nonetheless appropriately called friendships, since each of them has some of the central features of complete friendship. Here Aristotle turns to (2).

For the erotic . . . by his lover: This paragraph seems to be a parenthetical explanation of the contrast that Aristotle has just drawn between witty people who take pleasure in the same thing and erotic lovers who take pleasure in different things.

When the beloved's bloom is fading: 'Bloom' refers to the time in which an adolescent boy was thought especially desirable to an older man. Cf. note to x 4.§8; OCD, s.v. 'Homosexuality'.

Many, however, . . . accustomed to them: It is not clear whether Aristotle takes this fondness for character to indicate (a) friendship for pleasure (as in the witty people he has mentioned), or (b) transformation of friendship for pleasure into complete friendship.

§2 Those who exchange . . . less enduring friends: Aristotle adds another type of erotic friendship to those based on pleasure.

Those who are friends for utility . . . expedient for them: This follows awkwardly on the previous sentence. The connection of thought is clearer if we connect this sentence with the paragraph beginning 'With these [incomplete friends] also, . . . ' (1157a3), and treat the intervening two paragraphs as a parenthesis. (The sequence would be clearer if we deleted 'in their erotic relations' at the beginning of §2, and began this paragraph, 'For those who are friends for utility' [reading *gar* instead of the mss. reading *de*].)

(b) §2–3. Moreover, the instability of complete friendships results from their difference from complete friendship.

Clearly, however, . . . other person himself: The connection between complete friendship and concern for the other for his own sake is reaffirmed; cf. 3.§6 and note. Bad people can find some pleasure in features of each other (cf. 1159b10, 1166b13), but a bad person, Aristotle assumes, cannot find pleasure in the other person himself, but only in some nonessential property of him.

(c) §4–6. The degrees of similarity to complete friendship explain why other types of friendship count as friendship.

§4 Hence we must . . . than one: Aristotle does not say that the friendships are HOMONYMOUS. But his reasons for recognizing different species of friendship are similar to his reasons for recognizing homonymy; he wants to explain the common beliefs and to justify them as far as possible. His view here seems to be that there is one DEFINITION of friendship, which is fully satisfied only by complete friendship, and is only partly satisfied by friendships for pleasure and utility; see 1158b1–11. Cf. the relation suggested in *EE* 1236a7–32, b17–27.

On this view, . . . by similarity: The rest of the paragraph defends this claim. First, the sentence 'For insofar as there is something good . . . ' urges that the incomplete friendships really have something in common with complete friendship, and therefore should be counted as friendships. By contrast, the two sentences of §5 'But these [incomplete] types of friendship . . . very regularly combined' point out the differences from complete friendship, and show why the other types are friendships merely by similarity.

§6 Friendship has . . . species: This section sums up the argument of chs. 3–4.

These, then, are friends . . . similar to these: When A and B are 'friends coincidentally', A is not a friend of B himself, but of the pleasant or useful features that coincidentally (nonessentially) belong to B.

5

5.§1–5. The characteristics of friendship are fully present only in complete friendship.

(a) §1. Friendship requires both states and activities.

§1 Just as, . . . of friendship: The relevance of this discussion of STATES and their corresponding ACTIVITIES becomes clear only in §4; Aristotle is considering further recognized aspects of friendship that are fully present only in complete friendship.

(b) §2–3. The appropriate activities imply pleasure in living together.

§3 For nothing is as proper . . . solitary life fits them least of all: On the solitary life, cf. note to i 7.§6. Aristotle is not thinking of people living in the same house (which was not a very important center of a Greek man's life), but of shared activities; hence they 'spend their days' in the ways described in ix 12. Aristotle returns to this aspect of happiness in ix 9.§1–3.

(c) §4–5. Only complete friendship includes the right activities and attitudes.

§4 choiceworthy to . . . good or pleasant to himself: Instead of 'to' we might prefer 'for'. Cf. notes to iii 4.§4; x 3.§8, 5.§10–11.

§5 For loving . . . not their feeling: The argument implies that a good person wishes good because of his DECISION (5). Like the virtues, friendship is associated with the appropriate state and decision.

6

6.§1–7. The characteristics of friendship in the incomplete friendships

(a) §1. They are more typical of friendship for pleasure.

§1 Among sour . . . productive of friendship: There is no good reason to begin a new chapter here. Aristotle is carrying on his contrast between the actions and attitudes characteristic of complete friendship and those of incomplete friendships. See YOUTH.

(b) §2–3. Both types of incomplete friendship are superficial in comparison with complete friendship.

§2 for [complete . . . single individual: The supplement assumes that the comparison with excess applies both to complete friendship and to erotic passion.

Alternatively, one might take it to apply only to erotic passion; in that case, 'for . . .' would be a parenthesis.

On the right number of friends, see 1171a6.

§3 [To find . . . difficult: We should not begin a new section here, since the remark is closely connected with the rarity of good people. Since a person's goodness does not become clear at once, we need both experience (over some length of time) and familiarity (in many situations). Since it is difficult to have the right experience and familiarity with many people, the relevant kind of friendship cannot extend to many people.

for many people to please: Read *pollous areskein* (OCT: *pollois areskein*).

and the services take little time: This marks a contrast with the time and experience needed to form complete friendships.

(c) §4. Friendship for pleasure comes closer to complete friendship.

§4 Moreover, blessedly . . . sources of pleasure: A BLESSEDLY HAPPY person requires friendship as part of his life, as Aristotle argues more fully in ix 9.

no one . . . Good Itself . . . painful to him: This is probably a joke about the Platonic Idea discussed in i 6.

(d) §5–6. Friendships for pleasure and for utility do not often coincide.

§5 Someone in a position . . . not often both: This separation of pleasure from usefulness in friendships supports the claim that the friendships are different both from each other and from complete friendship.

For he does not seek . . . has both features: On wit, cf. 1128a4, 1176b14. These favorites of tyrants cannot be expected to have the virtue of wit; if their main object is to please the tyrant, they will tend to be buffoons. This is not the sort of condition a virtuous person would tolerate.

(e) §7. Conclusion on complete and incomplete friendships

§7 The friendships we have mentioned . . . pleasure for benefit: This section summarizes chs. 5–6 (following the summary at the end of ch. 4). In recalling the earlier reference to equality in exchange (in 4.§1), it also prepares us for the discussion of friendship between unequals in the following chapters.

7

7.§1–6. Friendship between unequals

(a) §1–2. Different types of friendship correspond to different roles and relations.

§1 rests on superiority: Lit., 'in accord with [*kata*] superiority'. The threefold division of friendships between equals is meant to apply to unequals too. Aristotle does not say so here, but see 1162a34–b4.

(b) §3–4. The equality and proportion that are proper to friendship

§3 Equality, however, . . . justice: The remark on equality in the previous sentence prompts Aristotle to guard against any misunderstanding. The type of EQUALITY relevant in friendship is not the proportional equality of 1131a11, but numerical equality; the friendship is in danger if this is violated too seriously. Cf. 1163b11.

(c) §5–6. The stability of friendship between unequals depends on the appropriate proportion.

§6 This raises a puzzle . . . god, for instance: The puzzle is this: (1) The greatest good is to be a god. (2) If you are a god you have no friends. (3) If I am your friend, I don't wish you to have no friends. (4) Hence I do not wish you to be a god. (5) Hence I do not wish the greatest good to you. Though (2) and (3) are not explicit in the text, they seem to be needed.

Aristotle's reply assumes a distinction between (1) and the claim: (1a) The greatest good for you is to become a god. Though (1) is true, (1a) is false, because you cannot both remain in existence and become a god. Becoming a god is the replacement of you by a god, not a further state of you. Since the only way for you to be a god would be to remain in existence and to become a god, and this is impossible, being a god is not a possible good for you; it could only be a good for the god who replaces you. Hence (5) does not follow from (4). See also 1166a20.

For . . . *he* will no longer have friends, and hence no longer have goods: Alternatively: 'For he will no longer be our friend, and hence will not be a good for us'.

since each person . . . to himself: On self-love, see ix 4, 8.

8

8.§1–7. Giving and receiving in friendship

(a) §1–2. In many cases, people choose being loved for its own sake.

§1 Because the many . . . to loving: This section seems to continue the discussion of proportion and equality in friendship. Here Aristotle considers the suggestion that people value their friends simply as a source of honor. The connection with the topic of friendship between unequals becomes clear only later (see note to §4–5 below).

For the flatterer . . . certainly pursue: Susceptibility to flattery is a sign that people value having friends (i.e., people who are friendly to them) as a source of honor. Love of HONOR (see iv 4) makes someone susceptible to the attention of flatterers (see iv 6). In the right conditions, one person's vices encourage further vices in others. This point might be usefully considered for the other Aristotelian virtues and vices, too (cf. 1121b3–12).

§2 Those who want honor . . . they are good: Aristotle answers the claim in §1 by arguing, first of all, that honor, taken without qualification, cannot be the end for which people want to have friends. For people want honor only with certain qualifications. On honor as a confirmation of virtue, cf. i 5.§5.

Being loved, . . . its own right: This is Aristotle's second argument against the claim in §1. Not only is honor the wrong end to explain people's liking for having friends; we do not need to refer to any ulterior end. Though having friends is sometimes a source of honor, people actually value this passive aspect of friendship (i.e., having people who are friendly to oneself) for its own sake.

(b) §3–5. But it is loving that is especially characteristic of friendship.

§3 But friendship . . . than in being loved: Aristotle now turns from the passive to the active side of friendship (from being loved to loving). While he has shown in §2 that people value the passive side of friendship for its own sake, he now argues that this is not enough to make them genuine friends, since a friendship requires the active side too.

A sign . . . finds in loving: On love by mothers, cf. 1161b26, 1166a5, 1168a25.

§4 Friendship, then, consists . . . virtue of friends: On those who love their friends (*philophiloi*), see the common belief reported in viii 1.§5. We now explain why friendship is a virtue and praiseworthy; its active aspect is a praiseworthy ACTIVITY.

§4–5 And so friends . . . can be equalized: Aristotle now applies his discussion of the passive and active sides of friendship to the topic of friendship between unequals. A genuine friendship between unequals can be formed only to the extent that the friends value the active as well as the passive side of their friendship.

(c) §5–6. The primacy of loving explains why virtuous friendship is stable.

§5 Equality and . . . is friendship: This (rather than the previous sentence) is probably the right place to begin a new section. Aristotle has just set out a general condition for genuine friendship between unequals. He now argues that—here as in friendship between equals—virtuous people best fit the general condition.

Vicious people, . . . each other's vice: For this contrast between virtuous and vicious people, cf. 1156b12, 1157a18. On the vicious, see 1166b6–29, 1172a9; *EE* 1239b11. For the vicious person's instability, cf. 1148a17, 1150a21, 1150b29. The vicious person has no reason to value his vicious friend's vice for its own sake as a good. He may find it pleasant because of the similarity to his own character. But this will be only one of the many pleasures the vicious person pursues because of his decision; his friend cannot rely on him when something pleasanter comes along. The virtuous person, by contrast, values virtuous actions as good in themselves.

§6 Useful or pleasant . . . pleasures or benefits: Lit., 'Useful and pleasant'. Probably this remark includes people who are not virtuous (and so do not love others for their character), but who are not vicious either (and so are not unreliable in the ways Aristotle has mentioned). (Virtuous people may also be included coincidentally, insofar as they form friendships for utility and for pleasure.) Less probably, the remark refers to vicious people who are both useful and pleasant, not just one of the two.

(d) §6–7. This makes it clear that friendship involves contraries only to a limited degree.

The friendship that seems . . . in return: This (rather than the previous sentence) is probably the right place to begin a new section. Aristotle's remarks about the active and passive aspects of friendship, and about pleasure and utility, prompt him to add a note on the dispute about whether friendship involves contraries (viii 1.§6).

Here we might . . . when he is not: This is a parenthetical comment on erotic lovers, who seem to provide a good example of love between contraries. The main argument resumes in §7.

§7 Presumably, . . . the intermediate: Aristotle has two answers to the suggestion that friendship is between contraries. (a) It is not strictly the contrary that is sought, but the 'intermediate'; we do not seek to go to the contrary extreme, but to fulfill some need or lack. (b) But even this model does not work for friendship in general; it works only for friendship for utility.

9

9.§1–6. Community and friendship

(a) §1. Both justice and friendship involve community.

§1 As we said at the beginning: See 1155a22. Cf. 1162a29.

The proverb . . . involves community: This proverb is attributed to the PYTHAGOREANS. It is often quoted by Plato (e.g., *Lys.* 207e, *Rep.* 424a).

§2 But, whereas brothers and companions . . . some less close: 'Companion' must indicate a relatively close and long-lasting relationship of habitual companions rather than, for instance, 'travelling companions' making just one journey together.

(b) §2–3. Different communities require different types of justice and friendship.

§3 Similarly, what is unjust . . . closer friends: Cf. 1130a5. Justice is concerned with the COMMON good of a community (1129b17), and the growth of friendship will increase the desire to treat other people justly. We might be inclined to see possible conflicts between the demands of friendship and the good of a community (suppose the good of the community requires the sacrifice of my friend's interests). Here Aristotle will see conflicts between two types of friendships. It is only in the best community that such conflicts will not happen; elsewhere the states of character required by the community will not be the same as those of the virtuous person (cf. 1130b29; *Pol.* iii 4).

(c) §4–5. But all these communities are subordinate to the political community and to its proper good.

§4 All the communities . . . political community: §4–6 mark a continuation of the argument of §1–3, and also a contrast with it. The emphasis of §1–3 has fallen on the difference between the communities characteristic of different types of friendship; this difference might lead us to think that we can say nothing general about the kind of community that is required for friendship. §4 corrects this impression by insisting that the political community has some superordinate place in relation to the other communities; this is a particular example of the role of the political community that he has mentioned at i 2.§5–8, vi 8.§1–4.

And the political . . . advantage: The comparison between the city and other communities begins with what they have in common: aiming at advantage.

for legislators . . . to be just: In mentioning the common advantage, Aristotle anticipates the contrast he will draw between the city and other communities. Cf. 1129b14–19. He does not say that the city aims only at advantage; hence he leaves room for the important further aim mentioned in *Pol.* 1280a25–1281a4.

§5 Now the other . . . partial advantage: This begins the contrast with the city.

tribe or deme: These were electoral districts in Athens; they also had governmental and religious functions. See OCD, s.v. 'Demes', 'Phylai'.

Some communities . . . companionship: OCT rashly deletes this sentence. If it is in the right place, it is a footnote to the list of communities aiming at advantage. Aristotle takes the opportunity to mention that communities aiming at pleasure are also subordinate to the city, as he explains in the following passage. Religious societies and dining clubs are mentioned together because the religious sacrifice of animals would be an occasion for a common meal.

But all . . . whole of life: The other communities are parts of the political community because each is affected by its relation to other social institutions; the city regulates them for the common good. The comprehensive character of POLITICAL SCIENCE corresponds to the comprehensive character of the political community; cf. *Pol.* 1252b27–31, 1278b15–30, 1280b23–1281a4. Partly, Aristotle is describing the activities of states he knows. But he also thinks these activities are essential for happiness, and hence wants them extended beyond their present scope; cf. 1180a24–9.

. . . [We can see . . . relaxations: Something seems to have been lost from the text here. The supplement suggests a possible connection of thought. The comprehensive concern of the city is shown by its regulation of religious festivals for advantage (by honoring the gods) and pleasure. By establishing religious holidays, the city fits the smaller communities into its comprehensive concerns.

For the long-established . . . whole of life]: The supplement suggests how this example is meant to illustrate the general point about the city. People would gather for religious observances and for enjoyment anyhow. But the city establishes these holidays (similar to the Lammas Fair) at harvest time because this is the best time—from the point of view of the larger community—for people to relax.

10

10.§1–6. Political systems and the corresponding communities

(a) §1–3. Different types of political systems and the characteristic deviations from them

§1 There are three . . . corruption of them: The relevance of ch. 10 becomes clear only in ch. 11. After having shown that the city regulates and organizes smaller communities within it, Aristotle argues that the different types of constitutions encourage different sorts of organization and different types of friendships. The particular effect of a city on the smaller communities within it depends on its constitution. Aristotle discusses these political systems and their changes in *Pol.* iii 7–8, 14–17; iv–vi. See also OCD, s.v. 'Democracy', 'Oligarchy'.

and since the third . . . polity: Aristotle uses *politeia* both for a political system or constitution in general and for what he calls the timocracy; see *Pol.* 1279a37.

(b) §4–6. The structure of these different systems can also be found in non-political communities.

§4 Resemblances . . . households: This section introduces a secondary purpose of the discussion of political systems. The social relations characteristic of the different systems can also be found in different households; hence, our understanding of these relations on the one level may help us to understand them on the other.

Homer . . . father: Frequent in Homer, e.g., *Il.* i 603.

Among the Persians, . . . slaves: The basis of this claim about the Persians is not clear (cf. Herodotus i 136). On rule over SLAVES, see 1161b3; *Pol.* i 4, 1254b2–24, 1255b16–22.

§5 1160b35 commits: Or 'assigns' (lit., 'duly gives', *apodidonai*). Cf. note to ix 2.§3.

§6 Democracy . . . dwellings without a master, . . . free [to do what he likes]: A mere 'dwelling' (*oikēsis*) differs from a proper 'household' (*oikia*) in having no definite structure (which, in Aristotle's view, requires a head); a 'rooming house' might be an example. On FREEDOM—in Aristotle's view, a regrettable feature of democracy—see *Pol.* 1310a31 (associated with *eleutheria*; see GENEROUS). It is not a vice confined to democracy; cf. 1180a26.

11

11.§1–8. Friendships in different political systems and in the corresponding nonpolitical communities

(a) §1–5. Different systems and communities result in different types of friendship.

§1 Friendship appears . . . justice appears also: Aristotle suggests that a specific form of friendship is possible only to the extent that people are related in ways that would make the transactions characteristic of such a friendship just. If, for instance, a king is not superior to his subjects in the way that genuine kingship requires, an attempt to represent his attitude to a subject as 'kingly' friendship is a fraud.

Homer . . . peoples: Homer, *Il.* ii 243 (and often).

(b) §6–8. Deviant systems undermine community and so undermine friendship.

§6 In the deviations, . . . of friendship: In deviant systems, the beliefs on which genuine friendship would be based are false. The tyrant is not superior to his subjects in the way that a king ought to be, and so he is not entitled to expect the attitudes that would be properly directed toward a king. If the subjects have these attitudes toward him, they must be deceived; since the deception may be recognized, their attitude is unstable.

For where . . . no justice either: The mention of tyranny leads Aristotle into a further discussion of other relations where ruled and ruler have nothing in common. He comes back to the main point about constitutions in §8.

This is true for a craftsman . . . soul . . . body: The SOUL uses the body as its instrument. See *DA* 412b10–413a3; *PA* 642a12; *Pol.* 1254a34, b4. At the end of this sentence, the mss. and OCT add *kai despotē(i) pros doulon* ('and for a master in relation to a slave').

there is neither friendship . . . inanimate things: See 1155b31, 1157b29. We can benefit these, since things are good and bad for them. But they have no aims and desires for us to consider and to share; hence we cannot respect or advance their aims by justice or friendship.

For master . . . without a soul: Cf. *Pol.* 1253b32. To be a slave is to be treated purely instrumentally, not as deserving anything in one's own right. The reason for treating a slave well, insofar as he is a slave, is always derived from the interests of the master; cf. the remark on wine in viii 2.§3.

§7 Insofar as he is a slave, . . . insofar as he is a human being: The implications of these two qualifications are not clear. One might take them in either of two ways. (i) Since a slave is in fact a human being, friendship with him is possible, and so he must not be treated solely as an instrument. (ii) Since he is in one respect a human being and in one respect a slave, the friendship and noninstrumental treatment that would be appropriate to him if he were not a slave is inappropriate because he is a slave. We might seek to resolve the unclarity here by reference to Aristotle's doctrine of natural slavery in *Pol.* i 4–6; cf. esp. 1254b20–4, 1255b12, 1260a10. There Aristotle argues that the natural slave is not just like an animal, but nonetheless lacks a proper human soul. Our present passage, however, contains no trace of a doctrine of natural slavery. In the *Politics* Aristotle insists that many actual slaves are not natural slaves; since these clearly are human beings, friendship for them seems to be appropriate.

For every human being . . . and agreement: Given the moral importance of this claim, it is remarkable that Aristotle says so little to explain it (cf. viii 1.§3). This clause by itself leaves open the possibility that some human beings are not capable of law and agreement; but the next clause excludes that possibility.

to the extent that . . . is a human being: The Greek has no expressed subject for 'is a human being'. The supplement suggests that Aristotle continues his claim about the relations of one human being to everyone. Alternatively one might supply 'a slave' as subject.

'To the extent that' (*kath'hoson*) might be equivalent to 'insofar as' (*hē(i)*) above, or it might introduce a possible clarification or restriction, leaving open the possibility that some beings are human beings only to some degree.

Some translators take Aristotle to be claiming that justice and friendship with all human beings is possible. Such a claim seems significantly weaker than the one he actually makes; he seems to imply that in some way all human beings are friends to all others.

12

12.§1–8. Friendships in families

(a) §1. They form a distinct type of friendship because they do not rest on voluntary agreement.

§1 But we should . . . companions: We set them apart because they do not clearly involve a COMMUNITY in quite the same way as the others do. See next note.

The friendship of citizens . . . some sort of agreement: The contrast with the previous cases suggests that it is more natural to speak of a 'community' when some voluntary agreement is required than in, e.g., families. Aristotle discusses the sort of agreement that is needed for a political community at *Pol.* 1280a25–1281a4.

(b) §2–3. Paternal friendship.

§2 Friendship in families . . . coming from him: On family friendships, cf. 1134b11, 1167b33; *MM* 1211b18–39. The father identifies the child's interest with his own because he regards the child as his own in something like the way his tooth or foot is his own. The natural and social relation of father to child causes the father to extend his self-concern in these ways, and (to a lesser degree) causes the child to extend his self-concern to his parents. The love of children for parents is important in education. See 1180b6.

A parent knows . . . a lesser degree: 'Regards as his own' translates *sunoikeiousthai*, cognate with *oikeion* (see PROPER). 'Is attached' or 'becomes close' might also be adequate. Some reference to beliefs and attitudes seems implied by the remarks about knowledge and perception. These remarks also justify 'because he regards (they regard)' in 18, 19, 29, where the Greek is simply 'as' (*hōs*).

And this also makes it clear why mothers . . . fathers do]: In the light of this claim about mothers, it is surprising that all these friendships are said to depend specifically on paternal friendship.

§3 For what has come . . . separate: 'Separate' explains what makes the child other. 'Himself' insists that the child is still the father himself; John Smith's son is another John Smith. Cf. 1170b6; *EE* 1245a29–35; *MM* 1213a12.

(c) §3–4. Fraternal friendship and the types of friendship derived from it

the same thing for both of them: Lit., 'the same for each other', i.e., the same blood, etc. An alternative translation, 'the same as each other', is less probable, since this claim seems to be inferred in 'Hence they are . . . '.

(d) §5–7. Family friendships include friendships between unequals and between equals.

§5 The friendship of children . . . superior: Aristotle connects family friendships with his earlier division; some involve unequals, and some equals.

§6 This sort . . . life in common: In saying that the friendship of parents and children 'also' includes pleasure and utility, Aristotle implies that (1) it is primarily complete friendship, which is friendship for virtue, and in which (2) each has goodwill to the other for the other's own sake. It is easier to see how the familial relations he has described satisfy (2) than to see how they satisfy (1).

Friendship between brothers . . . similar: Because of their similarity and their shared lives and pursuits, brothers will find it easy to take the sort of interest in each other that complete friends take in each other. The origins of the friendship are different, but the sorts of attitudes and actions expected seem to be similar.

(e) §7. Different types of friendship may be found in husbands and wives.

§7 The friendship of man and woman . . . among the animals: On the natural character of couples and families, cf. *Pol.* 1252a26.

Human beings, . . . in their life: Cf. *Pol.* 1278b17–30, 1280a13. Aristotle is thinking of living well, not merely of staying alive and satisfying natural desires.

For the difference between them implies that . . . : Or perhaps, 'From the start . . . ' (lit., 'immediately'; the Greek may have either a temporal or a logical sense).

And it may also . . . enjoyment for them: Here again (see note to 12.§6) Aristotle refers to his threefold division of friendship. On women's virtue, cf. *Pol.* 1260a13.

(f) §8. Different friendships involve different obligations of justice.

§8 How should . . . a classmate: On justice and friendship, see 1155a22, 1159b25. The remark on justice leads naturally into the discussion of disputes among friends.

13

13.§1–11. Disputes in friendships between equals

(a) §1. Different types of friendships lead to different sorts of disputes.

§1 There are three . . . superiority: Aristotle begins a long discussion of casuistical issues about friendship, and especially about the disputes that arise in it, which continues to the end of ix 3. The division of this discussion between two books (following the mss.) is quite misleading. The discussion of disputes (i) clarifies the nature of the different types of friendship (cf. note to §2 below); (ii) shows the types of character that support and undermine different friendships; and (iii) offers the sort of practical help that Aristotle has promised (cf. ii 2.§5, ix 2.§2). He begins by summarizing his previous discussion, making it clear (as he did in his discussion of familial friendships) that his threefold division is meant to apply to unequal as well as to equal friendships.

(b) §2–4. Friendships for utility easily lead to disputes.

§2 Accusations . . . for utility: The discussion of disputes is a further defense of the claim of complete friendship to be complete. It avoids the conflicts and quarrels that make the others fall short of complete friendships; cf. 1156b17, 1157a20, 1159b4. This is partly because virtuous friends have more reasonable expectations of each other, partly because they are more reasonable in judging each other's success or failure in fulfilling these expectations; see 1163a21–9, 1164b1.

and if this is what they strain to achieve, . . . or fights: 'Strain to achieve' (*hamillasthai*) seems to imply that each aims at this result rather than at any result that may involve competition or conflict with the other. Cf. ix 8.§7.

(c) §5–8 Disappointed expectations about reciprocal benefits are especially likely to lead to disputes.

§5 on rules: Or 'legal' (*nomikē*, cognate with 'law', *nomos*, above).

§6 Friendship dependent . . . explicit conditions: Within rule-governed friendship Aristotle distinguishes two types. One requires immediate repayment. The other allows postponement of repayment, and so involves trust in the character of the other person.

§8 If one party . . . accuse the other: If we begin a new paragraph here, we make this a general comment on both kinds of friendship for advantage; it picks up the last sentence of §5. If we do not begin a new paragraph, we make this a comment specifically on the kind of friendship just mentioned in §7.

This happens . . . decide to do what is beneficial: DECISIONS are concerned with what promotes ends. Ordinary people may wish for FINE things, but when they have to act on some wish, the wish that forms their decision is not their wish for the fine, but their wish for some other pleasure or good to themselves. The virtuous person is different because his wishes for what is fine are not ineffective; they are focused by deliberation on decisions to do fine actions.

(d) §9. To avoid disputes, we must make a fair return for benefits.

§9 We should, . . . willingly: In a2 retain *kai hekonti* (OCT deletes).

(e) §10–11. In friendships for utility, a fair return must correspond to the benefit received.

(f) §11. A different standard applies in friendships for virtue.

§11 Rather, the decision . . . in decision: Since the aim of friendships based on virtue is not some particular profit or pleasure, but the sharing of a life based on virtuous character, the important thing for measuring mutual benefits is the aim of the friend conferring the benefit. Aristotle does not suggest that fair exchange of benefits is unimportant in friendship based on virtue, but only that the basis for determining fair exchange is different.

14

14.§1–4. Disputes in friendships between unequals

(a) §1. Disputes arise from the conflicting expectations of the superior and the inferior party.

§1 [The superior party . . . right in a friendship: This analogy from business partnerships is also used in a political sphere by those who defend oligarchy as just; see *Pol.* 1280a25–40.

(b) §2–3. Sometimes these expectations are unreasonable; reasonable expectations in reward for public service

§2 Rather, the superior . . . supplies need: HONOR is the reward that the magnanimous person expects for his benefits to others; see 1124b9 (though he does not benefit others only for the sake of honor, he will form friendships for honor with some people). On honor as a reward for service, cf. 1134b6.

§3 for distribution . . . as we have said: On WORTH, cf. 1158b27, 1159a35, 1162b2. The point here is consistent with 1158b29. The friend's worth determines what sort of good he should get, and friends of different worth will be due different goods. But the quantity of one good should be equal to the quantity of the other, as far as this is determinable and possible; that is what prevents friendship from collapsing into entirely one-sided 'public service' (1163a29).

If we benefit from them in money or virtue: This seems to mean 'if we become richer or better'. Less probably, 'if we benefit from their money or virtue'.

(c) §3–4. Sometimes honor is the only possible return for benefits; illustration from the relation of father and son

§4 it might seem: Or 'it would seem'. It is not clear whether Aristotle endorses this view. He agrees that a father is free to disown a son but a son is never free to disown his father, if the relation between father and son is simply that between creditor and debtor. But he does not say whether he accepts the antecedent of this conditional. He alludes to a recognized practice of disowning sons in Athenian law (which, in Plato's view, allows the father too much freedom to disown; *Laws* 928e).

Book IX

1

1.§1–9. Disputes arising between friends with dissimilar expectations

(a) §1–4. The disputes arise when aims conflict.

§1 In all friendships . . . and the others: There is no break between Books viii and ix. Aristotle continues the discussion of the casuistry of friendship, begun in viii 13. On proportion in exchange, see 1132b31, 1133a31, 1163b11.

§3 For if the friendship . . . which was unstable: See note to viii 3.§2.

friendship in itself: Probably this abbreviates 'in which each loves the other in himself, not coincidentally, i.e., for what he is'; cf. note to viii 3.§6.

§4 pleasure in return for pleasure: One had the pleasure of listening to the music, and the other the pleasure of anticipating payment.

common dealings: This translates *koinōnia*, usually rendered 'COMMUNITY'.

(b) §5–7. To settle disputes, friends must agree on the value of their services.

§5 Who should fix . . . received it: The supplements assume that Aristotle is talking about cases such as those he has just described, where people have made no explicit agreement in advance, and the question about appropriate return arises after the benefit has been given.

This is what Protagoras . . . collect: On PROTAGORAS' way of collecting his fees, see Plato, *Pr.* 328bc.

Payment to a man . . . : Aristotle quotes the beginning of Hesiod, *Works and Days* 368. The passage is: 'Payment to a man who is a friend should be promised and paid. Be cordial with your brother, but [make a bargain with him] before a witness. For faith and faithlessness alike have ruined men.' Aristotle alludes to Hesiod as support for a practice of agreeing in advance about repayment.

§6 But those . . . agreed to: These people not only make an agreement in advance of the promised service, but actually exact payment in advance, and then fail to do what they have been paid for.

§7 And presumably the sophists . . . accused: It is not surprising that SOPHISTS (Protagoras is an exception) require payment in advance and then disappoint their pupils. Since they cannot fulfill their extravagant promises, they would never get paid if they agreed to defer payment until they had done what they promised to do.

(c) §7. In the best type of friendship, the value of services is fixed by the giver's intention.

And the return . . . and to virtue: See 1162b6, 1163a31–3.

And it would . . . gods and parents: The outlook and DECISION of the philosopher are different from those of the sophist, and so deserve the response appropriate to friends for virtue. Aristotle speaks of his philosophical colleagues in the Academy as friends (1096a13); cf. 1172a5, 1177a34.

(d) §8–9. In other types of friendship, the measure must be the benefit received.

§9 Presumably, however, . . . before he got it: On the right time for fixing the price, cf. 1133b1. These transactions between friends are intended to follow the principles of justice in exchange.

2

2.§1–10. Conflicts resulting from different types of friendships for different people

(a) §1–3. The specific obligations arising from different types of friendship must usually be respected.

§1 Or must . . . be general: These are cases in which one seems to have reasons for limiting obedience to one's father. (Obedience to one's father was a recognized source of dissension; cf. 1149b8.)

Similarly, should . . . do both: 'Similarly' seems to refer to the second alternative just mentioned. Aristotle suggests that giving preference to friends over virtuous people, and to benefactors over companions, is similar to recognizing MEDICAL and military experts as the appropriate authorities. In each case, different people, according to their different previous relations to me, have different claims on my attention in different circumstances.

§2 Surely it is . . . exactly: These casuistical questions illustrate what Aristotle has in mind in some of his comments on exactness; cf. ii 2.§3–5, and §6 below.

the fine and the necessary: Cf. iv 6.§6.

§3 Still, it is clear . . . companion: Aristotle's recognition of inexactness does not prevent him from offering rules to guide conduct. He affirms that different spheres of activity and different relations generate distinct obligations that should not be overridden by a single obligation to, for instance, one's father.

The verb translated 'render' here (*apodidonai*) is also translated 'return' in the rest of the chapter; it may mean 'give back' or 'duly give' (cf. Plato, *Rep*. 330c; *Luke* 20:25), and Aristotle exploits both senses.

(b) §4–6. This rule needs to be qualified.

§5 As we have . . . gift to B] instead: Aristotle's examples here show why he thinks EXACT and useful ethical rules cannot be found. The USUAL rules we can find are liable to exceptions reflecting the fine or expedient consequences of violating the rules. Cf. note to ii 9.§3.

§6 As we have often . . . to Zeus: According to this division of paragraphs, §6 repeats §2–3, and reaffirms Aristotle's claim that lack of fixity does not preclude some definite prescriptions. Alternatively, we might attach the first sentence to §5 and the second to §6.

(c) §7–10. Different benefits are owed to different people.

§8 nor accord . . . wise person or a general: Aristotle answers the question raised in §1; here 'wise person' (*sophos*) refers back to the doctor.

3

3.§1–5. The dissolution of friendships

(a) §1. Friendships for pleasure and utility are easily dissolved.

(b) §1–2. Special difficulties arise if one friend is mistaken about the basis of the friendship.

(c) §3–4. If one friend sharply changes character, for the worse or the better, that may cause the dissolution of the friendship.

§3 But if we accept . . . still love him: Here we face the difficulties that may arise in the best types of friendship. Since this is concerned with the friend's character, the friendship is threatened when the character changes. Aristotle urges that only deterioration to incurable vice (cf. 1150b32) should break the friendship. The importance of shared activities and characters in the best friendship makes it unreasonable to continue a friendship with someone who has become vicious beyond recovery.

The bad . . . similar: In this discussion, 'base', 'bad', and 'VICIOUS' seem to be used interchangeably.

§4 But if one . . . as a friend: Probably Aristotle does not mean here that the inferior person is really virtuous; if he were, then could the superior person not still admire his character and share his activities? Probably we are to suppose two developing characters (as suggested in 1157a10, 1162a9–15), one of which develops into a virtuous character while the other does not.

(d) §5. The dissolution of a friendship does not cancel all special relations.

§5 Then should the better . . . causes the dissolution: Even when a friendship is justifiably dissolved, the friend's present character is not all that matters; we should still be concerned about him because of the past interactions. Aristotle does not explain why, given his theory of friendship, it is reasonable for us to retain this concern.

4

4.§1–10. Self-love as a pattern of friendship

(a) §1. The defining features of friendship

§1 The defining . . . toward oneself: It would be better to begin a new book here than at ix 1. Aristotle now turns from his casuistical discussion to examine more general issues about friendship and its relation to the virtues. In chs. 4–9 he describes the different attitudes that belong to friendship, and argues that they are both psychologically intelligible and rationally defensible in a virtuous person. In ch. 4, he derives the features of friendship from features of the good person's attitude to himself. This derivation is important because it shows: (1) Self-love is sometimes good, since the virtuous person has it (ix 8). (2) The friend is another self (1161b28, 1166a31), insofar as we treat him as we treat ourselves. (3) We can justify friendship if we can justify treating other people as other selves (ix 7, 9).

For a friend . . . these features: Aristotle lists five marks of friendship. (1) A wishes and does goods or apparent goods to B for B's sake. (2) A wishes for B's life, for B's own sake. (3) A spends his time with B. (4) A makes the same choices as B. (5) A shares B's distress and enjoyment.

(b) §2–6. Each of these features is characteristic of the self-love of the virtuous person.

§2 As we have said, . . . standard in each case: Cf. 1113a29, 1176a15.

§3 For the excellent . . . whole soul: In §3–5 Aristotle finds the marks of friendship (discussed in the order 4, 1, 2, 3, 5—see note for §1 above) in the virtuous person's relation to himself.

He wishes . . . each person seems to be: The good person has a coherent and steady outlook on his life that gives precedence to his reason and understanding; see 1168b30, 1178a2. Here Aristotle does not mean that all the good person wants to do is think, but that he wants to actualize his reason in directing his desires and actions; hence he wants to act on his virtuous decision.

his rational part: Lit., 'that by which he thinks rationally' (*phronei*). The verb *phronein* is cognate with *phronēsis*, usually translated 'PRUDENCE'; here it seems to have a more general sense.

§4 And no one chooses . . . by a god]: The example about god makes the point suggested in the note to viii 7.§6. Concern for myself requires concern for me as the sort of being that I essentially am. In a21 retain *ekeino to genomenon* (OCT deletes).

§5 This . . . regrets [what he has done]: The good person will surely be sorry if things have gone wrong, if, for instance, his children (like Priam's sons; cf. i 9.§11) have all died, or his friend was crippled in an accident. However, he will not decide he should change his principles, or that he could reasonably have made past decisions different from those he made. Hence he will have nothing to blame or reproach himself for. The major component of happiness is acting virtuously; and this does not require success in the results it aims at. See note to i 10.§13.

§6 But is there . . . friendship to oneself: Even if we cannot properly speak of Smith's friendship to Smith, we can speak of friendship between different parts of Smith's SOUL (cf. 1138b15), corresponding to his different DESIRES.

(c) §7–10. Vicious people, however, are incapable of self-love and of friendship.

§8 Indeed, . . . have them: Aristotle has contrasted (i) the many, who are base (see VICIOUS) and (ii) the utterly base and unscrupulous. Now he returns to (i). He argues that the marks of friendship (see notes to §1, 3) are absent in vicious people's attitude to themselves. He discusses these marks in the order 4, 1, 2, 3, 5.

For they are at odds . . . another, as incontinent people do. For they do not choose . . . harmful; and cowardice . . . themselves: Alternative rendering: 'For they . . . another. This is true, for instance of incontinent people (for they . . . harmful). And cowardice . . . themselves.' The preferred rendering implies only a comparison between vicious and incontinent people. The alternative rendering implies that incontinents are included among vicious people (contrary to Book vii).

If the preferred rendering is correct, what sort of psychic conflict does Aristotle ascribe to vicious people, and how are they similar to incontinents? See 1149a17; 1150a21, b32. If the vicious person has the wrong first principles, how can he regret his pursuit of pleasure? He is simply following his principles. In 1166b7–10, 18–22 Aristotle perhaps suggests the answer. An intemperate person (a) has a conception of his good that requires him to satisfy his strongest appetites for pleasure; to do this he will plan prudently to make money, form friendships, etc. But (b) he also has strong appetites for immediate pleasures that will disrupt his more prudent plans; hence his appetite and his wish will conflict. In these cases, if the appetite is strong enough the intemperate person's initial wish gives way, and he forms a new rational plan. Since he has strong appetites and aversions, it becomes rational for him to act on them, if the pain resulting from their frustration will be greater than the pain resulting from their satisfaction. Hence he will act on his rational wish and decision; but since the rational choice he acts on is different from the one he would have acted on if he had not had such strong particular appetites, he will regret the necessity for acting on the choice he does act upon. He will suffer conflict no less than the incontinent person suffers it, but it will be a different conflict with different results.

hate and shun life: In b12 read *pepraktai dia tēn mochthērian, misousi te kai* (OCT: *pepraktai kai dia . . . misountai kai*).

§9 one part . . . another . . . each part . . . tearing him apart: 'Part' is supplied.

§10 Even if . . . full of regret: Unlike the virtuous person, the vicious person does not value acting on the right decision for its own sake; he values it only as a means to the satisfaction of appetite. Hence he will be disturbed by failures that will not disturb the virtuous person; and these failures will multiply if his decision is liable to change in the way suggested above.

5

5.§1–4. Goodwill and friendship

(a) §1–2. Goodwill is not sufficient for friendship.

§1 Goodwill . . . not friendship: See 1155b32, 1157b18, 1158a7.

§2 but goodwill . . . for contestants: This is the wish without decision that was mentioned in 1111b24.

(b) §3. It is a beginning of friendship.

§3 Goodwill, then, . . . erotic passion: 'Beginning' renders *archē*; see PRINCIPLE.

for when they have goodwill . . . trouble for him: Concern for someone's good for his own sake is not enough for regarding him as a friend or other self. This requires time and familiarity (1157a10, 1162a12), which will also produce the FONDNESS that is found in friendship (1126b21).

grow accustomed: See note to viii 3.§8.

(c) §3–4. It is present only in the best kind of friendship.

It does not, . . . goodwill either: See note to viii 3.§1. Here Aristotle seems to answer the question we raised about the presence of goodwill in incomplete friendships.

For a recipient . . . some use to them: Probably Aristotle is contrasting goodwill, as the just and proper reaction to being benefited, with the calculating expectation of future benefits that belongs to friendship for utility. Why, however, does friendship for pleasure not produce goodwill? Probably Aristotle means that such friendship implies no desire for the benefit of the other, whereas friendship for utility at least implies a desire for his benefit as a means to one's own benefit.

6

6.§1–4. Concord and friendship

(a) §1–2. Concord requires agreement about the distribution of goods.

§2 or to make Pittacus ruler, when he himself is also willing: Pittacus was elected sole ruler of Mytilene (early sixth century B.C.). He resigned after ten years; hence Aristotle's 'when he himself . . . '. The concord ended when Pittacus himself dissented from his being ruler.

But whenever . . . in conflict: 'Wants' might also be rendered 'wishes' (*boulesthai*; see DESIRE). Cf. Kant, *Critique of Practical Reason*, Ak., p. 28. Euripides' *Phoenissae* is about the bitter and uncompromising struggle (see, esp., 588–624) between Eteocles and Polyneices for absolute power in Thebes.

the common people and the decent party: These terms (*ho dēmos* and *hoi epieikeis*) are often used for the democratic and the aristocratic side in the political conflicts in a Greek city. See DECENT.

Concord, then, . . . [as a whole]: On political friendship, cf. 1160a8–14.

(b) §3–4. Genuine concord is confined to virtuous people.

§3 This sort of concord . . . same mind: Concord, resulting from a community that aims for a common good, is a foundation of justice and of a stable friendship. This is easier for virtuous people (see note to 1162b6; 1164b1); for they are not concerned with getting some good at the other's expense, but with virtuous action, which benefits all of them. Contrast the OVERREACHING attitudes of the vicious friend with the attitudes of virtuous people described in 1169a6–11, 28.

like a tidal strait: Lit., 'like the Euripus'. This is a tidal strait between Boeotia and Euboea (near Chalcis, where Aristotle's mother was born, and where Aristotle himself lived between 323 and his death). Cf. Plato, *Phd.* 90c.

7

7.§1–7. Active benevolence and friendship

(a) §1. A common view regards benefactors as purely selfish.

(b) §2–4. The common view is false: Active benevolence realizes the capacities of the benefactor.

§1 Now Epicharmus . . . point of view: Epicharmus (Sicilian comic poet, early fifth century B.C.), fr. 146 Kaibel.

§2 However, . . . not even similar: The active aspect of friendship was mentioned in 1159a27. Aristotle now seeks to prove what he earlier assumed, that the active aspect is valuable for its own sake. He presents and rejects the common view that assumes a person values for its own sake nothing but states of himself alone that do not essentially involve the states of another (cf. note to ix 8.§4). On this view, the benefactor cares only about the return he hopes for. Aristotle argues that active friendship is a NATURAL tendency of human beings even apart from any hope of reward.

§2–3 Benefactors, . . . acquired a soul: Cf. 1120b13, 1134b10, 1161b18. Though he does not say so, Aristotle here applies the explanation of parents' love for their children to active friendship in general. 'Product' here translates *ergon*, normally rendered 'FUNCTION'; the connection between the two senses is important in this argument.

§4 The reason . . . his own being: The argument is this: (1) Being is choiceworthy for all. (2) We have being insofar as we live and act. (3) Hence we have being insofar as we are actualized. (4) The product actualizes the producer. (5) Hence the producer has his being in the product. (6) Hence the producer loves the product.

'Actualization' here translates *energeia*. The usual rendering 'ACTIVITY' is unsuitable here, since the product itself, as well as the action resulting in it, is treated as an *energeia* of the producer (contrast 1094a4–5). Both the exercise of skill in the productive activity and the product resulting from this exercise actualize the agent's capacities, and so express his being. See also 1176a3.

'Now the product . . . actualization' might also be rendered 'the producer in his actualization is, in a way, the product'. The product is only the actualization in a way, not without qualification (*haplōs*—see UNQUALIFIED). It is the exercise of productive skill that is the primary actualization of the producer; that is the actualization 'indicated' by the product. Since the agent values the exercise of his capacities, he values the product (or, in the case of friendship, the beneficiary) that expresses the actualization. This is a source of pleasure to him, for the reasons explained in 1174b11.

This account of love for a beneficiary of one's benevolence does not explain all the special features of friendship for a person—those that reflect his being another self valued for his own sake. These features are relevant in ix 9.

(c) §5–6. Active benevolence is both fine and pleasant.

§5 At the same time, . . . fine for him: This explains the attitude of the magnanimous person (1124b9).

(d) §7. Active benevolence reflects one's own effort.

§7 This is also why mothers . . . children are theirs: On mothers, see 1159a28, 1161b26.

8

8.§1–11. Self-love and selfishness

(a) §1. A common view condemns self-love as selfish.

§1 There is also a puzzle . . . shameful: This chapter is complementary to ch. 7. Aristotle examines these common views: (1) Our underlying motive for active benevolence is selfish (ch. 7). (2) Virtue requires unselfish benevolence. (3) Self-love is selfishness. (4) Hence actions characteristic of virtue cannot proceed from self-love. The combination of these views implies that we cannot acquire the unselfish motive expected of the virtuous person. Aristotle agrees with (2), but rejects (4), because he rejects (3). He therefore agrees with (1), as long as 'self-love' is substituted for selfishness.

The puzzle discussed in ch. 8 results from (a) the common belief that self-love is bad (*Rhet.* 1389b35, cf. 1168b25; *Pol.* 1263b1; Plato, *Laws* 731e), and (b) Aristotle's claim in ix 4 that the virtuous person's self-love is good. In his defense of (b) Aristotle argues that (a) is too sweeping, because it overlooks some relevant examples, though it is right for the examples it considers (see ETHICS [7]).

[for any end apart] from himself: This expansion of 'from itself' is suggested by 'disregarding his own [interest]' at the end of the next sentence, applied to the decent person. Alternatively, we might take this to mean 'of his own accord', implying that the vicious person does nothing willingly and spontaneously, without calculating his own selfish interest, but benefits others only under compulsion (cf. 1167b15).

(b) §2–3. The demands of friendship, however, justify friendship, and hence love, for oneself.

§2 The facts, . . . not unreasonable: The 'facts' (*erga*; see FUNCTION) that Aristotle mentions seem to be other common opinions about friendship. He gives them the status of 'facts' because he has already discussed and defended them.

since we have said . . . to others: Aristotle refers back to ch. 4, on self-love, to justify his confidence in these claims.

All the proverbs . . . shin': For the first proverb, see Euripides, *Orestes* 1046 (a play in which friendship is prominent).

(c) §4–5. The bad form of self-love results in selfishness, because it rests on a false view of the self.

§4 That is why . . . contested: Goods that are contested (or 'fought over') are the goods pursued in competition. See 1169a21; *Pol.* 1271b8; Plato, *Rep.* 586b–c. Since my gain, in these cases, is necessarily your loss (cf. 1167b4), self-love directed to these goods results in OVERREACHING, and is harmful for other people, and hence (cf. 1121a29, 1123a32; FINE [4]) regarded as vicious (cf. 1169a6–11).

§5 eager above all to do: Less probably 'eager to excel everyone in doing' (taking *pantōn* as masculine rather than neuter). Here and in the rest of the chapter Aristotle describes the virtuous self-lover in noncompetitive terms, to distinguish his attitude from the competitive attitude that expresses OVERREACHING, and excessive love of HONOR. Cf. iv 3.§27, note (on the magnanimous person), note to v 9.§9.

(d) §6. The good form of self-love is unselfish, because it rests on a true view of the self.

§6 And just as a city . . . gratifies this part: Cf. 1166a17, 1178a2. A complex system is most of all its most CONTROLLING (or important) part because this part represents the interests of the whole; the direction and fortunes of the whole depend on this part. The rational part controls a human being insofar as its condition and outlook both reflect and determine the state of the whole person by the way it controls or fails to control his actions.

Similarly, someone is called continent . . . what each person is: Aristotle refers to the connection between continence, *enkrateia*, and mastery or control, *kratein*. I have mastery over my appetites when my understanding has mastery over them, since my understanding is to be identified with myself.

Moreover, his own voluntary . . . reason: Though Aristotle allows VOLUNTARY action on nonrational DESIRES, he thinks it is most voluntary when it results from rational desire and DECISION. For this is most of all *my* own voluntary action, in which the origin is most of all in *me*.

He differs . . . guided by feelings: Cf. i 3.§7, iv 9.§3. Here Aristotle does not connect guidance by feelings especially with impulsive or incontinent action. He is thinking of people whose nonrational desires set the ends they pursue and the DECISIONS they form; these include VICIOUS people.

and as much . . . seems advantageous: Read *oregesthai tou kalou* (OCT: *oregesthai ē tou kalou*). The virtuous person aims at the FINE (see note to viii 13.§8), since he cares about an action's being praiseworthy and advancing the common good. The vicious person cares about something's being good in itself, as certain pleasures are, in his view. But he does not care about its being fine and praiseworthy (see note to viii 1.§5).

(e) §7–8. Hence it leads to virtuous actions.

§7 And when everyone strains to achieve . . . of virtue: In saying that people 'strain' (*hamillasthai*; cf. viii 13.§2) to achieve fine actions, Aristotle contrasts this attitude (focused on the fine, not on surpassing other people) with the attitude of those who fight over 'contested goods' (§4 above). Cf. 1122b22, 1168b28. His confidence that the common good is achieved when everyone strains to do fine action is intelligible if this is the aim of fine action.

(f) §9–11. These virtuous actions include unselfish action aiming at the fine.

§9 It is quite true . . . fine for himself: In 'It is quite true . . . ' we return to the recognized examples of virtuous action that seemed (§1 above) to show that the virtuous person sacrifices himself in ways that are incompatible with the primacy of self-love. Aristotle answers that the virtuous person's self-love will make him want to do virtuous and fine actions; these are the actions required by the best sort of friendship and by the COMMUNITY that the virtuous person belongs to. Hence self-love is not only the paradigm of friendship (as ix 4 has argued); it is also the basis for friendship, since the virtuous person's self-love will move him to the fine actions that are expected of friends. The actions that Aristotle mentions here are characteristic of the magnanimous person (1124b6–9, 23–6) displaying bravery (1116a10–15, 1117b9–10).

§10 It is also . . . do it himself: This principle is followed in 1171b19.

§11 In everything praiseworthy, . . . ought not to be: Clearly the virtuous person's attitude to his friend's good is not entirely selfless and self-forgetful. But Aristotle takes it to be consistent with concern for the friend's good for his own sake. It is because this sort of concern is fine that the virtuous person thinks it is part of his good. Hence the virtuous friend never 'sacrifices himself', if that implies sacrifice of his own interests to another's; but he is no less concerned for the friend's good for the friend's own sake than a 'self-sacrificing' person would be. That is why, in Aristotle's view, the virtuous person is a self-lover without being selfish. In assigning 'more of the fine' to himself, he assigns to himself more of the fine than of other goods, as §10 has said. Aristotle does not say that he assigns more of the fine to himself than to his friend.

9

9.§1–10. Why does the happy person need friends?

(a) §1. According to one view, the happy person is self-sufficient, and hence does not need other people.

§1 There is also a dispute . . . friends or not: This is a third puzzle about self-love and friendship, following on those discussed in chs. 7 and 8. This puzzle arises from Aristotle's position in ch. 8. He has argued that the virtuous self-lover will be concerned with his friends because he is concerned with the fine. But what is fine about concern for friends? Are they not just an instrumental good, and hence not fine, but dispensable for a happy person? Aristotle answers this question here.

'When the god . . . of friends': Euripides, *Orestes* 667 (cf. note to 8.§2 above).

(b) §2. We need friends so that we can benefit them.

§2 It would seem absurd, . . . greatest external good: Aristotle does not mean that if someone is HAPPY and BLESSED without friends, he needs friends as well. He is claiming that someone cannot be happy without friends, so that friends are necessary for happiness, and that some of the happy person's activities are essentially shared with friends.

And if . . . for him to benefit: Here and in the rest of this chapter, Aristotle several times follows his common practice of incorporating a whole argument into a single Greek sentence. It is difficult to break his one sentence into several English sentences without obscuring the logical structure.

The importance of active beneficence has been discussed in ix 7. The role of friends in good and bad FORTUNE is discussed in ix 11.

(c) §3. The happy person cannot be solitary.

§3 Presumably it is . . . live together with others: On the solitary life and the political nature of human beings, see i 7.§6, viii 5.§3, notes.

(d) §4. To show that the happy person needs friends, we must distinguish the friendship of virtuous people from the other types of friendship.

§4 Then what are those on the other . . . useful people who are friends: The false belief underlying one side of the puzzle is exposed. As in ix 7 (cf. 1167b17), the objection assumes friendship is only an instrumental good, because it recognizes only friendship for advantage or pleasure. When we recognize the best sort of friendship, we can also see why this kind of friendship can be an intrinsic good.

for since his life . . . imported pleasures: Cf. 1099a16.

(e) §5. We can observe the actions of virtuous friends.

§5 Now if being happy . . . friend are of this sort: The argument of these two sentences is this: (1) Happiness is activity. (2) The activity of the good person is excellent, and pleasant in itself. (3) What is our own is pleasant.(4) The actions of virtuous friends are our own. (5) Hence a good person finds pleasure in the actions of virtuous friends. (6) Hence, the blessed person needs virtuous friends.

In 1169a35 read *hai tōn spoudaiōn dē* (OCT: *spoudaiōn de*).

Aristotle assumes that the good person enjoys his own virtuous activities, and hence enjoys his friend's too. The different uses of 'his own' (see PROPER) are important here. In b35 our friends' actions are not our own, since we do not do them ourselves. But in 1170a3–4 our friends' actions are our own, for reasons explained in 1170b5.

(f) §5–6. Friendship is a source of pleasure in virtuous activity.

§5 Further, . . . pleasantly: This seems to begin a new argument. Aristotle is still concerned with pleasure, as in the previous argument, but now he is concerned with the pleasure that the virtuous person takes in his own actions (rather than in observing his friend's actions).

(g) §7. Friendship encourages virtue.

§7 Further, . . . Theognis says: Theognis 35; Plato, *Meno* 95d.

(h) §7–10. Friendship realizes human capacities, through shared rational activity.

If we examine . . . [human] nature: Cf. 1167b29. Aristotle explains how the preferences of the virtuous person, described in §5–6, are not his arbitrary inclinations, but the expression and realization of natural tendencies. Aristotle's argument from nature occupies the rest of the chapter. We may understand it (with some simplification) as follows. (1) What is good by nature is good and pleasant in itself for a good person. (2) For human beings living is perceiving or understanding. (3) Life is good and pleasant in itself. (4) What is good by nature is also good for the good person. (5) If we are perceiving or understanding, we perceive it. (6) Perceiving that we are perceiving or understanding is the same as perceiving our being alive. (7) Perceiving that we are alive is pleasant in itself. (8) Living is choiceworthy for a good person. (9) The good person is related to his friend in the same way as he is related to himself. (10) Therefore, his friend's being is choiceworthy for him. (11) To perceive his friend's being, he must share conversation and thought. (12) Therefore, his happiness requires these activities of friendship.

For animals, life . . . perceiving or understanding: On life, see 1097b33, and SOUL. Here as in 1168a5 the natural preference for life makes intelligible the preference for ACTIVITY over mere CAPACITY.

for it has definite order, . . . good: Life has a definite order (lit., 'is defined'; cf. note to x 3.§2) insofar as human capacities fit each other in a mutually supporting and fulfilling way. The virtuous person does not invent an order, but develops the order that is already present in the natural capacities (as complete virtue does in vi 13), whereas the vicious person perverts and destroys the natural order by misusing his natural capacities; cf. note to 4.§8 above.

§8 But we must not . . . what follows): This is a parenthesis, justifying the claim that life is naturally pleasant, and pleasant in itself. The claim is not refuted by the experience of a life that is diverted or corrupted from its natural character. Aristotle refers forward to the discussion of pain in x 1–4. Pain prevents the full actualization of our capacities; cf. iii 12.§2, 1153b16, 1175b17.

§9 Now someone who sees . . . are understanding: Self-awareness (see *DA* iii 2) is a further good that depends on the goodness of the activity we are aware of.

§10 The excellent . . . another himself: On the friend as 'another oneself', cf. 1156b17, 1161b28. The best kind of friend is referred to here, since he is the one whom the virtuous person regards as he regards himself. Since he regards his friend as he regards himself, he will want to be aware of his friend's activities as he is aware of his own.

Aristotle has argued that if I have a friend, then the friendship with him is a part of my good. But how does this show that I have reason to acquire friends, or that I could not be happy without them? Aristotle needs to make it clear that I am better off if I have a friend to whom I take this attitude (cf. 1169b33, 1170a5). I extend my concerns and interests more widely, in a wider range of fine and virtuous activities, if I share them with a friend; hence I am better off if I have a friend than if I never have one; hence having friends is a part of my happiness.

He must, then, perceive . . . live together . . . conversation and thought: See 1095b30, 1097b9, 1157b18.

If, then, for the blessedly . . . also be choiceworthy: This conclusion recalls the statement in §7 of the conclusion to be proved ('an excellent friend would seem to be choiceworthy by nature for an excellent person'), showing that the intervening text is meant to be a continuous argument.

What is choiceworthy . . . lack something: Aristotle appeals to the COMPLETE and SELF-SUFFICIENT character of happiness, taking it to include everything good and choiceworthy; cf. 1097b6, 16–20.

10

10.§1–6. How many friends are needed for a happy life?

§1 Then should . . . as possible: Since the end of ch. 9 has insisted that 'living together' with friends is needed, the questions naturally arise: How many friends are needed for 'living together'? What sorts of obligations and activities should be involved in living together?

'have neither many nor none': Hesiod, *Works and Days* 715.

(a) §2. We need only a limited number of friends for utility and pleasure.

(b) §3–5. The requirements of a shared life limit the appropriate number of friends for virtue.

§3 For a city . . . hundred thousand: On CITIES, see *Pol.* 1326a5–b25. If 'people' (lit., 'HUMAN BEINGS') refers to the total population of a city, Aristotle is denying that classical Athens is a city. If, however, 'people' refers to citizens (the only ones who are really parts, as opposed to necessary conditions, of a city), the number will exclude resident aliens, women, children, and slaves. A city of a hundred thousand citizens (exercising political functions) would indeed be abnormally large.

§4 Clearly you cannot . . . distribute yourself among them: On the difficulty of having many friends, see 1158a10.

(c) §5–6. We cannot have the right kind of friendship if we have too many friends.

§6 By contrast, . . . ingratiating: See note to iv 6.§9. Ingratiating people show to many people the attentions that are appropriate only to close (*oikeios*; see PROPER) friends, and so try to secure the favor due to close friends. They do not know what is required for the right sort of close friendship, and in fact all they have is the friendship of fellow citizens, despite their efforts to make it look like something more.

11

11.§1–6. Friends in good and ill fortune

§1 Have we more . . . ill fortune: This question was raised in 1169b13.

(a) §2–4. Good people want to avoid causing pain to friends.

§3 For a friend . . . dexterous, . . . pleasure and pain: Cf. 1128a17. Here as before, dexterity requires someone to say the appropriate things, knowing the circumstances and the feelings of the people involved. Here would be one occasion for the PRUDENT person to display CLEVERNESS.

§4 That is why someone with a manly . . . his pain: This MANLY attitude is also a sign of magnanimity, 1124b9, 1125a9.

(b) §5. But they want their friends to share their good fortune.

§5 We should . . . trouble to themselves: Here the friend inviting help follows the principle of 1169a32–4. Presumably, however, the friend who gives the help will do something finer if his help is more difficult for him to give. Aristotle does not seem to pursue the full implications of his own views here.

(c) §6. They show proper consideration for friends in good and ill fortune.

12

12.§1. Shared activity in friendship

(a) §1. The best friendship requires shared activity.

§1 For friendship is community, . . . we seek: Here Aristotle summarizes the argument of 9.§7–10.

(b) §2. This shared activity includes the sharing of valued pursuits.

(c) §3. Virtuous friends have the best life.

§3 But the friendship . . . they meet: Virtuous people's stability is contrasted with vicious people's instability. See 1156b12, 1166b6, 1167b4. When virtuous people practice their virtues, and express their characters toward each other, they benefit each other and so strengthen the friendship, while the opposite is true for vicious people.

Could someone take the virtuous person's attitude to his friend, and yet be intemperate and unjust in his attitude to everyone else? And could two people be friends on this basis, each admiring the virtue of the other as far as it goes? Aristotle might answer: (1) Vice involves perverted affections and appetites, which are not easy to restrain at will; can such friends trust each other to restrain the vice from its natural development (cf. 1140b12)? (2) If someone really understands the value of virtuous friendship, will he not also see the value of justice and temperance?

(d) §4. Transition to the discussion of pleasure

§4 So much, . . . pleasure: This is the second reference forward to a treatment of pleasure; cf. 9.§8.

Book X

1

1.§1–4. The right approach to pleasure

(a) §1–2. The importance of pleasure

§1 For it seems . . . pleasure and pain: On the importance of pleasure, cf. ii 3, 1152b4.

§2 Least of all, then: Read *huper dē* (OCT: *huper de*).

For some say . . . altogether base: As in Book vii, Aristotle discusses common views about pleasure. In Book vii he concentrates on answering the view that pleasure is not a good. Here, by contrast, he explicitly defines his position by contrasting it with the extreme hedonist view (pleasure is not only a good, but the good, i.e., the supreme good) and the extreme antihedonist view (pleasure is not a good at all). He makes it clearer than he made in Book vii that he rejects both extreme views.

Others, however, . . . intermediate condition: This second group of extreme opponents of pleasure seem to rely on the sort of practical advice that Aristotle himself offers in 1103b26, 1109b1–12.

(b) §3–4. We should not commit ourselves to exaggerated and unrealistic views of pleasure.

§3 Surely, however, . . . the arguments]: Aristotle answers the second group of extreme antihedonists who have, in his view, misappropriated his advice. In his view, the practical aim of ethics does not justify pious frauds. These are self-defeating since the facts (*erga*; see FUNCTION) make the extreme theories incredible.

For if someone blames . . . make distinctions: Someone who insincerely says pleasure is base will not be able to avoid pursuing it himself on some occasions; since he cannot live by the implications of his theory, the many will neither believe in his sincerity nor take his theory seriously. Cf. note to 8.§12 below. (Alternatively, we might take this remark about failure to live by one's theory as an objection to both antihedonist positions.)

2

2.§1–5. Eudoxus' defense of pleasure

(a) §1–2. Eudoxus' arguments to show that pleasure is the good

§1 Eudoxus thought . . . is the good: EUDOXUS argues: (1) All animals seek pleasure. (2) What is choiceworthy is good (*epieikes*, usually rendered 'DECENT'), and what is most choiceworthy is the supreme good. (3) Each thing finds its own good. (4) Hence, pleasure is best for all. (5) Hence, pleasure is the good. His argument looks more plausible when the ambiguity of CHOICEWORTHY is remembered.

§2 to be avoided: Or 'object of avoidance'. The term (*pheukton*) shares the ambiguity of *haireton* ('CHOICEWORTHY').

(b) §3–4. His arguments do not show that pleasure is the good.

§3 This [last] argument, . . . to be the good: Aristotle begins by answering Eudoxus' last argument, and briefly stating his own position about pleasure. He uses Plato's reply, *Phil.* 20d–22b, to the hedonist arguments. His assumption—that if x is the good (i.e., the highest good) nothing can be added to x to make the result a better good than x—underlies the argument in i 7.§8 (cf. ix 9.§10 end).

combined with prudence: Here 'PRUDENCE' (*phronēsis*) may be used in the broader sense (present in Plato's *Phil.*) that extends to theoretical as well as practical reason.

(c) §4. A mistaken objection to Eudoxus' argument from universal pursuit of pleasure to the conclusion that pleasure is a good

§4 But when some object . . . what they say: Aristotle turns from rejecting Eudoxus' argument to show that pleasure is the good, to correct a possible misunderstanding. As well as rejecting the argument for hedonism, he rejects the extreme antihedonist claim that pleasure is not a good at all.

For if things . . . are [good]: Aristotle endorses a universal belief about something's being a good. He does not commit himself to endorsing all universally agreed common beliefs; see ETHICS (4). A less likely translation: 'Things that seem [true] to everyone we say are [true]'.

desired these . . . objection: In a2, read *ōregeto* (OCT: *oregetai*). In a3, read *to legomenon* (OCT: *legomenon*).

if prudent [animals]: The sense of 'PRUDENT' may be broader than its usual Aristotelian sense; see note to §3 above.

superior to themselves: Delete *phusikon agathon* (retained by OCT). Cf. 1153b11.

(d) §5. A mistaken objection to Eudoxus' argument from the badness of pain to the goodness of pleasure

§5 The argument . . . incorrect: As in Book vii, Aristotle answers some of the antihedonist objections. Here, however, his answers are explicitly focused on replies to Eudoxus' hedonism; in contrast to Book vii, the present discussion makes it clear that the extreme antihedonists are right to reject hedonism; it prepares us for Aristotle's positive account in ch. 4.

3

3.§1–13. Pleasure is a good, but not the good.

(a) §1. Further mistaken objection: Pleasure is not a quality.

§1 Again, if . . . not a good: Aristotle passes from antihedonist arguments specifically directed against Eudoxus to more general arguments to show that no pleasure is a good. This is a reason for marking a new chapter here. However, he clearly regards this as part of his discussion of common views about pleasure; see the last words of this chapter.

For virtuous . . . qualities either: The opponents assume that a good must be in the category of quality (see note to i 6.§3). Aristotle agrees with this for 'good' as in 'good person', but not for 'good' as in 'good for a person'.

(b) §2–3. Further mistaken objection: Pleasure admits of degrees, and hence is indefinite.

§2 They say . . . more and less: On definiteness and goodness, cf. note to ix 9.§7.

If their judgment . . . with the virtues: This first argument about definiteness relies on the fact that the experience of pleasure admits of degrees, so that we can be more or less pleased.

If, on the other . . . are mixed: This second argument relies on the fact that different types of pleasures admit of degrees, so that pleasures taken in one sort of object are more pleasant than pleasures taken in another sort of object.

(c) §4. Further mistaken objection: Pleasure is a process.

§4 It would seem, . . . not even a process: Aristotle replies to Plato's a criticism of pleasure (*Phil.* 53c–54c). In 1153a7 he only discussed the view that pleasure is a becoming. Here he seems to distinguish the generic notion of process (or change; see MOVEMENT) from the specific sort of process that is a becoming (*genesis*; see *Phys.* 225a12). According to this conception of a becoming, something's becoming is its coming into existence, as opposed to its destruction, which is its passing out of existence.

It is possible, . . . pleased quickly [or slowly]: Even if I am enjoying watching a game that happens quickly, my enjoyment itself is not quick or slow.

(d) §5–7. The relation of pleasure to pain shows that pleasure is not a process.

§6 They do indeed say . . . becoming]: The view is probably derived from Plato, *Phil.* 31e (though it is not necessarily the same view; see next note).

This does not seem . . . becoming empty: Aristotle assumes that pleasure is a condition of the SOUL, not a purely bodily condition, since it requires awareness (and Plato recognizes this, *Phil.* 34a). In b12, read *kenoumenos* (OCT: *temnomenos*).

(e) §8–10. The fact that some pleasures are bad does not show that pleasure is not a good.

§8 To those who cite . . . not pleasant: In §8–10 Aristotle continues his discussion of the extreme antihedonist position. But in discussing the relevance of bad pleasures, he also states his own qualified position about pleasure more fully. Here he offers three accounts of bad pleasures. (1) §8: They are not pleasant, except for people in a bad condition. (2) §9: The pleasures themselves are good, but they should not be chosen when they come from these sources. (3) §10: Pleasures differ in species, according to their sources, and those that come from bad sources are bad.

For if things are healthy . . . except to these people: 'Pleasant to S' translates the Greek dative case, which might also be rendered 'pleasant for S'. Aristotle might mean (a) x seems pleasant to S, even if x is really not pleasant, or (b) x is really pleasant for S, even if x would not be pleasant for someone else. Cf. notes to iii 4.§4; viii 2.§2; x 6.§10–11.

§9 Or else we might . . . anything and everything: This second account of bad pleasures depends on the distinction between 'choiceworthy without qualification' (see UNQUALIFIED) and 'choiceworthy in these conditions'. Here Aristotle allows that the pleasures themselves are good, but insists that they ought not to be chosen when they come from the wrong sources.

§10 Or perhaps pleasures differ . . . other cases: On the just person's pleasures, cf. 1099a7–21. This third account of bad pleasures is more restrictive than the second. Instead of saying (as the second account says) that sometimes pleasures are good, but ought not to be chosen because they have the wrong sources, Aristotle now suggests that the wrongness of the sources makes the pleasures themselves bad.

(f) §11–13. Pleasure is not the only good, or the ultimate good.

§11 The difference between . . . differ in species: The discussion of specifically different pleasures in §10 leads Aristotle back to the question that he took up in 2.§3 in his discussion of Eudoxus. There he rejected one of Eudoxus' arguments for identifying pleasure with the good, but did not state his own position on the question. Now he answers the question more directly. Contrast 1153b9–14, where he neither endorsed nor explicitly rejected the Eudoxan position. On flatterers, see 1127a8.

§12 And no one would . . . pain for it: Cf. 1176b22, 1177a6; *EE* 1215b22. Aristotle relies on the general assumption (already used against a version of hedonism in i 5.§3) that we are concerned to exercise distinctively human FUNCTIONS.

Moreover, there are many . . . resulted from them: Aristotle uses a counterfactual test (cf. 1097b3) to show that we do not always choose things for the sake of pleasure. We can see that pleasure is not our only end, because we would still choose some actions even if (contrary to fact) they did not result in pleasure. Aristotle makes it clear that he does not take his own account of pleasure as 'necessarily following' on activity to imply that pleasure is the highest good.

§13 It would seem . . . that are not]: This is the conclusion from the discussion in §11–12. Aristotle affirms his rejection of hedonism.

Let this suffice, . . . and pain: This sentence should be separated from the rest of §13, since it concludes the discussion (introduced by the last words of ch. 1) that has occupied chs. 2–3. As the previous sentence shows, Aristotle does not take himself to have simply raised prima facie objections to different views. He thinks he has established some positive conclusions about pleasure, which he incorporates into his own account in ch. 4.

4

4.§1–4. Pleasure is an activity.

(a) §1. Pleasure is complete at any time.

§1 What, then, . . . beginning: Aristotle signals his own positive account of pleasure, anticipated at 1173a29, 1153a7–17. He relies on the distinction between processes, which are incomplete ACTIVITIES, and complete activities; see also ACTION and PRODUCTION. Pleasure is not a process that has only an external goal; hence the arguments that rest on treating it as a process are irrelevant.

And pleasure . . . longer time: On form, see CAUSE. Here the form is closely connected with essence and DEFINITION; something achieves its form to the extent that it acquires the character that makes it the kind of thing that it is. The building of a temple takes time to acquire all that makes it a complete building of a temple;

hence it takes time to achieve its form. An enjoyment does not take time to acquire all that makes it a complete enjoyment. Though certainly I might prefer my enjoyment to be prolonged, it is no more an enjoyment by being prolonged.

(b) §2–3. A process consists of dissimilar parts, and is not complete at any time.

§2 constructing a building: In a20, read *oikodomia* (OCT: *oikodomikē*).

or, [in other . . . it takes]: In a21, read *chronō(i) toutō(i)* (OCT: *chronō(i) ē toutō(i)*).

Moreover, each process . . . from one another: Lit., 'And in the parts and in the time they are all incomplete, and they differ in form from the whole and from each other'. The words 'they are all' must apparently refer to (a) processes such as temple building; and 'they differ in form' must refer to (b) the parts of (a). The next sentence relies on the distinction between (a) and (b).

but the production . . . incomplete . . . of a part: Even when any one of (b) is finished, it looks forward to a further production. This explains why the whole production (a) is incomplete at any time when it is still going on.

Hence . . . differ in form; . . . a process complete in form . . . time [that it takes]: 'Differ in form' refers to (b), and 'a process' to (a) (see previous note).

§3 For if locomotion . . . And besides . . . differences in walking itself . . . in different places: First Aristotle considers locomotion as an example of (a), and then various possible examples of (b) (see note above). Then ('And besides . . . ') he takes walking, e.g., from London to Glasgow, as an example of (a), and its parts (e.g., walking from London to Birmingham, from Birmingham to Preston, etc.) as examples of (b).

Now we have . . . elsewhere: See, e.g., *Phys.* v 1–4.

(c) §4. Therefore pleasure is not a process, but an activity.

§4 for what is present in an instant is a whole: 'Instant' translates *nun*, usually rendered 'now'; cf. *Phys.* 218a6, 220a18. An instant is unextended; it is not a duration or an interval, and hence is not a part of time. Anything that is wholly present in an instant takes no time to come into being, and hence does not come into being at all; this is why Aristotle says it is a whole. There is no coming into being of pleasure because coming into being requires the parts to come into being one after the other, and pleasure is present as a whole all at once.

This also makes . . . process or a becoming: In 3.§4–7 Aristotle considered the claim that pleasure is a process (*kinēsis*) and a becoming (*genesis*). Having now offered his own alternative account of pleasure to explain why it is not a process, he goes on to explain why it is not a becoming.

4.§5–11. Pleasure completes an activity.

(a) §5. The best activity is the most pleasant.

§5 Every perceptual capacity . . . perceptible objects: 'Perceptual capacity' translates *aisthēsis*, lit., 'PERCEPTION' or 'sense', exercised in the ACTIVITY of perceiving. The 'object' (lit., 'perceptible' or 'thing perceived', *aisthēton*) is the special sensible (sight, sound, etc.; b27; cf. 1142a27) or common or coincidental sensibles.

(b) §6–8. Pleasure completes an activity by being a consequent end.

§6 But the way . . . health and the doctor . . . same way: The doctor is the efficient CAUSE, and health the formal cause, of being healthy. This does not mean that Aristotle intends the different ways of completing an activity (or 'bringing it to its goal', *teleioun*; see COMPLETE) to be efficient and formal causes. On the contrary, they seem to be different final causes.

§7 Clearly a pleasure . . . both present: §7 seems to interrupt the sequence of thought; §8 follows more naturally on §6. §7 seems to go better between §8 and §9.

§8 Pleasure completes . . . consequent end . . . on youths: Probably Aristotle here distinguishes two types of final CAUSE, which are two ways in which an activity can achieve its END. (1) Perceiving is good as an end in itself, as the activity of a desirable capacity or state; the action has the state 'present' in it insofar as that is the state it actualizes. (2) The pleasure is a further end, another good in itself, which is consequent on our choosing the action as a good in itself. It is an extra good added to the good of the action as the 'bloom' of youth (i.e., the attractiveness of a youth that made him an object of desire and pleasure to an older man (1157a6–10)) is added to his youth. See also 1153a6. A 'consequent end' (or 'supervenient end'; cf. 1104b4) is contrasted with the inherent or intrinsic end of the activity—i.e., the realization of the desirable state, which is an end in itself.

(c) §9. This explains why pleasure is not continuous.

§9 For nothing human . . . the activity: See 1154b20, 1170a6.

(d) §10–11. This also explains why we desire pleasure.

§10 Why does . . . being alive: More literally: 'One might think all desire pleasure because they . . . '. The translation seeks to make it clear that 'one might think' goes with 'because they' rather than 'desire pleasure'. Aristotle takes it for granted that people desire pleasure.

§11 But do we choose life . . . completes every activity: Though Aristotle sets aside this question about pleasure and life as ends, his answer to it emerges from 1174a4 and from what he has just said. We do not choose life and its activities purely for the sake of pleasures; we choose for their own sakes the activities that constitute our living (cf. 1168a5). Nor do we choose pleasure purely for the sake of living; it is one of the desirable activities that constitute our living. See note to 5.§7.

5

5.§1–5. Pleasures differ in kind, and especially in goodness and badness.

(a) §1–2. Different activities are completed by different pleasures.

§1 Hence pleasures . . . species: Aristotle accepts the third account of pleasure that he proposed in 3.§10, claiming that pleasures differ in species. Just action and sunbathing are not two sources of a qualitatively uniform sensation in the way that two cows are sources of the same milk; we cannot ask how much sunbathing we would need to replace the pleasure lost by failing to do just actions. Since pleasures differ in species, Aristotle insists that the virtuous person must get the specific pleasure of virtuous action. He must enjoy it because it is virtuous; and that enjoyment will require him to value it as virtuous for its own sake. Cf. 1099a17, 1104b3. 'Species' translates *eidos*, also translated 'form'. See note to 4.§2, DEFINITION.

(b) §2. The proper pleasure promotes an activity.

§2 This is also . . . completes: This seems the right place to begin a new paragraph. Aristotle passes from the claim that different activities have different proper pleasures to the fact that the proper pleasure has a characteristic and distinctive effect on the activity that it is proper to.

(c) §3–5. An alien pleasure impedes an activity.

5.§6–11. Which pleasures are goods?

(a) §6–7. The goodness of an activity determines the goodness of the pleasure taken in it.

§7 Still, pleasure would seem . . . appear the same: Aristotle makes it clear—clearer than he made it in Book vii—that the pleasure of fishing, for instance, is not simply the unhindered activity of fishing itself, but a further activity (cf. 1153a12–15, 1153b10; this is not clearly inconsistent with Book x). Though Aristotle does not say exactly what the extra end is, it is natural to think of the feeling of pleasure that is taken in a valued activity. Once we distinguish the activity and the pleasure, we can see that we do not choose life and its activities purely for the sake of pleasure; see note to 4.§11.

(b) §8. The function of a given kind of animal determines the proper activity and the proper pleasure.

§8 as Heracleitus . . . than gold: DK 22 B 9.

(c) §9–11. The human function determines the proper human pleasure, measured by reference to the virtuous person.

§10 But in all such . . . what he enjoys: On the good person as standard, cf. iii 4.§5, note, PROTAGORAS. Here the good person is the standard not only of what is a good pleasure but of what is really a pleasure.

§10–11 It is not pleasant, . . . corrupted people: Here Aristotle seems to accept the account of bad pleasures that he mentioned in 3.§8. Since vicious people are mistaken in their views about what is pleasant, they mistake what appears pleasant to them for what is really pleasant. They are even wrong about what is really pleasant for them; for what seems pleasant to them in their depraved condition is not what would be pleasant for them in a healthy condition.

6

6.§1–8. Happiness consists in activities in accord with virtue.

(a) §1–2. Happiness is an activity that is choiceworthy in itself.

§1 We have now . . . of pleasure: This summary places the discussion of pleasure after friendship, omitting the discussion of pleasure in Book vii. However, the summary is too compressed to decide whether or not Aristotle is describing a treatise that includes the books common to the *EE* and *EN*. See Introduction (3); x 9.§1 and note, below.

§2 We said, . . . said before: See 1095b31, 1153b19.

Some activities are necessary, . . . other end: On types of activities, see 1097a30–b11; HAPPINESS (2–3).

For happiness . . . self-sufficient: The 'for' is a little puzzling here. A self-sufficient end (a) is pursued for its own sake; and (b) is not pursued for the sake of anything else. Here Aristotle says correctly that self-sufficiency implies (a), and that virtuous actions satisfy (a). Virtuous actions, however, do not satisfy (b); see note to 7.§5.

(b) §3. Many suppose that pleasant amusements are the appropriate sorts of activities.

§3 But pleasant . . . own right]: Aristotle deals with the claim of pleasure to be the highest good more fully than when he briefly dismissed it 1095b19. He has now discussed the nature and varieties of pleasure, and can explain what error someone makes if that person identifies pleasure with happiness and does not (a) specify the type of pleasure, and (b) see that the value of the pleasure depends on the value of the activity that is the source of the pleasure.

That is why people who are witty . . . the tyrant requires: On witty people, cf. 1128a4, 1158a31. The people mentioned here do not have the virtue described in iv 8, but are more like the ingratiating people and flatterers of iv 6. Powerful people admired for their happiness have no more understanding of it than their imitators have; cf. 1159a12–17.

And so these amusements . . . people in supreme power . . . in them: On the example set by powerful people, cf. 1095b11.

(c) §4–5. But popular opinion is a poor guide; the virtuous person is the standard.

§4 Further, these powerful . . . bodily pleasures: On most people's lack of relevant experience of pleasure, cf. Plato, *Rep*. 582a–583a. On 'civilized' (or 'free') as opposed to slavish pursuits, cf. 1177a7; SLAVE.

Hence, . . . to boys and to men, . . . decent people: Cf. 1174a1.

§5 As we have often said, . . . excellent person. . . . and pleasant]: To rule out amusement as a candidate for happiness, Aristotle appeals to the excellent person as the standard for selecting the worthwhile activities and pleasures; see 1176a15.

(d) §6–8. Happiness must involve serious and worthwhile activities, not merely amusements.

§6 Rather, . . . Anacharsis says: Anacharsis was sometimes counted as one of the Seven Sages. See DK 10 A 1.

§7 Besides, . . . taken seriously . . . serious and excellent . . . of happiness: The different uses of *spoudaion*, translated 'serious' and 'EXCELLENT', are closely related here.

§8 Besides, . . . even a slave, . . . for happiness]: On SLAVES, cf. notes to iv 3.§29, viii 11.§6–7. They lack the capacity for life in accord with reason, and so are incapable of happiness; see 1099b32, 1178b27.

Happiness, then: In a9 read *ouk ar'* (OCT: *ou gar*; 'For happiness . . . ').

7

7.§1–9. Happiness: The supreme activity is theoretical study.

(a) §1–2. This is the best activity.

§1 The best . . . natural ruler and leader: This seems to refer to the practical functions of understanding. But Aristotle's next remarks refer to STUDY, not practical thought, as the activity of reason that is to be identified with its proper virtue. Perhaps he has two points in mind. (1) The ruling functions of reason show it is our best capacity. (2) Hence the best activity of all is the best activity of the best capacity; this is the activity of study. See also note to 7.§9.

Hence complete happiness . . . proper virtue: Aristotle need not mean that complete happiness is exclusively this activity. He may mean that if happiness is to be complete it must include this activity. The same applies to 'in accord with the supreme virtue' in a13. Cf. note to 8.§8.

and we have said . . . study: It is not clear what Aristotle is referring back to. He has not explicitly said that the relevant activity is study; but cf. 1139a6–17, 1141a18–22, 1143b33–1144a6, 1145a6–11. Aristotle does not say here that the activity of understanding that constitutes happiness is exclusively concerned with study.

§2 This seems . . . the truth: The rest of this chapter is a series of arguments for this claim. Aristotle appeals to his previous criteria for happiness, and argues: (1) Study is the single activity that best fits the criteria for happiness. (2) Hence, if happiness must be some single activity, study is the best candidate. (3) If happiness includes more than one activity, study will be the most important. These conclusions do not imply: (4) Study is the whole of happiness. It is open to dispute whether Aristotle accepts (4).

Further, it is the most continuous . . . continuous action: Cf. 1100b11, 1175a5.

(c) §3. It is the most pleasant.

(d) §4. It is most self-sufficient.

§4 Moreover, the self-sufficiency . . . more than in anything else: Since Aristotle says only that study is more self-sufficient than anything else (or self-sufficient above all [*malista*]), he does not say that the life of study meets his conditions for self-sufficiency in 1097b6–21. A life consisting of study alone contains the most valuable single good; but it does not contain all the goods needed to make the life lack nothing; cf. 1169b4–8.

(e) §5. It aims at no end beyond itself.

§5 Besides, study . . . beyond having studied: Cf. note to 6.§2. Study is not chosen for any end wholly external to it. Aristotle's remarks here do not show that it cannot also be chosen for the sake of happiness (i.e., as a part of happiness). Cf. 1097b2. (An alternative translation, 'it is the only virtue chosen because of itself', is less well supported by the next clause.)

(f) §6. It consists in leisured activity, and does not include actions aimed at some further end.

§6 Besides, . . . in leisure; . . . deny ourselves leisure . . . at peace: When Aristotle speaks of LEISURE, he does not refer to idleness or inactivity, but to action that we gladly take on for its own sake. When we 'deny ourselves leisure' (lit., 'are unleisured', *ascholein*), we take on actions that we engage in reluctantly, for the sake of some further end.

But the actions of the politician also deny us leisure; . . . it is different: These actions 'deny us leisure' (lit., 'are unleisured'; see previous note) because of their disagreeable and instrumental character, as explained in the latter part of the sentence.

(g)§7.Comparedwithactivitiesofothervirtues,theoreticalstudybestsatisfies the conditions for happiness.

§7 and are choiceworthy for something other than themselves: Lit., (1) 'and are choiceworthy not because of themselves' or (2) 'and are not choiceworthy because of themselves'. Since (2) appears to conflict with Aristotle's frequent claim (e.g., at 1176b8), (1) is preferable. Aristotle points out that virtuous action has two aspects. Campaigning against racism, for instance, is (a) a just action, and hence fine and choiceworthy in itself, and (b) aimed at a result wholly external to it, the passage of a law and its success in eliminating some racism. Aspect (b) distinguishes these virtuous actions from pure theoretical study, and hence makes the morally virtuous person dependent on external circumstances. Cf. note to vi 5.§4.

Hence a human being's . . . complete span of life, . . . proper to happiness: On a 'complete' length of life, cf. 1098a18, 1101a16.

(h) §8. This is a godlike life.

§8 Such a life . . . divine element in him: Study is the activity of the most divine element or part ('element' is supplied in the next two paragraphs; the Greek has only a neuter adjective) of a human being, and hence offers him a life that is more than merely human; cf. *Met.* 982b28–983a11.

And the activity . . . the compound: Probably Aristotle refers to the compound consisting of the understanding and the other parts of the SOUL. Less probably, he might refer to the compound of soul and body. Cf. 1178a20.

the makers of proverbs . . . mortal': See Euripides, TGF fr. 1040; Pindar, *Isthmians* v 16 (and others).

Rather, as far . . . power and value: The term rendered 'be pro-immortal' (*athanatizein*) is probably modelled on the terms used for supporters of the Medes (i.e., Persians) and Laconians (i.e., Spartans) (*mēdizein, lakōnizein*). Less probably, it might be rendered 'make oneself immortal'. 'Go to all lengths': lit., 'do all things'.

(i) §9. It realizes the supreme element in human nature.

§9 Moreover, each person . . . his controlling and better element: Or 'if it (i.e., understanding) is the controlling and better element in him'. See note to ix 8.§6. §9 adds to the claim in §8 that the life of study is (in one respect) superhuman the further claim that it is (in another respect) most truly human. Previously Aristotle has identified a person with his understanding because of its practical role; cf. note to 7.§1. He now suggests that if we identify the understanding with a person, we must identify the theoretical understanding with the person.

if understanding, . . . human being: 'More than anything else' suggests a qualification to the claim that theoretical understanding is to be identified with the person.

8

8.§1–13. Theoretical study and the other virtues

(a) §1–3. The virtues concerned with action are human, not divine.

§1 The life . . . are human: The Greek has no adjective qualified by 'in a secondary way'. 'Happiest' is the most appropriate one to supply, given the end of ch. 7. Less probably, one might supply 'happy'. Aristotle now supports his defense of the superiority of study as part of happiness. The activities of the other virtues depend on the human and nondivine parts of the compound (see note to 7.§8), and hence are subject to some of the limitations of human beings and their external circumstances. In particular, the virtues of character need external goods more than study needs them, and hence are more vulnerable to FORTUNE.

§3 Besides, prudence is inseparable . . . prudence: The claim that prudence is inseparable from (lit., 'is yoked together with') virtue of character was defended in vi 13.

(b) §4–6. Theoretical study is less dependent on external goods.

§4 Moreover, it seems to need external supplies . . . needs them: On happiness and external supplies, see GOOD.

Similarly, the brave person . . . virtue requires: Bravery requires me to stand firm, but if I am so feeble that I am immediately overpowered, I will never manage to stand firm. If I never find anything that would appeal to my appetites, I lack the FREEDOM or opportunity (*exousia*) to do intemperate actions, and so cannot do what temperance requires. Aristotle does not say that I cannot be brave or temperate in these cases, but only that I cannot achieve the results aimed at by the virtues.

§5 Moreover, . . . decision or action . . . on both: Aristotle usually takes decision to be the crucial aspect of virtue; see 1111b5, 1163a21, 1164b1.

Well, certainly . . . the complete [good] depends on both: If 'good' is the right supplement here, Aristotle is referring to the complete good that requires virtuous action, not merely virtue; that is why he goes on to refer to actions in the next clause.

§6 Insofar as he is a human being, . . . accord with virtue: When he refers to the political nature of human beings (cf. 1097b9), Aristotle seems to concede that a human being's happiness includes the activity of other virtues, and hence the virtues themselves, besides understanding devoted to study.

(c) §7–8. Traditions about the gods support the supremacy of theoretical study.

§7 For we traditionally suppose that the gods . . . trivial and unworthy of the gods: On the GODS, see 1101b18, 1145a26; *Pol.* 1253a26. The gods do not suffer from the human limitations that make virtues of character necessary and praiseworthy for human beings. There is no point in praising them for not having base appetites, as we would praise the temperate person (1119a11–20); for the gods were never in danger of having them, and did not need to train themselves.

And so the human activity . . . happiness: 'Most akin' and 'more than any others' imply a comparison between study and other human activities (cf. note to 7.§9 above). They stop short of identifying study with happiness.

§8 A sign of this . . . in study at all: On the capacity for happiness, see 1099b32. Aristotle may be making the same point here, if understanding in study and in practical thought are the same capacity; cf. notes to 7.§1, 9.

And so . . . of study: In 'some kind of' (*tis*), Aristotle may be drawing back from a complete identification of happiness with study; cf. note on §7 above.

(d) §9–10. Human beings also need external goods for happiness, but only at a moderate level.

§9 But happiness will need external . . . services provided: Aristotle returns to the point he considered in §6 above, about the importance of external goods in happiness. He argues that since we do not need a large supply of external goods, our need for them need not control our lives in ways that conflict with the role he has ascribed to study.

§10 Moreover, we can do fine . . . accord with virtue: Probably we ought to mark a new paragraph here (contrary to the OCT punctuation). §9 has recognized that we need some external goods for life and action in general. §10 moves on to a different role for external goods, as resources for FINE and virtuous action. Here, as in §6, Aristotle maintains that the happy person who gives the proper role to study in his life will not be exclusively concerned with study; he will also be concerned with fine actions that ACCORD with virtues of character. See *Pol.* vii 2–3.

(e) §11–12. Traditional views support us, but they must be tested in practice.

§11 Solon . . . temperately: See Herodotus i 30.

And Anaxagoras . . . the many: See DK 59 A 30.

§12 Hence the beliefs . . . arguments: On beliefs of the WISE, see ETHICS (4).

Hence we ought . . . by applying it to what we do and how we live: Lit., ' . . . from actions [or 'facts', *erga;* see FUNCTION] and lives'. We must pass the test stated in 1172a35, showing that we can apply our principles in practice. Aristotle thinks that some consistent ideals of life are so hard for a normal person to act on that they cannot be taken seriously.

(f) §13. Those who engage in study are loved by the gods.

§13 The person whose activity . . . the gods: This does not seem to be closely connected with §12. It fits well, however, at the end of §8, since it continues the description of the godlike character of the life of study, and infers that someone living such a life will be befriended by the gods.

9

9.§1–17. Ethics, moral education, and legislation

(a) §1–5. Since arguments alone do not make people virtuous, we must study the different means of moral education.

§1 We have now . . . pleasure also: This summary follows the order of the *EN;* cf. above 6.§1, note.

On the contrary, . . . act on our knowledge: Aristotle reasserts the practical aim of ETHICS (1103b26) and returns to the beginning of the *EN*. Having found what happiness is, and especially that it requires virtue of character to be acquired by moral EDUCATION (1104b11), we must now turn our attention to that. At the same time we return to explicit concern with the political community; see 1094b7, 1102a7, 1103b2, 1113b21, 1141b23, 1152b1. A design for happiness must extend beyond the person to the city he belongs to, and in particular the city must direct moral education.

§3 Now if arguments . . . Theognis says: Theognis 432.

§5 For it is impossible, . . . habits: This explanation suggests that it is the bad habits of the many that make them unreceptive to moral reasoning, as though good upbringing would have made them receptive. But in b11, 'naturally obey . . . ', Aristotle suggests that their nature was defective from the start; even with the right habituation they apparently could not reach complete virtue. In b17, read *ethesi*, 'habits' (OCT: *ēthesi;* 'characters').

what we seem . . . decent: Lit., 'through which we seem to become decent'.

(b) §6–8. Nature, habit, and rational argument are all needed for virtue; moral education is needed to form character and habit.

§6 The [contribution] of nature . . . fortunate ones: On nature, cf. iii 5.§17; note to vi 13.§1.

Arguments and teaching . . . nourish seed: When Aristotle says that arguments do not 'prevail' (*ischuein*), he does not mean that they have no influence; he means that their influence is not always effective. He uses 'prevail' similarly in the following paragraphs. On the need for a good upbringing, cf. the related but different reasons given in 1095a2, b4.

(c) §8–13. Formation of the right character requires legislation; hence states ought to be concerned with moral education, though many states neglect this task.

§8 for the many, . . . a temperate and resistant way: On resistance to pain, cf. 1150a31.

§9 For the many . . . compulsion . . . sanctions more than to the fine: Compulsion is distinguished from force (1179b29); see note to iii 1.§7. The role of punishment explains the relevance of iii 1, 5 and v 8. The distinctions drawn there will presumably be used in determining the proper treatment of different offenders.

§12 and law is reason . . . understanding: On the rational character of LAW, cf. *Pol.* 1287a28–32.

§13 And yet, it is only in Sparta, . . . like a Cyclops: On neglect of moral education, cf. note to viii 10.§6. Aristotle's approval of Spartan concern for moral education does not imply approval of Spartan moral education. See *Pol.* 1333b5–35. Aristotle quotes Homer, *Od.* ix 114 on the prepolitical Cyclopes (also quoted by Plato, *Laws* 680b–c). The context (paraphrased): 'They have no assemblies to deliberate and no rules but they live in caves. Each lays down rules for his children and wives, and [these heads of households] have no concern for one another.' (Aristotle has 'wife' instead of 'wives'.)

(d) §14–17. Legislative science is useful both for individuals and for states.

§14 But if the community . . . decide to do it: Aristotle offers second-best advice (characteristic of parts of the *Pol.*, e.g., iv 1) for someone who is not living in the right community; he advises systematic education by individuals, if the community will not do its part. In a32, read *orthēn [kai dran auto dunasthai]*, adding the phrase that stands in a30 in the mss. (OCT deletes the phrase in a30, and marks a lacuna after *orthēn* in a32.)

1180a33 legislative science: 'Science' is supplied from here on.

1180b6 for his children . . . fond of him . . . to obey: This is an expression of friendship in families; see 1161b19.

§15 For though generally . . . on everyone: 'Generally' translates *katholou*, translated 'universally' in b14, 21. The patient who does not benefit is not exactly an exception to the general rule. Insofar as he is feverish he may benefit from the normal treatment; but since he has other conditions too, the normal treatment may not, everything considered, be best for him, even though it is always best for fever, considered by itself.

§16 Admittedly someone . . . anyone else at all: We ought not to begin a new paragraph here. Aristotle concedes the possibility of some practical success without scientific knowledge, but insists that scientific knowledge is nonetheless necessary for proper understanding.

Nonetheless, . . . sciences are about: Though experience may make someone competent in a restricted range of cases, general competence and understanding require the grasp of the universal. The features of the virtuous person referred to in 1137a9 and 1144b3 are relevant here in distinguishing the expert craftsman from the merely experienced practitioner.

9.§18–23. Who should teach legislative science, and how?

(a) §18–19. Some apparently suitable teachers lack theoretical understanding, whereas others lack practical experience.

§18 Next, then, . . . part of political science: Like Plato (e.g., *Meno* 99–100), Aristotle is dissatisfied with politicians and with those who profess to offer instruction in POLITICAL SCIENCE. The practical politicians simply rely on experience, while its instructors overlook its importance.

Instead, those who practice it are the political activists, . . . rather than thought: The political activists (*politeuomenoi*) are professional politicians, who are popularly regarded as overactive busybodies; cf. 1142a2.

For evidently . . . friends of theirs: This paragraph is intended to justify the claim at the end of the previous paragraph, that practical politicians are not guided by thought (*dianoia*), but by EXPERIENCE.

(b) §19–21. Both experience and theoretical understanding are necessary.

§19 Nonetheless, . . . familiarity with politics: This paragraph corrects any misunderstanding that might have arisen from the previous paragraph. Though practical politicians lack political science, and cannot teach it, their experience is nonetheless important and relevant for political science. In a11, read *sunētheias mallon* (OCT: *politikēs sunētheias*).

§20 By contrast, those of the sophists . . . it is about: Aristotle returns to the sophists whom he introduced in §18, and accuses them of neglecting the point about experience that he made in §19. He insists that practical experience is no less necessary in political science than in prudence as a whole; cf. 1143b7.

§21 And yet doctors . . . must be treated: As in §19, Aristotle tries to avoid the kind of misunderstanding that might result from one-sided attention to what he has just said. Political science, like MEDICINE, will be practically relevant only if it rests on experience; but it is not to be confined to mere reports of experience.

(c) §22–23. The right approach to legislative science

§22 Since, then, our predecessors . . . we are able: On predecessors, cf. *Top.* 183b14. Aristotle does not deny that his predecessors have made particular suggestions about legislation (some are discussed in *Pol.* ii). He claims they have left the general area 'uncharted' (or 'unexamined'), with no systematic survey of the data, and no account of the proper method.

§23 First, then, . . . particular topics: Aristotle announces the program of the *Pol.*, in the order of the surviving treatise. This sentence applies to Book ii.

Then let us study . . . some badly: This sentence applies especially to *Pol.* iv–vi. The 'collected political systems' are the 158 descriptions of different constitutions, compiled by Aristotle's school. (See ROT pp. 2453–7.) Only one of them, the *Constitution of Athens*, largely survives.

For when we have . . . should follow: This applies especially to *Pol.* vii–viii. After studying the experience of different political systems and practices (following the advice in §20), we will be in a better position to evaluate different systems, and to apply the ethical principles of the *EN* in an account of the best system.

GLOSSARY

accord, in accord with, *kata* The Greek preposition *kata* means 'according to', and includes both (a) actual guidance (I build a shed *kata* the design if I consult the design as I work); (b) mere conformity (bodies fall *kata* the laws of nature without consulting these laws). When Aristotle speaks of action *kata* virtue, decision, etc., it is often both important and difficult to decide if he means (a) or (b) or something intermediate between them (see, e.g., note to v 2.§10).

account See REASON (4).

achievable in action See ACTION.

achievement See FUNCTION.

action, *praxis* There are three main uses. (1) Aristotle uses *praxis* and the cognate verb *prattein* broadly for all intentional actions (translated 'do' or 'achieve in action'). What we can achieve by *praxis* (the *prakton*, usually translated 'achievable in action') is what we can achieve by our own efforts (1096b34, 1147a3). Probably a *praxis* must be VOLUNTARY. In this sense children and nonhuman ANIMALS are capable of action (1111a26). Such action has a DESIRE for some END as its efficient CAUSE; the desire is focused on a PARTICULAR situation by further beliefs, and it is a particular action that is done (1147a5, 1110b6) and that we are responsible for. (2) More strictly, *praxis* is confined to rational action on a DECISION. Nonhuman animals are incapable of this. See 1094a5, 7; 1139a20; *EE* 1222b20, 1224a29 (cf. 1111b8). (3) Most strictly of all, *praxis* is confined to rational action which is its own END, and is not done exclusively for the sake of some end beyond it. It aims at 'doing well' (or 'acting well', *eupraxia*), for itself (see notes to i 4.§2, vi 2.§4, 5.§4). Action may also have some end beyond it. HAPPINESS is an end beyond virtuous action, which nonetheless is chosen for its own sake: 1097b1–5; 1174a7–8. In this sense action is contrasted with PRODUCTION: 1139a35–b4, vi 4–5; note to ii 4.§3. It is a complete ACTIVITY, and not just a MOVEMENT.

It is not always clear (e.g., at 1094a1) how strictly Aristotle uses *praxis*. The three uses above perhaps do not mark three different senses of the word. They may be (cf. Aristotle's view of the three types of FRIENDSHIP in viii 3–6) more and less complete specimens of action. The first two types share some of the features of the third; the first is voluntary and goal-directed, the second is also rational, and the third is complete.

activity, actualization, *energeia* A subject's *energeia* realizes its CAPACITY; hence the *energeia* of a CRAFT (such as shoemaking) and of the craftsman includes both the activities involved in the exercise of the craft and the product (the shoes) that is aimed at in the exercise (cf. notes to 1094a3, 1168a6; FUNCTION).

The scope of *energeia* is sometimes narrowed by contrast with *hexis* and by contrast with *kinēsis*: (1) In *DA* 412a22–8, Aristotle contrasts 'first' activity with 'second'. Someone is in first activity in relation to his knowledge of French if he has learned French and can speak it on the right occasions, but at the moment is asleep or thinking about something else. He is in second activity when he is actually speaking French (1146a31). To have a SOUL is to have a first activity. In the *EN* a first activity is called a STATE. When Aristotle defines HAPPINESS as an activity of the soul, he is requiring it to include second activities, not merely states (1095b32, 1178b18–20). (2) In 1174a14 ff., *Phys.* 201a9, *Met.* 1048b18, Aristotle draws a further contrast. (a) A MOVEMENT is an incomplete activity. The degree of activity is consistent with the retention of the capacity realized in the activity, where the complete activity implies the loss of the capacity. The movement of house-building, for instance, is going on when the bricks and stones have incompletely actualized their capacity to become a house; when they completely actualize that capacity and the house exists, they no longer possess that capacity, since a house is not still capable of becoming a house. (b) A complete activity, however, does not imply the loss of the capacity that is actualized in the activity. Seeing or living, for instance, does not imply the loss of the capacity to see or live. A movement is incomplete because it aims at some end beyond itself (e.g., the building process aims at the house being built) whose achievement makes that movement impossible to continue (we cannot keep building the house when it is already built), whereas a complete activity is its own end. Hence complete activity is identical to ACTION in Aristotle's narrowest sense. This is the type of activity that PLEASURE is (1153a10, 1174a14). Activities of virtue; see VIRTUE. Activity and FRIENDSHIP; see 1168a5, 1170a18.

agapan LIKE

agathos GOOD

aidōs SHAME

aischros shameful; see FINE.

aisthēsis PERCEPTION

aitia, aition CAUSE

akolasia intemperance; see TEMPERANCE.

akrasia INCONTINENCE

akribes EXACT

anankē NECESSITY

anger, *orgē* Anger is a FEELING (1105b22) especially associated with spirit (see DESIRE). The proper treatment of anger is discussed in iv 5 (see note to iv 5.§1). See also 1103b19, 1110b26, 1111a26, 1117a6, 1130a31, 1135b29, 1138a9, 1149a24–b33, 1150a29; *Rhet.* 1378a30.

animal, *zōon* Aristotle normally uses *zōon* for the genus to which insects, dogs, and human beings all belong (*Pol.* 1253a3, 8). Sometimes he uses it for those he also calls 'the other animals' (1111b9), excluding HUMAN BEINGS (1099b33); these animals are also called 'beasts' (*thēria*, e.g., 1139a20, 1147b4). Some of the differences between human beings and other animals are these: (1) Other animals have a SOUL defined by PERCEPTION. They live by perception and APPEARANCE without REASON (1098a2, 1139a20, 1147b4, 1149a10, 1170a16). (2) They share with human beings nonrational DESIRE (1111b12, 1178b27) but not rational desire. Hence they act VOLUNTARILY, but not on a DECISION (1111a25, b8). (3) They are not capable of HAPPINESS (1098b32, 1178b27) or of the VIRTUES of character (1149b31; cf. 1141a26; *EE* 1240b32), since these require decision.

animate See SOUL.

aporia puzzle; see ETHICS.

appear, appearance, evident, apparent The verb *phainesthai*, 'appear', has two constructions in Greek: (a) with the participle ('being wise, he appears so', i.e., 'he is evidently wise'), endorsing what appears (this is also the sense of the adjective *phaneron*, 'evident'; (b) with the infinitive ('he appears to be wise'), neither endorsing nor denying what appears. Sometimes, however, the verb is used without either participle or infinitive, and hence is indeterminate between (a) and (b). These cases are translated by 'is apparently'. This translation may mislead if it suggests that Aristotle is tentative or noncommittal in his assertion; this may, but need not, be true just as what is apparent may, but need not, be misleading or dubious. 'Would seem' normally translates *eoike* (lit., 'it looks like, or 'is like', a translation also sometimes used), which may, but need not, be less committal than 'seem', *dokein*.

Hence, when Aristotle reports what appears, or sets out the appearances (1096a9, 1145b3) only the context shows whether he endorses or rejects (e.g., 1113b1) or neither. The same applies to his use of 'seem' (*dokein*, cognate with *doxa*, 'belief'), which is equivalent to 'appear' in the *EN* (e.g., 1095a30, 1113a21; note on iv 3.§3, 34). The appearances include commonly accepted beliefs; Aristotle takes these as the material for arguments in ETHICS.

The condition I am in when something appears to me is *phantasia*, 'appearance' (1113b32, 1141a32). The appearance may result from PERCEPTION or from REASON (*DA* 434a5–10), and ANIMALS who have perception without reasoning are directed by perceptual appearance (1147b5); a HUMAN BEING may act on this contrary to reason (1149a32, 1150b28).

appetite, *epithumia* See DESIRE.

archē PRINCIPLE

aretē VIRTUE

argument See REASON (3).

athlios MISERABLE

attend, attention Usually this renders *epimeleisthai* and cognates (e.g., 1099b20, 1114a3, 1180a25), indicating systematic practice and training. When attending is contrasted with CAPACITY or potentiality (in 1147a33) the Greek is *theōrein*; see STUDY.

autarkēs SELF-SUFFICIENT; see HAPPINESS.

avoid See CHOICEWORTHY.

axia WORTH

bad See VICIOUS.

base See VICIOUS.

beautiful See FINE.

becoming, *genesis* See note to x 2.§4.

bia FORCE; see notes to iii 1.§3, 7.

blessed, blessedly happy, *makarios* We might expect this to be especially closely associated with the life of the GODS (cf. *EE* 1215a10; 1178b9), in which happiness is entirely stable and immune to the limitations of the human condition. In fact, however, the *EN* seems to use the term interchangeably with 'HAPPY'. Unless the terms are interchangeable, the argument in i 10.§13–16 is difficult to follow.

***boulēsis*, wish** See DESIRE.

***bouleusis*, deliberation** See DECISION.

bravery, *andreia*; cowardice, *deilia* *Andreia* is cognate with *anēr*, MAN, and with *andrōdēs*, 'manly'. It refers to the behavior and traits that were often thought to be the supreme display of a man's virtue, and proof of his devotion to his city (cf. Thucydides ii 42). These assumptions about bravery affect Aristotle's treatment of the virtue, and especially his focus on the display of bravery in battle (contrast Plato, *Laches* 192c–e). They do not, however, control his conception of bravery (see note to iii 8.§1).

Apart from the full discussion of bravery in iii 6–9, see also 1102b28, 1103b17, 1104b8, 1119a21, 1123b31, 1129b19, 1130a18, 1137a20, 1144b5, 1166b10, 1167a20, 1169a18, 1177a32, 1178a32.

capacity, capable, power, powerful, *dunamis, dunatos* If x has the capacity to F, x is capable of F and x will F in the right conditions. If fire has a capacity to burn, it will burn unprotected flesh close to it; this is a nonrational capacity. If Smith has a capacity to build, he will build when he chooses to build in the right conditions for building; this is a rational capacity. See *Met*. ix 1–7, esp. 5. Hence a capacity is what is realized in an ACTIVITY.

Capacities include CRAFTS and branches of STUDY (1094a10, 26) and also the natural capacities from which the VIRTUES are developed (1103a25, 1106a6, 1144a23, b1). *Dunamis* is also applied to power over things and people (1099b2, 1161a3 [see also FREEDOM], 1178a32). HAPPINESS is not a capacity; see 1101b12. Virtue requires not only capacity, but also DECISION (1127b14).

category See note to i 6.§3.

cause, reason, responsible, *aitios, aitia* In *Phys*. ii 3 Aristotle explains the doctrine of the four causes. Reference to an *aition* (neuter of adjective *aitios*) or *aitia* answers the question 'Why?'. Different 'why' questions about an object (e.g., a statue) can be answered by different types of explanations: (a) MATTER ('because it is made of bronze'); (b) form, *eidos*, stating its DEFINITION and essence, and hence the species (also *eidos*) it belongs to ('because it is a bust of Pericles'); see note to x 4.§2; (c) the efficient cause, the PRINCIPLE of MOVEMENT ('because the sculptor made it'); see 1110a15, note to vi 2.§4; (d) the final cause or END (*telos, hou heneka*, 'that for the sake of which') e.g., 'to represent Pericles'.

Aristotle's four types of explanation include more than those we commonly call causal explanations. Sometimes, therefore (e.g., 1100a2, 1137b27) 'reason' is appropriate. 'Cause' also renders the preposition *dia* ('because of'). See notes to i 4.§7, viii 2.§3–4.

In legal contexts the adjective *aitios* often indicates not only causation but also blameworthiness, and correspondingly the abstract noun *aitia* indicates both the cause and also the ground of accusation. Hence 'responsible' is sometimes apt, e.g., 1110b13, iii 5 (see note to iii 5.§7). See also CONTROLLING, VOLUNTARY.

change See MOVEMENT.

character, *ēthos, ēthikos* The *EN* is about the formation of VIRTUES of character. These are the STATES resulting from (a) early habituation, to acquire the right DESIRES, FEELINGS, PLEASURES, and PAINS (1104b11, 1179b24); hence Aristotle connects character closely with habit (1103a14–26); (b) the correct use of rational deliberation that marks a prudent person who makes the correct DECISION. The formation of the right character requires the EDUCATION of the nonrational parts of the SOUL (1103a3). But since they are to be trained to act according to correct REASON, training in reasoning and deliberation is also needed. It is someone's character that makes him the 'sort of' (*hoios*) person he is. Hence 'character' often translates *hoios* or the cognate *poios*.

The actions appropriate to a person's character are those said to be 'proper to him' or those he 'is the sort' to do (e.g., 1120a31, 1146a6, 12, and 'not for him', a32). All these phrases translate the Greek genitive case, i.e., 'is not of the generous (etc.) person'.

charieis CULTIVATED

child, *pais* In the *EN* children are regularly mentioned together with nonhuman ANIMALS because they still lack REASON and rational DESIRE (1100a1; *Rhet.* 1384b23). They need primary moral EDUCATION (1104b11, 1119a33–b15).

choiceworthy, *hairetos* This includes the GOOD, the FINE, the PLEASANT, and the expedient (see 1104b30, 1155b18; *Top.* 118b27). The term is an adjective formed from the verb *haireisthai*, 'choose' (a part of *prohaireisthai*, 'decide'; see DECISION) with a verbal adjective ending, which is ambiguous between (a) actually chosen, (b) capable of being chosen, and (c) deserving to be chosen. Which Aristotle means in a particular context is not always clear. Similar questions arise about the opposite of *hairetos*, 'to be avoided' (*pheuktos*; e.g., x 2); about *boulētos*, 'wished', in iii 4; about *philētos*, 'lovable', in viii 2; about *gnōrimos*, 'known' in i 4; about *phoberos*, 'frightening' (note to iii 6.§2), and about *epainetos*, 'praised' or 'praiseworthy' in iv 5 (esp. §14). See esp. 1172b9–28, where (c) is required at some stage, but we might suppose that (a) is assumed at the beginning. Our view about this ambiguity will affect our view on the relation of GOOD (1) to choice; cf. 1097a18–b6.

city, *polis* A *polis* is a COMMUNITY of free citizens (*politai*) governed by a political system, *politeia* (or constitution); see *Pol.* i 1–2; iii 1–3, 8–9. A *polis* differs from a monarchy (1115a32) in having a political system and LAWS that assign some rights and functions to the citizens even if, as under a tyranny (1160b10), these rights and functions are temporarily ineffective. When Aristotle speaks of a *polis*, he has in mind; something much smaller than most modern states; see note to i 2.§8, 1170a31; *Pol*. 1276a22–30. But the *polis* is a sovereign political unit, making alliances on its own initiative (1157a26), and with the functions of a modern state.

civilized See GENEROUS.

clever, *deinos* This is also rendered 'terrifying' (e.g., 1103b15, 1115a26, 1116b35). It is used for anything remarkable or formidable, and hence is used, as Aristotle uses it, for cleverness (1144a23, 1152a10, 1158a32). Cleverness is not said to be a deliberative capacity, but to be a capacity for finding what is needed to fulfill an end—which need not always require deliberation (a clever debater will be able to find the telling reply on the spur of the moment). See note to vi 12.§8.

coincident, *sumbebēkos* The term (often translated 'accident') is derived from *sumbainein*, 'come about together', which often just means 'happen' or 'turn out'. *Sumbebēkota* include many things that are not, in the ordinary sense, accidents or coincidences. F is a coincident of x if (a) F belongs to x, but (b) x is not essentially F (is not F IN ITS OWN RIGHT), and x's being F does not follow from the essence of x. See note to v 8.§4; *Met*. 1025a14–16; *Top*. 102b4–9.

common, shared, *koinos*; community, *koinōnia*; member, *koinōnos*; share, *koinōnein* The general sense of *koinon* is the basis of some more specialized uses. (1) A UNIVERSAL is common because it is shared by the instances that it belongs to (1096a28, 1107a30, 1141b26, 1180b15). (2) 'Common good' renders *koinon* at, e.g., 1122b21, 1123a5, 1162a23. (3) People who share some common pursuits and goals are members, *koinōnoi*, in a community. A *koinōnia* may involve a loose and temporary connection (as in a business transaction) or a close long-term relation (as in a family or a city); sometimes 'common dealings' represents *koinōnia*, where 'community' would be misleading; see v 5, viii 9, 1164a20, 1170b11; *Pol*. 1252b12–34. The common pursuit of a common good in a *koinōnia* is the foundation of FRIENDSHIP and of JUSTICE (1129b17, 1155a22).

compel See NECESSARY.

complete, *teleios* This is cognate with *telos*, 'end' (see final CAUSE). It applies to something that has reached its *telos*, and hence it applies to a mature, adult organism (1102b2; *Met*. 1072b24). Aristotle explains completeness in *Met*. v 16. He attributes it to HAPPINESS, 1097a25–b21, 1098a18, 1101a13, and to the CITY, *Pol*. 1252b27–30 (cf. 1281a1). 'Final' and 'perfect' are other possible translations of *teleios*; our choice of translation is connected with our view on some complicated questions about the relation of happiness to other ends. See, esp., 1094b8, 1095b32, 1097a25–b21, note to i 7.§3, 1098a18, 1099a15, 1100a4, 1101a14, 1102a1, 1103a25, 1129b26, 1153b16, 1154a1, note to vii 14.§8, 1156a7, 1174b15–33, 1177a17, 1178b7.

condition See STATE.

consideration See PARDON.

content See FOND.

continent See INCONTINENT.

controlling, in control, important, full, *kurios* (1) If someone is *kurios* over me, he controls me and my actions (1110a3, 6); hence the *kurios* is often a commander or ruler (1116a30, 33). To be *kurios* over an event is to be in control of whether it happens or not. Insofar as I am *kurios*, I am the PRINCIPLE and CAUSE of an ACTION, the action is up to me and VOLUNTARY, and I am responsible for it (1113b32, 1114a32; *EE* 1222b21). (2) Since what controls and rules a process is the most important thing about the process, determining whether it happens or not, *kurios* is also used more generally to mean 'important'. Often both control and importance are suggested (1143b34, 1145a6, 1168b30, 1178a3). (3) If a property is found in degrees, the application of the term to the complete instance controls its application in partial instances. Hence the *kurios* F is F most completely, and 'F' applies to it more fully than to things that are partially F or less F. Here *kurios* is rendered 'full', e.g., at 1098a6, b14, 1103a2, 1115a32.

convention, conventional See LAW.

conversation See REASON (6).

correct, *orthos* The verb *katorthoun*, translated 'be correct' (1098b29, 1104b33, 1106b26, 31, 1107a14, 1142b30), might also be translated 'succeed'. *Orthos* indicates success in pursuing an END or correctness in picking it (1144a20), as opposed to error (*hamartia*, 1135b18; sometimes 'fail' would also be suitable). Like 'right', *orthos* is applied to right angles and to straight lines; it is not confined to moral rightness. The virtuous person is guided by correct REASON insofar as he has the true conception of the end and its constituent ACTIONS (1142b32, see DECISION); then he does what is FINE and RIGHT.

corrective treatment, *kolazein* Aristotle applies two terms to punishment, *timōrein* ('exact a penalty') and *kolazein*. Though they are sometimes used together (1126a28, 1180a9), Aristotle conforms to the distinction drawn at *Rhet*. 1369b12. Hence, *timōria* is concerned with satisfaction for the harm done and so often involves revenge (1126a21, 28; 1149a31). *Kolazein*, by contrast, is forward-looking, concerned with restraining (or 'tempering'; see 1119a33, note to vii 7.§2, and TEMPERANCE) and improving the offender. See 1104b16, 1109b35, 1113b23, 30, 1114a1, 1132b30, 1180a11; *EE* 1214b33, 1230a39; *Rhet*. 1374b30; OCD, s.v. 'Punishment'.

cowardice See BRAVERY.

craft, *technē* See vi 4. A craft is a rational discipline concerned with PRODUCTION. Hence Aristotle sometimes speaks of it as SCIENCE (1094a1, 7), though it does not meet the strictest conditions for a science (1140b2, 34). Craft involves inquiry and deliberation, and so Aristotle often uses its methods to illustrate the procedures of VIRTUE and PRUDENCE. Still, there is a basic difference. For prudence, unlike craft, is concerned with ACTION (1140b3, 1153a25), not production. Moreover, it requires the correct use of a capacity, whereas a craft is a capacity that can be correctly or incorrectly used. Hence the virtuous person does not simply practice a craft, and the *EN* itself is not the exposition of craft knowledge. See 1104a5–11, 1106b5–16, 1112a34–b31, 1120b13, 1122a34, 1133a14–16, 1141b14–22, 11146b31–1147a10, 1152b2, 1167b28–1169a19, 1174a19–21, 1180b7–23. Craft and nature: 1099b20–3, 1106b14, 1140a15; *Phys*. 192b8–33.

cultivated, gracious, *charieis* The cultivated (or 'sophisticated') person may be the one who has gone more deeply into his particular craft or discipline (1102a21), or, more generally, the one who has a more discriminating view of life than the MANY have (1095a18, b22, 1127b23). In this sense being cultivated is an aspect of being civilized (see GENEROUS). See 1128a15, 31; notes to v 5.§7, viii 13.§2.

currency See LAW.

death See 1100a10, 1115a26, 1117b9, 1124b8, 1138a9, 1169a18.

decent, *epieikēs* This is cognate with *eikos*, 'likely', and means 'plausible, reasonable, respectable' (as we say 'a likely lad' or 'a reasonable candidate for the job'). Hence it is used more generally for a decent person, and hence interchangeably with 'GOOD' in the right contexts, as Aristotle remarks at 1137a35. (Cf. 1102b10, 1168a33; and for the political use, which is a feature of most of Aristotle's moral terms, cf. *Pol.* 1308b27.) In some contexts the term suggests someone who will do the decent thing even when the law does not require him to. This is the sort of decency (some translators use 'equity') discussed in v 10. See also 1143a20 (for its relevance to PARDON); *Rhet.* 1374a18–b22; *Top.* 141a15.

decision, *prohairesis* A decision is the result of (a) a wish, i.e., a rational DESIRE for some GOOD as an END in itself (1111b26, 1113a15); (b) deliberation, i.e., systematic RATIONAL CALCULATION about how to achieve the end (1112b15, vi 9). These result in (c) the decision, which is a desire to do something here and now, the action that deliberation has shown to be the action required to achieve the end (1112b26, 1139a21–b5).

Some results and difficulties of this account: (1) Not any desire followed by deliberation results in a decision—spirit and appetite do not (1142b18). Hence the INCONTINENT's incontinent action is not the result of his decision; his decision is correct, because his rational wishes are correct (1150b30, 1152a17). (2) Deliberation, and hence decision, are not about ends, but about 'things toward' or 'promoting' them (1112b1; see notes to iii 2.§9, vi 5.§1, viii 13.§8). These 'things toward ends' are not confined to instrumental means, i.e., to efficient causes of the end that neither wholly nor partly coincide with it (so that shopping for food is an instrumental means to eating dinner). They may also show us what counts as achieving the end, so that we find its components (eating the main course is 'toward' eating the meal because it is part of eating the meal). See PRUDENCE. (3) We can therefore explain why Aristotle says that the virtuous person decides on virtuous action for its own sake (1105a32, 1144a19). (4) A virtuous person shows his virtuous decision especially clearly in emergencies that allow him no time to deliberate afresh, 1117a17–22 (cf. notes to vi 9.§2, vii 7.§8). The deliberation about this type of situation must have been done earlier, and its result is available without further lengthy deliberation. (5) The correct decision is necessary for virtue of character and ACCORDS with a person's virtue. See 1106a36, 1110b31, note to iii 2.§1, 1117a5, 1127b14, 1134a17, 1135b25, 1139a23–6, 1144a13–22, 1145a2–6, 1157b30, 1163a22, 1178a34.

Etymologically, *prohairesis* suggests 'choosing (*hairesis*) before'. For Aristotle the 'before' has a temporal sense (1113a2–9), though no doubt also a preferential sense. Many translators use 'choice' to translate it; but this is a misleading rendering, since Aristotle allows choice (*hairesis*) without deliberation or decision, and such choice does not count as *prohairesis*.

decree, *psēphisma* From the late fifth century onward, Athenian legal procedure distinguished (a) LAWS, *nomoi*, not confined to a particular occasion, and made by a commission of legislators, from (b) decrees, directed to a particular occasion, and enacted by a majority vote of the Assembly of citizens. See note to v 7.§1; 1141b27, 1151b16, 1152a20; *Pol.* 1292a6, 32.

define, *horizein*; define, distinguish, *dihorizein* (1) These terms are derived from *horos*, 'limit, boundary' (see note to vi 8.§9; cf. 'definition' derived from the Latin *finis*), and often *dihorizein* is translated 'distinguish' (e.g., 1099a25). Similarly, *horizein* is associated with limiting, bounding, and determining (1170a22). (2) Often, however, the terms indicate definition, also expressed in the account of something (see REASON [4]), telling us what the essence of something is (*to ti ēn einai*, or *ousia*, 'SUBSTANCE'; 1107a6; *Top.* vi 4, *Met.* 1029b13–22). When we define functionally organized things, either artifacts or natural organisms, the definition specifies their FUNCTION and END (e.g., 1107a6). Aristotle seeks a definition for happiness, the virtues, friendship, etc. He is not looking simply for a verbal equivalence, a phrase that can replace the word being defined while preserving truth. Such a formula for defining happiness does not satisfy him (1095b18). He wants an account that will explain and justify the common beliefs (1098a20, b9). (3) The canonical form of definition places something in its species, *eidos* (see CAUSE), by stating its genus and the differentia of the genus that isolates the species: e.g., 'Man is a biped (differentia) animal (genus)'. Aristotle does this with virtue of character (1105b20, 1106a15; cf. *Top.* vi 5–6). Often the genus is associated with the question 'What?' (e.g., 'What is a man?' 'An animal'), and the differentia with 'What sort of?' (e.g., 'What sort of animal is a man?' 'A biped animal'). See 1098a31, 1105b19, 1106a14, 1174a13; *Top.* 128a20–9, 144a15–22.

dein RIGHT

deinos CLEVER

deliberate See DECISION.

demonstration See SCIENCE.

desire, *orexis* Aristotle normally recognizes three types of desire, corresponding to Plato's tripartition of the SOUL in *Rep.* 435 ff. (See 1138a5–13.) The three types are these. (1) Rational desire, wish, *boulēsis* (see DECISION) is for an object believed to be good. (See 1111b26; note to iii 3.§19, 1113a15, 1114a14, 1136b5, 1155b29, 1156a31, 1162b35, 1178a30.) (2) Appetite, *epithumia*, (sometimes rendered 'urge') is nonrational desire for an object believed to be pleasant. (See 1103b18, 1111a31, 1117a1, 1118b8, 1119a14, 1136b5, 1155b29, 1156a31, 1162b35, 1178a30.) The most striking examples of appetites are desires associated with basic biological needs, but appetite is not confined to these (e.g., 1111a31). The virtuous person has his appetites trained, but he does not lose them; he transforms them into good appetites. (3) Spirit, *thumos*, is nonrational desire for objects that appear good, not merely pleasant, because of the agent's spirited FEELINGS; see 1149a15 on the relation of spirit to reason. Aristotle regularly attributes to *thumos* the self-assertive feelings involved with pride and (when frustrated) with ANGER. Hence 'temper' might be a suitable rendering in 1105a8, 1111b18, 1116b23, 1135b26.

The different forms of appetite and spirit are FEELINGS, whereas rational desires are not. For this division elsewhere, see *DA* 414b2, 432b4–7; *EE* 1223a27; *Rhet*. 1368b37–1369a7; *Top*. 126a3–13. While it is not so explicit in the *EN*, it is often assumed. See 1095a2–11, 1098a3–5, 1102b13–1103a3, 1111a27, 1111b10–30, 1116b23–1117a9, 1119b3–8, 1135b19–1136a5, 1136b6, 1147a31–b5, 1149a24–b3, 1166a33–b25, 1168b28–1169a6.

dianoia THOUGHT

differentia See DEFINE.

dikaiopragein DO JUSTICE

dikaios just; see JUSTICE.

discussion See REASON (6).

disgraceful See FINE, SHAME.

distinguish See DEFINE.

distress See PLEASURE.

divine See GOD.

do See ACTION, PRODUCTION.

do justice, *dikaiopragein*; do injustice, *adikein* Aristotle defines these terms narrowly to mark the distinctions he thinks significant; see 1135a8–23. They are confined (with the cognate abstract nouns 'act of injustice' and 'just act') to voluntary actions, which need not result from a just or unjust DECISION, and hence from a just or unjust CHARACTER. The passive forms 'suffer injustice' and 'receive justice' indicate voluntary action by the agent from whom we suffer or receive it. Sometimes Aristotle coins or uses terms to mark the same distinction with other virtues, indicated by, e.g., 'unjust or intemperate action' (1114a12, 1172b25).

dokein seem; see APPEAR.

dunamis CAPACITY

education, *paideia* This is cognate with *pais*, 'child' (1161a17), and Greek states normally considered it appropriate for childhood (see OCD, s.v. 'Education, Greek'). Plato and Aristotle (following the SOPHISTS) are pioneers of what we regard as 'higher education'. The types of education relevant in the *EN* are these: (1) Moral education assumes that someone has the right sort of NATURE, and it trains him by habituation, *ethismos* (1098b4, 1099b9; 1103a10, b16; 1119a27, 1121a23, 115la19, 1152a29; 1180a3, 15) until he acquires the right habits (*ethos*; 1095a4, 1103a17, note to ii 1.§8, 1148b17, 34; 1154a33, 1179b21, 1180b5, 1181b22). These habits are patterns of action, acquired by training that uses pleasure and pain as incentives. But, equally important, they include tendencies to feel pleasure and pain, and to have other FEELINGS, in the right way, which is a precondition for genuine virtue. (See PLEASURE [4], 1103a33, 1152b4, 1172a20, 1179b25.) (2) However, childhood instruction is not enough. Training must continue with adults, to make them as virtuous as possible (1130b25, 1180a1). This is why moral education concerns POLITICAL SCIENCE. (3) The educated person will be cultivated, so that he acquires the tastes and outlook of the civilized (see GENEROUS) rather than the

SLAVISH person. (4) In the most specialized sense, the educated person is the one who has learned enough about different branches of knowledge and methods of inquiry to understand the right demands to make of ETHICS (1094b23; *PA* 639a5; *Met*. 1006a5). (5) Aristotle does not say how PRUDENCE is related to education. But since education aims at producing virtue of character in those capable of it (1099b19, 1180a5–15), and virtue requires prudence, prudence must be the result of moral education. It follows that this education must include the sort of intellectual training that produces the correct deliberation (vi 10) and DECISION required for prudence.

eidos species, form; see CAUSE.

eleutheros GENEROUS

end, goal, aim, *telos* The *telos* of a process is its final CAUSE, a state (a) that benefits some being with a SOUL; (b) that is caused by the process as efficient cause; and (c) whose occurrence, in particular the benefit it causes, explains the occurrence of the process. In this sense, cutting steak is the end of a steak knife, pumping blood is the end of a mammal's heart, and winning the game is the end of playing chess. The FUNCTION of an artifact or organism is also its end, 1097b24. See *Phys*. ii 8; 1097a18, 1110a13, 1111b16; 1113a15, b5; 1115b20, 1139a36; 1140b6, 16; 1144a32, 1151a16, 1174b33.

Some comments: (1) Every ACTION in the broad sense has something good or pleasant for its end (i.e., its intended goal). Every rational action based on rational DESIRE and DECISION has some good for its end, iii 4. (2) Every action in the narrowest sense has an internal end, so that it is chosen for its own sake, 1094a3, 1140b4–5. An external end makes an event or sequence of events a PRODUCTION. Internal and external ends distinguish MOVEMENTS from ACTIVITIES (in the narrow sense), and CRAFT from PRUDENCE. (3) Deliberation and decision are concerned with what promotes ends, not with ends themselves. Prudence is deliberative, but is a true supposition about the end (see DECISION [2]). (4) Though several things (virtue, pleasure, etc.) are ends, only one thing, HAPPINESS (2), is a complete (*teleion*) end. (5) Sometimes *skopos*, 'target, goal', is used, sometimes in a consciously metaphorical way (1094a24, 1138b22, 1144a25), with no obvious distinction in sense from *telos*.

energeia ACTIVITY

enjoy See PLEASURE.

enkratēs continent; see INCONTINENT.

enpeiria EXPERIENCE

eoike would seem; see APPEAR.

epieikēs DECENT

epistēmē SCIENCE

epithumia appetite; see DESIRE.

equal, *isos* What is *isos* is neither more nor less—either because (a) it is neither more nor less than a given amount, (e.g., an inch), or because (b) it is neither more nor less than the RIGHT amount. *Isos* shares the ambiguity that Aristotle points out in 'intermediate' and 'MEAN' (1106a26). Hence when *isos* is associated with JUSTICE, Aristotle means not that justice always requires numerical equality, but that it forbids having more or less than is right. Hence it forbids OVERREACHING. When Aristotle associates justice and 'equality', it is sometimes appropriate to think of fairness rather than what we would naturally call equality. On different types of equality, cf. 1131b31, 1157b36, 1158b29, 1162a35, 1168b8.

ergon FUNCTION

erotic passion, erotic love, *erōs, erōtikos* *Erōs* is one of the terms that might be translated 'love'; see FRIENDSHIP. Sexual desire is a component of, but not sufficient for, *erōs*. The mere appetite (see DESIRE) for sexual gratification (*ta aphrodisia*, cognate with Aphrodite; see 1149b15) need not include *erōs* (see 1117a1, 1118a31, 1130a25, 1147a15, b27, 1148b29, 1149b15, 1152b17, 1154a18). *Erōs* refers to the condition of those who might be said to be 'in love', though Aristotle in fact seems to restrict it in the *EN* to the desire of an older male for a younger (see OCD, s.v. 'Homosexuality'). Unlike simple sexual appetite, *erōs* includes intense interest in the beloved himself, desire for his presence and company (1158a11, 1167a4, 1171a11), and friendly feelings toward him. This is why it is a source of friendship. See 1116a13, 1156b1, 1157a6–13, 1158a11, 1159b16, 1164a3, 1167a15; 1171a11, b9, 31. The verb *eran* is rendered by 'long passionately' (1155b3) and 'heart's desire' (1098a28).

error See CORRECT.

essence See DEFINE.

ethics, *ēthika* 'Ethical' is derived from *ēthikos*, the adjective cognate with *ēthos*, 'character'. Hence ethics is the part of POLITICAL SCIENCE that studies HAPPINESS; since virtue of character is a major component of happiness, this part of political science studies character; hence the traditional name of the *EN*. In the work itself, Aristotle calls this discipline 'political science', not 'ethics' (see also *Rhet*. 1356a26–7); but 'ethics' is used at *Met*. 987b1, *APo* 89b9, *Pol*. 1261a31, *MM* 1181a25–1182a1.

The methods and aims of ethics: (1) It is concerned with ACTION, not only with knowing and STUDYING the truth, 1095a5, 1103b27 (cf. *EE* 1216b11–25, *MM* 1182a1–7), 1179a35. Knowledge of the truth is not the end, but the means (though cf. *Pol*. 1279b11–15). This does not make the knowledge unimportant. (2) Because ethics is concerned with action, PRUDENCE and DECISION are important parts of it. (3) For the same reason, ethical truths are only USUAL (1094b21) and hence lack the EXACTNESS that would be needed for a SCIENCE in the strict sense. (4) The method of ethical inquiry is dialectical, described in *Top*. i 1–4, 10–12. Hence it begins from common beliefs, what seems or APPEARS to the MANY or the WISE (i 4, *EE* i 6). Aristotle takes commonly held beliefs very seriously (1098b27, 1153b31, 1173a14, 1179a16). But he does not regard them as unrevisable; often he criticizes the many (1095a22, b16, b19, 1113a33, 1153b35, 1159a19, 1163b26, 1167b27, 1172b3, note to vii 7.§1). He takes common beliefs as starting points because they are known (or 'familiar') to us. See 1095b3; *Phys*. 184a16; *APo* 71b33; *Met*. 1029b3; *Top*. 141b8 (and see CHOICEWORTHY). (5) Discussion of these common beliefs shows that they raise puzzles, *aporiai*, when we find apparently convincing arguments from common beliefs for inconsistent conclusions (*Top*. 145b16, 162a17). Aristotle stresses the importance of a full survey of the puzzles (*Met*. 995a27) and follows his own advice in i 10–11, ii 4, iii 4, v 9–11, vi 12–13, vii 2, 1155a32, ix 8–9, x 2–3. (Some of these are surveys of the common beliefs that also include reference to the puzzles.) (6) To solve (or 'loose', 1146b7) the puzzles, Aristotle looks for an account that will show the truth of the most and the most important of the common beliefs, 1145b5. This account will provide us with a PRINCIPLE that is 'known by nature' or 'known without qualification' (see UNQUALIFIED), not merely known 'to us' (see [4] above), because it justifies claims to knowledge. (7) A defense of a theoretical principle shows how it vindicates many of the common beliefs (1098b9). But it does not vindicate them all. Hence a proper defense should also show why false common beliefs appear attractive and rest on explicable misunderstandings; see 1154a22, 1169b22, notes to iii 8.§1, v 9.§6, vi 5.§5. (8) Practically useful exact rules about particular cases are impossible (see [3] above). Aristotle does not intend his general principles and his account of the virtues to constitute such rules; see 1094a25, b20; 1098a20, 1101a27, 1104a1, 1129a11, 1179a34. For PARTICULAR circumstances, PERCEPTION, and EXPERIENCE are needed, though some general rules will also help, 1109a30, 1126b2, 1164b27, 1165a34. (9) Since ethics is to guide action (1105b12–18), it should be addressed to those who are capable of guiding their action by it, and hence to those whose upbringing has not made them incapable of acting on ethical instructions (1095a2, b4, 1104b11, 1179b4–31).

These different features of ethics might be regarded as aspects of (a) the moral principles and moral deliberation of the virtuous and prudent moral agent, or of (b) the theories and arguments of the moral philosopher. Aristotle, however, seems not to accept any sharp distinction between (a) and (b). The *EN* is a part of political science, and hence of prudence, using dialectical method. It is both a contribution to moral theory and the account of a process of practical deliberation (see, e.g., 1168b26).

ethos habit; see EDUCATION (1).

ēthos CHARACTER

eudaimonia HAPPINESS

Eudoxus He was a leading mathematician and astronomer as well as philosopher (c.390–c.340 B.C.). His hedonist views may underlie some of the argument in Plato's *Philebus*. He is cited or alluded to at 1094a2, 1101b17, 1172b9.

exact, *akribēs* A CRAFT and its products (1094b14, 1112b1) are called exact when they are finished and complete in details (cf. 1141a9); the most exact craft gives accurate detailed instructions, leaving nothing to chance or guesswork, and so produces a product that has every detail right. Hence an exact statement is correct and accurate in detail, and can be applied to particular cases without any further restriction or reservation (see UNQUALIFIED). It may be exact in either of two ways. (1) It is a general statement that applies to every case without the need of any qualification, e.g., 'The angles of a triangle add up to 180 degrees'. (2) It is a suitably specific statement in which all the necessary qualifications have been made, e.g., 'This train runs every day, except Sunday'. When Aristotle compares one discipline with another for exactness, he sometimes has just one of these aspects in mind, sometimes both. When he denies exactness to ETHICS, he intends both points (1094b13, 1098a27, 1102a25, 1103b34–1104a7, 1112b1; 1141a9, 16; 1164b27).

The generalizations are not true without exception, but only USUALLY, true, and the exceptions cannot usefully be listed in an exhaustive and helpful qualified generalization. This lack of exactness means that ethics cannot meet Aristotle's strictest criteria for a SCIENCE.

excellent, *spoudaios* A *spoudaios* matter is a serious matter requiring us to take it seriously (*spoudazein*). Aristotle regularly uses the term as the adjective corresponding to 'virtue', and hence as equivalent to 'good'. The association with 'taking seriously' is exploited at 1177a1–6, where 'serious' renders *spoudaios*; cf. 1125a10.

exousia FREEDOM

expect, reasonable to See REASONABLE.

experience, *empeiria* Aristotle sharply distinguishes experience from CRAFT and SCIENCE (1180b20, *Met.* i 1; cf. Plato, *Gorg.* 465a). Experience of PARTICULAR cases may allow us to form rules of thumb (e.g., in medical treatment) that yield some practical success. But science and craft know why something works, and do not merely believe that it works (cf. 1095b6). They can provide a general explanation and justification, and deal successfully with unfamiliar types of cases. Nonetheless, Aristotle insists that experience is important. Varied PERCEPTIONS and experience are the material for reasonable induction (see INFERENCE; *APo* 100a3). We need experience to make reasonable decisions in cases requiring perception (1109b20). Hence experience is an important aid to PRUDENCE; 1141b18, 1142a15, 1143b11, 1147a21. Cf. 1103a16, 1154b4, 1116b3, 1158a14, 1181a19.

facts See FUNCTION.

feeling, *pathos* *Pathos* is cognate with *paschein* ('undergo', be affected, 'suffer') and indicates a mode of passivity rather than activity (e.g., 1132a9, 'suffering'). Hence 'be affected' is sometimes (e.g., at 1147a14) the appropriate rendering. Usually 'feeling' is fairly close; for Aristotle regularly restricts *pathos* to conditions of the SOUL that involve PLEASURE or pain (1105b21; *EE* 1220b12; *Pol.* 1342a4; *Rhet.* 1378a19). These include the DESIRES and feelings belonging to the nonrational part of the soul (1111b1, 1126b33, 1135b21, 1136a8, 1168b20, 1178a15), presumably because these appear to be passive in certain ways, as reactions to external stimuli. 'Passion' (based on the philosophical Latin rendering of *pathos* by *passio*) would also be a suitable translation, though perhaps misleading to the modern reader (since not every *pathos* is passionate). A virtuous person does not lack feelings altogether (1104b24), and some feelings are both natural and necessary for a human being (1115b7, 1135b21, 1136a8, 1149b14). But he will not be controlled by his feelings; control by feelings is characteristic of the young (see YOUTH) and the incontinent; 1095a4, 1128b17, 1144b9, 1150a30, b214; 1151a20, 1156a32, 1179b13, 27; *Pol.* 1312b25–34.

fine, beautiful, *kalos* What is *kalos* deserves admiration; the term is applied to aesthetic beauty (e.g., 1099b3), and its opposite *aischros* ('shameful') to ugliness (e.g., 1099b3). *Aischros* is usually translated 'shameful', but sometimes by 'disgraceful' in contexts where its cognate *aischunē* ('disgrace') and *aidōs* ('shame') are being used; see iv 9. Sometimes the adverb *kalōs* just means 'well'. But often, as in 'judging finely' and 'deliberating finely' it has its narrower force (e.g., 1099a23,

1112b17, 1114b8, 1140a26, 1143a15, 1169a23, 1170b27). Doing something finely is connected with doing it RIGHTLY (1116b2, 1119b16, 1121a1) and CORRECTLY (1119a29).

In its narrower use, *kalos* is especially connected with virtue. The virtuous person DECIDES on actions that are fine, and he acts 'for the sake of the fine'; the fineness of actions causes him to decide on them (1115b12; 1116a28, b2–3; 1117b9, 14; 1119a18, b16; 1120a12, 23; 1122b6, 1123a24, 1136b22).

Acting for the sake of the fine is contrasted with acting under compulsion (1116b2), and with acting only for some further end to which the fine action is merely instrumental (see DECISION [2], 1123a25); hence the fine is contrasted with the pleasant and the expedient (1104b31, 1162b35, 1169a6; cf. 1155b19), and associated with LEISURE (*Pol.* 1333b1). Doing x because x is fine is not to be opposed to doing x for its own sake. Hence the virtuous person's concern with the fine does not conflict with his deciding on virtuous actions for their own sake (1105a32, 1144a19). He decides on them for their own sake insofar as he decides on them for the sake of the fine.

The *EN* is not completely clear on the relation between the fine and the noninstrumentally good (cf. *Rhet.* 1364b27, 1385b36). But it does not call an intrinsic good—such as health—fine, and does not suggest that if I enjoy sitting in the sun as a good in itself, it must be fine to sit in the sun. Probably Aristotle accepts the extra condition imposed in *EE* 1249b19 and *Rhet.* 1366a33 (cf. note to viii 1.§5) that the fine is the intrinsic good that is praiseworthy (cf. i 12, 1109b31). It must be something that the agent can be praised for, as a result of his own VOLUNTARY action expressing his CHARACTER and DECISION.

Actions are normally praised for being virtuous in ways that benefit others (cf. 1155a29); this partly explains why sacrificing one's life is fine (1169a18–b2). Here 'fine' might reasonably be taken to refer to the moral value of the action.

How, then, can Aristotle suppose that the virtuous person concerned with his own HAPPINESS will choose virtuous actions for the sake of the fine? This depends on what motive a virtuous person will have for being concerned with others for their own sakes. Aristotle considers this question in his account of FRIENDSHIP, esp. ix 9.

fond of, *stergein* Sometimes (cf. LIKE) *stergein* has a fairly weak sense ('be content', 1162b30). Usually, however, it indicates the FEELING associated with FRIENDSHIP and love (1126b22, 1156a15, 1157a11, 28; 1161b18, 1162a12, 1164a10, 1167a3, 1168a2, 22; 1179b30, 1180b6). Aristotle seems to think *stergein* is necessary for friendship (1126b22), but it is not clear if all the types of friendship he recognizes include *stergein*; perhaps they include it to different degrees.

force See notes to iii 1.§3, 7.

form See CAUSE.

fortune, *tuchē* *Tuchē* (cognate with *tunchanein*, 'happen'; hence 'chance', 'luck') is discussed in *Phys.* ii 4–6. As the *EN* understands fortune, x is a matter of fortune for S if and only if (a) x benefits or harms S; (b) S's DESIRE or DECISION does not CONTROL x. Fortune is involved not only in events entirely uncontrolled by S (if, e.g., S's uncle leaves S a legacy) but also in processes initiated by S in which something outside S's control is needed for success (e.g., S's building a house is the result of his decision, but it is vulnerable to ill fortune, since a storm might blow down the half-built house).

GOODS of fortune affect HAPPINESS (1096a1, 1098a31–b8; 1100a5, b22; 1101a28, 1129b3, 1140a18, 1153b17). Hence they contribute to the exercise of some virtues (1124a20). Still, happiness should not be identified with good fortune. Goods of fortune are actually bad for a VICIOUS person; and a virtuous person's happiness depends primarily (though not exclusively) on his virtuous character, which is not subject to fortune. Hence the virtuous person's primary aim will be to act virtuously, not to achieve the goods of fortune (1099b9–25, 1100b7–1101a31, 1120b17, 1124a12; *EE* viii 2).

freedom, *exousia* *Exousia* is not the legal status of a free citizen as opposed to a slave; see GENEROSITY. It is derived from *exeinai*, 'to be open, possible', and indicates the condition of someone who has open options. Hence 'free to' (1114a16, 1163b19), 'freedom' (1161a9, 1178a33), 'could have' (1163a13) all render *exeinai* and cognates. Since power over others leaves the ruler with more options about how to treat others, *exousia* often indicates the position of a ruler—hence 'power' (1095b21, 1158a28, 1159a19).

friendship, *philia*; love, *philein*; beloved, friend, *philos* *Philia* is discussed at length in viii–ix. While 'friendship' is the best English rendering, it lacks a cognate verb, and 'love' has to be used. *Philia* is different from what we might expect friendship to be. (1) It includes the love of members of families for each other. (2) It includes the favorable attitudes of business partners and associates and of fellow citizens for each other. (3) The attitude of some *philoi* toward each other is different from what we might expect. In the best kind of friendship one virtuous person admires the other's objective merits, his virtuous CHARACTER (cf. esp. 1165b13). (4) In general, these differences reflect the smaller role of purely idiosyncratic preferences, inclinations, and choices in *philia* than in friendships we might be used to. Some *philiai* are made appropriate by my family circumstances, some by the usefulness of the other, some by his objective merits—not by my whims and inclinations. Aristotle's *philia* for pleasure is probably the nearest to modern ways of thinking about friendship.

Still, *philia* has aspects that make it recognizably friendship. It requires some degree of goodwill and mutual recognition (1155b32–1156a10, 1158a7, ix 5) and shared activities (1157b19). It also requires some FEELING, actual FONDNESS for the other, not mere goodwill and benevolence (1126b20–8, 1166b32).

Aristotle classifies different types of relations that meet the conditions for *philia* to different degrees (1158b5). He distinguishes: (1) the three species with three objects (a) the good, (b) the useful, and (c) the pleasant; (2) friendships between (a) equals and (b) unequals; (3) friendships in different types of COMMUNITIES, e.g., families, clubs, cities (1161b11). The relation between these different divisions is not always clear. For instance, how many in (3) conform to (1a)? Sometimes Aristotle suggests only virtuous people are capable of (1a), 1156b7; how does this affect *philia* in families?

More of the *EN* is devoted to friendship than to any of the virtues. It is a necessary component of HAPPINESS, not merely instrumental to it. (See DECISION [2]; 1097b10; 1155a3–29; 1157b20, 1162a17, 1169b3, 1170b14, 1177a34, 1178b5; *Rhet.* ii 3). The study of friendship is equally important to POLITICAL SCIENCE (1155a22, viii 9–11).

full, fully See CONTROLLING.

function, product, result, achievement, *ergon* The best single translation for *ergon* would be 'work'. These different uses (sometimes closely related; see notes to i 7.§11, ii 6.§9, ix 7.§3) can be distinguished: (1) process of PRODUCTION, or productive task to be undertaken (1109a25, 1124b25); (2) product, result of the process (1094a5–6, 1106b10, 1133a9, 1167b34); (3) achievement, not involving any product (1100b13, 1101b16, 1120b13; note to iv 2.§6); (4) action, more or less equivalent to ACTIVITY (e.g. 1104b5); (5) contrasted with *logos* (see REASON [6]); hence 'facts' (1168a35, 1172a35), 'what we do' (note to x 8.§12); (6) function, characteristic task, ACTIVITY, and END (1097b25, 1106a16, 1139a17, 1144a6, 1162a22, 1176a3; see PLEASURE). A thing's *ergon* is connected with its essence (see DEFINE) and its VIRTUE; in animate beings the *ergon* corresponds to the type of SOUL.

generous, civilized, *eleutherios* This is cognate with *eleutheros* ('free'), indicating the status of a free person rather than a SLAVE (1131a28, 1134a27; see also FREEDOM). The *eleutherios* has the outlook appropriate to a free citizen (hence 'liberal' is a suitable translation). Aristotle understands this in a wider and a narrower sense. (1) The wider sense is rendered by 'civilized', to indicate the contrast with boorishness and SLAVISHNESS. The civilized person has the right sort of EDUCATION, and hence is concerned with the virtues and with the sorts of PLEASURE that are appreciated only after training and cultivation (see also CULTIVATED). The civilized person avoids any narrow-minded, calculating attention to bodily needs and the satisfaction of nonrational desires; for such an attitude is characteristic of the slavish person, who cannot use LEISURE correctly, but goes in for 'degrading' (*aneleutheros*, lit., 'unfree') activities (1121b33; at 1123a16 'paltry' renders *aneleutheros*). See 1118b4, 1125a9; 1128a25, 31; 1176b20; 1179b8. (The wide and the narrow senses of *eleutherios* are perhaps both exploited in 1158a11, 1168b27.) (2) In its narrow sense, *eleutherios* indicates the particular virtue described in iv 1 (cf. 1115a20, 1130a19; 1178a28, b14), the appropriate generosity in giving money and the appropriate restraint in taking it. Here 'generous' is the best translation.

Though Aristotle does not say so, he might have regarded these two types of *eleutherios* as HOMONYMOUS. They are clearly connected. The virtue of generosity is called *eleutheriotēs* because it is a particular manifestation of the more generally civilized character. Aristotle says less about the broader type of *eleutherios*, because it is really virtue as a whole (i.e., the appropriate nonslavish attitude to happiness) viewed in a particular way (in this respect, it is similar to general JUSTICE, 1130a10); it is especially clearly displayed in magnanimity.

genesis becoming; see note to x 2.§4.

genos See DEFINE.

gnōrimos known; see note to i 4.§3.

goal See END.

god, divine, *theos, theios* In the *EN* Aristotle does not try to describe the nature of the divine, as he does in, e.g., *Met*. xii 7–10. He speaks of it in these ways. (1) He notices the ordinary use of 'divine', to indicate something marvellous, beyond normal human capacities, 1145a21. (2) He refers to traditional views of the gods as objects of worship, prayer, and sacrifice (1122b20, 1160a34) without endorsing these views. (3) He refers to common views of the gods influencing the FORTUNES of human beings. *Eudaimonia* ('HAPPINESS') by its etymology suggests 'having a good *daimōn*' (divine spirit, translated 'god', 1169b8), and so suggests some belief in the role of gods (cf. 1099b9). Aristotle suggests there is something plausible in these views (1179a24). (4) Something divine, not very clearly articulated, can be seen in nature and in the natural desires and tendencies of natural organisms, (1153b32, 1173a4; cf. *DA* 415a29; *Phys*. 192a16; *DC* 271a33; *PA* 658a9). (5) Aristotle rejects some common anthropomorphic views of the gods. They cannot have anything like human personalities or characters, (1104b18, 1178b8). When a human being becomes a god, the change is so radical that he ceases to exist (1145a23, 1159a5, 1166a19). (6) But he is not agnostic about the divine. He recognizes a divine being that has a rational SOUL, but no FEELINGS or nonrational DESIRES; it is self-sufficient (see HAPPINESS [3]), and needs nothing, and hence has no need of virtues of character. The divine is unchanging, a permanent and essential feature of the universe (see 1134b28; note to vi 7.§3, 1154b26). Hence a god never passes from CAPACITY to ACTIVITY, but is always in activity. The god's activity is STUDY, and this is the object of divine PLEASURE (1154b26, cf. 1175a3). (7) These features of the god make it an ideal for our own pursuit of happiness. Insofar as each of us has the capacity for rational study, and insofar as the activity of this capacity is the single activity that best fulfills the criteria for happiness (x 7) we have reason to imitate the god as far as possible, and pursue study (1177b26). See HAPPINESS (5).

good, *agathos* The main uses: (1) The good aimed at by x is the result that x rationally aims at (1094a1, 1097a16). What I regard as a good is what I regard as achieving my aim. In this sense there will be many goods corresponding to my many rational aims (1097a15–22). I have a further rational aim, to satisfy each of these aims to the right extent and in the right relation to each other. When I have a conception of the right extent and relation, I have a conception of my complete good, which is my HAPPINESS (1097a22–b21), discovered by REASON (1). See also CHOICEWORTHY. (2) Things are 'good for' a result insofar as someone aiming at the result has reason to aim at them. They are good for a person insofar as they contribute to aims it is rational for him to have (exercise would still be good for me even if I were irrational enough not to aim at health). Hence Aristotle contrasts UNQUALIFIED goods (good for anyone, or for people with the right aims) with goods 'for someone' (good only for those in special conditions with particular aims). See 1113a22, 1129b2, 1152b26, 1155b24, 1157b26. (3) 'A good F' (1098a8, 1106a15). A good horse is a good specimen of horses. Its goodness is determined by the FUNCTION of horses, i.e., what they characteristically do and can be expected to do. Hence a good person does well (1098a12) what persons can be expected to do, and has the VIRTUE appropriate to persons.

These three uses are related. What makes a knife a good knife (3), depends on what good (1) we want the knife to achieve, and that will depend on what the knife is good (2) for. Similarly a good (3) person will be able to achieve goods (1) that depend on what is good (2) for a person—his final good or HAPPINESS.

We might object that what makes a person good depends on what (if anything) a person is used for, just as what makes a knife good depends on what a knife is used for; hence if a person is not used for anything, Aristotle's account of good (3) will imply that there are no good persons. Aristotle answers this objection by arguing that a person is not an artifact or an organ, and his goodness,

VIRTUE, is not to be measured by his use, but by his own noninstrumental good, i.e., his HAPPINESS.

On goods of body and soul and external goods, see 1098b12, 1099a31, 1129b2, 1153b21, 1178b33. Cf. FORTUNE. On good and PLEASANT, see 1111b17, 1113a34, 1140b13, 1153b7, 1155b19, 1156b15, 1157a1; 1172b9, 28; 1173b20–1174a12, 1176a15–29.

gracious See CULTIVATED.

habit, *ethos* See EDUCATION (1).

hairetos CHOICEWORTHY

hamartanein be in error; see CORRECT.

haplōs UNQUALIFIED

happiness, *eudaimonia* Aristotle follows common beliefs in identifying the highest human GOOD with happiness, also identified with 'living well' or 'doing well' (1095a18; cf. 1139b3, 1140a28, 1140b7). He argues for the identification in 1097a15–b21, appealing to common beliefs about happiness in support of his account (1096a1, i 8, 1153b14, x 7; see also GOD [3]). 'Happiness' is a misleading rendering of *eudaimonia* if we identify happiness with pleasure. If Aristotle understood it this way, the question about what happiness is (1095a1–8) would hardly be puzzling. For a hedonist account would make it difficult to see any real question about the identity of pleasure and *eudaimonia*. But Aristotle not only thinks there is a question; he denies the identity of the two (1175b34). Moreover, a hedonist account should make the agent's feelings and opinions decisive about whether he is *eudaimōn* or not. But such a view would make nonsense of the puzzles in i 10–11, and, more generally, of Aristotle's account of the VIRTUES. He thinks the virtues he describes are necessary for *eudaimonia*; he does not mean that they are necessary to make someone pleased or contented.

Happiness is the COMPLETE end, the only one that does not promote any other end. It is complete because it is the most comprehensive; there is no more comprehensive end for it to promote. Aristotle makes the same point in calling happiness self-sufficient, *autarkēs*, because it lacks nothing (i.e., no reasonable object of desire). See 1097b6, 1134a27, 1160b4, 1169b3–8, 1170b17, 1177a27; *Pol.* 1252b29, 1253a26, 1256b4, 1275b21, 1280b34, 1326b3, 1328b17. A person is self-sufficient (1125a12) to the extent that his complete happiness depends on himself, and not on external conditions (cf. 1177a27–b1). The virtuous person wants to make himself as self-sufficient as is compatible with the self-sufficiency of happiness. Since happiness is complete, including all types of goods, and some goods depend on FORTUNE, happiness must partly depend on fortune. But its major components—the virtues—do not depend on fortune. See BLESSED.

Since it is complete and comprehensive, happiness includes other ends that are pursued for themselves. To find what happiness is is also to find what these ends are (1097b2, 1174a4). The task of finding them belongs to PRUDENCE, which deliberates about them (1140a28) and finds what it is RIGHT to do. The result is the virtuous person's DECISION to pursue virtuous action for its own sake (1105a31, 1144a19; see FINE, LEISURE).

In x 6–8 Aristotle argues that STUDY has some special place in happiness. Does he mean (a) that it is the whole of happiness, or (b) that it is the single most important component? See 1145a6, 1177a12–18, 1178a2–9; 1178b5, 28.

hēdonē PLEASURE

hekousios VOLUNTARY

hexis STATE

homonymous, *homōnumos* Two things are homonymously F if and only if they share the name 'F', but the account (see REASON) of F is different for each. If the account is the same, then they are synonymously F. Hence we might say that the chest of an animal and a tea chest are homonymously chests. See 1096b27, 1129a17, 1130a33; *Catg.* 1a1–12; *Top.* i 15. Aristotle also refers to homonymy when he says that Fs are spoken of or so called 'in many ways' (*pollachōs*; 1096a23; 1125b14, cf. 1118b22; 1129a25, 1136b29, 1142b17, 1146b31, 1152b27), and when he says that some Fs are so called 'by metaphor' (lit., 'by transference'; 1115a15, 1119b3, 1137b1, 1138b5; 1149a23, b32; 1167a10). He is concerned to preserve the common beliefs (see ETHICS) and the common use of names, as far as is reasonable (cf. *Top.* 110a14–22, 148b16–22). Hence he wants to avoid the assumption that one name corresponds to one nature (so that everything to which the name is truly applied is synonymous). If in fact several natures of F correspond to the name 'F', the assumption that there is only one nature of Fs will lead us to dismiss as non-Fs all those Fs that fail to fit one account, so that we wrongly dismiss many of the common beliefs (*EE* 1236a25–32; cf. 1157a25–33, 1158b5). By recognizing homonymy, we avoid this premature dismissal of the common beliefs. Aristotle puts this general principle into practice in, for instance, his discussion of JUSTICE.

honor, price, *timē* *Timē* reflects other people's judgment of someone's WORTH—of his useful or FINE or GOOD qualities (1095a22–30, 1159a12–27). The English 'honor' suggests primarily the attitude of esteem and admiration. *Timē* includes this, but also includes the expression of this attitude in 'honors', i.e., the awards given to recognize worth (1123b1–24, 1124a4–25, 1134b6, 1163b5). We can show how highly we estimate something's worth and how highly we honor it by how much we will pay for it. Hence 'price' or 'value' and the cognate adjectives are suitable at, e.g., 1123a15, 1133b15, 1164b17, 1165b12 (see also note to vi 7.§4). This aspect of *timē* explains why a *timokratia* (lit., 'rule of honor') is a political system that restricts active citizenship by a property qualification, based on the value of a citizen's property (1160a34).

Aristotle rejects the single-minded pursuit of honor, since he takes happiness to include goods that depend on the agent himself, not on other people's attitude to him. But he also rejects the extreme view that honor is unimportant and irrelevant to happiness. He devotes iv 3–4 to the virtues concerned with the proper attitude to honor.

horismos, horos DEFINITION

hubris WANTON AGGRESSION

hulē MATTER

human being, *anthrōpos* This refers to the human species (Latin *homo*, as opposed to *vir*). Sometimes Aristotle may use the plural just to mean 'people'. But often it indicates some characteristically human features, either (a) of human beings as opposed to other ANIMALS (1097b25, 1148b20, 1150a2, 1170b13); or (b) of human beings and their circumstances, as opposed to GODS (1100b9, 1101a21, 1141a34, 1178b33); or (c) of human nature in general (1110a25, 1113b18, 1115b8, 1121b14, 1178b7). Some examples can be understood in more than one of these ways. Adult human beings are capable of virtue and vice because their desires are capable of being directed by DECISION; hence their VOLUNTARY actions are responsible, properly open to praise and blame. The exceptions are bestial people and those overcome by madness (vii 5; 1149b27–1150a8). See also CHILD, MAN, PERSON, POLITICAL SCIENCE, SLAVE, WOMAN.

hupolēpsis SUPPOSITION

important See CONTROLLING.

in itself, in its own right, *kath'kauto* If x is F in its own right, x is F because of what x is and not COINCIDENTALLY. Virtuous friends, e.g., are good in their own right (1156b19). Something that is good in its own right is not good just as a means to something else (1096b10); it is a good for its own sake, i.e., a noninstrumental good. Choosing something in its own right is choosing it without regard to conditions that make it a means to some other end, and hence implies choosing it for its own sake (1110a19, 1151b2). Something that exists in its own right is independent of any relation to something else (1095a27, 1096a20; hence 'by himself', 1177a33).

inanimate See SOUL.

incontinent, *akratēs* The incontinent—as opposed to the continent, *enkratēs*—lacks 'control' or 'mastery' (*kratein*) over himself, and specifically over his nonrational DESIRES (1168b34; cf. 1138b5–14, 1148b32; Plato, *Gorg*. 491d, *Prot*. 352bc, 355b, *Rep*. 430e431d). The incontinent has the correct DECISION (1152a17), but acts on appetite instead. Incontinence is fully discussed in vii 1–10; see, esp., the notes to vii 3.§10. See also 1095a9, 1102b14–28, note to ii 3.§1, 1111b13–15, 1114a13–16, 1119b31, 1136a31–b9, 1142b18–20, 1166b6–11, 1168b34, 1179b26–9.

individual The Greek (e.g., at 1094b7) just means 'one'.

induction, *epagōgē* The Greek means 'leading on'. Aristotle uses it to refer to the process of leading us from PARTICULARS to UNIVERSALS. It begins with particular facts, observations, or examples, and proceeds to a universal conclusion (1098b3, 1139b27, 1143b4; *APo* 84b23; *Top*. i 12). In the broad sense of 'INFERENCE', induction is a type of inference; but when 'inference' is used in the narrow sense, to refer to deductive reasoning, it is often contrasted with induction.

inference, *sullogismos* Inference is the exercise of REASON and of RATIONAL CALCULATION (in a wide sense) in combining propositions or beliefs to reach others. More narrowly, a *sullogismos* is the deductive form of inference commonly called 'syllogism', described in *APr* 24b18. *Sullogismos*, translated 'deductive inference' in vi 3, is required for demonstrative SCIENCE. In this sense it is contrasted with INDUCTION.

When Aristotle mentions *sullogismos* about action (1144a31) he cannot have in mind a syllogism in the full technical sense (since *sullogismos* about action, unlike a strict syllogism, has a particular premise); the translation 'inference' (cf. 1149a33) avoids assuming too much. 'Practical syllogism' is a term often used by critics, but not by Aristotle, for the type of inference described in 1147a15. Aristotle does indeed speak of the conclusion (1147a27) and of a premise (1147b9; cf. 1143b3).

intemperance, *akolasia* This term for the vice of excess—opposed to temperance—is derived from *kolazein* ('punish, correct'), and so indicates someone whose desires lack the CORRECTIVE TREATMENT they need to make them subject to correct REASON (1119a33–b19, 1150a21, 1180a11).

intermediate See MEAN.

involuntary See VOLUNTARY.

isos EQUAL

justice, *dikaiosunē* Aristotle treats justice as he treats some other virtues (see TEMPERANCE, GENEROSITY) that in ordinary beliefs have a wide scope; he narrows them so that each virtue is concerned with a distinctive range of feelings and actions. In v 1, he narrows the scope of justice by claiming that it is HOMONYMOUS; the name is applied to general and to partial justice. In v 3–5 the types of partial justice are described; but v 6 ff. seems equally relevant to both types of justice.

Aristotle thinks two types of justice must be recognized because general justice is not a distinct virtue. General justice is what is prescribed by correct LAWS of a city for the COMMON good: correct laws are concerned with all the virtues; hence it looks as though justice is the whole of virtue in relation to others (1129b25). Aristotle sees, however, that some unjust actions are the result of OVERREACHING for more than is fair and EQUAL. Since not all vicious actions are caused by this desire, the injustice resulting from OVERREACHING cannot be the whole of vice; hence there must be another type of justice and injustice besides general justice and injustice. Aristotle takes partial injustice to result from love of gain (1130a24). It is only general justice that is correctly identified with the whole of virtue in relation to others.

We can see why Aristotle thinks 'general justice' is too wide to be a specific virtue; it is also wider than what we would normally describe as justice. But his partial justice seems narrower than we would expect. If, for instance, I act viciously to avoid my share of a fairly distributed burden, I am acting unjustly and unfairly in a way recognizable to Greeks and to us, but not clearly included in Aristotle's partial injustice (though cf. note to v 9.§9).

kakos VICIOUS

kalos FINE

kata ACCORD

kath'hekaston PARTICULAR

kath'hauto IN ITS OWN RIGHT

katholou UNIVERSAL

kinēsis MOVEMENT

know See SCIENCE.

known, ***gnōrimos*** See note to i 4.§3.

koinos, koinōnia COMMON

kolazein CORRECTIVE TREATMENT

kurios CONTROLLING

lack See RIGHT (2).

law, convention, ***nomos*** *Nomos* is cognate with *nomizein* ('think, believe, recognize', as we speak of recognizing a government) and *nomisma* ('currency'; the connection with *nomos* is exploited in 1133a30). *Nomos* includes laws enacted by some legislator, but also includes less formally enacted rules, habits, conventions, and practices. The wide scope of *nomos* should be remembered at 1094b15, 1129b11, 1134b18; cf. *Rhet*. 1373b1–18.

Aristotle regards legislation as part of the general task of POLITICAL SCIENCE (1141b25). The happiness of the citizens requires virtue; and virtue requires moral education, which is best managed by legislation (1179b34). Hence moral training is the proper concern of the legislator, and a city that neglects this will undermine its political system and harm its citizens (1102a7, 1103b3, 1129b19, 1180a24; *Pol.* 1289a11, 1310a12, 1337a11). Though Aristotle insists that virtue includes more than mere conformity to law (1144a13), he thinks it will develop and flourish only in a city where it is supported by legal enforcement. He rejects the view that law should allow the maximum individual freedom; he takes this view to involve serious errors about happiness (*Pol.* 1310a28).

Aristotle refers to an old debate in Greek ethics about whether principles of JUSTICE are the product of NATURE or of *nomos* (1094b16, 1129b11). The defenders of *nomos* (e.g., PROTAGORAS) maintain not merely that different laws affect beliefs about justice, but that there are no facts about justice apart from the beliefs of different societies about it. In 1129b11 Aristotle rejects this denial of objectivity for justice (see also v 7). He rejects it for other virtues also (FINE things are mentioned at 1094b14).

See also DECREE. On law and DECENCY, see v 10. On law and general justice, see notes to v 1.§2, 2.§10.

leisure, ***scholē*** The correct use of leisure is the mark of the civilized (see GENEROUS)—as opposed to the SLAVISH person—and of the well EDUCATED person. Someone is at leisure when he is free of NECESSITY in some significant area of his life; he need not devote all or most of his time and energy to securing the means for staying alive and satisfying his most immediate and basic desires (1177b1; *Pol.* 1333a30–b5, 1334a11–40). Though leisure is mentioned only briefly in the *EN*, it is part of the background. For Aristotle addresses someone who lives in a city, a political COMMUNITY aiming at the good and not only at the necessary (*Pol.* 1252b29, 1279a10, 1280b33), someone who has the necessities he needs. He can choose to accumulate superfluous stocks of necessities, as the slavish person does (1118a25, 1147b23), or he can choose to pursue new goals that he regards as FINE. Aristotle urges someone to choose the second option, and tells him what to regard as fine. The virtuous person is not restricted to the exclusively utilitarian calculation of expediency and instrumental value that restricts the unleisured and slavish person. This freedom is shown in BRAVERY, GENEROSITY, and magnanimity.

like, *agapan* Sometimes its sense is fairly weak; hence 'be satisfied' at 1094b7, 1171a20. Often, however, the sense is stronger, and it is closely connected with FRIENDSHIP (1156a13, 1165b5, 1167b32). It lacks the special associations of other terms of endearment (cf. FOND, EROTIC) and is readily used for nonpersonal objects (1096a9, b11; 1118b4).

line of inquiry, *methodos* The term is used not only for an approach or procedure, but also for the branch of study or inquiry that embodies that procedure; hence 'discipline' would sometimes be suitable. See 1094a1, b11, 1098a29, 1129a6.

logos REASON

lovable See CHOICEWORTHY, FRIENDSHIP.

love See FRIENDSHIP.

magnanimity See note to iv 3.§1.

makarios BLESSED

man, *anēr* This refers to an adult male human being (1149b10, 1165b27, 1171b10, 1176b23). Often this is associated with the CHARACTER expected of a 'manly' (*andrōdēs*) person; the term is cognate with *andreios*, 'brave' (1109b18, 1125b12, 1126b1, 1171b6). More generally, Aristotle speaks of an EXCELLENT man, where we might expect 'person' (1098a14, b28; 1101b24; 1130a2, b27; 1143b23, 1145a28, 1176a27). He evidently assumes that being a man is a necessary condition of fully manifesting the VIRTUES of a human being. See also HUMAN BEING, PERSON, WOMAN.

many, most people, *hoi polloi* The opinions of the many are accepted as the starting point, though not the unrevisable basis, of ethical argument (see ETHICS [4]). *Polloi* is sometimes used in a statistical sense, rendered by 'most people' (e.g., 1150a12, 1151a5, 1152a26). But sometimes it has a more pejorative suggestion (e.g., 1095a16).

matter, *hulē* See CAUSE. By a natural extension it is also applied to the subject matter of a discipline. This consists of the actions or events or states of affairs that the discipline must study (1094b12, 1098a28, 1104a3, 1137b19).

mean, *mesotēs* This is the abstract noun cognate with *mesos*, 'intermediate'. Aristotle explains in ii 6 the sense in which he thinks VIRTUE of character is a mean, and the limits of the quantitative analogy (cf. EQUAL). The point of the doctrine of the mean is indicated in 1107a1. Each virtue is a STATE, not merely a CAPACITY or FEELING; for it requires training and rational control of one's feelings and capacities by PRUDENCE. The mean Aristotle has in mind is the state in which feelings are neither indulged without restraint nor suppressed entirely, and in which external goods are neither pursued without limit nor totally rejected; in each case the right extent must be determined by reason and PRUDENCE (1138b18–34, 1144b21). This doctrine is applied to the individual virtues of character in ii 7 and in iii 5 through v 11, to show that the same principles apply to each genuine virtue, even when this does not look obvious. To show that the doctrine applies in nonobvious cases, Aristotle isolates and names means and extremes that have been overlooked (1107b2, 30; 1108a4, 1115b24, 1119a5, 1121a16, 1125b1–29, 1126b11–20, 1133b29–1134a16).

medical science, *iatrikē*, medicine The practice of medicine is often cited in the *EN* as an appropriate example of a CRAFT that shares some of the lack of EXACTNESS that we find in ethics, and as a rational discipline that needs to be applied to practice. The frequency of Aristotle's references to medicine may reflect the fact that his father Nicomachus was a doctor (see Introduction [1]). It also reflects the fact that Greek medicine was the most obvious example of theory applied to practice; other crafts did not rely on any body of written theory parallel to the Greek medical writings (e.g., the 'Hippocratic' corpus, going back to the fifth century B.C.; see OCD, s.v. 'Medicine'). See, e.g., i 6.§16, ii 2.§3, 3.§4, 4.§6, iii 5.§14, iv 7.§13, v 1.§5, 9.§16, vi 7.§7, 12.§2, ix 2.§1, x 9.§21.

mesotēs MEAN

metaphor See HOMONYMY.

miserable, *athlios* A miserable person or condition is contrary to a HAPPY one (1100a9, 29, b5, 34; 1101a6, 1102b7, 1105b5, 1166b27). It appears from 1100b34 and 1101a6 that being miserable is not simply failing to be happy; some people lose happiness and are in a miserable condition without themselves becoming miserable (1100a9, b34). A miserable person is to be pitied for his bad circumstances, but also to be despised for having managed his life badly, contrary to his interests, when it was up to him to manage it well; this is the result that the virtuous but unfortunate person avoids. Hence, Aristotle believes, a miserable person is also VICIOUS (though this does not seem to be part of the meaning of the term). See, esp., 1166b27.

mochthēros VICIOUS

movement, change, process, fluctuation, *kinēsis, metabolē* A *kinēsis* may be any difference in a thing's condition between two different times. Only something absolutely stable and invariant is exempt from *kinēsis* (1154b26). More specifically, it refers to the types of change distinguished in *Phys.* v 1. In the discussion of PLEASURE (see notes to x 3.§4, 4.§2), Aristotle contrasts *kinēsis* (here translated 'process') with ACTIVITY (2).

Change and variation are necessary features of human life (1134b28). But the virtuous person achieves the desirable degree of stability that is compatible with these human limitations (1100b15, 1101a8, 1140b29, notes to viii 3.§6, ix 4.§5).

must See RIGHT.

natural virtue See note to vi 13.§1.

nature, *phusis* Things that have a nature have an internal PRINCIPLE of change (or MOVEMENT) and stability. They include all living organisms (1140a15; *Phys.* 192b8–33; *DA* 412a11, b15; *Met.* v 4). Nature in general is discussed in the *Physics* (i.e., 'On Nature'). Both the material and the formal CAUSE can be ascribed to something's nature (*Phys.* 193a9–b21). There are two important aspects of nature in the *EN*. (1) A thing's nature is its original constitution or tendency apart from human intervention; hence it is contrasted with LAW and EDUCATION (1094b16, 1103a19, 1106a9; 1134b18, 33; 1144b3, 1149b4, 1151a18, 1179b20). (2) A thing's nature indicates its FUNCTION and the final cause or END to which it tends. In ETHICS our task is to develop the natural tendencies so that they achieve the appropriate natural end (1097b11, 1103a25, 1152b13, 1153a12, 14, b32, 1162a16, 1170a14, 1173a4; *Pol.* i 1–2). The aspects of nature that are developed and realized include some original tendencies, but not all (1109b1–7).

When Aristotle discusses something 'from nature' or 'from the natural point of view' (*phusikōs*) he refers either to (a) appeals to general theories of nature (1155b2) or to (b) appeals to human nature, especially to human psychology (1147a24, 1167b29, 1170a13). The *EN* avoids (a), but regularly relies on (b).

necessity, *anankē* This is sometimes rendered 'compulsion'. (See *Met.* v 5.) Main uses: (1) The objects of demonstrative SCIENCE are necessary truths, about necessary, not merely USUAL, states of affairs. Since these are always the same, no matter what we do about them, we do not deliberate or decide (see DECISION) about these (1112a1, 1139b20). (2) The necessity involved in the 'mixed' actions described in iii 1 is conditional or 'hypothetical' (*Met.* 1015a20). In such cases, if I am to stay alive or to avoid some catastrophic evil, I must do something unwelcome (1110a26, 1115b8, 1116b16; 1121a34, b26). Similarly, pleasant things that are 'necessary' are those that are necessary for life or for a reasonably healthy life (1147b23). Freedom from exclusive concern with these sorts of necessities is LEISURE. (3) Necessity is also found in psychological states and in actions. Aristotle claims there is a set of beliefs, desires, and inferences that necessitates action. For, once they occur, a given action is necessary, because nothing but that action can now happen (1147a27). This is distinct from the necessity in (1), since it depends on previous particular conditions (the state corresponding to the minor premise of the inference).

need See RIGHT.

nomos LAW

nous UNDERSTANDING

observe See STUDY.

oikeios PROPER

old See YOUTH.

open to See FREEDOM.

opportunity See FREEDOM.

orexis DESIRE

orgē ANGER

orthos CORRECT

ought See RIGHT.

ousia SUBSTANCE

overreaching, *pleonexia* This is difficult to translate, because it is not completely clear what Aristotle has in mind. 'Greed' and 'graspingness' are unsuitable, since these motives might belong to a miser who is not necessarily unjust, whereas *pleonexia* always involves injustice (in the 'partial' sense; see JUSTICE). *Pleonexia* involves more than a mere desire to accumulate resources; it also includes a desire to have more than I am entitled to, so as to get the better of someone else. See Hobbes's description of the law of nature: 'that . . . no man require to reserve to himself any right, which he is not content should be reserved to any one of the rest. . . . The Greeks call the violation of this law *pleonexia;* that is, a desire of more than their share' (*Leviathan* ch. 15). See notes to v 9.§9, ix 8.§4.

paideia EDUCATION

pain See PLEASURE.

pardon, *sungnōmē* This is derived from *gnōmē*, 'mind' or 'judgment'. It is the exercise of judgment and consideration that finds in an action circumstances (as we say, 'special considerations') that exempt the agent from the blame USUALLY attached to that type of action. In the discussion of VOLUNTARY action, *sungnōmē* is translated 'pardon' (1109b32, 1110a24, 1111a2, 1126a3, 1136a5, 1146a2, 1149b4, 1150b8). In 1143a19–24, however, Aristotle plays on the etymological connection with *gnōmē*; 'consideration' is needed. The connection is not merely etymological; for the DECENT person's judgment often finds something pardonable in cases where the inflexible application of a rule that is only USUALLY true would result in mistaken blame.

particular, *kath'kekaston, kath'hekasta* Particulars include individual objects—e.g., this man or this tree—but also particular actions (1110b6, 1135a7, 1141b16, 1143a32) or situations (1109b22, 1126b3). What I actually do when I act is not just killing, e.g., but a particular token of that type—killing in a definite way at some definite place and time (cf. 1110b32–1111a21). Particulars are the objects of PERCEPTION, not of SCIENCE.

When we describe a particular we form a more specific and determinate description, adding to our description of the UNIVERSAL. Hence Aristotle also speaks of particulars when he refers to more specific and determinate descriptions. Hence, at 1107a29 the particulars are not particular action-tokens at definite times and places, but the specific virtues; cf. 1141b22. Here the particulars are not spatio-temporally located individuals, but simply more determinate types or general properties. In vi–vii (e.g., 1143a32; 1147a3, 26) it is not always clear which sort of particulars Aristotle has in mind.

Aristotle stresses the importance of studying particular cases or subdivisions that fall under a general account or definition. They allow us (1) to understand the general account, by seeing what it implies, (2) to apply it more successfully in practice, and (3) to test and confirm it, by showing that it fits the cases it is supposed to fit. See 1107a28, 1141b14 (PRUDENCE [2]), 1180b7; *Pol.* 1260a25; *Rhet.* 1393a16.

penalty See CORRECTIVE TREATMENT.

perception, sense, *aisthēsis* The verb *aisthanesthai*, translated 'perceive', refers to the exercise of any of the five senses, each with its special object (color, sound, etc.; see note to vi 8.§9), or of the common sense (see *DA* ii 5–iii 2). See 1103a29, 1118a1–26, 1149a35, 1174b14. Such perception is characteristic of the animal SOUL. Hence perception and nonrational DESIRE are contrasted with rational desire and DECISION (1095a4, 1098a2, 1111b18, 1139a20, 1147b5, 1149a9–10, 1170a16; cf. FEELING).

Aisthanesthai may also, however, indicate noticing or being aware of something (as in English 'I see') without any very specific reference to the five senses, and with no suggestion that everything noticed is a feature that is noticed by the senses. This sort of perception is important in applying ethical principles that are USUAL and may have exceptions in PARTICULAR cases. Actions are concerned with particulars (1107a31, 1110b6, 1135a7, 1147a3), and perception is what makes us aware of these (1109b20–3, 1113a1, 1126b24, 1147a26). We need perception to notice the facts of the situation. Aristotle seems to believe that we also need it to notice the moral features of a situation ('This isn't harmless teasing, but wanton cruelty', or 'Giving him the book would be a kind thing to do'). Aristotle distinguishes this awareness of particulars needed by PRUDENCE (1141b14–22) from ordinary perception (1142a20–30) and calls it a type of UNDERSTANDING, though also (because of its reference to particulars), a type of perception (1143b5). The trained judgment of a prudent person can identify the perceptual features that are morally relevant.

person This corresponds to no Greek word. It is used on the many occasions when Aristotle uses the masculine definite article with an adjective or participle to refer to an agent or a possessor of a virtue or affection or state. 'MAN' would be misleading here, since it would lead to confusion with *anēr*. But no doubt the people Aristotle has in mind are primarily men; hence the translation, Notes, and Introduction use masculine pronouns.

phainesthai, phaneros APPEAR

phaulos VICIOUS

philia FRIENDSHIP

phronēsis PRUDENCE

promote See DECISION.

phusis NATURE

Plato (427–347 B.C.) Aristotle was a member of Plato's Academy for nearly twenty years, and the *EN* reflects both what he learned from Plato and what he rejected. *EN* i 6 on the Form of the good (cf. note to 1158a14) criticizes Platonic metaphysics. Some of the discussion of pleasure as a process or becoming may reflect Aristotle's objections to arguments in Plato's *Philebus* (see note to x 3.§4). Still, Aristotle agrees with Plato on some important principles (see 1095a32, 1104b12, notes to v 11.§9, x 2.§3). Moreover, the general aim and conclusion of the discussion of virtue and happiness in the *EN* follows Plato's *Republic* quite closely. Like Plato, Aristotle maintains that the virtuous person is happier than anyone else even if he does not achieve complete happiness. Aristotle shows his familiarity with Plato himself by using the Greek imperfect tense to refer to Plato's oral remarks (see note to i 4.§5; SOCRATES).

pleasure, *hēdonē* This is the abstract noun corresponding to the verb *hēdesthai* ('take pleasure, be pleased') and to the verb *chairein* ('enjoy, find enjoyment'). Its opposite is *lupē* or *algos* (both rendered 'pain' or 'distress'). Aristotle's way of distinguishing pleasures shows that he does not think pleasure is some introspectively uniform state, or that its different sources ('pleasant things') are merely different and interchangeable instrumental means to the same end. The pleasures of dice-playing, sunbathing, and music are different in kind, not merely in origin (iii 10; 1147b24–31, 1154a7–b5, x 5; see also FUNCTION).

Aristotle is not a hedonist about good, since he does not identify good with pleasure. But he also rejects the extreme antihedonist denial that pleasure is any sort of good at all (vii 13; 1172b26, 1173b31–1174a8). The extent to which pleasure is good is explained by Aristotle's account of pleasure. It is an ACTIVITY, not a MOVEMENT or process; and it is consequent on some other activity. The pleasure is good if and only if, and because, it is consequent on a good activity (1153a9, x 4–5). Pleasure is not identical to HAPPINESS, but it is an important part of it (1095b16, 1096a1, 1098b25, 1099a7, 1153b14, 1172b26–1173a5, 1176a26, 1177a2).

Pleasure is the object of appetite (see DESIRE, 1111b17). Hence nonhuman ANIMALS have an APPEARANCE of the pleasant, though not of the GOOD (see REASON [1]). Human beings are guided by pleasure insofar as they follow their FEELINGS. Pleasure is important, therefore, in moral EDUCATION. Pleasure can mislead us about the good (1104b30, 1109b7, 1113a33) and destroy our conception of the good (1140b13, 1144a34). Even if we have the right conception of the good, a desire for pleasure that conflicts with this conception may cause us to be INCONTINENT. Hence moral education requires the right pleasures and pains (ii 3). The virtuous person must take pleasure in being virtuous and in the actions prescribed by the virtues (1099a7–21, 1104b3, 1117a35–b16, 1119a11–20, 1120a23–31, 1166a23–9, 1170a19–b8, 1175a19). This is the natural result of his DECIDING on these actions for their own sake and because they are FINE.

pleonexia OVERREACHING

poiein PRODUCE

poios CHARACTER

political science, *politikē* 'Political science' translates the adjective *politikē*; the noun understood with it is usually not expressed. Since political science is concerned with ACTION, and hence with the USUAL, it is not strictly a SCIENCE. Since it deliberates and DECIDES about happiness, it is the same STATE as PRUDENCE (1141b23–1142a10). It is the application of prudence to political questions about the good of a CITY. Aristotle argues that the proper concern of the state and of political science is to achieve HAPPINESS for all the citizens of the city (1094a26–b6, 1152b1–3, note to viii 9.§4–6). To discover this we must know what happiness for a human being is. That is the task of the *EN*. A human being is political by nature (note to 1097b9) because only a political community develops his nature so as to achieve his complete happiness; hence the inquiry in the *EN* is part of the inquiry continued in the *Politics* (see ETHICS).

politician, *politikos* The politician is an active participant in political affairs (1142a2, 1181a1), not a 'professor of politics' or 'political scientist'. But Aristotle thinks the 'true politician' (1102a8) will have PRUDENCE, and hence will be guided by his knowledge of POLITICAL SCIENCE and the human good. That will make him superior to contemporary politicians (1180b13–28). See also ETHICS. Since happiness requires virtue, the prudent politician wants the citizens to be virtuous (1102a7–10, 1103b2, 1180a5–12). He is concerned with moral EDUCATION, and with the motives and rewards that are part of it (1152b1–8, 1172a19–26). He seeks to punish vicious actions and to reform those who commit them, by CORRECTIVE TREATMENTS and penalties (1104b16, 1109b30–5, 1113b21–1114a3, 1180a12). See also LAW.

polloi MANY

ponēros VICIOUS

popular works, *exōterika, enkuklika* Aristotle might refer (a) to his own works written for more general circulation than the lectures that have been preserved, or, less probably, (b) to other people's works. See notes to i 5.§3, 6; 1102a26, 1140a3.

praxis ACTION

price See HONOR.

principle, beginning, *archē* *Archē* is cognate with *archein*, meaning both 'begin' and 'rule' (cf. the use of English 'lead' and 'first'). Often an *archē* is just a beginning or starting point. But the term has more specialized uses (see *Met*. v 1). (1) Each of the four CAUSES is an *archē*—especially the efficient cause (1110a15, 1113b20, 1114a19, 1139a31). (2) In the growth of knowledge there are two types of *archai*—the beginnings, known 'to us', and the principles, known 'by nature' (see ETHICS [4]). The beginnings—the *archai* we start from—are common beliefs (1095b6, 1143b4). The *archai* we seek to discover are the principles of a theory explaining the common beliefs (1098b2, 1140b34). In ethics our knowledge of these principles provides us with a conception of the END—the good to be pursued—for deliberation and DECISION (1140b16, 1144a32).

process See MOVEMENT.

produce, production, do, *poiēsis* Sometimes the verb *poiein* is used broadly for doing something or acting in general (sometimes where we would expect 'ACTION', e.g., 1147a28; cf. 1136b29). But its restricted use is explained in vi 4, 1140b6. It belongs especially to CRAFT, aiming at some end separate from the sequence of production itself. Insofar as a sequence of events is a production, it aims at an end outside itself, and hence satisfies the conditions for a process or MOVEMENT (1174a19–b5). This is why virtuous activity cannot be merely production, but must be ACTION. For 'product', see FUNCTION (2).

prohairesis DECISION

proper, own, close, akin, suitable, *oikeios* This is cognate with *oikos* ('household') and indicates the sort of closeness expected in one's relations with oneself and one's own family. Sometimes it may be rendered 'one's own'. But often (esp. in viii–ix) it indicates the recognition of closeness resulting from shared concerns and interests; hence kinship and closeness help to explain FRIENDSHIP (1155a21, note to viii 12.§2, 1165a30, 1169b33). On 'proper' or 'appropriate' arguments, see note to 1155b1. On actions 'proper to' the virtuous person, see CHARACTER.

pros to telos See DECISION.

Protagoras Protagoras (?485–415? B.C.) was a leading SOPHIST (cf. 1164a20). He maintained that 'a human being is the measure of all things', meaning that 'as things appear to each person, so they are to him' (Plato, *Tht*. 152a). Aristotle rejects the Protagorean view of moral properties, by affirming that the good person, not just anyone, is the measure of what is good and bad. See 1094b16, 1113a29, notes to v 7.§2–5, 1166a12, 1170a21, 1176a16.

prudence, *phronēsis* The verb *phronein* indicates intelligent awareness in general (1096b17, 1152b16, ix 4.§3 note; *DA* 417b8; Plato, *Gorg.* 449e6), and the noun *phronēsis* is used in this general sense by both Plato and Aristotle. In the *EN*, however (unless 1096b24, 1172b30 are exceptions, when Aristotle refers to Plato), *phronēsis* is applied to the practical prudence described in vi 5, 1141b8–1142a30. Prudence is good deliberation about things that contribute to one's own HAPPINESS in general (1140a25–8), resulting in a correct supposition about the END (1142b33) which in turn is the PRINCIPLE of further correct deliberation (1140b11–20, 1144a31–6). A good translation for *phronēsis* would be 'wisdom' if that were not already needed for *sophia*. 'Prudence' (from the Latin rendering *prudentia*) is a good rendering, since it suggests good sense about one's own welfare, but it may mislead, if we identify prudence with narrow and selfish caution (Aristotle rejects this identification at 1142a6–10). The 'prudence' in 'jurisprudence' comes closer to Aristotle's use of *phronēsis*.

Since it is deliberative, prudence is about things that promote ends (1144a20–9, 1145a5–6). But it is also correct supposition about the end. The explanation of Aristotle's similar claims about DECISION (2) explains his view of prudence too.

Prudence finds the right actions to be done, and hence requires a grasp of PARTICULARS, since this is needed for a successful conclusion of deliberation (1141a8–23, 1142a23–30, 1145a35). This is why prudence needs CLEVERNESS (1144a18–9, 1152a10–14), PERCEPTION, and UNDERSTANDING. Since it is concerned with action, and hence with USUAL truths, and with particulars, it cannot be SCIENCE, in the strict sense.

Prudence is both necessary and sufficient for complete VIRTUE of character (1107a1, 1138b18–34, 1144b14–1145a2, 1178a16–19). Since it is practical, someone cannot both have it and fail to act correctly. Hence a prudent person cannot be incontinent (1145a4–9, 1152a6–14).

psuchē SOUL

public service See note to iv 2.§1.

puzzle See ETHICS (5).

Pythagoreans Pythagoras (?c.530 B.C.) soon became a subject of legend and fable; Aristotle ascribes specific doctrines only to 'the Pythagoreans'. He attributes to them an elaborate account of reality in numerical terms, and takes it to anticipate some aspects of PLATO's Theory of Forms. See 1096b5–7, 1106b29–30, 1132b22; *Met.* 985b22–986b8, 987a13–27; DK 58 B 4.

ratio See REASON (5).

rational calculation, *logismos* This is the exercise of reason in rational INFERENCE and thought. (Greek often uses *logismos* esp. for arithmetical calculation or reckoning.) Aristotle narrows the use of the term to exclude the sort of inference required in SCIENCE, involving NECESSARY truths. He confines it to the area of deliberation (see DECISION), concerned with the USUAL (1139a11).

reason, reasoning, account, argument, discussion, conversation, speech, words, ratio, *logos* *Logos* is cognate with *legein* ('say'); it is what is said, or the thought expressed in what is said. The main relevant uses are these: (1) *Logos* as reason belongs to HUMAN BEINGS as opposed to other ANIMALS, and to the rational part of the SOUL as opposed to the nonrational DESIRES; hence an adult human being can be guided by reason rather than by FEELING. See 1095a10, 1098a3, 1102b15, 1111b12, 1119b11, 1147b1, 1150b28, 1169a1, 5, 1172b10. Reason makes human beings aware of the GOOD, not merely of the PLEASANT (1170b12; *Pol.* 1253a7–18). Awareness of the overall good requires comparison of present and future (*DA* 433b5–10, 434a5–10) in a single APPEARANCE, and the comparison of one desire against another to find what is good on the whole. This sort of deliberation is characteristic of reason. (2) Virtue is often said to ACCORD with CORRECT reason; See 1103b31; 1107a1; 1115b12, 19; 1117a8; 1119a20, b18; 1125b35; 1138a10, b20–34; 1144b23–8; 1147b3, 31; 1151a12, 22; *EE* 1220b19, 1222a8, b5. Here *logos* might refer to the activity of reasoning or to its product, the rule or principle discovered by the activity of reasoning, or to both the activity and the product. (3) When Aristotle speaks of reasoning, premises, and conclusions, *logos* is translated 'argument' (1094b13, 1095a30, 1104a1, 1144b32, etc.). (4) Sometimes rational understanding of something is expressed in a DEFINITION of what it is; here 'account' translates *logos* (e.g., 1096b1, 1103b21). (5) In geometrical contexts, the *logos* is the ratio between quantities (e.g., 1131a31). (6) In its broadest use, *logos* refers to more or less organized speaking, and hence is translated 'discussion', 'conversation', 'speech' (e.g., 1126b11, 1170b12, 1181a4). (7) *Logos* is sometimes contrasted, as mere words, with actions. See FUNCTION, 1105b13, 1168a35, 1172a35, 1179a22.

reasonable to expect, *eulogos* A *eulogos* state of affairs is one that we have some good reason or argument (*logos*) for expecting, without having a conclusive reason. Similarly, a *eulogos* claim is plausible without being conclusively supported. Since ETHICS is not a SCIENCE and relies on USUAL truths, many of its arguments have to be plausible and reasonable without being certain (1097a8, 1098b28, 1120b18; *GA* 763a4).

require See RIGHT.

responsible See CAUSE.

right, must, require, need, *dein* The best uniform translation of *dein* would probably be 'must'. The difference between *dein* and *chrēnai* (translated 'ought') and the gerundive form of a verb (translated 'should') is not clear in the *EN*. The main uses are these. (1) What the GOOD person must do is what is NECESSARY to achieve his happiness; hence it is what is CORRECT (1122b29) and what is FINE or expedient (*Top.* 110b10; *Rhet.* 1360b12). 'Right' is suitable for the use of *dein* in the rules that expound the doctrine of the MEAN, e.g., at 1106b21 (notice the connection with 'well'). Aristotle assumes that what is right and required of us is up to us to do, and that we can justly be praised for doing it and blamed for not doing it (1111a29, 1113b34). *Dein* sometimes indicates actions that are valuable for their own sakes; in these cases, it belongs to FINE actions. Hence, in the right contexts, it may convey awareness of an unqualified duty. (See also notes to iii 1.§24, vii 6.§1.) (2) What I must have for my survival or other ends is what I need. The verb 'need' translates *dein*, but the noun (in, e.g., 1133a27) translates *chreia*. (This seems more suitable than 'demand', since need may not be expressed in any actual demands.) When I have not gotten what I need, I am *endeēs*, 'lacking'. (3) Sometimes it is not clear whether *dein* refers to an actual need or to a claim that I need something and hence to a demand, request, or appeal for it (e.g., 1125a10, 1162b17). To reflect the ambiguity, 'require' is used for *dein* here.

science, knowledge, scientific knowledge, *epistēmē* This is a cognitive STATE of the soul, contrasted with mere *doxa*, 'belief'. When this is the primary contrast, 'knowledge' is used (e.g., in vii 2–3). But, unlike 'knowledge', *epistēmē* is found in the plural. The different *epistēmai* are the different sciences with their different subject matters. The state we are in when we grasp one of these sciences in the right way is *epistēmē*, rendered (e.g., in vi 3) 'scientific knowledge'.

An *epistēmē* may be any systematically organized, rationally justifiable and teachable, body of doctrine or instructions. *Epistēmai*, therefore, include CRAFTS (1094a28) such as medicine or gymnastics (1180b16; cf. 1106b5, 1112b1), and exclude pursuits that proceed by mere EXPERIENCE, rules of thumb, maxims, and hunches that cannot be rationally explained and justified (1180b17; *Met*. 981a1–20; Plato, *Gorg*. 465a). For this reason 'political science' and 'legislative science' are used in the translation where the Greek has only the adjectives 'political' and 'legislative'.

In *EN* vi, however, *epistēmē* is often confined to knowledge of scientific laws, to necessary and invariant truths about necessary and invariant states of affairs (vi 3, 5; cf. *APo* 71b9–72a14). The knowledge must be the conclusion of a demonstration, a deductive INFERENCE in which the premises are necessary truths explaining the conclusion, and are themselves reached either by UNDERSTANDING or by further demonstration ultimately derived from understanding. In this narrower sense, sciences include mathematics and some disciplines that study the natural universe. But they do not include productive crafts or political or legislative science (which lack EXACTNESS). Hence PRUDENCE cannot be a science.

seem See APPEAR.

self-sufficient See HAPPINESS.

sense See PERCEPTION, UNDERSTANDING.

serious See EXCELLENT.

sex See EROTIC PASSION.

shame, *aidōs* See iv 9. *Aidōs* indicates modesty and restraint in behavior; someone who has it is scrupulous in observing his standards and ideals, and prone to shame if he violates them. Aristotle associates shame closely with the sense of disgrace (*aischunē*). Though he sometimes commends shame (1115a14, 1179b11), he denies that it is a virtue. He thereby rejects a long Greek tradition (see also *EE* 1233b27).

shameful See FINE.

share See COMMON.

should See RIGHT.

sign, *sēmeion* We call x a sign of y if x is easier to notice than y (or the occurrence of x is less controversial than the occurrence of y), and noticing x makes it REASON-

ABLE to expect y, without giving a certain proof of y. See 1104a13, b3, 1159a21; *APr* ii 27; *Rhet*. 1357a34–b21.

simple See UNQUALIFIED.

slave, *doulos, andrapodon,* slavish, *andrapodōdēs* Aristotle is not completely clear about the similarities and differences between a slave and an adult human being. He can hardly deny that slaves are human, but he has to say that natural slaves have souls different enough to justify treatment of them as tools or instruments (*Pol.* i 4–7, 13; but cf. note to viii 11.§6–7). The slavish person is the one who cares about nothing beyond the satisfaction of his nonrational desires. He does not deliberate about changing them, but simply plans for their satisfaction. That is all a slave can do, and all a slavish person wants to do. His narrow range of desires and concerns makes him lack self-esteem, so that he will accept any humiliation to avoid pain. See 1095b19; 1118a25, b26; 1126a8, 1128a21, 1177a8, 1179b10. His opposite is the civilized person (see GENEROUS). See note to iv 3.§29. Cf. OCD, s.v. 'Slavery, Greek'.

Socrates Aristotle's specific remarks about Socrates (469–399 B.C.) in the *EN* can all be traced to PLATO's dialogues, but he often implies that the doctrines belong to the historical Socrates (by the use of the Greek imperfect tense; see notes to vi 13.§3, vii 2.§1). He distinguishes Socrates from Plato (1127b25; *Met*. 987b1, 1086b3; *Top*. 183b7). The ethical doctrines ascribed to Socrates in the *EN* are familiar from Plato's *Laches* and *Protagoras*. See 1116b4, 1144b18, 1145b23, 1147b15. For other probable allusions, see notes to i 5.§6, vi 5.§7.

softness, *malakia* See note to vii 7.§4.

sophia WISDOM

sophist, *sophistēs* *Sophistēs* is cognate with *sophos*, 'wise', and the sophists (who first appear in the mid-fifth century B.C.) were primarily concerned with higher education, especially for public life. See 1164a31, *Pol.* 1280b11; Plato, *Pr.* 310a–314c. Sometimes Aristotle uses 'sophist' to refer to those who use fallacious arguments that seem convincing when they are not; see 1146a21. He is unimpressed by the claims of sophists to give moral and political instruction; see 1164a30–3, 1180b35–1181a12.

sōphrosunē TEMPERANCE

soul, *psuchē* In *DA* ii 1 Aristotle defines the soul as the first ACTIVITY of a living body. If an axe were alive, then chopping (i.e., its characteristic activity or FUNCTION) would be its soul. In a living organism, the soul is the characteristic functions and activities that are essential to the organism and explain (as formal and final CAUSE) the other features it has. Compare 'The axe has a sharp edge for cutting' with 'Animals have hearts for pumping blood' and 'Human beings have senses and limbs for rational activity'. Aristotle takes the three explanations to be analogous. This conception of the soul underlies the arguments in 1097b34–1098a5, 1170a16, and 1178a9–22. (Cf. note to viii 10.§6.)

Since all living beings have functions, they all have souls (hence *apsuchos*, lit., 'soulless', translated 'inanimate', and *empsuchos*, lit., 'ensouled', is sometimes translated 'animate'); this broad scope of 'soul' explains some of the argument in i 7 and i 13.

The soul is divided into rational and nonrational parts (i 13, vi 1–2, 1144a1, 1145a3, 1166a16, 1168b30, 1178a2). See DESIRE, PERCEPTION.

Aristotle does not regard soul and body, as Plato does, as two separable SUBSTANCES; the soul is no more separable from the body than the axe's cutting FUNCTION is separable from its MATTER (*DA* 412b6). In the *EN* Aristotle is careful to avoid any commitment to separable parts of the soul in which he disbelieves (1102a28 is consistent with *DA* 433a11 ff.). Still, one part of the soul, the UNDERSTANDING that is capable of theoretical STUDY, has a special status, giving it the special place in HAPPINESS described in x 6–8 (where it is contrasted with the 'compound'; see note to x 7.§8).

species See DEFINE.

speech See REASON (6).

Speusippus Speusippus (?407–339 B.C.) was Plato's successor as head of the Academy. Aristotle refers to his metaphysical doctrine (1096b7) and to his views on pleasure (1153b5). His views may be Aristotle's targets elsewhere in the discussion of pleasure. See note to ii 3.§5.

spirit See DESIRE.

spoudaios EXCELLENT

state, *hexis* This means literally 'having, possession'; see note to ii 5.§2. This literal sense is exploited at 1146b31. A *hexis* is a first actualization or ACTIVITY, and hence, in relation to complete activity, a type of CAPACITY (*DA* 417a11–b16). In the *EN* Aristotle discusses the sort of state that is disposed to do F because it includes a tendency to do F on the right occasions because the state has been formed by repeated activities, i.e., by habituation in the regular practice of F actions (1103a26–b25, 1104a11–b3, ii 4). Because it has been formed by training, VIRTUE is a state rather than a mere capacity or FEELING (ii 5) and it is firmer and more stable than a mere condition (*diathesis*; cf. *Catg*. 8b26–9a13). A state is not merely a tendency to behave. If it were only that, two people who displayed the same behavior on the same occasions would have the same state. Aristotle, however, denies that the same behavior implies the same state. Someone's state also includes his desires, feelings, and DECISION. That is why 'habit' and 'disposition' are misleading translations of *hexis*.

study, observe, attend, *theōrein, theōria* *Theōrein* is cognate with *theasthai* ('gaze on') and indicates having something in clear view and attending to it. The main uses: (1) *Theōria* of a question or subject is looking at it, examining it carefully, and seeing the answer (1098a31, 33; 1100b19, 1104a11). (2) *Theōrein* is the ACTIVITY of the CAPACITY of knowledge. I may know Pythagoras' theorem even if I am not thinking of it; Aristotle regards that as knowing in capacity. The capacity is actualized when I consciously observe or attend to (*theōrein*) the theorem (1146b33). (3) In Aristotle's most specialized use, *theōrein* refers to the contemplative study that he identifies with HAPPINESS, or with a part of it. This is study in the sense in which I 'study' a face or a scene that I already have in full view; that is why the visual associations of *theōrein* are appropriate. Aristotle is not thinking of the inquiry needed to find answers; he probably thinks of surveying the deductive structure of a demonstrative SCIENCE, seeing how each proposition is justified by its place in the whole structure (1177a26). In x 7 Aristotle explains why he thinks study is the ACTIVITY that comes closest to meeting the conditions for complete happiness. (4) *Theōria* does not actually mean 'theory' as opposed to 'practice'; but the origins of this contrast are clear in 1103b26, 1177b2. In the *EN*, *theōria* is contrasted with ACTION (1177b2; but cf. *Pol.* 1325b16–30).

substance, *ousia* This is the first category (also called 'what-it-is'; see note to i 6.§3), including subjects (e.g., men, horses) as opposed to their qualities and other nonessential properties (1096a21; *Catg.* 2a10–19; *Met.* v 8). *Ousia* is also used as equivalent to 'essence' (1107a6; see DEFINE).

suffering See FEELING.

sumbēbekos COINCIDENT

sungnōmē PARDON

supposition, *hupolēpsis* This is the generic term for cognitive states, including both knowledge (see SCIENCE) and belief (*doxa*). It need not, therefore, indicate something tentative or conjectural. See 1095a16, 31, 1140b13, 31, 1145b21, 26, 1147b4.

syllogism See INFERENCE.

synonymous See HOMONYMOUS.

target See END (5).

technē CRAFT

teleios COMPLETE

telos END

temperance, *sōphrosunē* The traditional rendering 'temperance' indicates correctly that the concern of this virtue is moderation in the satisfaction of bodily desires. But it may mislead. (1) Aristotle's restricted conception of *sōphrosunē* (iii 10–11) tends to conceal the cognitive aspect of the Greek term, which sometimes indicates good sense, and the moderation resulting from it. See note to vi 5.§6 (a more probable etymology than Aristotle's derives the term from 'sound (*sōs*) mind (*phronein*)'; he is right to see some connection with *phronēsis*, 'PRUDENCE'). (2) Temperance does not require total abstinence from bodily pleasures, but the right extent of indulgence. (3) Temperance requires not merely abstinence, but abstinence without severe pain (1119a1–20). The temperate person is not merely continent (see INCONTINENT; 1104b5, 1120b35).

term See note to vi 8.§9.

thought See UNDERSTANDING (1).

timē HONOR

transfer See HOMONYMY.

tuchē FORTUNE

tyrant, *turannos* A tyranny is a deviation from kingship, and, in Aristotle's view, the worst form of government altogether (viii 10.§1–2). In contrast to a king, who rules in accordance with law and tradition, a tyrant is an extraconstitutional ruler. In Greek cities, a tyrant often rose to power in times of political and constitutional crisis. To call a ruler a tyrant is to refer to his constitutional position; it is not necessarily to imply that he is a cruel or oppressive or unpopular ruler. Nonetheless, tyranny is cited as an example of arbitrary and coercive power (1110a5, 1134a35–b8). It tends to corrupt and distort FRIENDSHIPS, encouraging flattery and subservience. See 1120b25, 1122a5, 1160b27–32; 1161a30–2, b9; 1176b15; *Pol.* iv 10, v 11–12.

ugly See FINE.

understanding, sense, *nous* This is used in both looser and stricter senses (cf. SCIENCE). (1) It is applied generally to rational thought and understanding, not distinguished from *dianoia*, 'thought' (1139a26, 32, 35, b4–5, 1144b9, 12, 1168b35, 1170a19, 1178a7, 1180a20). (2) In one idiomatic use, it is fairly represented by the English 'sense'. Someone with *nous* has common sense; he understands what is going on and reacts sensibly (1110a11, 1112a21, 1115b9). (Cf. the archaic use in 1116a34, where 'notice' translates *noein*.) (3) In its most restrictive use, *nous* is confined to true rational thought and understanding not resting on further justification. At 1143a35 Aristotle describes this as theoretical *nous*, applied to the first principles of demonstrative SCIENCE; this is of necessary truths (*APo* 100b5–17). (4) Practical *nous* (1143a35) grasps the relevant features of particular cases. Probably Aristotle means that *nous* shows that what is happening is a theft, and so I can see that some general principle about trying to stop thefts applies to this occasion. See PERCEPTION. Probably the use of *nous* for good sense, in (2) above, encourages Aristotle to use *nous* to refer to this practical insight.

universal, *katholou* A universal (or 'common' property; 1096a23, 1180b15) corresponds to every natural kind (e.g., dog, human being) and to every SCIENCE (1180b15; *Met.* 980a21–981b13). Hence a science studies universals (1139b29, 1140b31). ETHICS studies them too, as far as it can , though often it can only reach USUAL truths. Universals must be grasped by REASON (1147b4; see ANIMAL), and grasp of them is an important part of deliberation leading to DECISION, since that applies universal principles to PARTICULAR situations (1141b14, 1142a20, 1144a32; 1147a2, 25).

Aristotle criticizes the Platonic Form of the good in i 6 because he thinks it rests on the mistaken belief that a single universal corresponds to 'good' (1096a23). He insists on the recognition of HOMONYMY, to discover more than one universal corresponding to one term (1129a16).

unqualified, without qualification, simple, *haplōs* The adjective *haplous* means 'simple, uniform' (i.e., not compound or complex; e.g., 1154b21). The adverb *haplōs* indicates a statement made without qualification or reservation, or a property that belongs to a subject without restriction or qualification. Hence doing F *haplōs* is simply doing F, as opposed to doing F only in certain circumstances or with certain conditions (1106a8; note to iii 1.§5). The 'simple incontinent' is the one who is just incontinent, not incontinent in a particular, limited way (1146b3).

Sometimes when we speak *haplōs*, we speak inexactly, and conditions or qualifications must be added to produce an EXACT statement; it is the task of dialectic (see ETHICS [4]) to find these appropriate additions (*Top.* 115b3–35, 166b22,

166b37–167a20). If I say water is good to drink, that is true *haplōs*, but to be more exact I should mention the conditions in which it is and is not good to drink. See 1095a1; 1097a33, 1098a10, 1104b25, 1105b33; 1110a9, b1; note to v 1.§9, 1129b26, 1130a19; 1147b20, 32; 1148b8, 1151b2, 1156b13.

Sometimes, however, the *haplōs* statement is true and exact without qualification, even though it is true in some definite circumstances. Virtues, e.g., are good *haplōs* because they are good for the good person in the normal condition of a human being (1115b21, 1176a15). See 1095b3 (for 'known without qualification' see ETHICS [4, 6]), 1113a24, notes to vi 2.§5, 9.§7, 1147b24, 1152b27, 1155b24, 1157b27; *EE* 1227a18, 1234b31; 1236a9, b27; 1237a27; 1238a3, b5; 1248b26, 1249a17.

unwilling See VOLUNTARY.

up to us See VOLUNTARY.

urge, *epithumia* See DESIRE.

usual, *hōs epi to polu* A usual truth is a universal judgment that is true for most of the cases it applies to, but not for all (e.g., 'Men go gray in old age', *APr* 32b5). The state of affairs corresponding to this judgment is also called usual. ETHICS is concerned with the usual, not only with the UNIVERSAL and the NECESSARY (1094b21; cf. 1110a31, 1129a24, 1161a27). That is why deliberation (see DECISION) is important in ethics (1112b8) and why PARTICULAR cases must be judged by PERCEPTION (1109b20–3, 1126b24). Since principles of JUSTICE are only usual, they must be adjusted by DECENCY (1137b14). Aristotle's casuistry reflects reluctance to offer exceptionless rules (ix 2, esp. 1164b31). Concern with the usual deprives ethics of EXACTNESS, and prevents it from being SCIENCE.

Ethics has to offer usual truths if it is to guide action, as a practical discipline should (1103b26–1104a11). Aristotle does not say that all ethical truths (e.g., 'Bravery is finer than cowardice') are only usual. He means that those giving relatively specific practical advice (e.g., 'Stand firm in the battle-line' or 'Keep promises') are only usually true. He does not try to add the exceptions to make a more complex rule with no exceptions (e.g., 'Keep your promises except in conditions A, B, C'). He might argue that such rules will be so complex as to be unlearnable and useless; he prefers the agent to use deliberation, perception, and UNDERSTANDING to see what different moral principles apply to a situation, and how they affect each other. This is what the PRUDENT person can see because of EXPERIENCE and familiarity with particular cases.

vicious, bad, base, *kakos, phaulos, ponēros, mochthēros* It is hard to see any clear distinction in Aristotle's uses of these terms, which are all used for the contrary of GOOD and EXCELLENT. Cf. ix 3.§3 note. (In 1148b2–4, 'vice' renders *mochthēria*, and 'bad' renders *phaulos*. This might suggest that *phaulos* is sometimes weaker than *mochthēros*; but this is not generally true.) Like many Greek moral terms (see DECENT), these terms also have a social and political use; they are applied especially to the lower classes, the MANY, in contrast to the decent and respectable upper classes.

virtue, *aretē* If x is an F (e.g., a knife), then the virtue of x as an F is that STATE of x that makes x a GOOD F (in a knife its virtue will be cutting well, durability, etc., that make it a good knife). Hence x's virtue will reflect its good performance of the

FUNCTION of Fs (see Plato, *Rep*. 352d–353e). Aristotle's conception of virtue, therefore, is wider than moral virtue. In some cases 'excellence' may be the best rendering of *aretē* (e.g., 1122b15, 1141a12). Aristotle develops his conception of a good person from excellence in a CRAFT (see notes to 1098a12, 1106b8). This does not mean, however, that he has no conception of a moral virtue, or that he thinks virtues of character are just craft knowledge. He distinguishes being good at something from being a good person (1148b7); the good person is the person who has the virtues aiming at FINE and RIGHT action.

Virtues are divided into virtues of thought (see UNDERSTANDING) and virtues of CHARACTER. In his account of the individual virtues, Aristotle relies on common beliefs about their scope. But he often reforms common usage; he ascribes to each virtue a distinctive range of actions, motives, and CAPACITIES (see GENEROSITY, JUSTICE, TEMPERANCE, PRUDENCE, WISDOM; notes to iii 10.§8, vii 9.§4). To articulate the virtues clearly, he gives names to states of character that have not been recognized explicitly as virtues, but are shown to be virtues with the help of the doctrine of the MEAN (1107b2, 1108a16, 1125b23–8, 1126b19, 1127a13).

See also DECISION, DESIRE, EDUCATION, HAPPINESS, INCONTINENCE, REASON (2), SOUL, VOLUNTARY. On virtuous ACTIVITIES, see 1100b12, 1103a27, note to iii 5.§1, 1115b20, 1177a10, b6. On natural virtue, see note to vi 13.§1. On the unity of virtue, see note to vi 13.§6.

volatile, *melancholikos* See note to vii 7.§8.

voluntary, willing, *hekousios, hekōn* Aristotle seems to treat these two terms as synonymous. In ordinary Greek they both suggest absence of compulsion and of reluctance, as we speak of willing helpers, volunteers, and voluntary (as opposed to compulsory) service. Aristotle, however, regards unwilling, reluctant, and non-volunteered actions as *hekousia*; that is the point of 1110a4–b17. For this reason 'intentional' has sometimes been suggested instead of 'voluntary'. But 'voluntary' is still preferable in suggesting a reference to the agent's DESIRES and preferences. See 1110b12, 1111a32, 1169a1, notes to iii 1.§3, 13. Voluntary actions belong only to agents with desire, and are those caused by desires (see, esp., 1110b18–24). Since ANIMALS and children have desires, they act voluntarily, though they lack rational desire and DECISION (1111a25, b8). Hence, in Aristotle's strict use of 'ACTION' (2), not everything done voluntarily counts as an action (1139a19).

Aristotle seeks to identify voluntary actions, so that he can determine when praise and blame are appropriate for an agent (1109b30); he is defining conditions for holding agents responsible for their actions. Voluntary action justifies us in holding agents responsible if they are capable of DECISION (cf. 1149b30–1, 1150a1). Aristotle assumes that an action is voluntary and results from decision if and only if it is 'up to us', *eph'hēmin* (1113b6). It is up to us if and only if the PRINCIPLE of the movement (i.e., the efficient CAUSE) is in us (1110a15) or (in other words) we are the cause and CONTROL what happens (1113b21–1114a7, 1114a21–31). To avoid odd results, 'in us' must be taken to mean 'in our beliefs and desires'. For a perhaps different view of 'up to us', see 1135a23–b2; *EE* 1225b8.

Apart from the main discussion of voluntary action in iii 1, 5 and v 8, see also 1119a24–33, 1128b28, 1131a34, 1132b13, 1136b5, 1138a12, 28, 1140b23, 1152a15, 1153b21, 1163a2, 1164b13, 1169a1, 1180a16.

wanton aggression, *hubris* An act of *hubris* involves attacking or insulting another, but in a special way, so as to cause dishonor (see HONOR) and SHAME to the victim (*Rhet*. 1378b23) for the agent's pleasure (1149b20). See 1115a20, 1124a29, 1125a9, 1129b32, 1148b30 (sexual assault), 1149a32.

what, what sort See DEFINE (3).

wife See WOMAN.

willing See VOLUNTARY.

wisdom, *sophia* *Sophia* has a fairly broad use, as *phronēsis* ('PRUDENCE') has, in ordinary Greek. Any sort of expert could be called wise, in a CRAFT (1127b20, 1141a9–16) or in giving practical advice (e.g., Solon and the Seven Sages [*sophoi*], 1095a21, 1098b28, 1130a1, 1179a20). In Aristotle's narrower use, however, wisdom excludes both craft and prudence, and is confined to the best kind of knowledge (vi 7). Since neither craft nor prudence can achieve the degree of exactness needed for demonstration, neither can be SCIENCE, which alone can constitute wisdom. Hence wisdom must be concerned purely with STUDY, not with ACTION.

wish See DECISION, DESIRE.

woman, wife, *gunē* This refers to the adult female. Her natural differences from a MAN, leading to a FUNCTION different from a man's, are assumed in the *EN*. See 1162a19–27, note to vii 5.§4; *Pol*. 1259b28–1260a24, 1277b20. Greek uses the same words for 'man' and 'husband' (*anēr*) and for 'woman' and 'wife' (*gunē*). In viii 10–12 Aristotle is plainly concerned with relations between husband and wife. But 'man' and 'woman' are often the preferable translations; the roles of husband and wife are taken to be explained by the different natural capacities of men and women.

words See REASON (6).

worth, *axia* Sometimes 'value' and 'desert' might also be suitable. See 1119b26, note to iv 3.§3, 1131a26, 1133b24, 1158b27, 1159a35, 1160b33.

youth, young people, *neos* Youths are excluded from the study of ETHICS (1095a2) because they follow their FEELINGS. A youth is older than a child, but Aristotle does not say when, for these purposes, someone stops being a youth. Perhaps he is thinking of people under eighteen (see OCD, s.v. 'Epheboi'). Aristotle associates the different periods of a person's life with different traits of character, and hence with tendencies to virtue and vice; hence the young and the old have their contrasting traits. See 1119a33–b18, 1121a16–30, b13, iv 9, 1154b9, 1156a14–b6, 1158a1–10 (cf. 1126b16); *Rhet*. ii 12–14; OCD, s.v. 'Age'.

FURTHER READING

This list contains only a few of the main items likely to be useful to those beginning detailed study of the *EN*.

ARISTOTLE: GENERAL

The standard English translation:

1. Barnes, J., ed. *The Complete Works of Aristotle*, 2 vols. (Princeton, 1984) ('Revised Oxford Translation', cited as 'ROT').

A clear, stimulating, short account of Aristotle:

2. Ackrill, J. L. *Aristotle the Philosopher* (Oxford, 1981).

A fuller summary of the contents of Aristotle's works:

3. Ross, W. D. *Aristotle* (London, 1923).

Books covering several aspects of Aristotle's thought, including ethics:

4. Lear, J. *Aristotle: The Desire to Understand* (Cambridge, 1988).
5. Irwin, T. H. *Aristotle's First Principles* (Oxford, 1988).

For readers who know Greek, an indispensable work:

6. Bonitz, H. *Index Aristotelicus* (Berlin, 1870).

An attempt to construct an index to the Oxford Translation:

7. Organ, T. W. *An Index to Aristotle* (Princeton, 1949).

Volume 2 of ROT contains a brief index.

ETHICS: GENERAL

The standard edition of the Greek text ('Oxford Classical Text', cited as 'OCT'):

8. Bywater, I., ed. *Aristotelis Ethica Nicomachea* (Oxford, 1890).

Other editions:

9. Susemihl, F., ed. *Aristotelis Ethica Nicomachea* (Leipzig, 1882).
10. Rackham, H., ed. and trans. *Nicomachean Ethics*, ed. 2 (London, 1934).

The classic English translation:

11. Ross, W. D., trans. *Nicomachean Ethics*, revised by J. L. Ackrill and J. O. Urmson (Oxford, 1980).

The best commentary on the Greek text:

12. Gauthier, R. A., and J. Y. Jolif. *Aristote: L'Ethique à Nicomaque*, ed. 2, 4 vols. (Paris and Louvain, 1970).

The main English commentaries:

13. Stewart, J. A. *Notes on the Nicomachean Ethics*, 2 vols. (Oxford, 1892).

14. Burnet, J. *The Ethics of Aristotle* (London, 1900).

15. Joachim, H. H. *Aristotle: Nicomachean Ethics* (Oxford, 1951).

The most important medieval commentary:

16. Aquinas, T. *in decem libros Ethicorum . . . Expositio*, ed. R. Spiazzi (Turin, 1949).

17. ———. *Commentary on Aristotle's Nicomachean Ethics*, trans. C. L. Litzinger (Chicago, 1964).

The most helpful general guide to the *EN* is:

18. Hardie, W. F. R. *Aristotle's Ethical Theory*, ed. 2 (Oxford, 1980).

Books covering several aspects of the *EN*:

19. Broadie, S. W. *Ethics with Aristotle* (Oxford, 1991).

20. Kraut, R. *Aristotle on the Human Good* (Princeton, 1989).

21. Reeve, C. D. C. *Practices of Reason* (Oxford, 1992).

Collections of essays:

22. Barnes, J., M. Schofield, R. Sorabji, eds. *Articles on Aristotle*, vol. 2 (London, 1977).

23. Rorty, A. O., ed. *Essays on Aristotle's Ethics* (Berkeley, 1980).

24. Irwin, T. H., ed. *Classical Philosophy, vol. 5: Aristotle's Ethics* (New York, 1995).

25. Sherman, N., ed. *Aristotle's Ethics: Critical Essays* (Lanham, 1999).

26. Cooper, J. M. *Reason and Emotion* (Princeton, 1998), chs. 8–19.

27. McDowell, J. *Mind, Value, and Reality* (Cambridge, Mass., 1998), chs. 1–4, 9.

28. Owen, G. E. L. *Logic, Science, and Dialectic* (Ithaca, 1986).

29. Ackrill, J. L. *Essays on Plato and Aristotle* (Oxford, 1997).

On the relation of the *EN* to Aristotle's other ethical works:

30. Kenny, A. J. P. *The Aristotelian Ethics* (Oxford, 1978).

31. Kenny, A. J. P. *Aristotle on the Perfect Life* (Oxford, 1992).

It is often instructive to compare the *EN* with the other ethical works. A recent edition of the Greek text of *EE*:

32. Walzer, R. R., and J. M. Mingay, eds. *Aristotelis Ethica Eudemia* (Oxford, 1991).

Translation and notes:

33. Woods, M. J. *Eudemian Ethics I, II, VIII*, ed. 2 (Oxford, 1992).

Fuller bibliographies will be found in [18], [22], and:

34. Barnes, J., ed. *The Cambridge Companion to Aristotle* (Cambridge, 1994).

35. Everson, S., ed. *Companions to Ancient Thought 4: Ethics* (Cambridge, 1998).

The Aristotelian Approach to Ethics

Some idea of the influence of Aristotelian ideas in modern moral theory can be gained from:

36. Prichard, H. A. 'Does Moral Philosophy Rest on a Mistake?', 'Duty and Interest', and 'Moral Obligation', in *Moral Obligation* (reissue, Oxford, 1968).
37. Green, T. H. *Prolegomena to Ethics* (Oxford, 1883), Book 3, ch. 5.
38. Falk, W. D. 'Morality, Self and Others', in *Ought, Reasons, and Morality* (Ithaca, 1986), ch. 10.
39. Anscombe, G. E. M. 'Modern Moral Philosophy', in *Collected Papers*, vol. 3 (Oxford, 1981).
40. Foot, P. R. *Virtues and Vices* (Oxford, 1978).
41. Geach, P. T. *The Virtues* (Cambridge, 1977).
42. Wallace, J. D. *Virtues and Vices* (Ithaca, 1978).
43. Von Wright, G. H. *The Varieties of Goodness* (London, 1963).
44. Hampshire, S. N. *Two Theories of Morality* (Oxford, 1977).
45. Crisp, R., ed. *How Should One Live?* (Oxford, 1996).
46. Crisp, R., and M. Slote, eds. *Virtue Ethics* (Oxford, 1997).
47. Williams, B. A. O. *Ethics and the Limits of Philosophy* (Cambridge, Mass., 1985).
48. Heinaman, R., ed. *Aristotle and Moral Realism* (London, 1995).

Historical Background

The most convenient work of reference for historical events, dates, details of authors' lives and works, and conventions of reference to Greek texts is:

49. *Oxford Classical Dictionary*, ed. 3 (Oxford, 1996).

A short account of Greek philosophy:

50. Irwin, T. H. *Classical Thought* (Oxford, 1989).

Fragments of the pre-Socratics are collected in:

51. Diels, H., and W. Kranz, eds. *Die Fragmente der Vorsokratiker*, ed. 6 (Berlin, 1951) (Cited as 'DK').
52. Kirk, G. S., J. E. Raven, and M. Schofield. *The Presocratic Philosophers* (Cambridge, 1983) (in Greek and English).

On the history of Greek ethics before Aristotle:

53. Adkins, A. W. H. *Merit and Responsibility* (Oxford, 1960).
54. Dover, K. J. *Greek Popular Morality in the Time of Plato and Aristotle* (Oxford, 1974).
55. Irwin, T. H. *Plato's Ethics* (Oxford, 1995).

It is especially useful to read some of Plato's dialogues, in particular the *Laches, Charmides, Protagoras, Gorgias, Republic* i–ii, iv, viii–ix, the *Philebus*, and parts of the *Laws*.

Method

56. Owen, G. E. L. '*Tithenai ta phainomena*', in [28].
57. Barnes, J. 'Aristotle and the Methods of Ethics', in [24]. From *Revue Internationale de Philosophie* 34 (1980), 490–511.

58. Irwin, T. H. 'Aristotle's Methods of Ethics', in *Studies in Aristotle*, ed. D. J. O'Meara (Washington, 1981). See also [5], ch. 16.
59. Reeve, C. D. C. [21], ch. 1.

HAPPINESS

60. Cooper, J. M. *Reason and Human Good in Aristotle* (Cambridge, Mass., 1975), chs. 2–3.
61. Ackrill, J. L. 'Aristotle on Eudaimonia', in [23], [29].
62. McDowell, J. 'The Role of Eudaimonia in Aristotle's Ethics', in [23], [27].

Happiness and external goods:

63. Cooper, J. M. 'Aristotle on the Goods of Fortune', in [26].
64. Irwin, T. H. 'Permanent Happiness: Aristotle and Solon', in [25].
65. White, S. A. *Sovereign Virtue* (Stanford, 1992).
66. Annas, J. *The Morality of Happiness* (Oxford, 1993).

The function argument:

67. Whiting, J. E. 'Aristotle's Function Argument: A Defence', in [24]. From *Ancient Philosophy* 8 (1988), 33–48.
68. Nussbaum, M. C. 'Aristotle on Human Nature and the Foundations of Ethics', in J. E. J. Altham and R. Harrison, eds., *World, Mind, and Ethics*, (Cambridge, 1995).

The relation between Aristotelian *eudaimonia* and happiness:

69. Kraut, R. 'Two Conceptions of Happiness', *Philosophical Review* 88 (1979), 167–97.
70. Griffin, J. *Well-Being* (Oxford, 1986).

Conceptions of happiness in *EN* Book i and Book x:

71. Cooper, J. M. 'Contemplation and Happiness', in [26].
72. Keyt, D. 'Intellectualism in Aristotle', in [24]. From *Essays in Ancient Greek Philosophy*, vol. 2, ed. J. P. Anton and A. Preus (Albany, 1983).
73. Kraut [20].
74. Lawrence, G. L. 'Aristotle on the Ideal Life', *Philosophical Review* 102 (1993), 1–34.

VIRTUE

Many of the works cited under The Aristotelian Approach to Ethics (above) are also relevant here:

75. Dent, N. J. H. *The Moral Psychology of the Virtues* (Cambridge, 1984).
76. Frankena, W. K. 'Prichard and the Ethics of Virtue', in *Perspectives on Morality*, ed. K. E. Goodpaster (Notre Dame, 1976).
77. Burnyeat, M. F. 'Aristotle on Learning to Be Good', in [23], [25].
78. Urmson, J. O. 'Aristotle's Doctrine of the Mean', in [23].
79. Hursthouse, R. 'A False Doctrine of the Mean', in [24], [25].
80. McDowell, J. 'Virtue and Reason' and 'Some Issues in Aristotle's Moral Psychology', in [27].

81. Sherman, N. *The Fabric of Character* (Oxford, 1989).
82. ———. *Making a Necessity of Virtue* (Cambridge, 1997).
83. Cooper, J. M. 'Some Remarks on Aristotle's Moral Psychology' and 'Reason, Moral Virtue, and Moral Value', in [26].
84. Irwin, T. H. 'Aristotle's Concept of Morality', in *Proceedings of the Boston Colloquium in Ancient Philosophy* 1 (1985), 115–43.

It is sometimes interesting and amusing to compare and contrast the *EN* with a work by Aristotle's pupil and successor:

85. Theophrastus. *Characters*, ed. 2, ed. and trans. J. S. Rusten (London, 1993).

Voluntary Action and Responsibility

86. Furley, D. J. *Two Studies in the Greek Atomists* (Princeton, 1967). Partly reprinted in [22].
87. Kenny, A. J. P. *Aristotle's Theory of the Will* (London, 1979).
88. Sorabji, R. R. K. *Necessity, Cause and Blame* (London, 1980).
89. Irwin, T. H. 'Reason and Responsibility in Aristotle', in [23].
90. Meyer, S. S. *Aristotle on Moral Responsibility* (Oxford, 1993).
91. Ackrill, J. L. 'Aristotelian actions', in [23], [29].
92. ———. 'An Aristotelian Argument about Virtue', in [29].

Justice

93. Jackson, H. *EN Book V* (Cambridge, 1879). Greek text and commentary.
94. Allan, D. J. 'Individual and State in the Ethics and Politics', in *La Politique d'Aristote* (Fondation Hardt, Entretiens 11, Geneva, 1964).
95. Williams, B. A. O. 'Justice as a Virtue', in [23].
96. Feinberg, J. 'Justice and Personal Desert', in *Doing and Deserving* (Princeton, 1970).
97. Sachs, D. 'Notes on Unfairly Gaining More: *Pleonexia*', in *Virtues and Reasons*, ed. R. Hursthouse, G. Lawrence, and W. Quinn (Oxford, 1995).

Aristotle's views on justice are closely related to the political theory expounded in the *Politics*. English translations of this work include:

98. Barker, E., trans. *Politics*, rev. R. F. Stalley (Oxford, 1995).
99. Reeve, C. D. C., trans. *Politics* (Indianapolis, 1998).

Practical Reason, Deliberation, and Prudence

Greek text and commentary.

100. Greenwood, L. H. G. *EN Book VI* (Cambridge, 1909).
101. Cooper, J. M. [60], ch. 1.
102. Engberg-Pederson, T. *Aristotle's Theory of Moral Insight* (Oxford, 1983).
103. Anscombe G. E. M. 'Thought and Action in Aristotle', in [22].
104. Wiggins, D. 'Deliberation and Practical Reason', in [23].

105. Sorabji, R. R. K. 'Aristotle on the Role of Intellect in Virtue', in [23].

106. Charles, D. 'Ontology and Moral Reasoning', in [24]. From *Oxford Studies in Ancient Philosophy* 4 (1986), 119–44.

Practical Reason and Incontinence

The items under the previous heading are relevant here also.

107. Raz, J., ed. *Practical Reasoning* (Oxford, 1978). See especially the contributions by Anscombe, Von Wright, Kenny, and Harman.

108. Charles, D. *Aristotle's Philosophy of Action* (London, 1984).

109. Dahl, N. O. *Practical Reason, Aristotle, and Weakness of the Will* (Minneapolis, 1984).

110. Davidson, D. 'How Is Weakness of Will Possible?', in *Essays on Actions and Events* (Oxford, 1980).

111. Watson, G. 'Scepticism about Weakness of Will', *Philosophical Review* 86 (1977), 316–39.

112. Wiggins, D. 'Weakness of Will, Commensurability, and the Objects of Deliberation and Desire', in [23].

113. Bratman, M. *Intentions, Plans, and Practical Reason* (Cambridge, Mass., 1987).

Friendship

114. Vlastos, G. 'The Individual as Object of Love in Plato', in *Platonic Studies*, ed. 2 (Princeton, 1981).

115. Nygren, A. *Agape and Eros*, trans. P. S. Watson (London, 1953).

116. Cooper, J. M. 'Aristotle on the Forms of Friendship' and 'Friendship and the Good in Aristotle', in [26].

117. Annas, J. 'Plato and Aristotle on Friendship and Altruism', *Mind* 86 (1977), 532–54.

118. Bradley, F. H. 'Selfishness and Self-Sacrifice', in *Ethical Studies*, ed. 2 (Oxford, 1927).

119. Price, A. W. *Love and Friendship in Plato and Aristotle* (Oxford, 1989).

120. Whiting, J. E. 'Impersonal Friends', *Monist* 74 (1991), 3–29.

Pleasure

121. Ackrill, J. L. 'Aristotle's Distinction Between *Energeia* and *Kinesis*', in [29]. From *New Essays on Plato and Aristotle*, ed. R. Bambrough (London, 1965).

122. Penner, T. 'Verbs and the Identity of Actions', in *Ryle: A Collection of Critical Essays*, ed. O. P. Wood and G. W. Pitcher (London, 1970).

123. Owen, G. E. L. 'Aristotelian Pleasures', in [22], [28].

124. Gosling, J. C. B., and C. C. W. Taylor. *The Greeks on Pleasure* (Oxford, 1982), chs. 11–17.

125. Gosling, J. C. B. *Pleasure and Desire* (Oxford, 1969).

Terence Irwin is Susan Linn Sage Professor of Philosophy and Humane Letters, Cornell University. Born in Enniskillen, Northern Ireland, he received a B.A. from the University of Oxford in 1969 and a Ph.D. from Princeton in 1973. He taught at Harvard from 1972 to 1975 and has taught at Cornell since 1975. He is the author of *Plato's Gorgias* (translation and notes, 1979), *Classical Thought* (1988), *Plato's Ethics* (1995), and *Oxford Reader in Classical Philosophy* (1999), all published by Oxford University Press, and (with Gail Fine) of *Aristotle: Selections* (translation and notes, 1995) and *Aristotle: Introductory Readings* (1996), both published by Hackett.